D1607243

DICTIONARY OF LANDSCAPE ARCHITECTURE AND CONSTRUCTION

DICTIONARY OF LANDSCAPE ARCHITECTURE AND CONSTRUCTION

Alan Jay Christensen

McGraw-Hill

New York   Chicago   San Francisco   Lisbon   London
Madrid   Mexico City   Milan   New Delhi   San Juan
Seoul   Singapore   Sydney   Toronto

*The **McGraw·Hill** Companies*

Library of Congress Cataloging-in-Publication Data

Christensen, Alan Jay.
   Dictionary of landscape architecture and construction / Alan
Jay Christensen.
      p.   cm.
   ISBN 0-07-144142-5
   1. Landscape architecture—Dictionaries.   I. Title

SB469.25.C48   2005
712'.03—dc22   2004066199

ISBN 0-07-144142-5

The sponsoring editor for this book was Cary Sullivan, the editing
supervisor was Danielle Lake, and the production supervisor was
Pamela A. Pelton. It was set in Goudy by North Market Street
Graphics. The art director for the cover was Anthony Landi.

Printed and bound by RR Donnelley.

McGraw-Hill books are available at special quantity discounts to use as
premiums and sales promotions, or for use in corporate training
programs. For more information, please write to the Director of Special
Sales, McGraw-Hill Professional, Two Penn Plaza, New York, NY
10121-2298. Or contact your local bookstore.

This book is printed on recycled, acid-free paper
containing a minimum of 50% recycled, de-inked fiber.

This document was made possible through the kind and understanding patience of my dear wife, Terry, and six wonderful children while most of my spare time for one year was spent in research, writing, illustrating, and photographing. Thanks to each of them.

In my opinion, McGraw-Hill provides a great service to the seeker of knowledge, understanding, and wisdom in providing progressive, substantive, educational material.

Through the process of writing and going to final copy many people should be thanked, but I would be especially remiss not to give written appreciation for Cary Sullivan, who through her vision persisted in pursuing this book to its fruition; and Danielle Lake, who was most helpful through the editing process.

PREFACE

This publication represents research and analysis compiled, edited, and written by the author. In that effort, the following information may be helpful to the user for better understanding of this dictionary:

1. Words applicable to landscape architecture but most commonly understood are not defined within this work (i.e., water).

2. Most entries with multiple words do not have the words individually listed and defined so as to avoid redundancy and conserve space (i.e., crop coefficient, or cross connection).

3. Many conglomerate entries (multiple word entries) that are listed and defined as separate words and retain the given meaning of each word are not listed because the meaning is obvious with the meaning of each defined word (i.e., turf irrigation system).

4. Many words, such as definitions of abbreviations, have obvious and universal meaning with almost no variation from source to source. These are recorded without embellishment.

5. Many word definitions are modified, edited, or recorded from the standpoint of a landscape architect.

6. Definitions specific to the landscape industry that are less understood, or those affecting the health, safety, and welfare of people, plants, or other organisms are often expanded and expounded upon with more than a simple definition.

7. Words with the same definition that are commonly interchangeable are given identical definitions so that the user does not have to be referenced to another word before obtaining a definition. However, when there are interchangeable words or terms with one being more acceptable than the other, a reference is made from the less common term or word to the more common word or term for the definition.

8. Some definitions are newly recorded with no available references for gaining an understanding, but instead insight to the landscape industry and its evolving or new individualized jargon afforded the definition (i.e., setting heads).

9. The definitions in this work may be time-sensitive as meanings change over time and may also vary with circumstances. Care has been taken to provide the best definitive information available, understood, and researched by the author from his available sources at the time of writing. This document does not constitute a legal or binding list of definitions.

ABOUT THE AUTHOR

Alan Jay Christensen, a member of the American Society of Landscape Architects, the American Nursery & Landscape Association, the Irrigation Association, the American Institute of Certified Planners, and the International Ecological Engineering Society, has more than 27 years' experience in landscape architecture and landscape construction. In successfully operating several businesses for 23 years in the landscape industry, he has performed and managed landscape design, construction, and maintenance. His well-rounded experience in landscape and construction from New York to Hawaii has led him to obtain licenses as Landscape Architect, Irrigation Auditor, Landscape Contractor, Residential Construction Contractor, Commercial Construction Contractor, and Demolition Contractor. The holder of a patent for a method of planting trees that targets contaminants in brownfields, he has taught land planning at Brigham Young University and conducted research at Harvard University. He has special interest in debunking fallacies and misconceptions common in landscape architecture and is the author of several articles for professional landscaping publications.

DICTIONARY
OF LANDSCAPE
ARCHITECTURE AND
CONSTRUCTION

A

A, a **1.** Abbreviation for **acre**. The more common abbreviation for acre is **ac. 2.** Abbreviation for **ampere**(s). **3.** Abbreviation for area. In landscape applications, area is often expressed in **square feet**, **square yards**, or **square meters**. **4.** In botanical terms, a prefix meaning not; different from; away from; without.

A1 horizon A soil layer that is a **subhorizon** of the **A horizon**, distinguishable by its darker color from the rest of the **A horizon** due to a higher content of organic matter.

A2 horizon A soil layer that is a **subhorizon** of the **A horizon**, distinguishable by its lighter color from the rest of the **A horizon** due to a lack of organic matter because of leaching or eluviation.

A3 horizon A soil layer that is a **subhorizon** of the **A horizon**, similar to the **A2 horizon**, but also transitional to the **B horizon**, with visually distinguishable changes from either.

AAA Abbreviation for the American Arbitration Association.

AAN Abbreviation for the **American Association of Nurserymen** (now known as the **ANLA**).

AAN Standards The *American Standard for Nursery Stock,* as published by the **American Association of Nurserymen** (AAN).

AARS Abbreviation for **All-American Rose Selections**.

AAS Abbreviation for **All-American Selection**.

abacus A slab or division that forms the uppermost portion of the **capital** of a **column**, usually wider than the column.

abandonment A word often used in contract law to describe the failure of both parties to abide by the terms of a contract.

abate Removal of material, usually in making a design or producing a product from wood, metal, stone, etc. In metal work, this may be descriptive of the beating or pounding of a design into the material.

abat-vent Angled members with some space between them in an opening of an exterior wall or **fence** used for access to light while blocking wind and screening views. *See also* **louver**.

abaxial In botanical terms, the side away from the axis.

ABC **1.** Abbreviation for **aggregate base course. 2.** A reference to a type of soil profile. (*See* **ABC soil**.) **3.** Abbreviation for Associated Builders and Contractors.

ABC soil A mature soil profile that contains the three major **soil horizons**.

aberrant A descriptive term given to individual plants or species different in some way from the group they are associated with.

abiotic Not living.

abortive In botanical terms, an imperfectly developed portion of a plant.

Abram's law The strength of concrete is directly influenced by the ratio of water to cement.

abrasion The act of wearing away by friction.

abrasive A substance harder than the material it is used against in rubbing or grinding to create

abrasive surface

friction and wear away the softer material. Examples of useful abrasives are diamonds, carbide steel, metal shot, and sand (as with sandpaper).

abrasive surface A surface that is roughened for safety, such as the front **tread** of a stair.

abrevoir A space, gap, or joint between stones that is filled with cement or mortar.

abscisic acid A growth-inhibiting plant hormone, which also promotes leaf fall (**abscission**), the formation of potato tubers, and the change to dormancy in leaf buds.

abscission The natural separation of fruit, leaves, or flowers from a plant at a special area of tissue.

abscission layer The layer of tissue in a plant that facilitates the dropping of fruit, flowers, and leaves that cease to function.

absolute pressure In pumping references, the total pressure above absolute zero.

absorbed moisture Water that has been absorbed into the pore spaces of a solid such as soil or wood.

absorber **1.** That portion of a solar collector that collects and absorbs radiant heat energy. **2.** A material that collects and holds pollutants such as oil from water runoff, usually within a catch basin or an oil separator. **3.** A device used to arrest the shock of **water hammer**.

absorbing well *or* **dry well** *or* **waste well** A well collecting surface waters, providing for the water to be dispensed and absorbed into the ground.

absorption **1.** A process by which a gas and/or liquid enters into a solid material. This occurs through pores in a porous solid material. This process is usually accompanied by a chemical and/or physical change of the solid material. **2.** The process by which radiant energy is con-

verted to other forms of energy. **3.** The increase in weight of a solid material due to the process described in (1.) **4.** The increased weight of a tile or brick when immersed into boiling water or cold water for a determined period of time. This weight change is usually expressed as a percentage of the weight of the dry weight. **5.** A process where one substance adheres to the surface of another.

absorption bed An excavation that is filled with coarse aggregate and has a piping system for distribution of septic tank effluent.

ABS plastic *or* **ABS pipe** A plastic of **acrylonitrile butadiene styrene** often used to make pipe that is resistant to impact, heat, chemicals, and freeze-thaw. It is softer than **PVC** plastic and usually black.

abut **1.** To make contiguous or to make a contact point. **2.** In real estate, two properties with a common property line.

abutment The part of a structure such as a bridge or an arch that bears the weight of the span and is usually made of masonry or concrete.

abuttals Those boundaries of one piece of land that are in common with adjacent pieces of land.

abutting joint A joint between two pieces of wood, where the direction of the grain in one piece of wood is at an angle (usually 90°) to the grain in the other.

AC, ac, a-c, a.c. **1.** Abbreviation for **acre**(s). **2.** Abbreviation for **alternating current**.

ACA Abbreviation for **ammoniacal copper arsenate**. A thorn-like or spike-like protrusion.

acaulescent In botanical terms, a plant or leaf that is without a **stem**, or appears to be without a stem.

ACC Abbreviation for **acid copper chromate**.

accelerated erosion The movement of earthen particles in water runoff increased by human activities influencing the land. Activities causing increased erosion include removal of vegetation, loosening of soil, concentrating areas of runoff, or interruption of natural drainage patterns.

accelerator A material or substance added to concrete, grout, or mortar to increase its rate of hardening, and/or decrease its **set**ting time.

access A way of vehicular, pedestrian, or other approach, entry, or exit.

access door A door that provides access to equipment for maintenance, inspection, or repair.

access panel

access panel *or* **access plate** A removable panel or plate (usually secured with screws or bolts) in a frame that is usually mounted in a ceiling or wall and provides access to concealed items or equipment. It permits inspection of an otherwise inaccessible area. Wires and/or pipes for irrigation systems or pumps are sometimes concealed behind these panels in buildings.

They are also sometimes designed into park restrooms and pavilions for infrequent access to areas in ceilings or behind walls.

accessibility standards Parameters and recommendations regarding accessibility of handicapped persons to walks, structures, etc. *See* **Americans with Disabilities Act** and **Uniform Federal Accessibility Standards**.

accessible **1.** Easily accessed. **2.** Reachable by removal of a cover, panel, plate, or similar obstruction. **3.** Easily accessed by those disabled in wheelchairs or walkers.

accessible means of egress A path of travel, usable by a person who has impaired mobility, that leads to a **public way**.

accessory building A building with a secondary use to that of the main building located on the same plot. Refer to local jurisdictional agencies for their definition.

accessory structure A subordinate structure detached from, but located near, a principal building. Accessory structures usually include garages, decks, fences, sheds, etc.

acclivity A slope above; an upward slope.

accouplement Placement of posts, columns, or pillars in sets of two (paired).

accrescent A botanical term, something that increases in size with age.

ACD Abbreviation for an automatic closing device.

ACE Abbreviation for **Agricultural Conservation Easement**.

acerose In botanical terms, a plant part shaped like a needle or having a needle-like tip.

acetone A highly volatile solvent often used in lacquers, paint removers, thinners, etc.

acetylene

acetylene A colorless gas, that when mixed with oxygen, burns at a temperature of about 3500°C; used in welding.

acetylene torch A metal-cutting and welding instrument that operates on compressed acetylene (a colorless hydrocarbon) and oxygen.

achene In botanical terms, a small, dry, one-celled, one-seeded, **indehiscent** fruit. In technical terms, it does not include those fruits with specialized features such as a **samara, caryopsis, nut,** or **utricle.**

achlamydeous A flower without a **perianth** (outside envelope, **calyx, corolla**).

achromatic color White light; a color that does not elicit hue.

ACI Abbreviation for American Concrete Institute.

acicular In botanical terms, needle-shaped.

acid 1. In reference to soil, this indicates a pH below 7.0 (neutral). 2. A chemical substance capable of releasing excess protons (hydrogen ions).

acid copper chromate (ACC) A water-borne salt preservative for wood. Wood must be pressure treated for this preservative to be effective. It is highly recommended by experts as it is odorless, clean, does not leach, and its color can be masked easily when dry by painting or applying a solid color stain. This stain is not only good for preserving wood above grade, but can also be used for preservation of wood to be placed underground.

acid etched A reference to a metallic surface, glass, or concrete that has been treated in an acid bath to provide a rough surface or to remove a portion of its surface.

acidic 1. Soil or water with a **pH** less than 7.0.

Some only consider acidic to be 6.6 or less. 2. Igneous rocks containing more than 65% silica.

acidity The measure of a substance's **pH** below neutral (7.0).

acid rain Any rain that contains sulfur dioxide.

acid soil **Soil** having an acid reaction. It is usually in reference to a soil having a **pH** value of less than 6.6, but is technically applicable to any value lower than 7.0, which is neutral. These soils are common in areas of high rainfall. The most common cure for highly acidic soils is the addition of lime.

acisculis An old term for a small mason's pick, with a flat face and pointed peen.

ACM Abbreviation for asbestos-containing material. Any material with over 1% asbestos content.

AC pipe Asbestos-cement pipe that was commonly used for buried pipelines. It combines strength with light weight and is immune to rust and corrosion. It is no longer made because of the health hazards associated with asbestos.

acquiescence 1. An act of concurrence by adjoining property owners that resolves a boundary dispute or establishes a common boundary, where the definite or more accurate position of same has not or cannot be defined by survey. 2. The tacit consent of one owner, by not making a formal objection, to what might be an encroachment by an adjoining property owner over a questionable boundary.

acre English or U.S. measurement of area equal to 4840 sq yd; 43,560 sq ft; 0.405 **hectare**; 4046.85 sq m.

acre-foot 1. A reference to a quantity of water required to cover one acre to a depth of one foot.

2. A quantity of any material equal to the amount required to cover an acre one foot deep.

acrid Sharply bitter, unpleasantly pungent, or harsh in smell or taste.

acropodium **1.** A raised pedestal bearing a statue. **2.** The lowest member of a pedestal of a statue.

acrylonitrile butadiene styrene (ABS) A plastic formulated into piping that is used primarily in landscape work for drainage systems, storm sewers, irrigation systems, and underground electrical conduits. It is softer and much more bendable than **PVC**.

ACS Abbreviation for actual.

AC soil An immature, incomplete soil profile with only the **A** and **C horizon**s present, and no **B horizon**. These young soils commonly develop from alluvium or on slopes.

actinomycetes A group of soil microorganisms intermediate between fungi and bacteria. They may be filamentous much like fungi, and yet produce spores similar to bacteria. They are microscopic in size and are usually the source of the fresh, uniquely pleasant odor of newly tilled soil. They are active in decomposition, especially of cellulose.

activated sludge **1.** A recycled, dried product of municipal sewage treatment plants. It has higher concentrations of nutrients than composted sludge with a rating of approximately 6-3-0.5 for **primary nutrient**s. It is usually sold in a dry, granular form as a general-purpose fertilizer that does not burn, and is slow to release its nutrients. The long-term effects of using sewage sludge are still under investigation. Heavy metals such as cadmium may be present in the soil where sewage sludge has been used, and they may build up over time. There are possible negative effects depending on the content and origin of the sludge used. **2.** Sewage within aerated wastewater treatment basins and its associated complex variety of living microorganisms. After settling, a portion of this microbial sludge is recycled to influent of the treatment system. Microbes there continue to grow. The remaining activated sludge is removed from the treatment system and disposed of another way.

active earth pressure The horizontal pressure of retained earth in a horizontal direction.

active layer The surface layer in climates where permafrost exists. It is characterized by freezing and thawing.

active open space Land designated or reserved for recreational facilities such as swimming pools, ball fields, court games, picnic tables, exercise courses, playgrounds, ice skating, etc.

active pressure The force exerted by retained earth.

active recreation Athletic activities, or those activities of leisure requiring physical effort and often requiring equipment. This type of activity usually takes place at prescribed places, sites, or fields. It includes such activities as swimming, tennis, other court games, baseball, other field sports, golf, playground activities, jogging, rowing, etc. *See also* passive recreation.

active sludge A sludge that is rich in destructive bacteria; useful in breaking down fresh sewage.

active solar energy system A system that collects solar energy and distributes that energy by mechanical devices such as fans or pumps that obtain their energy from a conventional source (not from solar energy).

Act of God

Act of God   An unexpected event not controllable by human influence.

actual   This word is often used in specifying weight amounts of a specific nutrient in a fertilizer to be applied. This can be determined by taking the percentage of the specific nutrient in the fertilizer mix and multiplying it by the weight of the fertilizer being used.

actual start of construction   The first placement of a permanent construction fixture on site.

aculeate   In botanical terms, prickly or beset with prickles.

acuminate   In botanical terms, sharply tapering to a slender point. (Compare with **retuse, cuspidate, aristate, emarginate, acute, mucronate, obtuse**.)

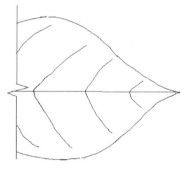

acuminate leaf tip

acute   In botanical terms, pointed, or ending in a point less than a right angle. (Compare with **retuse, cuspidate, aristate, acuminate, emarginate, mucronate, obtuse**.)

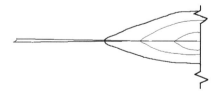

acute leaf base

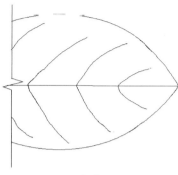

acute leaf tip

acute angle   Any angle measuring less than 90°.

acute arch *or* **lancet arch**   A sharply pointed arch whose centers are farther apart than the width of the arch.

AD, ad   **1.** Abbreviation for air dried. **2.** Abbreviation for **access door**. **3.** Abbreviation for **area drain**. **4.** Abbreviation for as drawn. **5.** A designation of the surface grades of two sides of a piece of lumber, especially plywood. **6.** A Latin prefix used in botanical terms meaning to or toward.

ADA   Abbreviation for **Americans with Disabilities Act**.

adapt   To make suitable for a particular purpose, requirement, or condition, by means of modifications or changes.

adapter   **1.** A fitting or part that facilitates different types (copper, **PVC, polyethylene, galvanized**) or sizes of pipe to be connected together. **2.** A device manufactured for the purpose of connecting tubing or equipment (especially electric) that is of different size, connection type, or design.

adaptive use   The extensive alteration, restoration, and/or renovation of an existing structure or building so that it will serve a new purpose.

ADD, add   **1.** Abbreviation for **addendum**. **2.** Abbreviation for **addition**.

addendum   A change or revision to drawings, specifications, or other information on a project out for bid, which has an effect on bids. It occurs before receipt of bids, and is usually stated in letter form that ethically should be delivered to all bidders (in fairness) with the drawings or papers indicating the change so as to allow understanding in comparison of bids. These changes become a part of construction documents for contract purposes.

addition   **1.** Construction that increases the height or floor area of an existing building or adds such items as a porch or attached garage. **2.** The increase to an existing contract amount. The professional procedure for accommodating such a change is a **change order**.

additive   A substance added to another substance to improve its characteristics such as those used in paints, plasters, mortars, etc. *See also* **admixture**.

additive alternate   An option on a bid for more services or materials not in the **base bid**, showing increased costs, if any, associated with the option.

ADF   Abbreviation with reference to shipping lumber meaning after deducting freight.

ADH, adh   Abbreviation for **adhesive**.

adhesion   The physical attraction of unlike substances to one another. This is the force that holds water molecules in soil-to-water interfaces so that all water does not drain from soil after saturation. This water is held in **mesopores** and **micropores**, but there is not enough adhesion force to hold water in the larger **macropores**.

adhesive   A substance that bonds to materials placed together, holding them in place.

Adj., adj   Abbreviation for adjustable.

adjoining grade elevation   The average elevation of the **finish grade** adjoining all exterior walls of a building or structure calculated from grade elevations taken at intervals (usually 10 ft or 3 m) around the perimeter of the building.

adjustable hanger   An apparatus for holding pipes or equipment hung from structures, which has the ability to change the elevation of the pipe or device held without detachment of the apparatus from the structure.

adjustable wrench   A wrench with an adjustable portion of its jaw movable by a knurled screw to facilitate grasping objects of varying sizes (e.g., **pipe wrench**, crescent wrench).

adjusted sodium adsorption ratio   An index of permeability problems with regard to water quality.

admixture   A material or chemical added to a concrete mix to accelerate cure, retard curing, repel water, or change its normal properties.

adobe   **1.** Clay used in making adobe brick. **2.** Any unfired brick.

adobe brick   Clay and straw molded into bricks, sun-dried and used in constructing structures. Adobe brick walls can be coated with lime to improve weather resistance.

adpressed   In botanical terms, pressed against another part.

ADR   Abbreviation for **alternative dispute resolution**.

adsorption   Liquids, gases, or suspended matter adhering to the surfaces of, or in the pores of, an adsorbent material (without a chemical reaction or bonding).

ADT   Abbreviation for **average daily traffic**.

advanced irrigation control system A **smart controller** that controls irrigation by monitoring the weather and/or the soil moisture. They adjust **station** run time(s) and/or the frequency when there are changes detected in the soil moisture and/or the weather. Some will monitor wind, rain, and/or temperature. Another feature of some of these controllers is that they can monitor flow in pipes to determine if there is a break in the line. The features of these controllers are not all the same, but they include some method of automatically adjusting their schedules through the seasons of the year in an attempt to keep the optimum amount of moisture in the soil. These controllers are quite helpful in preventing waste of irrigation water, but their accuracy and usefulness is only as good as their monitoring devices and monitoring locations.

advanced wastewater treatment (AWT) Treatment of wastewater more than the secondary treatment level.

advance ratio In furrow irrigation, a ratio of the time for the water to reach the end of the field to the total set time for irrigation.

advance time **1.** The time required for a selected stream of irrigation water to move from the upper end of a field to the lower end. **2.** The time required for a selected surface irrigation stream to move from one point in the field to another.

adventitious In botanical terms, developing in an unusual or irregular position, usually in reference to roots.

adventitious roots Roots growing from the stems of plants, usually sporadically. They may be a natural component of the plant, such as with *Hedera helix* (English ivy), which attaches itself to walls, plants, cliffs, etc. with these small rootlets. They are also sometimes developed in response to flooding. Flooding may cause these roots to develop on stems when belowground roots are in **anaerobic** soils.

adventive A plant type that has been introduced to an area, but not **naturalized**, or a plant that is only locally established.

adverse impact *See* **negative environmental impact**.

advertisement for bids A request made for **bids** for public entities. There is usually a legal requirement that this must be a public solicitation with notices easily available to the public (usually in newspapers) in the area of jurisdiction.

A/E Abbreviation for **architect-engineer**.

aerate Mixing air into soil, water, or other substances as a natural process or designed effort.

aerated concrete *See* **cellular concrete**.

aeration **1.** Infiltration or mixing of air with a substance. **2.** In landscaping, it usually refers to a portion of the **micropores**, **mesopores**, and **macropores** in soil being filled with air. The surface soils (to about 3 ft deep) usually have sufficient aeration for plant growth. **3.** In landscape maintenance, it refers to loosening the soil to add air by puncturing it with mechanical means. Some gas-powered aeration machines remove a small round core of soil. This practice not only provides air to roots, but also allows for better percolation of water to roots. This generally improves plant growth. **4.** In water treatment and cleaning, providing higher oxygen concentrations for chemical and microbial treatment processes.

aeration capacity The volume fraction of air-filled pores in a particular soil at field capacity.

aerial cable Any cable (especially electric) suspended overhead.

aerial photograph *or* **aerophoto** A photograph taken directly above the earth's surface.

aerial photomap An aerial photograph or **aerial photomosaic** map with information such as place names, boundaries, and so on.

aerial photomosaic A combination of aerial photographs fit together, showing a portion of the earth's surface.

aerobic Indicates the presence of oxygen and/or organisms living or active in the presence of oxygen.

aerophoto An **aerial photograph**.

aesthetic **1.** The visual appearance or look of an object, view, etc. **2.** The theory of beauty or sense of color.

aestival Appearing or blooming in summer; pertaining to summer.

A-frame A structural frame shaped like an upright capital letter A.

AG **1.** Abbreviation for above grade. **2.** Abbreviation for against the grain.

agaric In botanical terms, a mushroom or having a form like one.

AGC Abbreviation for Associated General Contractors.

agency **1.** A relationship by which one party, usually the **agent**, is empowered to enter into binding transactions affecting the legal rights of another party, usually called the **principal**. For example, an agent may enter into a contract or buy or sell property in another's name or on another's behalf. **2.** An administrative branch of government (federal, state, or local).

agent One who is empowered or authorized to enter into binding legal transactions on behalf of another, for a principal, or for an entity.

Agg. Abbreviation for aggregate.

agglomeration Collecting tiny suspended particles into a mass of larger size.

AGGR Abbreviation for **aggregate**.

aggradation **1.** The addition of a material to the ground surface to produce a uniform grade or slope. **2.** The filling of a stream channel with sediment. This may occur because of low or slow flows, and/or heavy sediment loads in the water.

aggregate **1.** In soils, a group of primary soil particles that cohere to one another more strongly than to other surrounding soil particles. **2.** Any of several hard, inert materials such as sand, gravel, or slag. **3.** Inert materials (2) individually or a mixture of them placed for weight-bearing stability of pavements, walls, footings, etc. **4.** A loose mixture of sand and crushed stone used to mix with **cement** to create a concrete.

aggregate base course A layer of **aggregate** material placed beneath a pavement, structure, etc., for bearing and stability.

aggregate fruit A fruit formed of two or more pistils, such as a raspberry.

aggregate strength The strength of an object determined by adding together the breaking strengths of the individual members of which the object is made up (i.e., individual strand members of a wire cable).

aggregation In soils, groups of individual soil particles, held together naturally and consisting of particles of sand, silt, and clay separated from each other by pores, cracks, or planes of weakness.

aggressive solids Soils that may be corrosive to cast-iron and ductile-iron pipe.

agitating truck A truck carrying a drum that mixes **hydromulch**, concrete, etc., capable of being mixed while moving.

agitation The process of mixing mulches, seed, liquids, and/or concrete. In mixing concrete, it must be agitated sufficient to prevent segregation, aggregation, or loss of plasticity.

agitator   **1.** A mechanical device used to mix various liquids and powders contained in a vessel. **2.** A device for mixing and maintaining plasticity while preventing segregation of the components of concrete.

AGL   Abbreviation for above ground level.

agricultural district *or* **agricultural preserves** *or* **agricultural security areas** *or* **agricultural preservation districts** *or* **agricultural areas** *or* **agricultural incentive areas** *or* **agricultural development areas** *or* **agricultural protection areas**   A legally recognized geographic area designed to preserve agriculture with a boundary formed by one or more landowners (including government landowners) and approved by at least one government agency. They are usually created for fixed, renewable terms. Enrollment is voluntary; landowners receive a variety of benefits including eligibility for reduced tax assessment, limits to annexation and eminent domain, as well as protection against excessive government regulation and private nuisance lawsuits.

agricultural protection zoning (APZ)   Any local land-use regulation protecting agricultural operations and/or their closely associated uses (e.g., limiting non-farmland uses, prohibiting high-density land development, requiring houses to be built on small lots, restricting subdivision of land into parcels that are too small to farm, etc.).

Agriculture Conservation Easement   A legal agreement usually recorded at the county (U.S.) restricting development on farmland. Easement is restricted to farming and open space use. (*See also* **conservation easement**.)

agronomic   The application of soil and plant science to crop production and soil management.

A horizon   The upper, darker **soil** layer (horizon) in a **soil profile**, comprised of materials that include **organic matter**, and characterized by high biotic activity. This is **topsoil**, which is the best soil for sustaining plant growth without the aid of **fertilizer**s. It is ideal for growing plants when comprised of approximately 45% mineral material, 5% organic matter, 25% water, and 25% air. In some soil profiles, this topsoil layer may be well developed and further divided into **subhorizon**s of **A1**, **A2**, **A3**, etc., or it may not be present (deserts, above timberline, etc.). The only layer that may be present above this layer is the **O horizon**.

AIA   Abbreviation for the **American Institute of Architects**.

AICP   Abbreviation for American Institute of Certified Planners.

air break   In a drainage system, a piping arrangement in which a drain from an appliance, device, ground surface area, or fixture discharges into the open air and then into another fixture, receptacle, or interceptor. This is used to prevent **back siphonage** or **backflow**.

air compressor   A machine that compresses air, creating higher pressures than the atmosphere and usually storing it in a tank for use. This pressure may be used to inflate objects, blow water out of pipes, operate pneumatic tools, etc.

air-dried lumber   Wood cut to particular dimensions and air-dried in stacks to remove moisture. This drying produces a straighter product of true size, better at holding nails, and not likely to shrink, split, or warp. Lumber is usually marked as follows: S-GRN for green unseasoned lumber with a moisture content of 20% or higher; S-DRY for lumber with a moisture content of 19% or less; MC 15 for lumber that is dried to 15% or less, etc.

air drill   *See* **pneumatic drill**.

air-entrained concrete   Concrete mixed with air-entraining **cement** or agents to improve its workability and resistance to frost. It incorporates minute air bubbles into the mix.

air-entraining agent   Any substance or material added to concrete, mortar, grout, etc. that produces air bubbles during the mixing process. These agents make the mixture easier to work and increase resistance to freezing.

air gap   In a drainage system, the vertical space between the outlet of a drainpipe and the high water elevation of the container into which it flows.

air lance   A rod-shaped device that shoots compressed air for cleaning surfaces.

air layering   In gardening, a **propagation** method of forcing a branch to root by making a slanting cut or removing a ring of bark below a node, dusting with rooting hormone, wrapping the cut and node in moss, and enclosing in plastic tied tightly to the branch. Roots appear in several months, then the branch can be cut free with its roots and transplanted.

air-lift pump   A pump used for raising water from a well that is comprised of a compressed air delivery pipe surrounded by a larger pipe that delivers water from below because of pressure from the smaller pipe.

air purge valve   A device that removes trapped air from pressurized pipes.

air release valve   A valve that releases air from a pipe or device under water pressure.

air vessel   An enclosed chamber with a volume of air connected to a water system in which air is compressed to varying degrees as water pressures fluctuate. This assures a more uniform flow. It also deters water hammer by air compression when water shutoff occurs abruptly.

AISC   Abbreviation for American Institute of Steel Construction.

AISI   Abbreviation for American Iron and Steel Institute.

AITC   Abbreviation for American Institute of Timber Construction.

AL   Abbreviation for aluminum.

alameda   A shaded walkway or promenade.

albedo   The reflective power of a material indicated by the percentage of incident radiation reflected by a material. In landscape work, this is usually important to consider with regard to light and heat reflected and/or radiated from large windows or light-colored surfaces on the sunny side of walls or fences. It may cause damage to landscape plants (including lawns).

alburnum   The wood of a tree between its heartwood outer ring and the bark (sapwood).

ALCA   Abbreviation for **Associated Landscape Contractors of America**.

alder   A hardwood from alder trees having a light color that darkens a bit toward brown as it dries, and is comparatively lightweight.

alfalfa valve   An outlet valve attached to the top of a pipeline riser with an opening equal in diameter to the inside diameter of the riser pipe. Includes an adjustable cover to control water flow.

algae   A group of microscopic **autotrophic** plants that are unicellular or multicellular, do not flower, lack true stems or roots, and grow in water or humid conditions.

algae bloom   In water features, the rapid growth of algae instigated by an increase in temperature and the presence of nutrients.

algicide   A product used for controlling algae in water.

alidade An instrument on a table useful for determining the directions of distant points. It was often used in mapmaking before the use of **GIS**.

alien A reference sometimes made to a plant that is native in one region but is then planted in another region by human activity instead of natural means.

alienation Transfer of title by one person to another in real estate.

alignment In highway and other linear ground designs, this is a drawing plan depicting horizontal direction as distinguished from a profile drawing that depicts the vertical components.

alkaline **1.** Composed of a base. **2.** Soil or water with a **pH** higher than **7.0** (neutral).

alkaline soils **1.** Soils having a **pH** greater than 7.0 (neutral). These soils are common in areas of light annual rainfall. **2.** Soils having an exchangeable sodium percentage greater than 15%. **3.** Soils having a sufficient exchangeable sodium (alkali) to interfere with plant growth and cause dispersion or swelling of clay materials within the soil.

alkalinity The amount of a substance's **pH** above neutral (7.0). In water, it is a measure of the capacity of water to neutralize acids. It accomplishes this through one or more bases in the water. Those bases can be one or more of carbonates, bicarbonates, hydroxides, borates, silicates, or phosphates.

alkali soils Soils with an excess of sodium often having a **pH** of over 8.5 and not suitable for the growth of most plants. The common remedy used to prepare alkali soils for planting is to apply gypsum and leach the soil heavily with water.

All-American Rose Selections A nonprofit association of rose growers and introducers dedicated to introducing new rose types and promoting existing exceptional rose types. Since 1938, the AARS seal of approval has annually been awarded to outstanding new rose varieties.

All-American Selection (AAS) Plants recommended (and awarded) annually by an organization as tested, new, previously unsold varieties of flowers and vegetables, giving recognition to those considered outstanding. They have growing facilities in the United States, Mexico, New Zealand, and Canada. Categories include field-grown flowers, vegetables, and bedding plants. The first varieties were chosen in 1932. The candidates are grown and tested at trial gardens located at seed companies, universities, and botanical gardens. There are two types of medals awarded. The gold medal signifies exceptional merit and is seldom awarded. The normal award is given to plants with outstanding characteristics. Because these plants are judged by a panel of experts, credibility is also awarded to the winners.

allée of trees

allée A wide walk, drive, etc., with trees or tall shrubs on either side. This is a French term used for referencing a walk of gravel, sand, or turf, bordered by **palisades**, hedges or trees usually with branches trained to meet and interweave overhead, shading the surface below (*allee cou-*

verte). The French sometimes used them in geometrically designed gardens or parks. (Compare to **avenue**.)

allelopathy   A condition in which a plant produces antibiotic chemicals that repress its growth or the growth of other plants.

Allen wrench   A hexagonal bent bar used to tighten and loosen screws or bolts that have a hexagonal indentation for insertion.

Allen wrench

all-heart lumber   Lumber that is completely heartwood with no sapwood.

alliaceous   A plant onion-like in odor or other aspects.

allochthonous   Substances (usually organic carbon) produced outside of and flowing into a wetland from the surrounding environment.

allopatric   **1.** A botanical term to describe plants occupying different geographical regions. **2.** In botanical terms, occupying well-separated habitats in the same region. (Compare with **sympatric**.)

allotment garden   A privately or publicly owned garden divided into sections and assigned to individuals for their use.

allowable depletion *or* **allowable soil depletion**   **1.** The portion of plant-available water that is given for plant use prior to irrigation based on plant and management considerations. **2.** The amount of water depleted from the soil between irrigation cycles, including that which is lost to drainage and percolation. **3.** That part of soil moisture stored in the plant root zone managed for use by plants. This is usually expressed as an equivalent depth of water in inches per acre, or inches. **4.** Allowable soil depletion or allowable soil water depletion before wilting point occurs.

allowable load   The maximum weight safely budgeted for a structural member spanning between two points.

allowable stress factor (K_{as})   The percentage of **evapotranspiration** in the landscape that can still produce an acceptable plant quality. In some cases, applications as low as 40% of evapotranspiration have allowed a marginal but acceptable plant quality. This is a management decision, and the effects of these adjustments must be closely monitored.

alloy   A combination of two or more metals, or of a nonmetallic substance with metal, usually for some improved quality.

alluvial fan   Sediment deposited by a stream in a fan shape (when viewed from the air), usually at the bottom of a slope. This is a common land feature in dry regions at the base of slopes where streams slow, allowing their sediment to settle and deposit.

alluvium   **1.** Any material deposited out of water that has been carried from another place. **2.** The soils of floodplains and alluvial fans comprised mostly of **detrital** material.

alpine   **1.** Growing on slopes above timberline. **2.** A term loosely used in reference to rock garden plants. **3.** A plant native to alpine or **boreal forest** regions. They are often referenced and used in ornamental plantings.

ALS   Abbreviation for American Lumber Standards.

ALT, alt.

ALT, alt. 1. Abbreviation for alternate. 2. Abbreviation for altitude.

alternate In botanical terms, any plant parts (leaves, buds, branches, etc.) arranged singly at the stem nodes (not on opposite sides). They alternate which side of the branch they emerge from.

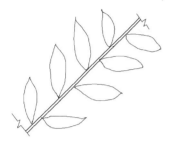

alternate leaf arrangement

alternate bid An optional bid to the base bid that deducts or adds services or materials and usually increases or decreases the **base bid** accordingly.

alternate host Either of two plants that a fungus or insect finds necessary to sustain its life. Some insects or diseases must alternate from one plant type to another in their life cycle. These diseases and insects can be eliminated if a large enough area does not have one of the necessary host plants. For example, the wooly apple **aphid**, which depends on both elms and apple trees; some rust diseases that are dependent on barberry and wheat; or rust diseases dependent on juniper and white pine.

alternating current Electrical current regularly alternating its direction of flow (at a fixed rate) in opposite directions. Power companies use this current to facilitate transmission over long distances.

alternative dispute resolution The resolution of a dispute without litigation.

ALTN Abbreviation for alteration.

alum. Abbreviation for aluminum.

aluminum 1. A silver-white, malleable, metallic element with good thermal and electrical conductivity, resistance to oxidation, and high reflectivity when polished. 2. A metal pres-ent in most soils, but more prevalent in acid soils. It becomes more soluble, more available, and more likely to cause toxicity to plants as soil acidity increases. In strongly acidic soils (5.5 pH or below), this is often a detriment to plant growth and can be toxic to them.

aluminum brass Brass with some aluminum added to increase its corrosion resistance.

aluminum bronze A copper-aluminum alloy having good corrosion resistance.

aluminum plate Flat aluminum sheet material.

aluminum-silicon bronze A copper alloy with aluminum and silicon added to increase strength and hardness.

aluminum sulfate An **inorganic fertilizer** that is **acidic** and lowers **pH**. Aluminum can be toxic to plants if overused.

ALY Abbreviation for alloy.

ambient pressure *See* **working pressure**.

ambient sound The noise level in a space that contains only the noise out of one's control such as rushing water, or street traffic, or motors, etc. It is any combination of sounds from external sources close by or far away.

amendment *See* **soil amendment**.

amenity Aesthetic characteristics or other features of land development that increase its desirability or its marketability. Amenities may include such things as a unified building design, recreational facilities, security systems, views, landscaping, attractive site design, adjacent open space or water bodies.

ament In botanical terms, an indeterminate spike-like (**spicate**) arrangement of flowers on a stem (**inflorescence**) having scaly bracts and unisexual flowers with no petals (**apetalous**).

amentiferous Descriptive of a plant bearing aments.

American Arbitration Association A non-profit association founded in 1926 to study benefits and techniques of arbitration; offers neutral arbitrators.

American Association of Nurserymen A trade organization that has now changed its name to the **American Nursery and Landscape Association**.

American Institute of Architects (AIA) A professional organization of architects.

American National Standards Institute (ANSI) Previously known as the American Standards Association. This is an organization of nearly 400 trade associations, technical societies, professional groups, and consumer organizations that establishes standards for materials and devices.

American Nursery and Landscape Association A trade organization providing education, research, and public relations for its members who grow and sell plants or install landscapes. Their web site is www.anla.org (previously known as AAN, American Association of Nurserymen).

American Society for Testing and Materials (ASTM) An organization that performs tests and establishes standard specifications for materials; their standards are usually referred to as ASTM.

American Society of Consulting Arborists An organization with members dedicated to the protection of the **environment** by promoting

tree and plant life for safety, functionality, and beauty.

American Society of Landscape Architects (ASLA) A national (U.S.) professional organization of **landscape architects** promoting the analysis, design, management, and stewardship of the natural and built environments through education, advocacy, communication, and fellowship. Their web site is www.asla.org.

Americans with Disabilities Act (ADA) A federal law requiring public facilities to be accessible for those with physical disabilities. (*See also* **Uniform Federal Accessibility Standards**.)

ammeter An instrument that measures electric current in **amperes**.

ammoniacal copper arsenate (ACA) A waterborne salt preservative for wood. Wood must be pressure treated for this preservative to be effective. It is highly recommended by experts as it is odorless, clean, does not leach, and its color can be masked easily when dry by painting or applying a solid color stain. Besides being good for preserving wood in weather aboveground, this stain can be used for wood placed in water and underground.

ammonia nitrogen A reduced type of nitrogen made as a by-product of organic matter decomposing and synthesizing.

ammoniated superphosphate A compound **chemical fertilizer** containing 2 to 4% **nitrogen**, and 14 to 49% available phosphoric acid (**phosphorus**).

ammonification Bacterial decomposition from organic nitrogen to ammonia.

ammonium nitrate A nitrogen fertilizer with 15% nitrogen (15-0-0). Also known as nitrate of ammonia. It has 32.5 to 34% immediately avail-

ammonium sulfate

able **nitrogen.** It must have ventilation or it can catch fire or explode. It cakes easily in storage.

ammonium sulfate   A **nitrogen** fertilizer with 21% nitrogen (21-0-0). *See* **sulfate of ammonia**.

amp.   Abbreviation for ampere.

ampacity   A word combining **ampere** and capacity that expresses the current-carrying capacity of electrical conductors in amperes.

amperage   Electric current expressed in amperes.

ampere, amp   The standard unit for measuring electrical current that is based on the number of electrons flowing past a given point per second. One volt acting across a resistance of one ohm provides a current flow of one ampere. Many devices and components of wiring systems are rated for the amount of amperes they can safely carry.

amphibious   Plants able to live in water or on land.

amphitheater, amphitheatre   An outdoor theater, usually semicircular or elliptical, with a stage or area for performances surrounded by seats that rise above the area allowing participants a view of the action, speaker, or displays.

amplexicaul   A botanical term referring to some kinds of leaves clasping a stem at their base.

ampliate   A botanical term meaning enlarged or dilated.

an-   Greek prefix in botanical terms meaning not, from, or without.

anaerobic   **1.** Any environment low in oxygen or free of it. **2.** Living or existing without air. **3.** In landscape work, this usually refers to soils that are waterlogged or need **aeration** to support most plants. **Root rot** is a common problem in anaerobic soils. *See also* **backfill**.

analysis   Separation, examination, investigation, and determination of constituent parts, including detailed aspects of a situation, condition, or phenomenon.

anastomosing vein   The veins in a leaf forming a complex network. *See also* **dichotomous vein, simple vein**.

anchor   Something that holds a member or element securely in place.

anchor bolt   Usually an L-shaped bolt set in concrete or masonry with its threaded end exposed and pointing upward for fastening materials, structures, or equipment.

anchoring cement   Grout placed in sleeves to anchor pipes or tubing in place within them.

anchor roots   The roots of plants that give stability to the plant so that it can stand upright and withstand wind.

androecium   A botanical term referring to all of the stamens of a flower, considered collectively.

anemometer   A device for measuring wind speed. These instruments and the information they produce assist in determining water needs of plant material. They usually consist of cuplike devices held on arms arranged radially around a point where they spin in the wind, allowing recording of speed through a wire.

anemophilous   A botanical term describing pollination by wind. (Compare with **entomophilous, ornithophilous**.)

angiosperm   The name of the **division** in the **plant classification** system indicating inclusion of all flowering plants with seeds that develop in an ovary. They are the most prolific vascular plants on earth. This division is made up of two classes: **monocotyledons** and **dicotyledons**. *See also* **taxon**.

angle dozer   A **bulldozer** with its blade angled to push the earth to one side.

angle iron   An L-shaped iron or steel piece.

angle of repose   The maximum slope at which a material can be piled or inclined without sliding or falling. This term is often used in reference to **clay** materials, piled **soil**, **gravel**, or wet **concrete**.

angle valve   A valve for adjusting, turning on, or turning off a flow. This type of valve is configured with its water outlet oriented 90° from its water inlet. It delivers water on a 90° angle from the direction of water entering it.

angular aggregate   Aggregate with more sharp edges than rounded edges. It is often produced by crushing.

anhydrate   A mineral calcium sulfate useful in Portland cement manufacturing to allow for controlling its set time.

anion   A negatively charged ion that is attracted toward the anode during electrolysis. The most common anions in soils and waters are bicarbonate, sulfate, carbonate, nitrate, and chloride ions.

ANLA   Abbreviation for the **American Nursery and Landscape Association**.

annexation   The legally binding or recognized inclusion of land into an existing community, city, township, etc., that results in a change in its boundary. Annexation generally refers to the new inclusion of properties just outside a city, town, municipality, etc., but it may also involve the transfer of land from one municipality to another.

annual   **1.** A plant with a life cycle of one year or less. These plants flower, set seed, and die within one growing season. A winter annual germinates in the fall and fruits the following spring or summer. **2.** Yearly or over a 12-month period.

annual rings   A woody (**dicotyledenous**) plant's annual circular growth marks of the **xylem** visible when branches or trunks are cut horizontally (to their longitudinal axis). This is a portion of wood formed in one year of a woody plant's growth. The rings are concentric and become wider and lighter colored with good moisture and sun, and darker and thinner otherwise.

annular nail   A **nail** with tapered rings along its shank, difficult to be removed from a material in which it is pounded. Also called a **ring nail**.

annulus   In plant identification, this means a little ring, and refers to the specialized, thick-walled cells encircling the sporangium of most ferns.

anod.   Abbreviation for anodized.

anodize   A hard, noncorrosive, electrolytic, oxide film on the surface of a metal.

anodized   A metal that has been submitted to electrolytic forces in forming a coat of protective or decorative film.

anoxic   The absence of oxygen (both free oxygen and chemically bound oxygen).

ANSI   Abbreviation for American National Standards Institute.

anther   The part of the **stamen** of a flower that produces pollen and consists of two pollen sacs with a connecting layer.

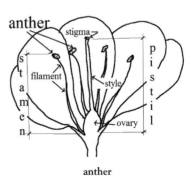

anther

anthesis The period during which a flower is fully expanded and functional.

anthocyanin A glycoside pigment producing blue or red colors in flowers, leaves, or plant parts.

anthracnose A plant disease caused by fungi that exhibit lesions of gray, tan, or dark brown on leaves, stem, fruit, or other parts of the plant. It is most common on ash, maple, elm, oak, sycamore, berry bushes, and many vegetable garden plants. On casual observance, this disease can be mistaken for leaf scorch. However, leaf scorch, also known as hot weather scorch, browns the edges of leaves first, and does not usually cause spotting or interior leaf damage. Wet or damp conditions promote this disease. It is treated by **fungicide** and/or pruning the affected portions of plants and destroying them (preferably by burning).

anthropomorphic **1.** In ecology, connoting human influence. **2.** In design, ascribing human characteristics to nonhuman things.

antidesiccant *or* **antititranspirant** A material sprayed onto plants to prevent excessive water loss from **trunks, foliage, branches, stems,** etc. It is sometimes sprayed onto plants before **transplant**ing to reduce moisture loss through **transpiration**. It can also be helpful during winter when evergreens have their roots frozen (prevents gathering water) or when root-pruning plants.

antislip paint A paint facilitating high friction for foot traffic, assisting in preventing slipping when dry. It has sand, dust, wood, or other material mixed in it.

antimicrobial A substance that kills microbial growth.

anti-siphon valve A device preventing removal or backflow of water or fluids.

ants Insects usually one half inch long or less with six legs and three distinct body portions. Their bite can be painful; they disturb seeded areas; they spread bacteria and spores; and they disfigure lawns or pavements with residue. Control is by spray, bait, or dust.

APA Abbreviation for American Plywood Association.

apetalous In botanical terms, a **flower** without **petal**s.

apex **1.** In botanical terms, this means tip; uppermost portion; narrowed; pointed; culminating point. **2.** The highest point, peak, or tip of any structure.

aphid An insect the size of a pinhead to about one-eighth inch. They are oval, soft, and can be red, green, gray, pink, or black. As they suck on plants, they secrete honeydew, sticky substance that attracts ants and can encourage **sooty mold**.

aphyllous A botanical term meaning without leaves, or not having normal leaves with blades.

apical In botanical terms, at the apex or summit of an organ.

apical dominance The suppression of side shoot growth by the terminal bud.

apiculate In botanical terms, tipped with a short and abrupt point.

apocarpous A term describing the **carpel**s of a flower being free from each other. (Compare with **syncarpous**.)

apophysis A botanical term referring to the expanded end portion of a cone scale of *Pinus* that is exposed when the cone is closed.

APPD Abbreviation for approved.

apple scab This is the most common disease of crabapples and apples. It is caused by the fungus *Venturia inaequalis*, which grows in cool, moist weather. Spores are carried by the wind in spring. It damages leaves, twigs, and fruit, and can cause fruit and leaves to drop early. To avoid this disease, plant resistant varieties, prune trees to improve airflow for drying after rain, and remove or discard fallen leaves on fruit.

application for payment An application or form prepared by a contractor for payment of work completed.

application rate In irrigation, the rate at which water is applied to a landscape, or the amount of water applied to a given area in one hour. *See also* **precipitation rate**.

appraisal A reasonable analysis determining the reasonable value. This is often a requirement on property when sold and is greatly affected by landscape architectural works in place.

appressed In botanical terms, lying close and flat against some other plant part.

approach grafting *See* inarching.

approved equal Materials, equipment, or methods approved for use in construction as an acceptable equivalent in essential attributes to that which was specified.

approving authority The agency, association, commission, department, or other organization created by law and authorized by the state, county, city, province, township, homeowners, etc. to administer and enforce design and construction requirements.

approx. Abbreviation for approximate.

APZ Abbreviation for **agricultural protection zone**.

aquaculture The hatching, raising, breeding, and harvesting of fish, or aquatic plants or animals in a natural or artificial aquatic environment that requires a body of water such as a pond, river, lake, estuary, ocean, or man-made water body.

aquatic Referring to watery environments. In hydrologic gradient, the aquatic environment begins at emergent wetlands. These environments are characterized by the growth of floating or submerged plants.

aquatic plant A plant that can grow in water whether floating or in saturated soil conditions.

aqueous Relating to water.

aquifer An underground bed or layer that is a water-bearing formation of permeable material capable of yielding groundwater to provide water to springs, wells, etc.

aquifer recharge area An area in which a significant amount of surface water runs into groundwater by: **1.** The infiltration into the soil or other rock materials that are directly below the surface: **2.** The downward movement of water through the materials that comprise the zone of aeration: **3.** The delivery of water into the zone of saturation where it becomes groundwater.

arable A term used to describe land that is capable of growing crops. It is tillable, with nutrients and sufficient other qualities to be suitable for agricultural efforts.

arbitration An effort for dispute resolution in which the involved parties agree to allow a neutral person to hear evidence from both sides and make a final and binding decision. This is nearly always a less costly and faster way to resolve a dipute than through the court systems.

arbor A cover over a walk, gate, patio, or passageway for pedestrians, or a shelter over a significant feature in a landscape made up of vines, branches, or climbing shrubs on latticework, **trellises**, or wire frames.

arborescent

arbor

arborescent In botanical terms, treelike in size or form, or becoming a tree.

arboretum An ornamental or functional garden for displaying trees, shrubs, and/or herbaceous plants for functional or educational purposes.

arboriculture The cultivation of trees and shrubs, usually for ornamental purposes.

arborist A person skilled and trained in the care and maintenance of trees.

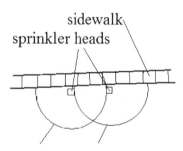

arc of radius of spray

arc **1.** In sprinkler irrigation, how far around in a circular pattern (usually expressed in degrees where 360° is a full circle) a sprinkler will rotate or spray. For example, a sprinkler with a 90° arc would spray a quarter-circle pattern. **2.** Something arched or curved. **3.** A continuous portion of a curved line.

arcade A covered walk with shops, arches, etc. on each side.

arch An overhead curved portion of a structure spanning an opening between two points of the structure.

arch

arch culvert An upwardly curved opening under a road, path, canal, or embankment usually constructed to allow passage of water, traffic, or pedestrians.

arching A term used in plant descriptions depicting a form that arches up and out. In grasses, this term refers to a grass that arches nearly as far to the side of its point of origin (at the ground) as it rises from its point of origin. (Compare with **mounded (2)**, **upright grasses**, **tufted**, **upright divergent grasses**, **upright arching grasses**.)

arching grass

architect **1.** A person trained in the design of buildings. **2.** A designation reserved by requiring licensure to perform architectural services.

architecture **1.** The art and science of designing structures. **2.** Structures.

architrave The lowest portion of classical architecture's entablature extending from column to column as a beam. *See* illustration under **entablature**.

arch ring In an arched structure, this is the curved portion carrying the load.

arcuate In plant identification and descriptions, a plant part curved into an arc of a circle.

ARC W Abbreviation for **arc weld**.

arc weld Melting metals together with an electric spark and molten metal from a metallic electrode.

area drain A receptacle or depression designed to collect runoff.

areole Specialized spot-like areas on a cactus stem. They have a rough, uneven, different color (from the rest of the surrounding area), a hard surface, and are usually covered with wooly hair. The spines and flowers of a cactus originate from these spots on the stem.

argenteous In plant identification and botanical descriptions, silvery in color.

argillaceous A botanical term describing something with the nature of clay.

arid climate A climate where precipitation averages less than 10 inches per year.

aril An outside appendage or covering that is formed by some seeds after fertilization as a growth from the ovule stalk.

arillate Pertaining to an **aril**.

aristate In botanical terms, having **awn**s, or being tipped with an awn or bristle, or being sharply pointed as in the tip of a leaf. (Compare with **retuse, cuspidate, emarginate, acuminate, acute, mucronate, obtuse**.)

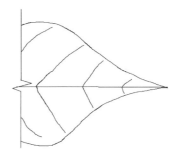

aristate leaf tip

armored cabling Electrical wires with a reinforced protective coating to protect the wires from destructive elements and keep safe those around the cable.

armyworms Larvae of caterpillars usually found in armies denuding plant material in their path. They are eaten by birds, toads, other insects, and skunks. Control with poison is available with bait across their path, sprays, or dusts.

arterial road A road having **collector roads** allowing traffic access and having more traffic than the collector roads.

artesian well **1.** A well made by boring into the ground to a point where an underground supply of water is reached with more pressure than needed to bring it to the surface. This creates a well that flows without the need of a pump. **2.** A deeply bored well.

article In construction specifications, the subdivision of a **section** that is usually then subdivided into paragraphs, subparagraphs, and clauses.

articulate, articulated In botanical terms, jointed.

artificial marble *See* **artificial stone**.

artificial soil mix Any mix for plants to grow in without soil as an ingredient.

artificial stone A mixture of rock portions bonded together.

artisan An individual skilled in an applied art; a craftsman.

AS Abbreviation for automatic sprinkler.

ASA Abbreviation for American Standards Association. *See* **American National Standards Institute**.

Asb. Abbreviation for asbestos.

ASBC Abbreviation for American Standard Building Code.

as-built A drawing(s) that shows the construction project as designed with any changes made during construction to give an accurate depiction of actual construction.

ASC Abbreviation for asphalt surface course.

ASCA Abbreviation for **American Society of Consulting Arborists**.

ASCE Abbreviation for American Society of Civil Engineers.

ascending A term often used to describe branches or other plant parts that angle upward from a plant's vertical trunk, stem, etc. (Compare with **spreading**.)

asepalous A botanical term describing a flower without **sepals**.

asexual In botanical terms, propagation without sex.

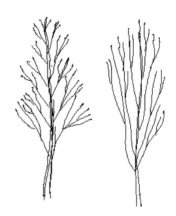

ascending branching

ash dump An opening in a fireplace through which ashes are swept into an ashpit.

ashes *See* **wood ashes**.

ashlar Stone produced for construction purposes having edges with more or less right angles, making it easier to stack. It comes in a variety of sizes.

ashlar brick *or* **rock-faced brick** A brick whose face has been beaten to resemble hewn stone.

ashpit A chamber below a fireplace for collecting and removing ashes.

ASI Abbreviation for Architects and Surveyors Institute.

ASLA Abbreviation for **American Society of Landscape Architects**.

aspect The direction in which a structure or slope faces with respect to the points of a compass.

aspect ratio In a rectangular configuration, an expression of the ratio of the long side to the short side of the rectangle.

asphalt **1.** A dark, cement-like material, solid or semisolid, made of bitumens that occur in nature or are refined in coal tar or petroleum production. **2.** A mixture of bituminous material with an aggregate for pavements.

asphaltic base course A layer of **asphaltic concrete** under various pavements, used for stability and spreading the load.

asphaltic cement, asphalt cement An asphalt for direct use in the manufacture of bituminous pavements.

asphaltic concrete *or* **asphalt paving** *or* **blacktop** A mixture of asphalt and aggregate used as paving material over a compacted base. It is usually placed and compacted while hot. For placement without heat, see **cold mix**.

asphalt joint filler An asphalt product for filling cracks and joints in pavements.

asphalt paper A paper material that has been coated, or impregnated, with asphalt to increase its resistance to wear and water.

asphalt pavement A pavement comprised of a surface mineral aggregate, coated and cemented together with asphalt cement on supporting asphalt layers.

asphalt pavement sealer A product applied to asphalt pavement to prevent deterioration.

asphalt prepared roofing A felt covered with asphalt and mineral material, available in rolls.

asphalt primer A material applied to waterproof surfaces to prepare them for asphalt application.

asphalt prime coat An **asphalt primer**.

asphalt seal coat A bituminous slurry or aggregate applied to the surface of pavement to waterproof, preserve, and prepare the surface.

asphalt shingle *or* **composition shingle** *or* **strip slate** Shingles composed of roofing felts coated with asphalt and mineral granules on the exposed surface.

asphalt-shingle nail *See* **roofing nail**.

asphalt soil stabilization The treatment of soil with liquid asphalt to improve load-bearing qualities and resistance to erosion.

asphalt surface course A top layer of asphalt pavement.

asphalt tack coat A thin coating of liquid asphalt on a pavement used to produce a bond between the old surface and the asphalt layer to be placed.

asphalt tile A floor tile comprised of asbestos fibers, mineral pigments, asphaltic binders, and finely ground limestone fillers that make a wear-resistant, inexpensive tile.

ASR Abbreviation for automatic sprinkler riser.

assembling bolt A bolt that temporarily holds parts of a structure so that it can be riveted.

associate In a design firm, this is a staff member with a special employment agreement.

Associated Landscape Contractors of America A trade association promoting business management and profitability for its members, consisting of mostly landscape maintenance firms, landscape installation firms, design/build landscape contractors, and interior landscape firms. Their web site is *www.alca.org*.

assurgent A botanical term describing something ascending (stems or branches, etc.).

astler Old term for **ashlar**.

ASTM Abbreviation for **American Society for Testing and Materials**.

astroturf Man-made, grass-like, outdoor carpeting.

AT Abbreviation for **asphalt tile**.

ATF Abbreviation for asphalt-tile floor.

atmospheric pressure The pressure of the weight of air at any particular elevation, usually

atmosphere

expressed in pounds per square foot. At sea level, the atmospheric pressure is 14.7 psi (33.9 **feet of head**), and the pressure decreases with increase in elevation. This is important when assuring water will move from a source to the pump for irrigation or water features as there must be more atmospheric pressure than suction loss *See* **net positive suction head available**.

atmosphere   **1.** A unit of pressure equal to the pressure of the atmosphere at sea level, which is approximately 14.7 lb/sq in or 101.325 pascals (760 mm Hg). At **field capacity**, water can be extracted by plant roots from soil **mesopores** with suction pressure (osmotic pressure) of about 0.1 to 0.3 atmospheres (1.4 to 4.41 psi). At wilting point, the pressure required to extract water from soil is approximately 15 atmospheres (220.5 psi). This is the point at which most plants can no longer extract water from the soil, causing wilting. **2.** A feeling or ambiance created by surroundings such as a formal landscape, waterfall, serene enclosed landscape, etc. **3.** The air surrounding the planet; the outer limit of the biosphere having influence on plants with its dust, pollution, humidity, wind movements, and/or temperature variations, etc.

atmospheric pressure *or* **barometric pressure**   Pressure exerted by the weight of the earth's atmosphere; at sea level, 14.7 lb/sq in (1.01 × 10⁶ pascals), decreasing with elevation above sea level.

atmospheric vacuum breaker   This device prevents back siphonage by allowing an atmospheric break in the pipeline. This is accomplished by a check seat, and an air inlet port within a 90° upright elbow area of a pipe. It is a **backflow preventer** consisting of a float, which moves up or down to allow atmospheric air into the piping system. It is always placed downstream from all shut-off valves. Its air inlet valve closes when the water flows in the intended direction. But, as water stops flowing, the air inlet valve opens, interrupting the possible back siphoning. This type of backflow device must always be installed at least 6 inches above all downstream piping and outlets that allow water to flow or it is not effective. Also, this assembly must not have shut-off valves or obstructions downstream as it cannot be under continuous pressure to be effective because it relies on the release of water pressure both up and downstream to allow the float check to fall admitting air to the pipes, thus preventing the back siphon of water. A shut-off valve would keep the assembly under pressure and allow the air inlet valve (or float check) to seal against the air inlet port, causing the assembly to act as an elbow instead of a backflow preventer. It must not be used for more than 12 hours in any 24-hour period. It may be used to protect against a pollutant, or a contaminant, but may only be used to prevent a back siphoning condition.

atriolum   A small atrium.

atrium   **1.** An open patio or plaza with a building surrounding it. It usually contains plants in pots or open planters. **2.** A glass enclosure attached to the side of a building. It usually harbors plants of interest, or is used for culinary purposes.

attached dwelling unit   Two or more **dwelling units** within the same detached dwelling unit structure. There is only one dwelling unit within a detached structure.

attenuate   In botanical terms, becoming narrow and thinner in width gradually, or a tapered portion of a plant part becoming gradually quite slender to a tip. It is more extreme and narrowly pointed than **acuminate**, or **acute**. (Compare with **cuneate, obtuse, cordate, auriculate, sagitate, hastate, truncate, oblique**.)

attenuate leaf base

attenuation Reduction of sound energy or intensity.

Atterberg limits *See* **liquid limit, plastic limit, shrinkage limit.**

Atterberg limits test A test of the water content that defines different states of consistency of plastic soils. This test is used to ascertain a soil's change with the addition of water to determine its tendency to become plastic or liquid.

auger **1.** The action of drilling or boring. **2.** A device used for boring or drilling wood, soil, etc. that may be handheld, hydraulically operated, or operated by gears with an engine or motor.

auger bit A bit used in a drilling or boring device.

auricles In botanical terms, small projecting lobes or appendages often at the base of a plant organ.

auriculate In botanical terms, earlike appendages or having one or more **auricles**. (Compare with leaf base descriptions of **cuneate, obtuse, cordate, attenuate, sagitate, hastate, truncate, oblique.**)

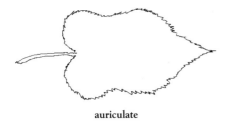

auriculate

AUTO Abbreviation for automatic.

automatic controller A timing device that turns on and off **automatic valves** or **valve in head** sprinklers at desired times and intervals without needing someone to be present to turn these sprinkler elements on or off.

automatic drain A drain in a sprinkler system that automatically closes when the sprinkler pipe is pressurized and automatically opens to drain the pipe when water pressure is released. They are spring loaded or use a ball that is forced by water into place where it blocks water flow out of the pipe. Some are only rated for **lateral lines** with intermittent **working pressure**, while others are rated for use on main lines where they can withstand constant **static pressure** without failing. They are used at low points on sprinkler pipes in temperate climates to prevent freeze damage to pipe systems.

automatic sprinkler system In landscape irrigation, a sprinkler system that is turned off and on by an **automatic controller** at times and intervals within its program capability. Automatic systems are usually controlled by electricity, but the first automatic systems were controlled by small tubes of water using changes in water pressure from the **controller** to the **valve**s.

automatic timer A timing device that turns on and off **automatic valves** or **valve in head** sprinklers at desired times and intervals without requiring someone to be present to turn these sprinkler elements on or off.

automatic valve In sprinkler systems, a valve that opens or closes when actuated by an **automatic controller**.

autotrophic Creation of organic carbon from inorganic chemicals such as in photosynthesis.

auxin A plant **hormone** used to stimulate root growth through cell elongation.

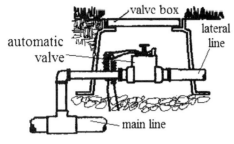

automatic valve

available water (AW) In a soil, the amount of water stored between **field capacity** and the permanent **wilting point**. The approximate amount of water capable of being stored in various soil types expressed in inches per inch is as follows: clay, 0.17; silty clay, 0.17; clay loam, 0.18; loam, 0.17; sandy loam, 0.12; loamy sand, .08; sand, 0.06.

avalanche protector A barrier protecting the tracks of excavation equipment from rocks or debris.

AVB Abbreviation for **atmospheric vacuum breaker**.

avenue 1. Usually a wide, tree-lined street. It is a term of French derivation, meaning an approach or access to a building, usually in the country with regularly planted trees along its length. But it currently describes a wide street with or without trees. 2. An access way.

average daily traffic (ADT) The average number of cars per day that pass over a given point.

AVG, Avg. Abbreviation for average.

AW Abbreviation for **available water**.

A/W Abbreviation for all-weather.

AWG Abbreviation for American Wire Gauge.

awl A pointed tool used for punching or gouging holes in leather, wood, hardboard, etc.

awl-shaped In botanical terms, sharp-pointed from a broader base.

awn A bristle-like appendage on a plant. In grasses or grains, one of the slender bristles that sometimes terminate the **spikelet**.

awns

awning A roof-like covering over a door, sidewalk, landscape element, or window, made of fabric, metal, glass, or canvas, etc. They are useful for protection from sun, wind, rain, and snow, but are also valued for aesthetics as decorative embellishments and used as signs. They usually project from a wall or roof.

AWPA Abbreviation for American Wood-Preservers' Association.

AWS 1. Abbreviation for all wood screws. 2. Abbreviation for American Welding Society.

AWWA Abbreviation for American Water Works Association.

ax hammer An ax for cutting or shaping rough stone.

axil In botanical terms, the upper angle (its point) between a leaf and the stem, or the point on a plant (being an angle) where a leaf, flower, or branch arises from a stem.

axillary   In botanical terms, something occurring in or at an **axil**.

axis   **1.** In botanical terms, the central line of any body or the organ around which others are attached. **2.** A straight line indicating the symmetrical center usually down the center of the longest dimension.

azimuth   In surveying, the horizontal angle measured clockwise from north to the direction of the object being located.

azonal soil   Earthen material in a **soil profile** characterized by not having discernable horizons and resembling the parent material.

B

baccate   A botanical term used in plant identification that means berrylike and pulpy.

bacillus popillae   Now known by the name of **paenibacillus popillae**. A biological (bacteria) control for the grub worms of Japanese beetles.

back charge   A monetary charge for damage, noncompliance with contracted construction design, or faulty construction by an owner, contractor, or subcontractor against any entity supplying or constructing a project.

backer strip   An asphalt-coated, water-repellent piece applied behind shingle joints.

backfill   **1.** Fill around the exterior of a structure, or around a foundation usually comprised of soil or gravel. The use of gravel or other porous material is meant to allow drainage away from the structure or foundation. **2.** Soil material used to fill a **planting pit**. Unmodified soil from the planting pit is usually deemed best for the plant's future growth and survival. **3.** Materials used to refill a ditch or other excavation. **4.** The process of placing backfill.

backfill amendment   This term refers to **amendments** being mixed with the **backfill** when planting. This practice is usually performed to provide more organic matter, fertilizers, and/or porous soil for the plant. This amendment has been found to create some difficulties for plant material. Changing the backfill creates a difference in the soil surrounding the plant pit and the backfill material within the planting pit. This interface between the soils tends to hold water, causing root rot, and also acts as an apparent barrier to root extension.

backfill concrete   A low-grade, nonstructural concrete mix used under structural concrete or to fill any area needing stability such as areas dug or disturbed under pavements or footings.

backfilled   The completion of **backfilling**.

backfilling   The action of placing **backfill**.

backfill mix   *See* **backfill amendment**.

backflow   The unwanted reverse flow of liquids in a piping system.

backflow connection   Any arrangement of pipes or plumbing devices that allows water to flow backward.

backflow preventer   In an irrigation system, a device installed between the point of connection and irrigation outlets that is designed to prevent the backflow of contaminated water into the potable water supply. These are usually only necessary on connections into potable sources. *See* **atmospheric vacuum breaker, double check assembly, pressure vacuum breaker,** or **reduced principle vacuum breaker**.

background plant   A tall plant (usually a shrub or tree) suggested for backdrops, assistance in enclosing a space, or for inclusion in mass plantings.

background planting   Plant massing at least to eye level that serves as a backdrop for a special feature, plant, or landscape element such as a statue, gazebo, etc.

backhoe   **1.** A tractor with a hydraulically operated arm and bucket capable of digging much like an arm and hand. Backhoes usually ride on rubber tires, whereas **trackhoes** ride on steel tracks. **2.** The portion of a machine that is shaped like an arm with a joint and having a bucket to dig with. This reference is not to the entire machine, but only to the implement.

backing

backhoe

backing **1.** Pieces of furring fit onto joists to provide a level surface for laying decking. **2.** Material for backfill in a retaining wall.

backing brick Broken pieces of brick or low-quality brick used as fill behind face brick or other masonry.

back nut A water-tight headed nut on a pipe or plumbing device.

back pressure **1.** Increase of pressure in the downstream piping system exceeding the supply pressure at the point of consideration which would cause, or tend to cause, a reversal of the normal direction of flow. **2.** Pressure in the opposite direction of intended flow within a sprinkler system.

backsaw A saw with a metal strip along its back to prevent the blade from bending. These types of saws are often used in miter boxes.

backshore The area of land between a beach berm and a distant landward slope.

backshore slope The bank or slope landward of the shore that is naturally formed.

backsight In surveying, viewing and/or measuring a previously established survey point.

back siphoning In irrigation, a reversal of water flow (backflow) due to reduction in system pressure, which causes a negative pressure to exist in the water system.

backup Overflow in a drain or piping system, due to being plugged.

back vent A vent for a plumbing fixture located on the sewer side of a **trap**, protecting against back siphonage.

bactericide An agent or compound used for killing bacteria.

bacteroid Irregularly shaped bacteria that form in the nodules of legumes.

badigeon Filler or patch material used in masonry or woodworks.

badminton A game played with one or two players on a team by hitting a small, feathered object.

bagasse A by-product from the manufacturing of sugar from sugar cane, which is somewhat **acid**ic and has a high water-holding capacity. It is used both as an **amendment** to **soil** and as a **mulch**.

bag plug An inflatable drain stopper that seals a pipe when inflated to seal a pipe.

bag *or* **sack** An amount of **Portland cement**: in the United States, 87.5 lb; in Canada, 112 lb; and in the United Kingdom and in countries with metric system measurements, 50.8 kg.

bagworms The larvae (caterpillars) of some kinds of moths with small individual tent-like bags. They are ¾ to 1 in long at full growth and may infest and devour foliage, enough to kill a tree. Control is by handpicking or insecticides.

baking soda A household product comprised of sodium or potassium bicarbonate. It is sometimes mixed with **horticultural oil** for application to plants for fungal protection.

balance pipe A pipe connected between two other pipes to average (equalize) the pressure in the two pipes.

balancing valve *or* **balancing plug cock**   A **valve** intended to control fluid flow in pipes, but not usually used to stop flow.

ballast   **1.** A sand and gravel mix used to make **concrete**. **2.** A stable layer under concrete of gravel, road base, etc.

ball-check valve   A spring-operated backflow preventer in a pipe system that forces a ball against a seat to stop backflow, but allows the ball to be pushed from the seat for flow in the intended direction.

balled-and-burlapped *or* **B&B**   This term refers to plants ready for planting that have root balls wrapped in an enclosure of burlap. They traditionally are prepared by digging completely around the roots of the plant and underneath, then wrapping the root ball with burlap, and tying twine around the ball to contain it. Balls could be planted by merely untying the top and pulling the burlap off the top of the ball because the twine and burlap would decompose. More often now, the plants are machine dug with a wire basket that the burlap-covered ball fits into, or some are dug and wrapped in both burlap and chicken wire.

balled-and-burlapped   This is a tree that is being planted in a balled and burlapped condition.

ball float   A floating piece that is used to operate a **ball valve**, which allows or prevents water to pass from a pipe supply line depending upon the elevation of the water. These are useful in sustaining the elevation of water in ponds.

ball peen hammer   A hammer with a head that has both a rounded pounding side and a flat pounding side.

ball peen hammer

ball-penetration test   An ASTM test method of wet concrete in which a rounded metal weight is placed on the smooth level surface of wet concrete to measure the depth that it sinks.

ball test   A test of piping or drains where a ball is rolled down the pipe to make certain the pipes are clear and will slope to drain.

ball valve   A valve with a handle (arm, lever) only requiring a quarter turn to turn completely on or off. It has a hollow ball with a hole through it that can be turned so that the hole in the ball is in line with the pipes to allow full flow or it can be turned to put solid sides of the ball toward the pipes to prevent flow.

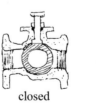

closed   open

ball valve

balsa

balsa *or* **corkwood**   A lightweight wood often useful in building scale models of projects.

baluster *or* **banister**   One of a number of short vertical members used to support a handrail.

balustrade   A rail or rails and their usually vertical supports (balusters) as a system along a deck, porch balcony, raised patio, etc. They are used for people's protection from falling, as a deterrent to access, an aesthetic treatment, etc.

band   In design, a horizontal flat projection or change in texture or color along a wall.

band clamp   A two-piece metal clamp used to hold riser pipes by bolting the two pieces of clamp together.

banding   The placement of fertilizers on the soil in narrow bands, usually at measured distances from the row of seeds or plants. The fertilizer bands are then covered by soil but are not mixed.

band saw   A power saw with a looped (endless) toothed steel belt.

bank   A mass of soil rising above a lower level or ground.

bank cubic yard   A cube of bank run material measuring three feet on all sides.

bankfull discharge   The flow of a river when it is full to the top of its banks.

bank material   Undisturbed, naturally in place, soil and/or rock.

bank-run   Earth (gravel and/or soil) materials taken from natural deposits without sifting, screening, etc. (directly from a bank of earth).

bank run gravel   Excavated material that is not screened and has generally a ¼ to 6 in diameter.

bank yards   The amount of cubic yards of earth material in its original place.

banner vane   A weather vane with a flat portion much like a banner.

bar   **1.** A long solid metal or wood product. **2.** A steel **reinforcing bar**. **3.** A unit of pressure equal to 14.5 **psi**, 1,000,000 dynes per centimeter, or approximately 1 **atmosphere**.

barbate   A botanical term used in plant identification that means bearded with long, stiff hairs.

barbed fittings   Pipe or tube fittings that are inserted into pipes or tubes and are held in place by the friction created by the barbs or clamps over the pipes into which they are inserted.

barbed wire   Twisted wire with barbs or sharp points along its length.

bar-be-que grill   A steel grate over a heat source used out-of-doors for cooking (esp. meat). They may be stationary, such as those made of masonry, or they may be mobile with wheels, such as many propane-heated grills.

bar-be-que grill

barbwire   *See* **barbed wire**.

bare root   Plants harvested for transplanting with no appreciable soil attached. **Deciduous**

plant material are generally more likely to survive this type of transplanting. Plants in this condition usually need to be kept cool, damp, and out of direct sunlight. They are not generally storable for long periods of time. It is best done while plants are **dormant**.

bar iron   Iron, available in the form of bars, which can be beaten into shapes to form tools, hardware, and decorative iron work. *See* **wrought iron**.

bark   The protective, tough exterior of a woody plant's stem, branches, and/or roots. Some plants have bark consisting only of **phloem** tissue, which grows and expands from the **cambium** layer outward, but in other plants their bark is also comprised of the phellogen (cork cambium), which grows and expands outside the phloem creating the outer bark.

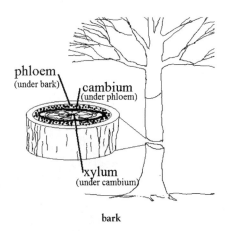

phloem
(under bark)

cambium
(under phloem)

xylum
(under cambium)

bark

bark pocket *or* **inbark** *or* **ingrown bark**   A small amount of bark surrounded (or nearly so) by wood within a tree or within a piece of the lumber it yields.

barley straw   The portion of the barley plant left after harvesting its grain. It is useful to bun-

dle and place in the water of enclosed water features to control algae.

barn   A usually enclosed farm building used for protecting grain, hay, farm animals, farm equipment, etc. from the weather.

barn-door hanger   A horizontal track hanger on the outside of a barn that holds one or two large sliding doors.

barn-door stay   A small wheel that rolls in a horizontal track, guiding the sliding of usually large exterior barn doors.

barred-and-braced gate   A gate having one or more diagonal braces to reinforce the horizontal members.

barred gate   A gate with one or more horizontal timber members.

barrel   **1.** A container capable of holding 31½ gal of liquid or material. **2.** An obsolete American weight measure of Portland cement amounting to 376 lbs. **3.** A portion of a pipeline having a constant inside diameter and wall thickness.

barrel arch   An arch formed by a solid piece of material as opposed to many or several portions of a material.

barrel fitting   A short piece of threaded pipe, such as a **nipple**, for making pipe connections.

barrens   A plant community with significantly small coverage or stunted individuals that would otherwise grow to larger specimens under favorable conditions.

barricade   An item or assemblage of items preventing or deterring passage or access of vehicles, people, etc.

barrier   **1.** A term used to describe a plant that deters or prevents passage. **2.** An item or items preventing access or passage.

barrier curb A steep-faced **curb** intended to prevent encroachments.

barrier dune A large mass of coastal sand dunes paralleling the shoreline.

barrow **1.** Soil or rock material obtained from another portion of a site or from another piece of land. It is usually in its original makeup without screening or separation of material (soil and rock) sizes. **2.** Abbreviation for wheelbarrow.

barrow run A temporary placement of wood or other materials to facilitate the passage of wheelbarrows on a construction site.

barrow-pit A hole or excavation in an embankment where material has been moved for use elsewhere.

bar scale A linear bar placed on a drawing, picture, model, etc. for reference to the **scale** of items or spaces in the drawing, picture, model, etc. in relation to the size in existence or as planned, designed, or perceived. For most people not familiar with design drawings or cartography, bar scales are better understood than written scales. This is because the bar scale can be measured with a ruler or **scale**. Also, when a drawing or picture is enlarged, bar scales stay true, whereas written scales do not.

bar schedule **1.** A tabulation of reinforcement iron bar used in reinforced concrete, such as in retaining walls, which indicates the number, size, and dimensions of each bar specified. **2.** A schedule on paper depicting the progress of a job with bars to visually indicate the duration of various tasks from one date or week to another.

bar screen A device made up of bars set at predetermined spaces for separating stone in various sizes and/or earth material from rock.

bar spacing With regard to reinforcing bars, the distance from the longitudinal axis of one bar to the center of another bar's longitudinal axis.

bar strainer A screening apparatus made up of a bar or many bars to prevent objects from entering a culvert or drain.

bar type grading A network of iron assembled with metal bars in one direction with iron spacers between them, forming a grid pattern or a grate.

basal **1.** Arising from the base of a stem such as where a fleshy portion of a leaf begins from the **petiole** (stem). **2.** Growing at the **crown** of a plant.

basalt An igneous rock of dark color used in paving.

base **1.** In paving, the prepared layer beneath the paving made up of crushed stone, gravel, or combinations thereof with sand. This layer is placed to distribute paving loads over the base and improve the load-bearing capacity. **2.** With regard to paint, the medium that is the main ingredient for the paint. **3.** The lower portion of a column that is wider and/or thickened. **4.** The lower portion of an item or structure.

baseball field An outdoor field for the game of baseball (hardball) that starts at a point (home plate) and travels out in two base lines at right angles to one another 90 ft to bases and bisecting that angle. Pitcher's mound is 60 ft, 6 in away from home plate. The outfield fence is about 250 ft from home plate. These dimensions are for understanding of scale, comprehension of shape, etc. and are for planning purposes only. Contact the appropriate league for their exact layout and dimensions required with current information and different types of play fields.

base bid An amount of money or trade items stipulated in return for services and materials offered, not including any **alternate bids**.

base coarse **1.** The lowest coarse in a masonry wall. **2.** The first layer placed in pavement construction. **3.** A layer of material placed on compacted subgrade for providing drainage, distributing weight loads, reducing the action of frost, etc.

base coat **1.** A layer of liquid material applied to a wood surface before staining or otherwise finishing. **2.** The first layer of paint applied to a surface (also called a prime coat).

base elbow A cast-iron pipe elbow with a flange for support.

base flashing A **flashing** at the point where a wall or vertical surface meets a roof. It is used to help prevent leakage of water through the roof at these critical areas.

baseflow The portion of stream flow attributed to groundwater. It is generally a more steady flow and often continues into or through droughts.

base line An established line (a line surveyed and staked or the edge of an object such as a building or road) from which measurements or surveys are taken.

base map **1.** A map of an area showing the important natural and man-made features, as well as unseen existing elements such as **right-of-ways** and property lines. **2.** A plan of proposed and/or existing features for a site, used as a beginning point for various other plans or maps of proposed and/or existing elements (lighting plan, planting plan, sprinkler plan, etc.) superimposed over it. Examples are city plans with a sewer, water plan, or drainage plan superimposed. Another example is a proposed plan for a building with electrical and plumbing superimposed as separate plans.

base-plate A metal sheet used to distribute a load that is not uniform over the area that is designed to carry the load more uniformly.

base tee A pipe tee with a flange supporting it.

basic intake rate In reference to soils and irrigation, the approximate percolation rate that can be expected in a soil before it reaches saturation. This approximate rate in inches per hour is as follows: clay, 0.10; silty clay, 0.15; clay loam, 0.20; loam, 0.35; sandy loam, 0.40; loamy sand, 0.50; sand, 0.60.

basic services For construction of a project, services, usually of a designer (**landscape architect, engineer, architect,** etc.), including schematic design, design development, construction documents, bidding advertisement and evaluations, negotiation, and contract administration.

basic slag A by-product of steel refining used as a phosphatic **fertilizer**, but highly **alkaline** and containing calcium. It is not for use on **acid**-loving plants or in alkaline soils. It contains 2 to 16% available phosphoric acid that is slowly released into soil.

basifixed A botanical term used in plant identification that describes something attached at the base. (Compare with **dorsifixed**.)

basin **1.** A depressed area of land identified by higher areas surrounding it or nearly so. **2.** Shallow, concave area meant for holding water or other liquids. **3.** An area to which all surface water drainage gathers to a selected point in a natural or man-made drainage area.

basin irrigation Irrigation achieved by flooding areas of level land surrounded by dikes. Used interchangeably with level border irrigation, but basin irrigation often refers to smaller areas.

basketball court A hard surface with at least one basketball standard for playing the game of basketball. A full-size basketball court has a standard at each end and measures 84 ft long by 50 ft wide for high school, and 94 ft long with the same width for college.

basketball standard A pole, backboard, and hoop standing erect as designed and intended for use in the game of basketball.

basketball standard

basket weave **1.** A checkerboard pattern made with bricks or rectangular pavers, usually laid three or four abreast and turned every three or four bricks to one side or the other. **2.** A fence with thin horizontal boards that are attached to posts and extended from one side of a post to the other side of the next post. Each horizontal board alternates as to which side of the post it passes on.

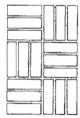 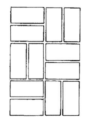

basket weave patterns

basswood In construction terms, a light-colored wood from the American linden tree. It has low density and its fine texture is mostly used for trim and plywood.

bastard ashlar *or* **bastard masonry** **1.** Ashlar stones roughly dressed at the quarry and not finished. **2.** Masonry material in thin blocks that is square-hewn and placed to resemble **ashlar**.

bat **1.** A brace made of a piece of wood. **2.** A piece of insulation of a specific size usually utilized in areas between studs in walls or between rafters. **3.** A portion of brick with one good end that has not been damaged.

batch A quantity of material mixed at one time.

batch box A container utilized for mixing concrete, mortar, plaster, or the like to insure proper portions by having space or spaces with the correct volume or volumes for those proportions.

batch plant A facility where the mixing of concrete or asphalt takes place.

batten **1.** A narrow, horizontal strip of wood. **2.** In roofing, a strip of wood used as a base for attaching tile shingles, wood shingles, etc.

batter A slant on a nearly vertical surface. This type of wall lays back slightly as it rises and is a common practice on boulder retaining walls to assure stability.

batterboard A device made up of boards set beyond the corners of a structure to be excavated, allowing one to pull strings from the boards to determine the exact location of a corner. These boards are two horizontal boards that are nailed at right angles to each other and staked to the ground.

battered wall A wall with a face having **batter**.

batt insulation A blanket-like thermal insulation that is flexible and used between studs or joists in frame construction. It usually comes precut in widths to fit industry standard spaces such as studs set on 16 in centers.

battlement The repetitive raising and lowering of the top edge of a wall with short spaces, originally designed for defense behind the wall by one throwing or shooting from the lowered space with wall protection on each side of the opening. The up and down repetition in the top of a wall or designs resembling that pattern is called a battlement design. *See also* **crenelated**.

bay **1.** A group of regularly repeated special items defined by ribs, joists, or beams and their supports within a structure. **2.** An alcove or recessed area defined by plants laid out in a design. **3.** A **parking bay** of contiguous parking stalls in a single row. **4.** A garland or crown of laurel representing excellence or victory. **5.** A compartment or stall in a barn. **6.** A portion of a larger body of water that projects into a land area with the land surrounding most of its perimeter.

B&B, b&b **1.** Abbreviation for grade B and better lumber. **2.** Abbreviation for **balled-and-burlapped**.

bbl. Abbreviation for barrel.

BC soil Any soil with only a **B** and **C horizon**. The most frequent reason for loss of the **A horizon** is erosion.

bcy Abbreviation for bank cubic yards.

BE Abbreviation for bevel end.

beaked In botanical terms, ending in a long narrow tip.

beam **1.** A ray of light or a group of nearly parallel rays of light. **2.** A relatively large structural member placed in a structure to carry loads (usually of joists, or girders). These members are usually metal or wood and carry loads from other transfer members such as joists, girders, etc. **3.** A long, heavy, wood member.

beam anchor A metal tie for anchoring beams to a wall or larger structural member.

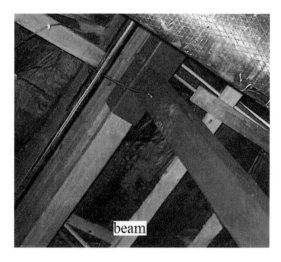

beam

beam compass An instrument used for drawing arcs that has a horizontal bar with a drawing instrument attached at one point and a pin or pointed instrument at the other point for the center of the radius. The pencil and the pin (one or both) must be movable along the bar to allow adjustment in drawing size of arcs.

bearclaw A large, sloped, heavy, steel screen for separating cobble or removing debris from soil by dumping it through the screen with a **front end loader**.

bearded A botanical term meaning that a plant part bears a tuft or ring of rather long hairs.

bearer **1.** A scaffold's horizontal member that bears the weight of the platform. **2.** Any horizontal member of a structure bearing a load, such as a joist or beam. **3.** The support for a winder tread in a stair or the support of a stair landing.

bearing In surveying, a measure of deviation from north or from south toward either east or west in degrees, minutes, and seconds.

bearing bar A load-carrying bar supporting a metal grate or grating material.

bearing capacity **1.** The weight load per unit area that a particular area of ground can support safely without failure (movement). **2.** The weight pressure that can be placed upon soil or rock without yield.

bearing plate A steel slab placed under columns, girders, or beams to distribute load from them to their supports.

bearing pressure The load on a bearing surface divided by the area in contact with its surface.

bearing strength The maximum load that a structural member can sustain divided by the bearing area.

bearing wall A wall designed to support vertical loads as well as its own weight. A structural wall or load-bearing wall.

bed **1.** An area of soil covered by plants or prepared for planting. **2.** A cultivated area of land.

bedding **1.** The mortar bed spread to lay bricks in. **2.** Any base prepared for paving. **3.** Areas of ground prepared for annual flowers **4.** The growing medium used for **annual**s. **5.** The method and/or materials used in backfilling pipes, conduits, structures, culverts, etc.

bedding mortar A mixture of sand and **cement** used in laying brick or paving stone.

bedding plant A plant (usually an **herbaceous annual**) suitable for mass plantings because of their colorful flowers or foliage for a decorative affect in landscaping. They are usually **annual**s or tropical plants grown for their outstanding aesthetic qualities in a short period of time. They are often changed from season to season.

bed joint **1.** The horizontal mortar layer or bed on which masonry units are laid. **2.** A crack in bedrock. **3.** One of the joints that are radial in an arch made of individual units (bricks, stones, etc.).

bedrock In-place solid rock at the earth's surface or underlying the soil layers. This rock is stable for the bearing of weight loads such as structures. Bedrock near the surface is a challenge to most landscape efforts and makes the growing of most plants more difficult because drainage, root space, and water-holding capacity are issues of concern.

bed shear stress The force of flowing water on the bed of a stream.

bed-type filter A filter made up of a porous medium through which water is forced to clean various sizes of suspended solids.

bee A flying insect much like wasps and hornets, except it has a mouth capable of sucking and/or chewing. They are useful in pollination.

beechwood In construction, a fine-grained, durable, strong hardwood often grown in Europe and North America. It is light colored or reddish-brown and is useful as flooring.

beetle **1.** An insect usually having a hard pair of wings covering their flying wings that open in flight. There are 250,000 species, many of which are destructive to plants by feeding on them or transmitting diseases. **2.** A hammer of mallet for driving stones into pavement, etc.

begging A hut covered with mud or turf.

behavioral connectivity In landscape ecology, the measure of the degree to which a landscape element is connected for a process such as the movements of deer, or frogs, or water through a space from one area to another.

belfry **1.** A tower with a bell in it. **2.** The supporting framework in a **bell tower**.

Belgian block curb A type of **paving** stone cut in a truncated, pyramid shape, laid with the base of the pyramid down.

Belgian fence espalier A pattern of **espalier**ed plants forming a Y in its branching pattern. Usually several plants are placed close enough to cross branches in forming a pattern.

Belgian fence espalier

bell-and-spigot joint *or* **bell-and-socket joint**   A connection between two pieces of pipe, one having a flared end sealed with caulking (sometimes using oakum and lead for cast-iron pipes) or a compressible ring or gasket.

bell *or* **bell end**   The flared end of a pipe made large enough to accept the end of another pipe of the same size so as to form a joint. It may also be called a hub.

bellows expansion joint   This is a joint formed with flexible metal bellows capable of compressing or stretching to compensate for linear contraction or expansion due to changes in temperature throughout the run of the piping.

bell tower   A structure that supports one or several bells usually placed higher than surrounding structures, if any.

bell tower

bell wire   A small diameter wire covered with insulating material capable of only carrying 30 volts or less.

belt coarse   A horizontal band of masonry extending across a wall of a different color or texture from the adjacent masonry.

belt loader   A machine used in excavation that removes material and conveys it on a belt where it is loaded into a container or a hauling device.

belvedere   A small ornamental structure often placed for an impressive view, distant or near. They are most often found in ornamental gardens of large homes and grounds or in parks.

bench   **1.** Anything made to accommodate more than one person sitting side by side; may be made of logs, metal, lumber, fiberglass, marble, concrete, etc. **2.** A level area of earth or a level land form.

bench

benched borders   *See* **border irrigation.**

benching   **1.** Concrete placed, as a safeguard against sliding, on unstable slopes, or slopes capable of being unstable. **2.** Concrete placed along pipes to prevent them from sliding on slopes or in unstable conditions.

bench mark   In surveying, a known reference, or permanent object (if surveyed in, usually a steel marker placed in concrete) having its elevation and/or exact location verified and usable as a point of reference. This is a point from which other areas can be surveyed for elevation and/or location.

bench sander   A power sanding machine, usually mounted on a stand or bench, used to smooth objects held against it with a rotating abrasive disk or belt.

bench terrace   A flat area cut or filled on a hillside.

bench vise   A vise mounted on a bench, truck bumper, or other heavy object to allow work of force on material held in the vise.

bending moment   A more accurate and descriptive term for the more succinct expression **moment**. The point at which bending is produced in a beam or other structural member.

bending strength   The ability of a structural member to bend without breaking.

beneficial impact   *See* **positive environmental impact**.

benefits with regard to employment   Benefits are those items not part of an employee's pay, which benefit an employee such as: sick leave, vacation, holiday, life insurance, pension plans, worker's compensation, disability insurance, etc.

bentomat   Waterproof material used to line ponds or planters that contain **bentonite**.

bentonite   **1.** Any **clay** that can prevent the penetration of water and may be used as a liner for ponds, or other man-made water bodies. **2.** A powder formulated from fossilized volcanic ash

that is often mixed with water and added to clay to make a water-resistant gel. **3.** A clay characterized by high absorption commonly swelling to several times its dry volume when saturated with liquid.

berm   **1.** A mound or wall of earth, gravel, sand, or rocks either naturally occurring or constructed in a landscape useful for screening, for aesthetic purposes, to protect (deflect wind, sound, etc.), and/or to allow planting above a high water table. **2.** A bank of earth piled against a wall. This is often used against a house to help stabilize its temperature. **3.** A shelf or terrace built into an embankment or slope, which breaks the continuity of the length of the slope or embankment.

Bermuda grass   A fine textured perennial grass used in warm climates as a lawn. It may also be thought of as a weed as it is difficult to eradicate. It spreads by rhizomes and by seed.

berry   **1.** Fleshy or pulpy fruit with one or more seeds, and not having stone seeds as in **drupes**. **2.** Edible fruits referred to as berries, but botanically are drupes or conglomerates of drupes, such as blueberries, blackberries, loganberries, mulberries, raspberries, strawberries, etc.

best efficiency point   With reference to pumps, the point on a **pump performance curve** with the highest efficiency for the pump to run. The highest efficiency point on the curve is also the best hydraulic operating point for the pump.

best management practice (BMP)   A structural or nonstructural management-based practice used singularly or in combination to reduce nonpoint source inputs to receiving waters in order to achieve water quality protection goals. These activities, prohibitions, practices, procedures, programs, or other measures are designed to prevent or reduce the discharge of pollutants directly or indirectly into natural waters. They are intended to reduce or avoid adverse impacts of development on the site's adjoining land, water, waterways, and water bodies. They are designed to control soil loss and reduce water-quality degradation caused by nutrients, animal waste, toxins, and sediment and should minimize adverse impacts to surface water and groundwater flow, circulation patterns, and to the chemical, physical, and biological characteristics of wetlands.

bevel   A chamfer; an angle between two surfaces that is not a right angle; often a 45° angle.

bf   Abbreviation for board feet.

bg. cem.   Abbreviation for bag of cement.

B horizon   The soil horizon found immediately below the **A horizon**. It is often referred to as part of the subsoil (*see* **C horizon**), as it contains little organic matter, and commonly has a high clay content. It has a darker color than the **C horizon** because clays, organic colloids, and/or leachable material from the A horizon are carried to it via water percolation. This layer of soil may be further divided into **subhorizon**s of B1, B2, B3, etc.

bhp   Abbreviation for **break horse power**.

B.I.   Abbreviation for black iron.

bib *or* **bibcock**   A water faucet that has its outlet bent downward from the valve.

bibcock   A water outlet valve operated by turning a handle.

bicolor   With reference to plants, having two distinctly different colors, usually in the fruit or flower.

bid   A proposal made in exchange for completion of work or for an item. Most proposals involve a stipulated sum of money or trade items.

bid bond   A bond secured by a bidder guaranteeing that the bidder will accept the project if

offered by the owner, and/or that the bidder will complete the project for the stipulated bid amount.

bidding documents   Documents given at the time of bidding including such items as instructions to bidders, a **bid form**, contract documents proposed, and/or any **addendum** issued.

bidentate   In botanical terms, two-toothed.

bid form   A form often provided to bidders to be filled out and delivered, as a **bid**.

bid opening   **1.** A time of opening all **bid**s submitted. With large projects the time of opening bids is usually specified in the **invitation to bid**. The opening and reading and/or listing of bids submitted that conform to prescribed procedures.

bid price   The amount in monetary value or trade that a bidder requests as payment for accomplishing work.

bid security   A certified check, a deposited amount of cash, a money order, or a **bid bond** submitted with a bid guaranteeing the owner that the bidder, if awarded the contract, will complete the work in accordance with the bid documents for the **bid price** (amount requested).

bid shopping   Requesting bids from subcontractors or others after the date all bids were accepted and/or negotiating a price lower than the lowest bid received on time for materials and/or work.

bid time   The time and date determined by the owner and/or agent of the owner (usually the designer) for receipt of bids.

biennial   A plant with a normal life cycle of two years. When grown from seed, these plants typically do not flower the first year, but in the second year they flower, set seed, and die.

bifid

bifid In plant identification and descriptions, more or less deeply cleft from the tip into two usually equal parts.

bifurcate In botanical terms, twice-forked.

bifurcation Dividing into branches or parts.

bigeneric hybrid A **hybrid** plant created by crossing parents from two different **genera**. *See also* **intergeneric hybrid**.

bike path *See* **bikeway**.

bike route *See* **bikeway**.

bikeway A trail, path, or marked area along a street or travel way, provided for the use of bicyclists.

bilabiate In botanical terms, **labiate** or having two lips as on the **corolla** of a mint.

bill of materials The compilation of materials needed to accomplish a particular work.

bill of quantities A list of the quantities of items needed to complete a particular work.

binder coarse **1.** A masonry portion of a wall used to bind an inner and an outer wall together. **2.** An asphaltic concrete paving course between two other courses (the base and the surfacing course) made up of aggregate and bituminous material.

binder soil A reference to soil of good binding ability made up primarily of fine particles of clay, silt, or even fine sand, and also having colloids (extremely small particles). This type of soil is easily compacted and useful in construction, but it is not conducive or favorable to plant growth and root extension.

bindweed A perennial weed (also known as morning glory) that is extremely difficult to eradicate. Seeds last for years and can grow from any portion of the root left in the soil. It is reported that roots can extend as deep as 20 ft.

Breaking or attempting to pull the plant is a lot like mowing a lawn; it will continually grow back. The best way to eradicate it is to be persistent and consistent with weed sprays. It is best to use a spray that will kill roots. This is most effective in the fall when the plant is storing food from the leaves into the roots. The author has found that using two combined weed sprays is most effective.

binomial With reference to a **scientific name** (**botanical name**), this means giving two names identifying a plant, usually the **genus** and **species** names. *See also* **monomial** and **trinomial**.

binomial nomenclature The naming of plants by the first name indicating the **genus** (its first letter capitalized), and the second name indicating **species** (lower case). Any further naming of **variety, cultivar**, etc. is optional. This system of naming and classifying plants (and animals) was developed by the Swiss botanist and naturalist, Carl von Linné. *See also* **botanical name**.

bioassay The use of living organisms for testing toxicity of wastewater.

bioavailability With regard to landscape and plant nursery work, the amount of substance readily available to plants as a nutrient or toxin.

biodegradable Material that can readily be decomposed (usually in the soil) by microorganisms.

biodiversity A reference to the number of various life forms on earth, on a continent, in a country, in a state, on a site, or other arbitrarily defined area, and usually referring to the number of species. *See also* **biological diversity**.

biodynamic gardening A movement taking on this name to promote practices much like those of organic gardening that does not use **pes-**

ticides, or at least those that will not leave residue, and improving soils through **organic** means, etc. It appears some of the substances recommended by the movement cannot be supported.

biofilter   A filter in a water feature or water treatment design that uses biological means (often bacteria) to remove contaminants.

biogeographical   A reference to the geographical distribution of a living organism.

biogeography   The portion of biological science that studies the geographical distribution of plants and animals.

biological diversity   The variety of life of any kind, including microscopic life such as viruses, bacteria, and including all plants, amphibians, aquatic life, animals, and humans. Three levels of diversity are considered: (1) within an ecosystem (no earthly ecosystem has definite boundaries fully contained); (2) diversity of species; and, (3) genetic diversity that occurs within a species.

biological oxygen demand   Oxygen requirements of aquatic organisms that deprive fish or other aquatic animals of necessary oxygen within a water body.

biological pest control   The use of plants, organic materials, naturally occurring chemicals, and/or beneficial insects to control pests and diseases in an area or on plants.

biomass   **1.** Living matter (living tissues of plants, animals, bacteria, etc.) present in an area. **2.** Living matter capable of being converted into usable energy through biological or chemical processes. **3.** The weight of organic material (living matter or matter produced by living things) within an area and sometimes a specific surface area (usually 1 sq m).

biomimicry   Mimicking naturally occurring designs.

biophilia   An appreciation for, or love of, life and the living world.

biosphere   **1.** The planet earth with all its living organisms and environments. **2.** In broad terms, a reference for all living organisms in combination with their environment. **3.** In landscape ecological terms, living organisms and their environment with reference to a large area such as a **landscape**, **region**, continent, or more often, the earth.

biotechnical stabilization   The conjunctive use of both live vegetation and a retaining structure. This also includes grass or ground covers planted in a mesh or mechanical system.

biotic   **1.** Living things. **2.** Related to life.

biotope   The area needed for a particular conglomeration of plants and animals to live. It may be an area larger or smaller than an **ecotope**.

bipinnate *or* **bipinnately compound**   In botanical terms, double or twice pinnate with the primary pinnate divisions once again being pinnate. (Compare with **simple, pinnate, palmate, trifoliate.**

bipinnate

bipinnatifid Botanically, being twice **pinnately compound**.

bipinnatisect In botanical terms, a three times' divided leaf-blade whose three parts are again divided several times.

birch In construction, a lumber of high density, moderately strong, yellowish-white, sometimes brown, that is mostly used for flooring veneers and wood products produced on a lathe.

birdbath **1.** In landscape ornamentation, usually a raised basin capable of holding a small amount of water, but enough water that a bird can bathe itself. They are commonly made of iron, stone, marble, or plastic and may be quite decorative. **2.** A shallow puddle of water at a low spot on pavements.

bird feeder A container used to hold seeds or other food intended for consumption by birds.

birdhouse Any artificial nesting site for birds.

birdhouse

bird netting An open weave material placed over plants as a shield to protect fruit from bird damage.

bird's-mouth A notch cut in a sloping timber of a structure allowing the sloping timber to rest upon a vertical wall and be attached thereto. These are commonly used on rafters to attach them to exterior walls.

bisexual In botanical terms, possessing perfect **(hermaphrodite)** flowers having both stamens and pistils.

bit A small, steel shaft with spiral cuts in it, which when placed in a drill or brace can be used as a tool to bore or cut a hole when it is rotated.

bit. *or* **bitum.** Abbreviation for bituminous.

bit-gauge *or* **bit-stop** A metal device temporarily attached to a drill, preventing a bit from drilling too deeply.

bitumen A substance derived from coal or petroleum such as coal, tar, pitch, or asphalt that is usually dissolved in a solvent or heated to a liquid state before application.

bituminized fiber pipe A pipe made of cellulose fiber and coal tar with an advantage of being lightweight.

bituminous cement A black, hydrocarbon material used in sealing flat roofs and also between joints or cracks in concrete or asphalt paving.

bituminous coating An asphalt or tar material placed over a finished pavement for a more protected surface.

bk. Abbreviation for backed.

BL Abbreviation for building line.

black spot A general term for fungal diseases causing black splotches on plants. *See* **leaf spot**.

blacktop A mixture of asphalt and aggregate used as paving material over a compacted base. Usually placed and compacted while hot. For placement without heat, see **cold mix**.

blade **1.** In botanical terms, the expanded, flat, thin portion of a leaf, not including its **petiole**. It is often veined. In grasses, it is long and narrow. **2.** The cutting portion of a knife. **3.** The flat portion of a trowel used for tooling or smoothing a surface. **4.** A main rafter member of a roof. **5.** A broad, slightly cupped, metal plate on the front of a tractor that pushes earthen material and can also be used to rip unconsolidated rock.

Blain test A test used for determining the fineness of cement.

blanch To make white or take the color out by excluding light.

blanching The practice of tying leaves over the head or leaves of a plant to produce a lighter color or milder flavor (as with cauliflower).

Blaney-Criddle method An air temperature method to estimate crop **evapotranspiration**.

blanket insulation A fibrous glass material with or without facings used as thermal insulation or sound insulation.

blasting The use of explosives, generally for fracturing and breaking bedrock.

bldg. Abbreviation for building.

bleaching A term used to reference the process of applying a liquid to something to cause it to lose color or become whiter. It is most often used in construction with reference to wood and is brought on naturally without the use of chemicals or water through extended exposure to sunlight. Water often aids naturally to the bleaching of wood and is evident where sprinkler heads overshoot onto siding, fences, or decks. If a bleach is to be applied to wood treated with a preservative, it should not be applied until at least 60 days after the preservative, and even then the bleach may not be as effective as desired due to discoloration.

bleed In plants, the loss of sap, usually at wound.

bleede A small drain valve used to allow fluid to drain from radiators, pipes, or tanks.

bleeder pipe A pipe (usually made of clay) that carries water from a drainage tile to a storm sewer.

bleeding **1.** The flow of water within, and/or the emergence of water on the surface of, newly placed concrete or mortar caused by the settlement of solid materials or sometimes brought about by overworking the material. **2.** The appearance of a color pigment from the subsurface through the finished paint coat. **3.** The loss of any or all electrical current in an underground wire due to damage to its coating.

bleed valve On an automatic valve that is normally closed, a small device on the valve which if turned enough will allow a bit of water to escape, which triggers the valve to open, allowing water to flow through the valve into the downstream piping. Its name comes from the small amount of water that escapes (bleeds) through the bleed valve to outside the water system while it is in operation. This is useful on an automatic sprinkler valve as it allows one to open the valve and operate sprinklers without use of the automatic controller. This option is useful when testing the valve for operation because of a lack of response from sprinkler controller operation, or when needing to turn on sprinklers without accessing the sprinkler controller.

blemish A minor appearance defect not affecting durability, function, or strength in a material such as wood, concrete, stucco, marble, steel, etc.

blight **1.** An indiscriminate term for many diseases of plants, but usually associated with a fungal disease causing plants to wilt or wither. **2.** A plant disease causing the general and rapid destruction of living tissue (stems, flowers, leaves, etc.).

blind

blind **1.** Descriptive of a plant that fails to produce flowers or fruit. **2.** A term describing a condition of **bulb**s or **shoot**s that fail to produce flowers. This can be caused by excessive heat, disease, dry soil, or by **forcing** too early. **3.** A condition when a bud stops developing. This happens to some tree species' **terminal buds** in transplanting.

blind drain A drain that is not connected to a drainage system.

blind flange A flange that closes the end of a pipe.

blinding **1.** The compaction of soil above drain tile to reduce the likelihood of soil moving into the tile. **2.** Completely covering piping with earth or other material. **3.** The placement or sprinkling of stone chips, sand, fine gravel, etc. on freshly placed asphaltic concrete or a freshly tarred road to provide a more suitable surface.

blind joint A joint that is not visible after completion of a project.

blind nailing **1.** Placing nails in such a way that their heads are not visible on the face of the work. **2.** Placing nails on a roof so as not to expose them to the weather.

blind nipple A short piece of pipe having a cap on one end.

blk. Abbreviation for block.

block **1.** A masonry unit commonly referred to as a concrete block. **2.** In stonework, a large piece of stone, usually squared, that is taken from the quarry to another site for sawing or further work. **3.** An area within a community, town, etc. that is completely surrounded by streets, or the length from the point of one street intersection to the point of the next street intersection.

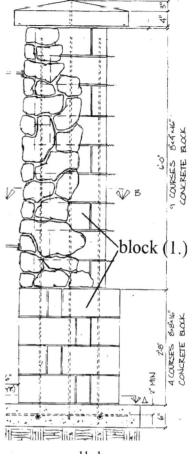

block

block and tackle A set of pulleys in a device that usually has a hook for attachment and allows chains or ropes to be drawn through them for use in raising or shifting heavy loads.

block bridging Short portions of boards fixed between joists to stiffen and strengthen them.

blocking Pieces of wood used in shimming, securing, joining, or reinforcing other wood members within a structure.

blocking chisel A wide, broad chisel used in masonry work made in various thicknesses, shapes, etc.

block insulation A rigid or semi-rigid slab of material used for thermal protection.

block plane A small, wood, planing device useful in cleaning up miters and end grains.

blood meal An organic fertilizer made of dried animal blood (usually cattle) with an acid re-action and an **NPK** ratio of approximately 15-1.3-0.7 Nitrogen ranges from 12 to 15%, with 15% most common.

bloom **1.** An open or showy flower. **2.** The flower of any plant. **3.** A whitish, or bluish-white powdery, glaucous, usually waxy coating on some fruits such as grapes and plums, and on the stems or leaves of succulents or cacti, etc. **4.** The action of a plant producing, displaying, and/or opening flowers.

bloomy A descriptive botanical term referring to a plant part that has a powder-like, waxy deposit on its surface.

blossom *See* **bloom** (1), (2), (4).

blotch A disease caused by **fungi**. *See also* **blight**.

blow count **1.** In soil boring, the number of blows required to force a sample spoon 6 or 12 in into the soil. **2.** The number of strikes or blows necessary to drive an object into a soil.

blue mottling A bluish discoloring of soil indi-cating that **anaerobic** conditions have been present.

blueprint **1.** A reproduction of a drawing made by contact printing where lines are defined on light-sensitive paper, and usually developed with ammonia fumes. The older blueprints were negatives with white lines and the remainder of the drawing being blue. Later blueprints were white with the lines being blue. **2.** Reproduc-tions of design drawings or working drawings used for communicating construction intent.

bm. Abbreviation for beam.

B/M Abbreviation for **bill of materials**, which is also called a **quantity survey**.

board **1.** A reference to any piece of lumber with the exception of laminated wood. **2.** A piece of lumber from 4 to 12 in wide and less than 2 in thick.

board fence **1.** Any fence made with lumber. **2.** A fence constructed with horizontal lumber attached to square posts.

board foot A unit measurement of lumber that is an amount of wood volume equal to 1 in thickness and 1 sq ft.

board meter A unit measurement of the amount of wood in a piece of lumber equal to the volume of an area 25 mm (2.5 cm) thick and 1 sq m.

boardwalk A walkway made of boards often used along shopping areas, at the edges of beaches, or in sensitive, environmental areas frequented by tourists.

bob *See* **plumb bob**.

BOCA Reference to the National Building Code (uniform building code) in the United States. This is prepared by the Building Officials and Code Administrators International whose address is 4051 West Flossmoor Rd., Country Club Hills, IL 60478.

BOD *or* **biochemical oxygen demand** The oxygen used during degradation of organic and inorganic materials in water.

body The outside enclosure of a sprinkler device such as a sprinkler valve or sprinkler head without the inner working parts.

b of b Abbreviation for back of board.

bog **1.** A wet ground area that is generally soft, having soil mainly made up of decaying organic

bog garden

matter. **2.** A temperate climate wetland usually exhibiting an acidic **pH**, and characterized by the presence of mosses, a diverse **plant pallet**, and an accumulation of **peat**.

bog garden   Land where the soil is permanently damp.

bog plant   A plant that will thrive in wet or saturated soil, but will not survive submerged conditions. If there is constant standing water, they should be referred to as **marginal plants**.

boil   A wet portion of material in an excavation.

bole   The portion of a tree stem (**trunk**) from the ground to the first branch.

bollard   A low post or many posts together set in a line to prevent access of vehicles to an area or to prevent vehicles from damaging a surface or structure. They may be made of stone, concrete, wood, marble, or steel pipes, and may be filled with concrete, etc. They are often decorative in appearance.

bolster   **1.** A horizontal, wood piece or large timber on top of a column or pillar providing an area for dispersing loads from above. It is usually decorative. **2.** In masonry work, a **blocking chisel**.

bolster chisel   A steel chisel with a wide blade for cutting brick, pavers, or blocks. It is used with a **club hammer** to strike it.

bolt   **1.** The premature production of seed. **2.** A metal shaft with a head and threads along a portion of the other end or all of the shaft. The head of the bolt is shaped to accept some type of tool to hold it in place, or it is shaped to be held firmly in place by the material it is placed in so that a device or nut may be turned on its threads to hold an item or items firmly in place or together. **3.** A fairly short section cut from a tree trunk ready for sawing into lumber. **4.** A roll of paper, etc. **5.** A phenomenon in annuals or vegetables when they grow quickly to the flowering stage at the expense of good overall development. This is caused by hot weather, planting late in the season, excessive fertilization, etc. It is especially detrimental to crops that flower before obtaining the desired size or producing the desired crop.

bolt head   The enlarged end of a bolt, usually held in place with a tool while a nut or object is tightened on the other end to hold materials together.

BOM   Abbreviation for **bill of materials**.

bona fide bid   A bid that meets the conditions of the bidding requirements and is signed by an authorized person representing the bidding party.

bond   **1.** In construction, a financial guarantee from an insurer that assures that the work required by the bid will be accomplished. **2.** Masonry units laid in a wall in a pattern that provides the wall with strength and stability. **3.** The union of materials.

bond beam   In block walls, a continuous opening between blocks where steel is placed and secured with masonry grout. This becomes a structural element to provide stability to the block wall.

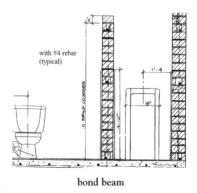

with #4 rebar (typical)

bond beam

bond coat   A primer coat to assure adhesion on a surface of another material, especially paint on a surface.

bond timber   A timber built into a brick wall or a stone wall, usually in a horizontal position for the purpose of giving it strength.

bonding capacity   The amount of monetary exposure a bonding company will extend. This is usually based on a contractor's prior performance and capabilities.

bonding layer   A layer of mortar laid on a masonry or concrete surface for bonding with another layer of masonry.

bone ash   Residue of calcined bones used in making pottery, glass, and as a **fertilizer**. It is **alkaline** and has an **NPK** of 0-35-0.

bonemeal   An organic fertilizer made from ground animal bones being slightly **alkaline** and having an **NPK** ratio of about 4-21-0.2. Steamed bonemeal is not as long-lasting as bonemeal and has an NPK of 2.5-24-0.

bonsai   A practice started in Japan of growing woody plants in a small container to keep them miniature and create a miniature landscape or tree. This requires meticulous pruning of branches and roots to create a fine specimen with a gnarled old look.

bonus and penalty clause   The portion of a contract that establishes an extra amount of money to be awarded for completion of a project prior to the agreed day of completion or a penalty for completion after the agreed upon date.

booster pump   A pump that increases the flow and/or pressure in a piping system over that which it normally maintains or produces.

boot   A metal flange around a pipe that passes through a roof, assisting in preventing leakage at the pipe penetration in the roof.

border   **1.** An **edge** or boundary of a planting area or paving. **2.** Plants delineating an **edge**.

border dike   Earth ridge built to guide or hold irrigation or recharge water in a field.

border irrigation   The practice of irrigating by flooding strips of land, rectangular in shape, cross-leveled, and bordered by dikes. Water is applied at a rate sufficient to move down the strip in a uniform sheet. Border strips with no down-field slope are referred to as level border systems. Border systems constructed on terraces are commonly known as benched borders.

bore   **1.** Larvae of insects that tunnel and eat into stems and trunks, causing extensive damage or death of the plant. **2.** The action of drilling or making holes. **3.** The diameter of the inside of a pipe or any fitting thereon.

boreal   A reference to the northern **biogeographical** region.

boreal forest   Arctic conifer forests dominated by fir spruce, and tamarack.

borer   An insect that bores into woody plants as a larvae or as an adult.

boring   **1.** The action of making a hole, usually by turning an instrument or using a drill. **2.** Auguring, usually horizontally underground, by rotating a bit to extend a pipe or such from one point to another.

boron   A micronutrient in soil necessary for most plants' optimum health and growth. In areas of high **pH**, this nutrient may be lacking. It plays a role in calcium utilization and without it death may occur in the growing portions of plants.

borrow   Fill material required for construction and obtained from other locations.

borrow pit   An area from which soil or other unconsolidated materials are removed to be used, without further processing, as fill for activities such as landscaping, utility **backfill**, build-

bosk

ing construction and maintenance, or highway construction and maintenance.

bosk, bosque The heads of trees or large plants intertwined into a mass, thicket, grove, etc.

boss **1.** A botanical term meaning a tight, rounded cluster, usually referring to stamens. **2.** In an employment setting, one who directs another's work. **3.** With regard to pipe systems, a protuberance on a fitting or pipe for strength, for fastening it to objects, to assist in alignment, etc.

bossing Soft sheet metal shaped to a three-dimensional surface to which it is applied.

botanical garden A public or private facility, park, or **open space** landscape with a variety of plant material on display for interest, observation, study, scientific research, and/or demonstration of the cultivation of flowers, fruits, vegetables, or ornamental plants. Ornamental botanical gardens usually seek to eventually display mature specimens and/or rare **species** or **varieties**.

botanical name The Latin name (**scientific name**) of a plant usually composed of **genus**, **species**, and sometimes, **variety**, **cultivar**, or **strain**. A plant may have several common names, but a plant may only have one botanical name. Plants requested by botanical name are more likely to be the plant desired. *See* **plant classification** and **taxon**.

botany The branch of biology concerned with the study of plants.

bottle brick Hollow brick shaped so it can be interconnected with similar bricks and possibly laid with steel reinforcement.

bottom chord A lower horizontal member of a truss.

bottomland Floodplain areas of lowlands. They may be wetlands and are often dominated by wetland tree species.

bough A branch of a tree, and especially main branches, and/or evergreen branches.

boulder **1.** A rock larger than 25 cm or 10 in in a dimension used in walls, foundations, or mortar. **2.** A single large rock native in a landscape or placed for enhancement in landscape construction.

boulder

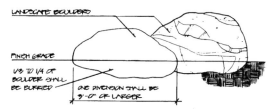

boulder detail

boulevard A wide, tree-lined street. Early French boulevards were intended as **promenade**s and not for heavy traffic as in recent years. The heavy-traffic, wide boulevards became a feature of city planning not only in France, but also in the United States where the term has come to be associated with a wide main thoroughfare.

boundary **1.** A separating line that establishes or indicates a limit to an area or an extent. **2.** A **property line**.

boundary survey A diagram that will mathematically close based on compass bearings, distances, and angles, usually prepared by a licensed land surveyor, and referenced to a bench mark or section corner, etc.

bow   With regard to lumber, a board with a curve in its length.

bow compass   A device for drawing arcs or circles made up of a bow with a pencil or a drawing device on one end, and a point on the other end placed at the center of the arc.

bower   In landscape gardening, usually describes a sheltered area or open structure within a garden. It can be a shelter of tree **bough**s or vines entangled together.

bowling green   A highly maintained portion of lawn that originated with the game of lawn bowling.

bow saw   A saw with a tubular frame roughly in the shape of a C holding a replaceable blade connected at each end of the frame.

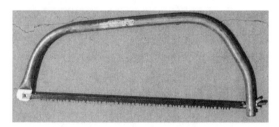

bow saw

box   *See* **boxed plant**.

box beam   A hollow beam.

box culvert   A culvert of reinforced concrete with a rectangular or square cross-section cast in place or made of precast sections.

boxed plant   A plant (usually a tree) grown in a wooden box. Wooden boxes are used on large plant material where other containers would be difficult to remove without disturbing the roots and endangering the tree in planting. The box is comprised of several boards on each of four sides and the bottom. The box is usually tapered with the top being wider. This allows the box to be suspended with a piece of equipment and chains or straps while the bottom boards are removed. The plant will not fall out if established because of the tapered box and the consolidation of the roots and growing medium. The sides of the box may be removed in the planting pit without the established root ball falling apart if the boards are removed as the planting pit is backfilled.

boxed plant

box garden   A garden with hedges of boxwood dividing it into sections or areas.

box nail   A **nail** with a wide, thin, flat-top head and slender, pointed shank for general construction purposes, especially for woodwork and thin materials. It is similar to a **common nail** except that its shank is not as thick as a common nail's shank.

box section   Referring to concrete pipe that has a rectangular cross-section.

box stall   An individual compartment in a barn or stable meant for an animal.

boxwood   In construction, dense, hard, fine-grained, white or yellow wood often used on a lathe for producing wood products or also for inlay.

box wrench   A wrench with two useful ends usually having a closed socket and an opened socket that fits nuts and bolts and is used to tighten them.

brace   **1.** A metal or wood member used to support a portion of a structure or a frame temporarily or permanently. **2.** A drilling tool with a handle crank and chuck that receives a bit so that it may be rotated to drill holes.

braced excavation   An area where earth has been removed and the perimeter banks are retained by wood, steel, or concrete sheets.

bracing   Elements of support. *See* **brace.**

brackish   **1.** A term used to describe saline water. **2.** A term less correctly used to describe stale or stagnant waters such as in swamps, etc. **3.** Anything salty, including soil.

brackish water   Surface or ground waters having a salt content greater than 0.5 parts per thousand.

bracts   Modified, reduced leaves just below a flower or cluster of flowers. Some bracts are not green and can be quite colorful such as on poinsettia, bougainvillea, or flowering dogwood trees.

brad   A small nail used for finishing with a head nearly the same width as its sides.

braided wire   Electrical conducting wire made of smaller wires braided or twisted together.

brake horsepower *or* **Bhp**   The horsepower actually needed for a **pump** to provide the required pressure and flow for a particular need. It may be found by multiplying the **total dy-namic head** by the gallons per minute needed, and dividing it by the product of 3960 multiplied by the efficiency of the pump (taken from a **pump performance curve** provided by the manufacturer).

bramble   Shrubs that are thorny or prickly and often bear edible fruit (blackberries, raspberries, etc.).

branch   **1.** A natural division of a plant stem. **2.** In plumbing, a pipe that starts or ends at a main, a riser, or a stack.

branch collar   A slightly swelled, sometimes wrinkled, area at the base of a branch where it meets the trunk. Cells in this area form the tree's defensive boundary where it attempts to prevent spread of damage by insects or disease. These cells will form the wound wood that covers and protects the area if a branch was removed. Branches should not be removed by cutting off the protective collar flush with the trunk. Cuts should be made next to it regardless of the size of branch being pruned.

branch fitting   A pipe fitting used to connect a branch pipe to a main pipe.

branch line   In irrigation pipe systems, this is any pipe that diverges or branches off from another pipe in the direction of water flow from a valve through the pipes.

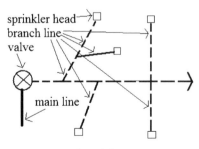

branch line

brashy   Wood that is weak and brittle.

brass   A copper alloy having zinc as its principal element.

brass pipe   A tubular metal manufactured from an alloy of 85% copper and 15% zinc.

braze   To join pieces of metal with metal alloy of nonferrous metal (solder) that melts at a temperature above 800F and provides a hardened connection.

BRC   Abbreviation for **bronze**.

break   A term sometimes used to describe a **mutant** plant.

breaker   **1.** A machine that crushes rocks. **2. Breaker switch**.

breaker box   **1.** A metal enclosure (box) housing **breaker switch**es. It also often houses a main electrical switch that will turn off all electricity.

breaker box

breaker switch   A switch in an electrical system that controls electricity flowing to **outlets**, lights, and/or electrical devices, and **flips** to the off position when there is a short in the line. This is a safety feature to assist in avoiding fire and/or shock.

break horsepower   The mechanical power supplied by an engine or motor determined by a friction break or dynamometer applied to the shaft or flywheel.

breaking ground   The start of excavation work that begins a construction project.

breakwater   **1.** An artificial earthen (soil, rock, concrete, rubble, boulders) barrier in a water body, extending above the water surface and perpendicular to the shoreline. It is generally used to change the natural littoral drift, to protect inlet entrances from clogging with excess sediment, or to protect a harbor area from waves created by boats, winds, or water currents. **2.** A overing of a shoreline area with heavy rock, boulders, concrete pieces, etc. to prevent erosion of the shoreline.

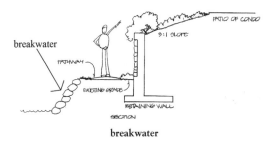

breakwater

breast drill   A hand-operated drill with an end that can be braced against one's chest for additional force.

breeching fitting   A symmetrical Y-shaped pipe fitting used to unite two parallel pipes.

breezeway   A covered passageway connecting two spaces.

BRG Abbreviation utilized on drawings for **bearing**.

brick A rectangular masonry unit made of clay treated in a kiln.

brick anchor *or* **brick tie** A metal strip used when facing a wall with brick to anchor the brick to a wall by having the strips attached to the back wall and placing the other portion of each strip in the mortar of the brick wall laid in front of it.

brick and brick The laying of brick where no mortar shows on the face as they are laid touching one another and then mortared from behind.

brick face The surface of a brick intended to be exposed on the front of a brick wall.

brick on edge A brick laid on its narrowest side in a wall.

brick trowel A metal, diamond-shaped blade with an offset handle used for spreading mortar. It has a narrow end called a point and a wide end called a heel.

brick trowel

bridal joint A joint where a piece of lumber is hollowed or shaped to accept the end of another piece of lumber that has been hollowed or shaped.

bridal path A path constructed and intended for equestrian use. These paths are usually barricaded if they intersect roads to prevent vehicles from entering where horses are being ridden. They are usually wide enough for two horses to pass one another.

bridge An elevated structure connecting two elevated points.

bridgeboard A notched board supporting treads and risers of a staircase.

bridge deck The slab or other surface forming the travel surface of a bridge.

bridging **1.** Installing braces between joists to help strengthen them and better distribute loads from above. **2.** Braces between joists.

brier A plant or mass of plants that are thorny or prickly.

bristle In botanical terms, a stiff, sharp hair or any very slender body of similar appearance.

British croquet A game played with mallets, different colored balls, and hoops for passing balls through on a lawn. The size is 84 ft by 105 ft. See also **lawn croquet**.

British Standard A publication by the **British Standards Institution** that itemizes grades, sizes, qualities, and other specifications of materials.

British Standards Institution An organization in Great Britain that establishes and publishes standards for specifications in that country.

British thermal unit The amount of heat necessary to change the temperature of 1 lb of water upward 1F.

brk. Abbreviation for brick.

broadax A type of ax having a broad blade used in roughly shaping timbers.

broadcast A method of application by scattering or dispersing a material such as seed, fertilizer, etc. over the ground. This can be done by hand, by a hand-cranked seed broadcaster, or by a tractor-drawn broadcaster. Mechanical broadcasters help assure evenness of application.

broadleaf Plants that do not have needlelike or scale-like foliage.

broadly spreading A term often used to describe tree crowns that are widely vase shaped with a narrow bottom and a wide top. (Compare with **round, columnar, fastigiate, oval, weeping, upright spreading, pyramidal.**)

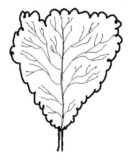

broadly spreading tree form

broad stone A stone produced for construction purposes having edges with more or less right angles, making it easier to stack. It comes in a variety of sizes.

broken joints Staggered, vertical, masonry joints where masonry units are not placed directly above one another. This pattern divides for a stronger wall as units are not placed directly above one another lining up joints.

broken-pitch roof A roof with more than one pitch on either side of its ridge as with many barn roofs.

bronze A mixture of copper and tin.

broom **1.** To lightly brush a concrete surface in its early cure stage, giving it a rougher texture. **2.** To make certain a roofing layer has bonded to the bitumen underneath it by pressing over its entire surface. **3.** The widening or spreading of the top of a post or pile pounded into the ground.

broom finish To lightly brush a concrete surface in its early cure stage, giving it a rougher texture that is more skid or slip resistant.

brownfield An abandoned, idled, or underused industrial or commercial facility where expansion or redevelopment is complicated by real or perceived environmental contamination.

brown rot A powdery, brown residue after a certain type of fungus destroys wood.

brownstone A sandstone used extensively in the eighteenth century in the United States that is dark brown or reddish.

BRS Abbreviation for **brass**.

Br Std Abbreviation for **British Standard**.

BRU Abbreviation for brick.

brush A tool with bristles held tightly together, used for painting or cleaning.

brushed surface A concrete surface stroked with a brush to give it a rough or textured look as in a **broom finish**.

BS **1.** Abbreviation for both sides. **2.** Abbreviation for **British Standard**.

BSI **1.** Abbreviation for British Standard Institution. **2.** Abbreviation for Building Stone Institute.

BSMT Abbreviation for basement.

BTB Abbreviation for bituminous treated base.

Btu, BTU Abbreviation for **British thermal unit**.

BTUH Abbreviation for BTU per hour.

bubble level A closed glass tube filled with liquid except for a small space where a bubble is formed and can be centered in the tube to determine horizontal or vertical lines or planes, as well as to determine direction of slope in paving surfaces or pipes to assure drainage.

bubbler An irrigation head that allows water to flow or bubble from it freely (not in a spray or drip) over a small area.

buck

buck A **sawhorse**.

bucket A portion of a tractor that digs or carries materials and is shaped for containment, somewhat like a scoop.

bucket-wheel excavator This is an excavating machine that moves under its own power, digs with a rotating wheel, and dumps earth onto a conveyer belt.

buckle Distortion, movement, or breaking of a wood or steel member or sheet.

buck scraper An earth scraping machine which fills with earth as it is moved, and then it is raised on each side (on runners) to release the load.

bud **1.** Flower buds that develop into blossoms. **2.** Leaf buds or growth buds that are at the ends or sides of stems and develop into leaves. **3.** To propagate by **budding**.

budding **1.** In gardening, a method of **propagation** by transplanting a bud to another plant by cutting a T-shaped slit in a stem of a plant, and removing a bud with a bit of wood from another plant to place it in the T-shaped cut. It is then bound in place. **2.** In reference to plants in general, a plant's buds swelling in the spring before leaves emerge.

bud union The enlarged knob just above the soil where top growth joins the rootstock.

budworms and budmoths Young caterpillars that feed on or in plant buds.

buffer **1.** A strip of land, compatible land uses, fence, or a border of trees, etc., between one use and another that somewhat **mitigates negative impacts** between uses. **2.** A visual screen. **3.** A strip of land with natural or planted vegetation intended to separate or at least partially obstruct the view of two adjacent land uses or properties from one another. **4.** A device that blocks scat-

tering of rock when blasting. **5.** The zone around the edge of a water body where disturbances and uses are limited to protect the water body from contamination or degradation.

buffering The resistance of a substance to an abrupt change in **pH** (**acidity** or **alkalinity**).

buffer strip In land use, the portion of a lot or a land area used to visually separate one use from another by way of vegetation, screening, and/or distance; to shield or obstruct such **negative impacts** as noise, illumination, poor aesthetics, or other incompatibilities or nuisances.

buffer zone An area of land separating two distinct land uses that is zoned, set aside, or required to provide softening or mitigation to the effects of one land use toward the other.

builder A company or individual responsible for construction.

builder's level A long straight piece of wood or metal alloy with bubble levels set within its frame.

Builder's Risk Insurance Insurance for coverage of construction work.

building code A construction document usually referred to after adoption by a government agency. It describes and identifies materials, methods, and/or procedures for building and/or construction practices.

building footprint The shape included within the surrounding exterior walls of a building as they are traced upon the ground.

building inspector An individual authorized by a government agency to inspect construction work making certain it conforms to applicable codes, regulations, and/or drawings approved by the jurisdiction.

building official An individual charged by a governing agency with administration and enforcement of **building codes** and rules. Also, one duly authorized by such an individual to be a representative.

building paper An inexpensive paper, usually asphalt covered, which affords some thermal insulation, a little weather protection, and a vapor barrier.

building permit A written document authorizing construction that is given by an official having jurisdiction over the area built upon.

building regulations A term sometimes used for **building code**.

built environment **1.** The elements of the **environment** that are generally built or made by people rather than natural processes. **2.** The whole of the human physical surroundings and conditions that have been constructed.

built-up beam A beam of wood or metal made of individual units bound, bolted, welded, or fastened together in some fashion forming a larger, stronger, structural member.

built-up roofing Roofing made of layers of roofing felts, asphalt, and/or cold tar pitch surfaced with either a layer of asphalt with gravel or cold tar pitch with gravel.

bulb With regard to plant material, a swollen or thickened storage organ just beneath the soil surface, which in season produces leaves, roots, stems, and flowers. It encompasses **true bulbs**, **rhizomes**, **tuberous roots**, **tubers**, and **corms**.

bulb

bulbil Small bulbs formed along stems in **axils** of leaves and flowers. Bulbils may be planted to form new plants.

bulblet Often called an **offset**. New bulbs are formed from lateral buds on the basal plate. These smaller bulbs can be separated and planted.

bulbous Growing **bulbs** or growing from a bulb.

bulk Material provided loose, and not in bags, boxes, or other containers. It is usually loaded for hauling with shovels or tractors.

bulk density A numerical reference to the measurement of whether a soil is friable or compacted. It is the weight of a unit volume of oven-dry soil, including the pore and solid volumes. A topsoil with a bulk density of about 1.33 **Mg/m** is considered the preferred density for a favorable rooting medium. Soil density exceeding about 1.6 Mg/m is considered unfavorable or greatly inhibiting to root penetration. *See also* **soil compaction** and **compact**.

bulkhead **1.** A structure including **riprap** or sheet piling, constructed to separate land and water and establish a permanent shoreline that will not erode. **2.** A structure or partition placed on a bank, a steep slope, or bluff to retain or prevent sliding of the land.

bullate In botanical identification and descriptions, covered with rounded projections resembling unbroken blisters.

bulldozer A heavy tractor moving on tracks with a horizontal curved blade useful in clearing land, road building, stripping soil, etc.

bull float A long-handled tool (4 to 16 ft, 1 to 5 m) with a wide (+/− 42 to 60 in, 100 to 150 cm) trowel-like head (+/− 8 in, 20 cm) made of wood, **aluminum**, or magnesium used in finishing concrete. Its handle usually has sections that can be added for reaching distant portions of new wet concrete pavements to smooth and even the surface. Most have the capability of interchanging the trowel head for different smoothnesses or finishes.

bullhead tee   In reference to pipes, a **tee** fitting that has smaller openings in line with each other and a larger opening to the side or the tee.

bullnose   In concrete work, the rounding of an edge or sharp angle in a surface of wet concrete, or a reference to the finished look of such rounding.

bull-nose block   A masonry unit or block having at least one rounded corner.

bulwark   A solid structure built for defense or protection as with a sea wall or breakwater.

bunch grass *or* **bunching grasses**   A grass that grows in tufts and is often called a bunch grass because it grows in separate bunches rather than in a mass or sod. These grasses can appear as sod if planted close enough together.

bund   A long, narrow wall or embankment along a body of water.

burl   Dome-shaped swellings on the trunks of some trees growing to as much as 2 ft in diameter.

burlap   A rough, woven fabric of hemp, jute, or such (sometimes flax), used for containing the balls of trees, for retaining water in curing concrete, for reinforcement in plaster, etc.

burnish   To polish and increase the glossiness of a surface.

burr   In piping, a piece of pipe or sliver of pipe left after cutting or threading still slightly attached to the pipe cut.

burst pressure   A reference to the maximum pressure a valve can sustain without rupturing.

bursting strength   With regard to pipe and fittings, this is the point at which there is enough internal pressure to finally cause the pipe and/or its fittings to come apart, crack, or disintegrate.

bush   A low shrub with many stems instead of a single stem.

bush fruits   All shrubs with fruits fit for human consumption.

bush hammer   A hammer having pointed shapes on its face for dressing stone or concrete. It is either used by hand or it may be power driven.

bushing   In piping, a fitting that facilitates joining a smaller pipe to a larger pipe.

butt-end treatment   The treatment of one end of a post or timber to assist in preserving it underground. Various preservatives may be used.

butterfly   Adult insects with large, usually colored, wings. They are similar to moths, but have wings closed when at rest, antennae with knobs at the end, and fly in the day. Some varieties are useful for transferring pollen as they sip nectar. The larvae of a few varieties are destructive to plants.

butterfly garden   A garden that provides plants that are attractive to butterflies and/or their larvae.

butterfly hinge   A decorative hinge having somewhat the shape or appearance of a butterfly.

butterfly valve   A valve with a disc hinged in the center of its opening, which controls the flow of fluids through the valve.

buttering   In masonry, the spreading of mortar on a masonry unit.

butt fusion   A method in piping of joining two plastic pipes together by heating their ends to a molten state and then pressing them together to form a bond.

butt hinge   A hinge that has two rectilinear shapes with one on either side of its center shaft.

butt joint A joint where two members are at right angles, flat, and square in their area of contact.

buttress The lower conical portion of some trees growing in response to flooded conditions. They may include distinct ridges that broaden and anchor the base of the tree. Some species typical of this phenomenon are cypress, black gum, and wetland oak.

butt splice A **butt joint** where the joint is strengthened or held in place by boards secured usually on two sides of the butt joint.

butyl A thick, strong, durable, rubber liner often used as a waterproof liner.

BV Abbreviation for **butterfly valve**.

bypass In piping, an optional water route through an extra pipe, diverting water and again delivering the water to where it connects downstream and thus allowing the passage of a portion of the pipe that normally facilitates flow.

bypass pruner A tool for pruning plants that has two handles and two blades that pivot on a pin, allowing one blade to pass by a curved, shaped blade to make a cut. These pruners are popular.

bypass valve A valve used to control flow through a **bypass**.

C

C   Abbreviation for **Celsius (centigrade)**.

cabana   An open structure or tent near a swimming pool, beach, etc.

cabinet file   A hand file that is rounded on one side and flat on the other side.

cable   **1.** Electrical conductors insulated from one another in a group. **2.** An electrical conductor made up of smaller diameter wires twisted together. **3.** A heavy rope or wire.

cablegation   A method of surface irrigation that utilizes gated pipe to transmit and distribute water to furrows or border strips. A plug moving at a controlled rate through the pipe causes irrigation to progress along the field and causes flow rates from any one gate to decrease continuously from a maximum rate to zero.

cable grip   A tool connected to the end of a cable to facilitate pulling the cable underground with a machine or through a conduit.

cable-pulling compound   A material used to reduce friction on a cable when being pulled through a conduit.

cable vault   An underground, enclosed space (usually a concrete, fiberglass, or plastic box) into which cables are spliced together.

Cactus and Succulent Society of America (CSSA)   A society dedicated to educating people regarding cacti and succulant plants, as well as to protecting and preserving these plant types.

CAD   Abbreviation for computer-aided drafting.

caducous, caduceus, caduceous   In botanical terms, used to describe portions that fall off early or before their usual time.

cairn   A heap or pile of stones placed as a landmark or memorial.

caisson   **1.** A watertight chamber for working on structures below a surrounding water level. **2.** A cylindrical concrete foundation penetrating through unstable soil and resting on rock or stable soil. **3.** An augured or drilled **piling**.

calcareous   Soil containing **calcium carbonate**. It is **alkaline** in reaction.

calcicole   A plant that thrives in **alkaline** soils.

calcifuge   A plant that does not grow in **calcareous (lime, alkaline)** soils.

calcined clay   A baked **montmorillonite** clay that does not shrink or swell when wetted or dried. It is sometimes added to a soil mix for plants to improve the air-water relationship.

calcite   A mineral form of calcium carbonate used in **Portland cement** manufacturing. It is also a constituent of limestone and marble.

calcium carbonate   A naturally occurring compound usually found as calcite and aragonite, in bones, plant ashes, etc. It is used in making **lime** and **Portland cement**.

calcium chloride   A product sprayed on dirt roads that holds dust down, but has a harmful effect on vegetation. Runoff from roads treated with this product should be directed away from vegetation.

calcium cyanamide

calcium cyanamide   *See* **cyanami**.

calcium magnesium carbonate   *See* **dolomite**.

calcium magnesium phosphate   *See* **calcium-magnesium phosphate**.

calcium metaphosphate   A **phosphatic** (53%) **fertilizer** that is nearly neutral in **pH**.

calcium nitrate   A nitrogen fertilizer with 34% nitrogen (34-0-0). *See* **nitrate of lime**.

calcium sulfate   *See* **gypsum**.

caliber   The internal diameter of a pipe.

caliche   A type of **hardpan** condition usually in desert areas. It is a deposit of calcium carbonate (**lime**) that "cements" soil particles together beneath the soil surface and does not allow hand digging, root penetration, or water percolation.

caliper   **1.** In horticultural practice, an instrument with two legs, pivoting at one end, and allowing a measurement of the diameter of a plant's stem (trunk) or branches between the other two ends. **2.** A measurement of the diameter of a plant's trunk or stem. This is primarily used in reference to trees. For trees less than 4 inches in diameter, the measurement is usually taken at 6 inches above ground level. For trees greater than 4 inches in diameter, up to and including 12 inches, the caliper measurement is usually taken at 12 inches above the ground level. For trees greater than 12 inches in diameter, the trunk is usually measured at breast height (**diameter at breast height** or **DBH**), which is 4½ ft above the ground. Typically, existing larger caliper trees are measured at breast height.

callus   A mass of cells that develops from and around wounded plant tissues.

calorie   The amount of heat necessary to raise the temperature of one gram of water one degree Celsius (**centigrade**).

calyx   The outer, usually green, enclosure (sepals) that surrounds a flower bud.

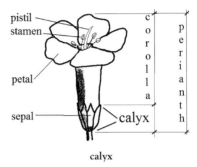

calyx

camber   **1.** A slight upward curvature in a beam or truss to improve appearance or prevent sag by compensating for loads placed upon it. **2.** A slight rise in curvature of a surface to accommodate water drainage of the surface (runoff).

camber beam   A beam curved slightly upward near its center.

cambium   On **dicotyledon**ous trees and shrubs (including all woody plants) this is the layer between the bark and the underlying tissue (sapwood) upon which they are dependant for growth of new wood by cell division. This is also where a plant forms its bark. This layer extends from the base to the plant tips. *See also* **xylem** and **phloem**.

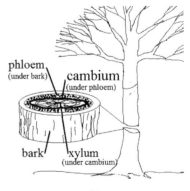

cambium

campanile   A free-standing bell tower.

campanulate   In botanical terms, a bell-shaped or cup-shaped flower with a broad base.

campanulated   Having a bell shape.

Canadian Standards Association   An organization that tests and publishes standards for the construction industry in Canada.

canaliculate   A botanical term indicating that a plant part has parallel grooves or channels.

candela   *See* **candle**.

candelabra   A pattern (form) of an **espalier**ed plant that resembles a candelabra with branches generally forking horizontally and turning upward.

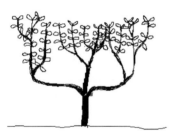

candelabra espalier

candle *or* **cd**   In lighting design, a luminous intensity. The description or standard for this intensity is one-sixteenth the luminous intensity of 1 sq cm of a black body surface at the solidification temperature of platinum. A light source of 1 candle (candela) emits 12.57 lumens.

candlepower   Luminous intensity of a source producing light expressed in **candela**s.

cane   The woody stem of a plant that only lives for two or three years (e.g., raspberries).

cane bolt   A cane-shaped metal bolt that is attached to a door or gate. It can be turned and pushed down so that the bottom portion of its shaft slides into a hole in a pavement to prevent the door from moving. These are often used in barns, stables, and warehouses.

canescent   This refers to a fine, close gray or pale **pubescence** on a plant or a plant part. (Compare with **argenteous**, **cinerous**.)

canker   A localized, diseased area mostly on woody plants where tissue has died due to the effects of fungi or bacteria, visible as lesions on trunks, branches, and other plant parts. These areas shrink, die, and crack, exposing tissue underneath. As they interfere with water uptake, the foliage often dies as do ends of twigs. Preventing cankers is best achieved by adequate water, **fertilizer**, and avoidance of injury. Prune cankers out while being careful not to spread the disease with pruning equipment.

cankerworm   Larvae of various insects, but especially of small moths, that defoliate trees and shrubs. They are often noticeable when lowering themselves by small threads.

canopy   A covered shelter for protection from sun, rain, snow, tree-litter, etc., that generally projects over a sidewalk, driveway, entry, window, or similar area. It may be wholly supported by columns, poles, or braces extending from the ground.

cantilever   **1.** Anything in design extended beyond its support. **2.** In framing and decking, a structural member that extends horizontally beyond its last vertical support.

cantilever wall   A reinforced concrete retaining wall with a footing extending underneath the slope to be retained, thus resisting overturning by the weight on this cantilever footing.

canvas   A closely woven material made of hemp, flax, or cotton.

cap

cap   **1.** A fitting or device used to close the end of a pipe. **2.** A top portion of a **retaining wall**, **pillar**, **column**, etc., different from the rest of the wall in its material, thickness, dimensions, etc.

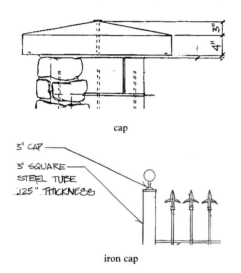

cap

3" CAP
3" SQUARE STEEL TUBE .125" THICKNESS

iron cap

capillary   In botanical terms, hair-like.

capillary action   The force resulting from water surface tension as well as attraction of soil particles to water molecules. This force, when combined with osmotic pressure from roots, causes water in the pores of soil to move. In clay soils, capillary force is higher and may move water as much as 30 ft vertically.

capillary capacity   The amount of water still held in the soil when the excess water that can be drained by gravity has drained out. *See* **field capacity**.

capillary fringe   The zone immediately adjacent to and above the **water table** in which all or some of the smaller gaps between soil particles are filled with water having less than atmospheric pressure. In this area, water is drawn up from the water table by capillary action. The smaller spaces in soil hold onto water tighter and draw it up higher than the larger pores. In gen-

eral, soils having smaller spaces between particles draw water higher along the fringe of the water table.

capillary movement   In soils, the movement of water due to unequal tensions of water developed under different degrees of curvature of the surface film of the water. As a root hair absorbs moisture from around two soil particles, the film curvature around those particles curves and the tension draws moisture from around other particles toward that point, causing the movement of water in the soil. This movement is very slow. A plant will usually wilt before an appreciable quantity of water can move within reach of its roots from any great distance.

capillary water   In association with soil, water that is retained in the pores of soil and not drained under the force of gravity. Capillary action holds water in the soil above the water table. This water is held in the capillary or small pores of the soil, usually with soil water pressure (tension) greater than ⅓ bar. Capillary water may move in any direction.

capital   The uppermost portion or member of a **column** or **pilaster** that is meant to distribute, accept, and bear the weight of the structure above it. It is the wider and often decorative portion at the top of a column.

capitate   In plant identification and description, this means head-like, formed into a head, or abruptly enlarged and making a head.

cap screw   A threaded screw with a chamfered point driven into a hole and then tightened into it (without a nut).

capsule   **1.** A seed case that splits open to release seeds when it is dry. **2.** In botanical terms, a dry **dehiscent** fruit made up of more than one carpel.

carbonaceous Containing organic matter.

carbon-arc welding A weld caused by an arc between a carbon electrode and a metal piece.

carbon disulfide Also called carbon bisulfide, a dangerous soil **fumigant**. Upon exposure to the atmosphere, it evaporates into a poisonous, explosive gas that is heavier than air and damages plants.

carbon:nitrogen ratio, carbon to nitrogen ratio The ratio (proportion) of carbon to **nitrogen** by weight in **organic matter** or **soil**. As the carbon (undecomposed organic matter) amount (first number) increases, the nitrogen used for **decomposition** increases, becoming unavailable to plants as it is robbed for the decomposition process. The **A horizon** in a soil usually stabilizes with a ratio of about 10:1 through 12:1. Forest litter with less decomposition may be 20:1, and other organic substances may be much higher (i.e., sawdust that is not decomposed). The higher the carbon in the ratio, the more nitrogen will be stolen from the soil to break down the material. Nitrogen stolen from the soil for decomposition often has a detrimental effect on plant growth. *See* **nitrogen deficiency**.

carbon steel Steel having a various amount of alloy elements.

cardinal temperature The minimal temperature at which growth occurs.

carotene *See* **xanthophylls**.

carpel The fertile portion (megasporophyll) of an angiosperm **flower**, which bears the ovules. One or more carpels join to compose a pistil.

carpel indehiscent In botanical terms, remaining closed at maturity.

carpenter's level A straight metal or wood bar used to determine horizontal or vertical lines for being true by use of a bubble in glass.

carpenter's level

carpenter's square A flat, steel, L-shaped tool with measurements (inches, centimeters) marked along its edge, used to mark perpendicular lines or check corners for being perpendicular (square) to each other.

carriage bolt A metal bolt with a flattened end threaded for accepting a nut with like threads; the other end has a wide, rounded top that is flat underneath and has no indents on its top surface for accepting a screwdriver, and no flat sides to accept a wrench for stopping it from turning when the nut is tightened. Instead, it has a square shoulder portion just under the rounded head's flat bottom that holds the bolt by being secured in a similarly sized square hole in the piece it is bolted to. Threads on the shank may extend the entire length or for only a portion of its length. It is useful to bind items together or secure items in place.

carriage bolt

cartilaginous In plant identification and description, tough and firm, but somewhat flexible, like cartilage.

caryopsis A small **indehiscent** one-seeded fruit with the seed fused to its surroundings (i.e., wheat, rye, corn).

casebearer Moths and larvae that feed on leaves, flowers, seeds, etc. and have portable tubes or pouches in which they live or hibernate.

case-hardened Steel or iron that has been hardened on the outside.

case-hardening **1.** In metal, a way of increasing durability and strength of steel or iron (*see* **case-hardened**). **2.** In timber, when drying and seasoning lumber if the outer layers dry too quickly this causes stress between them and the inner layers.

casing **1.** The exposed molding, framing, or trim around a door or a window. **2.** A portion of pipe used to line a hole. **3.** The housing that encases the impeller of a pump.

casing nail A small, slender **nail** with a slightly flared head that is not much larger than the nail shaft. It is often used in finished-surface woodwork. It is usually not desirable to allow a nail head to show on the finished material it is attaching. It can be driven into the material with a punch or the force of a mechanical nail gun, and covered with similar material to that which it is nailed so that its location is unnoticeable.

cast-in-place concrete Concrete poured on-site. It is designed to stay in the location where it is poured and finished. It is not brought in as **precast concrete**.

cast-iron An iron alloy with high carbon content (keeping it from being classified as steel) formed into shapes by pouring it into molds at high temperature in a molten state. It has a high compressive strength, but low **tensile strength**.

cast-iron pipe (CIP) A thick wall metal pipe mostly used on large water service lines. It is available in various wall thicknesses and pressure ratings.

castor pomace The dried pulpy residue of castor beans after extraction of oil. It is an acidic fertilizer with an **NPK** of 5 to 6, $1\frac{1}{3}$ to 2, $\frac{1}{2}$ to 1.

catch basin A container for surface drainage waters in which sediment settles out before water is drained out.

catch can *See* **catchment**.

catch can grid A defined pattern of cans or containers for catching water dispersed by sprinklers where the cans are spaced on 1–2 ft intervals. This is a method used by manufacturers, irrigation auditors, and testing facilities to obtain accurate **sprinkler profiles**.

catchment In irrigation auditing, a container that is set out to catch irrigation water as it falls from the spray of sprinklers. These containers are used to measure the water distribution of sprinklers. They are set out in a uniform pattern, the sprinklers are operated for a specific period of time, and the water they catch is measured for determining **distribution uniformity**, efficiency, and **precipitation rates**.

caterpillar An elongated, smooth, or hairy, wormlike larva usually of a **butterfly** or **moth**. They can be quite destructive as they chew and consume leaves and other plant parts.

cathodic corrosion Decomposition and destruction of metals caused by the electromechanical action of **electrolysis**. This occurs when two dissimilar metals (i.e., a galvanized fitting and a brass or copper fitting for pipes) are in contact with one another in the presence of water or another conductor. Dissimilar metals in a piping system should be separated by an insulator pipe or fitting, such as one made from plastic.

cathodic protection A way of defending or saving ferrous metals (containing iron) from **galvanic corrosion** when they are covered with moist soil or are under water. One method is to attach to the metal fittings or pipes to another piece of metal that is more electronegative to divert the **electrolysis**.

cation   A positively charged ion which during electrolysis is attracted toward the cathode. Sodium, potassium, calcium, and magnesium are the most common cations in waters and soils.

cation exchange capacity   The measure of the positively charged ions in a soil matrix.

catkin   In botanical terms, an **ament**, or something closely crowded with bracts. They look like drooping caterpillars.

cat's-eye   A knot in a piece of lumber smaller than ¼ in (0.6 cm).

cattle manure   *See* **cow manure**.

catwalk   A narrow pathway affording access to areas otherwise difficult to reach. They may be used in areas such as highly sensitive environmental sites, areas above excavations, or access to lights or signs high off the ground.

caudate   In botanical terms, having a tail or tail-like appendage.

caudex   **1.** The woody or persistent base of a perennial plant. **2.** The stem of a palm tree or a tree fern.

caulescent   A plant with an obvious leafy stem.

cauliflorous   In botanical terms, a production of flowers or fruit directly out of old wood portions of a plant.

cauline   A botanical term meaning on the stem or pertaining to the stem. Cauline leaves are attached to the stem above the ground in contrast to basal leaves, which originate at ground level.

caulk   Material used to fill joints or cracks in or between construction materials.

caulking gun   A tool used for applying caulk, usually allowing the caulk to be extruded under pressure by pumping a small handle with one hand. These guns are also available with extrusion being supplied by forced air (pneumatically).

cavitation   With regard to piping systems or **pumps**, the forming and collapse of air (vapor) bubbles through pressure changes in the water system or pump. This occurs when the pressure on a liquid falls momentarily below the vapor pressure for that liquid, causing a change from liquid to vapor, and then a pressure increase causes another change and the gas becomes a liquid again. This phenomenon can also occur in suction lines of pumps. *See also* **vapor pressure**.

cavity wall   A masonry wall of two **withe**s having a separation of air between them. The walls are usually connected by metal ties extended between the two withes.

cavity wall tie   A corrosion-resistant piece extending between two masonry walls tying them together as in a **cavity wall** or hollow wall.

CB   Abbreviation for **catch basin**.

C & BTR   With regard to lumber, this is a grade of "C and better."

C/B ratio   This abbreviation refers to the saturation coefficient for brick, which is the ratio of the percent absorption of a brick submerged in cold water for 24 hours to the absorption of a brick submersed in boiling water over a 5-hour period. The 24-hour cold water test is divided by the 5-hour boiling test. This is a strength value, which assists in measuring the durability of masonry units, which can also be measured by conducting freeze/thaw tests. This is of prime importance in landscape work as brick in the landscape is exposed on one or both sides to weather in nearly all cases. It is more important in areas of annual temperatures below freezing.

CCA

CCA Abbreviation for **chromated copper arsenate**.

ccf Abbreviation for hundred cubic feet.

C-clamp A C-shaped steel clamp where a threaded piece is screwed through one threaded female end of the C and extended to the other end of the C where it can be tightened against objects. This type of clamp is used to hold materials temporarily while being worked on.

CCW Abbreviation sometimes used for counterclockwise.

CD, cd **1.** Abbreviation for **candle** or **candela**. **2.** Abbreviation for grade of plywood face and back.

CDX Abbreviation for a plywood grade of C&D with exterior glue.

CEC (cation exchange capacity) The ability of a soil to bind positively charged ions.

cedar A softwood often used in outdoor applications because it is resistant to decay.

cedar-apple rust A fungus (*Gynosporangium*) that damages crabapple, hawthorn, mountain ash, red cedar, quince, and upright junipers. It alternates living on **pome** fruit-bearing trees one year and juniper cedar trees the next year. It causes swelling and gall on juniper-cedar and yellow or orange spots on apples or leaves. Resistant apple varieties include Freedom, Liberty, and Priscilla; varieties of resistant junipers are Chinese and Savin. It is wise to remove alternate hosts from the immediate growing area.

ceiling hook A hook with screw-like threads on one end designed to screw it into a wall, ceiling, wood, etc.

CELA Abbreviation for **Council of Educators in Landscape Architecture**.

cellar A room below grade or a portion of a building having more than half its height below grade.

cell pack *or* **cell tray** A modularized set of small square or rectangular planting containers fitting into a **flat**. They usually contain 96, 72, 48, 36, or 24 cells per flat.

cellular construction Concrete walls constructed with portions of their interior having voids.

cellular grid A method of retaining soil with a lattice-like array of structural members made of concrete, timbers, or polymeric web. These grids allow for the establishment of vegetation that becomes the main stabilizing element for retention.

cellulose A material of plant structures that is the main component of dried woods, flax, hemp, jute, etc. This type of material is often used as the mulch component in **hydromulch**.

Celsius, C Same as **centigrade**.

cem. Abbreviation for cement.

cement A fine gray powder of calcined limestone and clay for mixing with sand, gravel, or other elements to make concrete or mortar.

cementatio The process of cementing.

cement block An incorrect term for **concrete block**.

cement brick Brick fabricated from the mixture of cement and sand. It is not usually used on the face of walls or exposed to acid or alkaline conditions.

cement-coded nail Nails coated with cement. The dried, rough coating makes them stay in place better when pounded into wood.

cement mixer An apparatus for mixing concrete by a drum that mixes the materials by turning, which agitates the materials and mixes them thoroughly. *See* **concrete mixer.**

cement mortar *See* **mortar.**

CEM. MORT. Abbreviation sometimes used for cement mortar.

center bit A bit used for boring holes. It has a center piece on the end of the bit with threads or a sharp point to hold the bit in place once it starts to drill. It may also have projections at the outside edge of the bit to mark its circumference as it is applied to material to begin boring.

centering The materials used under an arch to support it while it is being built.

center island A parking island located between bays of parking and usually running the length of the parking bay.

centerline A line measured or marked on-site or drawn, representing the center of an object such as a road, pipeline, structural member, etc. It is usually indicated on drawings with a dashed line having a long dash and one dot or short dash. It may be labeled with a symbol of a small "c" and a capital letter "L" superimposed over the "c."

center punch Hand tool consisting of a short piece of metal rod with a point at one end, usually being case-hardened and useful in marking where a hole is to be drilled. When struck with a hammer from the opposite end of the point the mark made will usually indent enough for a drill bit to stay in place to begin drilling.

center-to-center Usually in reference to a distance between the middle point or line of two items of the same type (i.e., plants, joists, posts, paths, etc.).

centi A prefix indicating 100.

centigrade *or* **Celsius** *or* **C** A scale for measurement of temperature where 0° is the freezing point of water and 100° is the temperature at the boiling point of water. To convert centigrade (Celsius) to **Fahrenheit,** multiply the centigrade temperature by 9, divide by 5, and then add 32 to the result.

centimeter (cm) The metric measurement of $\frac{1}{100}$ **m** (0.01 m), or $\frac{39}{100}$ in (0.39 in).

centipede A long, segmented, many-legged insect. The garden variety is about ¼ inch long, but other varieties are over an inch long.

central A spine of a cactus where the spines originate from an **aerole**'s center instead of its periphery as they do in a **radial.**

central leader **1.** The main, central stem of a tree from which branches grow. **2.** The upper portion of a tree's or shrub's center stem or **leader,** which is dominant in growth and often extends above other branches and foliage.

central-mixed concrete Concrete mixed completely off-site or a significant distance away and transported to the point of placement.

centrifugal pump A **pump** having pumping action created by fluid passing through a high-speed, rotating **impeller** that builds pressure by centrifugal force caused by fluid being forced outward as it exits the center of the impeller with velocity and pressure. Water is directed by its casing. It produces a smooth, steady flow and is useful in pumping water and sewage with some solids such as gravel, sand, leaves. Types of centrifugal pumps include the **closed-coupled valute pump,** the **valute with flexible coupling pump,** the **horizontal split case pump,** and the **vertical turbine pump.**

cephalium In botanical terms, a woolly cap, usually at the apex of cacti.

cercinate vernation The simultaneous unwinding and growing of fern leaves.

cerogenous A botanical term, wax producing.

certificate of insurance A certification obtained as evidence to an owner, general contractor, etc. that a provider of construction services is covered by a particular type of insurance for a particular maximum amount.

certificate of occupancy A certificate granted by a government jurisdiction for occupancy of a facility and use of it as approved in design, completed in construction, and verified by the government agency.

certificate of payment A written document approving payment for work completed and materials provided.

certificate of substantial completion A verification by a designer or owner that a project is complete except for **punch list** items. At this point, a time of final payment and maintenance duration is usually established.

Certified Irrigation Contractor (CIC) An irrigation professional who has been tested and certified by IA (Irrigation Association) and whose principal business is to install, repair, and maintain irrigation systems.

Certified Irrigation Designer (CID) The IA (Irrigation Association) Certified Irrigation Designer produces professional irrigation designs by writing specifications and drawing designs for the construction of irrigation projects.

Certified Landscape Irrigation Auditor (CLIA) An irrigation professional who is certified by the IA (Irrigation Association) to be involved in the analysis of landscape irrigation water use. Auditors collect site data, make maintenance recommendations, and perform water audits. Through their analytical work at the site, these irrigation professionals develop monthly irrigation base schedules.

Certified Landscape Irrigation Manager (CLIM) An irrigation professional who is certified by the IA (Irrigation Association) as an irrigation professional familiar with all areas of turf irrigation design and construction management. They must be certified as **CIC**s, **CID**s (all specialty areas), and **CLIA**s. Certified Landscape Irrigation Managers have extensive experience in design, construction, construction management, and auditing of irrigation systems.

cespitose A botanical term, growing in dense, low tufts.

cesspool *or* **leaching cesspool** *or* **pervious cesspool** An excavation in the ground that is covered and lined for receiving domestic sewer discharge, surface waters, storm system water, or drainage system waters and is designed to retain organic matter or solid materials while allowing the water or liquids to seep through the side and bottom surfaces. The bottom of the enclosure is either open to earth or a gravel layer, or has holes to allow the escape of liquids from the bottom of the cesspool.

cf **1.** Abbreviation for cubic foot, or cubic feet. A cubic foot is a volume that measures 1 ft long (12 inches) along all edges and is comprised of 144 **s.i. 2.** Abbreviation for 100 ft.

cfm Abbreviation for **cubic feet per minute**.

chaff In botanical terms, small scales or bracts on the receptacle of compositaceae; the **glume**s of grasses, etc.

chaffy In botanical terms, furnished with chaff; of the texture of chaff.

chain **1.** A measuring instrument used in surveying made up of 100 links. In the United States, the links are 1 ft long. **2.** A unit of measurement equal to 66 ft (20 m). **3.** A length of interlocking metal links. Large chains are used with tractors for lifting, with block and tackle, on trencher booms with teeth to dig, or for holding equipment while in transport, etc. Smaller chains are used on chain saws or between pulleys in transferring force from an engine, etc.

chain-link fence A fence made of heavy, interwoven, steel wire to make a fabric that is usually galvanized for durability. This mesh is stretched between posts to provide a barrier fence. It can be made more aesthetically pleasing by coating with plastic vinyl, etc., in colors such as brown, green, or black, and by sliding colored slats through the fabric.

chain saw A handheld, power cutting tool with a rotating **chain** and embedded teeth that cut through wood.

chain trencher A machine used for digging trenches, with a rotating continuous metal **chain** outfitted with teeth blades that dig.

chalk **1.** An **alkaline** soil composed of decomposing and fossilized shells. It is whitish, grayish, or yellowish in color. **2.** Used in a **pull-string** (**chalk line**) to mark materials for cutting or for placement. **3.** A calcareous, light-colored limestone that is soft.

chalk line A string covered with chalk stretched tightly over a surface, pulled and then let go at the center to snap a line on the surface marked with the chalk. This line is often used for cutting or marking a place of attachment.

chamfer A symmetrical beveled cut or beveled edge. It is usually on a right-angled edge and is a 45° angle surface to the other main surfaces.

champaign A term used mostly by the French to describe a large, open, fairly flat countryside.

change order A document showing change in the work or cost of a contract.

channel The deeper portion of a water flow way that has faster current, water flow, and pressure.

channel bar *See* **channel iron**.

channel block A hollow masonry unit with openings to accept a continuous steel reinforcement and grout.

channeled In botanical terms, hollowed out like a gutter, or marked with one or more deep, longitudinal grooves.

channel iron A metal rod with a U-shaped cross section.

channelization The creation of a channel or channels producing faster water flow, a reduction in hydraulic residence time, and less contact between the water and solid surfaces under the water body.

charcoal A partially burned wood piece that absorbs gases filling pore spaces from decaying matter and keeps soil sweet smelling. It is useful in containers, pots, or confined planters.

charette A concentrated design effort in an academic atmosphere to complete a project within a time limit.

chartaceous In plant identification and description, papery in texture.

chase A groove or recess in a wall provided for piping or other utilities.

check A small crack in wood that has been dried too quickly or steel that has been cooled too quickly. Checks in wood run parallel to the grain and across growth rings.

check valve A valve that automatically permits liquid to flow in just one direction. May be used to prevent water in the landscape from entering the city water main where it would

chelate

contaminate the water supply. They are also useful in preventing pumps from losing their prime when the pump is turned off.

chelate   An organic substance holding micronutrients in a form available for absorption by plants. These are **fertilizers** with an extra metal ion, making the fertilizer available to plants. They are also known as **metal-organic complex** fertilizers. **Iron** chelate is used in alkaline soils to overcome **chlorosis** as it makes iron available to the plant. Chelate **micronutrient**s such as iron or **zinc** may be prevalent in the soil but unavailable to plants because they are locked as insoluble compounds. When a chelating agent is added, the nutrient elements are made available to plants.

chemical fertilizer   *See* **inorganic fertilizer.**

chemigation   Application of chemicals or **fertilizer**s to plants through an **irrigation system** by mixing them with irrigation water.

cherry wood   A rich, red-brown wood, which when finished takes on a high luster and is a fairly high density.

chestnut wood   A medium-hard wood that has a coarse grain and is useful in ornamental woodwork.

chicken manure   *See* **poultry manure.**

chinch bugs   A small, black and white, soft-bodied bug that is longer than wide and destructive to grasses and grains. The young are red or yellow, marked with brown, and suck plant juices. They are fond of sunny, warm areas.

chink   A crack in a wall.

chinking   Material placed between logs in a log wall.

chipper   A motorized machine that chips and grinds branches, stems, and woody material into

various sizes. This chipped material is often used as mulch in planting beds to prevent excessive evaporation from the soil, discourage weed growth, and provide a finished appearance.

chisel   A hardened steel rod with a flat end and a flat nose making a stout metal blade used in shaping wood, stone, and metal when pounded with a hammer.

chisel pattern   A pattern of shingles on a roof in which the bottom edges are clipped on an angle.

chlorine   A **micronutrient** necessary in plant growth that is very seldom lacking in soil. It is a regulator of osmotic pressure necessary in **evapotranspiration.**

chlorophyll   A green, organic compound produced by plants in **photosynthesis** and is the receptor for photosynthesis.

chloroplast   Granules of chlorophyll protoplasm within plant cells. They are green, and through **photosynthesis** manufacture carbohydrates (starches and carbohydrates) for the plant.

chlorosis   A condition in plants caused by a deficiency in **iron**, or sometimes **zinc**, evidenced when newer leaves turn yellow. Some refer to chlorosis as any condition where there is lack of green caused by malnutrition or disease. It is most often used in reference to a plant's inability to take up iron from the soil. In its mild form, yellow areas can be seen between the veins of the leaves, which remain dark green. In severe or prolonged cases, the entire leaf will turn yellow, usually with the exception of the veins. In most soils where chlorosis occurs, there is usually enough iron in the soil, but the presence of another substance, such as **lime**, makes the iron unavailable to plant roots. Iron sulfate or iron **chelate** can be applied to the soil to overcome this condition. Iron can also be provided to the plant by spraying leaves with **foliar** sprays.

chord **1.** The distance between two points on an arc or curve. **2.** The distance from one side of an arch in a structure to the other side. **3.** A significant member of a truss extending along its upper or lower edge that resists bending and is attached to other members.

C horizon An infertile mineral layer of the soil below the **solum** (**A** and **B horizons**) in an ideal **soil profile** extending to the bedrock (**R horizon**) and often referred to as the subsoil. It is weathered rock disintegrating into sand and clay particles. It may be further divided into **subhorizons** of C1, C2, etc.

choropleth map A map showing areas of various sizes and shapes representing qualitative or quantitative information.

chromated copper arsenate (CCA) A waterborne salt preservative for wood. Wood must be pressure treated for this preservative to be effective. It is highly recommended by experts as it is odorless, clean, does not leach, and its color can be masked easily when dry by painting or applying a solid color stain. Besides being good for preserving wood in weather aboveground, this stain can be used for wood placed in water and underground.

chromated zinc chloride (CZA) A waterborne salt preservative for wood. Wood must be pressure treated for this preservative to be effective. It is highly recommended by experts as it is odorless, clean, does not leach, and its color can be masked easily when dry by painting or applying a solid color stain.

chromium plating A protective finish able to take on a high polish that is corrosion resistant and extremely hard.

C.I. Abbreviation for cast-iron.

c.i. *or* **cu. in.** *or* **i³** Abbreviation for cubic inches. It is a volume equal to a cube measuring 1 inch along each edge.

CIC Abbreviation for **Certified Irrigation Contractor**.

CID Abbreviation for **Certified Irrigation Designer**.

ciliate In botanical terms, the **margin** of a leaf with a fringe of hairs. (Compare with **entire, pectinate, cleft, lobed, dentate, denticulate, serrate, serrulate, double serrate, incised, crenate, crenulate, parted.**)

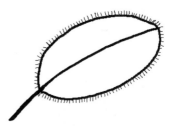

ciliate leaf margin

cinder block A masonry unit that is lightweight and most often used for interiors. It is made of **cinder concrete**.

cinder concrete A lightweight concrete made with cinders instead of aggregate.

cinders Material from volcanoes or blast furnace slag.

cinerous Derived from or resembling cinders in composition or color (gray, usually tinged with black).

CIP Abbreviation for **cast-iron pipe**; and **cast in place**.

circinate In botanical terms, rolled inward from the end, like some umbrella handles.

circuit 1. An electrical conductor made of two or more wires through which current may flow to an electrical device and back again. 2. The area covered by sprinkler heads operated by a single valve.

circuit breaker A safety switch installed in a **circuit** that will automatically switch off when electrical current exceeds a predetermined amount, or when a short circuit is experienced. They can be manually reset when their switch is automatically flipped off.

circular saw A power-driven saw with a circular blade and a cutting edge along the rim of the circular blade.

circular saw

circulation 1. Systems, structures, and physical improvements for the movement of people, goods, fuel, water, air, sewage, or power by such means as streets, highways, railways, waterways, airways, pipes, and conduits, and the handling of people and goods by such means. 2. The movement of objects, living things, liquid, or gas, especially in a patterned flow. 3. A pattern of movement of people, cars, water, etc.

CIR BKR This term is sometimes used on drawings to abbreviate circuit breaker.

cistern A container for storing water with an opening to an atmosphere. These are often used for storing rainwater from roofs.

citronella Oil derived from *Cymbopogon nardus* (**common name:** lemon grass) and other plants. This oil is often used for burning in containers outdoors as it is thought to repel insects.

city planner An officially designated city employee charged with the responsibility for interpreting and administrating the zoning codes and other land development ordinances adopted by a city.

city planning The decision-making process and design process by which goals and objectives are established, existing resources and conditions are analyzed, strategies are developed, and controls are adopted to achieve goals, plans, and objectives for cities or towns.

civil engineer An engineer whose primary emphasis is the occupation of designing public works (roads, water, sanitary sewer, storm sewer, etc.) projects as well as subdivisions, and the overseeing of those construction projects.

civil engineering Application of the knowledge of forces of nature, principles of mechanics, and the properties of materials to the evaluation, design, and construction of civil works for the use of mankind.

cladode A descriptive botanical term referring to a flattened leaf-like **stem**.

cladophyll A flattened stem closely resembling a leaf.

clamp A tool for holding materials in place while working on them (e.g., for welding, grinding, gluing, etc.).

CLARB Abbreviation for the **Council of Landscape Architectural Boards**.

class 1. A designation of a pipe or component's maximum design pressure, which increases with wall thickness. Class 200 pipe has a pressure rating of 200 psi. Plastic pipe is often identified by class. They are solvent-welded or slip joint pipes because their thickness is not generally enough to thread. **2.** A major category of **taxon**omy ranking above the **order** and below the **division**.

claw   In botanical terms, the narrow or stalk-like base of some petals.

claw hammer   A hammer with a head that has a striking side and a side that is curved for pulling nails.

claw hammer

clay   1. Earth with **soil** particles of a size less than $\frac{1}{12,500}$ in (0.002 **mm**) in size, often made up of **silicate**s and **aluminum**. It is the smallest of soil particles from the mineral fraction and greatly assists in loam soil structure formation by encouraging aggregation. Clay is plastic-like when wet and hard when fired. It is used for brick, tile, and pottery. **2.** A soil textural class comprised of approximately 40–100% clay, with 0–40% **silt** and 0–45% **sand**. It is a fine-textured soil, usually forming very hard clods when dry, but is easily moldable and sticky when wet. When it is moist, it can be pinched between the thumb and fingers. It usually forms a long, flexible "ribbon." An exception to this is when the clay is high in colloids. When a soil is classified as clay, it is usually easily compacted and has poor drainage. However, some clay is essential in the best soils to prevent leaching of nutrients, allow for root penetration by forming granules,

contribute to the fertility status, and assist with water retention. Clay also has properties of surface charges for adsorption of water, gas, and nutrients. Clay has a potential for shrinking and swelling.

clay brick   A solid clay masonry unit warmed and then heated in a kiln to harden.

clay loam   A **soil** textural class comprised of 27–40% clay, 15–43% silt, and 20–45% sand. This fine-textured soil usually forms clods when dry, and when moist and pinched between the thumb and forefinger it forms a thin "ribbon" that will readily break and can barely sustain its own weight. If squeezed when moist, the cast will bear much handling without breaking. Kneading it will work it into a heavy compact mass that will crumble readily.

clay masonry unit   A masonry unit that is larger than the normal brick size.

clay pipe   A **vitrified-clay pipe**.

clay tile   1. A tile used in flooring. **2.** A roofing tile made of clay, hardened through a heating process.

clean aggregate   Aggregate material that has been washed to be free of organic compounds, or earth.

cleanout   1. A pipe fitting with a plug that can be removed for placing a device down into the main piping system for cleaning or inspection. **2.** An opening at the base of concrete forms for removing debris before concrete is poured. **3.** The task of removing soil from a trench by hand after a machine trencher has initially dug the trench.

clear   To remove all trees, shrubs, and other plant material from an area of ground. Also see **grub**.

clear-cutting Removal of an entire stand of trees or vegetation.

clearing Removing vegetation and their roots from an area.

clear lumber Wood without any knots or defects.

clear span The distance along a member or structure from one of its supports to the next nearest support.

clear vision area The triangular area bounded by the street property lines of corners and a line joining points along the street lines a determined number of feet from their point of intersection. This area is kept free of visual obstructions from street to street to provide an open view of the intersection, providing more safety for those traveling toward the intersection so that they can avoid intersecting traffic.

clear vision triangle *See* **clear vision area**.

cleft In botanical terms, having a natural cut or indentation halfway down or more. With regard to leaves, the measurement is from the leaf edge to the midrib. (Compare with **ciliate, pectinate, centire, lobed, dentate, denticulate, serrate, serrulate, double serrate, incised, crenate, crenulate, parted**)

cleft leaf margin

cleft timber Wood that has been split along its grain and sold by approximated dimensions.

clevis A horseshoe-shaped or U-shaped piece of steel that receives a bolt or pin through the two ends of the U shape.

CLIA Abbreviation for **Certified Landscape Irrigation Auditor**.

climate The temperature, humidity, cloudiness, solar intensity, daylight hours, precipitation, wind, etc. over an area of the earth.

climber Vines or weak-stemmed shrubs (as with some roses) that have a tendency to climb.

clinging In reference to plant materials, the tendency of a plant to wrap around or attach itself to other plants or objects by **twining** or attaching (especially with **tendrils** or **adventitious roots**). Examples of vines that cling by attachment are English Ivy and Boston Ivy.

clinometer A handheld instrument for measuring vertical angles and slopes by focusing one eye on the instrument window and another eye on a point the same distance above the ground as the point on the slope. The angle and degrees are shown in the instrument window.

clip joint A joint in a masonry wall that is thicker than the usual joints. This is often done to bring a masonry coarse to its proper dimension.

clock A term sometimes used in reference to an **automatic controller**.

clock valve A type of **check valve** with an interior piece that opens on a hinge, allowing water flow in one direction and closing when flow is reversed.

cloister A covered walkway surrounding a courtyard.

clone   A plant from a series of plants reproduced by asexual methods producing genetically uniform plants. These genetically identical plants are usually produced vegetatively (asexual propagation) by **grafting**, **cuttings**, **budding**, and **divisions**. These methods produce cloned plants.

closed canopy   A tree cover thick enough that it does not allow one to observe the sky from beneath it or to observe the ground from above it.

closed-coupled volute pump   A **centrifugal pump** with the distinctive feature of the pump being a part of the motor casing and frame. The pump is mounted directly to the motor shaft.

closed forest   **1.** A forest where undergrowth reaches from the ground to the lower canopy of trees. **2.** A forest with a cover of interlinking tree **crown**s.

closed impeller   A pump having an impeller closed by two discs (a shroud), one on either side of the impeller. This type of pump is usually more efficient for a longer period of time than an **open impeller** pump, but it does not pass objects well.

closed string   A board along the outside edge of stairs that extends down their length and covers the stair risers and treads from side views. The steps are then closed to view when viewing them from the side. *See also* **open string**.

closed water-piping system   An irrigation system or water system that does not allow water to reverse flow and return back to its source. This is usually facilitated by installation of a backflow preventing device.

close nipple   A pipe **nipple** having threads along its entire length, which is the shortest possible length permitted in standard practice to facilitate tightening on each end.

closer   The last stone, brick, or block laid in a horizontal course sometimes cut to fit the space available.

clout nail   A large, flat-headed nail used for fastening asphalt roofing, metal sheeting, plaster board, etc.

club hammer   A heavy mallet-type hammer used with a bolster chisel to cut brick, pavers, or block.

club root   A disease of wallflowers such as allyssum, candytuft, vegetables, etc. caused by a fungus. It is sometimes called "finger and toe." It misshapes and enlarges roots, and causes plants to wilt in the day while partially recovering at night. This can be controlled by having a **pH** over 7 or by having well-drained soil.

CLUG   Abbreviation sometimes used for **caulking**.

clump   **1.** Trees that are grown (naturally or forced) with many stems or trunks growing from the ground. **2.** A hard lump of soil. A dirt clod.

clump forming   **1.** A grass or **herbaceous** plant that forms separate crowns from the parent and does not form a thick sod. **2.** A tree that tends to naturally form many trunks (as opposed to naturally forming one single trunk) from a fairly central point. **3.** A shrub that tends to form a mass as several plants grow together in a colony.

clumping grasses   A grass that grows in tufts and is often called a bunch grass because it grows in separate bunches rather than in a mass or sod. These grasses can appear as sod forming if planted close enough together.

cluster development   *See* **clustering**.

clustering   **1.** A land development concept grouping buildings and roads closely together usually in groups or clusters, and usually keeping the total development density at that which could be constructed on the site under conventional zoning and regulations leaving surrounding land without paving or buildings. This is a common method of preserving natural land features, agriculture, sensitive land areas, etc. The open space area is often developed for recreational use. **2.** The grouping of plants, especially of the same type.

cluster (residential) **1.** The layout of residential buildings or dwelling units in such a way as to provide less area of disturbance to the land, allowing more area to remain in agriculture or a natural condition, or as a developed open space. **2.** The placement of more than one residential building on a single lot or parcel of land for the purpose of constructing single-family residential dwelling units, whether in an attached or detached construction arrangement.

cluster subdivision A wholly or principally residential subdivision that permits a reduction in lot area, setback, or other site development regulations, provided there is no increase in the overall density permitted for a conventional subdivision in a given zoning district. The remaining land area is used for common space as a visual or functional amenity or as a means of ecological preservation.

cm Abbreviation for **centimeter**(s).

cmp Abbreviation for corrugated metal pipe.

CMU Abbreviation for **concrete masonry unit**.

CN ratio Abbreviation for **carbon to nitrogen ratio**.

CNRC Abbreviation for Canadian National Research Counsel.

CO **1.** Abbreviation for **cleanout**. **2.** Abbreviation for **certificate of occupancy**. **3.** Abbreviation for **change order**.

coarse The portion of **sand** with particles 1/50 of an inch to 1/2 of an inch in size.

coat A single layer of paint, stain, etc. applied to a surface.

coated nail A nail with a coating of galvanization, cement, or other material meant to prevent it from coming loose.

cobble *or* **cobble stone** *or* **cobblestone** **1.** A rounded stone larger than a pebble or **gravel** but smaller than a **boulder**, especially when used for paving or construction purposes. **2.** A rock fragment or rounded rocks between 2½ and 10 inches (64 to 256 mm).

cobble

cob wall A wall made up of clay, straw, and gravel.

cocoon A protective coating secreted by an insect **larva** in which a **pupa** develops.

code This term is sometime used in the construction industry to reference any regulations imposed on design and work by governing agencies.

code of practice A document of standards outlining acceptable construction with various materials and workmanship.

codling moth A small moth whose larvae infest apples, English walnuts, quince, pears, etc. The larvae enter fruit as it starts to form.

coefficient of expansion The change in measurements of a material per unit of dimension per degree change in temperature.

coefficient of permeability An expression of the rate that water flows through the **soil**. It is also referred to as **hydraulic conductivity**.

coefficient of runoff A number representing storm runoff that varies depending on the type of ground surface, indicating the portion of a rainfall converted to **runoff**. It is a number between 0 and 1 with impervious surface having higher coefficients of runoff. It is used in the **rational formula**.

coefficient of uniformity (CU) A numerical water distribution indication in an area of irrigation based on a formula that averages the entire area without highlighting small problem areas; treats overwatering the same as underwatering. Its formula is CU = 1 − (average deviation/average **catchment**). It is a measure of the variability of water distribution (**precipitation rate**) for a specific irrigated area. Using a catchment test in an irrigated area, it is a comparison of the average precipitation of all catchments and the deviation from that average. A perfect score of 100 states that the system is efficient and there is no variability of water distribution.

coetaneous In plant identification and descriptions, flowers that develop at the same time that leaves develop.

cofferdam A temporary, watertight enclosure from which water is pumped. Holds back surrounding water or water-logged soil, providing an area for performing construction.

cog joint A joint between two crossing structural wood members that have been notched to fit together.

cohesion The attraction of like substances to one another. This is an important feature of water around soil particles and facilitates or prevents movement of water.

cohesionless soil A soil that has little strength when air dried and little **cohesion** when submerged.

cohesive soil A soil that has **cohesion** when submerged and strength when air dried.

coir A fiber obtained from coconut and often used to prevent erosion, etc.

cold frame Simple small structures built to protect plants from full exposure to weather. They usually have some glass and are not artificially heated. *See also* **hotbed**.

cold joint A joint in concrete where the first pour is allowed to harden before the next batch is placed against it. This usually forms a poor bond between the two batches.

cold mix Asphaltic concrete placed without heat. It is not usually hard or durable as hot asphalt.

coliseum A large outdoor amphitheater.

collar **1.** The outer side of a grass leaf at the joint of the blade and the sheath. **2.** A **root collar** or **branch collar**.

collected plants Any plants gathered on-site, in the natural landscape, or on another site, etc. and transplanted from where they have grown. They are not grown in containers and are not grown by a **nursery**.

collector road A road that has more traffic than other roads, allowing access of traffic to it. *See also* **arterial road**.

colloid Any substance so fine that when it is dispersed in a liquid it stays suspended.

colonial A reference to design reminiscent of American colonial design.

colonize The multiplying of a plant type beyond its existing area of coverage.

colonnade Columns in a line. They may be independent, a part of a roofed structure, or a series of arches, etc.

colonnade

colony A group, clump, or stand of plants separated from others of their type.

colossal columns A column that is taller than one story of a building.

column

colosseum A large amphitheater that is usually outdoors.

column **1.** A tall narrow structure like a **post** or **pillar** that usually supports a structure above it, but may also stand as a feature without bearing any weight as a part of a building or wall. As ornamental building supports, they are often round with a base and a **capital**.

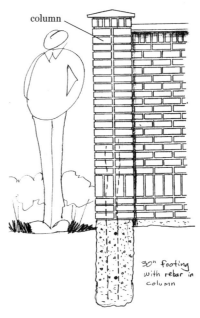

column

columnar A plant form that is upright, narrow, with nearly parallel sides and reminiscent of a column. Usually tall narrow trees or shrubs. (Compare with **round, weeping, fastigiate, oval, broadly spreading, upright spreading, pyramidal.**)

Com Abbreviation used in the lumber industry for common name.

comb Abbreviation sometimes used on drawings for combined or combination.

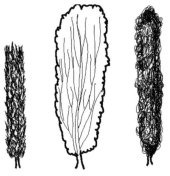

columnar tree forms

combination pliers   A tool capable of wire cutting and gripping with jaws having a hinge point and handles. The handles can be squeezed and the jaws can grasp or cut items. The hinge point has a slip point giving the jaws two adjustments as to size.

combination square   A tool that may be used as a square, a level, a marking gauge, a straight edge, or a plumb that has one leg of the square capable of sliding along the other for adjustment.

combined aggregate   A mixture of both fine and coarse aggregate for use in concrete mixes.

combined sewer   A piping system facilitating the drainage of both storm water and sanitary sewage.

comfort station   A toilet facility for public use.

commercial fertilizer   **1.** Any **fertilizer** commercially available. **2.** A **fertilizer** that is manufactured mostly from chemicals, then mixed (sometimes with inert materials to get the proper percentage), and bagged.

common nail   A **nail** with a wide, round, thin, flattop head and slender, sharply pointed shank for general construction purposes, especially for woodwork where finished wood is not critical. It is similar to a **box nail** except that its shank is not as slender as a box nail's shank. Often used for framing wood structures.

common name   The name a plant is ordinarily known by that is not its **botanical name (scientific name, Latin name)**.

common open space   Land of a **development**, not individually owned or dedicated for public use, and designed and intended for the common use or enjoyment of the residents of the development.

common wire   The ground wire in an electrical system. It completes the return path of electricity to the source.

commuter rail   The portion of passenger railroad operations that carries passengers within urban areas, or between urban areas and their suburbs. It differs from railroad in that railroad passenger cars generally are heavier, the average trip lengths are usually longer, and the operations are carried out over tracks that are part of the railroad system.

compact   **1.** In horticulture, a plant that has a tighter branching pattern or denser, more prolific foliage, and/or is shorter than other plants of the same species. **2.** In landscape and excavation, to compress and cause a reduction of voids by the pressure of heavy weight, regulated moisture, or vibration. In relation to **soil**, **aggregate** used in a base for paving. This can be accomplished and increased by mechanical compactors, by natural settling over time, or by traveling (driving or walking) over the material. Adding just the right amount of moisture will assist compaction efforts when the material is too dry. Too much moisture or too little moisture will prevent adequate compaction. Too much water will cause the soil to become plastic or

compacter volume

liquid-like, preventing compaction by mechanical means until dried sufficiently. The cyclical wetting by rain (or overhead irrigation) impact and drying generally increases compaction. Soil compaction is advantageous and usually essential to the stability of structures and paving, but is detrimental to plant growth. Plants find compacted soils adverse due to little aeration, little gaseous diffusion, difficulty in root extension and penetration, and the lack of water as it does not infiltrate well. The greatest cause of **established tree** deaths is compaction. **3.** A concrete that has been packed tighter by a process of vibrating or tamping when freshly placed to reduce the number and size of voids within the concrete mix.

compacter volume The volume of soil and rock material after compaction. There is usually a loss of volume through the compaction process.

compaction *See* **compact.**

compactor A machine or device used for accomplishing compaction by pressure of weight or vibration.

companion flange A wider portion or plate that is a part of a pipe or fitting suitable for connection to a flange of another pipe or fitting.

companion planting The practice of placing differing plants near one another for the beneficial effects to one or both plants (e.g., discouraging pests or diseases, improved growth qualities).

compass In design, an adjustable drawing instrument used for scribing circles.

compass saw A handsaw used for cutting circles or intricate shapes having a narrow blade and usually a wooden handle at one end.

compass timber Lumber cut from a branch of a tree having the shape desired for a construction member.

complete fertilizer Any **fertilizer** with all three of the primary nutrients for plants. Those ingredients and their chemical symbols are **nitrogen** (N), **phosphorus** (P), and **potassium** (K). They may be present in various grades and ratios. On many fertilizer bags there is no label of the ingredients, but the percentages of the ingredients are shown in the same order: N-P-K. A bag with 16-10-8 contains 16% **nitrogen**, 10% **phosphorus**, and 8% **potassium**.

complete flower A flower containing both male and female reproductive organs. It is also known as a **perfect flower**.

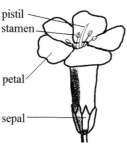

complete flower

completion bond A bond that guarantees a contractor will pay his obligations associated with a project, leaving it completely free of all liens or financial encumbrances.

completion date The date work is to be complete. In the **contract documents**, the date of completion is usually specified, otherwise there may be an agreement with the owner, usually in writing, as part of the contract.

compositae The daisy family of plants, which includes asters, dahlias, daisies, dandelions, lettuce, sunflowers, zinnias, as well as many other flowers, some shrubs, and even a few trees. It encompasses about 900 **genera** and about 20,000 species.

composite board **1.** Lumber comprised of more than one piece of lumber attached firmly together by fasteners, or glue, or both. **2.** Wood particles pressed and glued together to form a wood sheet or board.

composite plant A plant of the dicotyledonous family called *compositae*.

composite roofing *See* **built-up roofing**.

compost Decomposed or decomposing organic material (or mostly organic material) used as an amendment to soils in fertilizing land and improving the texture of soils. It may also be used as a surface mulch. Compost can be made of grass clippings, kitchen refuse, garden debris, leaves, sewage sludge, animal droppings, etc.

composted sludge This is a recycled, dried product of municipal sewage treatment plants. It is usually composted with wood chips, aerated and allowed to cure to various stages of stability and maturity. If it is cured to meet **EPA** standards of Grade A requirements, it is odor-free and nontoxic. It is usually incorporated into soil as an amendment with a low **primary nutrient** content of about 2, 2-3, 0 (varies). The long-term effects of using sewage sludge are still under investigation. Heavy metals such as cadmium may be present in the soil where sewage sludge has been used, and they may build up after a period of time. There are possible negative effects depending on the origin of the sludge used.

compound **1.** In botanical terms, having similar parts aggregated into a common whole. It often describes leaves that are completely divided to the midrib, forming two or more leaflets, or a branched **inflorescence**. (Compare with **simple**.) **2.** A mixture of elements or minerals, etc.

compound board *See* **composite board**.

compound leaf In botanical terms, having a **leaf** comprised of two or more blades (**leaflets**) growing from woody portions of a plant on the same petiole. (Compare with **simple leaf**.)

Comprehensive General Liability Insurance Insurance covering injury to persons or property in a broad range of construction activities.

comprehensive growth management A state, regional, county, or municipal government program meant and prepared to control the timing, location, and character of land improvements, land development, and building construction.

comprehensive plan *or* **master plan** *or* **general plan** A regional, county, or municipal document that contains a projection of land planning into the future determining how the community will grow and change along with a set of plans and policies to guide that vision of the future.

compressed In botanical terms, flattened on two opposite sides.

compression Stress force that tends to crush or shorten a structural member or to compact a material in the direction of its action.

compression fitting A **fitting** for pipe that may have a rubber gasket or has a soft material that can be tightened on a pipe by turning a large nut around the pipe or bolts into the fitting to form a tight joint that will prevent leaking of fluid under a reasonable (designed) pressure. These types of fittings are useful for repairs, especially on galvanized (or any metal) pipes. Some compression fittings are used for connections with plastic pipe, especially in drip systems. Pressure can push the pipes out of the fittings; therefore, pipes should be held firmly in place with hangers, thrust blocks, staples, etc., depending on the application and pressure.

compression coupler

compression test With regard to mortar and concrete, a test to determine **compressive strength** of the material.

compressive force Any force that tends toward shortening (smashing, compressing) a member. This force is usually from weight placed on a member. (Compare with **tensile force, shear force**.)

compressive strength The ability of a material to sustain and prevent **compressive stress** before failure. (Compare with **tensile strength, shear strength**.)

compressive stress The tendency of a material to shorten, smash, or compress when placed under **compressive force**. (Compare with **tensile stress, shear stress**.)

compressor A machine capable of compressing air. Useful in the operation of pneumatic tools. Compressors also have many other uses.

conc. Abbreviation for concrete.

concave In botanical terms, being or appearing hollowed out.

concealed flashing In roofing, a flashing completely covered by shingles.

concentrated load A load in a specific area of a structure not distributed over a large area but confined to a small area.

concentrated superphosphate This is different from **superphosphate** in that gypsum is removed from the reaction products to allow it to become 98% soluble and have a formula of 0-45-0. This product is often used for mixing **complete fertilizer**s.

concentration time *See* **time of concentration**.

concept plan A preliminary presentation plan of a proposed project showing basic layout and functions of uses or design types in a basic idea form with sufficient accuracy to be used for the purpose of discussion.

concolored, concolorous A botanical term, of uniform color, with both sides or all parts colored alike.

concourse **1.** A place where several roads or paths intersect. **2.** A large open area for accommodating crowds.

concrete A mixture of **cement, sand**, water, and small stones (**aggregate**, gravel) that dries to an extremely hard, durable surface. It is used in **foundation**s, **footing**s, abutments, walls, paving, etc.

concrete block A **concrete masonry unit**.

concrete flat-work *See* **flat-work**.

concrete hardener The mixture added to concrete to increase its strength by altering the rate of hydration.

concrete insert A material inserted in concrete while curing or by drilling after curing to receive a bolt or screw that will allow attachment of items or materials to the concrete.

concrete masonry unit (cmu) A block of concrete made of **Portland cement** and aggregate used in building masonry walls, usually having hollow portions formed through the block, which affords a lighter weight, and space for reinforcement, as well as space for power, plumbing, etc.

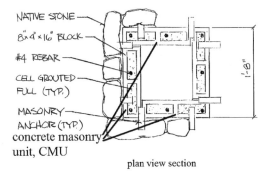

NATIVE STONE
8"x 4"x 16" BLOCK
#4 REBAR
CELL GROUTED FULL (TYP.)
MASONRY ANCHOR (TYP.)
concrete masonry unit, CMU

plan view section

masonry column

concrete mixer A machine that turns with paddles or ribs for use in mixing cement, aggregate, sand, water, or other materials for the formation of concrete. Concrete mixers come in various sizes. The most common referred to by this term is a drum for mixing that is capable of being tilted up when mixing or down for pouring, all by hand, and usually with the use of a lever and or electric switches.

concrete nail A nail with a large, thick, flat top and a thick shank or a flat, long, wedge-shaped nail with a blunt point used for pounding into concrete. They are thick and hardened to be capable of penetrating and being attached to concrete by a sharp blow or blows.

concrete pipe A pipe made of concrete often used underground for drainage or culverts.

concrete pump An apparatus with a pump that forces concrete to its location of placement through a pipe line or hose by force.

concrete retarder Material added to a mix of concrete to decrease its rate of hydration allowing a longer time of setting up and hardening.

concrete saw A machine-powered saw capable of cutting hardened concrete.

condemnation **1.** A declaration by a governing jurisdiction that a piece of property or building is unsafe or unfit for human use. **2.** The taking of private property for public use by a governing jurisdiction, which is compensated for by payment at an appraised value.

conditional stability A condition in the landscape where stability of a soil or slope is based on such essential factors as plant roots holding a steep slope in place.

conditions of acceptance Parameters specifying characteristics of the materials that they must fall within to meet the requirements of the **contract documents**.

conduction The exchange of heat by molecular kinetic energy within a material such as when a hot or high temperature area flows to a cold or low temperature area.

conductor **1.** A wire or cable having a low resistance to electrical flow and thus useful in conducting electricity. **2.** In landscape work, usually a reference to a vertical pipe intended for carrying rainwater from the roof of a structure. Erosion may occur at the outlet unless provisions are made to prevent it. **3.** A material useful in transferring or transmitting heat.

conductor shielding A metallic enclosure or sheath around an electric wire or cable.

conduit **1.** A **sleeve**. In pressure irrigation systems, wires and pipes are often both placed in sleeves under paving. **2.** A tube, pipe, or channel for accommodating the flow of water. **3.** In electrical work, a tube, duct, or pipe housing electrical wire. They are used to prevent electrical wiring from being damaged, or to facilitate rewiring or maintenance of wires where they can be pulled through these tubes or pipes. This is useful especially after construction to allow maintenance without removal or boring through walls, floors, pavement, or ceilings. In sprinkler irrigation work when **automatic timers** are placed in buildings, their valve wires are usually placed in conduits until they reach the ground. **4.** In landscape ecology, a **spacial** form in or on the earth used for movement of elements (plants, animals, water, soil, air, etc.).

cone   A woody seed bearing structure grown on some evergreen trees (those that are coniferous), especially those with needle-like leaves. In botanical terms, a mass of scales in a circular arrangement making a rounded structure with reproductive purposes as found on cycads or pines. An example is a pinecone.

cone of depression *or* **drawdown cone**   A roughly conical concavity (or depression) in the groundwater surface around a pumping well.

confining bed   A body of **impermeable** material in an adjacent geologic strata of one or more **aquifers**.

conglomerate   A description of pebbles, gravel, etc. embedded and bonded together in a natural cementing material.

conical   A term meaning cone-shaped with a broad base, narrowing toward the top. It is often used in plant descriptions, especially when describing the shape of the entire plant (i.e., some coniferous evergreen trees).

conifer   Mostly evergreen trees and shrubs with true **cones** or **arillate** fruit. Most have needles, but some have quite narrow leaves. Some conifers are pine, fir, spruce, yew, cedar, etc.

coniferous   Cone-bearing trees with true cones comprising mostly **evergreen** trees such as spruce, hemlock, pine, or fir. See **conifer**.

connate   In botanical terms, being united or fused together.

connective   A botanical term describing the tissue that connects the two pollen sacs of an anther in an **inflorescence**.

connectivity   In landscape ecology, the measure of the degree to which a **matrix**, a **corridor**, or a **network** is connected. The fewer the gaps or aberrations, the greater the connectivity.

consent of surety   A written permission from a bonding company for change orders to bonded work whether for a time extension or change in contract amount.

conservation   Preservation from harm or protection from loss or consumption. It is often descriptive of efforts to save natural resources such as soil, vegetation, water, animals, coal, etc.

conservation easement   A legally recorded, voluntary agreement that limits land to specific uses associated with conservation issues. Easements may apply to all or part of a property. They are usually permanent, but term easements may also be utilized, imposing restrictions for a specific number of years. Land protected by conservation easements usually remains on the tax rolls while it is privately owned and managed. Landowners donating permanent conservation easements are generally entitled to tax benefits. *See also* **Agriculture Conservation Easement**.)

conservatory   *See* **greenhouse**.

consolidation   **1.** The process of soil becoming compressed with less pores or smaller pores due to pressure. Compaction can be increased by walking over earth, driving equipment over earth, or with special compacting equipment that vibrates or place weight on the earth. **2.** The settling and compaction of green concrete to make certain there are no air bubbles around reinforcement, etc.

consolidation settlement   A settlement of earth material over a long period of time, usually years.

constraint   A feature or condition of the built or natural environment that poses an obstacle to design, planning, or construction.

constructed wetland   A wetland constructed in a non-wetland area.

construction   **1.** The way that something is built. **2.** The process of building or making an item or a change upon the land. Such work includes land clearing, excavation, erection of structures, assembly and installation of components, or equipment, etc.

construction bond   **1.** Usually refers to a **completion bond**. **2.** Sometimes used in reference to a **performance bond**.

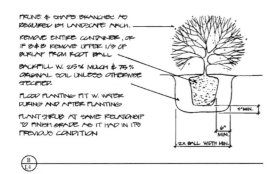

PRUNE & SHAPE BRANCHES AS REQUIRED BY LANDSCAPE ARCH.

REMOVE ENTIRE CONTAINER, OR IF B&B REMOVE UPPER 1/3 OF BURLAP FROM ROOT BALL

BACKFILL W. 25% MULCH & 75% ORIGINAL SOIL UNLESS OTHERWISE SPECIFIED.

FLOOD PLANTING PIT W. WATER DURING AND AFTER PLANTING

PLANT SHRUB AT SAME RELATIONSHIP TO FINISH GRADE AS IT HAD IN ITS PREVIOUS CONDITION

1" MIN.

6" MIN.

2X BALL WIDTH MIN.

B
L4

construction detail

construction detail   A drawing on a plan for construction work such as a planting plan or an irrigation plan, showing detailed information

about the construction of a particular item on the plan. It is usually referenced on the plan with a circle divided in half and an arrow or line pointing to the item or area referenced. One half of the circle will indicate the page number, and the other half usually indicates the number or letter of the detail on the sheet where it can be found. The details are usually placed in rows or columns either numbered or in alphabetical order on a drawing sheet. The construction detail usually has a label telling what the drawing represents along with a circle divided in half (as indicated above) showing how it ties into the plan.

construction dumpster   A large, very long **dumpster** (approx. 8 × 20 ft or more) used mostly in the construction industry because of the large amounts of debris it accommodates.

construction dumpster

construction envelope   One or more specified areas on a lot or parcel within which all disturbance of land such as construction of structures, driveways, parking, roads, landscaping, water surfaces, decks, utilities, walks, and improved recreation facilities are to be located. Some **agencies** omit areas restored with natural vegetation from being part of the construction envelope.

construction joint   **1.** An area along the two pours of concrete where they meet. **2.** An indented line in a concrete surface that is scored while finishing or sawed afterward to control areas where concrete may break or to afford a particular desired pattern.

construction loan A loan obtained for building a structure or landscape, etc. for the short duration of the construction period only.

consultant One hired to provide professional advice or design.

cont. Abbreviation for continuous or continued.

contact adhesive, contact bond Glue that is dry to the touch, but sticks and adheres upon contact.

contact splice A splice of reinforcement rebar where the two bars overlap and are in direct contact with one another.

container In landscape work, a confined, moveable space that is usually designed for the use of growing plants.

container-grown Plants cultivated in containers instead of in open ground or in a field grown.

containerized In the landscape or plant nursery industry, a plant material grown in a **container**. This term is usually in reference to plants in plastic containers larger than **flat**s. **Established** plants in containers can be sold all year without serious danger in **transplanting**.

containerized plants

contamination Usually in reference to water supplies, the introduction of a water source that is not potable, or a solid into a potable water piping system.

contingency allowance An amount of money set aside for unforeseen items in construction work.

continuous beam A beam that extends over three or more posts, supports, or columns.

continuous flushing emitter A **micro-irrigation** system **emitter** designed to permit passage of large, solid particles while operating at a trickle or drip flow. This reduces filtering requirements of the system.

continuous foundation A foundation that supports several independent loads.

continuous girder A girder having more than two supports.

continuous grading A description of a size distribution of earth material, such as aggregate, where the intermediate size fractions are present. *See also* **gap grading**.

continuous hinge A hinge that extends along the entire length of the material to which it is attached.

continuous truss A truss that distributes its load over at least three supports.

contorted Twisted, strained in appearance or bent.

contour **1.** A shape or form usually referring to a ground or land surface. **2.** A line depicting a constant elevation. (Same as **contour line**. Compare with **hachure**.) **3.** To shape, grade, or form (especially a ground surface).

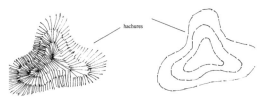

hachures

contours

contour interval The vertical distance between contour elevations.

contour line A line on the earth's surface connecting points of equal elevation on the surface of the ground. On a plan they are drawn to a definite scale and every part of the line is expressed as the same elevation above or below a given datum. Contours with a curve pointing uphill indicate a swale, while those pointing downhill indicate a ridge or rise. They can only intersect on paper in the extremely rare case of overhanging rock, and are the same line in plan view only when they are on the face of a wall, cliff, or other vertical surface. A contour that closes on itself within a drawing is usually a depression or a raised area (ridge). Equally spaced contour lines indicate a uniform slope, and closely spaced contours indicate steep grade. Those far apart indicate slight grade. It is important to note that water drains perpendicular to contours.

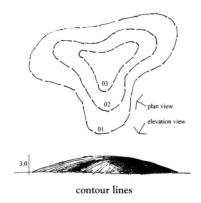

contour lines

contour map A plan showing **contour line**s as a visual understanding or description of a land area, site, etc.

contract documents All papers associated with a contract including the legally binding agreement itself as well as specifications, drawings, **addenda**, etc.

contracting officer The owner or someone duly authorized as a representative for a particular project.

contractor One who is responsible for, oversees, and directs the completion of a construction work. With regard to work on the land, this includes those engaged in the construction of buildings (residences or commercial structures) as well as heavy construction contractors engaged in activities such as paving, highway construction, **landscaping**, **excavation**, and utility construction.

contract sum The amount agreed to for a construction work.

contract time The amount of time specified, usually in contract documents, for completion of a work.

contractual liability The responsibility and liability of a contractor.

control joint A line of indentation in concrete, sawed after hardening, or tooled while still in a moldable state for design and also to control where future cracking may take place and avoid it from showing on the surface.

controlled burn A fire that is intentionally ignited and contained within a designated area to remove highly flammable undergrowth (reducing the risk of forest fire), or to prepare the site for planting.

controlled fill Earth material, gravel, rock, soil, etc. placed in layers and compacted, usually to a specified density, to make certain that the entire fill depth is stable.

controlled-release fertilizers Fertilizers that release their nutrients in regulated amounts. These are (1) fertilizers that very slowly dissolve in the soil, and (2) plastic-coated fertilizers through which water slowly penetrates, releasing the soluble fertilizer.

controller

controller **1.** A mechanical or digital timer operating valves or heads to allow irrigation to be automatic at programmed intervals for programmed periods of time. *See* **sprinkler controller**. **2.** Any device that controls other electrical devices as to when they operate.

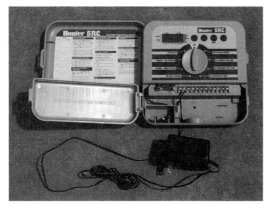

controller

controller program *See* **program**.

control valve In irrigation, the valve that allows water to enter distribution lines, may regulate amounts of flow, and also turns the flow of water off.

control wire **1.** Any wire connected to the **automatic controller** and extended to an **automatic valve** where it is connected to control the opening and closing of the valve. **2.** In an electrically operated, automatic **irrigation system**, there are two wires connected to each automatic valve, a common (ground) and an individual wire for each individual valve that is sometimes called the control wire or hot wire.

convection The exchange of heat by flowing liquid or gas such as air or water such that it conveys heat by transfer to other surfaces and tends to circulate as it heats and cools.

convenience outlet An electrical, **receptacle** outlet.

converted timber Wood sawed from lumber as boards.

convex In botanical terms, having the shape of the canopy of an upright umbrella.

conveyance zone The central route of drainage in a drainage basin where water concentrates into the base stream flow.

conveyor A belt that moves in a circle with its upper surface transporting material and dropping it at the other end where the belt loops back to the beginning.

cool season grasses Grasses that thrive in cool weather (daytime highs approx. 60 to 75 F). Most of these grasses are evergreen, but they may turn color slightly in the fall or winter. An example of this type of grass is bluegrass. The classification of grasses as cool or warm season is somewhat arbitrary as grasses perform differently from climate to climate. Grasses growing throughout the winter months in a mild climate may become completely dormant in a colder climate.

cool season plants Plants that thrive in cool weather (daytime highs approx. 60 to 75 F) such as some grasses, vegetables, and **herbs**.

Cooperative Extension Service A service in the United States offered through counties. Many have access to resources of agricultural colleges and all have access to the United States Department of Agriculture.

coping **1.** A protective top or ornamentation for a wall, column, etc. It is often used to direct water away from the face of the wall, as well as for aesthetic appearance. **2.** The top row of stones or brick in a wall that differ in shape from the rest of the stones in the wall (usually for a decorative effect) and are usually thinner with a slope to their upper surface to facilitate water drainage.

coping block   Solid-topped **concrete masonry units**, sometimes having a design, that are often used as a top for a masonry wall.

coping brick   Brick designed and created for the top coarse of a wall.

coping saw   A small saw with a thin blade and an extended handle, capable of cutting tight radii in wood or other materials.

coping stone   The stone used on the top surface of a wall.

copper   A **micronutrient** found in soils, necessary for plant growth. It assists in the formation of growth-promoting substances in plants.

copper alloy   A metal made up mostly of copper (the main metal, copper, at least 40% content), but not having over 93.3% copper content. Anything over 93.3% copper content is considered copper.

copper fitting   A fitting for copper pipe that may be soldered or threaded.

copper nephthenate   A wood preservative that is dark green, and is not usually toxic to plants or animals contacting it in wood.

copper plating   A layer of copper given to the surface of another metal.

corbel   A masonry design where the course directly above another course of brick protrudes slightly outward from it. Usually this overlap extends for several courses.

cordate   A botanical term describing a plant part (especially a leaf) that is shaped like a stylized heart with the notch at the base (indented **basal**). (Compare with **cuneate, obtuse, attenuate, auriculate, sagitate, hastate, truncate, oblique**.)

cordon   **1.** To prune a plant to a single main stem. **2.** An **espalier**, usually of a fruit tree, trained into a horizontal shoot or shoots.

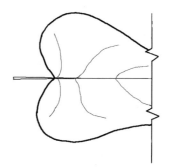

cordate leaf base

core   **1.** The open spaces in a **concrete masonry unit**. **2.** In a hollow stone wall, the filling between the two sides.

core-boring   Drilling and obtaining a sample from a hard earthen material or rock for testing.

core-drill   A piece of equipment useful for rotating through a rock, wood, steel, or hard earthen material to either obtain a sample or allow for some useful purpose or access.

core-test   A test performed on a piece of concrete cut from an **in-place** piece of concrete for a sample. The test is usually for compression.

coriaceous   In botanical terms, leathery in texture.

coring   Removing materials from masonry concrete or rock structures or surfaces for testing.

corm   A type of **bulb** usually broader than the tall swollen underground portion of the stem, covered with dead leaf bases arising from a basal plate. During growing season, new corms are formed from **axill**ary buds at the top of the old corm. Smaller corms forming are called cormels.

cormel   A **corm** in its early stage or formation.

corner angle   A post-attachment that is an angled piece of metal along with a portion that is a long piece of metal to be set in concrete while the upper angled portion sits on top of a concrete **footing**. The upper portion of the angled metal is bolted to the post.

corner clearance The triangular area bounded by the street property lines of corners and a line joining points along said street lines a determined number of feet from their point of intersection. This area is kept free of visual obstructions from street to street to provide an open view of the intersection and more safety for those traveling toward the intersection so that they can avoid intersecting traffic.

corner island A **parking island** located between two **parking bay**s and running the length of the parking bays.

corner lot A lot that has, on two adjacent sides, frontage to a street or path, etc. Often there is a definition by a governing jurisdiction of what constitutes a corner lot, giving further definition by requirements of the length(s) of either or both sides.

corner notch A notch cut in boards where they overlap at a corner, such as at a log cabin, etc.

corner return block *or* **corner block** This is a **concrete masonry unit** with two solid faces adjacent to each other so that it may be placed on a corner with the two solid faces exposed to view.

cornice Any projection or crown that is the top of a wall or structure, used most often as a decoration, but also sometimes as a means of directing water away from the wall below. It is also the uppermost portion of the classical **entablature** (*see* illustration at **entablature**).

corolla In botanical terms, the flowery envelope (usually showy) within the **calyx**.

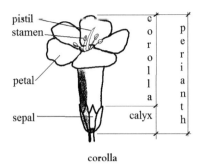

corolla

coroniform Like a crown.

corporation cock *or* **corporation stop** A valve used on water or gas service lines near their connection with a public (corporation) water or gas main.

corp stop *See* **corporation stop**.

corridor In **landscape ecology**, a narrow area or strip differing from its surroundings and usually facilitating the flow of animals, materials, elements, etc. along its length. It may differ from its surroundings in material composition, light, microclimate, cover, material, color, food availability, etc. Corridors may function as **conduit**s, **barrier**s, or **habitat**s, and may be **source**s, **filter**s, or **sink**s.

corrosion inhibitor Materials or chemicals used to inhibit the oxidation of metals.

corymb A flat or convex flower cluster, with branches arising at different levels and blooming from the outside toward the center.

corymbose In botanical terms, **corymb**-like.

cosmopolitan Distinctly urban or worldly; urbane.

costa The midrib of a **simple** leaf from the **petiole** where it meets the **leaf blade** to the leaf tip.

cost estimate An approximate deciphering of cost of construction or materials prior to bids, purchases, or construction commencement.

cotter pin   A pin with a vertical, circular head and an opening in the center. It has two side-by-side arms extending down the pin's length. It is made of a malleable metal so that it can be pushed through a hole, and the two arms that extend beyond the hole are then bent over to assist in securing items (e.g., nuts) in place.

cottonseed meal   Residue of cotton seeds after oil has been removed. It has an analysis of 7-3-2, is immediately available, and long lasting. It is acidic in reaction.

cotyledon   The first leaf (**monocotyledon**) or first of a pair or whorl of leaves (**dicotyledon**) developed by a seed of a plant. The **angiosperm division** of flowering plants is divided into two **class**es (**monocotyledon, dicotyledon**) by the number of leaves in their seed embryo.

Council of Educators in Landscape Architecture   (CELA)   An organization that began about 1920 concerned with the content and quality of professional education in landscape architecture. Its publication is *Landscape Journal.*

Council of Landscape Architectural Boards (CLARB)   An organization established in 1961 to facilitate exchange of information among state boards for licensing landscape architects and to produce and implement reciprocal licensing arrangements between states. In 1971 it was reorganized and its objectives broadened to include promoting high standards in landscape architectural practice, fostering the enactment of uniform laws pertaining to the practice of landscape architecture, and equalizing and/or improving the standards for examination of applicants for state registration.

counter-bore   To enlarge a hole so that it will receive the head of a nut or bolt in such a way that it is below or at the surface of the material it is placed in.

counterflashing   A strip of metal turned down over other flashing at a junction to prevent water from entering the joint.

countersink   **1.** To place a nail, screw, bolt, or rivet in material with its head flush with the material surface by preparing a depression for its head to be drawn into, or by tightening or pounding the head hard enough to cause it to bite into a softer material. **2.** A bit used in a drill or router that has a conical shape to its cutting point so that it may be used to make a depression in a material to allow a head of a bolt, screw, nail, rivet, etc. to have its head flush with the surface of the material when it is secured in the material.

countersunk bolt   **1.** A screw with the top of its head flush with the surface of the material in which it is secured and tightened into. **2.** A bolt with a circular, flat surface to its head that tapers to its shank so as to allow its head to easily be drawn into a soft material or into a countersink hole and provide a flush finish between the surface of the head of the bolt and the surface of the material it is secured into.

countersunk rivet   A **rivet** used in conjunction with **countersink** holes having its point pounded flat into the countersunk space while hot.

countersunk screw   **1.** A screw with the top of its head flush with the surface of the material into which it is screwed. **2.** A screw with a circular, flat surface to its head that tapers to its shank so as to allow its head to easily be drawn into a soft material or into a **countersink** hole and provide a flush finish between the surface of the head of the screw and the surface of the material it is secured into.

county agricultural agent One who works for the **Cooperative Extension Service**.

coupler In pipe work, a **fitting** accommodating the connection of the ends of two pipes in a straight line.

coupler

coupling In pipe work, a device that connects while covering over or inserting into the ends of two pipes or male projections.

court In reference to **spacial** definition, an uncovered space that is completely or mostly enclosed by walls, buildings, plants, etc.

courtyard Synonym of **court**.

cove A concave, curved edge between a ceiling and wall or a floor and wall.

cover **1.** With regard to reinforcement in concrete, the distance between the reinforcing bar and the concrete. **2.** In roofing, the portion of a shingle or tile that is covered with each **coarse**.

coverage **1.** In sprinkler irrigation, the area (as a shape on the ground) a sprinkler head or sprinkler system waters. **2.** In paint, the area that a gallon of paint (or a specified amount of paint) will cover on a particular surface type. **3.** In roofing, the area that can be covered by a particular amount of roofing.

cover crop Legumes (alfalfa, clover, cow peas, etc.) sown in fall and turned over in early spring to return humus and nitrogen to soil. Sometimes called **green manure**.

cover plants Usually those plants used to cover (grow on) soil that has been exposed in construction, planted to prevent erosion.

cow manure Feces of cows, dried and pulverized for a moderately slow-acting fertilizer (**NPK 2, 1.5, 2**).

cp Abbreviation for **candlepower**.

CPVC Abbreviation for chlorinated polyvinyl chloride.

crabgrass An annual weed grass that thrives in poorly drained soils, landscapes with frequent surface watering, and in lawns that are lacking nutrients. It germinates from seed in early spring, can root where stems touch the ground, and prolifically produces seed in the late summer. It can easily be recognized in late summer as it turns somewhat purple. Its fibrous roots make it difficult to pull, but it should be pulled before it goes to seed. Pre-emergent herbicide can be effective before seed germinates.

cramp **1.** A frame with a tightening screw useful in compression joints between wood pieces being glued together. **2.** Any device for holding a frame together during construction. **3.** A metal piece holding two abutting masonry units tightly together.

crandall A tool much like a hammer with many sharp, pointed steel rods as heads mounted in the slot in the end of a handle. This tool is useful in shaping and preparing stone for construction.

crane A machine with a tall boom and cable that is capable of being lowered from the top of the boom for lifting and moving heavy loads.

crenulate

crane

crawler tractor Any power-driven vehicle with tracks on rollers allowing it to move about. This type of locomotion is useful in muddy soils or loose material. It also is helpful in that it distributes the weight of the machine over a wider area.

crc Abbreviation for cold-rolled channel.

creasing Courses of bricks or tiles toward the top of a wall overlapping the course below it 1 to 2 inches.

creep **1.** With regard to land, a slow movement of earthen material or rock that is not easily perceived except over a long period of time. It is often only evidenced by the tipping of trees, etc. **2.** With regard to roof materials, a stretching or shrinking as a result of moisture or temperature changes. **3.** Water drainage flowing at the interface between a structure and the surrounding

soil or rock. **4.** The movement of structural materials due to stress and pressure over time.

creeper In botanical terms, trailing shoots rooting at intervals.

creeping (stems) In plant description, growing flat on or beneath the ground and rooting.

crenate A botanical term that describes rounded teeth on a plant part, especially a leaf. (Compare with **ciliate, pectinate, cleft, lobed, dentate, denticulate, serrate, serrulate, double serrate, incised, entire, crenulate, parted.**)

crenate leaf margin

crenelated Having a **battlement** design of repeated raised and lowered portions of a line or top of wall, etc.

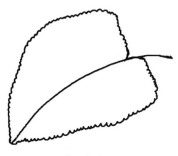

crenulate leaf margin

crenulate A botanical term describing a plant part, especially a leaf margin, that has a minutely **crenate** leaf margin. (Compare with **ciliate,**

pectinate, cleft, lobed, dentate, denticulate, serrate, serrulate, double serrate, incised, crenate,
entire, parted.)

creosote   A wood preservative made from coal
tar that is mildly toxic to plants and animals and
is insoluble in water. It is water repellant, stains
black (especially on clothes), and has a mild
aroma (offensive to some people) that returns
whenever temperatures heat the wood. It has
been most effective when wood is impregnated
with it by pressure treating. This may allow as
much as 40 years of protection. It has especially
been used in railroad ties as a preservative and
waterproofing material. Many have used these
salvaged or new ties in landscape construction
work, but recently they have been found to
cause potential detrimental health effects, and
the black sticky material comes off on clothing,
making it difficult or impossible to completely
clean.

crescent truss   A **truss** shaped in the form of a
crescent with bracing in between the upper and
lower curves.

crest   **1.** The ornamentation of the top of a wall
or roof. **2.** The top of a hill or ridge.

crested   In botanical terms, an elevated and
irregular ridge.

crest tile   Roofing tile that is made to fit on the
top ridgeline of a roof.

crib   **1.** A framework constructed of steel, concrete, or wood members interlocked and usually
forming a retaining wall. **2.** A stall or partial
enclosure for storing grain, hay, bark gravel,
mixed soil, etc.

crib wall   A retaining wall that consists of a hollow, box-like interlacing or interlocking configuration of timbers, reinforced concrete beams,
logs, or even steel beams filled with rock or soil.

cricket   In reference to roofing, a small raised
area with a slope to either side of its ridge used
behind an object protruding through the roof
(such as a tower or chimney) that would otherwise catch water drainage behind it. This causes
the water draining from above to be directed
around the object.

crimp   To bend, warp, or smash together.

crinite   A botanical term meaning bearded with
long, soft hairs.

critical angle   An angle or slope of stairs or of a
ramp that should not be exceeded as it would
otherwise be considered unsafe or uncomfortable. The angle not to be exceeded is considered
50° for stairs and a maximum of 20° on ramps.

critical path method   A way of planning and
scheduling a project by showing a sequence in
duration of operations that are critical to complete the project on time.

critical section   The portion of an element
considered most likely to fail.

critical slope   The steepest angle on which a
soil aggregate or other material will stand and
support itself before **sluffing** occurs.

crook   With regard to lumber, a piece that is not
straight from end to end.

crop coefficient   A numerical expression that
shows variation in moisture requirements of
plants.

croquet   A game played with mallets, different
colored balls, and hoops for passing balls
through on a lawn. *See* **lawn croquet** and **British
croquet**.

crosier   The leaf buds of ferns that expand in the
spring and then unfurl.

crossbreed   To **hybrid**ize by producing plants
from two separate varieties within a **species**.

cross bridging   Diagonal braces from the top of one joist to the bottom of the adjacent joist and vice versa, usually in pairs, placed to assist in preventing the twisting of joists.

cross connection   A connection between a **potable water** source and a water source that is contaminated (not suitable for drinking).

cross grain   Wood in which the cut is made not parallel with the grain lengths.

cross peen hammer   A hammer with the opposite side of the hammer head having a wedge shape.

cross section   A **section** through an object, building, device, site, etc., showing its shapes and attributes when cut through as in a crosswise cut.

cross slope   A slope in one direction (usually across a pavement or field) that facilitates surface water runoff.

cross valve   A valve on a pipe that connects two parallel pipes.

crosswalk   **1.** That part of a roadway at an intersection included within the connections of the lateral lines of the sidewalks on opposite sides of the road measured from the curbs, or from the edges or the traversable roadway. **2.** Any portion of a roadway at an intersection or elsewhere distinctly indicated for pedestrian crossing by lines, paving types, or other markings on the surface.

crown   **1.** The point on plants where the roots and the top of the plant's structure (**stem**) join. *See also* **root collar (root crown)**. **2.** The **basal** portion of herbaceous plants at soil level where new shoots are produced. **3.** The entire spatial area (head) of a tree, including its branches and leaves. **4.** The high point of a road, path, patio, etc. when viewed in cross section. These are usu-

ally created to provide drainage of water from the surface. **5.** The inside top of a pipe.

crozier   A plant structure with a coiled end as in the unfurling of a fern's frond.

cruciform   A botanical term meaning cross-shaped.

crushed gravel *or* **crushed stone** *or* **crushed rock**   **1.** Rock that has been mechanically crushed, having at least one face fractured. **2.** Rock that is sifted and crushed to a particular size gradation having some pass without crushing, but any oversized portions being crushed in the process.

crustaceous   In plant identification and description, hard, brittle, and breakable.

cryptogamous   In botanical terms, reproducing by spores without producing seeds or flowers.

crypt   A complex of chambers or passages underground.

CSI   Abbreviation for Construction Specifications Institute.

CSK   On drawings, an abbreviation for **countersink**.

CSSA   Abbreviation for **Cactus and Succulant Society of America**.

CtoC   Abbreviation sometimes used for center-to-center.

cts   Abbreviation for copper tube size.

CU, cu   **1.** Abbreviation for **coefficient of uniformity**. **2.** Abbreviation for cubic. **3.** Abbreviation for copper.

cubic feet *or* **c.f.** *or* **cu. ft.** *or* **ft³**   An English and U.S. measurement of volume equal to 1728 **cubic inch**es, or 0.0370 cubic yards or 0.028 **cubic meter**s, or when this is a volume of water it has a weight of 62.43 pounds.

cubic feet per minute A measurement of the amount of a liquid substance passing a given point. It is usually in reference to water flow because of its large volume.

cubic meter (m³) Cubic **meter**(s) or 1.307 cubic yards.

cubic yard bank measurement The number of **cubic yards** of earth material in its original place on a site.

cubic yards A cubic yard is equal to a cube with each side measuring 3 ft, comprised of 27 **c.f.**

cucullate In botanical terms, hooded, or hood-shape.

cul-de-loop A street that quickly turns into and reconnects with its main axis. The island created is often landscaped or used for parking.

cul-de-sac The **dead end** of a street, which is usually bulb shaped or circular allowing for the turning around of vehicles.

culinary water Any water fit for use in the kitchen and clean for human consumption. Within a municipality, this water is usually treated for purity.

cull **1.** To remove undesirable offshoots or plants from a clump or group of plants. **2.** A plant not suitable for selling or for its intended use. This is a relative term with many definitions, but generally cull describes plants that are undesirable or inferior in some way, in someone's opinion.

culm In botanical terms, plants having the peculiar hollow stem or stalk of grasses, sedges, rushs, and bamboo.

cultivar In botanical terms, usually a cultivated plant that would likely not survive (or at least not be true to type) by natural reproduction from seeds. It has distinguishable differences from the **species**, or is a plant with a variation that has originated in a cultivated state. It is a term that has replaced older terms of horticultural variety and garden variety to avoid confusion with botanical **variety**. The **International Code of Botanical Nomenclature** makes the distinction between variety and cultivar by the way they are written in a botanical name. But there is much confusion about this and few follow the instructions, and instead simply list a cultivar or variety after the species without identifying whether it is a cultivar or a variety. To most of those in the landscape industry, it is not important which it is as it identifies the ability to reproduce true to type in the wild.

cultivate To break up the soil surface for improvement of aeration, mixing of organic nutrients, improvement of soil texture, and improvement of water percolation.

cultivation The loosening of a soil with either a hand or mechanical-type implement for the purpose of controlling weeds, providing aeration, or tilling in amendments.

cultivator An implement for loosening the soil around plants.

culvert A tube, pipe, or opening made of steel, corrugated metal, concrete, masonry, aluminum, etc., where water flows through under a structure, transportation route, etc.

culvert

cuneate In botanical terms, cuneiform, wedge-shaped, or triangular, having the narrow end at the point of attachment. It is often used in describing the base of a leaf of this shape at the point of the **blade**'s attachment to the **petiole**. (Compare with **attenuate, obtuse, cordate, auriculate, sagitate, hastate, truncate, oblique**.)

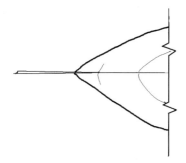

cuneate leaf base

cuniculus A low underground passageway.

cup With regard to lumber, a board that has a curve in its width or face.

cupulate A botanical term meaning cup-shaped.

cupule In botanical terms, a little cup, as with the cup of the acorn.

curb **1.** A wood, metal, stone, masonry, etc. low wall or slightly raised edge. Often used to contain a pavement, plants, water, etc. **2.** A concrete divider or edger used in landscapes to separate one material from another. It may be flush with the ground or have a raised edge.

curb appeal A term describing the initial impression of an individual viewing a property from the street area. It is the feeling or perception obtained when approaching a property for the first time. It is based on the appearance of a building and its setting with the surrounding landscape.

curb box, or **curb-stop box** This is a vertical sleeve providing access for a long key to be extended down and placed on a valve such as a **curb cock**.

curb cock or **curb stop** A valve on a water-line servicing a site or a structure, usually placed between the sidewalk and curb, which allows the water supply to be turned off.

curb cut A space along a raised curb line is flush with pavement, allowing for vehicle access.

curb line **1.** The line on a drawing representing the exposed vertical face of a street curb. **2.** The line at the edge of a concrete or stone curb, etc. and the edge of asphalt or paving surface.

curb machine or **curbing machine** A powered machine that extrudes a concrete or asphalt edge.

curb return A curved segment of curb found along a road at an opening of the curb that is made for **ingress** or **egress**. These curb openings usually have a return on each side of where driveways or future driveways will occur.

curing The hardening of concrete. Quality is influenced by humidity, temperature, as well as additives to the concrete mix.

curing agent Something added to a mix to increase its ability to harden.

curing compound A material or liquid applied to concrete, usually retarding water losses, while the concrete cures.

current **1.** The flow of electricity, measured in amperes. **2.** The flow of water in a narrow channel or within a large water body such as a lake.

curtain drain An intercepting drain.

cusp A botanical term referring to an abrupt, sharp, often rigid point.

cuspidate In botanical terms, tipped with a sharp and stiff point. (Compare with **retuse, emarginate, aristate, acuminate, acute, mucronate, obtuse**.)

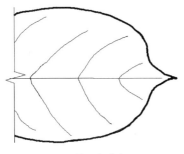

cuspidate leaf tip

custom-built **1.** Constructed on-site and not built at a factory or prefabricated. **2.** The design of a structure only built once or with specific changes for a user.

cut With reference to **excavation** work, the removal of rock or soil from a site or a part thereof.

cut and fill In excavating, this is the moving of material in digging or **filling**.

cut glass Glass that has been decorated, drawn on, or labeled on its surface.

cut nail A nail that is wedge shaped and has a blunt point cut from a piece of steel.

cutoff A structure intended to eliminate or reduce percolation of water through porous earth material.

cutoff valve A valve used to stop flow of water (or fluid, or gas).

cut stone Rock used in building walls or structures made to a specified size.

cutting In gardening, cut portions of plants used for **propagation**. Certain types of plants can be propagated by cutting off portions of the plant stems, roots, or leaves and planting or nurturing those cut portions to create a new plant.

cutting garden A small space, usually on a residential lot, where the owner grows flowers specifically for the purpose of cutting their blooms off to use for indoor decorating.

cutworm Hairless larvae of night-flying moths that feed at night and on overcast days, cutting off plants at the roots, and eating leaves. These can be particularly devastating in **lawn**s and **annual** planting beds.

CV, cv Abbreviation for **cultivar**.

CW, cw **1.** Abbreviation for clockwise. **2.** Abbreviation for cold water.

c.y., *or* **cu. yd.,** *or* **y³** Abbreviation for cubic yards. A cubic yard is a volume equal to a cube with each side measuring 3 ft × 3 ft. It is comprised of 27 **c.f.**

cyanami *or* **calcium cyanamide** A **chemical fertilizer** containing 21% nitrogen, with an **acidic** reaction. It is toxic to some plants. It loses its toxicity in most soils if it is applied a month or so before planting.

cybm Abbreviation for **cubic yard bank measurement**.

cycle **1.** In irrigation, this refers to one complete operation of a controller station or all stations. **2.** One complete reversal of alternating current from a forward flow (positive alternation) to a backward flow (negative alternation).

cycle and soak An irrigation controller feature that allows the controller to divide up station runtime with several short periods of irrigation to complete one watering **cycle**, allowing the soil sufficient time to absorb the water (rather than run off) before continuing irrigation. This helps prevent **runoff**.

cyme   In botanical terms, like a **corymb** (a flat-topped inflorescence), but blooming from the center outward.

cymose   In botanical terms, cyme-like, or bearing a **cyme**.

cypress   In lumber, a fairly strong and heavy wood. Its heartwood is often used on outdoor situations as it is decay resistant and durable.

CZA   Abbreviation for **chromated zinc chloride**.

D

d Abbreviation for **penny (pennyweight)**, which indicates a size of nail by weight. The higher the number indicated in front of this symbol, the larger the nail.

D1S Abbreviation for **dressed** one side.

D2S Abbreviation for **dressed** two sides.

D2S&M Abbreviation for **dressed** sides and matched.

D4S Abbreviation for **dressed** two sides and standard matched.

dado A rectangular cut across a piece of wood allowing another wood piece to place its end in the cut and form a joint.

damping off In horticulture, disease caused by a certain fungus in soil. Seedlings die immediately before or just after they break through the soil surface. Careful watering of seedbed soil, using sterilized soil, and careful sanitation practices can assist in preventing this disease.

dampproofing With regard to concrete and masonry, an application of a chemical (usually liquid) to concrete or mortar to repel water.

dandelion A weed or potherb (**genus** *Taraxacum*) usually 2 to 18 in tall with yellow flowers, producing many seeds in a seed head that disperse in the wind like tiny parachutes. It has a fleshy **taproot**.

dap Similar to dado, this is any notch in a timber made to accept another timber.

darby A **screed**.

dasycarpus A description for thick fruit.

date of substantial completion The date when a construction job is finished enough for the use for which it was intended as agreed upon by the parties involved.

daylight The term used to describe the point where a pipe or underground tunnel surfaces and is open to daylight.

day-neutral plant A plant with flower formation not being controlled by length of daylight.

dB Abbreviation for **decibel**.

DBH Abbreviation for **diameter at breast height**.

dc Abbreviation for direct current.

DDT A dangerous pesticide that passes from plant to animal and has harmful effects upon the body including harm to the reproductive system. It is not biodegradable and is harmful environmentally. It is prohibited from use in many countries.

dead **1.** In wiring, a wire not connected to a source. **2.** A pipe in a sprinkler system that no longer operates.

dead end **1.** A pipe with a plug or end cap at one end and not used. **2.** A street that only has one access point.

deadheading In botanical terms, the removal of spent flowers from a plant in order to prolong its blooming period. Removing spent blooms causes many plants to produce more flowers in a natural effort to reproduce through seed produc-tion. Removing flowers before seed is produced, which forces some plants to attempt reproduc-tion again.

dead load **1.** The weight of the members of a structure bearing on any given point on a struc-ture. **2.** The overburden above a pipe.

deadman **1.** A piece of a retaining wall extending from the wall backward being buried and assisting in anchoring the wall by the earthen material pressing upon it. **2.** A heavy object, or a wide object, or secured object buried in the ground as an anchor usually having a cable attached to hold something such as a large tree in place.

dead oil Another name for **creosote**.

deadwood Wood of a branch, trunk, or twig of a tree no longer capable of assisting the tree in life functions. A short time after dying, the wood dries, and bark usually exfoliates, making it eas-ily identifiable.

decibel A unit of measurement for loudness of sound or noise.

deciduous **1.** Plants with leaves that fall in autumn. **2.** Any plant that sheds all its leaves at one time once each year. Most broadleaf trees in the temperate zones lose their leaves before win-ter, and some plants in deserts lose leaves in the dry season. **3.** A description of a plant that has parts (e.g., **leaf** or **petal**) shedding naturally at a particular stage of growth or season of the year.

decimeter (dm) One-tenth of 1 **meter**, or 3.94 in.

deck **1.** The floor of a structure. **2.** In land-scape terms, a flat outside area with a durable surface (especially of wood) usually constructed for leisure activities. **3.** Any flat platform, as on

a roof, especially the upper flat or nearly flat sur-face of a mansard or curb roof. **4.** The structural surface to which a roof covering system is applied.

decking **1.** The boards used on the surface of a **deck** where people walk. **2.** A reference to any and all wood used in a **deck**. **3.** The boards placed as the flat portion of a flat roof.

decking

declined A botanical term meaning curved downward.

decompose To rot, decay, and break up into constituent parts by chemical processes. **Organic matter** is said to be mature in decomposition in the soil when it no longer inhibits plant growth in its use of **nitrogen** for decomposition.

decomposition The action of decomposing. *See* **decompose**.

decompound In plant identification and botanical descriptions, this means repeatedly (and often irregularly) divided and **compound** with numerous **leaflet**s.

deconstructed Disjointed, cut-up, or made of artificial materials.

decorative block A concrete masonry unit with special decorative design to be used in a visible area of a wall, etc. because of increased aesthetic appeal.

decorative fountain   A **water feature** indoors or outdoors that uses water as an aesthetic interest for its sound, humidity, reflections of surroundings in its surface, or interest of flow.

decumbent   **1.** A plant growing flat and close to the ground with the summit, apex, or extremity tending to rise. **2.** Any plant with a form that is flat or **prostrate** on the ground.

decurrent   In botanical terms, extending downward from the point of insertion.

decussate   In plant identification and botanical descriptions, arranged oppositely, with each succeeding pair set at right angles to the previous pair.

deduction   An option on a bid for less services or materials than those included in the **base bid**, showing a decrease in costs.

deductive alternate   An option on a bid for less services or materials than those included in the **base bid**, showing a decrease in costs.

deep phyto   A type of phytoremediation with trees, which allows the targeting of contaminants deep in the soil or in an underground water table. This patented method of remediation overcomes difficulties deep in soils of gaseous diffusion, aeration, compaction, and lack of nutrients. It prevents root development in favorable shallow soils and encourages root extension beyond the backfill of the drilled hole by compartmentalization of roots. This type of phytoremediation appears to be most effective with **phreatophyte**-type trees, though a water table is not necessary for optimum **remediation**. For further information, contact the author who is the owner of the patent.

deep soils   **Soil**s that are generally at least 40 inches deep from the surface to a **water table**, unweathered parent material, or **bedrock**.

defective work   Material or workmanship that does not perform to standards of the industry or that is less than the standards of contract documents.

deferred taxation   A form of property tax assessment that permits eligible land to be assessed only at its value for agriculture and not for its fair market value in development (highest and best current use) within the limits of its zone or legally allowable development. Taxes are based generally on how much money the land can produce in crops or livestock, instead of its speculative value for development. Taxation is only deferred until the owner converts its use to one that is nonagricultural, at which point landowners must pay some or all of the taxes that are excused. Taxes will usually assess the difference between taxes paid under differential assessment and taxes that would have been due if the land was assessed at fair market value.

deflection   **1.** Any bending or movement of a member under a load. **2. Deformation** of a structural piece under a load.

deflexed   In describing a part of a plant, this means bent abruptly downward.

deflocculation   The destruction of **aggregation** in a soil, especially the fine colloidal particles in clay soils. *See* **flocculate**.

defluorinated phosphate rock   A chemical **fertilizer** produced by heating **phosphate** rock. It supplies phosphate with an 8 to 24% availability and has a slightly alkaline **pH**.

defoliation   A plant's dropping, shedding, or loss of leaves either naturally or prematurely. Causes of premature loss of leaves can include lack of water, too much heat, cold temperatures, high winds, insect infestation, disease, chemicals, etc.

deformation   A change in the shape of a structure or a structural element due to a force or a load.

deformed bar

deformed bar *or* **deformed reinforcing bar** A steel bar used for reinforcing, having a pattern of raised areas on its surface to prevent it from moving in concrete with change in temperature or application of pressure.

degraded wetland A wetland negatively impacted by human action, impairing the wetland's physical or chemical properties, resulting in reduced functions such as valve for habitat or flood storage.

dehiscent In botanical terms, this often refers to fruit; opening at maturity to expose, release, or discharge the contents.

dehydration Loss of water. In plants, this is a critical problem leading to death if not corrected quickly.

dekameter (dam) The metric measurement equal to 10 **m**s, or 32.81 ft.

deliquescent A botanical term describing a condition of a plant or one of its parts when the central axis is not apparent as it branches irregularly into a series of smaller pieces. (Compare with **excurrent**.)

deltoid In botanical terms, shaped like the Greek capital letter delta. A triangular shape that is mostly equilateral with one of its sides as a base.

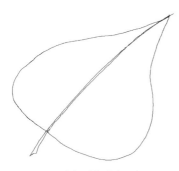

deltoid leaf shape

demand The flow of water required to operate a sprinkler system expressed in gallons per minute or liters per second.

demolish The act of **demolition**.

demolition The collapsing, dismantling, or destruction of materials, buildings, utilities, site furnishings, vegetation, pavements, structures, etc. (all or any part thereof) on-site and removing them for disposal or **salvage**.

demolition in progress

demonstration garden A garden built to show a method(s) of gardening, landscaping, irrigation, etc.

dendritic Branching like a tree as in the water drainage pattern of gullies or canyons or the **venation** of some leaves.

dendrology The study of woody plants or trees.

denitrification The reduction of oxidized nitrate nitrogen to nitrogen gas by **anaerobic** microbial effects.

dense-graded aggregate Aggregate sized to afford a minimal amount of voids and higher bulk density.

densiflorus Densely flowered.

density   *See* **development density.**

density bonus   The allocation of development rights allowing a parcel to accommodate additional square footage or additional residential units in excess of the maximum for which the parcel is zoned, in exchange for some provision such as the preservation of an amenity at the same site or at another location. Such amenities could be public open spaces, plazas, landscaping, etc.

density factor   In irrigation auditing, the vegetation density factor. Newly planted and sparsely planted landscapes often have less leaf surface area than mature, dense, or heavily planted landscapes and typically will use less water. A medium density factor is one with higher density being greater than 1 and low density less than 1.

density transfer   A way of providing or preserving open space by concentrating densities and leaving unchanged historic, sensitive, or hazardous areas. In some jurisdictions developers can buy development rights of properties associated with agricultural land, public open space (**sending zone**), etc., and transfer the development rights of additional density to the base number of units permitted in another zone or site proposed for development (**receiving zone** or site).

densogram   A graphical representation of irrigation precipitation rates within a studied area. It usually shades higher precipitation rates with darker areas and lower precipitation rates with lighter areas.

dentata   Coarsely toothed.

dentate   A botanical term usually referring to a leaf edge that is toothed with spreading, pointed teeth. Covered or edged with pointed projections, but wider than **serrate**, not pointing for-

ward, and not rounded as with **crenate**. (Compare with **ciliate, pectinate, cleft, lobed, entire, denticulate, serrulate, double serrate, incised, crenulate, parted**)

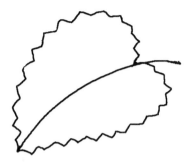

dentate leaf margin

denticulate   A botanical term usually referring to a leaf edge meaning that it is slightly or minutely toothed with small projections not pointing forward and not rounded. It is the diminutive (miniature or smaller size) of **dentate.** (Compare with **ciliate, pectinate, cleft, lobed, entire, serrate, serrulate, double serrate, incised, crenate, crenulate, parted.**)

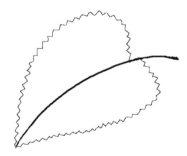

denticulate leaf margin

depauperate   A small or poorly developed plant or plant part that is in such a state because of unfavorable environmental conditions.

deposited metal

deposited metal   Metal used as filler in welding.

depressed   In botanical terms, flattened, or as if pressed down from above.

depression storage   Runoff held in shallow, low spots in the terrain.

desander   *See* **separator**.

desertification   The degradation of land within dry subhumid, semi-arid, or arid areas resulting in decreased vegetation and less ability of the land to support it, brought about by various factors including climatic changes, fires, diseases, human activities, etc.

desiccate   To dry up. A drying up of leaves when plants do not receive enough water. If water is present, they may not be able to utilize it due to disease or the presence of too much salt. Another common cause occurs to **broadleaf evergreen** plants in the **temperate** climate when on sunny days winter temperatures freeze the ground so that roots cannot gather water while the leaves are experiencing **photosynthesis** and need water.

desiccation   The act, process, or completion of drying up a plant. *See also* **desiccate**.

design   The process of taking ideas and producing a work of art, a work to complete, a visual or written instruction for completing a work, etc.

design flood   The relative size or magnitude of a major flood as expressed in the expected frequency of such a storm precipitation rate (i.e., 100-year storm). It reflects flood experience and flood potential as the basis of the delineation of a floodway or a flood hazard area.

design load   Total weight in the most severe case that a timber, bridge, deck, or other structure is designed to sustain.

design storm   A rainstorm of a given intensity and frequency used as the basis for designing and sizing storm water facilities.

design strength   The weight-bearing capacity (or amount below capacity) of a structural member.

design working pressure   **1.** The pressure assumed to be available in formulating a sprinkler design. **2.** In **class** type **PVC** pipe, the maximum pressure the pipe is expected to work under without failure.

detail   **1.** Intricate or minute portions of designs or elements. **2.** A drawing showing a particular portion of an element of a design depicting specifics about how it should be built, assembled, or constructed. See also **construction detail** for an example.

detention   In storm water management, this is the practice of temporarily detaining runoff **on-site** to be released later at a prescribed rate. Or, the practice of restricting its flow to off-site.

detention basin   A man-made or natural water collector facility designed to collect surface and subsurface water to impede its flow and release its water gradually and slowly into natural or man-made outlets.

determinate inflorescence   Inflorescence that stops growth of a stem when it flowers at its end.

dethatch   The removal of dead stems, leaves, and remains of grasses and some ground covers that collect on the surface of the soil as **thatch**. This removal usually results in a more vigorous, healthy growth of the live plants. This removal in lawns is usually done with a gas-powered dethatcher (vertical mower). Otherwise, dethatching is accomplished by hand or with a thatching rake.

Cool-season grasses are usually detached in early spring or in fall while warm-season grasses are generally detached in late spring.

detrital *or* **detritus** **1.** Dead plant material in the process of microbial decomposition. **2.** Any material produced by being disintegrated, or by being worn away, such as rock fragments, sand, etc.

developer The legal or beneficial owner or owners of any land included in a land development.

development A land planning or construction project involving substantial property improvement and often a change of land-use character within site.

development density In land planning efforts, the intensity of development or land use on the basis of area covered by impervious surface, population density, building floor area coverage, or number of dwelling units. It is most often understood as the permitted number of dwelling units per gross acre of land to be developed.

development regulation Governmental regulation of a use and development of land through zoning, subdivision regulations, site plan requirements, official maps, city planning, flood plain regulation, or other methods.

development rights Entitlement of property owners to develop land in accordance with local land use zoning and other regulations. These rights may sometimes be sold to public agencies, qualified nonprofit organizations, or other citizens. *See* **transfer of development rights**.)

dewater The removal of water from a work area or construction site by providing **drainage, well points**, or pumping.

dew point A point in temperature below which moisture in the atmosphere is condensed into minute drops, and deposited on surfaces.

D horizon The portion of a soil profile usually considered part of the **C horizon**, lying beneath any **O, A, B,** or **C horizon**s, that is comprised mostly of rock decomposing into clay and sand particles. It sits directly over bedrock (the **R horizon**).

di- A Greek prefix used in botanical terms meaning two.

DIA Abbreviation for diameter.

diabrotica A **beetle** often associated with cucumbers and referred to as the cucumber beetle, but destructive because it not only feeds on vegetables, but also many flowering plants. Its larvae feed on roots.

diag. Abbreviation for diagonal.

diam. Abbreviation for diameter.

diameter at breast height (DBH) A measurement of a tree trunk **caliper** (usually 12 inches or greater) at the approximate height of one's chest. *See also* **caliper**.

diameter of throw *or* **coverage** The average diameter of area wetted by a sprinkler operating without windy conditions.

diammonium phosphate A compound chemical fertilizer with 21% **nitrogen** and 53% **phosphorus**.

diaphanous A botanical term meaning thin and translucent or transparent.

diaphragm pump A **pump** much like a **piston pump** except that the piston is replaced with a diaphragm that is driven up and down by a rod that is attached at the center of the diaphragm.

diaphragm valve A valve commonly used in **irrigation systems** that opens and closes as pressure changes on a diaphragm. It can pass mud and small stones.

dias A raised area for seating people such as speakers, leaders, or dignitaries.

dibber *See* **dibble**.

dibble *or* **dibber** A handheld pointed tool to make holes in the soil for planting seeds, cuttings, bulbs, and seedlings.

dibble hole A depression (hole or cavity) formed in a container or in a planting bed generally the size and shape of the liner, pot, or tube containing a plant's root ball to be placed in it.

dicalcium phosphate A **chemical fertilizer** with approximately 40% available phosphoric acid.

dichlamydeous Having two kinds of **perianth** members such as **sepal**s and **petal**s.

dichotomous In botanical terms, forked or divided in two.

dichotomous vein In a leaf blade, veins that fork and fork again, but never cross.

dicotyledon An **angiosperm** plant (a **division** of flowering or seed plants) that grows from a seed producing two **cotyledons** to begin growth. In a **scientific name**, this is a **class of plants** that is one of two categories in the angiosperm division. *See also* **plant classification**, **taxon**, and **monocotyledon**.

didymous A botanical term that means developing in pairs.

didynamous A botanical term, four **stamens** in two unequal pairs, as with most *lamiaceae*.

die A tool used for making threads on pipe, etc.

dieback A condition in woody plants in which twigs or shoots begin to die from the tips, often continuing down the plant structure in progressive deterioration. This can be caused by insect infestation, fungus, inadequate water, inability to withstand climatic conditions, extreme weather, early or late frost, nutrient deficiency, etc.

dielectric fitting A special type of adapter used to connect a copper or brass pipe with an iron or steel pipe that prevents galvanic action that otherwise would allow corrosion.

dielectric union A pipe union having an insulator between the two sides of the union to reduce corrosion caused by galvanic action.

differential assessment A property tax relief program for agricultural properties allowing eligible farmland to be assessed at its value for agricultural use rather than its fair market value, or highest and best use.

diffuse In botanical terms, spreading widely and irregularly.

diffuse radiation Diffused or scattered solar radiation. As it passes through atmospheric molecules, water vapor, dust, and other particles, it appears to come from the entire sky. There is no defined shadow as on a hazy or overcast day.

diffusion The transfer of a gas or liquid from an area of high concentration to an area of lower concentration.

digital controller *or* **digital sprinkler controller** An electrically operated **sprinkler controller** with a small (usually) computer capable of being programmed to automatically turn sprinkler **valve**s on and off and keep track of time. It has a screen (various sizes) for reading programmed information regarding the operation of the valves on the sprinkler system. (Compare with **mechanical controller**.)

digitally lobed   In botanical terms, fingered and main veining radiating from more than one point.

digitate   A leaf shape that resembles the extended fingers on a hand. An example is the leaf of a horse chestnut tree. The leaflets are all borne on the apex of the **petiole**.

dimension   **1.** A measured or scaled length. A measure of something (especially an object) in one direction. **2.** A measurement on a drawing from point to point shown with indications of the portion measured and the amount measured being written. The amount measured has various methods of making certain one unfamiliar with the drawing will understand to which portion of the object it refers.

dimension ratio   The diameter of a pipe divided by the wall thickness.

dimension stone   Stone shaped or cut to desired shapes and/or sizes.

dimerous   All parts in twos.

dimidiate   A botanical term describing a plant part that appears halved as if one half were wanting.

dimorphic   A botanical term, of two forms.

dimorphous   A botanical term, occurring in two forms.

dioecious   In botanical terms, **stamen**s and **pistil**s in separate flowers on different plants, or plants having male and female organs on separate plants.

diplostemonous   A botanical term, a flower that has two cycles of **stamen**s.

direct cross-connection   A connection between a potable water pipe and a nonpotable water source with or without a valve on the connection.

direct current (dc)   An electrical current with a constant flow (as opposed to **alternating current**) rate and a constant **voltage**.

direct-gain system   A passive solar heating system in which sun enters and warms a house interior directly.

direct radiation   Light (radiant energy) directly from sun, capable of casting a shadow.

direct solar water-heating system   Solar heating of water that comes directly from a potable source to the collectors to produce a hot water supply.

dirt   *See* **soil**. This word is offensive to those working most closely with soil.

disbudding   Thinning flower buds to improve quality of flowers.

discharge pipe   **1.** Any pipe that facilitates water or another fluid to flow from its end. **2.** With regard to a pump, the pipe from the outlet of the pump to its point of outflow.

discharge pipe friction loss   The loss of pressure due to friction from a **pump** to the point of discharge.

discharge zone   An area where groundwater seepage or springs are concentrated.

disease   In plants, usually refers to insect infestation, proliferation of detrimental fungus, or an infection of a virus. These can be brought on by lack of water, excess water, lack of nutrients, excess nutrients, lack of sunlight, excess sunlight, excess or too little heat, frost, pollution in water or air, etc.

disease resistant A term describing a plant that has some ability to resist particular diseases (other varieties of the same plant may be susceptible). The resistance may occur naturally, or it may be the result of a breeding program designed to enhance the plant's resistance to specific disease(s).

disk, disc In plants with florets arranged in dense, rounded or flatish disc heads, the central part of the **flower** head made up of closely packed tubular flowers. An example would be the raised center portion of the flower of plants of the daisy family.

dispersion **1.** Scattering or mixing within a water or gas volume. **2.** With regard to soils, the breaking apart of soil structure so that individual soil particles behave as individual units.

dissected A botanical term, deeply (and often repeatedly) divided or cut into many small or slender parts, lobes, or divisions.

dissected leaves

distal A botanical term, toward or at the tip or end. (Compare with **proximal**.)

distichous In botanical terms, two-ranked or being in two vertical rows.

distilled water Water that has had all salts and other solids removed from it. Rainwater is naturally distilled through the process of evaporation. Bonsai plants are often watered with distilled water to avoid buildup of salts.

distribution uniformity (DU) The evenness of water distribution over an irrigated area. It is calculated using a **catchment** test. It is computed by dividing the average reading of the lowest one-quarter of catchments by the average reading of all catchments, and multiplying the answer by 100. An excellent percentage is 75 to 85%, while a good percentage is 65 to 70%. Wind, equipment damage, and interference with distribution by objects or plants will affect distribution uniformity.

distribution uniformity of the lowest quarter A coefficient of uniformity depicting water distribution in an area of irrigation based on a formula that treats underwatering as a more significant problem than overwatering. It is a method of rating the evenness of water applied over an irrigation area with perfect uniformity being 100%. Most landscapes have 55 to 75% distribution uniformity. It is the average water applied in 25% of the area receiving the least amount of water without regard to location, divided by the average water applied over the total area (multiply by 100 for percentage).

disturbance **1.** Something that has an effect on the environment. **2.** Something that negatively affects a plant. **3.** In landscape ecology, an event of natural phenomenon significantly changing the pattern of variation in structure or function of a system of the landscape.

disturbed wetland A wetland directly or indirectly altered by man or other natural force while keeping a defined area.

ditch **1.** A long, narrow excavation dug in the ground for accommodating water flow, a pipe to be buried, a foundation to be constructed, an electrical conductor to be placed, a sleeve to be buried, etc.

ditcher *or* **ditching machine** *See* **trencher**.

diurnal In botanical terms, daytime or pertaining to the day. It may often refer to flowers that only open in the daylight hours.

diurnal damping depth The maximum depth from the surface that soil experiences temperature change over a 24-hour (diurnal) period.

divaricate In botanical terms, very widely divergent or spreading from the **axis** or **rachis**.

divergent A term sometimes used in botanical descriptions to refer to a plant part that spreads.

divided In botanical terms, leaves cut into divisions extending approximately to the base or the midrib.

divided street *or* **divided roadway** *or* **divided highway** A street having an island or another barrier or open space separating moving lanes.

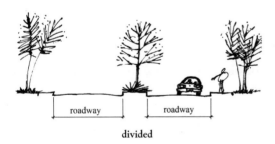

divided

dividing *See* **division**.

division **1.** In gardening, a method of **propagation** by dividing the roots of plants such as those with **rhizomes**, **tubers**, **bulbs**, clumping **perennials**, etc. In many cases, these plants are healthier after dividing. This is usually done in

fall (preferred) or early spring when they have expanded in growing for a year or more. **2.** In plant **taxonomy**, the broad category dividing a **kingdom** into categories. The subcategory under division is the **class**. *See also* **taxon**.

dk Abbreviation for **dekameter**(s).

dm Abbreviation for **decimeter**(s).

D&M In the lumber industry, the abbreviation for **dressed** and matched.

DOC (dissolved organic carbon) The total filterable organic carbon in a particular water sample.

dock A structure built over or floating upon the water and used as a landing place for boats as well as for other marine transport, fishing, swimming, etc.

dodge ball *See* **team dodge ball**.

dog run An enclosed outdoor area intended for the exercising, housing, or containment of dogs or similar animals.

dog-run (kennel)

dolabriform A botanical term, pick shaped and attached toward the middle, or at some point along the length rather than at an end.

dollar spot on lawns A fungus (*Sclerotinia homeocarpa*) encouraged by spring's warm, wet, weather and fall's wet weather with cool nights. Lawns low on fertilizer (esp. nitrogen), or poorly drained areas are most susceptible. This disease is recognized by small, round, brown spots later becoming straw colored. A white cobwebby fungus growth seen most easily in early morning before the dew dries; may cover dying leaf blades. The best options for preventing this fungus is to plant resistant varieties of grasses and to water deeply, infrequently, and in the morning.

dolomite *or* **dolomitic limestone** A mineral of calcium magnesium carbonate usually from compacted limestone beds. It is sometimes applied to growth mediums to supply both calcium and magnesium carbonates while raising the soil **pH**.

domestic well A water supply from a well for household use.

dominant With regard to **plant material**s, a **species** that is most characteristic of a **habitat**, or that tends to crowd out other plant species.

donor site *See* **transfer of development rights** and **sending site**.

door head **1.** In framing, the upper horizontal member of the frame for a door. **2.** In finish design, any projection immediately above a door that gives emphasis to the top of the door.

dormancy **1.** Plants or seeds that are alive, but not growing. **2.** A regularly occurring period when plant growth processes greatly slow down or growing ceases. This occurs in many species in the temperate region beginning in winter as cold days grow shorter and temperatures begin to lower; this ends in spring when plants are exposed to higher temperatures and longer days. Dormancy protects plants against extremes of temperature. It is usually best not to fertilize during dormancy.

dormant oil A highly refined oil used for spraying on deciduous shrubs and trees while dormant (preferably shortly before bud break) that kills eggs and or insects, usually by smothering. It can kill tender herbaceous **understory** plants, so it is best to cover them before spraying.

dormant spray A sprayed application of **fungicide**, oil, or insecticide during a plant's **dormancy**. This is a very effective way to assist in controlling disease. *See also* **dormant oil**.

dorsal In botanical terms, the back or outer surface of an organ.

dorsifixed A botanical term used in plant identification, attached on the back. (Compare with **basifixed**.)

dote *or* **doat** *or* **doze** A dull appearance in wood indicating decay has caused it to become weak.

double-acting pump A pump in which the up and down motion of a piston moves water as it moves in each direction.

double axe An axe having a blade on both sides of its head.

double check assembly A backflow device with two internally loaded, independently operating check valves together with tightly closing, resilient-seated shutoff valves upstream and downstream of the check valves with resilient-seated test cocks for testing of the assembly. It may be used to protect against a pollutant only.

double corner block *or* **pier block** *or* **pilaster block** A concrete masonry unit having rectangular end faces and rectangular side faces that are not indented but smooth and able to be exposed on any of these sides with a solid surface.

double-cut file   A file with two diagonal sets of cutting ridges, each set crossing the other.

double-cut saw   A handsaw with teeth designed to allow cutting both when the saw is pushed and when it is pulled.

double extra strong pipe   A steel pipe that has a thicker wall and twice the strength of a pipe of normal wall thickness.

double-faced hammer   A hammer having a striking face at each side of its head.

double flower   A flower with many petals densely arranged, not just in a flat, circular form, but three dimensional. Often used to accentuate a description of the ornamental aesthetic value of this type of flower.

double-head nail *or* **scaffold nail** *or* **form nail**   A **nail** with a head, and, a short distance down the shank, another head like an extended ring. This ring allows the nail to be pounded into material to that point where it is difficult to pound it in any further so that it can later be pulled from the material. These types of nails are often used in such work as making of forms for concrete so that the nails can be easily pulled when the forms are removed.

double manure salts   A fertilizer also known as **potassium sulfate** that supplies 30% water-soluble potash and up to 56% magnesium.

double serrate   A descriptive botanical term referring to a leaf with large teeth and small teeth that alternate along its **margin**. (Compare with **ciliate, pectinate, cleft, lobed, dentate, denticulate, serrate, serrulate, entire, incised, crenate, crenulate, parted**.)

double serrate margin

Douglas fir   A strong, fairly straight wood useful for structural members and for any framing. It is also used to manufacture plywood.

dovetail   The end of a piece of wood shaped like a fan (or dove's tail) with the widest dimension at its end, which is shaped to be placed within another piece of wood's joint formed to accept it. This forms a joint that is difficult to pull apart. The shape of the joint can vary greatly, and more than one interlocking piece may form the joint with many varieties having their own name (sometimes only locally recognized).

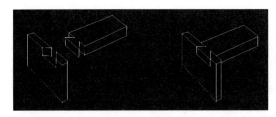

dovetail joint

dovetail saw   A small saw with a thin blade, fine teeth, and a protruding handle.

dowel   A small, usually cylindrical rod or piece used at a joint in metal, stone, dry-stacked masonry units, wood, etc., assisting in securing the joint by extending into holes prepared to accept it in each member and assist in resisting **shear** loads.

downpipe

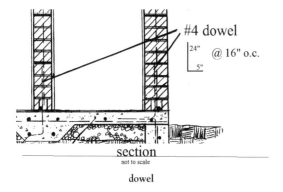

dowel

drafting brush

downpipe   *See* **downspout**.

downspout *or* **conductor** *or* **downcomer** *or* **downpipe** *or* **rainwater pipe**   A pipe or tube, usually exposed on the surface of a structure, and usually made of **aluminum**, plastic, or **tin**, for conveying precipitation or excess water from a roof or flat area of a structure downward.

downy   In botanical terms, being clothed with soft short hairs.

downy mildew   Any of a number of fungal diseases with a down-like white, gray, or lavender appearance; common to violets, Boston ivy, poppies, alyssum, and some vegetables. Unlike powdery mildew, these fungi extend through the plant tissue.

downzoning   A change in the zoning for a particular area, decreasing residential densities, decreasing allowable square footage of building, or restricting some or all uses previously allowed.

dozer   *See* **bulldozer**.

dpm   Abbreviation for damp proof membrane.

draft   **1.** To draw or design on a writing surface or with a computer. **2.** A fairly smooth, narrow edge cleaned around the face of a stone.

drafting brush   A flimsy haired brush with an extended handle used to brush away erasing debris, writing debris, etc. without marring the drawing.

drafting machine   A useful instrument that can assist one who drafts because of its ability to act as a T-square, protractor, scale, and triangle. It is attached to a large board or drafting table, usually at the top, and has a jointed arm, allowing it to be moved about.

drafting template   A stiff, fairly thin plastic sheet with shapes cut in it that can be traced onto drawings.

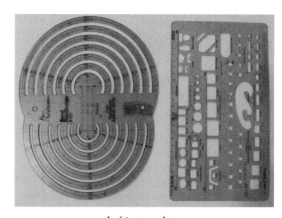

drafting templates

drag   A tool consisting of a steel plate having a finely serrated edge; used to dress stone by dragging it back and forth across the surface.

drain   **1.** A pipe, channel, or an appurtenance carrying waste water or storm water. **2.** A device

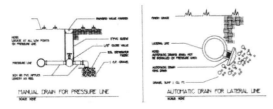

drains

in a pipe system (especially irrigation) that prevents water from escaping until automatically (when pressure is released) or manually opened. (See illustrations of installations (construction **details**) for manual and automatic drains on a sprinkler system.

drainage   **1.** In regard to land, the ability of water to remove itself from an area by **runoff**, or percolation through the soil. **2.** The ability or inability of soil to lose water when flooded by allowing air into the soil, alleviating **anaerobic** conditions. **3.** Water leaving an area by gravity.

drainage basin   The area defined by topographic flow boundaries that contributes storm water to a lake, pond, drainage system, estuarine waters, or oceanic waters.

drainage coefficient   The amount of excess water that must be removed (including irrigation water) from a land area by a drainage system to prevent damage to crops, vegetation, structures, etc.

drainage divide   The border between two drainage basins or watersheds.

drainage facility   Any component of a drainage system.

drainage fitting *or* **Durham fitting**   A threaded fitting, used on drainage pipes that has a shoulder affording a smooth, continuous interior surface that assists in avoiding clogs.

drainage fixture   A device in a **drainage system** that is manufactured off-site and put in place on a pipe, ditch, etc.

drainage network   A system or connection of stream channels that are usually connected in a hierarchical fashion.

drainage system   **1.** The system through which water flows from land, including watercourses, water bodies, and wetlands as a part of the **hydrologic cycle**. **2.** The water courses and piping network providing means of moving excess water away from a site, area, or structure.

drainage tile   *See* **drain tile**.

drainage well   A bed of stone or hole in the ground constructed for the purpose of trapping storm water for infiltration into subsurface materials.

drained wetland   A wetland in which the level or volume of ground or surface water has been reduced or eliminated by man-made or natural forces.

drainfield   Underground pipes or tiles through which wastewater is percolated into the soil.

drain hatch   A drain at a **dump station** with a cap that can be lifted by stepping on its handle with a foot. The cap helps prevent gases from

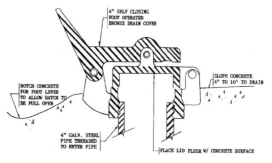

drain hatch detail

drain pocket

escaping, debris from clogging the sewer access, and animals from crawling in.

drain pocket In landscape irrigation, an amount of gravel (or similar granular material with voids for water to drain through) surrounding a **manual** or **automatic drain**. *See* illustration under **drain**. They allow water to easily flow from the drain and provide a larger area for water to filter into the surrounding soil. These are particularly useful in **heavy soil**s where the water may otherwise have considerable difficulty flowing from the drain.

drain tile A tile formed as a short pipe that has loose or open joints when pieces are butted together. It allows water to drain into or out of the pipe when buried depending on the situation. It can be used to drain water from soil, or to disperse water into a soil.

drawdown cone *See* **cone of depression**.

drawknife *or* **drawshave** A woodworking tool with a blade, and a handle at each end of the blade. It is useful in shaving wood by pulling it toward the user.

drawn finish A smooth, bright finish on metal tubing, wire, rod, bar, strips, etc.

dressed The finished, prepared face or faces of a brick, lumber, stone, etc. This finishing is usually to provide a more positive aesthetic effect for what is exposed to view in a completed structure. The finishing may be accomplished by sanding, rubbing, chiseling, or cutting the surface.

dressed and matched *or* **tongue-and-groove** In reference to lumber, wood members cut with a ridge on one edge and a recessed area on the other edge so that boards can be inter-locked for strength and tightness in **planking**, **decking**, etc.

dressed size The dimension of lumber after sawing and smoothing the faces.

DRG Abbreviation for drawing.

dried blood A product of a slaughterhouse, used as **fertilizer** with 12 to 14% **nitrogen**; causes an acid reaction. *See also* **blood meal**.

drier An additive that makes paint or varnish dry faster after application by absorbing oxygen.

drift **1.** A deposit of rock fragments and soils driven together by water, wind, or ice. **2.** With regard to irrigation, the change in a sprinkler application pattern due to wind.

drifter A rock drill driven by compressed air.

drift pin **1.** A device with a pin or steel post extending upward that is inserted into a post to attach it to a footing. This device must have its lower portion placed in a footing at the time of its pouring. **2.** A tapered, round rod used to align holes in pieces of metal. **3.** A round or square metal rod much like a nail. A hole is drilled smaller than the rod and the rod is then driven into it for a tight fit.

drift punch A punch tool with a tapered, blunt nose used for aligning holes.

drill **1.** A tool that rotates, being driven by hand or a motor and having various bits for boring, or for turning screws or bolts. **2.** A tiny furrow made with the corner of a hoe, a pointed stick, etc. for seed to be planted in. Vegetables grown from seeds planted in straight rows are sown in the drills. **3.** A machine usually pulled behind a tractor that lays down **seed** and covers it with soil, or pokes it into the ground to improve **germination** rates. Mechanical tractor implements for drilling are best used on large land areas. **4.** A machine used for boring holes in the ground.

drinking fountain A device that supplies water in such a manner that one may drink from a flow of water without the use of a container to catch it in. Most provide water for consumption by a slow-moving, usually arching water jet and a basin into which the spillage falls. The water emission device is metal, and the basin may be stone, metal, masonry, etc.

drinking fountain

drip edge A protrusion at the lower end of a roof or top surface of any structure or wall that keeps water off the upper wall face at its junction. It prevents water from running down the abutting vertical surface by allowing it to drop a short distance down its face and then be directed outward by a slight protrusion where it drips off instead of running down a wall or vertical surface below.

drip irrigation Water distributed to plants slowly, usually at low pressure, through small **emitters**. Its possible virtues include: decreased loss of water to wind, runoff, or evaporation; a high uniformity of water distribution per plant; usefulness in difficult terrain or where spray on adjacent areas or structures is undesirable; increased leaching of salts as it keeps soil moist; and in some plants, an improvement in growth and quality. The drawbacks of drip irrigation include: difficulty of maintenance as emitters are not easily observed to check operation; plants are not washed off; the soft tubing is easily damaged by rodents, dogs, or excessive weight placed over it; the tubing at or near the surface is easily displaced or vandalized; filtering is necessary to prevent or reduce clogging; and there is a possibility of salt buildup at the edge of the wetted area.

drip line **1.** A line drawn around a tree at the edge of the outermost ends of its branches. The line at the outside edge of a plant's head where water drips off the plant in an approximate line around the plant. **2.** A pipe carrying water to drip **emitters** or a drip emitter pipe with emitters integral to it or placed in it.

drive band A steel band encircling the head of a timber pile to prevent it from splitting when driven into the ground.

drive cap A steel cover placed over the top end of a **pile** to prevent damage to the pile while it is being driven into the ground.

drive island A **parking island** that is located between a **parking bay** and an access drive.

driveway **1.** A private way or road used for vehicles. **2.** A parking area in front of a garage, usually in private residences.

drop cloth A protective covering of plastic, cloth, or paper to spread over a floor, furniture, the ground, etc. when construction is underway.

drop hammer A heavy weight used for driving a **pile** into the ground.

drop manhole A **manhole** provided for inspection and maintenance of sewers where the incoming sewer pipe is considerably higher than the outgoing sewer pipe.

drop siding Cladding for walls in horizontal pieces that overlap when one is placed (dropped) upon another. It is usually made of vinyl, aluminum, or wood.

drop tee A **pipe tee** having lugs in its side, allowing it to be attached to a support.

drought A prolonged period when an area of land receives less natural precipitation than it historically has been accustomed to.

drought resistant Used interchangeably with **drought tolerant**.

drought tolerant A term often used to describe plants with low water requirements, the ability to withstand extended periods without water, or plants of a desert region. They usually have deep and well-developed root zones, waxy leaves, leaf hairs that reduce airflow over the leaf surface, shiny leaf surfaces to reflect light, or leaves that fold up or drop under stress conditions. This term is often inappropriate, or ambiguous because tolerance of drought varies with temperature, soil type, exposure to winds, exposure to sunlight, degree of establishment, age of the plant, size of the plant, depth of rooting medium, etc., and the degree of drought varies greatly.

drove A mason's chisel; its useful end is 2 to 4 in wide.

drove work Stone that has been finished with a **drove**.

drumlin A narrow ridge or hill, often curved, that was formed by glaciers and is composed of glacial till.

drupe In botanical terms, a fleshy, **indehiscent**, one-seeded (usually) or many-seeded fruit. When it contains more than one stony seed, it provides an **endocarp** to enclose each of the seeds.

drupelet In botanical terms, the diminutive (naturally much smaller, or not normal sized) of **drupe**.

dry density The weight of soil after all moisture is removed by an oven, usually at a temperature of 221F (105°C).

drying off Intentionally withholding water from a plant as it enters **dormancy** (usually to assist in becoming dormant).

dry lumber See **kiln-dried lumber**, or **air-dried lumber**.

dry masonry Brick, stone, concrete, masonry units, etc. placed and assembled together in construction without the use of mortar.

dry-pack Slightly moist, almost dry concrete capable of being rammed into spaces.

dry-rodded weight The weight per unit volume of an aggregate when compacted dry.

dry rodding Compacting dry aggregate materials with a rod in a calibrated container to measure the weight per unit volume.

dry rubble construction Rough stones of irregular shapes and sizes assembled together without the use of mortar.

dry well **1.** A well collecting surface waters from such areas as roads, roofs, basement floors, or foundations providing for the water to be dispensed and absorbed into the ground. **2.** A water well in the ground that is no longer capable of providing water. **3.** *See* **cesspool. 4.** *See* **absorbing well.**

DS   Abbreviation for **downspout.**

DU   Abbreviation for **distribution uniformity.**

dual programmable   A feature of some **automatic controllers** that allows them to turn on one set of valves or heads separately at completely different times or days from another set of valves or heads. This is essential where there are valves operating lawn areas requiring a significant amount of water and shrub areas requiring little water.

dub   To strike, cut, rub, or finish, making a surface smooth, or of an equal height.

duckboard   A wooden walkway over muddy ground.

duck tape   *See* duct tape.

ductile-iron pipe   Pipe fabricated of cast-iron alloys in which graphite replaces the carbon that is in **cast-iron.** It is stronger than cast-iron, but more expensive.

duct tape   Thin, strong, cotton or synthetic material made in a roll with one side that is very sticky and adherant to most any clean dry surface. It is usually gray and 1½ to 4 in wide.

duff   Partially or completely decomposed organic matter on the ground, usually beneath an organic litter layer.

DU$_{LQ}$ Abbreviation for **distribution uniformity of the lowest quarter.**

dump station   A place provided for recreational vehicles, camp trailers, etc. with contained sewage to dump their sewage into the sanitary sewer.

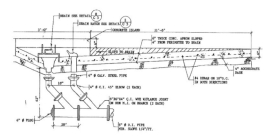

dump station apron and drains

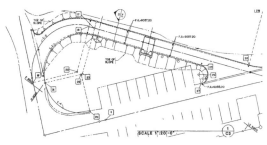

dump station plan

dumpster   A large metal container used for refuse and dumped only by a large truck or motorized device able to lift it. It may be dumped on-site into the truck, or, with a larger dumpster container, it may be hauled off-site for dumping.

dump truck   A truck that has a body capable of lifting to slide its load out.

dump truck

dumpy level A surveying instrument for measuring differences in elevation.

dung 1. Feces. 2. To spread manure for fertilization purposes.

duplex A structure containing two **dwelling units**.

duplex nail A **nail** with 2 heads, one like an extended ring a short distance down the shank. This second head allows the nail to be pounded into material to that point where it becomes difficult to pound it in any further so that the nail can later be pulled from the material. These types of nails are often used in such work as making forms for concrete so that the nails can be pulled easily when the forms are removed.

duplex outlet *See* **duplex receptacle**.

duplex receptacle An electrical device having **receptacles** for mounting in an **outlet box**.

Durham system A waste water system using recessed **drainage fittings**. This prevents waste from catching on connection joints in the pipe.

dust Fine particulates deposited from the air that can block stomata in leaves and block gas exchange.

dusting Applying powdered **fungicides** or insecticides to plants.

Dutch door A door with two separately hinged portions such that one is above the other and each can be opened or closed independently. These are especially useful in barns, etc.

Dutch elm disease Disease caused by the fungus (*Ophiostoma ulmi*), spread by elm bark beetles. It affects American and European elm trees. This disease is best prevented by planting resistant varieties and keeping them healthy.

Dutch lap A method of laying shingles, slates, etc. on a surface in which each one overlaps the one directly below it and one to the side.

dwarf With regard to plants, a **variety** of a particular plant that is lower and more **compact** than other plants of the same species.

dwarfed *or* **dwarfing** Plants that are kept from becoming their normal size at maturity through cultural practices or abnormal environmental conditions. This can be induced by elevation, size of container, lack of water, pruning roots or tops, removing leaves, restricting stems with wires, grafting to a **dwarfing stock**, etc.

dwarfing stock An **understock** that causes a plant grafted upon it to become dwarfed.

dwelling unit Usually a space providing complete, independent living facilities for one or more persons, including provisions for living, sleeping, eating, cooking, and sanitation. Different jurisdictions may define this differently.

dwg Abbreviation for drawing.

dynamic head The pressure in any water system when in use and flowing.

dynamic penetration test A soil test facilitated by pounding a testing device into the soil. In pile driving, the resistance of a pile to further penetration expressed in blows per unit depth of penetration.

dynamic pressure In a **sprinkler system**, the pressure measured at a point inside the system while it is in operation with water in motion and flowing.

dynamic pump A **pump** having pumping action created by a dynamic action taking place between some mechanical element and a fluid. Examples of this pump type are **centrifugal pump**s, and jet pumps.

E

E   A symbol for an elbow (90°) used in a pipe system.

e- *or* **ex-**   A Latin prefix used in botanical descriptions meaning without, from, or away from.

E.W.   Abbreviation for each way.

E/A   Abbreviation for **engineer/architect**.

ea.   Abbreviation for each.

early maturing   A descriptive term applied to certain vegetables that mature faster than others of the same species. Faster-growing varieties tend to fit into this category.

earth   **1.** In landscape terms, the loose material mainly composed of minerals on or near the surface of this planet. **2.** A **soil**. **3.** The surface of the ground.

earth berm   *See* **berm**.

earthen   Of or relating to **earth** or ground.

earthing up   Mounding the soil against the main stem of a plant to **blanch** or otherwise prevent light from affecting its crop. Leeks, potatoes, and celery are often blanched in this manner. Too much light on potato tubers may turn them green and poisonous. Mounding against woody plants is ill advised. *See* **root collar** and **mulch**.

earth pressure   The horizontal pressure exerted by earth that is retained.

earthwork   **1.** Any work dealing with the moving of earthen material, especially that of **excavators**. **2.** A construction work of earth such as an embankment, mounds, etc.

earthworms   Members of the class *Oligochaeta* and mostly the family *Lumbricidae*. They move through the soil improving aeration and excreting organic matter valuable in creating topsoil. They assist in maintaining soil fertility and enhancing soil composition. Mucoprotein is produced within earthworms and appears in castings, which contributes to stability of soil aggregates. It also can be used by other organisms as an organic material to provide energy. They tend to move lower in the soil profile when the upper portion of the soil is hot and dry, and rise to the surface or move elsewhere when the soil is saturated with water.

earwig   Any of many long insects with jointed antennae, and appendages at the end of the body resembling forceps. They feed at night on flowers, leaves, and other insects. During the day, they hide in soil or dark places.

eased   A slightly rounded edge of a construction element, such as stair nose.

easement   A designated part of a property owner's land authorized by the property owner for use by another for a specified purpose. These areas of easement may be for right of travel, access to facilitate installation, maintenance of utilities, drainage facilities, conservation, agriculture, etc.

east elevation   **1.** A drawing, usually to scale, showing the east-facing portion of a structure or element as it would be seen by one standing east and facing west to view it. **2.** The **elevation** of a portion of ground, paving, or structure situated east of the remainder of it.

eastern elevation

eastern elevation   *See* **east elevation**.

eastern exposure   **1.** A slope that from top to bottom slopes downward toward the east. **2.** The east-facing portion of a structure. **3.** The area to the east of any nearly vertical surface that has a changed microclimate effected by it with regard to heat or cold, or brightness of sunlight or shadow.

eastern red cedar *or* **aromatic cedar**   An aromatic, decay-resistant, fine-textured wood having a reddish color with white streaks. It is often used in outdoor applications such as fences and **decks**.

east-malling stocks   **Understocks** used for **grafting** apples.

easy elbow   In pipe work, an elbow that makes a sweeping bend (as opposed to an abrupt bend) of 90°. These elbows are usually installed as conduits to facilitate pulling wire through them.

eave   In structures, the portion of a roof projecting outward and overhanging the wall below.

eaves channel   *See* **rain gutter**.

eaves gutter   *See* **rain gutter**.

eccentric fitting   Any pipe having its center offset from the center of the run of pipe.

eceptacle   The end of a flower stalk on which the floral organs are borne.

echinate   In botanical terms, with prickles.

echinulate   Diminutive of **echinate**.

eclectic   **Design** utilizing a variety of historical styles.

ecological impact   A modification or change in processes effecting living things or their environment that could result in the disruption or loss of normal processes of habitat, vegetation, air quality, soil, water resources, or an increase in ambient noise levels, or other positive or negative changes to other ecological elements.

ecology   **1.** Interactions of organisms with the physical environment as well as with each other and the results of those interactions. **2.** The study of living things in their environment, or the interdependence between life forms and their habitats.

ecosystem   **1.** An area of living organisms and the associated nonliving things with which they interact. **2.** In a selected area, the system of interactions between all living and nonliving things. **3.** An area of similar appearance and function with the group of organisms associated with that area interacting with their environment. This area may be a small piece of land (e.g., **patch, corridor, matrix**) or a large-scale area.

ecotone   **1.** A boundary between ecosystem types adjacent to one another. It can include environmental conditions that are common to both of the adjacent ecosystems, and it can have higher or lower species diversity. **2.** A smaller area than an ecosystem with a variance in environmental conditions.

ecotope   The smallest unit of land that is mapped with generally homogeneous vegetation and ecosystem functioning.

ecotype   Plants of the smallest taxonomic subdivision (subspecies, strains, or varieties) that are adapted to a restrictive set of environmental conditions.

ectomycorrhiza   A type of **mycorrhizae** that forms a symbiotic relationship with plant roots.

edaphic   Relating to the soil or being influenced by it rather than by climate.

edema   Swelling of plant tissues with excess water; any watery swelling of plant parts usually showing as small blisters that can burst and leave a small rusty brown spot. They are most often found on undersides of leaves but also appear on **petiole**s, cacti, etc. The most common cause is abundant, warm soil water and a cool, moist atmosphere. These conditions cause the roots to absorb water at a rate faster than transpiration, which creates a loss of water on the plant's surfaces. Water accumulates in the leaf or plant tissue in excess of its storage capability, some cells enlarge and block the **stomatal** openings, which usually vent water vapor from the plant, and this contributes to increased water retention. As this condition continues, rupture occurs in plant tissue. The raised, crusty brown or light-colored older spots are areas of past epidermis rupture.

edge In landscape ecology, an area which when viewed from above is at the outer portion of a **patch** or **corridor** where environment differs significantly from the inner portion (**interior**). It is the portion of a mostly homogeneous shape on the earth's surface at its outer limits where the environment (sun vs. shade, cool, dampness, plant differences, animal differences, etc.) is different from the interior of the shape. It may be a lake, a grassy area, a patch or corridor of forest or heavy vegetation near the boundaries where environment becomes different and so favors different organisms than those further within the shape. **2.** In a designed landscape, *see* **edging** (**2**).

edger **1.** *See* **edging**. **2.** A tool used to cut low-growing plants (grass, ground covers) along the edge of sidewalks, curbs, gutters, or edging.

edge trimmer A mechanized device usually with a string but sometimes with a blade that is rotated at high speed so that one may direct it at grass or other thin plant material to cut it; a part of maintenance.

edger

edging **1.** In a landscape, the strip of steel, fiberglass, concrete, plastic, wood, etc. used in a linear form, whether straight, curved, or contrived, used as a border, boundary, or aesthetic dressing and separating two types of ground coverings such as lawn, bark, rock mulch, shrubs, etc. They not only have an aesthetic function, but they also keep one plant (usually grass) from overrunning another, or acting as an edge for a mower to run over and near a vertical surface. This prevents having to come back to trim long grass that otherwise could not be reached by mower blades adjacent to vertical surfaces. **2.** A planting placed at an edge in a landscape for a physical barrier, a visual barrier, a dressing, a visual delineation, a windbreak, etc. Items used to create such a border, edge, or boundary include trees, shrubs, flowers (most commonly plants for small borders) or indeed, just about any plant types arranged in a row. **3.** A strip of metal, wood, etc. used to hide or protect edges. **4.** In concrete finishing, the effort of rounding edges to improve the finished edge, to prevent cracking and chipping of an edge, or to prevent tripping. **5.** The act of trimming grass, ground covers, or other plants along a hard surface edge.

edible landscaping Landscapes wholly or mostly comprised of **edible plant**s.

edible plant

edible plant A plant with some portion of it that may be eaten. It may be the leaf, root, flower, stalk, or the fruit.

effective span The distance between supports measured from center to center of vertical supports.

efficiency curve With reference to pumps, an indication on a **pump performance curve** showing the best ranges for a pump with regard to head-capacity performance. It is expressed or measured as a percentage, and is created from a ratio of liquid output horsepower to the input horsepower.

effluent Liquid or gas flowing from a process or treatment system. Effluent is a waste water and may be termed as such after any level of treatment. Discharge from a septic tank or a sewage treatment facility is effluent.

egress An exit.

EIR Abbreviation for **environmental impact report**.

ejector pump *See* **sump pump**.

elastomeric coating A closely adhering neoprene, rubber, or silicone-based coating that forms a watertight, tough, skid-resistant surface.

elbow In pipe work, a fitting facilitating a change in direction of a pipe. The most common elbows are 90° and 45°.

electric-discharge lamp A man-made light source with a glass enclosing a gas that produces light when electricity passes through it.

electric remote control valve A **valve** with a **solenoid** and attached wires that allow operation by an electric sprinkler **controller** from a location remote to the valve.

electric sign An electrically illuminated element with words or symbols conveying information or attracting attention.

elbow

electrolysis Reducing dissolved or fused chemical compounds to a simpler form by passing electricity through them in the presence of an electrolyte or a conductor of electricity other than metal. In piping systems, this occurs with the water being the electrolyte when two dissimilar metals are in contact with one another, especially a galvanized fitting or pipe and a brass or copper fitting or pipe. This leads to corrosion and decomposition of the metals.

electrolytic corrosion Decomposition of materials caused by electrolysis. This occurs when two quite dissimilar metals are touching one another in the presence of water or another electrical conductor. This is a cause of deterioration and corrosion of metal fittings when copper or brass is in contact with galvanized metal in a piping system.

electrolytic protection A way of defending or saving ferrous metals (metals containing iron) from **galvanic corrosion** when they are covered with moist soil or when they are under water. One method is to attach to the metal fittings or pipes another piece of metal that is more electronegative to divert the **electrolysis**.

electroplated A metal surface having a thin electrochemical deposit of brass, zinc, copper, cadmium, tin, or nickel.

elephant trunk   A hopper with a long tube for assisting in placing the concrete in deep shafts or forms.

elevated planter   A **planter** with an elevation higher than the grade beneath it. The planting soil is contained and held aloft by poles, cables, or other points of attachment.

elevated planter

elevation   **1.** The measured amount above or below sea level of an object or area. It is usually expressed in feet or meters. **2.** The measured amount above or below a given base point on a drawing or site. This base point is usually a floor elevation, a paving elevation, or a known surveyed **benchmark**. **3.** A drawing showing the view of, or appearance of, something as seen from a specific side projected to a vertical plane without any vanishing points (not a perspective drawing).

elevation view   *See* **elevation** (3).

elliptic   In botanical terms, elliptical, oval, or oblong, with the ends regularly rounded. It may describe a leaf shape, tree **crown** shape, etc. A tree of this shape is more tall than broad with its widest point near the middle of the height of its crown.

elliptical arch   An arch having the shape of an ellipse.

elliptic

elm   In lumber, a tough, strong, hardwood of brown color. It has been used for veneer, piles, and decking, but is difficult to obtain.

elongate   Drawn out in length, often used in descriptions of plant parts.

elongation region   The region of the root in which existing cells undergo elongation. These cells are thin walled and help to absorb water and nutrients.

eluviation   Movement of dissolved or suspended substances in soil when water input exceeds evaporation.

emarginate   In botanical terms, notched or indented at the summit, tip, or apex. (Compare with **retuse, cuspidate, aristate, acuminate, acute, mucronate, obtuse.**)

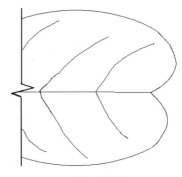

emarginate leaf tip

emboss

emboss A raised or indented design or message.

embryo In botanical terms, a young seed plant still within a **seed** and capable of becoming a mature plant.

emergent plant **1.** An **herbaceous** plant standing erect, rooted in shallow water but having most of the plant growing above the water's surface. **2.** A rooted plant that grows on land that is periodically or permanently flooded, and, when flooded, has portions of the plant (stems and leaves) extending above the water surface.

emery A granular form of impure carborundum. It is used for grinding and polishing.

emery cloth A cloth coated with emery, often used for polishing metal.

eminent domain The power or right of a governing jurisdiction to obtain private property for public use while making certain the property owner is reasonably compensated.

emission uniformity The index of uniformity of emitter discharge rates throughout a micro-irrigation system. It considers both variations in emitters and variations in the pressure to operate emitters.

emitter In **drip irrigation**, a small device placed on a low-pressure pipe that allows water to be provided only in small droplet amounts, usually measured in gallons per hour or liters per hour instead of per minute as with sprinkler irrigation. (Compare with **orifice emitter, turbulent flow emitter, pressure compensating emitter, vortex emitter, laminar flow emitter, continuous flushing emitter.**)

emitter tube A plastic tube intended for distribution of water to or from one **emitter**. It is usually about ¼ in in diameter.

emitter tube stake A plastic or metal stake to hold plastic **micro-irrigation** tubing in place.

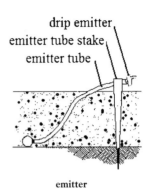

emitter

EMT Abbreviation for Electrical Metallic Conduit; Thin Wall Conduit.

emulsifier A dispersant or something that holds in suspension; usually a liquid.

enamel A paint composed of finely ground pigments and a resin binder that dries to form a hard, smooth, glassy surface.

enation An outgrowth on the surface of a plant as a result of a virus.

encorbelment The projection of any course of masonry over the course immediately below it.

encroachment The unauthorized extension of any portion of a structure or land.

encumbrance A restriction of the use of **real property**.

end dump A long trailer with at least one set of tandem dual wheels pulled by a large semi truck capable of holding large amounts of bulk materials such as rock, topsoil, bark mulch, etc. for delivery and dumping by raising from the front end high enough to allow the material to slide out the back.

end island A **parking island** of landscaping located at the end of a row or bay of parking stalls that is not connected to any other landscaping.

end dump trailer

endangered species A species in considerable danger of extinction in all or a significant portion of its range.

end lap The amount of overlap at the end of a roll of material such as roofing felt.

endemic A **native plant** in a restricted region, or being restricted to a particular region.

endless saw *See* **band saw**.

endocarp The inner layer of a **pericarp** of a fruit of a plant (as with an orange or apple), which contains two or more layers of different texture or consistency.

1 seed
2 endocarp
3 mesocarp ⎤ pericarp
4 exocarp ⎦

peach (cutaway illustration)

endocarp is the stone

endogenous A botanical term referring to something originating internally.

endomycorrhiza A type of **mycorrhizae** that forms a symbiotic relationship with plant roots.

endosperm Food storage tissue in a seed.

engineer/architect A reference to the designer of a project, most often found within contract documents; **landscape architect, architect, civil engineer,** or mechanical engineer.

engaged bollard A low post, partially embedded into a wall or column, so as to prevent motor vehicles from damaging the surface.

engineer's chain A distance measuring device used in land surveying consisting of a series of links, the length of which is 100 ft.

engineer's level Precision leveling instruments used to determine differences of elevation.

engineer's scale A ruler or straight edge divided uniformly into multiples of 10 divisions per inch facilitating drawing or measuring scaled drawings with decimal values for distance. For example, a drawing may be drawn at a scale of 1 in equal to 20 ft (1 in = 20 ft, or 0.20 in = 1 ft).

English bond A brickwork pattern alternating courses of **headers** and courses of **stretchers**. This makes a stronger wall than offset stretchers.

English garden An informal garden deliberately lacking symmetry. These gardens attempt to mimic nature with winding paths, naturally shaped ponds, plantings in informal masses, etc. This design is the opposite of the **formal garden**.

enhanced wetland An existing wetland with certain functions that have been increased or enhanced by human influences.

ensiform A botanical term, sword-shaped (e.g., leaves of iris).

entablature In Classical architecture the horizontal bands of moldings in mass, supported by a column and composed of (from lowest to highest) the **architrave**, the **frieze**, and the **cornice**. This design has sometimes been used in formal design of **colonnade**s and **pavilions**.

entire

ensiform leaves

entire leaf margin

entire In botanical terms, a leaf with smooth margins. They are not at all toothed, notched, or divided. (Compare with **ciliate, pectinate, cleft, lobed, dentate, denticulate, serrate, serrulate, double serrate, incised, crenate, crenulate, parted**.)

entomology The study of insects.

entomophagous A term used to describe a plant that is insect-eating.

entomophilous A flower relying mostly on insects for pollination.

entablature

environment The complete surroundings of either an organism, a portion of an organism, or an organism's community.

environmental assessment A preliminary study of a proposed land use development and the effects it may have on the environment. These assist in determining whether there is a need for a detailed **environmental impact report**.

environmental impact The results of impelling change by one or more forces in an environment upon other elements within the same environment whether climatic, geologic, biotic, edaphic, anthropomorphic, etc. The force may benefit other environmental elements (**positive environmental impact**), or it may be detrimental to other environmental elements (**negative environmental impact**). Most changes in the environment affect more than one organism or its environment, and what may be a positive impact for one may be positive to several others, but it is often a negative to others.

environmental impact report A report required by government agencies that assesses all the significant and known environmental characteristics of an area and determines what presently understood effects or impacts will result if the area is altered or disturbed by a proposed action.

environmental inventory Gathering and categorizing data and information on natural and human features in an area proposed for a planning project.

environmentally friendly Said of a process or product that is beneficial to, or not destructive of, the environment.

enzymes Substances (organic catalysts) produced by living cells that may bring about or speed up chemical reactions.

EPA The Environmental Protection Agency of the United States.

EPDM Abbreviation for ethylene propylene diene monomer, a synthetic rubber liner often used to line water features, roofs, or roof planters because it is waterproof and more stretch resistant and UV resistant than PVC liner.

ephemeral **1.** Plants with flowers that last one or two days. **2.** Short-lived plants that may grow more than one generation per year. **3.** Lasting one day. **4.** Lasting a short time. **5.** A spring-blooming **herb** usually found in **mesic deciduous** forests.

epi- A Greek prefix used in botanical terms meaning upon; often used to mean outer or outermost.

epicarp *See* **exocarp**.

epigynous Joined to the ovary. A botanical term meaning the **perianth** and **stamens** are attached to the top of the ovary instead of beneath it. (Compare with **hypogynous, perigynous**.)

epipetalous A botanical term describing a plant part attached to the **petals** or **corolla**.

epiphyte A plant that obtains its nutrients and water from the air and grows sitting on the surface of another plant, but receives no nourishment from the plant that supports it. They are often incorrectly thought of as parasites. Examples of these types of plants can be found amongst ferns or orchids.

epistyle, epistylium An **architrave**.

epithedes The upper member of the **cornice** of an **entablature**.

epoxy resin finish A waterproof surface most often applied to wood. It is usually applied in three coats and is ⅛ to ¼ in thick.

equestrian **1.** Related to horseback riding. **2.** One who rides a horse.

equilibrium A term used in structure design to describe a condition where the sum of all the **moments** are equal to zero; sometimes referred to as the law of equilibrium.

equinox A point in the year when the sun is at the equator causing the length of days and nights to be equal both south and north of the equator. This occurs at approximately March 21 and September 23.

equipment ground In electrical wiring, a connection from the exposed metal parts of equipment housings and from the grounding port of outlets to provide a ground.

erodibility The susceptibility of a soil to erosion by water or wind.

erodibility factor A value used in the **universal soil loss equation** representing relative erodibility of the soil.

erose In botanical terms, something with an irregular shape appearing as if it were gnawed.

erosion The detachment and movement of soil or rock fragments, or the wearing away of the land surface or subsurface by water, wind, ice, or gravity.

erosion control fabric A rolled or sheeted material laid over the **soil** surface or at a water body edge to prevent **erosion**. It is made of small intertwined wood strings, coconut fiber, plastics, jute, paper, etc.

errors and omissions insurance Insurance covering mistakes by a designer when preparing the contract documents.

escutcheon A pipe flange used to cover a hole through which the pipe passes.

esker A narrow, long ridge of coarse gravel deposited by an ancient stream flowing in a valley or tunnel walled with ice in a melting glacial ice sheet.

espalier **1.** A shrub or tree trained or pruned to grow flat against a wall, fence, etc. They may be trained into formal or informal patterns and are often trained with wire, sticks, or rods to guide the branching pattern. Typical formal espalier patterns include **candelabra, horizontal cordon,** and **Belgian fence espalier. 2.** A trellis, wire pattern, fence, etc. on which plants are trained to grow in an espalier pattern.

esplanade A relatively open area designed for walking or driving, while usually offering a view.

Essex board measure A chart listing the number of board feet in a board one inch thick and of various standard sizes. It is usually printed on a special carpenter's square.

est. Abbreviation for estimated.

established *See* **established plant.**

established plant **1.** A plant that has been transplanted long enough to extend roots outside the original root zone at the time of planting to the surrounding soil, or has become firmly rooted in existing soils surrounding the original planting pit. **2.** A plant that has been grown in a container of some type for a sufficient period of time so that it holds all the soil of the container when pulled from the container. Established plants have roots extending to the bottom of the container and should not leave significant growing-medium residue when

pulled from the container. **3.** A plant that has overcome transplant shock.

established shrub *See* **established plant.**

established tree *See* **established plant.**

estimate *See* **cost estimate.**

estuary The lower end of a river where the ocean tide has an effect.

ET Abbreviation for the word **evapotranspiration.**

ethnobotony The plant lore of a culture, race, or group of people.

etriolation A condition of being pale or feeble without natural vigor.

eu- The Greek prefix (used in some botanical terms) meaning true, real, or typical.

eutrophic Water having an excess of plant-growth nutrients that typically create algal blooms and feature high or low dissolved oxygen.

eutrophication The natural aging process of a water body whereby eventually the basin is filled in. This water-body aging is speeded up by increase of **biomass**, which occurs when nutrients (especially nitrogen and phosphorus) become more prevalent in the water, promoting algae and other aquatic vegetation. Eventually in the natural process, areas silt up and become bogs.

evaporation The change of water from a liquid to a gas in the process of vaporization as water molecules escape from surfaces to the atmosphere.

evaporation pan Standard U.S. Weather Bureau Class-A pan (48-in diameter by 10-in deep) for estimating a crop **evapotranspiration** rate.

evapotranspiration (ET) **1.** The process of water loss from soil by both **evaporation** and by

transpiration through plants growing in the soil. **2.** The amount of water needed by a plant. It is the sum of the amount of water lost through the evaporation of moisture at the soil's surface and the transpiration of the water through the plant. The daily evapotranspiration rate is used in scheduling the irrigation needs for plant material.

even-pinnate A botanical term, pinnately compound, but without a terminal leaflet; typically there is an even number of leaflets. (Compare with **odd-pinnate**.)

everbearing A term usually associated with berry plants indicating they bear fruit more or less the entire growing season.

everblooming Flowering more or less continually throughout the season of growth.

evergreen A plant that does not naturally lose its leaves yearly, all at once. These types of trees hold their leaves over winter or longer until new ones appear.

everlastings Plants that retain form or color when dried, often being used in dry flower arrangements.

ew Abbreviation for each way.

excavation   **1.** The mechanical removal or digging, piling, scraping, leveling, compacting, etc. of earth material for utilities, roads, paths, pipes, buildings, landscapes, features, large plants, etc. **2.** The work or livelihood made of **cut**ting or **fill**ing soil or rock from an area of the earth.

excavator   **1.** A company or person who performs **excavation** for their vocation. **2.** Power-driven machines that dig, move, or transport earth gravel, etc.; especially a machine with tracks, a hydraulically operated arm, and a bucket at the end of its arm.

exceedance probability The likelihood of a storm occurring during any one year equaling or exceeding the rainfall rate used as a basis for the design of a storm-water drainage system.

excessively drained soil Soil in which water is removed very rapidly. These soils are porous, shallow, or steep. Optimum amounts of soil moisture for plant growth are seldom present in these soils. Irrigation is usually required.

excess joint A space between units (bricks, stones, etc.) in masonry work where more than enough mortar is placed between units, causing it to project beyond the wall face.

excess runoff   **1.** Surface runoff not satisfactorily accommodated by natural or planned drainage systems. **2.** Any water moving from a site surface and not being detained or infiltrated on-site.

exchange time The time it takes to completely replace water in a lake or other water body at the rate of inflow.

excurrent In botanical terms, projecting beyond the apex, or a tree trunk continued to the very top, or with an apparent central axis from which lateral branches arise. (Compare with **deliquescent**.)

exempt meter Where sewer fees are based on water usage, this is a water meter placed on a waterline where the water will not be entering the sewer (such as for landscape use) and is exempt from being considered as water for determining sewer fees.

exfoliating A descriptive botanical term referring to a plant part (especially bark) peeling off in thin strips or sheets.

exfoliation   **1.** Peeling, swelling, curling up, or scaling of a surface. **2.** The loss of leaves from a plant.

EXIST.   Abbreviation for existing.

exfoliating bark

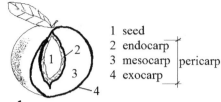

peach (cutaway illustration)

1 seed
2 endocarp
3 mesocarp } pericarp
4 exocarp

exocarp is the outer skin

existing conditions   In reference to land, this includes anything present on the land or site, and anything affecting the land or site. These conditions may or may not be visible. They are myriad and complex in their interrelationships and effects. Examples are soils, geology, elevations, vegetation, wildlife, avalanche hazard, prevailing winds, views, archeological elements, air drainage, water drainage, average temperature, hazardous waste, slopes, structures, pavements, utilities, easements, social influences, economical influences, historical importance, etc.

existing grade   The surface of a site prior to construction efforts of cutting or filling any of its area.

existipulate   A botanical term meaning without **stipules**.

exocarp   The outermost layer of the **pericarp** of the fruit from a plant (such as a cherry or peach).

exogenous   A botanical term describing something that originates externally.

exotic   **1.** In **horticulture** and **ecology**, this refers to organisms that are introduced into an area (by wind, ocean current, water drainage, birds, or humans) other than that which they are considered native. This may apply to plants, animals, bacteria, all living things. **2.** A plant or animal species that has been intentionally introduced by human intervention, that does not naturally occur in a region. **3.** A plant from a foreign part of the world. It is not indigenous and not capable of prolonged survival under local regional climatic conditions without aid or protection.

exp.   Abbreviation for expansion.

expanded metal   Metal mesh made from a steel plate and sometimes twisted between openings to provide roughness or traction (e.g., for walking upon, etc.).

expanded slate   Slate enlarged and made porous by heating. This material is lightweight and sometimes used as an aggregate where weight is critical. It is often used in soil mixes for roof structures to limit weight loads.

expansion bolt   A bolt in an expandable sleeve that is inserted into a material (concrete, drywall, brick) until the sleeve is flush with the surface. The bolt is then screwed and tightened into the sleeve, causing it to expand and be held tightly in place. These types of bolts are useful in anchoring items to existing masonry, concrete, etc.

expansion joint   A joint in paving that is filled with a material that can expand or compress as the paving on either side expands or contracts due to heat, cold, or loads. This prevents paving from cracking or damaging structures it abuts.

explanate A botanical term meaning spread out flat.

exposed-aggregate finish A finish of concrete where rock embedded in the concrete can be seen on the surface. The aggregate can be mixed in concrete before pouring or sprinkled on its surface and lightly pounded into green concrete. Before the concrete sets, the concrete film on the rock must be washed off. This is usually accomplished with a spray nozzle on a hose.

exserted In botanical terms, protruding out of (e.g., the stamens out of the **corolla**).

ex-situ Something out of place or off-site. It can refer to groundwater or earthen material removed or hauled off. It may also refer to the propagation and care of rare plants on a site or area where they are not native.

ext. Abbreviation for exterior.

extension agency, cooperative extension, county extension service, extension service In the United States, an agency in each state that has the responsibility of providing information to citizens of its local state and county regulations regarding agriculture, soil conditions, historic climatic conditions, expected plant diseases and remedies, etc.

external grip A reference to the type of attachment on the outside of a pipe for a machine to pull the pipe underground.

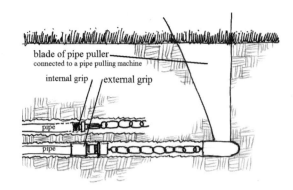

external grip

extra An item or task in construction not a part of the original agreement and usually calling for extra compensation.

extrastaminal A botanical term meaning outside of the **stamen**s.

extrorse In botanical terms, turned outward, or facing outward. (Compare with **introrse**.)

extruded concrete edger A linear piece of concrete extruded from a machine used as an edge between landscape ground finishes (i.e., lawn, rock mulch, ground covers, and bark mulch).

eye In botanical terms, an undeveloped growth bud capable of producing a new plant or more growth.

eyebolt A bolt with a head that forms a circle with a hole for accepting wire, rope, hooks, chain, etc.

F

F **1.** Abbreviation for **Fahrenheit. 2.** Abbreviation for female (useful in describing a **fitting** end). **3.** Abbreviation for fill.

F 1 hybrid In botanical terms, a first generation **hybrid** obtained by artificial cross-pollination between two dissimilar parents, each from a pure line or race, and each bearing hereditary factors.

F 2 hybrid *or* **F 2 generation** In botanical terms, the second generation from a cross, usually obtained through self-pollination within F1 **hybrid**s; not expected to be true to the form of their parents.

FAB Abbreviation for fabricate.

faboid A botanical term meaning bean-like.

façade **1.** A building's exterior face. The exterior wall of a building exposed for public view. **2.** That portion of any exterior elevation on a building or structure extending from ground level to the top of the **parapet**, wall, or **eave**s and including the width of the building elevation.

face **1.** Any exposed surface. **2.** The widest surface of a board. **3.** The surface of a hammer used for pounding nails. **4.** The act of placing one building material over another, usually to improve the finished look.

faced A building material surfaced with another material to improve its finished look, or to make it more durable.

face stone Stone used on a surface exposed to view.

facia *See* **fascia.**

facing brick *or* **face brick** Brick made with attention given to its aesthetic appeal.

Fahrenheit (F) A measurement or scale of temperature in which boiling water occurs at 212° above 0 and freezing of water occurs at 32F. The temperature in F degrees may be converted to **centigrade** (Celsius) by subtracting 32 from the Fahrenheit temperature value, then multiplying by 5, and then dividing by 9.

fair-faced brickwork A tidy, clean-looking surface of brickwork.

fairway The usually manicured lawn area between the golf **tee** and the **green** with its hole.

fairy ring A fungus causing dark green rings in lawns caused by mushroom-like fungi and spreading in a circular ring that enlarges to sometimes several **yard**s (**meter**s) across.

falcate In botanical terms, curved like a hand sickle or hawk's beak.

fallout shelter A structure, usually below grade, for use as protection against radioactivity in the event of a nuclear blast or accident.

fallow **1.** Agricultural cropland allowed to be idle during the growing season to restore productivity through the accumulation of water, nutrients, or both. **2.** Description of land not planted for a season. **3.** Plowed land.

family In plant classification, a grouping of related plant **genera** that are distinctly different from other genera. As a group of related plants, they form a category ranking in the plant classification system (**taxonomy**) that is a subcategory of an **order**, and ranks between it and the **genus**

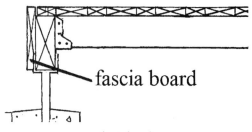

fascia board

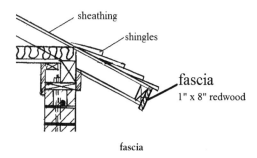

sheathing

shingles

fascia
1" x 8" redwood

fascia

(a subcategory of it). A plant family category is most often made up of several or many genera (in some cases it may contain only one genus and species). Examples of common plant families are the rose family and the pea family. *See also* **taxon**.

FAR Abbreviation for **floor area ratio**.

farinose A botanical term meaning covered with a meal-like powder.

Farm Bureau A U.S. nonprofit organization for farmers, often with information about assistance with growing plants, etc. They have chapters in every state and some counties.

fascia, facia A flat horizontal member usually covering and attached to other structural members, as on the eave of a roof.

fasciate A broad, flattened stem.

fasciation A growth defect causing a flattening or spreading of a stem.

fascicle A botanical term meaning a close cluster or bundle.

fascicled Growing in bundles or tufts.

fastigiate **1.** A plant with upright, erect branches; narrow at the top or somewhat **columnar**, but narrower in form. (Compare with **round, columnar, weeping, oval, broadly spreading, upright spreading, pyramidal.** *See also* illustration.) **2.** A description of plant parts crowded close together, more or less parallel, and most often erect.

fastigiate tree forms

fastigiated (branches) In botanical terms, close; parallel.

fast track Construction being undertaken while design is still being finalized.

fatigue In construction materials, the repeated application and removal of loads or pressure on a metal or other material causing a structural change that can lead to cracks or failure.

faucet *or* **water tap** A water outlet valve operated by turning a handle.

fc Abbreviation for **footcandle**.

FCAP Abbreviation for **fluorachrome arsenate phenol**.

FD, fd Abbreviation for floor drain.

feathering This often means to slightly change. Two edges not flush often need feathering. Shutting a valve off slowly, or turning it on slowly can be feathering.

fecal Relating to, pertaining to, or constituting feces.

fecundity The potential reproductive capacity of a plant, taking into consideration the number of viable seeds produced.

feeder roots These plant roots are mostly within about 12 to 18 inches of the soil surface and absorb most of the nutrients and water for a plant. They are relatively short lived. *See also* **anchor roots**.

fee simple Land ownership encompassing all property rights, including the right to develop the land.

feet of head One foot of head is equal to the pressure at the bottom of a column one foot tall. That pressure expressed in pounds per square inch is 0.433.

feet per second In reference to pipes, ditches, or rivers, the speed (**velocity**) that water flows.

female A pipe **fitting** or device that either has inside threads or an inside socket for acceptance of a **male** end; used for the connection of pipes or devices.

female plant A plant that produces fruit or seed without producing pollen.

female thread A thread inside a fitting, plumbing fixture, sprinkler head, valve, etc.

fen A freshwater wetland on low ground dominated by herbaceous and shrubby vegetation. The soil is usually organic peat, and it is partly or totally covered with water.

fence An upright enclosure or barrier, such as wooden posts, wire, iron, etc., used as a boundary, means of protection, privacy, screening, or confinement, but not including hedges, shrubs, trees, other natural growth, or landforms.

fenestration An opening or openings in a wall.

fermate *or* **ferbam** Ferric dithiocarbonate used as a **fungicide**.

fermentation layer The layer of the **O horizon** where most decomposition takes place. See **Oe layer**. It is comprised of unrecognizable organic material physically disintegrated into pieces and decomposing.

ferns In botanical terms, plants without **flowers** or seed, and having **frond**s.

ferrous metal Metal having iron as the principal element.

ferruginous A descriptive botanical term referring to a plant part with a rust color.

fertile **1.** Regarding soils, *see* **fertility**. **2.** A plant bearing functional reproductive structures capable of producing seeds.

fertility With regard to soils, the ability of a soil to sustain plant life. A soil that is fertile for one plant may not be fertile for another plant. Fertility is generally thought to encompass only the nutrient content of the soil. But, in reality, soil fertility (its ability to sustain plant life) includes drainage, physical condition, aeration, acidity or alkalinity, moisture, presence of any diseases and pests, toxic substances, and depth to a solid surface, etc.

fertilize **1.** The process where pollen is applied to the female portion (pistil) of a flower, allowing for the formation of seed. **2.** To apply nutrients (naturally or by human intervention) to a plant or the ground in proximity of a plant's roots for use by the plant.

fertilizer In landscape work, material or chemicals that supply needs (other than air, water, space, and stability) of plants in the soil. The **primary nutrient**s of most fertilizers are **nitrogen**

(N), phosphorus (P), and potassium (K). They are usually listed on containers of fertilizer in the foregoing order as a percentage of each (i.e., 5-10-8 or 5% nitrogen, 10% phosphorus, 8% potassium). *See also* **secondary nutrients**, **complete fertilizer**, and **micronutrient**s.

fertilizer analysis The breakdown usually labeled on fertilizer products showing the minimum percentages of nutrients included.

fertilizer burn This is a burning or wilting of leaves caused by salts commonly found in fertilizers (especially nitrogen fertilizers), which changes **osmotic pressure** in the soil thereby preventing water from entering roots. **Leaching** salts from the soil with excess watering can move the salts from the root zone. **Fertilizers** have a salt index number that can be helpful in determining the amount of fertilizer that can be applied without excessive salt application.

fertilizer ratio The amount of **nitrogen** (N), phosphorus (P), and **potash** (K) present in a fertilizer by percentage. It is usually listed as three numbers always in the order of N, P, K.

fertilizer spike A hardened fertilizer in the shape of a spike that can be pushed or lightly pounded into the soil. Concentrations at the spike can sometimes burn roots.

fertilizer tablet A hardened **fertilizer** in the shape of a large tablet (or pill) that can be buried in the soil. Concentrations at the tablet can sometimes burn roots. It is meant to slowly decompose and leach into the soil where it can feed roots.

festoon A decorative chain, strip, or banner hung between two points, or a festive pendant hung from a point, etc.

fetch The distance of water surface across a water body. This is an important factor in determining wave sizes.

fetid An offensive odor.

fiberboard A board made of glue and wood chips formed into sheets.

fiberglass reinforced pipe A pipe fabricated from glass fibers and resins for durability and strength.

fiber optic A communication cable comprised of glass or plastic fibers with protective cladding, strengthening material, and an outside cladding. Lasers or diodes transmit light through these fibers. They are better for communication cables because they do not have electromagnetic interference problems or grounding problems, they are small in diameter, lightweight, and have a large transmission bandwidth. These may be encountered when digging underground, and it is important to locate them before digging commences because they are expensive to repair and more expensive to compensate for any necessary costs associated with loss of service. (Damaged large lines have been known to be expensive enough to put a reputable excavation or landscape company into bankruptcy, even with insurance.)

fiber-reinforced concrete Concrete with fiberglass filaments mixed in to add strength and resistance to cracking.

fibrous In botanical terms, made up of fibers, or thread-like parts.

fibrous concrete Concrete having fibers in its mix, to reduce its weight and improve its tensile strength.

-fid A botanical suffix meaning deeply cut.

fiddlehead The unfurling of a fern **crosier**.

fiduciary An overseer or one in a position of trust.

field capacity The amount of water held in **soil** when gravitational force on the water equals the retentive force. After saturation, the soil pore spaces are filled with water, but the larger pores drain due to gravity and the smaller pores are left with water retained. Field capacity is determined by the amount of water in the soil or the moisture condition of the soil at that point. Expressed as a percentage, it may be calculated by subtracting the **oven dry weight** of a soil sample from the wet weight of a soil sample, and dividing that difference by the oven dry weight of the soil sample.

field check   **1.** To observe or measure on-site.

field drain   A buried, perforated pipe used to drain an agricultural field.

field grown   A term referring to nursery stock grown directly in soil in the field as opposed to being grown in **containers**.

field order   A minor change in construction work not increasing or decreasing the cost to the owner.

fieldstone   **1.** Loose rock found in soil or on its surface. **2.** Flat or rectangular rock easily placed and fit in masonry.

fieldwork   Efforts not in an office, but outdoors, or especially on a site.

filament   In botanical terms, the thread-like stalk of an **anther** or **stamen**.

file   A metal handheld tool with ridges, or small teeth, useful in **feathering** or smoothing metal, plastic, wood, etc.

filiform   In botanical terms, thread-shaped, very slender, or stringy.

fill   With reference to **excavation** work, the placement of soil or rock material.

filler   A small aggregate used to improve the wearing surface of an asphalt coating.

filler coat   A primer paint coat.

fillet   **1.** A slender band, square in section, used as ornamentation. **2.** A narrow space, concave between two surfaces.

filling   In work related to land, the depositing on land whether flat or in trenches or holes, whether submerged or not, of gravel, earth, or other materials.

fill pump   A pump that supplies a tank with water.

filter   **1.** In irrigation this is a device that removes debris or small particles of soil from flowing water to prevent irrigation devices (i.e., heads, emitters, etc.) from clogging. They must be cleaned periodically. Most of them are cleaned manually, but there are a few that can be cleaned automatically from the **sprinkler controller**. **2.** In landscape ecology, this is a penetrable change in the landscape that causes a change in the numbers or amounts of output of organisms, or materials that penetrate the landscape change. The change in landscape may be a road, a clearing, a rocky area, a forested corridor, etc.

fimbriate   In botanical terms, fringed.

fimbrillate   A botanical term that is the diminutive of **fimbriate**.

final grade   *See* **finish grade**.

final plan *or* **finished plan**   A map, layout, or construction design to **scale** and ready for implementation of the designed project.

fine grade   **1.** The act of grading, raking, etc. to prepare a finished landscape surface, usually in preparation for **sodding**, **seeding**, **planting**, or placement of surface **mulch**. **2.** The finished surface of a ground ready and prepared for **seed, sod, mulch**, or **plant material**.

fines   The by-product of rock processing, being fragments of rock from powder size to sand size.

fine sand   The portion of **sand** with particles 1/500 to 1/250 in in size.

fine-textured soil   A soil containing 35% or more **clay**, also known as **heavy soil**.

finish carpentry

finish carpentry The application of wood trim to structures, as well as the installation of doors, windows, etc.

finish grade *or* **finished grade** **1.** The final grade, slope, shape, and elevation of all surfaces (lawn, walks, patio, etc.) at the completion of an outdoor project. This may be the surface of **sod**, soil, **mulch**, pavement, a wood **deck**, etc. **2.** The smooth completed grading of soil prior to seeding, **planting**, **sodding**, etc.

finishing Smoothing, brushing, troweling, treating, etc. to give a green concrete surface its final appearance.

finishing machine A motorized machine used to give a finished surface to green concrete.

finishing nail This is a **nail** with a small head just slightly larger than its shank. The head is slightly rounded at its edges, or is a consistent diameter from the top of its head surface to its shank (this is a very short distance compared to its shank length). It is used where it is not desirable for a nail head to show on the finished material. It can be driven into material with a punch or the force of a mechanical nail gun so that it can be covered with similar-looking material to that which it is nailed into so that its location is concealed.

fir A softwood useful in the framing of structures.

fire blight Disease common to flowering pears, pyracantha, and other plants. It is identified by blossoms and leaves shriveling, turning a blackish brown, and dying. Bark becomes dark brown and may form cankers. For preventing, plant resistant varieties, avoid poorly drained soils, and avoid too much fertilizer. Cut off dead twigs 1 ft below affected area and discard (do not use in compost or mulch).

firebrick *or* **fired brick** A ceramic brick containing a high percentage of silica capable of withstanding high temperatures and useful in chimneys, bar-b-que structures, etc.

fire hazard area Land where, due to slope, fuel, weather, or other fire-related conditions, the potential loss of vegetation, habitat, life, and property from a fire necessitates special fire protection measures.

fire hydrant A point of connection for fire-hose and a valve to turn the water on and off.

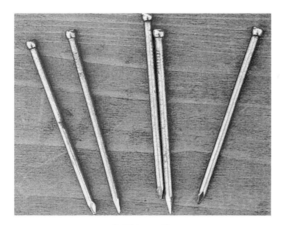

finishing nails

fire hydrant

142

fish meal   A complete organic **fertilizer** made of dried, ground fish or fish parts containing 8 to 10% **nitrogen**, 4 to 9% **phosphoric acid**, and 2 to 4% **potash**.

fishplate   A wood or metal piece attached by nails or bolts to the ends of two abutting ends of lumber.

fish tape   A long, thin, stiff metal strip used to extend through a **conduit** or **sleeve** and then attach to an electrical **conductor** to pull it through.

fistulose, fistulous   A botanical term meaning hollow.

fitting   Pipe connectors (devices for connection of pipes) such as elbows, tees, couplers, reducer bushings, unions, etc.

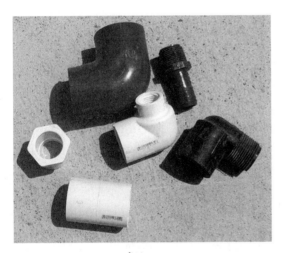

fittings

fix   With regard to soils, formation of a compound that is stable, stationary, and available to other organisms or plant roots (e.g., bacteria that fix nitrogen). *See* **rhizobium** and **nitrogen fixation**).

fixation   The process of changing a soluble or exchangeable nutrient form to a relatively insol-uble form, which may have a negative effect on plant health and may even cause death.

flabellate   A botanical term meaning fan-shaped.

flaccid   A botanical term meaning weak, soft, flabby, or hardly, if at all, capable of supporting its own weight.

flag   **1.** A synonym of **wilt**. **2.** A common name for plants with sword-like foliage such as iris. **3.** Any fabric or other flexible material attached to or designed to be flown or dangled from a flagpole, staff, or structure. **4.** The act of **flagging** a sprinkler system with small flags (**sprinkler flag**) on wires or plastic staffs, or the flags themselves. **5.** *See* **flagstone**. **6.** A symbol or symbols represented on material, or even on a plain piece of material, usually triangular or rectangular, that represents an entity (country, state, company, etc.), advertises a product, or is hung in celebration of a holiday, etc.

flagelliform   A botanical term meaning very slender and elongate, with the form of a flagellum.

flagging   **1.** The layout of a sprinkler system on a site with small flags at each head location. **2.** A **flagstone** pavement or the setting of flagstone.

flagpole   A freestanding structure or a pole attached to a building or to the roof of a building and used for the purpose of displaying flags.

flagstone, or flag, or flagging   A flat stone, about 1 to 6 in thick, used in making patios, walkways, or stepping stones.

flambeau   A luminaire mimicking a flaming torch.

flange   A projection or ring on a shaft or pipe.

flanged joint   A pipe joint with an extended ring at its end or ends allowing it to be bolted to a companion ring (flange) of another fitting. It is prevented from leaking by use of a gasket between the flanges.

flagpole

flange union A **flanged fitting** in two pieces, each of which is screwed onto the end of a pipe and then bolted together.

flap valve With regard to piping, a **check valve** made of a hinged disk that permits flow in only one direction.

flashboards Boards used to control water levels that may be removed.

flashing A thin waterproof material to prevent drainage and seepage between a roof and a wall or over exterior door openings and windows. It extends under shingles or roofing and is bent to cover an intersection as with another surface at 90° (e.g., a wall or parapet).

flat In the nursery industry, hollow boxes or trays fitted with small containers for raising plants from **seed**, **cutting**s, or **set**s.

flat grain A reference to lumber that is cut from a tree with its end's shortest dimension nearly parallel to the growth rings. This produces a grain in the face (largest dimension) of the board that is marbled and with lines changing direction. Looking at the end of the board one will see grain lines perpendicular to its shortest dimension, which is parallel to its widest flat side. *See also* **vertical grain**.

flathead wood screw This screw has various indented shapes in its head for accepting a tool (screwdriver) to drive (turn) it into wood. The top of its head is flat with either a threaded taper from its flat-head surface to its more slender pointed shank, or it is a slender shank of a constant diameter continuing to its threads where it then tapers with threads to its point. Its tapered head allows it to be drawn flush with the surface it is driven into.

flat washer *See* washer.

flatwork Concrete construction work associated with areas where concrete has more horizontal flat surface than other surfaces and usually requires a finished surface.

Flemish bond A pattern of brick in a wall made by alternating **stretchers** and **headers** with each header centered on the stretcher immediately above and below it.

flexible diaphragm/compensating emitter *See* **pressure compensating emitter**.

flexible liner A material that comes on a roll, is waterproof, and is used in lining ponds or planters.

flexuous A descriptive botanical term referring to a plant part having a wavy or zigzag pattern.

flight A continuous run of steps without a landing.

float **1.** A tool or device for smoothing a surface. **2.** An apparatus in a water feature that controls the elevation of a water body and the inflow of water from an outside source by means of a floating device that raises and lowers and opens or closes the water supply line.

float check The float used in an atmospheric vacuum breaker, preventing water flow when water pressure drops.

floating foundation A thick, reinforced concrete slab used instead of wall or column footings or foundations to support and distribute the load of a structure to a soil having low-bearing capacity. It is also called a **raft foundation** or **mat foundation**.

float switch An automatically actuated switch turned off or on by a float on a liquid surface.

float valve *or* **float-controlled valve** A **valve** controlled by a float riding on a liquid surface allowing water to flow when it drops to a preset level and stopping water flow when it rises to another level. These are often used in water features.

floccose In botanical terms, composed of or bearing tufts of woolly or long, soft, fine, loosely arranged, and more or less tangled hairs. (Compare with **tomentose**.)

flocculate The aggregation of fine particles together. This is important in clay soils for the colloidal portions because they fill the pore spaces preventing aeration, gaseous exchange, or penetration of roots or water. Liming acid clay soils and the freeze-thaw process tend to encourage clay's ultramicroscopic particles to cling together in larger aggregates or crumbs allowing for freer water and airflow, etc. This texture can be destroyed by working the soil while wet, repeated walking over the soil, or equipment driving over the soil.

flolicaceous In botanical terms, leaf-like.

flood control Processes or constructed elements for the conveyance, control, and dispersal of flood waters.

flood elevation The elevation flood waters should reach at a particular site during the occurrence of a specific flood period. For example, a 100-year flood elevation is that elevation flood waters are expected to rise to in the event of a 100-year flood.

flood frequency The probability of a flood of a given magnitude occurring in a given year.

flood irrigation A method of watering plants where the area containing plants is flooded until the soil is soaked.

floodplain **1.** Areas of rivers that are flooded periodically by the lateral overflow. **2.** In hydrology, the entire area that is flooded every 100 years (average). **3.** A land area susceptible to inundation by water as a result of a flood. This may be evident by land forms and may be defined by such, or it may be calculated by a flood frequency along with measurement of the drainage channel capacity to determine the elevation or extent of flooding along the drainage path.

floor area ratio (FAR) The floor area of a building or buildings on a lot divided by the total lot area.

floral structure The elements comprising a **flower**.

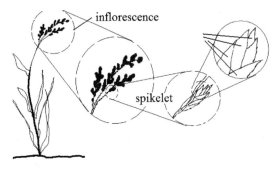

florets

floret An individual flower in a cluster. This pertains to a spike or panicle of grasses, or to tiny flowers composing the head of a composite plant or crowded flower head. They are individual flowers making up a large flower head. Though grass flowers and others are mostly green or brownish, they are flowers made up of florets or a floret. Examples of some other flowers containing many florets are daisies, dandelions, and thistle.

floriculture   A branch of ornamental horticulture concerned with the study, cultivation, management, and marketing of flowering plants, cut flowers, or potted plants. The broadest meaning of the term includes all aspects of growing flowers.

floriferous   A descriptive botanical term referring to a plant that bears flowers. It is most commonly used to describe a plant with abundant flowers.

florist   One who deals in cut flowers.

floristic system   The botanical classification system. Under this system plants are categorized into divisions, each of which is subdivided into smaller and smaller groups arranged according to relationships and similarities or dissimilarities among plants. *See also* **botanical name**.

flow   The movement of fluids through pipe, fittings, valves, or other devices or equipment generally measured in gallons per minute (gpm), gallons per hour (gph), cubic feet per second (ft³/s), cubic meters per hour (m³/h), liters per minute (l/m), or liters per second (l/s).

flow control   A device, usually on an automatic valve, which allows for manually increasing, decreasing, or shutting off water flow potential.

flower   **1.** A **blossom**; **inflorescence**. It is the reproductive structure of flowering plants (**angiosperm**s, Greek for seed in a vessel). Complete flowers are comprised of **stamen**s, **pistil**s, **petal**s, and **sepal**s. An incomplete flower lacks one of these items. The illustration shows a complete flower; though each flower is unique in some way, this depicts the major components as they may be found. **2.** To **bloom**.

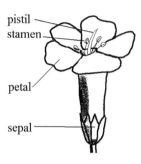

flower

flower bed   An area utilized for the planting of flowers.

flower bud   A **bud** on a plant that will produce a **flower**. (Compare with **leaf bud**.)

flow pressure   *See* **working pressure** or **dynamic pressure**.

flow range   In irrigation, the minimum and maximum water flow required for an automatic valve to turn off or on.

flow sensor   A device that monitors or senses the water flow past a given point.

fluorochrome arsenate phenol (FCAP)   A waterborne salt preservative for wood. Wood must be pressure treated for this preservative to be effective. It is highly recommended by experts as it is odorless, clean, does not leach, and its color can be masked easily by painting or applying a solid color stain when dry.

fluorescent light   A **luminaire** that gives off light by lighting a phosphor coating.

flush   **1.** Two surfaces even with and immediately adjacent to one another, neither extending beyond the other. **2.** To wash out, as with a filter on irrigation systems. **3.** In sprinkler or drip irrigation systems, the process of running water through the lines before attaching **heads**, **valves**,

emitters, or other devices that could become clogged with debris (rocks, sand, etc.) left in piping systems during construction fitting (especially when work has been done in a trench).

flush-cut joint *or* **flush joint**   A joint in masonry work where the joint of mortar is made **flush** with the brick or masonry unit face. This is not often used out-of-doors, especially in temperate climates, as moisture tends to eventually enter the joints and cause damage when freezing.

flush-head rivet   A **rivet** that is placed in material with its head **countersunk**.

flushing   Cleaning out debris and sediment from pipes by the force of moving liquid, usually water.

flush plate   The small metal, plastic, or wood finishing covering an electrical receptacle on a finished surface with holes if necessary to allow switches, or points of plug in, etc.

flush valve   A **valve** in an irrigation system, water feature, etc. that can be opened to run water backward through a filter to remove (flush out) debris that has accumulated during normal use.

fly rafter   A rafter in the overhang of a gable-type roof.

foamed concrete *or* **foam concrete**   A relatively lightweight concrete made by adding foam or gas while still in a liquid state.

FOB   Abbreviation for free on board. It means the price of an item not including the freight to ship it.

focal point   A noticeable area or spot of attention, activity, or attraction. It may be such a spot because many paths, views, rays, walks, etc. converge or it is of a different color, texture, height, width, brightness, etc.

fodder   Tracing paper (translucent paper) usually sold on rolls of various lengths and widths in a yellowish or whitish color.

foetid   An offensive odor.

fogger   A device that creates a water fog when in operation. These seem to be most often used indoors in **greenhouse**s.

fogging   A term sometimes used to describe a **sprinkler irrigation system** that has too high of an **operational pressure** (**dynamic pressure**) causing the individual **sprinkler head**s to not only spray water but to disperse some water to the air as a mist (fog). This is a detrimental situation because water in the form of mist is most often lost to wind or **evaporation**.

FOK   Abbreviation for free of knots.

folding rule   A rigid ruler with measuring units, and joints for folding it to a small size, allowing convenience in hand-carrying and storage.

foliaceous   A botanical term meaning leafy in texture.

foliage   Plant leaves. This term usually refers to the leafy material of the entire plant **head** or sometimes a portion of leaves of a plant or the leaves of many plants.

foliar   Of or relating to leaves.

foliar feeding   Supplying nutrients to plants through their leaves. This is a benefit, but not a substitute for soil nutrients. It is sometimes used for immediate results.

foliar fertilizing   The application of **fertilizer** (usually mixed with water) to plant leaves in a fine spray.

font   A style of lettering.

food chain or web   The interconnected group of plants and animals in an ecosystem. One living organism is food for another, which is food for another, which is food for another, etc. Contaminated food may have a chain reaction.

foot

foot, (ft), (') English or U.S. length equal to 12 **in**, or 0.3333 **yd**, or 30.48 **cs**.

footbridge Any bridge built and intended for pedestrian use.

footbridge

foot-candle (fc) A measure of illumination on a surface that is everywhere 1 ft from a uniform point source of light of one **candle** and equal to 1 **lumen** per sq ft. It is equal to 10.76 lux. Natural outdoor light intensity may vary from 10,000 fc or more to 2,000 fc or less depending on cloud cover, time of day, obstructions, and time of year.

footing In terms of construction, that portion of a structure placed at the lowest part to prevent settling; usually under a **foundation**, **post**, wall, **pier**, or **column** and enlarged (especially wider) so as to bear and distribute the load from above by dispersing it to the earth material it contacts. It is usually wider than the portion of the structure attached to its upper surface for stability and has increased area to transmit weight (load).

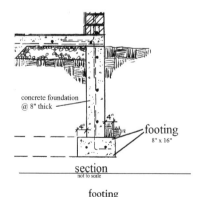

concrete foundation
@ 8" thick

footing
8" x 16"

section
not to scale

footing

footpath A walkway.

footprint With regard to construction and land, the horizontal area of a structure or element as seen in plan, measured at the outside of all exterior portions where it meets the ground. It is formed by an outline where a structure or any object meets the ground.

foot valve With regard to pumps, a **valve** that is placed on the end of a **suction pipe** and only opens when the pump is in operation. It is only needed when the center of a pump's suction entrance is higher than the water source.

forb A nongrassy plant that does not form wood. It may be an **annual**, **perennial**, or **biennial**. Often used to describe plants of meadows or prairies.

force account Construction work on a time-and-materials basis that may have a limit set by money available.

forced bloom *See* **forcing**.

forcing Bringing flowers, vegetables, and fruits to maturity out of season.

forecourt An entry space.

foreman A specially trained individual that leads, works with, and is responsible for the actions of a crew.

forest **1.** A biological community dominated by trees and other woody plants covering land. Also, any large area where trees are predominant. **2.** An area designated by a governing agency as a forest.

forestry Generally, a profession involved with the science, business, and art of creating, conserving, or managing future use of forests.

forklift truck A motorized vehicle with two extended steel prongs capable of lifting and moving heavy materials or objects.

form Boarding or sheeting of plywood in place temporarily to hold a shape for poured concrete, etc.

formal garden An outdoor area for human use, enjoyment, leisure, aesthetic pleasure, etc. comprised of such elements as plants, benches, patios, decks, walks, water features, fountains, etc. organized into symmetrical shapes or geometric patterns or forms (definitely having a human influenced and perhaps even engineered appearance).

formal plant A plant that is dense, rigid, or compact or one that can be pruned to shape. See **topiary**.

formaldehyde This toxic gas is sometimes used as a soil **fumigant**. It is colorless, suffocating, tear provoking, and deadly to plants.

form nail A double-headed nail that can be pounded into a **form**, etc. to its first flange or head and then later be pulled out easily with a **claw hammer**.

form release agent A substance sprayed in **forms** to facilitate easy removal with less sticking or chance of damage to the concrete when removed.

form stripping agent See **form release agent**.

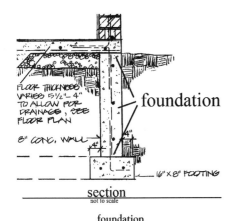

foundation

foundation **1.** The masonry or concrete portion of a structure usually below surface grade that transmits weight (load) from the structure above. **2.** The earthen material or rock upon which a structure transmits its load and depends upon for stability.

foundation bolt A usually L-shaped bolt set in concrete or masonry on a foundation tip with its threaded end exposed pointing upward for fastening materials, structures, or equipment.

foundation planting Individual shrubs or massing of shrubs or other plants at the base (foundation, where they meet the ground) of buildings, or structures.

fountain **1.** An artificially manufactured place where water comes forth for aesthetics (see also **decorative fountain**) or for drinking (see **drinking fountain**). **2.** The source or point from which something is supplied. **3.** The device or structure from which an artificial source of water arises. **4.** A natural spring of water coming from the earth.

foxfire A greenish, phosphorescent glow produced by a fungus that infects the roots of oak trees or rotting wood.

foxy timber Structural-sized wood members having portions with a reddish color indicating the beginning of possible wood decay.

fpm Abbreviation for feet per minute.

fps Abbreviation for **feet per second**.

fpt Abbreviation for **female** pipe thread.

fragipan A hard, dense soil layer that has been compacted to a point that roots cannot penetrate it and water cannot penetrate it easily.

fragmentation The process by which the **landscape** with its various spatially identifiable habitats is divided into smaller and smaller areas, **patch**es, or **corridor**s as a result of land use development, or natural processes.

frame

frame An assemblage of wood and/or steel supports as structural members.

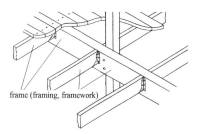

frame (framing, framework)

frame construction Structures made of wood or steel members providing form and support for all sheathing of the structure.

framework *See* **frame**.

framing **1.** *See* **frame**. **2.** The actions of constructing the framework of a structure.

framing anchor A thin steel device with holes for bolts, nails, or screws, shaped to hold or attach to wood members at their joints as a way of joining them together.

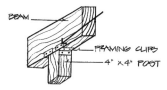

framing anchor

framing clip *See* **framing anchor**.

frass Excrement from insects.

freeboard **1.** The distance between the expected maximum water level and the top of a tank. **2.** In water features, the vertical distance between an expected high water level of a water body and the elevation at which it will overflow.

freeze damage **1.** In irrigation work, damage to pipes, valves, heads, etc. due to water being left in them and freezing. The expansion of the water when it freezes will even break metal pipes and valves if they are full of water. An insignificant amount of water in pipes can freeze without damage to them. In the temperate zones piped irrigation systems should be drained before freezing temperatures arrive. **2.** With regard to plants, any damage to them caused by temperatures below 32**F** (degrees **C**, the point at which water freezes). Plants can endure various amounts of cold temperatures. As the temperature drops, so does the number of plant species able to withstand the colder temperature. One should always check historic temperatures of a site and plant hardiness before specifying or planting plants.

freezeless faucet A valve at the end of a long pipe with a handle and spigot (faucet) at its top that allows one to pull the handle up to release water from the valve. After water is turned off, the pipe and faucet drain to prevent the water from freezing and breaking the pipe or faucet.

freezeless faucet

French drain *or* **boulder ditch** A trench filled with loose rock, rubble, or gravel for carrying away excess runoff or any excess water.

Fresno scraper An earth scraping machine that fills with earth as it is moved, and then as it is raised on each side (on runners) releases the load.

friable A condition of **soil** when its **aggregates** are easily hand-crumbled to their smallest size when dry. It is normally moist but not wet, and when it is wet, it is not sticky and does not flow. It is not hard when dry.

friction factor (Christiansen Procedure) The coefficient used in the Christiansen Procedure to determine pressure loss in a multiple outlet system.

friction loss **1.** In general terms, the loss of pressure (reduction of **gpm** or **cfm**) or loss of water velocity due to resistance to flow from friction with the walls of the surfaces surrounding the flowing water. **2.** In irrigation systems, the total amount of pressure (usually expressed in gpm) lost as water flows through the water meter, pipes, fittings, valves, and other equipment of an irrigation system. As the velocity of water flowing through the irrigation system increases, friction loss will also increase. These losses can be used to calculate the approximate dynamic (working) pressure at any given point of the irrigation system.

frieze In Classical architecture, the portion of the **entablature** between the **architrave** and the **cornice**. *See* illustration under **entablature**.

frits Small glass beads bound to a metal micronutrient of questionable value in most landscapes, but thought to be effective in growing citrus.

fritted trace elements Soft glass infused with **micronutrients** that slowly dissolve in soil or plant growth medium, thus releasing the nutrients slowly.

frog A hollow portion in a brick or block mortar face allowing for more mortar, forming a better bond and a more stable structure.

frond **1.** The leaf-like portion of a fern. **2.** Any relatively large leaf.

frontage The length of a parcel of land adjacent to another element such as a street, boardwalk, water body, pipe, or another parcel of land.

front-end loader A tractor with a bucket at its front capable of holding, lifting, and moving heavy objects or materials.

front-end loader

front lot line A line separating the lot from a street. For corner lots, a line separating the narrowest frontage of the lot from the street is usually considered the front.

frost Minute crystals of water formed or deposited on surfaces when water vapor **freezes**.

frost action The influence upon materials, pipes, and irrigation devices, plants, etc. by the forces of water (or water-based fluids) being frozen and thawing. In temperate climates, this action may occur on a daily basis in spring, winter, or fall depending on the weather. It is often the cause of breaking pipes and devices in outdoor irrigation systems not properly drained.

frost-free-days   The number of days in warm months that an area historically can expect under normal conditions to have weather not producing **frost**. This is always approximate, and most areas will have **frost pocket**s freezing sooner than other adjacent areas.

frost hardy   A term describing a plant capable of enduring **frost** and associated temperatures.

frost line   The approximate lowest elevation below ground level where frost is expected or freezing actually occurs during winter.

frost pocket   **1.** A portion of soil that is frozen within a soil that is not frozen. **2.** A low-lying area where cold air sits and frost is more prevalent than the surrounding area.

frost tender   A plant that is easily damaged by frost.

fructescence   The maturing or ripening of fruit.

fructify   To bear fruit.

fruit   **1.** The ripened ovary of a seed plant and its contents. **2.** The edible reproductive portion of a seed plant. **3.** The process of a reproductive body of a plant ripening.

frutescent   In botanical terms, becoming shrubby.

fruticose   In botanical terms, shrubby.

fry   Recently hatched or young fish.

fs   Abbreviation for forged steel.

ft, (')   Abbreviation for foot or (plural) feet.

ft2   Abbreviation for **square foot** (feet).

ft3   Abbreviation for cubic foot, or cubic feet. A cubic foot is comprised of 144 sq in.

ft. lb.   Abbreviation for foot pound.

FTG, ftg   **1.** Abbreviation for **footing**. **2.** Abbreviation for **fitting**.

ftng   Abbreviation for fitting.

fugacious   A botanical term meaning fleeting or lasting only a short time.

full-circle head   A **sprinkler head** that distributes its water over an area in a full circle (360°). It may have a stationary spray that covers the circular area or it may be a rotating spray or stream. *See* **rotor head**, **spray head**, **impact head**.

full-open valve   A valve capable of shutting off a pipe, but when open having a cross section of at least 85% the size of pipe.

full sun   A term used in describing a location for a plant or the requirement of a plant to have no shade during the day; sometimes meant to describe at least 5 to 6 hours of direct sunlight.

fulvous   A term used in botanical descriptions meaning tawny, dull yellow.

fumigant   Smoke, vapor, or gas that can control insects.

fumigation   Saturation of air or soil with smoke, vapor, or gas to control insects, **pest**s, or **fungi**.

functional connectivity   In landscape ecology, the measure of the degree to which a landscape element is connected for a process such as deer movements, frogs movements, or water movement.

fundula   An old term for a dead-end street.

fungicide   Chemicals or compounds applied to plants for controlling fungal diseases.

fungus (fungi, plural)   Microscopic or small **heterotrophic**, plant-like organisms without

chlorophyll. They do not have roots, stems, or leaves and usually grow in dark or moist environments. Long filamentous hyphae compose this organism. These microorganisms may invade or penetrate organic materials, which brings about rapid decomposition. They are one of the few organisms that are able to decompose lignin, which is highly resistant to decomposition.

fungus gnats Small flies (*Sciaridae* family) whose maggots feed on **fungi**, plant **roots**, plant **stems**, and decaying **organic matter**.

funiculus A botanical term referring to the stalk of an **ovule**.

funnelform A botanical term meaning shaped like a funnel.

funny fittings *or* **funny coupler** *or* **funny tee** *or* **funny elbow** Those fittings with barbs on at least one end used to connect **funny pipe** to a **sprinkler head**, or a **pipe fitting** in a **lateral line**, or two funny pipes together, or three funny pipes together, etc.

funny pipe with tee and coupler

funny pipe Polyethylene pipe, usually ½ in, connected with barbed fittings. This pipe was originally and currently used to connect sprinkler heads to a sprinkler system's lateral lines.

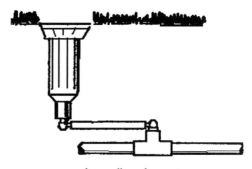

funny elbow, funny pipe

furcate A botanical term meaning forked.

furring Small wood spacers used in leveling a vertical or horizontal floor, ceiling, wall, etc.

furrow A narrow, long depression in soil made by a single ripping device (i.e., plow), or many depressions made by an attached series of ripping devices (i.e., harrow or discs) pulled or pushed through the soil. Usually they are made in parallel rows throughout a field or across a site to be planted, or to prevent erosion (perpendicular to the slope).

furrow dike A small earth dike formed in a furrow to prevent water translocation.

furrow irrigation A method of watering plants by running water into a narrow, shallow trench next to a row of plant material and allowing it to soak the soil containing the roots.

fusarium wilt A **fungus** that kills seedlings.

fuscous A term used in botanical identifications and descriptions referring to a gray-brown color.

fuse A device in an electrical system protecting against an overload of current that cuts off electrical flow by melting a gap (blowing) when it receives excess current. Fuses cannot be reused when blown.

fusiform In botanical terms, spindle-shaped (both ends taper from a wide middle).

fxm Abbreviation describing the ends of attachment of a pipe system component (esp. **fittings**); female by male.

G

g   Abbreviation for **gram**(s).

ga.   Abbreviation for gauge.

gabion walls   A retaining wall made of rectangular containers (baskets) fabricated of heavily galvanized wire, which are filled with stone and stacked on one another, usually in tiers that step back with the slope rather than vertically.

gable   The end of a pointed roof with two sloping sides of equal length meeting at a ridge point.

gable roof   A roof having two sides of continuous slope meeting at a ridge point.

gain   A groove or notch cut into one wood member to receive another wood member shaped to fit.

gal   Abbreviation for **gallon**(s).

galeate   Helmet shape.

gall   Abnormal growths on leaves, stems, trunks, or branches usually caused by an infestation of insects, fungi, bacteria, or viruses.

gallery   **1.** A long, covered area used as a corridor. **2.** An underground passageway usually for servicing. **3.** The highest, usually enclosed, seats in a stadium.

gallon   English or U.S. capacity measurement comprised of 4 **quart**s, 231 cubic inches, or 3.785 **liter**s.

gallon can *or* **gallon container**   A loose term describing the size of a plant container (usually plastic or metal) that varies in volume from ½ to 1 gal.

gallons per minute   The number of **gallon**s per minute passing by a point of reference. This is the usual U.S. (English) volume flow measurement for sprinkler irrigation calculations in pumping, pipe sizing, and irrigation regulation and distribution devices (sprinkler heads, emitters, meters, valves, etc.).

gal./min.   Abbreviation for gallon per minute. *See* **gpm**.

GALV, galv   Abbreviation for **galvanized**.

galvanic corrosion   The decomposition of metals through electromechanical action (**electrolysis**) in the presence of two dissimilar metals (galvanized steel and copper or brass, etc.) in contact and a compound capable of carrying electrical current such as water. This action causes decomposition and corrosion in metals.

galvanized   A metal object covered with zinc to protect it from rusting.

galvanized iron   Zinc-coated iron for use where there is exposure to water.

galvanized pipe   Steel or iron pipe that has a zinc coating to resist corrosion. This is especially helpful in preventing corrosion when the exterior of a steel pipe is to be exposed to water, soil, or weather. The fittings for this type of pipe are normally threaded, but may also be compression fittings.

game   In the ecosystem, animals harvested from the wild by hunters.

gamopetalous   A description of a flower with united petals.

gamophyllous A botanical term identifying a plant with **connate** leaves, petals, etc.

gamosepalous With the **sepal**s **connate**, at least toward the base.

gap grading A measurement of particle sizes in earthen material where intermediate-size particles are completely lacking. *See also* **continuous grading**.

garage A building, or a portion thereof, used or designed to be used for the parking and storage of vehicles.

garden **1.** An ornamental outdoor landscape. This type of garden is almost always near a building or in a city and is highly maintained. It may be a **formal garden** or **informal**. **2.** A landscape near a building or, indeed, any land space that is enjoyed. It is a place used in leisure enjoyment and/or to enjoy viewing. It is pleasant to the eyes and gladdens the heart. "God Almighty first planted a garden; and indeed it is the purest of human pleasures; it is the greatest refreshment to the spirits of man; without which buildings and palaces are but gross hand-works . . ." (Francis Bacon, *Of Gardens*, 1625 A.D.) **3.** A piece of ground for growing edible plants, especially vegetables, but also fruits, or any plant with edible parts. It is usually of a small size and capable of supplying some food for a single family or a neighborhood.

garden apartment An apartment building located on a lot, either singly or together with other similar apartment buildings, generally having a lower density of population than other apartment complexes and having substantial landscaped or natural open space adjacent to the dwelling units.

garden hoe A tool with a long handle and a small metal plate at its end at nearly a right angle to it that is useful in weeding, making furrows, etc.

garden hose The common hose used for attachment to a hose bib, or water spigot, for distribution of water, usually in ⅝ or ¼ in.

garden hose

gardening trowel A small, short shovel, usually less than 14 in long with handle included, for small plant placement, digging in seeds, etc.

garden rake A long-handled tool with a 12 to 18 in head of tines useful in raking up rocks, clods, debris, etc.

gargoyle A water spout or drainage opening projecting from a roof, or the **parapet** of a wall or tower, or a fountain opening on a wall, with the essential element being a human, an animal, etc. carved into a rather odd figure.

garden rake or steel rake

garland A structural ornamentation in the form of a border, wreath, or a **festoon** of leaves, fruits, vines, or flowers.

garland drain A ditch or trench of small proportions used to prevent runoff or other surface waters from reaching an excavation.

garth An open courtyard area surrounded by a covered walkway or building. These spaces historically were often grassed areas.

gas concrete Concrete made lightweight by generating gas in its mix before hardening.

gasket In piping (cast-iron, steel, some PVC, etc.), a rubber ring or other resilient material used in coupling together some types of pipes to prevent leakage.

gasketed pipe *See* **gasket**.

gas main A pipe from a gas utility company that supplies gas to the consumer's pipes.

gate A portion of a fence, wall, or other barrier that may be opened to allow passage.

gate valve A valve that has a wheel-type handle for turning off or on by raising or lowering a gate in the path of fluid flow. Gate valves have a brass to brass seat and are not recommended for frequent use.

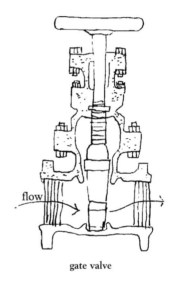

gate valve

gateway 1. A narrow opening for passage. 2. An entrance to a city, community, valley, or other large-scale space or an area of ecologically changed **landscape**. 3. An opening in a wall, fence, or other vertical man-made barrier. 4. An entrance **gate** that, along with the barrier of which it is a part, offers privacy, protection, ornament, or seclusion.

gauge, gage 1. A number designating the thickness or size of wire, metal, screws, etc. 2. A template showing a thickness (or depth) for a material layer or depth (sand, trench, asphalt,

gauge pressure

etc.) used to keep its thickness or depth constant. **3.** The portion of a slate, shingle, etc. that is exposed after placement in roofing.

gauge pressure   Water pressure minus the value of atmospheric pressure at a particular elevation above sea level.

gazebo   A small, free-standing, roofed structure open on all or some sides, usually placed in a landscape or garden for seating or standing out of sun or rain, for observing appealing views, or for its aesthetic value.

gear-driven head   In **irrigation**, a rotating spray or stream **sprinkler head** operating via a set of gears in the head. Their operation is usually smooth and quiet as opposed to the noise created by an **impact head**. See also **rotor head**.

geminate   A botanical term referring to plant parts in pairs.

genera   Another term for **genus** or the plural of genus.

general contractor   The contractor directing and responsible for a construction project. They often employ subcontractors.

general plan   See **comprehensive plan**.

generator   A machine used for converting mechanical power into electrical power.

geniculate   A botanical term meaning abruptly bent or twisted.

geniculum   In botanical terms, having a thickened joint or **node** of a **stem**.

genus   In botanical terms, a group of plants that closely resemble each other and are distinctly different from other genera. In classification it is the rank between a **family** and a **species**. A genus may have one or more species. Botanical names first give the genus then the species. For the **botanical name** *ginkgo biloba* the genus is ginkgo and the species is biloba. The gingko genus only

has one species. Other genera have many species such as with *prunus*. Genera are established for plant material based on botanical publication in accordance with the internationally established procedures. See also **taxon**.

geodetic survey   A survey of land where the curvature of the earth is considered in calculations. This type of survey is only necessary on very large land parcels needing precise points of controlling other surveys.

geographic information system (GIS)   A program of computerized, spatially explicit, land-related information digitally stored and capable of efficient analysis, comparisons, and correlation in a computer system. The geographic data is useful in spatial analysis, and because it is rectified with specific points on the earth its interpretations can be useful in analysis. Geographic maps and special information can be acquired from a variety of sources for computer analysis. It may use topographical maps, soil maps, aerial photographs, vegetation distribution maps, etc. This information can then be used to create spacial maps for record-keeping and decision-making. GIS systems may be used to maintain maps of protected land, regulation distribution, suburban sprawl, etc.

geomorphic system   A natural system comprised of an association of landforms linked together by the flow of water, air, or ice.

geomorphology   The relief features of the earth.

geotropism   The response of a plant to gravity. Roots tend to grow toward the center of the earth's gravity while stems grow away from it. Root growth directions are also extremely influenced by aeration, compaction, nutrient presence, etc., while stems are influenced by light. See also **phototropism** and **tropism**.

germinate   To sprout or begin to grow.

germination   *See* **germinate**.

germination rate   The percentage of seeds that can be expected to grow when properly planted and receiving adequate nutrients, light, water, etc.

GFCI   Abbreviation for **ground fault circuit interrupter**.

GFI   Abbreviation for **ground fault interrupter**.

GFRC   Abbreviation for **glass fiber reinforced concrete**.

GI   Abbreviation for **galvanized iron**.

gibberellic acid   A plant **hormone** used to encourage larger plants or fruits or to promote grapes without seeds.

gibbous   In botanical terms, more swollen at one place than another.

gimlet   A small tool having a sharp, threaded point used to bore holes into wood by hand.

girder   **1.** A large steel, wood, or reinforced concrete member supporting other structural members with concentrated loads (from **beam**s, joists, etc.) at various points along its length. **2.** A large **beam**, especially one that is built of several elements.

girdle   *See* **girdling**.

girdling   **1.** Removal of bark completely around a branch, trunk, or stem. **2.** Something tied (staking attachment, etc.) around a woody portion of a plant that has been left long enough to become embedded into the plant. **3.** A condition when roots cross and grow upon one another. As they increase in size they cut off circulation and become a weak point in root structure.

GIS   Abbreviation for **geographic information system**.

glabrate   In botanical terms, becoming **glabrous** with age, or almost glabrous.

glabrous   In botanical terms, smooth; having no hairs, bristles, or other **pubescence**.

glacial till *or* **boulder clay**   Unstratified deposits of glaciers that usually contain mixes of clay, sand, silt, cobble, boulders, etc.; often useful in sustaining loads from structures.

gladiate   A botanical term meaning sword-shaped with a straight or somewhat curved shape.

gland   In botanical terms, a secreting surface or structure; any protuberance or appendage having the appearance of such an organ.

glandular   A descriptive botanical term referring to a plant part having secreting organs.

glass-fiber–reinforced concrete   A concrete mix with an **admixture** of short alkali-resistant glass fibers to give it strength.

glasshouse   *See* **greenhouse**.

glaucescent   A botanical term referring to a plant part that becomes **glaucous**.

glaucous   A fine, whitish, grayish, or bluish, powder-like covering or thin waxy substance on plant parts that usually rubs off easily, like that on a fresh plum or grape. It is sometimes found on leaves or other parts of plants other than just fruits, and may be more or less waxy or powdery in appearance.

glaze   **1.** Installing glass in windows, doors, etc. **2.** To make a hard surface on a brick, tile, pottery item, etc. by adding a ceramic coating or extra firing in a kiln.

glazed   A description of a material with a very hard surface, a glossy finish, or a surface covered with a glossy or glassy film.

glazing   **1.** The act of placing glass in an opening. **2.** A glass surface for seeing through.

gliding The application of a precious metal such as gold in flakes or leaf to a surface as a finish, or the finish itself.

global coordinate system The network of east–west and north–south lines measured as degrees, minutes, and seconds to locate points on the earth's surface.

globe valve **1.** A valve configured with its water outlet oriented 180 degrees from its water inlet. This valve allows a pipe to continue in a straight line. **2.** A valve with a somewhat round shape and a wheel-like handle capable of moving a shaft with a washer type seat to regulate the amount of flow or completely stop the flow of water, or other liquid.

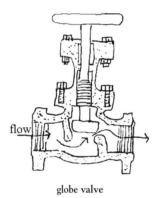

flow

globe valve

globose In botanical terms, a spherical shape or nearly so.

glochid In botanical terms, having barbed hair, or bristles, as is common in cacti.

glochidia A botanical term meaning hair-like outgrowths with barbs at the tip.

glochidiate A Latin word used in botanical descriptions meaning barbed at the tip.

glomerate A botanical term meaning densely compacted in clusters or heads.

glomerule A botanical term meaning a small, compact, dense cluster.

glued-laminated *or* **glue-laminated timber** A beam, girder, joist, or other wood timber comprised of several boards (four or more) bound together by an adhesive. Each board is usually less than 2 in wide.

glue-lam Abbreviation for **glued-laminated**, a type of lumber formed by glueing smaller boards together.

glume In botanical terms, either of two empty bracts at the base of the **spikelet** of grass seed heads.

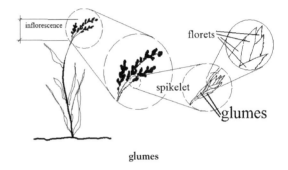

inflorescence

florets

spikelet

glumes

glumes

glutinous In botanical terms, sticky.

go-devil An item used to clean out pipes by placing it in a pipe near the source and forcing it through the pipe with water pressure.

golden ide *See* **golden orfe**.

golden orfe A fish (*Leuciscus idus*) native to Europe that may grow 1.5 to 2.5 ft long, gold, silver, orange, or blue, and sometimes used in **water feature**s. It is a slender, bullet-shaped schooling fish that sometimes has black dots on its head and back. It survives winters in the temperate climate, helps control mosquito larvae and snails, and can survive somewhat **brackish** waters.

goldfish A small fish usually 2 to 8 in long of a brown, black, orange, gold, or white color(s), useful in water features for interest and for assisting in keeping water clean.

golf course A tract of land laid out with at least nine holes for playing a game of golf; consists of greens, fairways, and hazards.

gooseneck In pipe work, any section with a U shape.

gopher *See* **pocket gophers** or **ground squirrels**.

gouge A chisel with a curved blade.

GOVT Abbreviation for government.

gpd Abbreviation for **gallon**s per day.

gph Abbreviation for **gallon**s per hour.

gpm Abbreviation for **gallons per minute**.

gps Abbreviation for gallons per second.

GR Abbreviation for grade.

grade **1.** The amount of **slope** of an area of ground surface. It is usually expressed in a percentage derived by the rise in elevation being divided by the length. **2.** The action of smoothing, raking, or shaping the surface of the ground. **3. Grading 4.** The **elevation** of a point on the ground. **5.** The lay of the land, its form and shape.

grade beam A foundation that carries the weight of the outside wall and extends a short distance beneath the soil to distribute the load.

graded aggregate Aggregate sorted for size.

grade line A staked line with indications marked for elevations referring to common datum.

grade ring A concrete ring made to various thicknesses for use under a manhole and placed by itself or with others to achieve the needed elevation for the manhole cover.

grader *or* **towed grader** A large, usually six-wheeled, machine (unless towed) used in earthwork for leveling, spreading, side casting, or for light stripping operations.

grades In connection with drainage or the shaping of earth, an amount of **slope**.

grade stake A stake marking a specified elevation for earthwork operations.

gradient The amount of inclination or rate of slope of land surface, paved surface, pipe, etc. between two points, expressed as a constant percentage of grade. It is arrived at by dividing the vertical distance between elevations by the horizontal distance between them.

grading **1.** In land work (**excavation**), removing (**cut**ting) earth, **fill**ing, or usually a combination of both on a site. **2.** Moving soil to form a shape or obtain a smoothness. **3.** The classification of **plant material** according to quality or size.

graffiti An inscription, word, figure, marking, or design that is marked, etched, scratched, drawn, or painted on any building, structure, fixture, vehicle, trailer, or other property, whether permanent or temporary, which has the affect of defacing the property.

grafting In gardening, a method of propagating certain varieties of plants by removing twigs from one plant and cutting them into branches or onto root stock of another plant.

grafting wax A substance used for placement on fitted parts of a new graft.

grain **1.** A grass-like plant with a hard seed. **2.** In landscape ecology, the texture of land when viewed from the air. Land with small patches makes a fine-textured landscape, and land with large patches makes a coarse-textured landscape.

gram (g) The metric weight measurement of 1 or 0.035 oz.

grandstand A raised area or structure allowing spectators to observe activities at ball fields, race courses, stadiums, gatherings in parks, etc.

granolithic concrete A hard surface concrete usually with granite aggregate suitable for finished floor surfaces.

granular fertilizer *or* **granular herbicide** A fertilizer or herbicide incorporated with particles usually about ¹/₁₀ inch diameter, or with any material that has a coarsely ground carrier suchlodicule as coal, corn cobs, or **calcined clay**, that is applied dry and incorporated into the soil by watering it in.

granular material Gravels, sands, or silts.

granular structure In soil science, one of the six types of soil structures. Characterized by rounded, porous heads with large macropores. This soil's structure forms under conditions of frequent wetting and drying with high organic matter and organism activity. This type of soil structure has a great deal of pore space with many macropores, which affords a high infiltration rate and ease in root penetration, with favorable gaseous diffusion. These soils are usually found in the A horizon.

graphic In **landscape architectural** work, any drawing or drafting work.

grapple A hydraulically operated steel jaw on a tractor bucket that clamps down on the bucket assisting in picking up demolished materials, large branches, boulders, etc.

grass Mostly herbaceous plants with slender leaves, jointed stems, and flowers in **spikelet**s of **bract**s (the **palea** and the lemma bracts).

grasshopper A plant-eating insect (*Orthoptera* order) with large hind legs for leaping, sometimes with wings. They can be highly destructive to plants as they are ravenous eaters. They sometimes gather for migratory movement, which may completely denude vegetation in their path.

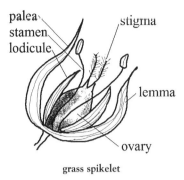

grass spikelet

grassland Land that has grasses as its predominant vegetation type (e.g., prairies or meadows).

gravel An accumulation of small stones or crushed stones close to the same size without much fine material or larger stones. It is larger than **sand** and smaller than **cobble**. This term is usually applied to aggregate passing a 76.1 mm (3 in) sieve, but being retained by a 4.76 mm (No. 4) sieve. It is useful in mass, usually facilitating **drainage** or providing stability, leveling, etc. under **structure**s or paving.

gravel

gravel board *or* **gravel plank** A board (usually treated for resistance to decay or a decay-resistant board) attached at the bottom of a wood fence to prevent the rest of the fence planking from contacting the ground where the planks would decay faster.

graveling-in The process or action of spreading gravel on **built-up roofing**.

gravel stop A raised edge on a gravel roof to prevent gravel from falling from the roof.

gravity wall A heavy concrete wall prevented from overturning mainly by its own weight.

gray water Water having been used for other purposes than those associated with human waste, and not being highly contaminated. This water is more easily treated and reused. Water wasted from home use is often termed gray water (except for sanitary sewer water), but one should test it before using directly on plants as it is often high in salt from the soaps included.

grease cap A plastic cap for waterproofing the joint of two or more **conductors** (wires). They usually enclose or cover **wire nut** connectors and contain grease or a grease-like substance. They usually accept a wire nut when it is pressed into the cap through its base. The wires extend out of

grease caps

the cap and the grease-like substance prevents water from accessing the wire nut. This prevents shorting out the wires.

grease trap *or* **grease interceptor** An underground enclosure for removing and retaining (trapping) grease from waste water, sewage, or runoff of pavements, etc. The grease is usually allowed to float to the top of the trap, where it is held or soaked up by material, and later removed.

great house The main residence or largest building of a large estate or plantation.

green **1.** An open lawn area. **2.** An open space available for unstructured recreation, its landscaping consisting of grassy areas and trees. **3.** In golf, the area of manicured very short grass (usually bent grass) around a golf hole where one uses a putter to move the golf ball toward the hole.

green area Land not covered with buildings or paving, and devoted to plant material.

greenbelt A series of connected **open spaces**, or any tract of vegetation in urban or rural areas that is somewhat linear. It may be an area of open space such as agriculture parks, undeveloped land, etc. usually surrounding or cutting through a city, neighborhood, or community. They often follow natural features such as ravines, creeks, or streams.

greenfield **1.** This term in land planning and landscape architecture is used in reference to land planned for a use that is in a natural, agricultural, or pristine state, not having prior land development. *See also* **brownfield**. **2.** Farmland and open areas where there has been no prior industrial, commercial, or intense residential activity, and where the threat of contamination is much lower than in urbanized areas.

greenhouse

greenhouse *or* **conservatory**   A building or structure constructed chiefly of plastic, glass, glass-like or translucent material, cloth, or lath, which is devoted to the protection or cultivation of flowers, vegetables, ground covers, or other tender plants. In these structures where the climate is modified or completely controlled, the climate is improved for the growing of plants. They may have artificial means (natural gas heater or electrically powered humidifier, etc.) of controlling temperature, light, or humidity. They can also extend the growing season, winter over tender plants, start annuals early, raise vegetables and flowers out of season, or grow plants that could otherwise not be grown in the hardiness zone where the greenhouse is located.

green lumber   Lumber with 20% or higher moisture content that should be dried (seasoned) on-site before use.

green manure   Legumes (alfalfa, clover, cow peas, etc.) sown in fall and turned over in early spring to return humus and nitrogen to soil. It is referred to as green manure because the crop is turned under while still green.

green thumb   Someone good with growing and caring for plants.

greenway   A linear park, strip, or belt of vegetated open space land, or open space conservation area that provides passive recreational opportunities, pedestrian or bicycle paths, or the conservation of open spaces or natural areas. They are also often valued for aesthetic relief, buffering between land uses, or to provide a corridor for wildlife or people.

grinder pump   A pump that is capable of solids-handling; designed for grinding sewage solids or such to produce slurry capable of pumping.

grip   **1.** A temporary ditch removing rainwater from a foundation while a structure is being constructed. **2.** The length of a fastener or rivet measured within the materials it binds or fastens together.

groin   **1.** A wall or barrier built from the beach into the surf zone to slow or stop movement of sand. **2.** The intersection and formation between two **vaults**.

groove   A cut or indentation as a line across wood grain. When a similar cut is made parallel with the grain, it is a **plow**.

grooved joint   A coupling device sometimes used to connect steel or iron pipes. It is comprised of a split, circular clamp with an elastomeric gasket that fits around the joint and can be bolted tightly in place to prevent leakage.

gross acreage   The total acres encompassed within a parcel of land. (Compare with **net acreage**.)

gross area *or* **gross volume**   The area or volume in its entirety, without omitting any portions.

gross precipitation rate   The total flow of water through a sprinkler station that does not account for the losses of water between the sprinkler nozzle and landscape. Or, the rate at which water is applied over an area of irrigation without considering losses that occur between the point of discharge and the ground (wind, fogging, blockage, evaporation, etc). It is expressed in an amount of depth per hour or minute. The most common use is gpm, and the factor for converting **gpm** per area to inches per hour is 96.3. The formula then for gross precipitation rate is the quantity flow in gpm multiplied by 96.3 and divided by the area.

gross section   A term used for the area of a cross section through a structural member without deducting any holes in the area of the section. (Compare with **net section**).

grotto A cave or a recessed area made to resemble a cave. When artificially created, they often include waterfalls or fountains with decorations or representations of sea shells or sea creatures, etc.

ground **1.** Any solid portion of the earth including soil, rock, or minerals. **2.** A reference to the surface of the earth as in "placed on the ground." **3.** A **conductor** that facilitates electric current being connected to the earth (ground) through the conductor(s) and used as a common return for an electrical circuit.

ground bark The bark of trees ground into pieces for use as **mulch** in landscaping. It can be ground coarsely to be used as top dressing or to a fine texture more suitable for mixing with other components to create a growing medium for plants.

ground cover **1.** Any mulch or plant covering the ground. Landscape uses may include decoration, erosion prevention, weed control, etc. **2.** Plant material used to cover the ground and usually in reference to plants not seen as individual shrubs when mature, but as a mass to cover the ground.

ground fault circuit interrupter *or* **ground fault interrupter (gfi)** A device that turns off electrical power when it detects a short or contact with water. It is a fast-acting circuit breaker that senses slight imbalances in a circuit caused by current leakage to a ground and, in as little as $\frac{1}{40}$ of a second, it shuts off the flow of electricity.

ground floor The first floor of a building, not including a cellar or basement.

grounding conductor A **conductor** that **ground**s electrical equipment or an electrical circuit, but does not carry current during normal operation. It returns current to the source to open a **circuit breaker** or **fuse** if a metal component accidentally becomes electrically charged.

grounding rod A metal rod in contact with the ground, acting as a **grounding conductor**.

ground layering In gardening, a method of **propagation** by forcing a branch to the ground, cutting halfway through the lower portion of the branch and covering it with soil until it grows roots when it is cut off and transplanted.

ground squirrels A squirrel that lives in burrows 2 to 4 ft underground. It is a landscape nuisance when it eats bulbs, nuts, roots, flowers, bark, fruit, vegetables, etc.

ground sun angle The angle between a beam of solar light and the slope of the surface that it encounters in the landscape.

groundwater Water beneath the earth's surface; usually refers to water concentrated to an **anaerobic** state in the soil. However, the water may be fresh with a groundwater flow. This may also refer to water in the ground occupying micropore or macropore space. Its level in the ground varies with wet weather, irrigation, and mechanical extraction.

groundwater divide A vertical, imaginary, impermeable boundary that, in an ideal groundwater system, coincides with the ground surface ridges or high points from which water flows in opposite directions.

groundwater recharge The process of infiltration and percolation of rainwater or snow melt from land areas or water bodies through permeable soils or rock into water-holding rocks, soils, or cavities that provide underground water storage serving as a replenishment or recharge for **aquifer**s.

ground wire *See* **grounding conductor**.

grout A rich, strong **mortar** containing more water than normal, allowing it to be more liquid and useful in filling cracks, spaces, and joints of **masonry**, **paver**s, **tile**, etc.

grower   A plant farmer who grows and sells **plant material** mostly to wholesale nurseries, but also to retail outlets or even the general public.

growing medium   *See* **growth medium**.

growing-on   Plants in a nursery that are kept in order to be grown to a larger size or specific shape before selling.

growing season   The season or portion of year when a plant is not dormant, and has its active growth period. Different areas on the earth and differing climates affect this period with seasonal changes in temperature, moisture, or available daylight. Commonly this term is used in reference to the period of growing from spring to fall, especially in the **temperate** climate regions. There it is the period of time between the last frost of spring or winter and the first frost of fall or winter.

growth habit   With regard to plants, the expected natural form an entire plant displays in three dimension. It usually refers to a mature plant.

growth media   The plural of **growth medium**.

growth medium *or* **growing medium**   **1.** The natural or artificially made rooting material sustaining a plant's growth and usually the base of its support. **2.** The **soilless** artificial mix or pure material such as ground pine bark or peat used by nurserymen in **propagating** plants in containers.

growth regulators   Synthetic or natural organic compounds affecting plant growth. Some examples of these are indoleacetic acid, **gibberellic acid**, abscisic acid, 2.4-D, naphthalene acetic acid. In dilute amounts they will promote, inhibit or change plant growth. Other names they are known by are **auxin**s, plant **hormone**s,

and phytohormones. These hormones affect such growth phenomenon as regulation of leaf drop, root initiation, bud dormancy, bending of plants in response to light, as well as other growth characteristics.

growth retardants   Chemicals that produce compact, stunted, or greener growth on some plants.

growth rings   The annual growth colorations visible as circular rings when branches or trunks of **dicotyledenous** plants are cut perpendicular to their longitudinal direction. They are concentric rings wider and lighter colored with good moisture and sun, and darker and thinner otherwise. Darker rings are usually winter with slower growth, and lighter rings are usually summer with faster growth.

grozing iron   A tool with a hot tip used by plumbers to finish soldered joints.

grub   **1.** To dig in the ground, especially for looking for something. **2.** A small, soft, thick, worm-like larvae of an insect, usually found in the ground or decaying material. **3.** Clearing an area of ground by removing from the ground roots, stumps, etc. It generally does not include removal of rock materials, buildings, utilities, etc. unless specified. See also **clear**.

grub axe   A tool for digging and chopping roots of vegetation, etc.

guano   The waste product of sea birds and bats yielding 9% water soluble phosphate and 13% nitrogen. This type of phosphate is very soluble and useful to plants, but is in short supply. A fast-acting **fertilizer** with an **NPK** ratio of 13-12-2.5.

guarantee   In construction work, a legally binding commitment by a company or individual for their finished work, or installed or delivered materials, to be of good quality, and if found inferior stating that they will be replaced or reconciled with the owner at no extra cost.

guardrail A short safety fence or barrier at the edge of a vehicular passageway protecting vehicles from danger of any kind off the edge of the road.

gully **1.** A small trench formed by **erosion** that is big enough not to be removed easily by a farm tractor's implements. This is a sign of heavy erosion. **2.** A small gulch or narrow ravine on the land. In natural areas these are usually well-established, fairly stable natural water channels. They are usually several feet deep and wide, but not of great concern for erosion potential. **3.** Any linear depression of the natural ground facilitating drainage from the size of a canyon to the size of a **swale**.

gully erosion *See* **gullying**.

gullying Soil **erosion** identified by the formation of narrow, steep-sided channels fed by runoff rivulets (small streams of water). This is an indication of serious erosion.

gunite **1.** Concrete material applied by being pumped through a hose. It is useful on water features and amorphous designs. **2.** A proprietary name of **shotcrete**.

gusset plate A flat steel plate used as a connecter between structural members or as a stiffener.

gutter **1.** A lower area along a roadway that is usually paved with concrete or asphalt where water from the road is drained and carried away. **2.** A shallow channel along the edge of a roof to convey water away.

guy A stabilizing or supporting wire, rope, cable, etc. anchored on one end and attached to an object (such as a tree) on the other end to assist in giving the object stability.

guy anchor A buried object to which a **guy** is attached for stability. When planting trees, these are sometimes buried in the outer areas of the planting pit.

guying *See* **tree guying**.

gymnosperm Naked seeds. A plant in which the seeds are not enclosed in an ovary. Examples are **conifer**s and **podocarp**s. (Compare with **angiosperm**.)

gynodioecious A botanical term referring to plants that produce female flowers and perfect flowers on separate plants.

gypsum Calcium sulfate used in landscaping as an **inorganic** soil amendment to lower **pH** or to assist in the improvement of the texture of clay soils. One of its soil-enhancing qualities is that it can facilitate the leaching of salts that otherwise bind clay particles.

H

h   Abbreviation for hour.

ha   Abbreviation for **hectare**(s).

habit   With regard to plants, the natural form, growth style, or natural growth tendency of a specific plant type. Examples are **upright**, **columnar**, **prostrate**, **weeping**, **trailing**, **clinging**, **ascending**, etc.

habitat   **1.** The ecosystem surrounding and interacting with an individual, species, or a group of species. **2.** An area of land inhabited by any individuals of species or population. **3.** The local environment that an organism uses to live in or with. It is variable in size, content, and location as long as it meets with organism's needs.

hachure   One of many adjacent parallel or nearly parallel lines sometimes drawn on topographic maps in the direction of slope indicating relief or steepness of land. Steeper slopes have heavier shading with these lines by being more closely spaced.

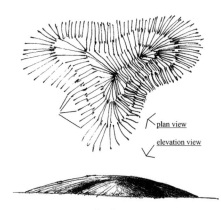

plan view
elevation view

hachures

hacking   **1.** Brick laid with their lower edge set in (indented) from the face of the wall. **2.** Stone courses in a wall changed into courses of different heights.

hacksaw   A saw with a handle at its end perpendicular to the blade (or nearly so) and an adjustable frame that holds thin blades with small teeth suitable for cutting metal.

hacksaw

ha-ha *or* **haw-haw**   A fence concealed from view below a slope or in a depressed area (ravine, trench, etc.).

half-cut notch   A way of joining timbers at a corner by cutting off the end halfway through the timber and just enough of the end length to allow it to be placed over another timber at 90° and fit snugly.

half-hardy   **1.** A condition with plants in which they may or may not survive a winter climate of an area (depending on the year and the severity of weather), but in some cases, with some winter protection they may survive. **2.** An annual plant that will withstand cold temperatures, but will not survive frost or freezing.

half header   A half piece of block or brick useful for ending a course.

half-ripe   The condition of current season shoots of trees and shrubs that are somewhat beyond the softness of actively growing young stems and fully firm wood. In this condition a plant is often preferred as a cutting in propagation efforts.

half standard   A woody plant with a tree form, having a **head** that starts its branching about 2½ to 4 in above ground. This term is often used for trees that normally **branch** to the ground, but have been **prune**d to do otherwise, or for shrubs that are **graft**ed, pruned, or trained to have a tree form with a single trunk and a head formed above the ground.

halophyte   Plants adapted to growing in salty soils.

halophytic   Plants that are accustomed to (or prefer) growing in saline soils. They are usually **xerophyte**s.

hamate   A botanical term describing a plant part that is hooked at the tip.

hammer   A hand tool with a slender handle and a metal head forming a T, and at least one side of the head has a surface for pounding. It is used to pound nails, pull nails, or for flattening and shaping materials.

hammer drill   A rotating power device that also pounds as it turns and is useful in making holes in concrete, stone, or masonry.

hammock   A place for lying down, usually outdoors, that is made of netting, canvas, etc.; long enough to lay on, tied at each end, and then tied to a support (tree, pole, sand, etc.) beyond each end. It is usually not tied to make the canvas or netting taught, but is allowed to hang slightly.

hand compactor   **1.** A heavy metal plate with a long handle attached upward from its center above the plate, allowing the plate to be lifted and dropped or thrown to the ground, causing compaction beneath the plate where it is pounded. **2.** A compaction machine that is operated by hand without riding upon it, but instead, is walked behind or pulled. *See* **compact** and **compactor**.

hand level   **1.** The act of **grading** an area with hand tools such as shovels and rakes. **2.** An instrument like a telescope with crosshairs and a bubble to indicate when it is level. This instrument is useful in **drainage** and **grading** work.

hand pump   A type of **piston pump** with a handle for accomplishing pumping by hand.

handrail   A rail provided at stairways, ramps, the edge of dangerous heights, etc. for people to grasp with their hands, assisting them with stability and protection from danger or harm, and sometimes to prevent them from damaging sensitive items outside the rail.

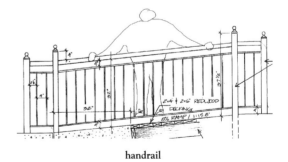

handrail

handsaw   A saw used for cutting wood that has a handle to grasp while manually pushing and pulling it to cut.

hammock

hanger **1.** A device used to suspend one item from another, such as a pipe, conduit, etc. from a structural member (joist, bridge, beam, etc.) overhead. **2.** Any device used to suspend one object from another.

hard compact soil According to OSHA, earth materials not classified as running or unstable.

hardening Slowing growth, reducing water, lowering the temperature, decreasing fertilizer, or slowly shifting the plants from a much sheltered area to a less sheltered area. This is done to increase chances for plant survival at transplantion.

harden off **1.** A process (usually a week or more) of gradually adapting a plant that has been grown in protective shelter to withstand light, temperatures, or other environmental factors of full exposure outdoors. **2.** The process of a plant becoming adapted to colder weather in the fall, and becoming able to withstand cold.

hard freeze *or* **hard frost** Generally, a description of freezing temperatures that drop below 32**F** and remain there for several hours, killing all unprotected annuals and other plants not hardy to freezing. However, some sources indicate the temperature must be below 28F, while others indicate that the temperature must be at least as low as 26F for a period of at least 4 hours.

hard hat A hat usually made of plastic with space between straps on the head and the hard

hard hat

plastic outer surface that is often worn for safety on construction projects in an effort to protect the head. It is often required on construction jobs by **OSHA**.

hardiness The capacity of **plant material** to adapt to a given climate.

hardpan A hardened soil layer preventing or greatly hindering drainage and hand excavation. It is often hidden under topsoil, and restricts or prevents water percolation. In desert soils, it is usually caused by a **caliche** (calcium carbonate) layer of weathered soil where particles have been cemented together by minerals. They may also be cemented together by iron and aluminum compounds. Plant roots in hardpan are restricted to the shallow soil layer above it. This may stunt shrubs and trees. The poor drainage may bring on disease, and trees are subject to wind throw.

hardscape The hard surface elements of a planned (designed) landscape that give it definition (sometimes called the bones of a landscape) and style, including walks, driveways, **edger**s, walls, buildings, **fence**s, and large ornamental or sculptural pieces.

hardware A general term for metal and plastic fittings, devices, tools, equipment, etc. used in construction.

hard water Water most often found in alkaline areas containing minerals, usually salts such as calcium and magnesium, carbonates, and bicarbonates, etc., that often collect inside metal pipes, causing **incrustation**, etc. This water is not good for **acid**-loving plants.

hardwood The wood of a deciduous tree. This term does not refer to the relative hardness of the wood.

hardy With regard to plant material, an indication of ability to withstand the normal temperature changes and other climatic features of an area. It does not mean that it can withstand all (i.e., soil pH, drought, etc.) conditions of the area.

hardy plant **1.** A plant that can be planted before the last killing frost in the spring. **2.** When applied to plants in the temperate zone, it means the ability to resist frost, or long freezes. **3.** To plants in general, it refers to a plant's ability to survive the climate, microclimate, soils, or other conditions of the place they are or will be planted. **4.** A reference to whether a plant is likely to survive a designated climate zone or hardiness **zone**.

harrow **1.** An attachment for a tractor (or anything that can pull it, even horses) that has many downward pointing prongs used to break up, pulverize, or smooth soil that has been plowed to prepare it for planting. **2.** To break up, pulverize, or smooth.

hasp A device for holding a door, gate, drawer, etc. closed by a metal loop on a hinge that fits over another loop at 90° and can be secured with a paddle lock.

hasp assembly A door or lid fastener with a hinged metal strap that fits over a loop and is recurred in place by a paddle lock or pin.

hastate In botanical terms, a shape like an arrowhead, but with the basil lobes pointing outward,

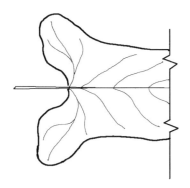

hastate leaf base

nearly at right angles. (Compare with **cuneate, obtuse, cordate, auriculate, sagitate, attenuate, truncate, oblique.**)

hatchet A tool for chopping wood and pounding that has a head with a sharp edge on one side and a flat side on the other. It is about the same size as a hammer, but is much like a short wood ax.

hatracking Pruning a tree by flat topping it, cutting its central leader, or stubbing off mature wood.

haunch **1.** The portion of an arch between its apex and a point of support. **2.** The lower-third portion of the circumference of a pipe.

haunching Placing pipe bedding material such as sand or cement around and under the lower one-third of the pipe.

hayloft An upper area of a barn where hay is stored.

hazardous waste Any refuse or discarded material in solid, semisolid, liquid, or gaseous form that cannot be handled with routine waste disposal because it presents a hazard to human health or the health of other living organisms due to its chemical, biological, or physical properties.

hazards In golf, those areas adjacent to **fairways** where if golf balls enter it is difficult to recover a ball. They include areas such as sand traps, water features, plants, or very tall grass.

Hazen-Williams Formula A formula developed for calculating the pressure loss in large pipes. The information obtained from using this formula for various pipes is usually available from the pipe manufacturer in a chart. It takes into account pipe length, pipe roughness, pipe **inside diameter**, and **velocity** of water.

H-beam A steel beam that when viewed from the end or in section is shaped like an H; commonly used in earthwork as retaining structures or as pilings.

hdr. Abbreviation for header.

head **1.** Generally the top, end, or upper portion of a structure or part. **2.** A **sprinkler head**. **3.** *See* **static head**. **4.** *See* **head pressure**. **5.** The entire leaves and branches above the ground of a woody plant. **6.** The upper horizontal piece of a door or window jamb forming the top of the frame. *See* **window head** or **door head**.

header **1.** A brick laid crosswise in a wall with its end(s) exposed. **2.** A masonry unit placed with its ends exposed and overlapping two or more adjacent withes of masonry in tying them together. **3.** A framing member that crosses and supports the ends of joists, rafters, etc., transferring weight to the parallel joists, rafters, etc.

header pool The pool that is highest in elevation in a recirculating water feature.

heading back A method of pruning in which 1-yr old shoots are cut back to buds, or an older branch or a stem is cut back to a stub. Shearing is a form of heading back. This type of pruning ruins the natural shape of plants, especially trees, and promotes weakly attached new growth. **Thinning** is a better method of pruning trees.

head pressure *or* **head feet pressure** An expression of pressure as related to the height of the surface of a column of water (or other liquid) above an elevation, indicated in feet of water. It is equivalent to 0.433 psi per foot of water. The term head is usually understood to mean **static head** and not **dynamic head**.

head-to-head coverage In sprinkler irrigation, a layout design of sprinkler heads with the radius or limit of coverage of one head reaching to the next head. As most sprinkler heads do not provide even coverage throughout their radius of reach, this allows a much more even distribu-

tion of water to the coverage area. Common methods of spacing of sprinkler heads for head-to-head coverage include **square spacing** and **triangular spacing**.

headwall A masonry or concrete retaining wall around the outlet or entrance of a drain pipe or culvert. These provide protection against erosion of the surfaces around pipe entrances or exits where water is turbulent.

heart rot A disease usually in old trees caused by fungi that normally rot dead wood. It affects ornamental trees. This disease may be evidenced by yellowish to brown mushroom-like or woody growths on the tree bark exterior. Invisible beneath them is internal decay. Hard growths are called conks.

heartwood *or* **duramen** Nonliving wood at the center of a tree that is generally darker, much more durable than sapwood, and more decay resistant than sapwood.

heat exchanger A device that transfers heat from inside to outside air, or from fluid, or from solid to solid, without allowing direct contact between the two.

heat-fusion joint A special pipe and fitting that is heated and placed together to form a bond and a leak-proof joint.

heat gain The net temperature increase in an area or material.

heath Open, level, uncultivated land with poor soils, usually acid, and usually having poor drainage.

heat island The microclimate, area, or patch of warmer air that forms in and over urbanized areas because of paved or **impervious** surfaces, reflection from upright structures, and buildings gathering heat or generating it and then releasing it.

heat loss

heat loss The net temperature decrease in an area or material.

heat transfer The flow or exchange of heat between gases, solids, or liquids, through conduction, convection, or radiation.

heave The upward lifting of soil caused by expansion due to frost, moisture absorption, etc.

heaving The lifting of plants, rocks, or structures in soils (esp. some clays) from the actions of freezing and thawing.

heavy soil Any **soil** with a significant amount of **clay**, making it more difficult to work, more sticky, and slower to warm in the spring. They are not necessarily heavier than other soils.

hectare A metric measurement of area comprised of 10,000 sq **m**s. One hectare is approximately 2½ **ac**.

hectometer (hm) A metric measurement of 100 **m**s or 328.08 ft.

hedge A row or line formed by shrubs, bushes, small trees, or any kind of plant being planted closely together, forming physically or visually a boundary, fence, decorative line, or barrier. They are often pruned to a symmetrical shape that is flat or cube shaped, etc., forming a natural-looking wall.

hedgerow A tall row of vegetation that separates lower vegetation or open lands, configured in a line and usually on a boundary (not necessarily straight) of fairly constant width such as between fields or along ditches. In landscape ecology, they include fencerows, shelterbelts, **hedge**s, **windbreak**s, and plants along many water **corridor**s. They are sometimes planted for wind and water **erosion** protection in agricultural areas, but are more often found along roads or fields seeded by wind, water, birds, etc.

-hedral A Greek suffix, often used in botanical terms to describe something relating to a surface.

heeling-in A method for storing bare root plants temporarily by burying or covering their roots with moist material such as sawdust or soil to prevent them from drying out.

heirloom garden A landscape designed and installed with plant material used in a particular area at a particular period of time in the past. These gardens have a historical style of planting design and materials.

helistop An area to be used for the landing, takeoff, or parking of a helicopter.

hemi- The Greek prefix meaning half, sometimes used in botanical descriptions.

herb **1.** An **annual**, **biennial**, or **perennial** that produces seed and does not develop woody tissue. Herbs die at least back to the ground at the end of a growing season. **2.** An **annual**, **biennial**, or **perennial** that has culinary value and is prized for use in cooking.

herbaceous **1.** Having the characteristics of an **herb** with little or no woody tissue and lacking a persistent live stem aboveground. **2.** Plants that die to the ground and grow a new stem each year.

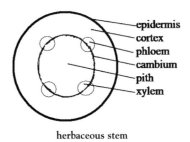

herbaceous stem

herb garden   A small plot of land usually near a residence and close to the kitchen where herbs are grown for culinary purposes.

herbicide   **1.** Certain chemicals or compounds in liquid or granular form used on ground surfaces to prevent germination of seeds. This is particularly helpful in control of weeds. **2.** An agent (usually a chemical) used to kill plants that it comes in contact with directly upon application or through translocation to roots in the soil. *See also* **selective herbicide** and **nonselective herbicide**.

herbivore   An animal that eats plants or parts of them.

hermaphrodite   In botanical terms, having both sexes present; **stamen**s (male) and **pistil**s (female) in the same flower.

heroic   A golf hole design style with two routes for approach of a hole, with the safer route taking at least an extra stroke over the risky and difficult route. The risky route is very difficult to negotiate. *See also* **strategic** and **penal**.

herringbone   A pattern sometimes used in placing brick or rectangular objects where pieces are at right angles to one another, but the end of one piece is placed adjacent to an end of a side of the other.

herringbone pattern

Hessian canvas   A British term for **burlap**.

hetero-   The Greek prefix meaning unlike, or of differing sorts, sometimes used in botanical descriptions.

heterogeneity   **1.** The state of being **heterogeneous**. **2.** In landscape ecology, having variety, being uneven, not spatially configured in any given way, yet not random.

heterogeneous   Made up of dissimilar or diverse parts.

heteromorphic   A botanical term meaning of two or more forms or types.

heterosporous   Producing two different kinds of spores, one of which produces male gametophytes, the other female. The opposite of **homosporous**.

heterotrophic   A description of organisms that live on organic carbon compounds.

hewn   Roughly shaped, usually with hand tools.

hewn stone   The American term for **ashlar**.

hexa-   The Greek prefix meaning six, sometimes used in botanical terms.

hidden nailing   Nailing that is covered when construction is finished.

high-density polyethylene   A type of polyethylene, often used to make pipe and other irrigation components.

highest and best use   A phrase generally promoted in real estate as the use of property that will bring to its owner the greatest profit if offered for sale.

high hazard   According to the National Standard Plumbing Code, a situation where backflow of water in a system is an actual or potential threat to health or the purity of the potable water supply.

high-water mark That mark on reservoirs, ponds, lakes, and streams that is the elevation of the highest normal water level. In natural systems, this normally occurs annually. Although the annual water mark varies, it can usually be found by examining the banks and ascertaining where the presence of waters is so common and so long continued in ordinary years, as to mark the soil or rock with a character distinct from that of the abutting land surface.

hilling up The practice of mounding soil up, usually several inches at the base of plants. This is beneficial to some vegetables, roses, and a few shrubs, but it is detrimental to trees.

hillside Generally, a portion of a hill between its crest and the base where it no longer slopes in the same direction.

hillslope processes The geomorphic processes that shape slopes, including soil creep, landslides, and runoff.

hilum A botanical term referring to the scar on a seed at its point of attachment.

hinge A device attached to a lid, door, cover, etc. and a frame or wall that swings or pivots, allowing opening for access. Most hinges have two plates with screw holes for mounting and cylinders on one edge that fit together allowing a pin to slide through them to hold the hinge together and allow pivoting.

hippodrome A modern sports arena.

hip roof *or* **hipped roof** A roof that slopes upward from all four sides of a building.

hirsute In botanical terms, hairy with coarse, stiff-like, or beard-like hairs, often bent or curved. It is coarser than **villous**, but less firm and sharp than **hispid**, and not pungent (penetratingly painful).

hispid In botanical terms, bristly; beset with stiff hairs.

historic district An area related by historical events or themes, by visual continuity or character, or by some other special feature that helps give it a unique historical identity. May be designated a historic district by local, state, or federal government and given official status and protection.

historic preservation Preservation of landscapes or structures because of the value of understanding the past.

hm **1.** Abbreviation for **hectometer**(s). **2.** Abbreviation for hollow metal.

hoary In botanical terms, grayish or whitish in color.

hod A container for carrying mortar or bricks.

hoe **1.** A tool with a small metal plate at the end of a long handle at nearly a right angle that is useful in weeding, making furrows, etc. *See also* **garden hoe**. **2.** A **backhoe** or **trackhoe**.

hoe

hoes   A tool with a thin blade on a long handle used to dig or cut weeds, or to **cultivate** or loosen the soil.

holding bed   A location where plants are temporarily stored until planting them permanently.

holiday   In construction, an area skipped in painting, coating, staining, or otherwise finishing a surface.

hollow masonry wall   A masonry wall of two **withe**s having a separation of air between them. The walls are usually connected by metal ties extended between the two withes.

homeowner's association   A nonprofit organization operating under agreements through which each lot or home developed or other described land area is automatically a member and each lot is automatically subject to a charge for a proportionate share of the expenses for the organization's activities such as maintaining, managing, and preserving common property and landscaped areas held in common.

homogeneity   Being homogeneous.

homogeneous   Of a similar nature or kind or of a uniform structure throughout.

homomorphic   A botanical term meaning each with the same form.

homosporous   Producing only one kind of spore, which produces both male and female.

honeydew   A sticky secretion deposited on leaves from sap-sucking insects. It often becomes a nuisance when there are masses of insects infesting trees as it drips from them.

hook bolt   A bolt with a hook on an end.

hopper   A bin with a funnel shape for holding construction materials such as sand, gravel, or green concrete.

hopscotch   A game usually played by children where players throw an object into successive spaces outlined in a figure on the ground and then hop through the continuous adjacent spaces, picking up their object on the way back. This is repeated so that players continue through each space of the figure. The figure is usually drawn on the ground with chalk in a rudimental fashion by children, but the standard figure has 10 spaces and measures 12 ft 6 in long by 5 ft wide.

horiz.   Abbreviation for horizontal.

horizon   **1.** In **soil** science, the reasonably distinct layers of soil or a land's underlying material in a profile as observed, studied, or found in a vertical section of land. Horizons are created by differentiation of particles, chemicals, organisms, or moisture movement within the soil profile. They are usually distinguishable by their change in color or texture. Each layer or horizon is determined not only by color and texture, but also by **soil structure** type, **pH**, **root**s, and **organism**s. The master soil horizons are the **A horizon**, **B horizon**, and **C horizon**. *See also* **soil horizon** and **subhorizon**. **2.** In the **landscape**, this refers to the apparent line where sky meets the earth or objects upon it.

horizontal   A term used in describing a plant form common to **ground cover** plant materials; their growth spreads laterally across the ground.

horizontal plant material

horizontal control In surveying, this is established horizontal positions that have been accurately located.

horizontal cordon A pattern in **espalier**ed plants with branching being horizontal and usually on opposite sides of the center plant stem. These horizontal branches in some plant types can run for significant distances.

horizontal cordon espalier

horizontal split case pump A **centrifugal pump** with the distinctive feature of the pump having two separate cases for the motor and the pump. It is mostly used for large water needs at 700 **gpm** or above.

hormone A growth-regulating substance much like vitamins, with effects on different portions of plants and their growth characteristics. Minute amounts usually have dramatic effects that can be favorable or unfavorable.

horn and hoof meal Ground hooves and horns of animals, usually from slaughterhouses. It is a slow-release **fertilizer** with an **NPK** ratio of about 14-1-0.

horseshoe arch or **Arabic arch** or **Moorish arch** An arch narrower at its base than at its widest point.

horseshoes A game in which horseshoe-shaped metal pieces are tossed at pegs usually mounted in sand. Points are scored after tossing by measuring if they are close enough to pegs or if they encircle (ringer) the peg. The pegs are usually set 50 ft apart for men, 40 ft apart for women, and 30 ft apart for boys and girls.

horticultural oil or **dormant oil** or **superior oil** A highly refined oil that is sprayed on plants to smother or disrupt membrane functions of insects or their eggs. The type used on plants in leaf is different from that used on deciduous plants that are dormant. The type used on dormant plants is more often called **dormant oil**. Sulfur products used on plants within a few weeks can combine with this product to make a phytotoxic substance.

horticultural species A plant species that is not indigenous to an area of concern.

horticulture The science or art of growing or cultivating ornamental plants, vegetables, flowers, and fruits.

hose bib A water outlet **valve** operated by turning a handle and having **male** threads at its point of outlet for attaching it to a garden hose.

hose thread A thread size used for a common garden hose that is 12 threads per inch in the popular ¾ in size.

host plant Any plant that furnishes sustenance for another plant or animal. Any plant that a bug or disease thrives on. Generally this term describes a plant that commonly supplies sustenance. For example, cabbage plants are host plants to the harlequin plant bug; and wheat and corn are hosts to chinch bugs in the South.

hotbed **1.** A low enclosure for protection of tender plants, growing vegetables, out of season, or **forcing** bedding plants. They are useful where temperatures drop below freezing. **2.** A planter heated from below.

hotcaps Small, tent-like devices used to shield young plants from wind or frost.

hot-dip A surface obtained on ferrous metal by dipping it in molten zinc to form a protective coating.

hothouse   A heated **greenhouse** capable of growing **tropical plant**s.

hot wire   An electrically charged wire that is ungrounded and usually identified by black or red insulation, but may be other colors.

housed joint   *See* **dado**.

house trap   A sewer pipe with a low sweep bend for keeping a collection of water and preventing the sewer gases from accessing the interior of a structure through the pipe.

hovel   An open-sided shelter for farm produce or livestock.

hp   **1.** Abbreviation for horsepower. **2.** Abbreviation for high pressure.

HPT   Abbreviation for high point.

hr.   Abbreviation for hour.

ht.   Abbreviation for height.

hub   The flared end of a pipe made large enough to accept the end of another pipe of the same size in forming a joint.

humectant   A moisturizing agent.

humid climate   A climate in which precipitation averages more than 40 in per year.

humidity   The wetness of the atmosphere or dampness of air. *See* **relative humidity**.

hummock   A clump of vegetation raised up within a wetland.

humus   A dark brown or black material derived from living things in its last stage of decomposition. This material is full of nutrients for plants. It is mostly found in the **soil's** **A horizon**.

humus layer   The humus layer of the **O horizon** made up of highly decomposed organic matter. *See* **Oa layer**. This is a residue as the decomposable components of the soil have been affected by physical and chemical processes.

hvy.   Abbreviation for heavy.

hw   Abbreviation for hot water.

HWY   Abbreviation for highway.

hyaline   In botanical terms, transparent or nearly so.

hybrid   With regard to plants, this term was historically used to describe a plant bred from two plants, each of which were of the same **genera**, but were of distinctly different **species**. Plants with parents of different genera were appropriately called **bigeneric** or **trigeneric** hybrids. Plants of the same genus, and species, but of a different variety were termed **crossbreed**s. But more recently geneticists are accepting the term hybrid for any individuals with parents that differ genetically in at least one gene. Under this definition plants that were formerly defined as crosses or as crossbreeds are now also defined as hybrids.

hybrid controller   A sprinkler controller that combines both mechanical control features, and digital control features.

hybrid solar energy system   A solar energy system that uses a combination of different types of energy collection or distribution systems such as an active solar energy system, a passive solar energy system, or a conventional energy system.

hybrid system   A term used to describe a solar heating system that combines active and passive techniques.

hydathode   An epidermal plant structure (often ending a vein) that exudes water.

hydrant   A device for directing water to flow out from a main water line through a hose, valve, nozzle, etc.

hydraulic conductivity   The ability of water to be transferred through a **soil**.

hydraulic control A reference in **phytoremediation** to control of groundwater through plant transpiration also known as **phytohydraulics**. It has the ability to contain groundwater-borne contaminants and prevent them from underground migration.

hydraulic gradient **1.** The change in elevation (slope) of a groundwater surface from one point to another horizontally. **2.** The change in water's **head** pressure per unit of distance in a given direction within geologic strata or within a flowing water system.

hydraulic hammer An attachment for a tractor with a heavy point that impacts under pressure and is used to break up rock, concrete, etc.

hydraulic hammer

hydraulic jack A jack operating by pistons with oil or another liquid.

hydraulic mortar A mortar that is capable of hardening under water.

hydraulic radius **1.** The ratio of the cross-sectional area of a stream to its perimeter in section. **2.** The ratio of the cross-sectional area of fluid flow in a pipe to the wetted perimeter of the inside of the pipe.

hydraulic radius

hydraulics The branch of science that analyzes and utilizes the effects of water and other liquids in motion.

hydraulic sprinkler system *or* **hydraulic system** In the beginning of automatically operated sprinkler valves, hydraulic tubes were used to operate valves by change in pressure instead of wires. This refers to such a sprinkler system with a hydraulic control of valves.

hydraulic test A test under pressure for any leaks in a plumbing line.

hydric Associated with, characterized by, or necessitating a considerable amount of moisture.

hydric soil A soil having experienced wet conditions much of the time and having been developed under those conditions. They have developed anaerobic conditions, and usually have organic content.

hydrograph **1.** A graph of a stream or pipe outfall or discharge rate over time. **2.** A record of the rise and fall of water levels during a given time period.

hydrograph method A way of forecasting stream flow by using a **hydrograph** to depict the changes in runoff of a drainage basin throughout a rainstorm.

hydrologic cycle The ongoing circulation of water between ocean, atmosphere, and land.

hydrologic equation The proportion of the amount of surface runoff on a piece of ground to the precipitation amount minus **evapotranspiration** loss, plus or minus changes in groundwater or soil water.

hydrologic response The properties, distribution, and circulation of water.

hydrology A science of properties, distribution, and circulation of water underground, on the surface, and in the air.

hydrometer method A method to determine clay content of a soil by dispersing the soil particles in water and drawing off samples at determined time intervals.

hydromulch A mixture of mulch with water or other ingredients in a machine that shoots the mixture through a hose, pipe, or nozzle. Other ingredients of the slurry may include **seed**, fibers, **tachifyer**, **fertilizer**, or other ingredients. Reference may be made to it in a slurry state or after dried in place.

hydromulcher This refers to a machine capable of mixing and distributing hydromulch over the ground.

hydromulching The action of applying **hydromulch**.

hydrophyte A plant adapted to water or bogs.

hydropneumatic pressure system A water supply system where the pressure in a tank or piping system is kept at a specified pressure and the pump begins operation when the pressure drops below an acceptable predetermined pressure. Pressure within the system controls the pump operation. This eliminates the need of a controller in an irrigation system to start the pump when any valve in the system is in operation.

hydroponics **1.** Growing plants in water and nutrients without soil or an inert medium for support. **2.** The growing of plants in water containing nutrients rather than soil where water is pumped through gravel, fiberglass, or other inert media that anchors the plants.

hydroseed A mixture of seed with water or other ingredients in a machine that shoots the mixture through a hose, pipe, or nozzle. Other ingredients of the slurry may include cellulose mulch, fibers, newspaper mulch, **tachifyer**, fertilizer, or other ingredients. Reference may be made to it in a slurry state or after dried in place.

hydroseeding The action of applying **hydroseed**.

hydrostatic barrier The use of plants to control movement of groundwater. In **phytoremediation** this is used to control the flow of contaminants.

hydrostatic head Pressure expressed as the number of vertical feet necessary for a column of water to exert pressure.

hydrostatic pressure The pressure exerted by water, especially standing water due to gravity.

hydrostatic test Usually refers to testing a closed pipe system under a required amount of fluid pressure while not allowing any movement of the fluid within the system. Any liquid movement or drop in pressure indicates leakage from the system. In irrigation work, if there are any leaks while performing this test one can often find the wet spots in the soil, allowing easy location of the leak for repair. (Compare with **operational test**.)

hydrozone A portion of a landscaped area having plants with similar water needs that are watered by one irrigation valve, or a set of valves with the same irrigation schedule.

hygroscopic Absorbing moisture from the air; plants taking up and holding moisture from the air. They sometimes swell, shrink, or change in position with the humidity.

hygroscopic water **1.** Water bound tightly by soil solids at potential values lower than minus 31 **bar**s. **2.** Water tightly held by soil particles. It will not move with the influence of **capillary action** or gravity, and is normally unavailable to plants.

hypertufa A **concrete** mix utilizing some organic matter to promote the growth of moss and algae on its surface for an old or antique effect. Used to make planting containers, sometimes formed to resemble stone. It is made of various materials based on the basic mixture of one part each of Portland cement, peat moss, builder's sand, and water. The materials are molded over a form and dried.

hypo- A Greek prefix often used in botanical terms meaning beneath.

hypogynous A botanical term referring to the **perianth** and **stamen**s being attached directly to the receptacle. (Compare with **epigynous**, **perigynous**.)

I

I.A.   Abbreviation for Irrigation Association.

IAA   Abbreviation for **indole-3-acetic acid**.

IAL   Abbreviation for International Association of Lighting Designers.

IB   Abbreviation for **I-beam**.

I-bar   Steel or iron bar with a cross section resembling an I.

I-beam   A metal beam with a cross section in the shape of an I.

ICBN   Abbreviation for **International Code of Botanical Nomenclature**.

ICE   Abbreviation for the Institution of Civil Engineers, London.

ice dam   Accumulation of snow and ice at the eaves of a sloping roof.

iconic   Of or relating to architecture.

ID, id   **1.** Abbreviation for inside dimension. **2.** Ab-breviation for identification. **3.** Abbreviation for **inside diameter**.

ide *or* **idus**   *See* **golden orfe**.

IEE   Abbreviation for Institution of Electrical Engineers, London.

IEEE   Abbreviation for Institute of Electrical and Electronics Engineers.

IERI   Abbreviation for Illuminating Engineering Research Institute.

IES   Abbreviation for the Illuminating Engineering Society of North America.

igneous rock   Rock formed from the cooling of molten magma (molten material from the earth), having a temperature in excess of at least 1000F, which then cools to a solid.

illuminance   The brightness of something luminous.

imbricate   In botanical terms, overlapping as with fish scales, snake skin, or roof shingles; arranged in a tight, shingled spiral.

immarginate   In botanical terms, without a leaf **margin**.

immature soil   Earthen material in a **soil profile** characterized by not having discernable horizons, much resembling the parent material.

impact   **1.** In ecology or environmental terms, to have a significant or major influence or effect for change. **2.** In construction terms, to strike forcefully.

impact fee   A payment of money imposed by a government agency on development activity as a condition of granting development approval or a building permit to assist in payment for the planned facilities needed to serve new dependent growth and development activity. Impact fees generally do not include a reasonable permit fee, application fees, administrative fees for collecting and handling impact fees, the cost of reviewing calculations, or the administrative fees required for appeal.

impact head *or* **impact sprinkler**   A **sprinkler head** that irrigates with a stream of water impacted by an arm that bounces off the stream and is returned by a spring. The impact action turns the head. Impact heads usually allow adjustment of arcs without nozzle change but require nozzle change for adjustment in water quantity output. They are noisier than a **gear-driven head**.

impact load The weight and effect of a momentary contact to a structure of another body.

impact resistance The capability of a material or product to sustain a hard, sudden blow or shock without damage or failure.

impact wrench An air-driven or electrically driven wrench delivering regular impulses of successive torques to remove or tighten items by rotation.

imparipinnate In botanical terms, pairs of **leaflet**s on opposite sides along a central stem, with a single leaflet at the end.

impeller In a **pump**, a rotating wheel receiving water from its center with vanes causing fluid to be forced outward to the housing (**valute**) in which it is encased, creating pressure and flow.

imperfect flower A flower that does not have both female (**pistil**) and male (**stamen**) parts.

impermeable A term applied to soil or pavements not allowing the easy draining of water through them.

impervious Not penetrable by water or other fluids; often used to describe pavements or surfaces that prevent most water from percolating through them or even being absorbed by them, such as asphalt, concrete, etc.

impervious surface Any surface covered or hardened so as to prevent or greatly impede the percolation of water into the underlying soil.

impervious surface ratio A ratio derived by dividing the amount of the site that is covered by any man-made material that substantially reduces or prevents the infiltration of **storm water** by the total horizontal area of the lot.

impetus The span of a roof or arch.

imposed load The load on a structure or member of a structure not including its own weight (the dead load).

impost A sometimes decorative masonry unit or course at an end of an arch.

impoundment A body of water confined by a dam, dike, pipe, floodgate, or other barrier.

impregnation In the lumber industry, wood having preservatives, fire retardants, etc. forced into them under pressure.

impressed A term used in botanical descriptions to indicate something sunken, such as veins.

in (″) Abbreviation for **inch**.

in² Abbreviation for **square inch**.

inarable Ground that is too hard, too rocky, or in any condition not allowing tilling or plowing.

inarch A method of **grafting** sometimes referred to as approach grafting in which a strong-rooted sapling is planted adjacent to the bottom of a tree with need of assistance (understock), and the end of the sapling is grafted into the **understock** plant. This method of grafting is used to improve the health of damaged trees (especially those damaged at their base), assist trees with weak root systems, or give support to a weak lower crotch in a tree.

inbreeding In reference to plants, a situation describing **pollen** of the same plant fertilizing its own **pistils**.

incan. Abbreviation for incandescent.

incandescent daylight lamp An incandescent lamp with a glass bulb colored a blue-green to absorb part of the yellow and red light and give off a whiter light. Its efficiency compared with a normal incandescent light drops by about 35%.

incandescent lamp *or* **incandescent filament lamp**   An electric light source made of a glass bulb from which a light is emitted by electric current heating a metal (usually tungsten) filament.

incandescent lighting fixture   A **luminaire** (complete light apparatus) that makes light by passing electricity through a tungsten filament that glows.

incarious   Grayish or whitish in color.

incense cedar   A moisture-resistant wood with a fragrant resinous odor.

incentive zoning   The awarding of bonus credits to a development in allowing more intensive use of land if public benefits are included in a project. Such benefits may include preservation of greater than the minimum required open space, provision for low and moderate-income housing, or plans for public plazas and courts at ground level.

inch, (in) (″)   English or U.S. length measurement equal to 0.083 **ft**, or 6.453 sq **cm**s.

inchworm *or* **looper**   Any of a number of small, hairless caterpillars, usually of small moths that defoliate trees and shrubs. They are often noticeable either inching along (moving by a looping movement made in alternating the clasping of a surface with the front and back prongs), or lowering themselves by small threads.

incipient decay   Lumber in the early stages of decay not yet affecting its strength.

incised   In botanical terms, cut rather deeply and irregularly. (Compare with **ciliate, pectinate, cleft, lobed, dentate, denticulate, serrate, serrulate, double serrate, entire, crenate, crenulate, parted**.)

incline   A sloping surface that is somewhere between horizontal and vertical.

incised leaf margin

incomplete fertilizer   A fertilizer with only two of the three components (**NPK**) of a complete fertilizer, such as 10-6-0 or 0-6-8.

incomplete flower   A flower that is missing any of the following: a **pistil, stamen, calyx,** or **corolla.**

incrustation   **1.** The depositing of materials on the interior of pipes or equipment from chemicals in the water. **2.** A decorative surfacing of better materials applied over more common or less aesthetically pleasing materials.

indehiscent   A fruit that remains closed at maturity, or a plant that does not naturally release its seed; not splitting.

indemnification   One person or company agreeing to assume liabilities and hold harmless another for certain items or acts.

indemnify   An agreement to hold harmless an individual, group, or entity from liabilities or losses.

indent   A gap left by leaving out a stone, brick, or block in a course of masonry to allow for bonding of future masonry.

indenter bar   *See* **deformed bar.**

independent programming   A feature of some **automatic controllers** that allows them to turn on one set of valves or heads separately at

indeterminate

completely different times and days from another set of valves or heads.

indeterminate **1.** A stem that continues to grow without being limited by a terminal **inflorescence**. **2.** A sequential flowering beginning with the lateral or basal flowers, and continuing to the upper or central flowers.

indigenous **1.** Originating, living, occurring, or growing naturally in an area. **2.** A term used to describe plants that are native, or natural to an area, site, region, or environment at some point in time. Opposite of **exotic**. *See also* **native plant**.

indirect expense Overhead expense not directly chargeable to a specific project.

indirect lighting Illumination distributing 90 to 100% of the emitted light upward to a surface so as to provide reflected light rather than direct light.

indirect luminaire A **luminaire** emitting 90 to 100% of its total light above a horizontal plane.

indirect solar water heating system A solar water heating system utilizing a closed circulation loop through a **heat exchanger**. The fluid flowing through the **solar collector** is isolated from the water to be heated.

indirect sunlight Light from the sun that is not direct, but diffused or reflected. This term usually refers to the light needed to sustain a plant when direct sunlight may damage it. Most often used in reference to indoor plant locations.

indirect waste pipe A drainpipe with an air gap between it and the rest of the drainage system, preventing siphonage backward.

indole-3-acetic acid A naturally occurring **auxin** produced in the apical **meristem**s of roots and shoots.

indumentum A descriptive botanical term referring to a plant part having a dense, hairy covering.

indurated In botanical terms, hardened.

indusium The thin covering over clustered sporangia of a fern sori.

industrial waste Waste in water from industrial uses.

inert Inactive, deficient in active properties, or lacking the anticipated biological or chemical action. This term is often used in reference to seed or fertilizer material that is just excess filler without the properties desired by the user.

inferior ovary In botanical terms, an **ovary** that is below the **calyx** leaves.

infertile **1.** Soil that lacks nutrients necessary for healthy plant growth. **2.** Plants that do not flower, do not bear fruit, or do not have functional reproductive organs. **3.** Anything infertile or unproductive.

infill Development or redevelopment of land that has been bypassed, remains vacant, or is underused in the continuing urban development process.

infiltration **1.** A gas or liquid passing into or through a substance such as soil by penetrating its pores or interstices. **2.** The movement or seepage of water from the surface to the subsoil or groundwater. Its rate is normally expressed in terms of inches (or **mm**) per hour. **3.** Water entering an excavation, hole, drainpipe, or sewage pipe, etc. from surrounding earth.

inflated In botanical terms, turgid and bladdery.

inflexed A botanical term that means bent inward.

inflorescence A botanical term that refers to the arrangement of flowers on the stem or the flower cluster as a whole.

inflow **1.** Water flow entering a sewer pipe from sources other than seepage from surrounding earth. *See also* **infiltration**. **2.** Water in a sewer system, other than waste water, that enters (including sewer service connections) from sources such as, but not limited to, roof drains, cellar drains, catch basins, drains from naturally wet areas, manhole covers, cross connections between storm sewers and sanitary sewers, cooling towers, and surface runoff.

influent Water, waste water, or other liquid flowing into a water body or treatment unit.

informal Often used to describe a design, plant, or a garden that is more natural appearing than contrived, more free-flowing than rigid, more asymmetrical than symmetrical, more oriented to interest or variety than to formality and repetition. *See also* formal **plant** or **formal gardener**.

ingress An access or entry point or entrance.

initial set A partial hardening of mortar, cement, etc. This is usually a point at which it is hard enough to walk upon it without causing damage, hard enough to allow one to get on boards to finish its surface, hard enough to substantially resist penetration of a weighted test needle, or hard enough not to be affected by touch. This term is obviously variable, but the consensus is that it is descriptive of a partially hardened concrete.

inlet An opening for intake.

in-line pump A pump mounted directly within a pipeline that is often supported by the pipe and usually mounted vertically.

inner court An open space surrounded by walls, buildings, structures, etc.

inorganic Anything not originating from plants or animals.

inorganic fertilizer, chemical fertilizer Any fertilizer not of plant or animal origin. They generally supply readily available nutrients, but are not long-lasting (except those that are coated). *See* **slow-release fertilizer**.

inorganic nitrogen Nitrogen combined with other elements, not in animal or vegetable form. Calcium nitrate is an example.

in place Constructed or located where it is designed or desired to remain.

insecticidal soap A mixture (sometimes homemade) that is effective on most soft-bodied insects by removing or making ineffective the coating on them that assists in their retaining moisture, causing them to dehydrate.

insecticide Certain chemicals and compounds capable of killing or repelling particular insect pests.

insectivorous A term describing plants that consume insects for nourishment.

insertion In botanical terms, the place or mode of attachment of an organ to its support.

inside diameter (ID) With regard to pipes, the greatest distance inside the pipe from one wall to another.

inside micrometer A device for accurately measuring the inside dimension of a pipe.

inside thread The threads (angled circular slicing) on the inside of a pipe or device.

in situ In **landscape architecture, land use planning, phytoremediation**, or **landscape construction**, an activity taking place on-site and not at another location. It is usually in reference to remediation of pollutants in or on the ground.

insul. Abbreviation for insulation/insulated.

insulated flange A **coupling** that prevents electrical charges from continuing in piping or devices. When connecting pipes, this prevents or interrupts the electrical transmission path that otherwise would be facilitated. This type of connection assists in preventing damage from **electrolysis**.

insulation **1.** In electrical systems, a material not conducting electricity. Wire is often covered (sheathed) with this to prevent shorting to ground or harm to those who may come into contact with it. **2.** Material used to prevent infiltration of heat or cold (thermal transfer).

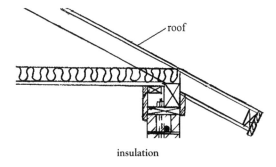

insulation

intake door An opening for water (or another fluid or gas) to enter a tank, pipe, etc.

intake rate *or* **infiltration rate** The measurement of the speed by which water is absorbed into the soil.

integral waterproofing A term for waterproofing of concrete by an additive during mixing.

integrated pest management A preventive management of pest activity and infestation by providing proper waste management, structural repair, maintenance, control techniques (biological, ecological, mechanical, etc.), and application of pesticides.

intercepting chamber A **manhole**.

intercepting sewer A sewer that receives flow from branch sewers.

interception With regard to precipitation, the amount of rainfall or snow intercepted by vegetation before it reaches the ground.

interceptor A device that collects debris, preventing its entering a drainage or sewer system.

interface The common boundary or surface, often a plane, between two bodies or materials.

interflow Water from rainfall and snow melt that moves laterally through soil and seeps into stream channels. In forested areas, this is the long-term source of water in streams.

intergeneric In botanical terms, a **hybrid** between **genera**.

intergeneric hybrid A **hybrid** of two different but closely related **genera**. *See also* **bigeneric hybrid**.

interior A spatial term used in landscape **ecology** to describe the part of **patch**es or **corridors** wide enough to have a significantly different environment from that near the **edge**. In this area, wind or air currents, sun or shade, organisms, or processes common to the edge no longer have a significant influence. This can be the inner portion away from the edge of a lake, city, wooded area, grassland area, polluted area, etc.

interior lot A building lot having a street on only one side.

interior-type plywood Plywood composed of glue not suited to durability when exposed to water, and thus not intended or promoted for exterior use.

intermittent stream Natural stream channels that carry water part of the year but are otherwise dry.

internal drainage In soil science, the relative rate of saturated water flowing through a soil profile.

internal grip A reference to the type of attachment on the inside of a pipe for a machine to pull the pipe underground.

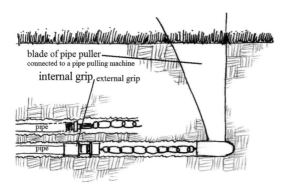

blade of pipe puller—
connected to a pipe pulling machine
internal grip, external grip

pipe

pipe

internal grip

internal manual bleed A feature that allows an automatic valve to open manually (without a controller) by releasing water from above the diaphragm to the downstream side of the valve. It is useful during installation and maintenance operations.

International Code of Botanical Nomenclature (ICBN) An internationally recognized code intended to promote uniformity and stability within botanical nomenclature. The code provides a method and record for naming taxonomic groups, avoiding names that could cause error, ambiguity, or confusion. These difficulties are a significant detriment, plaguing communication and understanding in the use of **common name**s. The code is adopted by the International Botanical Congress, and is updated from time to time. The code adopted in 1993 by the 15th congress in Yakahama, Japan, was known as the Tokyo Code. The most recent publishing of this dictionary was adopted in 1999 at St. Louis, Missouri, by the 16th International Botanical Congress.

internode In botanical terms, the part of a stem between two **node**s, or joints.

interpolation The process of determining or plotting the elevation and location of unknown

points on a site, map, or drawing from the location of points of a known elevation.

interspecific hybrid *or* **interspecies hybrid** To **hybrid**ize by producing plants from two separate varieties within a **species**.

interstice A narrow or small space between objects such as brick or stone in a wall, or the minute space between soil particles.

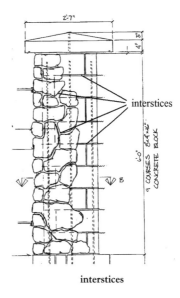

interstices

intrinsic permeability A measure of the relative ease with which an earthen material can transmit a liquid. It is a property of the material independent of the nature of the liquid and the force causing movement.

introduced A term descriptive of a plant moved to a location where a plant of the same variety is not found. It could be moved across a neighborhood, town, county, mountain range, river, continent, or ocean. It appears that the only truly non-introduced plants are those that are growing where another identical plant type once grew. But, then, one wonders when the first plant of that type was introduced to that location.

introduced species   Any species not presently (or previous to some arbitrary date) found native to a particular site or area.

introrse   In botanical terms, turned or facing inward or toward the **axis** of the **flower** or growth. (Compare with **extrorse**.)

intuitive design   Quick and ready insight or knowledge about design without rational or burdensome thought.

invasive   A term used to describe plants that vigorously spread, propagate, have rapid unchecked growth, or invade a surrounding landscape area. Any plant tending to spread prolifically.

invert   The bottom inside elevation of a pipe, channel, culvert, etc. at a selected point along its length, at its entrance, or at its exit.

invitation to bid   A written or verbal request or invitation from an owner, general contractor, etc. for a proposed price, bid, work, or materials.

involucrate   In botanical terms, with an **involucre**.

involucre   In botanical terms, a **whorl** or set of **bract**s around a flower, **umbel**, or fruit. It usually describes bracts overlapping at the base surrounding the flower or supporting it.

involute   In botanical terms, rolled inward from the edges, usually toward the upper surface.

IP, ip   Abbreviation for iron pipe.

IPM   Abbreviation for **integrated pest management**.

IPS, ips   **1.** Abbreviation for international pipe size. **2.** Abbreviation for **iron pipe size**. **3.** Abbreviation for inside pipe size

IPT, ipt   Abbreviation for iron pipe threaded.

IR   Abbreviation for inside radius.

iron   A **micronutrient** found in soils, necessary for plant growth and chlorophyll synthesis. A deficiency causes iron **chlorosis**. As soil alkalinity increases, the iron in soil becomes less soluble and less available to plants.

iron cement   A cement including cast-iron filings used in repair of cast-iron parts.

iron chelate   An iron **fertilizer** bound with a metal ion not easily converted to a form unavailable to plants. It is also known as an iron **metal-organic complex** fertilizer. Iron is a necessary micronutrient for plants to develop chlorophyll. Without it, the leaves of plants yellow. Iron is sometimes present in a soil, but bound and not available to plants. Chelated iron is available to plants immediately.

iron deficiency   *See* **chlorosis**.

iron fence   *See* **wrought iron fence**.

iron pipe size   The dimension of an iron pipe from the farthest points (opposite sides) on its outside surface. Other types of pipe, plumbing, or sprinkler components often carry this designation so that one may know they can be joined easily when the **nominal IPS** is called out.

irregular flower   A flower with **petal**s sometimes dissimilar in form or orientation. (Compare with **zygomorphic**.)

irrigation   The application of water to germinate seed, or sustain **plant material** growth or life by means other than natural rainfall.

irrigation cycle   One complete operation of each station on a **program** of an **automatic controller**.

irrigation efficiency   The care in irrigation to provide minimum water use for maximum results. It is effected by distribution uniformity and management practices such as run times.

irrigation head A device in an **irrigation system** attached to pipes for distribution of water in the system.

irrigation schedule A combined legend and table on an irrigation plan referencing symbols on the plan to identify the parts they represent. It usually includes the symbol of the part, the name of the part, the manufacturer, its size, its type or materials makeup, and remarks about how it is installed, where it is installed, etc.

irrigation system A method, apparatus, piping, ditching system, watering system, etc. designed to convey, transport, and distribute water to plants.

irrigation water **1.** Water used in an irrigation system whether potable or dirty. **2.** Untreated or unclean water used for irrigation purposes.

island **1.** Any land, designed and constructed or naturally occurring, that is completely surrounded by water. **2.** In **landscape ecology**, any **patch** completely disjointed from a similar patch. **3.** In traffic design of roadways and parking lots, a raised planting completely surrounded by pavement and usually surrounded by a **curb**. They are placed to guide traffic, provide aesthetically pleasing surroundings, separate lanes, limit paving, preserve existing vegetation or other features, etc. *See also* **center island**, **corner island**, **drive island**, **end island**.

isolation joint An expansion joint or any joint where the two materials or portions separated by the joint do not touch.

isometric drawing A type of three-dimensional drawing with all principal planes parallel to corresponding axes where vertical lines stay vertical and horizontal lines are on an angle (often 30°).

isotropy In water hydraulics, the condition in which all significant water properties are independent of direction.

ISR Abbreviation for **impervious surface ratio**.

ITE Abbreviation for Institute of Transportation Engineers.

J

jackhammer A heavy hammer driven by air and standing about waist high with pointed or chisel bits. It forces its bit up and down with the full weight of the machine upon it. It is useful in breaking up concrete, rock, etc.

jack rafter Any rafter shorter than the rest in a roof.

jackscrew A jack that raises by twisting a large rod with threads.

jamb A vertical member on the side of a door, window, etc.

Japanese beetle A small, metallic green and brown **beetle** (*Popillia japonica*) introduced into the United States from Japan. It is highly destructive, feeding on grass roots and decaying vegetation as a grub and then as an adult eating foliage and fruits.

jardiniere A large decorative pot or stand for plants.

JB, jb Abbreviation for **junction box**.

jealous glass Glass that is not transparent.

jerry-built A description of poor construction.

jetting With regard to pipe laying, shooting water under pressure to settle and compact soil around a pipe, etc.

jetty An artificial, narrow land (rock, concrete, stone, etc.) projection or barrier to water, extending above the water surface and out into the water body. They are usually approximately perpendicular to the shoreline and are placed in twos, approximately parallel to each other. At some distance from the shore, they often turn to form a narrow entrance for watercraft to enter their protected area. They are generally used to change the natural littoral drift, protect inlet entrances from clogging with excess sediment, or to protect a harbor (dock, boats, etc.) or shore area from waves created by boats, winds, or water currents.

jib A crane.

jitterbug A compactor that jumps up and down.

job site The area of construction.

joggle joint Interconnecting pavers or masonry units with shapes other than square or rectangular.

joint With regard to plants, the points on woody plants from which the leaves arise.

jointed In botanical terms, composed of joints, or having joints.

joint compound In drywall construction, a compound used for finishing joints, etc.

jointing compound A material used on threads of pipe to assist in sealing.

joint shingle A wood shingle attached by nailing edge to edge rather than overlapping shingles.

joint venture A coalition of two or more persons or companies combined for a project.

joist A small wood or metal structural member of a **deck**, ceiling, floor, roof, etc., usually arranged parallel to one another, that directly supports the **decking**, **planking**, floor, ceiling, etc. and that in turn is supported by **beam**s, **girder**s, walls, etc.

joist anchor

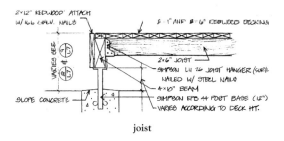

joist

joist anchor   A metal tie for anchoring joists to a wall or larger structural member.

joist hanger   A metal connector plate cut and bent to accept a joist end while also being flush against a timber and having holes to accept **bolt**s, **screw**s, or **nail**s to attach joist ends to timbers (**beam**s, **stringer**s, etc.).

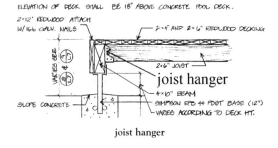

joist hanger

journeyman   An experienced, reliable worker who is competent in a trade and is an employee.

juglone   A substance found in the roots of black walnut trees that is harmful to some plants (i.e., roses, azaleas, rhododendrons).

junction box   In electrical wiring, a box housing connections of **conductor**s (wire splices). In sprinkler irrigation work, the splices must be waterproof. Various devices can enclose and protect the splices, but the most common is a **grease cap**.

jute   A fiber made of durable plants, used to manufacture erosion control matting, carpet backing, etc.

jutty   A **jetty**.

juvenile   A young individual plant. It may differ from mature plants by its soft growth, vigorous increase in size, foliage shape, foliage size, or whether flowers or fruits are present. **Cutting**s from juvenile plants generally root faster than from mature plants.

juvenile form   A plant with a leaf that is so different on young plants that to compare a mature plant to a young one it is not apparent they are the same species. An example of this is English ivy as it has markedly lobed or angular leaves in youth, and is vine-like without any flowers, but in maturity it has flowers, leaves that are ovate or heart shaped, and erect portions of stems.

K

k- Prefix for kilo, or 1000.

K The symbol for **potassium**. This is the third percentage listed on a **complete fertilizer** bag.

kainite A slow-acting chemical **fertilizer** containing 12 to 22% soluble **potash** and about 20% magnesium. It may be harmful on clay soils.

kame A small, cone-shaped hill or ridge of gravel and sand deposited when glacial ice sheets converged.

K_c Abbreviation or symbol for the **crop coefficient** in irrigation auditing.

KD Abbreviation for **kiln-dried**.

keel In botanical terms, a projecting ridge on a surface, like the keel of a boat; the two anterior petals in the bean family.

keeper *See* **strike plate**.

kelp A plant that grows in the ocean and is sometimes used as an organic fertilizer. It has a **NPK** ratio of about 1-0.5-9.

kennel **1.** A shelter or enclosure for a dog or cat. *See also* **dog run**. **2.** A facility boarding and breeding cats or dogs.

kevel *or* **cavel** *or* **cavil** A stone mason's ax for shaping stone.

key A joint, indentation, hole, slot, channel, etc. that another member or material (wood, steel, concrete) fits into in order to hold it in place and prevent movement.

key fruit A dry, indehiscent, winged, and often one-seeded fruit also called a **samara**.

key valve A **valve** operated by a key.

keyway A channel or slot in masonry or concrete between portions built at different times. This affords a stronger, more stable bond between the portions.

kg Abbreviation for **kilogram**(s).

kicker A piece of lumber or wood attached to another piece or to a frame to take a thrust force for it or steady it.

kickout The failure of an excavated vertical surface, **shoring**, or a **braze**.

killing freeze A description of temperatures below 32F (0°C) that remain there for several hours, killing unprotected annuals, and other plants not hardy to freezing temperatures. Each plant type differs as to its hardiness or survivability when temperatures fall below the point of water freezing. Young plants or very old plants may be more susceptible than others of the same type. The lower the temperature drops, the more plant types may not survive. If plants have some protection or a different microclimate (more sun, near a warm building, or protected from wind) they may survive while other plants of their type without some protection do not. For new plants that are marginally hardy, planting before temperatures begin to drop in the fall may make it more likely they can **harden off** and sustain colder temperatures in the winter.

killing frost Any frost that kills plants. *See also* **hard freeze** and **killing freeze**.

kiln-dried *or* **hot-air dried** A term often used to describe lumber dried in a kiln. *See* **kiln-dried lumber**.

kiln-dried lumber

kiln-dried lumber Wood cut to particular dimensions and placed in a kiln (heated enclosure) to remove moisture. This produces a straighter product of true size better at holding nails, and not likely to shrink, split, or warp. Lumber is usually marked as follows: S-GRN for green unseasoned lumber with a moisture content of 20% or higher; S-DRY for lumber with a moisture content of 19% or less; MC 15 for lumber that is dried to 15% or less, etc.

kilogram (kg) The metric weight measurement of 1000 g or 2.2046 lb.

kiloliter (kl) The metric volume measurement of 1000 l or 1.31 c.y.

kilometer (km) A metric length measurement equal to 1000 m or 0.62 mi.

kilovolt An electrical force equal to 1000 **V**.

kilovolt-ampere Electricity equal to the product of **amp** and **voltage** divided by 1000.

kilowatt (kw) Electrical power equal to 1000 **W**s, or about 1.34 hpr.

kingdom In **taxonomy** the five broad categories containing all living and extinct things. The kingdom of plants is called *Plantae*. The next category or unit of differentiation is the **division**. *See also* **taxon**.

king post A vertical board or timber in a truss extending from its ridge to a beam below.

kiosk **1.** A small structure with a roof and at least one open side, usually found in a garden, a park (for weather protection), or in a busy pedestrian area (for selling items). **2.** A small structure that cannot be occupied, with closed sides or faces, standing in a pedestrian mall, at a historic site, etc. that posts or shows information, directions, maps, posters, notices, and announcements.

kip A unit of weight measurement equal to 1000 lb or 4448 Ns.

kl Abbreviation for **kiloliter**(s).

km Abbreviation for **kilometer**(s).

km² Square **kilometer**(s) or 1,000,000 sq **m**s, or 0.3861 sq miles.

knapping hammer A steel hammer used to break stone. It is useful for splitting cobbles, for shaping paving stones, or for producing roughly sized material.

knobbing *or* **knobbling** In stone work, the knocking off from stone the most obvious portions extending beyond desired dimensions.

knoll A small hill or mound.

knot **1.** A swelling on a plant. **2.** The base of a woody branch where it meets the stem and is enclosed therein. **3.** In lumber, a usually darker round (or nearly so) portion of wood or a spot where the grain forms concentric rings. This is usually where there was a branch. These are usually harder than the surrounding wood and after drying can become loose and easily dislodged, especially in some woods. They tend to weaken the board by not being integral to the grain. In most cases, they ruin the surface appearance although some wood with knots is sought after for its knotty appearance. *See* **knotty pine**.

knot garden An intricate, ornamental, small garden space, usually formal, with color, hedges, and points of interest.

knotty pine Wood of a pine tree cut to provide knots that do not loosen and are considered decorative.

knuckle A part of a normal door hinge that usually has more than one cylindrically shaped projection that fits into another and through which a pin is passed to hold the hinge point together.

koi A decorative, freshwater fish (colorful carp) used in ponds, having colors of brown, black, orange, gold, or white, useful in water features for interest and for assisting in keeping water clean. These fish can become over 1 ft long when they reach maturity and are often highly prized for their various colorations and size.

ksi Abbreviation for kilopounds per square inch.

kV Abbreviation for **kilovolt**.

kVA Abbreviation for **kilovolt-ampere**.

k-value The time rate of heat flow through a material of a particular dimension from one of its faces to the other.

kw Abbreviation for **kilowatt**.

kWh Abbreviation for kilowatt hour, which is a unit of energy equal to 3.6 megajoules.

kyanize, kyanise The preservation of wood by steeping it in a mercuric chloride.

L

l. **1.** Abbreviation for **liter**(s). **2.** Abbreviation for linear.

L.A. Abbreviation for landscape architect.

labiate In botanical terms, **bilabiste**, or having the limb of a tubular **corolla** or **calyx** (as with mint plants) divided into two different sized portions with one overlapping the other.

labor and material payment bond A monetary guarantee by an insurance company to an owner that a contractor will pay for all labor and materials of a contracted work or, in the event that the contractor does not, then the surety will pay for those debts holding the owner harmless financially and the contractor responsible to pay the debts back to the bonding company.

labyrinth **1.** A **maze** sometimes made of hedges in gardens. These garden features are comprised of convoluted paths outlined by hedges, usually above eye level, and with the usual design goal to make negotiating them to their entrances or exits difficult and confusing.

lace bug *See* **lacewing**.

laced valley *or* **woven** In roofing, the interlacing of roofing materials at a valley (inside angled intersection).

lacerate A descriptive botanical term referring to a plant part that appears torn or irregulary cut or cleft.

lacewing An insect with large, translucent wings with dark veins, long antennae, and brilliant eyes. They are serious plant pests as they creep on undersides of leaves, sucking their juices. They generally fly at night and are fond of

azaleas, chrysanthemums, rhododendrons, and photinias.

laciniate In botanical terms, slashed or cut into deep, narrow lobes or usually unequal segments.

lacquer A liquid, usually enamel, applied to surfaces where it dries to a glossy finish.

lacrosse A goal game played on a lawn where players throw and catch with long-handled devices. The playfield space required is 330 ft long and 180 to 210 ft wide.

lacustrine Pertaining to or growing around lakes.

lactiferous A botanical term meaning bearing a milky latex.

ladder A device used to climb up or down having slender steps (rungs) between two rails.

ladybird *See* **ladybug**.

ladybug Small, rounded, usually brightly colored, beetles of the family *Coccinellidae* that feed on other insects. They feed on these insects both in the larval stage and as adults. They often help control small sucking insects such as **aphids** on plants.

lag bolt A metal, threaded, pointed bolt with an expanded flattop portion, flattened to accept a wrench for tightening. Similar to a **wood screw**, but can be tightened with more force and generally of a larger size. The shank of this bolt differs from the shank of a machine bolt or carriage bolt in that the threads of this bolt start from a pointed base and are wider apart with a greater angle to their rise for piercing and grasping wood or a similar substance. Threads on the shank may extend the entire length or for only a portion of its length.

lagging **1.** Thermal insulation of pipes, tanks, ducts, etc. **2.** In excavation, the use of boards placed side by side along an excavated bank of earth.

laitance The fines (fine particles) and water in excess on a concrete surface that is usually the result of too much working of the surface. This material is weak and will usually crack off in the future. *See also* **spalling**.

lake sand Rounded instead of sharp sand particles.

lamina The flattened portion of a **leaf** that does not include the **petiole**, often called the leaf **blade**.

laminar Thin and flat, often describing a leaf blade.

laminar flow This term usually refers to the flow of water along or near a hard surface or solid surface.

laminar flow emitter In **drip irrigation**, an **emitter** that regulates water flow (usually into droplets) having a small narrow path, causing loss of pressure due to friction as water travels the path. Examples of laminar flow emitters are spiral paths, capillary tubes, and microtubes. Elevation differences, friction loss in pipe distribution, small particles that plug the small laminar flow tubes, and temperature differences (changing water viscosity and flow) can affect the output of these emitters. Used with proper application, they can be reliable, and are inexpensive. *See also* **emitter**.

laminate A material made of two or more layers bonded together as in plywood, etc.

lamp A manufactured light source often referred to as a tube or bulb. It does not include any other elements associated with a light fixture such as the reflectors, attachments to wiring, bulb holder, ballasts, or decorative portions (**luminaire**).

lamppost An upright support of a luminaire (light fixture).

lanate A botanical term meaning woolly.

lanceolate In botanical terms, lance-shaped, or narrow and long.

lanceolate leaf shape

land The earth's surface not under water.

land clearing Any activity that removes the entire vegetated ground cover of an area. This term does not generally refer to agricultural harvests, mowing, trimming, pruning, or removal of vegetation to maintain it or other nearby vegetation in a healthy, viable condition.

land cover **1.** Materials such as vegetation, mulches, and concrete that cover ground. **2.** Land uses covering a general area of land (i.e., agricultural, commercial, suburban). **3.** The vegetative cover of land.

land degradation **1.** The loss in capacity of a land to produce crops or biomass for livestock. **2.** The pollution of land or reduction of its ability to sustain life. With regard to land's reduction of ability to sustain life, this term is often relative to life forms most prized; while some life forms are decreased, sometimes others are increased.

land development Any improvement to a land. In most government jurisdictions, it applies only to buildings, roads, utilities, walks, parks, etc. in creating an **urban** or **suburban** area.

land evaluation and site assessment (LESA) A numerical system for assessing the quality of farmland. It is generally used to select tracts for agricultural protection or to determine lowest quality farmland to allow development. This information is useful to nursery operations, topsoil, acquisition, sod farms, etc.

landfill **1.** The collection of garbage, refuse, and trash buried under layers of earth. **2.** Managed waste disposal sites that bury debris.

landform A feature of the earth's surface.

land grant university A university or college designated by its state legislature or congress to receive grants from the Morrill Acts of 1862 and 1890 in teaching agriculture, military tactics, and the mechanical arts. They each established an **extension service** for assisting local agricultural efforts, etc.

landing A larger space between runs of stairs for resting, or intersection with other paths.

landmark An item on the land of special interest or note.

landscape **1.** An area planted within urban surroundings, near a building, near pavements, or as a park, etc. **2.** The landforms of an area. **3.** In **landscape ecology**, a **mosaic** where a group of contiguous ecosystems is repeated in similar form for an area miles wide with recognizable boundaries of the land or the elements thereon. Examples are desert landscapes, swamp landscapes, cultivated landscapes, suburban landscapes, and forested landscapes. **4.** Improving, covering, or repairing the ground in any way including construction of pavements, structures, **irrigation systems**, or **planting**, **seeding**, **grading**, etc.

landscape architect **1.** A professional licensed to perform services in **landscape architecture**. **2.** A professional performing **landscape architecture** by designing changes in land and features thereon for human enjoyment and by planning effective placement of structures, vehicular and pedestrian ways, plantings, earthwork, drainage facilities, buildings, land uses, etc., and producing construction documents for the building of such. Concerned with stewardship of natural, constructed, and human resources in providing environments that serve useful, aesthetic, safe, and enjoyable purposes.

landscape architecture A profession encompassing both the natural and built environments. It involves a multidisciplinary design work composed of some understanding of soil science, civil engineering, landscape ecology, architecture, **horticulture**, **arboriculture**, botany, irrigation systems, land planning, transportation planning, environmental issues, art, drafting, etc. Those adequately trained in this profession have a well-rounded knowledge of the natural and built environment useful in managing multidisciplinary developments or land planning efforts.

landscape buffer An area of landscaping separating two distinct land uses, or a land use and a public **right-of-way** intended to mitigate or soften differences between them.

landscape construction Work in constructing such items as (including but not limited to) walls, paths, **sprinkler system**s, drainage systems, outdoor lighting, **water feature**s, trails, paths, driveways, paving, **deck**s, and **patio**s. These are professionally designed by **landscape architect**s and constructed by **landscape contractor**s.

landscape contractor A construction business principally engaged in the decorative or functional alteration of grounds, or elements thereon or buried therein. They contract and perform construction of landscape elements including but not limited to walls, paths, **sprinkler system**s, drainage systems, outdoor lighting, **water feature**s, trails, paths, driveways, paving, **deck**s, and **patio**s. That which is designed by a landscape architect is brought to existence and fruition by a landscape contractor.

landscape design The drawings, models, or action of laying out structures, land activities, recreational facilities, vegetation, land cover, erosion protection, watering methods, etc.

landscape ecology The study of interactions among organisms and their environment usually on the scale of a landscape.

landscape element 1. Any item within a **landscape. 2.** In **landscape ecology**, a relatively homogeneous spatial element when viewed from the air. It can be a **patch**, a portion of a **matrix**, a **corridor**, etc.

landscape fabric *See* **weed barrier fabric**.

landscape fabrics Various plastic or fibrous materials, usually on rolls, used to cover the ground in control of weeds, erosion, or for increased soil stability. Most of them are staked into place and covered with mulch to keep them from moving. Some are also buried in trenches at the edge (especially on slopes) to further ensure their remaining in place.

landscape improvement An improvement to real estate by landscape work.

landscape planning The decision-making, technical, and design processes associated with the assignment, configuration, and compatibility of land uses and their operations.

landscape planting area An area on a **site** or a **site plan** that is devoted to the growing of shrubbery, trees, grass, or other plant material. They are usually delineated by surrounding **impervious** surfaces, areas unsuitable for plant growth, or property lines.

landscape rake A long-handled tool with a fan-shaped, thin, flat-fingered portion for dragging over the ground in gathering up leaves or light debris.

landscape waste All debris from landscape areas including but not limited to grass, shrubbery cuttings, leaves, tree limbs, fruits, and other materials accumulated as the result of the care of lawns, shrubbery, vines, and trees.

landslide Historic or present earth mass movement characterized by surface flows of rock, soil, or debris on slopes. They most often occur with heavy rain, snow melt, earthquakes, excavation, or earth filling.

land survey A survey of land establishing or reestablishing lengths and bearings (directions) of boundary lines.

land tie A **deadman**.

land tile Porous clay tile pipe laid with butt joints that allow water in or out, and draining land or dispersing water.

land trust A private, nonprofit land conservation organization formed to protect farm land, forest land, natural areas, historic structures, recreational areas, etc. Land trusts generally accept donations of land for conservation **easements**. They usually offer the public education about the need to conserve land.

land use The use (past, present, or future) of land (i.e., agricultural, industrial, residential, natural, recreational, commercial, etc.).

land-use plan A map showing existing or future uses of land areas. When compiled by a city it will usually include designations such as commercial, industrial, agricultural, single-family residential, multifamily residential, etc.

land use planning Making plans for the uses of land that will over a long period best serve the general welfare of people together with facilitating the ways and means to accomplish them.

land-use survey A gathering of information to produce a map of existing land uses.

lane **1.** A portion of a road accommodating a single line of vehicles and usually painted with lines to define its limits. **2.** A narrow road or path usually bounded by a vertical element (shrubs, trees, fence, buildings, etc.) on one or both sides.

lantern flies *See* **leafhopper**.

lantern skylight A small **skylight**.

lanuginous In plant identification and description, a botanical term meaning woolly or cottony.

lap **1.** To overlap at least a portion. **2.** The length to which structural members, sheeting, etc. overlaps.

lap adhesive An adhesive used to seal the overlaps of a jacket around an insulated pipe.

lap cement An asphalt adhesive used between overlaps of rolled roofing.

lap joint The area of overlapping materials. This is usually in reference to rigid materials such as wood or steel overlapped and secured together to afford support to one or both pieces.

lapies Usually a deeply trenched bedrock beneath the soil surface that has been affected by limestone, gypsum, or other soluble rock.

large knot A knot in lumber greater than 1½ in (3⅘ cm) in diameter.

larry A **hoe** useful in mixing mortar that has a hole or holes in it.

larva A stage of some insects when they are active, immature, wingless, and have been hatched from an egg. They usually live by eating plant material.

latch A device with at least two separate parts mounted on two adjacent disconnected items (objects) that facilitates an interconnection between its parts, by movement of a portion of it to fasten the two items (objects) together, but not lock them together.

latch plate The thin metal piece protecting the area of a door around a **latch**.

lateral **1.** In botanical terms, born on the side of a structure or organ. **2.** A **lateral line**.

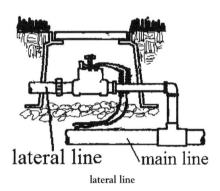

lateral line

lateral bud A bud on the side of a stem or branch and not at an end of either.

lateral force A force or load usually acting in a horizontal direction. Examples of these forces are earthquakes, wind, and pressure exerted by soil or water against a wall that retains it.

lateral line *or* **lateral pipe** A pipeline in an irrigation system that distributes water from

valves to **sprinkler head**s or points of discharge. Any pipe downstream of an irrigation valve.

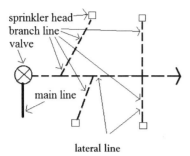

lateral line

lateral sewer   A portion of a sewer line that has no other sewer discharging into it.

latex   An emulsion of minute, dispersed particles of rubber or plastic material in water obtained by polymerization and often used for coatings and adhesives.

latex paint   A paint of latex with pigments and other binders.

lath   **1.** In landscape work, a structure for partial covering overhead to reduce or prevent damage to plants from excess sunlight or frost. **2.** A 3 to 4 ft long thin (½ in or less) stake used most often in surveying to mark the location or an offset to another shorter survey marker stake. Also sometimes used with plastic caution tape strung between them at their tops to alert pedestrians not to stray onto landscaping that may have newly planted sod, wet conditions, etc.

lathe   A machine that rotates a piece of wood or metal for shaping.

lath house   Structures with partially open roofs or sides giving plants some shade, and protection from wind. They are also often used to get plants adjusted to weather after moving them from indoors or a distant area of variant weather.

Latin name   The **botanical name (scientific name)** of a plant usually composed of **genus**, **species**, and sometimes variety or **strain, cultivar**, etc. A plant may have several common names, but a plant may only have one botanical name (genus and species). Plants requested by Latin name are more likely to be the plant desired. **Common name**s are often confused with different plants, as sometimes different plants have the same common name and some plants have more than one common name, especially from one region to another. *See also* **plant classification** and **taxon**.

latitude   **1.** An amount of variation allowed. **2.** With regard to surveying, the north and south directions.

latrine   A toilet.

lattice   A diagonally crossed network (forming a net pattern) that is usually made of metal, plastic, or wood strips that is useful as decorative screening or for other ornamental construction. It can often be purchased in preconstructed sheets of 4 × 8 ft.

lattice fence   A fence made with **lattice** to afford some privacy yet allow some light and air to flow through.

lattice girder *or* **lattice beam**   A web of diagonal pieces arranged like latticework between horizontal members comprising a beam.

latticework   A **construction** with **lattice** or in the fashion of lattice.

lavatory   **1.** A toilet. **2.** A water container for washing that has an open top and drainage piping. **3.** A room with a basin for washing hands and face, as well as having a toilet.

lawn   In landscape, a grassy area kept substantially free from other plant material, and usually kept mowed for aesthetic purposes or for recreational use. Typical lawn grasses are bluegrass (*Poa*), Bermuda grass (*Cynodon*), bebt grass (*Agrostis*), St. Augustine grass (*Stenotaphrum*), wheatgrass

(*Agropyron*), blue grama grass (*Bouteloua*), buffalo grass (*Buchloe*), fescue (*Fescue*), ryegrass (*Lolium*), and zoysia grass (*Zoysia*).

lawn croquet A game played with mallets, different colored balls, and hoops for passing balls through on a lawn. The size is 75 by 40 ft. (*See also* **British croquet**.)

lawn mower A machine that cuts grass evenly to a desired height. *See also* **reel mower** and **rotary mower**.

law of reflection A law that holds true of reflected sound, light, and radiant heat stating that the angle of incidence (reception) is equal to the angle of reflection.

lax A term sometimes used in botanical descriptions referring to a plant part appearing loose.

layering In gardening, the practice of **propagation** of a plant by developing roots on a branch before removing it. It is generally more successful than the **cutting** method of propagation. The two methods of layering are **ground layering** and **air layering**.

layout A plan showing a scheme for an arrangement of objects and/or spaces.

lb Abbreviation for **pound**(s).

LCM, lcm Abbreviation for **loose cubic meter**.

L&CM Abbreviation for lime and cement mortar.

LDG, ldg Abbreviation for **landing**.

leachate Fluids associated with decomposing waste in a **landfill**.

leaching A process of liquids flowing through or contacting the surface of a solid and mobilizing constituents from the solid through the actions of physical transport and dissolution. This process washes out soluble products such as calcium, salts, ammonium, chloride, nitrates, etc. Soils are sometimes given abundant water to facilitate the removal of materials in solution by the passage of water seeping through soil. This process can leach out harmful soluble agents such as salts. But in leaching out harmful chemicals one may also lose essential nutrients such as nitrogen, as it tends to move through the soil with water.

leaching cesspool An excavation in the ground that is covered and lined for receiving domestic sewer discharge, surface waters, storm system water, or drainage system waters designed to retain any organic matter or solid materials while allowing the water or liquids to seep through the side and bottom surfaces.

leader **1.** A downspout. **2.** With regard to trees or shrubs with a single trunk, the central **stem**. It especially refers to the top portion and is often referred to as the central leader.

leader head *or* **conductor head** A widened portion of a water drainage **leader** (or downspout) top where runoff is collected or received into the leader.

lead pipe A pipe made of about 99.7% lead.

lead wool A fibrous material made with thin strands of lead used as caulking in pipe joints.

leaf (plural: leaves) That part of a plant that manufactures food for a plant from elements

leaf blade

leaf blight

obtained from air, soil, etc. through the process of photosynthesis with the influence of light. Leaves are appendages of stems of various lengths and shapes. Most leaves are flat and thin, but their size and shape are both considerably variable, sometimes on the same plant.

leaves

leaf blight *See* **blight**.

leaf blister Any of several diseases causing blister-like deformities on plants.

leaf blotch Diseases caused by fungi, looking much like **leaf spot**, except that this damage is irregular and generally larger.

leaf bud A **bud** on a plant that will produce a **leaf**.

leaf burn A drying of a leaf that starts at the edges because of excess light, chemicals, strong or drying winds, or lack of water. *See* **leaf scorch**.

leaf curl A descriptive symptom of a condition caused by fungi, environmental conditions, insects, or bacteria. Curled leaves can also be caused by herbicide sprays drifting from nearby areas.

leaf cutters Any caterpillar that feeds by neatly cutting out parts of leaves.

leaf-cutting bees These insects damage leaves of plants as they cut portions of leaves and some-

times flowers to obtain nest-building materials. Though they are a nuisance to gardeners and landscapers, they are also beneficial in pollination. They are particularly efficient at pollinating alfalfa. Plants particularly susceptible are rose and bougainvillea.

leafhoppers A sucking insect sometimes called a plant hopper, or lantern fly. They are any of numerous fast-moving greenish or brownish insects of the family *cicadellidae* that suck the juices of plants from the underside of leaves causing white stippling on the upper leaf surface. They sometimes spread virus diseases. They can be controlled by insecticides.

leaflet This is one of the divisions or blades of a **compound leaf**. The fleshy portions of a compound leaf arising from the same petiole are completely separated into these portions of leaf and are found on the same petiole, which may also be divided.

leaflet

leaf miner Any of various small insects (moths or dipteran flies) that lay eggs on leaf surfaces and whose **larva**e burrow into and eat the **parenchyma** of leaves resulting in an unsightly serpentine effect on the leaf.

leaf mold   Decaying leaves often used as an amendment to soil.

leaf rake   A long-handled tool with a fan-like piece attached for dragging leaves or such into piles. The fan shape is usually made of thin, flat, stiff, and bendable bamboo, metal, or plastic strips.

leaf rollers   A moth (*lepidopteran*) having larvae that damage plants by rolling in a leaf to make a nest. It prefers oak or fruit trees. They have a number of insects that usually hunt them and keep populations down, but when found, remove the leaf and destroy it. If infestations are heavy, chemical sprays can effectively control them.

leaf scar   The mark left on a branch, stem, twig, etc. when a **petiole** becomes detached and the leaf falls. It is very noticeable on some plants.

leaf scorch   The partial or complete **desiccation** of a **leaf** due to lack of water supply to the leaf. This may be caused by lack of irrigation, frozen roots, damage to roots, drying winds, etc. Precautions can be taken by planting shade-loving plants in shade, using drought-tolerant plants in areas of heat or low irrigation, watering plants adequately, adding mulch around plants to prevent evaporation, and by controlling insects and diseases.

leaf skeletonizer   Any caterpillar that eats the fleshy portion of leaves so that a skeleton-like leaf is left.

leaf spot   *See* **anthracnose**.

leaf tiers   A term given to caterpillars that feed on leaves and tie them together with silky threads.

lean concrete   Any concrete with low cement content.

ledger   In framing, a horizontal element of lumber supported by a post, wall, etc. and having joists attached to it.

ledger board   A horizontal board joined by vertical supports, as in fence construction.

ledger strip   A strip of wood nailed along the bottom of a beam to assist in supporting joists.

leggy   Plants with stems unnaturally long from lack of light, high temperatures, excessive nitrogen, etc. Their lower areas usually have few leaves.

legume   A **family** of plants with roots that contain nitrogen-fixing bacteria (e.g., **rhizobium**). This family includes some herbs, shrubs, and trees. Important food and forage plants belonging to this family include clovers, beans, and peas.

leguminous   Pertaining to legumes.

lemma   In a grass flower **spikelet**, the lower of two **bracts** enclosing the flower. It has its back at the outside of the spikelet.

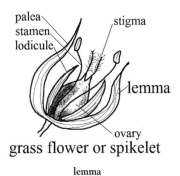

grass flower or spikelet

lemma

lens   Glass or plastic enclosing the bulb of a **luminaire**, allowing light to be transmitted through it.

lentic   Having to do with wetlands, ponds, or lakes that are not flowing waters.

lenticel A group of loose corky cells formed beneath the epidermis of woody plants, rupturing the epidermis, and admitting gases to and from the inner tissues and atmosphere. They appear as many regularly spaced, slightly raised spots or elongated bumps on the woody portions (especially smooth bark) of some plants. *Betula nigra* is an example of a plant with visually pronounced lenticels on its bark.

lenticels

lenticular In botanical terms, lens-shaped, both sides convex.

lepidote A botanical term that means scaly or covered with small scales.

LESA Abbreviation for **Land Evaluation Site Assessment or Agreement**.

letter of intent A letter indicating one will enter into a contract with another.

levee **1.** A mound of sediment along a riverbank deposited as a result of periodic flooding. **2.** A dike to contain the waters of flood irrigation. **3.** A spot on a river for landing boats. **4.** Any man-made embankment constructed to prevent flooding. They are most often made of earth and are meant to contain, control, or divert the flow or rising of water or protect property and lives.

level **1.** Any instrument used to measure whether a surface is horizontal, level (perpendicular to a line pointed to the center of the earth), or sloped. They are of two types: handheld and mounted. A handheld level is a surveying instrument usually comprised of a telescope with a bubble. A mounted level is a surveying instrument usually comprised of a telescope with a bubble used to level it on a tripod support, on which it rotates in shooting elevations and determining slopes, etc. **2.** A **spirit level**. **3.** The position of a line or plane when perfectly horizontal (perpendicular to a line drawn to the earth's center).

leveling **1.** In landscape work, making the ground evenly smooth (almost always with some **slope** for drainage), usually in preparation for planting, irrigation work, placement of mulch, etc. **2.** The act of moving or securing an object or structure to a position as described under **level** (**3**).

leveling rod *or* **leveling staff** A rod with measurements marked upon it for measuring differences in grade elevation.

l.f. Abbreviation for lineal **feet**.

LFT Abbreviation for linear foot.

lg. **1.** Abbreviation for long. **2.** Abbreviation for length. **3.** Abbreviation for large.

lgth In the lumber industry, abbreviation for length.

LH Abbreviation for left hand.

liability insurance Insurance that protects the insured against physical or financial injury to the person or property of someone else.

liana   A botanical term referring to a climbing or woody vine.

license   A written permission given to engage in an activity, as required by law or agency rule.

lien   *See* **mechanic's lien**.

life-cycle cost   The cost of a material, or piece of equipment, structure, etc., including its initial cost and maintenance costs during its lifetime.

lift   **1.** A layer of compacted fill material. This earthen material is used in filling operations placed at various thicknesses to facilitate some end such as a degree of compaction. A compacted, stable **fill** is comprised of lifts of a certain thickness (as necessary for various materials and aggregates to facilitate compaction) that have each been compacted. **2.** A scaffold frame above another scaffold frame. **3.** Concrete poured between two construction joints. **4.** A portion of vertically formed concrete poured at one time. **5.** An amount of grout or mortar placed at one time in a structure such as a wall. **6.** A bench in a multilevel excavation. **7.** A forklift.

liftgate   A gate opening by moving it vertically, as opposed to a gate that swings open on a side edge.

lifting   Digging plants up for storage or for **transplanting**.

lift latch *or* **thumb latch**   A bar on a door (small or large) that must be lifted at one or both ends to allow the door to open.

light   **1.** A pane of glass. **2.** An artificial source of illumination.

lightbulb   *See* **incandescent lamp**.

light globe   Most often this refers to an **incandescent lamp**.

lighting   **1.** Various methods, equipment, etc. used to provide light; illumination. **2.** The coverage, distribution, and intensity of any artificial light. **3.** Any devices supplying artificial light.

lighting fixture   An electrical device that holds a lamp, usually has a lens, and often is decorative.

lighting panel   An electrical box containing fuses or circuit breakers protecting branch circuits serving lighting fixtures.

lighting unit   A **lighting fixture**. Also a **luminaire**.

lightning arrester   A device protecting electrical wiring and devices from the affects of lighting.

light pole   Any pole holding aloft a light source. They are usually made of metal or wood and contain a hollow portion where wires or pipes can be concealed.

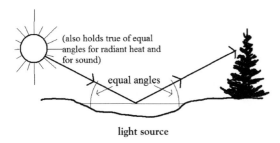

light source

light pole

light shade

light shade   Filtered shade or shade during part of the day.

light soil   A term used loosely without specific definition to describe **soils** that are easily worked and not compacted, are mostly **sand**y (having little **clay**), full of lightweight organic matter, or made up of large particles. This term does not refer to its color or weight.

ligneous   Wood, wood-like, or resembling wood.

lignification   The process of making something woody. This takes place by the depositing of **lignin**.

lignin   The woody cell walls of plants and the material between them that bonds them. The woody portion of plants.

ligulate   In botanical terms, furnished with a **ligule**.

ligule   A botanical term literally meaning a little tongue. It is often applied when describing the flattened part of the ray corolla in *Asteraceae* and to the appendage on the inner (upper) side of a leaf at the junction of the **blade** and **sheath** in many *Poaceae* and some *Cyperaceae* (grass-like plants).

limb   **1.** A large branch of a tree. **2.** The expanded part of a **sympetalous corolla** above the throat. The expanded portion of any **petal** or **leaf**.

lime   **1.** With regard to soils, CaO, **calcium carbonate**, or its application. It comes in several forms from limestone-derived materials and is beneficial for increasing **pH** (neutralizing acidic soils), for making **clay** soil more granular (less sticky) and porous, for assisting sandy soils in retaining water and becoming more compact, as well as for improving soil nutrient availability. In **acid** soils, it will assist in breaking down humus and making available more **phosphorus**

and **potash** otherwise not available to plants (unless applied too heavily). **2.** A fruit of *Citrus aurantifolia*.

lime concrete   Concrete made from mixing lime, sand, and gravel.

limestone   A sedimentary rock of calcite or dolomite useful as building stone or crushed-stone aggregate.

limit of disturbance   One or more specified areas on a lot or parcel within which all disturbance of land such as construction of structures, driveways, parking, roads, landscaping, water surfaces, decks, utilities, walks, or improved recreation facilities are to be located. Some **agencies** omit areas restored with natural vegetation from being part of the limits of disturbance.

limnetic   The portion of a wetland void of **emergent** vegetation because of deep water. Here light does not penetrate to the bottom of the water.

lineament   **1.** Straight features in the landscape, usually in reference to revealing some feature of the subsurface such as a geologic change or fault. **2.** A distinguishing or characteristic feature of the land.

linear   In botanical terms, a leaf that is narrow and flat with the **margin**s parallel.

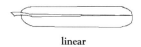

linear

linear pit   A trench large enough for planting trees together in a linear alignment along a street, walk, **promenade**, etc. where they will share rooting space. It is useful to provide extra rooting space and stability for the tree structure where the space would otherwise be limited by urban features (walls, foundations, curbs, pavement, etc.) or other materials unfavorable to rooting.

line level   A small **spirit level (bubble level)** enclosed in a metal or plastic case with hooks that can be hung on a string. When the string is pulled tight the bubble indicates proximity to level by its proximity to being centered. This is useful in determining grades for drainage, checking bottoms of excavations, the **slope** of a **pipe** or ditches, or in construction or placement of objects and structures, etc.

line of sight *or* **line of collimation**   **1.** A line seen through a surveying instrument when looking toward an object or point. **2.** A direction of observation by one looking at an object, especially in the landscape. **3.** A visual path from a particular vantage point.

liner   A small, propagated, immature plant usually made available by nurseries, to grow in containers to a larger size more suitable for sale. They are often grown in flats or trays with small planting soil cups.

lintel   A horizontal member above an opening that usually carries weight of materials and loads above it.

lip   In plant identification and descriptions, a projection or expansion of a plant part.

liquefaction   The change that comes about in some granular material (earthen material) from a solid state to a liquid state in an earthquake due to vibrations and shaking.

liquidated damages   Any amount specified to be paid by a contractor to an owner as compensation if a contracted work should extend its completion beyond the date agreed upon at the time of signing the contract for the work.

liquid fertilizer   Plant nutrients applied in a water solution.

liquid limit   A term used in reference to a soil condition where, with any more water added to the soil, the soil would change from a plastic to a liquid.

liquid manure   A **liquid fertilizer** made by soaking manure in water and then removing the solid portions.

liter (l)   The metric measurement of 1 l, 61.02 **c.i.**, 0.908 dry quarts, or 1.057 liquid quarts.

litmus   An organic chemical strip of paper useful for indicating **acidity** or **alkalinity**. It becomes red when placed in something having **pH values** below 4.5 and blue for **pH values** above 8.3.

litmus strip   *See* **litmus**.

litmus test   A procedure, situation, or experiment that reveals information or truth. *See also* **litmus**.

litoral   *See* **littoral**.

litter   Waste materials such as bottles, glass, cans, scrap metal, plastic, garden rubbish, junk, paper, disposable packages or containers, and all other similar materials, and any other substance that is a nuisance to the public, or that creates a public health, fire, or safety hazard.

litter layer   The **Oi layer** within the **O horizon** of a **soil profile**. It is comprised of undecomposed and recognizable organic matter such as leaves, sticks, and other living organism residue. If it is present, it is the surface layer.

littoral, litoral   **1.** The shoreward zone of a lake or wetland. **2.** The area where water is shallow enough in a lake or wetland to allow **emergent** vegetation. **3.** Growing on or near a shore. **4.** The zone on a shore between high and low water marks.

littoral transport   Movement of sediment along a coastline.

live load **1.** Any load on a structure that is not permanently existing as a force on the structure. **2.** The weight load expected or existing on a structure, including people, furniture, equipment, and appliances. It does not include the influence of wind, earthquake, etc. **3.** Any and all loads imposed on a building, deck, bridge, or other structure due to use or occupancy.

live stake A live, woody, long-stem portion of a plant, usually without any branches, roots, or leaves still attached, pounded, or placed into the ground as a planting procedure. If suitable plant material is used, and they are prepared and placed correctly, they will root and leaf out. In the illustrations, two types of stakes are shown. One is pounded into the ground. The others are of small diameter and are planted by punching a hole with a prong on a tractor or by excavating and backfilling.

living unit A dwelling providing living facilities for one family including provisions for living, sleeping, eating, cooking, and bathroom facilities.

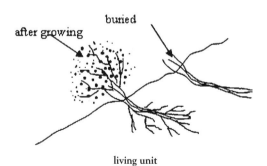

living unit

lm Abbreviation for **lumen.**; abbreviation for lineal meters.

lm/sf Abbreviation for **lumen** per square foot.

lm/W Abbreviation for **lumen** per watt.

load **1.** A force (especially by weight) or system of forces, applied to a structure, a structural member or foundation, etc. of a structure. **2.** The power delivered to an electrical device or piece of equipment.

loader A motorized machine of various sizes having a front bucket and arms for scooping earth or materials, lifting them, transporting them on wheels or tracks, and dumping.

loading dock A raised area (dock) that a truck or train can be backed up to being about the same elevation as the vehicle or trailer bed elevation to be unloaded. This allows for easier unloading or loading.

loam The textural class name for **soil** having a moderate (or relatively even) amount of **sand**, **silt**, and **clay**. It is comprised of 7 to 27% clay, 28 to 50% silt, and 23 to 52% sand. This is the ideal soil for most plants, and the term loam is used to describe soil rich in **organic matter**, not easily compacted, and able to drain well. It is mellow with a slight gritty feel but fairly smooth and a little plastic-like. When it is squeezed while dry, it forms a cast that will not break with careful handling, but when squeezed while moist can be fairly readily handled without breaking.

loamy sand A **soil** textural class comprised of 0 to 15% **clay**, 15 to 30% **silt**, and 70 to 90% **sand**.

lobe In botanical terms, any projection or division by indentation (especially a rounded one)

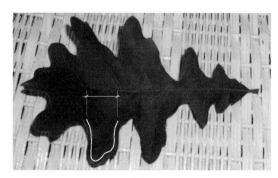

lobe

lobed leaf margin

of a leaf, etc., especially when not extending more than halfway to the midvein or base.

lobed In botanical terms, a plant part, especially a leaf, with cuts or indentations usually less than halfway to its base or **midrib**. (Compare with **ciliate, pectinate, cleft, entire, dentate, denticulate, serrate, serrulate, double serrate, incised, crenate, crenulate, parted.**)

lobed leaf margin

locknut **1.** A **nut** with a design (various types) that creates friction against the bolt it is fitted to, or against the surface it is tightened to, causing resistance to rotation and loosening. These types of nuts are made so as to not loosen without extra force when they are tightened. **2.** A

nut used against another nut to tighten and hold fast each nut and prevent loosening.

lock washer A **washer** with various designs for binding against a bolt head and the surface it is forced against, causing resistance to removing the bolt by rotating.

locule A **compound** ovary of a plant.

locust Coarse-grained, strong wood of a locust tree. It is hard, decay-resistant, and durable; often used for posts.

lodicule One of the tiny scales in the inflorescence of grasses.

loess A wind-deposited accumulation of uniformly sized, **silt**y material, or any silt deposits usually of a buff or yellowish brown color thought to have been accumulated by wind.

logo A stylistic design, emblem, or representation used for identifying or representing an object, firm, development, etc. Many developments have logos designed by **landscape architect**s. It may or may not contain words, letters, or numbers.

logo

longitudinal section A drawing of a subject as if viewed from a **plane** that intersects the object lengthwise.

long-radius *or* **sweep radius** *or* **sweep elbow**
A term for a bent pipe portion or **fitting** changing a pipe's direction with a large sweeping radius assisting in avoiding pressure loss to resistance, improving flow characteristics, or facilitating easier pulling of wire through it.

longshore transport Movement of sediment parallel to the coastline.

long ton The weight of 2240 lb (1016 kg).

looper *See* **inchworm**.

loose cubic meter Material not in a compacted state and measuring one cubic meter in volume. Usually refers to soil as it has a significant difference in volume between its loose and compacted states (difference in volume depends on type of soil with variations according to presence of sand, rock, organics, etc.).

loose material Soil or rock in a blasted, broken, **friable**, or loadable state.

lopper A long-handled pruner with jaws that either bypass each other or cut against an anvil jaw.

lost-head nail A nail with a small head intended to be pounded beneath a surface and lost to view.

lot A contiguous parcel of land used or set aside for use as the site of one or more buildings or other definite purpose.

lot coverage Usually refers to a measure of intensity of land development by examining the land area of a site that is **impervious**.

lot frontage That part of a lot contiguous (in control) with a street, easement, etc.

lot line The defined property boundary on the land.

louver An assembly of sloping, overlapping blades or slats often used in overhead structures outdoors to allow some sun to reach a surface below and prevent some (or all sun at a particular time of day) from reaching that surface. They are also used in fences to allow light and air while providing some screening. *See also* **abat-vent**.

low bid In analyzing a number of bids submitted, this is the one that proposes to perform the required work or provide the materials at the lowest price compared to the other bids.

low-carbon steel Steel comprised of less than 0.20% carbon.

low-density concrete Concrete with an oven-dry weight of less than 50 pounds per cubic foot (800 kg/m^3).

lowest responsible bidder *or* **lowest responsive bid** *or* **lowest qualified bidder**
The bidder with the lowest price that meets all requirements of the bid, which may include licensing, bonding, experience, proper forms, correctly filling out forms, and so on.

low-flow irrigation *See* **micro-irrigation**.

low hazard According to the National Standard Plumbing Code, a situation in which a backflow of water in a system would be a nuisance or objectionable, but not a health hazard.

low-head drainage The drainage flow of water left over in pipe and equipment through a low elevation sprinkler head (or heads) after a valve is turned off.

low-pressure mercury lamp A **mercury-vapor lamp** that obtains no more than 0.001 **atmosphere** during operation.

low-voltage lighting This is usually an outdoor lighting system with **luminairies** that operate on low voltage converted from single phase (120 **volt**s) or sometimes supplied by solar **photovoltaic** collectors with batteries for storage.

low-voltage wire In irrigation systems using **solenoid**s on valves, operated by low-voltage electricity (24 **volt**s drawing 2.3 to 10 **amp**s), the wire associated with such a system is referred to as low-voltage wire.

LPS   Abbreviation for **low-pressure sodium**.

L.S.   Abbreviation for lump sum.

LT, lt   On drawings, abbreviation for **light**.

LULU   Abbreviation for locally unwanted land use. This phrase is often used with regard to proposed development projects heavily opposed by local residents.

lumber   Parts of logs (woody portions of trees); any wood that is split or sawed. It is prepared for use in construction, building, etc., and is usually thought of as smaller than **timbers** and larger than wood pieces.

lumen   A unit of luminous flux. One **footcandle** is a measure of one lumen per square foot on a surface.

luminaire   A complete light fixture for attachment to electrical wiring including the bulb or tube for production of light, any reflectors, housings, and any decorative embellishments.

luminance   The luminous intensity of a surface.

luminosity   The ration of light expressed in lumens per watt.

lump-sum agreement   A contract to complete work for a set amount agreed upon before the work begins.

lunate   In botanical descriptions, crescent-shaped.

lustrous   In botanical descriptions, shiny or shining.

L.V.   Abbreviation for low voltage.

lyrate   In botanical terms, lyre-shaped. It can be an **obovate** or **spatulate pinnatifid** leaf with the end **lobe** large and roundish and the lower lobes small.

M

M, m **1.** Abbreviation for thousand. **2.** Abbreviation for male. **3.** Abbreviation for man-hour. **4.** Abbreviation for **meter**(s). **5.** Abbreviation for **mile**(s). **6.** On drawings, an abbreviation for **bending moment**. **7.** A mix of masonry **mortar** having 1 part cement, ¼ part hydrated lime, and an amount of water equal to 2 to 3 times the sum of their volume of cement and lime. It is for highly compressive and lateral loads, able to withstand frost action, and useful in below grade applications. *See also* **mortar** type **S** and **N**.

m³ Cubic meter(s) or 1.307 cubic yards.

machine bolt A metal bolt with a flattened end, threaded for accepting a nut with like threads, and the other end having a flat top and flattened sides (square shaped or hexagonal shaped) to accept a wrench for tightening. It is flat on the underside of the head, and its head has no indents for accepting a screwdriver. Threads on the shank may extend the entire length or for only a portion of its length.

machine bolts

macrescent In plant identification and descriptions, withering and persistent.

macroclimate A fairly uniform weather history over a large geographical area.

macronutrient Any of the three (**nitrogen, phosphorus, potash**) most essential nutrients for plant growth. These nutrients are usually listed (showing percentage of each) on fertilizer bags in the order NPP.

macrophyte Macroscopic (visible to the eye without assistance) vascular plants.

macropore A space or void between structural portions of **soil** that can contain water when soil is saturated, but is large enough or of a particular composition to allow water to freely drain by gravitational force and to become filled with air when at **field capacity** (there is moisture in the soil, but it no longer freely drains). Their minimum size is approximately 0.03 mm. (Compare with **mesopores** and **micropores**.)

maculate In plant identification and descriptions, spotted or blotched.

maggots Larvae of a variety of flies.

magnesium A whitish-silver metallic element common (eighth most common on earth) in soils and a necessary **micronutrient** for plants. It is found in chlorophyll molecules of plants as it assists in an electrochemical role during **photosynthesis** and also assists the plant structurally.

magnesium sulfate A colorless crystalline substance found in nature or manufactured and otherwise known as Epsom salts; used in making cements and fertilizers. It is approximately 10% **magnesium** and 14% **sulfur**.

magnetic bearing

magnetic bearing A line referencing from local magnetic north as found on a compass and changing over great latitudinal distances.

magnetic declination The angle, usually expressed in degrees, from **magnetic north** to **true north**.

magnetic north The direction a compass that points from a specific location to magnetic north. This direction is not the same as **true north**. True north may be found if one knows the **magnetic declination** angle for a location.

mailbox A box used to facilitate mail delivery.

mailbox

mailbox

main connection The point where a sprinkler system is connected to the city or public water line.

main line A pipe line in a **sprinkler system** that distributes water from a source to **valves**. Also

known as a **pressure line**. (Compare with **lateral line**.)

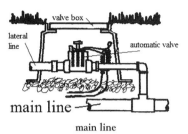

main line

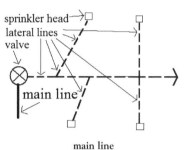

main line

main sewer A sewer line into which sewer branches dispense materials.

maintained Preserved in a condition or state of quality equivalent to that which was designed, constructed, or used in the past.

maintenance Upkeep of land, structures, plants, machinery, equipment, systems, etc. It includes but is not limited to mowing, weeding, tilling, pruning, sweeping, and replacement of defective parts in a manner that does not alter the basic design.

makeup water In irrigation, water supplied to compensate for losses by **evaporation** and leakage.

male A pipe **fitting** or device that either has outside threads or is an unflared pipe end, or a device with a protrusion of the appropriate size for acceptance into a **female** socket (glued, threaded, or compression tightened, etc). This is

218

the normal method for connection of pipes or devices.

male thread Pipe threads on the outside of a pipe or device. (Compare with **female thread**.)

mall A plaza, walk, or system of walks, often lined with trees and designed for pedestrian uses.

mallet A short-handled wooden or plastic headed hammer.

malm A **calcereous** soil with much chalk as fine particles.

management allowed depletion (MAD) With regard to scheduling of plants or landscapes, the maximum amount of plant-available water (expressed as a percent) that is allowed to be removed from the **soil** before **irrigation** occurs.

manganese A **micronutrient** necessary in soil for plants to grow that in excess can also cause their ill health. It is seldom lacking in soil (except **alkaline** soils) and becomes more soluble, more available, and more likely to cause toxicity as soil **acid**ity increases. If acidity is 5.5 or below, plant toxicity due to manganese is likely in many plants. In alkaline soils, manganese availability is reduced as is solubility of materials containing this nutrient.

manganese steel A very hard, brittle steel with 11 to 14% manganese and 1.5% carbon.

manhole **1.** A concrete vault, usually with a heavy cast-iron lid, capable of being driven over by vehicles. Manholes provide access for maintenance of sewers, water line devices, electrical equipment, etc. **2.** An access hole through which a person can gain access to an underground or enclosed structure. It usually is round with a heavy cover made of cast-iron. They are used for entering a utility vault (usually underground) or something similar.

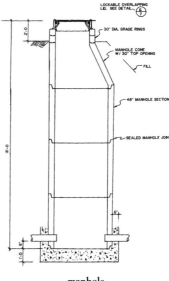

manhole

man-hour **1.** One worker toiling or persisting at a task for one hour. **2.** The work accomplished by a worker in one hour. **3.** A unit of measurement for scheduling or estimating costs of work and various tasks by using an average of the amount of work that one person can complete (on average) in one hour.

manifold A series of valves placed together with associated **fittings** and connections.

manlift A mechanical device used for lifting workers and materials, either on a boom that hydraulically extends, or on scissor lifts.

Manning formula A formula used to determine the velocity of flows of streams or pipes useful in engineering sizes of channels and pipes.

mantis *or* **mantid** *See* **praying mantis**.

manual angle valve A valve for adjusting, turning on, or turning off a flow. This type of valve is configured with its water outlet oriented 90° from its water inlet. It delivers water on a 90° angle from the direction of water entering it.

manual bleed

manlift

key handle

threaded outlet

cutaway section

manual angle valve

manual bleed On an **automatic valve** that is normally closed, a small device on the valve which if turned enough will allow a bit of water to escape, triggering the valve to open and allowing water to flow through the valve into the downstream piping. The small amount of water that escapes (bleeds) through the bleed valve to the outside water system while in operation is how it got its name. This is useful on an automatic sprinkler valve as it allows one to open the valve and operate sprinklers without accessing the **automatic controller**. It is useful when testing the valve for operation because of lack of response from **sprinkler controller** operation, or when repairing sprinklers and flushing lines.

manual drain A drain valve of various styles and types, useful in a sprinkler system where it is manually opened or closed (by hand or with a valve key) to allow water to drain from a pipe. It is useful at low points on sprinkler pipes in temperate climates to prevent damage to pipes, fitting, etc. from freezing when full of water. (Compare with **automatic drain**.)

manual operation Operated by hand instead of automatically. Sprinkler controllers have this option. Some sprinkler control valves are operated only by hand, but nearly all today are automatically operated with an option for manual operation (hand operation) by opening a bleed valve or by unscrewing some other part of the valve such as a **solenoid**.

manual system *or* **manual sprinkler system** A **sprinkler system** that requires **manual operation** by turning on and off valves by turning a handle, knob, etc. by hand or with a **sprinkler key**.

manual drain valve

manual valve   A valve (ball, angle, etc.) operated by hand or with a key that will allow one to turn on, or off, or adjust the flow of water. They were common in the operation of sprinkler zones before automatic valves became available. They are still used as drains on irrigation systems, allowing one to drain the system by opening the valve to prevent freezing. A manual **sprinkler system** is operated by these valves. Before **sprinkler system**s had the option for automatic operation, most sprinkler systems used **manual angle valves** that have a cross handle on top allowing one to slide a **sprinkler key (manual valve key)** over its intersection point and turn the valve off (closed) or on (open) while standing. These valves were usually brass and many are still in operation. They are still commercially available and used occasionally, usually as a necessity where there is no electrical service, or in replacement of existing manual valves.

manual valve key   A key as described in **manual valve** for turning off and on a particular type of sprinkler valve.

manual sprinkler valve key

manure   Generally the refuse from stables, turkey farms, and cattle yards, including both animal excrements and straw or other litter. It may be too high in nitrogen or ammonia until composted.

marble   A hard metamorphic rock or **limestone** that can be sawn into slabs, takes a high polish, and is often veined or irregularly colored by impurities. It is often used in statues, benches, cladding of structures, etc.

margin   In botanical terms, the edge of a **leaf** or **leaflet**.

marginal   In botanical terms (especially in describing leaves), the edge or around the edge.

marginal plants   Plants that grow partially submerged or in shallow water.

marginal shelf   An underwater shelf created for **marginal** plants.

maritime   In botanical terms, plants growing near the ocean or the seacoast and so influenced by salt water.

marker   **1.** A term (derived from Magic Marker) for felt-tipped pens of various colors and widths often used in coloring drawings especially before computers became so useful in this work. **2.** A plaque, monument, sign, flag, stake, or label that identifies a historic site, a surveyed line or corner, or a significant natural feature, etc.

marl   A naturally occurring soil **amendment** of **lime** with **clay** or with **silt** sometimes used in place of lime to raise the **pH** of **acid soils**. It is not as effective as lime unless applied in greater amounts to the soil.

marsh   A wetland dominated by monocotyledons (cattails, grasses) or other herbaceous **emergent** plant material.

masking tape   An adhesive-backed paper tape used in masking areas before painting.

masonry   **1.** Anything constructed with mortar holding pieces (clay, stone, brick, glass) together. **2.** The art and craftsmanship of placing and building structures with stone, brick, concrete block, etc.

masonry anchor   **1.** A metal device with an opening for accepting a threaded bolt or screw to firmly anchor elements to masonry. It is placed in masonry when masonry is formed, or it is drilled and pounded into masonry afterwards. **2.** A metal piece nailed to wood backing or mortared into a masonry back wall for attaching face masonry (brick, stone, etc.).

masonry cement

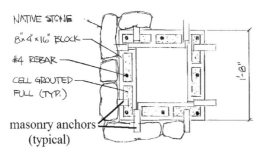

NATIVE STONE
8"x4"x16" BLOCK
#4 REBAR
CELL GROUTED FULL (TYP.)
masonry anchors (typical)

masonry column (plan view section)

masonry cement   Cement used in mortar.

masonry course   A horizontal row of masonry units in a wall.

masonry drill   A rotating, electrically powered drill with a bit suitable for making holes in masonry.

masonry nail   A hardened-steel, small nail with a fluted shank used for fastening items to masonry.

masonry unit   A natural or man-made building unit of stone, burnt clay, etc.

mason's hammer   A heavy-headed hammer with one face for pounding and the other side of the head shaped much like a chisel.

masonwork   See **masonry**.

mass balance   A balanced input and output of product in an ecological system or area.

mass movement   See **landslide**.

mass retaining wall   A **gravity wall**.

mass transfer   In **phytoremediation**, the conveyance of liquids, gases, or solid materials from one location to another, such as from groundwater to plant or from soil to plant.

mast arm   A piece of a lamp pole between the **luminaire** and the pole. It attaches to the pole and holds the luminaire (light fixture) over an area to illuminate it.

master plan   See **comprehensive plan**.

MASTERSPEC   A proprietary example or model of specifications for construction work produced by the American Institute of Architects and often used by the construction industry as a base for modifying to a specific job.

master switch   A single switch controlling supply of electricity to an entire site, project, structure, or building.

master valve   In irrigation, a valve that turns off water to the main line until irrigation is to occur and then turns water off at the conclusion of irrigation. With an automatic irrigation design using a master valve, one must make certain that a controller has a wire connection point for a master valve in order to operate it automatically.

mastic   **1.** A thick, putty-like substance used to seal between loosely fit concrete pieces, such as segments of a manhole placed atop another. It often comes in preformed thick strips covered with a protective paper or plastic strip that is stripped away as it is applied. **2.** A coating used on thermal insulation to make it more durable, especially to weather conditions.

matchboards   Boards that have a formed, raised bump along the length of one edge and a corresponding groove along the other length of edge. This allows them to be placed together (one inserted into the other) side-by-side to make a tight, strong fit. Also called **tongue-and-groove**, or **dressed and matched** boards.

matched precipitation   In irrigation, sprinkler heads under the same water pressure having flow rates proportional to the area of coverage. The area of coverage is dependant upon arc, radius (or length of throw), or pattern. In matched precipitation, one quarter-circle head

222

will allow to flow (gpm) one quarter the water that a full-circle head will allow to flow (gpm). This is usually achieved by using the same head with nozzles appropriately selected. In order for this matching of nozzles to be useful and assure matched precipitation over an area of irrigation, sprinkler heads must be placed to achieve **head-to-head coverage**. This condition assists in obtaining a more uniform and even distribution of water without wet and dry spots. For water conservation, this is important because when precipitation rates are not matched, one must water longer to assure adequate water to areas receiving less water.

matched precipitation rate   **1.** A system or zone in which all heads have similar **precipitation rate**s and are spaced with **head-to-head coverage**. **2.** Sprinkler heads and nozzles matched with flow rates proportional to the area of coverage. *See* **matched precipitation**).

matched roof boards   Boards used in roofing that are matchboards.

matched siding   *See* **drop siding**.

material safety data sheets   According to **OSHA**, detailed information prepared by a manufacturer or importer of a chemical that describes the physical and chemical properties, physical and health hazards, routes of exposure, precautions for safe handling and use, emergency and first aid procedures, and control measures.

mat foundation   A thick, reinforced concrete slab used instead of wall or column footings or foundations to support and distribute the load of a structure to a soil having low-bearing capacity.

matrix   **1.** Within a landscape **mosaic**, the background of ecosystems or land uses charac-

terized by a large area within a **mosaic** with high **connectivity**. **2.** With regard to **mortar** or **cement**, the material in which **aggregate** or **sand** is embedded.

maturation region   The area of a root characterized by the formation of root hairs arising from the root epidermis or from the cortex. This area becomes the **absorption** zone and is highly structured, accommodating the flow of water, nutrients, and vascular tissues. The water and nutrients are transported to the other parts of the plant from this region.

mature soil   A soil containing **A horizon**, **B horizon**, and a **C horizon**.

maturing   The process of hardening mortar, plaster, concrete, etc.

maturity   **1.** A plant that has reached its maximum size. **2. Organic matter** that has reached a point in decomposition in which it will not inhibit plant growth by robbing **nitrogen** through further decomposition.

matutinal   In plant identification and descriptions, of the morning or opening and functional in the morning.

maul, mall   A heavy-headed, short-handled hammer made of wood. *See also* **mallet** or **beetle**.

MAX, max.   Abbreviation for maximum.

maximum acceptable pressure   The highest pressure that the weakest component can withstand without damage, or without premature wearing and eventual failure of the component.

maximum demand   **1.** The greatest flow of water (or waste discharge) for all the fixtures, heads, outlets, etc. in a pipe system. This is usually for a specific time or the time of most use (most water flow). **2.** The most electricity required or expected in a system usually for a specific time.

maximum diameter solids With regard to **pumps**, the largest solid the pump can pass without clogging, or jamming.

maximum run time The amount of time a sprinkler can operate on a particular soil and vegetation type before it exceeds its infiltration rate into the soil. Each soil has a basic intake rate, and when exceeded, the extra water must run off the surface. This rate is expressed in inches per hour (clay, 0.10; silty clay, 0.15; clay loam, 0.20; loam, 0.35; sandy loam, 0.40; loamy sand, 0.50; sand, 0.60) can be divided by the **precipitation rate** and multiplied by 60 (to convert to minutes) for the maximum amount of time that sprinklers in an area with a specific soil type should be run to avoid **runoff**.

maximum size of aggregate With regard to concrete, the largest aggregate particles within the mix in sufficient quantity so as to affect the mix. This is usually determined by sieve size. It is common to allow about 5 to 10% of the concrete's weight to be made of this size.

maximum working pressure The maximum pressure at which piping materials and devices are safe to use.

maze *or* **planting maze** A fanciful planting scheme designed with a much contrived tortuous path between hedges with dead ends and many splits in the path making it difficult for one to find a way through the area on the path.

mbf Abbreviation for thousand board feet.

m.b.m., MBM In the lumber industry, abbreviation for thousand board measure (feet).

MC, mc **1.** Abbreviation for moisture content. **2.** Abbreviation for metal-clad.

MC asphalt Abbreviation for medium-curing asphalt.

mcf Abbreviation for thousand cubic feet.

MCM Abbreviation for thousand circular mills. *See* **wire size**.

meadow An area predominated by grasses or forbs and often associated with wildflowers. They are mostly thought of as openings in woods or forests, and have few if any trees within their area. Some seed companies have a seed mix they call by this name with plants common to such areas.

meager lime With regard to lime for mortaring, a low-purity lime containing 15% impurities or more.

mealybugs Scaly insects of the family *Pseudococcidae* having a white powdery covering. They have an oval-shaped body, with soft white plates that have the white cotton-like covering. Unlike most scales, these bugs can move, but very slowly. They can cause stunting or death of plants by sucking plant juices. One may find that if they have infested for a time there can be a black, sooty mold growing on the honeydew they secrete. Ants often feed on the honeydew. Spray plants off every two weeks or so to knock them off or use an insecticidal soap. Indoors they can be controlled by wiping with a cotton swab soaked in rubbing alcohol. Natural predators are ladybugs and lacewings.

meander A bend or loop in a water course; or a water course that bends and turns.

mean gradient Average **slope**.

measuring chain *See* **chain**.

mechanical connection Attachment of two or more elements with fasteners such as bolts, rivets, or screws, instead of with glue, or welding.

mechanical controller A sprinkler controller that has manual switches, dials, knobs, pins, etc. for setting irrigation control. (Compare with **digital controller**.)

mechanical joint With regard to pipe connections, a joint tightened with nuts and bolts. Some incorrectly refer to any pipe not glued at its joints as a mechanical joint.

mechanical pencil An instrument that clamps down its narrow, cylindrical drawing material when in use and can allow the drawing material's extension as it is used up in drawing or writing.

mechanic's lien A legal encumbrance placed upon a property by a contractor or one supplying goods and services that requires contracted labor or materials not paid for by an owner to be paid in full before the property is free and clear for sale to anyone. Mechanic's liens can be used to force the sale of a property to satisfy the lien and pay the debts.

median That portion of a divided highway separating lanes of traffic that is raised, landscaped, or left natural.

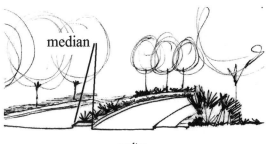

median

medio-variegated A term descriptive of leaves having a lighter center than the color of the **margin**.

medium-duty scaffold A scaffold capable of carrying a working load not in excess of 50 lb/sq ft (245 kg/sq m).

medium sand Sand with particles ⅟₂₅₀ to ⅟₅₀ in.

medullary ray *or* **pith ray** Horizontal tissues or tubes extending from the pith of a tree to the outer portions of the **stem** or **trunk**. These spaces are used to store and transport food.

megagram The measurement of 1,000,000 **gram**s.

membrane **1.** In construction work, a water-resistant or waterproof material or combination of materials used in water features, on flat roofs, around the outside of foundations, etc. **2.** In botanical references, a very thin covering or sheet separation.

membranous In botanical terms, a texture of a membrane that is thin, rather soft, and more or less translucent.

memorial park A cemetery.

MER Abbreviation for mechanical equipment room.

meristem Plant tissue that divides to produce new cells. Shoot or root tips have **meristematic regions** at their tips.

meristematic region The area of the root characterized by cell differentiation and little absorption.

mesh In construction work, usually a fabric of steel.

mesic **1.** Characterized by, relating to, or requiring a moderate amount of moisture. **2.** A temperate or moist **microclimate** that is not **xeric** or **hydric**.

mesocarp In the fruit of some plants, the middle layer of the **pericarp**.

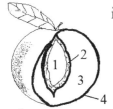

is the fleshy portion

1 seed
2 endocarp ⎤
3 mesocarp ⎟ pericarp
4 exocarp ⎦

peach (cutaway illustration)

mesocarp

mesopores   The pores in **soil** filled with water between **field capacity** and **wilting point**. *See also* **micropores** and **macropores**.

mesotrophic   Used in reference to a moderate amount of nutrients in water.

metal halide lamp   A lamp that uses an electric current to produce a light from a metal vapor such as mercury or sodium.

metal leaf   A thin coating of silver, gold, etc. to improve the appearance of a material.

metallophytes   Plants that preferentially colonize in soils rich with metals.

metal-organic complex   *See* **chelate**.

metastability   *See* **conditional stability**.

meter, metre (m)   An International Standard measurement unit of length equal to 39.37 in or 10 **dm**s.

metes and bounds   Description of property (land parcels) using measurements of distances and bearings in delineating and establishing edges, boundaries, or limits.

methyl bromide   A chemical **soil sterilant** often sold in cans under pressure. This is a dangerous gas that must be used and handled with care.

metre   *See* **meter**.

metric ton (t)   A metric weight of 1000 kilograms, 1,000,000 grams, 1.102 U.S. tons (short tons), or about 2205 pounds.

metropolitan planning organization   A local government having legal jurisdiction over a city area for land planning, transportation, and land uses.

metropolitan statistical area   An area established by the Bureau of Census for a county with a central city or adjoining central cities totaling 50,000 or more in population, and the surrounding suburbs that are strongly linked economically and socially.

Mg   Abbreviation for **megagram**(s).

mg   Abbreviation for **milligram**(s).

mgph   Abbreviation for thousand gallons per hour.

mh, m.h.   **1.** Abbreviation for **manhole**. **2.** Abbreviation for **metal halide**. **3.** Abbreviation for **man-hour**.

m/hr, m.h.   Abbreviation for man-hour.

mi²   Abbreviation for **square mile**(s).

micro-   A Greek prefix, meaning small, or male, often used in botanical terms.

microclimate   A reference to a fertilizer that is hardened into the shape of a stake so that it may be forced into the ground. It decomposes, and some materials leach, acting much the same as a **fertilizer tablet**. Any change in climatic conditions such as wind, sunlight/shade, temperature, humidity, etc. in a relatively small, distinctly different area or locality, as affected by man-made or natural elements such as buildings surrounding a city street, a hill protecting from wind or hot late afternoon sun, plants affording shade, a water body affording an increase in humidity, etc. Microclimates are created on each side of a building facing a different direction, or in areas protected by trees, or in a building's courtyard.

microclimate factor (K_{mc}) In irrigation auditing, a factor used to compute water needs. The average landscape has a factor of 1. A landscape with shade or wind protection is less than 1. A landscape surrounded by buildings, paved surface, fences, etc. will have a factor higher than 1 with higher water needs.

micro-irrigation *or* **low-flow irrigation** *or* **low-volume irrigation** A term used in reference to application of irrigation water at very low rates. The flow from each emission device is usually measured in gph (gallons per hour) rather than gpm (gallons per minute). Advantages of this irrigation over rotary or spray irrigation are water conservation (reduction in evaporation, loss to wind, less runoff, only essential areas covered), pipe size and strength requirements are reduced, weed growth between plants is reduced, system operation does not interfere with normal use of the land, reduced liability (no water on walks and driveways), less erosion on steep slopes, and no spray is allowed on building or fences when irrigation occurs at their base. Disadvantages are that they are high maintenance (small passageways may become clogged, filters must be cleaned), limited application (not for lawns and some plants), filtration and pressure devices are required, surface pipes or emission devices are subject to damage, no visible water leads to lack of user confidence, and users may not notice any poor operations.

micronutrient **1.** A trace element. **2.** An organic compound required for biological growth in relatively low quantities compared to the major growth nutrients. Example of micronutrients are **molybdenum, copper, boron,** cobalt,

iron, iodine, **manganese, zinc,** and **chlorine.** Many commercial fertilizers contain micronutrients. They may or may not be listed on a package with the **macronutrient**s. If they are applied in excess, some can be toxic.

microorganism An organism (plant or animal) such as bacteria, **algae, fungi,** or **virus**es too small to be seen with unaided vision.

micropores The smallest pores or gaps in a soil identified as those that, after rain, are still filled with water when a soil reaches **wilting point.** They are small enough and the water is held tight enough that it cannot be drawn out by plant roots. (Compare with **mesopores** and **macropores.**)

micropropagation The **propagation** of plants using tissue in a test tube or other container.

micro-spray, microspray Distribution of water to plants by very small spray devices on low pressure.

micro-sprinkler A sprinkler operated at low pressure, with a small distribution pattern.

midge Tiny two-winged flies sometimes called punkies or no-see-ums. Their larvae can cause plant **galls** as they tunnel into tissue.

midrib The midvein or the middle or main rib of a **leaf** or **leaflet.**

mildew A whitish **fungal** growth appearing on decaying organic matter or on **plant material,** etc. *See also* **powdery mildew** and **downy mildew.**

mild steel An iron made with a minimal amount of carbon (0.15 to 0.25%) that is often used in tanks and other areas where rust resistance is important.

mile (m) A measurement of 5280 ft.

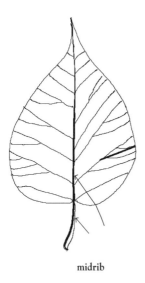

midrib

milky disease A bacterial infection that kills Japanese beetles and grubs that may be applied to lawns to control them.

mill construction Heavy timber works.

milligram (mg) The metric weight measurement of 0.001 **gram**s or 0.015 grains.

milliliter The metric measurement equal to 0.001 l or 0.061 in³.

millimeter (mm) The metric length measurement of one thousandth of one meter (0.001m), or 0.039 of an inch.

milling **1.** The processing of stone, or applying various cutting or shaping techniques to finished stone. **2.** The process of dressing a surface of metal with rotary cutters to produce a desired surface.

millipede A cylindrical, hard-shelled myrioped 1 to 2 in long and coiled when at rest and having two pairs of legs on each body segment. They generally only feed on dead or decaying material.

mill run Ungraded and uninspected products from a mill.

millwork Wood products made at a wood-planing mill ready for use as moldings, cabinets, door frames, etc.

min. Abbreviation for minute or minimum.

mineralization The conversion of an element from an organic form to an inorganic state as a result of microbial decomposition.

mineral soils Soils in which the mineral component predominates.

mineral spirit *or* **petroleum spirit** A flammable thinner obtained in petroleum distillation often used in paints and varnishes.

mini-excavator A small **trackhoe** useful for digging in small areas and for trenching.

mini-excavator

minimalist design A type of design where the use of decorative elements, including ornamentation and color, is kept to a minimum.

minimum acceptable pressure The lowest water pressure satisfactory for operation at the most hydraulically remote fixture or component in a piping system.

minor change   A change in construction work not involving an adjustment in the **contract sum** or **contract time**.

misalignment sensing probe   A device mounted in the casing of a pump **impeller** that monitors its wear and separation so that when it is worn it can be replaced before serious damage occurs.

MISC, misc.   Abbreviation for miscellaneous.

mission tile   A curved, red-clay roofing tile laid in courses, with adjacent tiles having their convex side laid alternately up and down. *See* **Spanish tile**.

mister   A device delivering a very fine spray or almost fog of water.

mite   A small arachnid that sucks plant juices. There are many varieties causing disease with a variety of symptoms on plants. Most are difficult to see with the unaided eye, but the damage is visible in striped leaves and small webs, especially on undersides of leaves.

miter box   A channel with grooves for guiding a handsaw at the proper angle in making a miter joint.

miter joint   An angled joint where two members meet.

miter, mitre   A beveled end or edge.

mitigation   Any option that will decrease the impact (negative or positive) of an action or occurrence on the natural or human environment. This is a practice that ameliorates environmental impact by replacement, restoration, or enhancement of functional values. In changes on the land, this refers to efforts to prevent, avoid, minimize, compensate for, or replace damaged land, water, air, plants, wildlife, economic impacts, social impacts, etc.

mitigation banking   With regard to wetland mitigation, accumulating acreage credits through replacement enhancement, restoration, or preservation of wetlands to be applied toward compensation for filling other wetlands as may be required by government agencies.

mixed bud   A bud that produces both flowers and leaves such as with a leafy branch having one or more flowers.

mixer   *See* **concrete mixer**.

mlf   Abbreviation for thousand linear feet.

mm   Abbreviation for **millimeter**(s).

moat   A broad, deep, usually water-filled trench surrounding a property or area.

model   **1.** A usually three-dimensional representation at a small scale of a full-scale project for purposes of study or to illustrate construction. **2.** A pattern of something intended to be reproduced. **3.** In land analysis, any method of problem solving.

moderately well-drained soils   Soils in which water is removed somewhat slowly, therefore, the soil profile is wet for a small but significant portion of time.

modification   **1.** A written amendment to **contract documents**. **2.** A **change order**.

modulus of rupture   A measure of the load-carrying capacity of a **beam** being expressed as the ration of the bending moment at rupture to the section modulus of the beam.

modulus of toughness   The amount of energy per unit volume absorbed by a structural material when subject to shock or impact without fracture.

moellon   Filling between stone facing walls made of stone rubble.

mold   A fungus on dead or living material.

molding In construction of structures, long decorative pieces added at edges, corners, etc. as an embellishment.

mole **1.** A long, metal, bullet-shaped, enclosed tube with an internal manner that is driven by forced air through a connected nose. It is used to hammer its way under pavements to provide paths for pipes, wires, etc. **2.** Burrowing insectivores (family *Talpidae*) with tiny eyes, concealed ears, soft fur, short forelegs pointing outward, flattened hands, and claws for digging. They primarily eat earthworms, larvae, and bugs, but will occasionally eat roots and nibble on greens. Tunneling near the surface can sever roots, heave plants, and damage lawns. Their tunnels are usually about 5 to 11 in underground and exits frequently are a raised saucer of earth with a depressed center where a hole may be visible. Trapping seems to be the most effective way of preventing damage from moles.

molybdenum A **micronutrient** necessary for plant growth. It allows the reduction of nitrates in plants. Symptoms of a lack of it in plants are interveinal **chlorosis**, stunting, and general plant paleness. It may be lacking in soils that are highly **acidic** (low **pH**). Raising the pH with lime generally assists in making it available unless it has been leached out.

moment A commonly used term for the more descriptive expression of **bending moment**. It is the force applied to a body tending to cause the body to rotate about a point or axis line. It is equal to the product of the force and the perpendicular distance of the point from the line of action of the force.

momentum The product of the mass of a body and its velocity.

monitor skylight A **skylight** on a roof ridge, or section of a roof.

monkey wrench A wrench with one fixed jaw and another movable jaw for grasping round objects.

monoammonium phosphate A fertilizer with 11% nitrogen and 48% phosphorus (11-48-0).

monocarpic **Plant material** that only **flowers** and fruits once and then dies. Some plants of this description live for many years.

monocot A shortened name for **monocotyledon**.

monocotyledon *or* **monocot** An **angiosperm** (division of flowering or seed plants) with seeds that have one **cotyledon** when they begin growth, and parallel veins in their leaves. *See also* **taxon**, **plant classification**, and **dicotyledon**.

monoecious Having both female and male reproductive organs on the same plant (**stamen**s and **pistil**s) in separate flowers. Examples are begonias and pines.

monolithic **1.** Shaped from a single block. **2.** Characterized by massiveness. **3.** Concrete cast in a single piece.

monomial With reference to a **scientific name** (**botanical name**), this means simply giving one portion of the name identifying a plant, usually the **genus** name. *See also* **binomial** and **trinomial**.

monomorphic A botanical term that means all alike in form.

monotypic Botanically this describes something of a single species or genus.

montmorillonite A common clay mineral that swells and becomes soft and greasy when wetted.

monument **1.** An object marking the corners, boundaries, or elevation of real property or establishing the location of a survey station. **2.** A stone, pillar, megalith, structure, building, etc. built in memory of the dead (as in a cemetery) or in commemoration of an event.

monument sign A relatively low sign with elements, features, and design causing it to appear as if it belongs to the landscape more than to the sky.

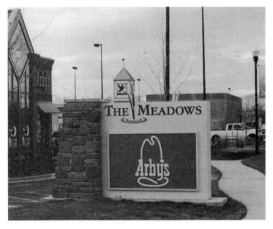

monument sign

moraine The material (**sand**, **gravel**, **cobble**, **boulder**s, etc.) carried and deposited by a glacier.

mormon board A metal plate attached to the teeth of a backhoe or trackhoe for grading soil smoothly without teeth marks in the soil.

morning glory *See* **bindweed**.

mortar A moldable mixture of cementatious material (**cement**, **lime**, **sand**, or water) used to secure **masonry unit**s, stone, brick, etc. after it hardens in place. It is used to cement items together, making them act as one masonry unit. **Mortar** must be of high quality when used outdoors to avoid moisture entering walls, low masonry strength, cracking, or disintegration of masonry. The best of mortar types for outdoor use are type **M**, **S**, and **N**. (Type **O** is not recommended for outdoor use.) Most mixtures generally have 1 part by volume of **Portland cement**, ¼ to 1 part by volume of hydrated lime, and a water amount not less than 2¼ to 3 times the sum of the volumes of cement and lime used.

mortar bed A thick layer of masonry mortar for setting a member or unit into.

mortise A hole, notch, or recess cut into a timber or other material.

mortise-and-tenon joint *or* **mortise joint** A joint between two members formed by fitting a **tenon** at the end of one member into a **mortise** in another member.

mosaic A repetition of **patch**es, **corridor**s, and **matrix** forming a pattern on a large area of land.

mosaic diseases Plant virus infections molting foliage and stunting plants.

mosquito Any of two-winged flies (*Culicidae*) with females able to puncture the skin of animals and suck blood. They are sometimes the carriers of serious diseases. They lay eggs on the surface of still water. The wiggly larvae live in water, and are eaten by fish. Prevent infestation by draining standing water or stocking with fish.

moth An insect much like a butterfly, but with wings usually proportionately smaller and usually with a duller color and stouter body. Their **larvae** eat plants.

mother plant A plant that is pollinated to create a hybrid seed.

motor grader A machine (usually diesel powered but sometimes towed) with a large blade usually mounted toward the middle of the machine used to move, scrape, or spread earth materials. Its adjustable blade makes leveling much easier.

mottled

motor grader

mottled A term used to describe spotted or discolored portions of leaves.

mound A **berm**; an area of raised ground.

mounded **1.** A description of an area of ground with an earthern mound or mounds. **2.** A descriptive term for ground covers (and some low **horizontal** shrubs), and grasses (or grass-like plants) that have a mounded form. In ground cover, mounded forms may be quite **prostrate**, but at the point of each plant center, the foliage is mounded higher. This form in grasses usually indicates a mounding form made of weeping foliage. The upper leaves cover the lower leaves. (Compare with **tufted, upright grasses, upright divergent grasses, upright arching grasses, arching**.) **3.** Any material or debris in a pile or heap.

mounded plant forms

mountable curb A low **curb** with a flat slope designed to be crossed easily by a vehicle.

moving lane Any traffic lane where traffic movement is the primary or sole function. (Compare with **parking lane**.)

mow **1.** To cut down or cut off plants, especially grass, to an even height. **2.** The hay storage area in a raised portion of a barn.

MPO Abbreviation for **metropolitan planning organization**.

MPR Abbreviation for **matched precipitation rate**.

mpt Abbreviation for male pipe thread.

MR Abbreviation for **mill run**.

MSA Abbreviation for **metropolitan statistical area**.

MSDS Abbreviation for **material safety data sheets**.

msf Abbreviation for thousand square feet.

muck **1.** Dark organically rich soil. **2.** Soft, moist, farmyard manure. **3.** Material removed in excavation. **4.** To clean up manure, mud, filth, etc.

mucronate In botanical terms, tipped with an abrupt short point. (Compare with **retuse, cuspidate, aristate, acuminate, acute, emarginate, obtuse**.)

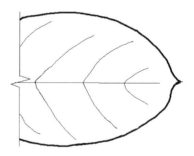

mucronate leaf tip

mucronulate A diminutive of **mucronate**.

mud **1.** Soil mixed with sufficient water to make it pliable. **2.** Masonry **mortar**.

mudflow The movement of a mass of weak, water-saturated soil downslope.

mulch **1.** A top dressing material spread over a planting bed, or around the base of a tree, usually made up of organic material (pine needles, shredded bark, hay, straw, grass clippings, etc.). Other materials used as mulch include crushed brick, crushed stone, river rock, cobble, and shredded newspapers. Mulch can be used to protect seed, plants, rhizomes, or bulbs from extremes in heat or cold, or from **erosion**. It can also be used to prevent weed germination, and when used for this purpose it is often placed over a **weed barrier fabric**. It may also be used for its aesthetic qualities, for moisture retention in the soil, to promote soil granulation, and to prevent the soil surface from becoming crusty. It is advantageous to pile mulch up around some herbaceous (or herbaceous-like) plants, but piling mulch against woody plants, tree **crown**s, or over the **root collar** is detrimental to the health of the plant. *See* **root collar** and **earthing up**. **2.** Organic material used in mixture with soil to produce a more favorable growing medium for plants. Roots growing from a soil mix into a surrounding soil usually face difficulty because of the **soil interface** where there is a change in soil consistency. Mulch also creates a soil more favorable to water retention, which can be helpful in retaining water for plants or detrimental in holding excess water because of the soil interface, promoting **root rot**.

mulching mower A lawn mower that cuts and then continues to chop lawn clippings as one mows, producing smaller pieces capable of decomposing faster in the lawn and assisting in preventing buildup of thatch.

mule A **hybrid** plant that is sterile.

mull A layer of forest soil rich in humus made of both organic matter and minerals.

multicapital A botanical term, many-headed.

multistem Plants that have several stems arising from the ground rather than one single stem.

multistem, single stem

municipal services Community services traditionally provided by local government entities such as water, sewer, roads, parks, schools, fire protection, police protection, etc.

muriate of potash *or* **potassium chloride** A **chemical fertilizer** with 48 to 62% potassium and about 15% sodium chloride. The salts can be damaging in some soils and to some plants. *See also* **potassium chloride**.

muricate A botanical term, beset with small, sharp projections, or a rough surface made of many sharp points.

mushroom compost A by-product of the mushroom industry that may be used as an **amendment** to soil, but should not be mixed at more than 50% by volume as it may contain toxic levels of accumulated salts. **Leaching** may be necessary.

mutant A plant with an inheritable change different from its parents that occurs in the genetics of the plant without external influence. It may be taller, shorter, more compact, hardier, hold its leaves longer, have larger flowers, a different colored flower, leaf, etc. These changes cannot be the result of soil conditions, disease, temperature, etc., but are actual changes in the genetics of the plant.

mutation In horticulture, a change in plant genes that produce offspring differing from the parent plant.

muticous   A botanical term, blunt without a spine.

mxm.   Abbreviation for male by male, which describes a nipple or other plumbing or irrigation device with outside threads on both of its ends.

mycelium   The mass of hyphae (branched filaments) produced by many fungi. This does not include the spore-bearing parts or organs of fungi.

mycorrhiza   A fungus that attaches to roots for a beneficial association. It unsheathes and attaches to roots with hyphae without apparent harm to the plant. Indeed with many plants it actually increases the effective diameter of the root and its absorptive surface. There is usually an enhanced nutrient and water absorption ability for the host plant. This is a symbiotic relationship where the fungus can decompose organic matter or absorb energy and nutrients for the plant in a manner that the plant cannot. Mycorrhiza also produces hormones having beneficial effects for the host plant. In return the mycorrhiza receives a steady supply of **photosynthate** from the host plant.

myd   Abbreviation for thousand yards.

Mylar   A thin, transparent plastic with a rough enough surface to be used for drafting or drawing upon.

N

N, n **1.** Abbreviation for north. **2.** The symbol for **nitrogen**. This is the first percentage listed on a **complete fertilizer** bag. **3.** Abbreviation for **nail**. **4.** A type of exterior **mortar** having 1 part by volume **Portland cement**, 1 part by volume hydrated lime, and water in the amount of 2¼ to 3 times the volume of cement and lime. It is mostly used for residential construction, masonry veneers, and interior construction. *See also* **mortar** types **M** and **S**.

NA, na **1.** Abbreviation for not available. **2.** Abbreviation for not applicable.

NAA Abbreviation for **naphthalene acetic acid**.

NAAMM Abbreviation for National Association of Architectural Metal Manufacturers.

nab The **strike plate** for a door bolt.

NAHB Abbreviation for National Association of Home Builders.

nail **1.** A slender, usually sharp, pointed fastener designed to be pounded into material for attachment of something. It holds better to material if it is pointed, but splits wood less if it is blunt. Those made of aluminum, stainless steel, or hot-dipped-galvanized steel are weather resistant. Those coated with zinc, cement, or other materials, or with spirals or rings formed in them, hold to the object they are pounded into much tighter. **2.** The act of pounding the fastener described in (1).

nailable concrete Concrete with lightweight aggregate, or sometimes also containing sawdust, into which nails can be driven easily.

nail claw An essentially straight, steel bar with a hooked, curved, or claw-like end with a flat tip and a slot in it. The slot is for fitting over a nail head and allows the nail to be pulled from material into which it has been driven. It is also useful in tearing apart structures, walls, etc. during demolition or remodeling. The flat tip can be driven between attached boards and used to pry them apart.

nail plate A metal plate fitting over two joining wood members having holes that allow nails to be driven through to secure the attachment of the two members.

nail punch A short, tapered, strong, steel tool with a slightly broadened top used to pound nails flush with a surface, or below a surface, or for marking a metal to start a drill bit in place.

nail stain A stain caused on a surface, which usually bleeds downward from the **nail** because the nail used was not weather resistant.

nailing strip A wood strip, attached to a surface as a base for attaching another material with nails.

naked A botanical term, a plant lacking various organs or appendages.

naked flooring The framework of flooring before floorboards are laid.

nanometer A measurable length of light wavelengths equal to 10^{-9} m or 10 angstroms (Å).

naphthalene acetic acid A synthetically produced **auxin**.

naphthenate A drying agent in paints that also includes lead, cobalt, calcium, or manganese salt.

napiform A botanical term that means turnip-shaped.

natatorium A swimming pool.

National Electrical Code A nationally (U.S.A.) accepted guide to safe installation of wiring along with its associated equipment.

National Electrical Manufacturers Association (NEMA) A trade group of electrical manufacturers providing standards of electrical construction and dimensional uniformity of equipment.

National Electrical Safety Code (NESC) Electrical rules prepared by the **NEMA** and approved by ANSI.

National Historic Landmark A historical marker or place of significance often with a structure, sign, kiosk, or expanded facilities explaining its significance to tourists.

National Register of Historic Places A U.S. government organization that maintains information on structures, objects, districts, and sites of national, state, or local historical significance.

National Resources Conservation Service (NRCS) A U.S. government agency, formerly known as the Soil Conservation Service (SCS) within the Department of Agriculture, providing leadership and administering programs to help people conserve, maintain, improve, and sustain natural resources and environment. It provides statistical information, maps, technical assistance, and funds soil conservation and farmland protection programs. NRCS has offices in all states and in most rural counties.

National Trust for Historic Preservation A nonprofit private organization chartered by the U.S. Congress to encourage preservation of historic buildings, objects, and sites in America. Address: 1785 Massachusetts Avenue, NW, Washington, DC 20036.

native plant **1.** A plant that can be found growing and reproducing without human assistance in an area. **2.** A plant that was found growing and reproducing in an area before recent (usually a point in time specified) human assistance in becoming established. Humans by nature have always moved seed from one location to another in clothing, food, domesticated animals, or their belongings, hence the necessity of specifying a time period.

native species Any species of living organisms that are found existing and reproducing naturally in a specific area. The difficulty is that nature rarely makes boundaries the same for living organisms, while most boundaries of states, counties, etc. are arbitrary in relation to ecosystems.

native vegetation Any indigenous plant adapted to soil and climatic conditions of an area.

natural-cleft A term used to describe stone split (cleaved) parallel to its stratification for an irregular, somewhat flat, surface.

natural convection Air or water movement due to differences in density resulting from variations in temperature causing movement or circulation.

natural drainage The flow of water over undisturbed existing surface topography of the earth.

natural environment The area surrounding a living organism including the area surrounding and influencing humans, but in most cases not including anything influenced by humans. This is because many believe humans are influenced by natural environment, but do not consider humans to be part of the natural environment. All organisms influencing the environment would include humans.

natural erosion The amount of erosion expected on undisturbed land, usually between 0.18 and 0.30 tons of earth per one acre per year. (Compare with **accelerated erosion**.)

natural features In terms of land, conditions produced by nature such as surface land forms, geology, slopes, vegetation, water, drainage patterns, aquifers, recharge areas, climate, microclimate, floodplains, aquatic life, wildlife, views, and **landscape ecological** patterns of **patch**, **corridor**, or **matrix**.

natural finish An application, varnish, water-repellent preservative, sealer, etc. that does not significantly affect the original color or grain, but often enhances and preserves the material to which it is applied.

natural grade The elevations and contours or land forms of the undisturbed natural surface of the ground of a site or land area.

naturalize Allowing a plant to reseed or spread with whatever random natural causes may affect its propagation and distribution in the landscape.

naturalized A plant that is thoroughly established and growing in an area, but originating from another area.

natural open space Land or water that is essentially unimproved.

natural sand A **sand** that is not crushed, but is the result of natural disintegration and abrasion of rock.

natural species Any species of organism natu-

rally found in an area. They may also include nonnative **species** of vegetation or wildlife that are adaptable to the climatic conditions of an area and are currently found living and propagating in an area without human assistance.

natural stone Rock from its native occurrence in the ground, not man-made imitation of rock as sometimes used in masonry.

natural ventilation Air movement within a greenhouse or building facilitating moving out stale air by natural forces, rather than by fans.

natural wetland A **wetland** that occurs naturally, without construction.

NBC, nbc Abbreviation for National Building Code.

NCM, ncm Abbreviation for noncorrosive metal.

necrosis A plant part that is dead and discolored.

nectary A descriptive botanical term referring to a plant's nectar-secreting gland that is usually a small pit or protuberance.

needle The slender, narrow, needle-like leaves of coniferous plants.

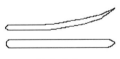

needle leaf shape

needle cast This disease of pine, fir, and spruce trees is caused by several fungi. Infected trees look scorched. It usually starts on lower branches with needles falling or sometimes leaving them with only green tips. Eventually it can kill the tree. Prevention is aided by avoiding poor drainage areas, and good air circulation around trees.

negative environmental impact Conse-quences in a realm involving interrelated or interdependent living things and their surround-ings having influences of a detrimental nature, or being influenced in a detrimental way. It is most often used in the context of an anthropo-morphic (human) cause of detrimental environ-mental changes, and focuses on the effects of those changes. However, what is viewed as a negative impact upon one element or organism may be a positive impact to another. *See* **envi-ronmental impact**.

needle foliage

negative impact *See* **negative environmental impact**.

negative-slump concrete A concrete mix having a **zero slump** before and after the addi-tion of water. *See also* **slump test**.

NEMA Abbreviation for National Electrical Manufacturers Association.

nematicide A pesticide used to control **nema-todes**.

nematode A microscopic, thread-like transpar-ent worm that feeds upon living and dead organic matter. Some are parasites that infest roots, bulbs, and leaves. These are the most abundant animals in the soil. They cause problems for arborists, agriculturists, nurseries, greenhouses, and new plantings. They are parasitic, in most cases living inside plant roots and usually deforming them. They extract cell contents, form knots, and galls on the roots of the host plant.

nemoral Of or pertaining to woods or groves.

neon lamp A cold-cathode glass tube lamp filled with gas. Some use neon gas and some have filters to control color. They are often used for sign lettering, etc.

neoprene A synthetic rubber with high resis-tance to sunlight and oil. It has been used for roof membranes, flashings, liners for water fea-tures, etc.

NEPA Abbreviation for National Environmen-tal Policy Act.

nerve In botanical terms, a vein (**nerve**), espe-cially a prominent longitudinal vein, of a leaf or other organ in a plant.

NESC Abbreviation for National Electrical Safety Code.

net acreage Gross acreage less any selected or necessary deductions of acreage in zoning land-planning computations.

net area *or* **net volume** The area or volume calculated with the omission of any portions not relevant, essential, or included as part of the area of concern.

net cross-sectional area With regard to masonry units, the gross cross-sectional area of a section through a unit not including empty **cores** or cellular spaces.

net cut With regard to earth-moving activities, the required **cut** of earthen material minus the required **fill** (if any) of material needed for a spe-cific project or site.

net fill With regard to earth-moving activities, the required earthen **fill** minus the required **cut** (if any) of a specific project or site.

net positive suction head (NPSH) *See* **net positive suction head available**.

net positive suction head available (NPSHA) The amount of pressure available for causing water to flow from its point of suction to the pump. It is calculated by taking the atmospheric pressure in feet at the elevation where the pump will be placed (33.9 ft at sea level) and then subtracting the following from it: the static height (in feet) of liquid below the pump centerline; the suction pipe friction loss (in feet of head); the entrance loss (in feet of head); the suction side miscellaneous loss (in feet of head); and the vapor pressure of water (at 60F, 0.2563 psi × 2.31 = 0.59 ft of head; this amount is almost insignificant but varies with temperature).

net positive suction head required (NPSHR) The **head pressure** necessary for a pump to be able to draw water from a source. It is usually indicated in feet. In selecting **centrifugal pump**s for irrigation or water features, it is helpful to know that as their flow or capacity increases, their NPSHR also increases. **Pump performance curves** charts supplied by manufacturers give the necessary NPSHR for the pump with variations in **impeller** diameter, etc.

net precipitation rate (NPR) A measure of the amount of water in a specific area of a sprinkler irrigation system that actually reaches the landscape. The net precipitation rate is the **gross precipitation rate** minus the losses to wind, evaporation, or interception, that occurs between the sprinkler nozzle and the landscape surface. It is necessary to use field **catch cans (catchment**s) to obtain this information. It may be calculated by multiplying the average catch volume, in cubic inches (or convert milliliters to cubic inches by multiplying by 3.66) and dividing it by the product of the amount of time sprinklers were run multiplied by the catch can (catchment) opening area in square inches.

net section A term used for the area of a cross section through a structural member including deductions for any holes in the area of the section. (Compare with **gross section**.)

net-veined In plant identification and descriptions, veins forming a network.

network In landscape ecology, an assemblage of interconnected corridors.

neutral With regard to horticulture, any substance or compound, natural or man-made, that has a **pH** of 7.0.

neutral flower In plant identification and descriptions, a flower with neither stamens nor pistils.

neutral soil A **soil** that has a pH value of 7.0 and so is neither acidic nor alkaline. Soil having a pH range from 6.6 to 7.3 is thought by many as neutral. In actuality, truly neutral soil has a pH of 7.0.

neutral wire The ground wire (**grounding conductor**) in an electrical system. It completes the return path of electricity to the source.

newel 1. The post around which a circular staircase winds. **2.** A taller post at the top or bottom of stairs assisting in supporting a handrail and often decorative.

new town Large planned communities with a pedestrian-friendly development pattern, and with open space connections and preservations. They generally are made up of community centers, housing, offices (or other employment opportunities), retail, recreation, open space, and public facilities.

NFC Abbreviation for National Fire Code.

NFPA Abbreviation for the National Fire Protection Association.

NGR stain *or* **non-grain-raising stain**   A liquid wood stain free of water with a base of alcohol or another solvent.

NIC   Abbreviation for not included in the contract.

niche   **1.** The area and materials needed by an organism for survival considering its habits and environment. **2.** A recess in a wall, usually masonry, that is often semicircular in plan view and sometimes contains an urn or sculpture.

nickel   A silver-colored metal alloy used with steel to assist in making it more resistant to corrosion and rust.

nickel steel   Steel made up of 3 to 5% nickel and 0.2 to 0.5% carbon.

nicotine sulfate   A broad spectrum botanical pesticide restricted in the United States because of its toxicity.

nidged ashlar *or* **nigged ashlar**   Stone having a surface with a sharp pointed tool.

NIMBY   Abbreviation for the phrase, not in my backyard. This phrase has been used in reference to those who do not want a particular activity or thing near where they live or spend time.

nippers   Hand cutters with jaws at the end used for cutting wire or thin metal rods.

nipple   A piece of pipe with threads on both ends for connecting threaded fittings or equipment.

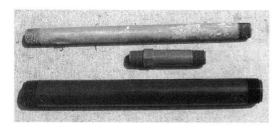

nipples

nit   A unit of **luminaire** equal to 1 **candela** per sq m.

nitrate of ammonia   Also known as ammonium nitrate, a chemical fertilizer that has 32.5 to 34% immediately available **nitrogen**. It must have ventilation or it can catch fire or explode. It cakes easily in storage.

nitrate of lime *or* **calcium nitrate**   This chemical **fertilizer** contains 15.5% immediately available **nitrogen**, and it slightly decreases soil acidity.

nitrate of potash *or* **potassium nitrate**   This **chemical fertilizer** contains about 13% immediately available **nitrogen**, and 44% water-soluble potash.

nitrate of soda *or* **sodium nitrate**   This compound chemical **fertilizer** contains about 16% immediately available **nitrogen**, and slightly increases **alkalinity**.

nitrification   In soils, the formation of nitrates and nitrites (forms available to plants) from ammonia (or ammonium compounds of **organic materials**) by microorganisms. Also, transformation through oxidation of ammonia nitrogen to nitrite or nitrate forms.

nitrogen   In **fertilizers**, the first percentage listed on a label. This is the nutrient most used by plants. They consistently need this nutrient to sustain growth. This nutrient is supplied in nature through dead plant and animal material decomposing and leaching into the soil.

nitrogen deficiency   A plant lacking the essential growing element of nitrogen. This can be recognized by smaller leaves, yellow leaves, and slow growth.

nitrogen fixation   The change of **nitrogen** into a compound useful to living things. There are three natural ways nitrogen may be made into a useful form fixed with other substances: (1) It is taken from the atmosphere at the time of lightening strikes by its electrical energy and changed to nitric oxide and nitrogen dioxide. It dissolves and comes to the earth as rain in a diluted form. (2) Certain **legume**-type plants through cooperation with bacteria (**rhizobia**) are able to convert atmospheric nitrogen into nitrogen compounds. (3) There is a metabolic assimilation of atmospheric nitrogen gas into ammonia or nitrogen compounds by soil organisms such as *Azotobacter chroococcum* and *Clostridium pasteurianum*.

nitrophoska   A compound **chemical fertilizer** containing approximately 12% **nitrogen**, 12% **phosphorus**, and 21% water-soluble **potash**.

nm   Abbreviation for **nanometer**.

nocturnal   With reference to plants, usually a flower that opens at night and closes during the day; or any plant part active or functional only at night.

node   **1.** In conceptual planning of outdoor spaces, a point of special interest or concentrated attention. This term is often used in landscape architectural planning of conceptual spaces. It assists in determining where to place a statue, or a plant of dynamic visual quality, or an area where people will gather. In corridor planning, it identifies a spot where paths, roads, trails, etc. intersect, creating interest and conflict for users. **2.** In electric wiring, a junction with several conductors intersecting and connecting. **3.** In framing, a point where members of a truss intersect. **4.** In botanical terms, the points on a stem where leaves are attached (or have been attached).

nodose   In botanical terms, knotty or knobby; used especially in describing roots.

nodule   A swelling in a leguminous root containing symbiotic bacterium (**bacteroid**s, **rhizobium**), assisting in fixing nitrogen. *See also* **nitrogen fixation**.

noggin piece   Filling between joints such as between logs in a cabin.

no-hub pipe   A pipe (usually cast-iron) fabricated without hubs or bell ends, joined to another section of pipe by a stainless steel or rubber fastener or coupler.

noise pollution   Continuous, annoying, or episodic excessive noise.

nomenclatural synonym   A name based on the same type plant specimen as another name (a plant with two common names).

nomenclatural type   In plant identification and descriptions, the individual specimen or other material on which a name is based, and to which the name is permanently attached.

nomenclature   To call a name. It is most often used in landscape work in reference to the botanical names given to plants. *See* **botanical name** and **Latin name**.

nominal diameter   A term used to call the size of a pipe, bolt, rivet, reinforcing, steel bar, or rod, not necessarily equal to the true diameter.

nominal dimension   A measure of a masonry unit with a dimension including the thickness of a mortar joint, in the United States, not exceeding ½ in (13 mm) added for the joint.

nominal pipe size   *See* **nominal size**.

nominal size   **1.** A reference to a piece of lumber's measurement before drying, seasoning, or planing for a smooth surface. A 2 × 4 does not actually measure 2 in by 4 in for this reason unless it is in its **rough sawn** state. *See* **dressed size**. **2.** A comparative reference to pipe size that is not actual dimensions. Pipes of the same nominal size have different wall thicknesses due to their material and pressure rating or schedule, but the outside diameter is the same in order to accept the same size **fittings**. The outside dimension of the pipe in actuality is often different from the nominal size. For example, a ½ in **PVC** pipe will have an outside dimension of 0.840 in and all ½ in PVC fittings will snugly fit that size. Also, a 2 in class 200 pipe will fit into the same fitting that a schedule 40 two-in pipe will fit into even though they have different wall thicknesses.

nominal strength   The strength of a structural member before the reduction by any strength-reduction factors.

noncombustible material   Any material that will not ignite, burn, or support combustion when subject to fire or heat.

nonferrous   Containing no (or very little) iron.

nonpoint source   Water pollution that does not originate from one point such as a pipe outfall.

nonpotable water   Water that is not fit for human consumption and has some form of contamination or lack of treatment.

non-return valve   A valve that allows fluid to flow in only one direction. *See also* **backflow preventer**.

nonselective herbicide   An herbicide that kills all plants that it contacts. It does not selectively allow any plant type to live. *See also* **selective herbicide**.

nonslip concrete   Concrete having a rough surface.

nonstaining cement   Cement used in masonry work containing less than a specified amount of water-soluble alkali.

nonstaining mortar   A mortar with a low free-alkali content.

nonvolatile memory   A feature in irrigation controllers that retains programmed information in an electronic memory during a power failure, without the need for a battery.

NOP   Abbreviation for not otherwise provided for.

normal-weight concrete   Concrete with a unit weight of approximately 10 lb/cu ft (2400 kg/cu m), having aggregates of normal weight.

Norman brick   A brick with nominal dimensions of 2⅔ in × 4 in × 12 in (8.5 cm × 10.2 cm × 30.5 cm).

north arrow   An arrow of direction on a plan view that indicates the direction of north. It is commonly found with or near the indication of scale for the drawing. The direction of north by tradition should point up or to the right where possible. It is traditionally found in the lower right corner of drawings. It is usually identified with "North" or an "N" designed into or on it.

north elevation   **1.** A drawing, usually to scale, showing the north-facing portion of a structure or element as it would be seen standing to the north of it and looking south to view it. **2.** The **elevation** of a portion of ground, paving, or structure situated north of the remainder of it.

northern elevation   *See* **north elevation**.

northern exposure   **1.** A slope that from top to bottom slopes downward toward the north. In the northern hemisphere, it receives less light, and in the southern hemisphere, it receives more light. **2.** The north-facing portion of a structure. **3.** The area to the north of any nearly vertical surface that has a changed microclimate effected by it with regard to heat, cold, or brightness of sunlight or shadow.

northern grasses   Cool season grasses.

no-see-ums   *See* **midges**.

nosing *or* **nose**   The protruding front edge of a stair tread extending in front of a riser, usually rounded.

no-slump concrete   Fresh concrete with **slump** of less than ¼ in (6 mm). *See* **slump test**.

notice of completion   A written document verifying that a project is complete and ready for occupancy.

notice to bidders   A notice in the bidding requirements informing prospective bidders of a project and explaining how to submit a bid.

notice to proceed   A notice given (usually a written directive) by an owner, **general contractor**, etc. to a **contractor, subcontractor**, etc. to proceed with the beginning of work of a contract.

noxious   Harmful or destructive to living things. Most weeds deemed noxious are in reality simply obnoxious, except to the extent they are harmful in using resources that could be used by more useful or pleasing plants.

nozzle   **1.** In **irrigation**, a small, usually interchangeable, emission device for water spray and stream patterns that is part of an irrigation distribution device such as a **sprinkler head**. They usually provide a spray pattern for a sprinkler head as water under pressure passes through them. The water spray patterns they produce vary in the distance they throw the water, the size of water droplets or streams produced, the application rate of water distributed over the area of coverage, and the evenness of coverage over the distribution

nozzles

area. They are usually not integral, and the head and various nozzles may be selected for inserting or attaching to the sprinkler head to change the water distribution patterns. **2.** A device at the output of a decorative fountain producing water spouting forth in a particular shape, style, or form. **3.** A device used on the end of a hose, usually with an adjustment for various spray widths, and fineness or coarseness of water spray.

NPK   The abbreviation often found on fertilizer bags, etc. for the three necessary components of a **complete fertilizer**. They are always in the order of **nitrogen, phosphorus**, and **potash** and are usually followed by the percentage of each found in the fertilizer.

NPL, npl   Abbreviation for **nipple**.

NPS, nps   Abbreviation for **nominal pipe size**.

NPSH   Abbreviation for **net positive suction head**.

NPSHA   Abbreviation for **net positive suction head available**.

NPSHR   Abbreviation for **net positive suction head required**.

NRCS   Abbreviation for **National Resources Conservation Service**.

NRS   Abbreviation for nonrising stem.

Ns   Abbreviation in regard to pumps for **specific speed**.

NTS, nts   Abbreviation for not to scale.

nt wt   Abbreviation for net weight.

nude   *See* **naked**.

nuisance   With regard to real property, generally a condition that damages (physically or by sight, sound, etc.) a property or persons.

nursery   In the landscape industry, a facility, area, or establishment **propagat**ing, cultivating, or growing plants for sale, transplanting, harvesting, or other use. It may be open land, or greenhouses of trees, shrubs, flowers, or other plants.

nut **1.** In botanical terms, a one-seeded fruit with a hardwood-like outer cover that does not spontaneously split. It is larger than an **achene**. **2.** Edible, hard-shelled, usually one-seeded fruits (exceptions are peanut, etc.). **3.** A short, metal piece with inside threads just larger in diameter than the bolt or threaded rod it screws onto. It may be twisted down the bolt shaft by hand and may have a rough surface for tightening by hand (thumb nut); but for more dependable torque tightening, most have a shape allowing a wrench to turn and tighten them.

nut

nutrient Elements and components necessary for growth and development of an organism. In **arboriculture**, any chemical or substance that provides a raw material necessary for growth of plants. **Macronutrients** essential for plant growth are **nitrogen, phosphorous,** and **potassium**. *See also* **micronutrients**.

nymph **1.** A larval form of some insects (grasshoppers, mayfly, silverfish, etc.) that resembles the adult form, but lacks fully developed and useful wings and genitalia. **2.** In classical mythology, a divinity of nature represented as a beautiful maiden. These are sometimes the inspiration or object of a sculpture.

nymphaeum A room for relaxation decorated with plants, sculpture (sometimes **nymph**s), or fountains.

O

oak A strong, hard, heavy, wood.

oak moth A lepidopteran insect that is pale brown or tan. Their larvae are caterpillars that eat foliage and are about an inch long. When full sized, the larvae have bulbous brown heads and olive green bodies with black and olive or yellow stripes. They mostly attack oak trees, and are only a significant problem when populations are heavy enough to defoliate trees. They will usually only have populations of this size for 2 to 3 years and then diminish in number. They are most active in climate **zone**s 7 to 9 and 14 to 24.

oak root fungus The *Armillaria* fungus causes this disease, breaking down root tissue, and girdling plants. It not only affects oak, but about 700 other species of plants. Infected plants' leaves turn yellow, wilt, and die. In fall or winter, clumps of mushrooms may appear at the plant crown or on soil near the plant. Planting resistant plants and avoiding sites with poor drainage will help prevent this disease.

Oa layer *or* **Oa horizon** The **humus layer** within the **topsoil**. It is highly decomposed organic residue. Here the decomposable components of the soil have been affected by physical and chemical processes until decomposition is essentially complete. At this stage nitrogen can be supplied from this horizon for plant growth instead of robbed for decomposition of materials.

obcordate A leaf that is inversely heart-shaped with the notch being at the apex (heart-shaped with small end basal). Compare with **cordate**.

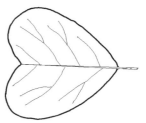

obcordate leaf

obelisk

obelisk A tall, four-sided shaft tapering to a pyramid at the top.

oblanceolate In botanical terms, leaves with the broad end near the tip and tapering or narrowing to the base from the tip.

oblanceolate leaf shape

oblique In botanical terms, slanting of unequal sides. (Compare with leaf base descriptions of **cuneate, obtuse, cordate, auriculate, sagitate, hastate, truncate, attenuate**.)

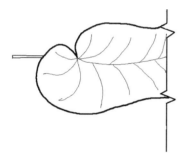

oblique leaf base

oblong In botanical terms, plant parts that are much longer than wide (usually two to three times), have parallel edges, and are more or less elliptic.

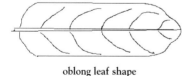

oblong leaf shape

obovate In botanical terms, inversely ovate, or the broad end toward the tip, shaped like an upside down egg.

obovate

obovoid Pear shaped.

obrotund Usually referring to a nearly round **leaf** shape.

observatory **1.** A room, lookout point structure, or place with a wide view. **2.** Any place used for observing the sky and studying stars, etc.

obtuse In botanical terms, a plant part that is blunt or rounded at the end or tip. It is especially used in describing blunt or rounded **leaf** tips. (Compare with leaf tip descriptive terms: **retuse, cuspidate, aristate, acuminate, acute, mucronate, emarginate**. Also, **cuneate, attenuate, cordate, auriculate, sagitate, hastate, truncate, oblique**.)

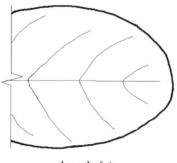

obtuse leaf tip

oc Abbreviation for **on center**; a measurement from the center of an element to the center of another element.

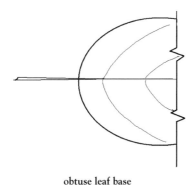

obtuse leaf base

occupancy In land and structure issues (usually according to building codes or planning ordinances), the use of land or buildings.

occupancy permit An allowance given by an **agency** for the right to use land or buildings after complying with their requirements. In the landscape industry, on new building sites there is generally pressure to finish landscaping as it often holds up this permit.

Occupational Safety and Health Act A federal law in the United States that regulates the activities of employers and employees to protect their health, safety, and welfare.

Occupational Safety and Health Administration Those employed by the federal government in regulating, inspecting, penalizing, and enforcing the rules and regulations as set forth in the **Occupational Safety and Health Act**.

OD, od Abbreviation for outside diameter. This refers to the actual diameter measured to the outside of the tube, cylinder, or pipe unless it is preceded by the word nominal. Piping outside diameter dimensions are usually given to three decimal places.

odd-pinnate In botanical terms, **pinnate** with an uneven number of **leaflet**s and always having a terminal leaflet. (Compare with **even-pinnate**.)

odiferous A term descriptively used for a plant with a strongly offensive or unpleasant smell.

Oe layer *or* **Oe horizon** The **fermentation layer** within the **O horizon** in some **soil profile**s being comprised of unrecognizable organic material physically disintegrated into pieces and decomposing.

offset **1.** A small new plant starting the base of a perennial or at the end of a stem from its base. Only some perennials propagate this way. Examples are hen-and-chicks (*Echeveria*) and strawberries. **2.** A bend in a pipe. **3.** A line parallel or following another, but being a constant distance away.

offset digging Trenching with a ditching machine whose boom is displaced from the center of the machine to one side. This allows digging near fences, walls, curbs, etc.

offset screwdriver A screwdriver having a head 90° to the shaft.

offshoot A lateral shoot from the main stem of a plant.

off-type Used in identifying a seedling or plant that is different in one or more traits from the **cultivar** it was derived from.

ogee (OG) A double curve, made by combining a convex and concave line, much like an S shape.

OH, oh Abbreviation for overhead.

ohm The unit of measurement for electrical resistance or impedance equal to a constant current of one ampere producing a decrease of one volt.

O horizon The layer in a **soil profile** that may be present above the mineral soils (**A, B, C, hori-**

zons) dominated by fresh or partly decomposed organic material and humus. It may be further divided into subhorizons. *See also* **Oa**, **Oe**, **Oi**, **horizon**s.

Oi layer *or* **Oi horizon** The **litter layer** sometimes present at the surface of a **soil profile** and a portion of the **O horizon**. It is comprised of undecomposed organic matter such as leaves, sticks, and other living organism residue.

oleoresinous varnish A varnish made of a drying oil and a hardening resin.

olericulture The culture of vegetables.

oligotrophic Water quality without sufficient nutrients for plant growth, but having abundant dissolved oxygen.

Olmsted, Frederick Law (1822–1903). Considered the foremost American landscape architect, but also an ecologist before the word existed. He headed the profession for a time and was largely responsible for establishing its status in the United States. He was an engineer, but worked first as a surveyor and tried framing before 1850 when he toured Europe, and was influenced by English Landscape Gardens. In 1858 he and Calvert Vaux won a design competition for New York's Central Park. He greatly assisted in establishing the profession of **landscape architecture**.

omnivore An animal that eats plants and animals.

on center Usually refers to a distance between the center points or lines of two items of the same type (i.e., plants, joists, posts, etc.).

on-grade Items at ground level or on the ground.

on-site Within the limits of a project or development.

opaque Not allowing visible light to pass through. Not able to see through.

O&P Abbreviation for overhead and profit.

open bidding Allowing **bids** from all parties desirous of bidding on a project.

open burning The burning of any matter in the open that emits its fumes or smoke directly into the atmosphere without passing through a stack, duct, vent, or chimney.

open cut An area where earthen material has been removed so that the denuded surface is open to the sky and vulnerable to precipitation that can cause erosion.

open floor A floor or deck with its joist visible from below.

open-graded aggregate An aggregate containing little or no small particles or having relatively large voids after compaction.

open impeller In a pump, an impeller without shrouds or discs to enclose the impeller veins. This type of pump is most useful in liquids that contain suspended solids.

opening of bids The opening of envelopes containing bids (if so enclosed) and reading them. If in a public opening, then the bids are read aloud as each one is opened.

open riser The distance between treads on a stair not having a solid portion between them.

open sheeting *or* **open sheathing** *or* **open timbering** In an excavation, planks or boards not butted together and having space between these boards expected to hold the earthen wall in place. This type of stabilization or protection is not suitable where there is groundwater or loose or very sandy earth.

open solar energy system A solar energy collection system with a storage tank open to atmospheric pressure.

open space Usually refers to green space within an **urban** or **suburban** setting, but it may also sometimes be used for paved plaza areas, etc.

Generally, it is any land or area not covered with buildings, roads, parking lots, or pavements, etc., whether a constructed or a natural landscape. It usually refers to a park, recreational area, or natural area. Various governing jurisdictions define this term differently.

open string   A board along the outside edge of stairs that extends down their length and is cut on its upper edge to fit the risers and treads. The steps' side edges are then open to view when viewing from the side. *See also* **closed string**.

open-timbered   A structure with its timber work exposed.

open woods   A forest or woods where the trees are not so heavily canopied as to prevent sunlight from having a beneficial effect on the forest floor.

operational pressure   The pressure within a system in operation.

operational test   Checking an **irrigation system** under normal water pressure while allowing its operation to determine if the water distribution devices receive enough water and pressure to perform to their designed activities. In sprinkler irrigation, one should check for proper length of coverage from the head, the proper arc coverage, and any **fogging** of heads (caused by excessive pressure).

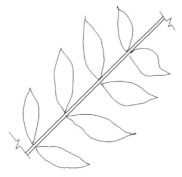

opposite leaf arrangement

opposite   In botanical terms, being directly on the other side, or straight across, as with leaf or branch attachments on some plants. (Compare with **alternate**.)

optical fiber cable   A communication comprised of glass or plastic fibers with protective cladding, strengthening material, and an outside cladding. Lasers or diodes transmit light through these fibers. They are better for communication cables because they do not have electromagnetic interference problems or grounding problems, they are small in diameter, lightweight, and have a large transmission bandwidth. These may be encountered when digging underground, and it is important to locate them before digging commences as they are extremely expensive to repair and more expensive to pay for any necessary costs associated with losses of service. (Damaged large lines have been known to be expensive enough to put a reputable excavation or landscape company into bankruptcy, even with insurance.)

orbicular   In botanical terms, a circular outline; usually in reference to a leaf or leaflet with a nearly circular shape.

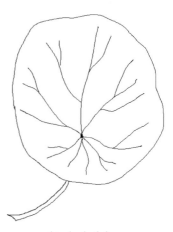

orbicular leaf shape

orbital sander   An electrically powered machine with a circular spinning wheel covered with sandpaper, used for flattening or smoothing surfaces by sanding.

orchard A group of fruit or nut trees; also used in reference to any tree harvested for its food value (i.e., sugar maple trees, etc.).

order **1.** A ranking in the plant classification system (**taxonomy**) that is a subcategory of a **class**, and ranks above a **family**, which is a subcategory of it. *See also* **taxon**. **2.** The broadest category in soil classification.

ordinance A law or regulation adopted by a local governmental or jurisdictional authority. Ordinances often have regulations for project landscaping, drainage, removal of vegetation, etc.

organic **1.** Derived from living organisms. **2.** Chemical compounds that contain reduced carbon bonded with hydrogen, oxygen, or a variety of other elements. Organic compounds are usually volatile, combustible, or biodegradable. They may include proteins, carbohydrates, fats, and oils.

organic fertilizer A **fertilizer** derived from living or once-living organisms. It may be from their remains or a by-product of their living functions. Examples are manure, cottonseed meal, bonemeal, etc. If packaged, they will usually identify the percentages of **complete fertilizer** ingredients. They are generally slower to release their ingredients than chemical fertilizers. They may have other helpful or harmful ingredients, and may also improve soil texture. Harmful effects can be an increase in **pH**, or addition of salts (as with some manure).

organic gardening Growing, cultivating, and otherwise caring for plant material by natural means without chemical **fertilizer**s, **pesticide**s, or **insecticide**s. It makes use of only natural organic fertilizer, soil amendments, and pest controls. Many believe this is best because it reduces risks (associated with chemicals) to people, animals,

and beneficial insects in the garden. It also minimizes impact to the environment. With edible plant products, this is preferred by many as they feel it produces the healthiest food possible.

organic material *See* **organic matter**.

organic matter Material originating from a living organism. This is the source of **humus** and is a natural soil improvement for plant growth.

organic nitrogen **Organic** compounds bound with **nitrogen**.

organic silt A **silt** soil having high organic content. These soils do not stay compacted well, and swell with water. They may be suitable growing medium, but are not suitable for underlying paving or structures.

organic soils **Soil**s in which the organic component predominates the soil.

organism A living thing.

organophosphate An organic derivative of phosphoric acid (or those similar to it) that is often used in pesticides (malithion, etc.).

orientation **1.** The direction a person, structure, or any upright feature with a face is directed, or facing. **2.** The direction from which something accepts or intercepts sunlight, drainage, wind, etc. **3.** The action of situating and placing a structure or any item in relation to the sun or the points of a compass.

orifice The hole on any irrigation device such as **nozzle**s and **emitter**s from which water emerges. The shape of the orifice in a nozzle and the angle of any baffle that the water strikes against determine the angle and density of spray.

orifice emitter In drip irrigation, an emitter of water droplets having a small hole (orifice) that controls the amount of water emitted. Elevation differences and friction loss in pipe distribution can affect the output of emitters. Those with built-in pressure regulators can assist in overcoming some difficulties with pressure change over distance. *See also* **emitter**.

orna. Abbreviation for ornamental.

ornament In design of a construction project, color, shape, etc. added as **aesthetic** attraction or embellishment. These adornments are not usually structurally essential.

ornamental **1.** A reference to a plant grown for its decorative qualities. **2.** A reference to any decorative element in design.

ornamental grasses Grasses and grass-like plants not utilized to sustain foot in a landscape as a **lawn** nor utilized for revegetative value, but rather chiefly for their ornamental qualities such as form, texture, color, or **inflorescence**.

ornamental ironwork Twisting, bending, cutting, or welding iron into shapes for pleasing aesthetics of an iron tubing or rod design.

ornamental tree A tree valued for its ornamental character (i.e., flowers, bark color, leaf type, colorful fruit, etc.).

ornithophilous Plants that are pollinated by birds.

orographic Mountainous terrain and its effects upon plants, soils, precipitation, wind, shadows, etc.

orthostate **1.** A stone taller than it is wide. **2.** A stone in the lower portion of a stone wall that is taller than the courses above it.

OSHA **1.** Abbreviation in the United States for **Occupational Safety and Health Act**. **2.** Abbreviation referring to those involved in the enforcement of the **Occupational Safety and Health Act**, usually employees of the **Occupational Safety and Health Administration**, Department of Labor.

osmocote A **slow-release fertilizer** coated with resin and used in soil mixes or on the soil surface to provide nutrition.

osmosis Materials in soils that become dissolved possess an osmotic pressure due to dissolved ions. Differences in these dissolved ions cause movement of a solvent (a dissolved mix in homogeneous solution) through a semipermeable membrane such as a cell of a root into a solution of higher solute (a dissolved solution) concentration that tends to equalize the concentrations of solute on both sides of the membrane. This is the process by which roots gain nutrients and water. *See* **osmotic pressure**.

osmotic pressure The pressure produced by the action of **osmosis**. Water moves from a solution with low osmotic pressure to a solution with high osmotic pressure. This pressure must be higher in a root cell for water to pass from the soil through the root cell membrane into the root. One of the causes of higher osmotic pressure in soil than in root cells is the excessive presence of salt in the soil. When the osmotic pressure in the soil exceeds that in the root cells, water may actually be pulled from the root into the soil, which harms or kills plants. *See* **fertilizer burn**.

ostiole A small entrance.

ostiolum A small opening or door.

ounce (oz) An English or U.S. weight of 16 drams, or 437.5 grains, or 28.35 **gram**s.

outbuilding **1.** A separate accessory building not physically connected to a principal building. **2.** A smaller building on the same site as a house or larger building, but smaller than the house or main building.

outfall **1.** The place of ultimate deposit of drainage or sewage waters from a conduit, drain, gutter, paved area, or stream. **2.** The dropping,

outflooding

flowing out, or discharging of water at the end of a pipe or conduit.

outflooding Flooding that occurs when a river or stream overflows and allows water outside of its banks.

outlet In an electrical wiring system, a point where a plug can be inserted to obtain electrical current to operate power tools, a controller, or other electrical devices. **2.** *See* **outfall**.

outlet box A component in an electrical wiring system that is a metal or plastic box housing one or more **receptacles** or **outlet**s for connection to fixtures that use electricity to operate.

outline lighting An arrangement of lamps or tubes outlining certain features such as the shape of a structure.

out-of-plumb Not vertical.

outrigger A beam near the ridge of a roof that extends beyond the end wall of the structure.

outrigger scaffold A **scaffold** supported by brackets fastened to the wall of a structure.

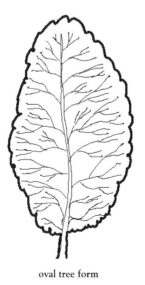

oval tree form

outside caliper A type of **caliper** gauge designed to measure the outside diameters of round or cylindrical objects such as tree trunks.

outside foundation line A line at the outer surface of a foundation wall.

ova A botanical term meaning the female germ cells of a plant.

oval In botanical terms, elliptical. It can describe a plant part, or especially, the shape of a tree's head. (Compare with **round, columnar, fastigiate, weeping, broadly spreading, upright spreading, pyramidal.**

oval-head wood screw This screw has various indented shapes in its head for accepting a tool (screwdriver) to drive (turn) it into wood. Its head is larger than the shank and is rounded at its top edges with a flat underside immediately around its shank. Its shank has either a threaded taper from the underside of its head surface to its more slender pointed shank, or it is a slender shank of a constant diameter continuing to its threads where it then tapers with threads to its point.

ovary The **ovule**-bearing lower part of a **pistil** enclosing the **ovules** (of **angiosperm**s) that ripen into a fruit. It is the expanded basal of a pistil.

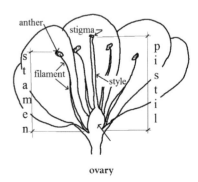

ovary

ovate In botanical terms, shaped like the section of an egg with the broader end basal. These leaf shapes are broadest near its base and taper toward its tip.

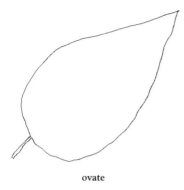

ovate

oven dry weight The weight of soil after all moisture is removed in an oven at a temperature of 221F (105°C).

overburden **1.** The weight or thickness of earthen material over rock or over a specific stratum. **2.** An undesirable top layer covering a useful material wanted for construction.

overcloak Sheet-metal roofing overlapping the adjacent sheet underneath.

overdesign Excess capacity planned for. This is important to consider in irrigation design, as water pressure and landscape areas change over time.

overdraft With regard to aquifers, an aquifer having more outflow than inflow.

overexcavate The process or act of removing more ground material than is necessary or normally necessary for a particular task. It may be used in reference to a foundation, a utility trench, or grading, but is most commonly used to describe the amount of soil to be removed beyond the minimum to place a plant in a hole.

overflow The water flowing out of a tank, bowl, detention basin, pond, etc. after it has reached a particular level.

overgrown An area where plants have become too large for the space they were intended to occupy.

overhaul **1.** The transport of excavated material farther from the distance for which it has been agreed that there are no hauling charges. **2.** The complete renovation or repair of a landscape, machine, or any item.

overhead In business, any costs not directly attributable to a job for materials, operations, or labor.

overhung impeller pump A **centrifugal pump** with an **impeller** mounted at the end of a shaft overhanging its bearings.

overland flow **Runoff** or stream flow.

overload **1.** Weight on a structure exceeding its designed weight load capacity. **2.** Excessive electrical power in wiring or a device beyond its safe capacity.

overplant **1.** Planting or seeding in an area already vegetated. **2.** Adding extra seed to assure a good stand of vegetation. Sometimes this will require thinning for survival, depending on the plant type.

overpotted A condition in which plants are grown in a container too large for their reasonable needs. The soil toward the edges of the pot becomes **anaerobic** and prevents roots from expanding there. This condition usually spreads so that the plant eventually looks sickly or dies.

overseeding To seed over an area already seeded, planted, or established with vegetation.

overspray Water sprayed by sprinklers beyond its intended coverage area.

overwinter A plant surviving through winter. Sometimes the likelihood of a plant overwintering is improved with assistance by adding mulch to cover the root zone, or covering the plant with glass.

ovoid In botanical terms, shaped like an egg when looked at in **section view**.

ovule An outgrowth of the **ovary** of a seed plant enclosing an **embryo** capable of producing a new plant.

owner With regard to landscape projects, whether design, maintenance, or construction, the person, persons, or organization that possesses (owns) the property that is being changed or is proposed for change.

owner's association A nonprofit organization operating under agreements through which each lot, home, or other described land area developed is automatically a member and each lot is automatically subject to a charge for a proportionate share of the expenses for the organization's activities such as maintaining, managing, and preserving common property, including landscaped areas held in common.

oxbow A bend in a river channel that over time becomes isolated from the river's main flow, which may contain water and wetland vegetation.

oxygenating A term used to describe underwater plants that release oxygen into the water.

oxygen demand *See* **biological oxygen demand**.

oz Abbreviation for **ounce**(s)

P

P   The symbol for **phosphorus**. This is the second percentage listed on a **complete fertilizer** bag.

packaged concrete   All the necessary dry ingredients for concrete included in a bag or package allowing one to simply mix the contents of the bag with water to produce concrete.

packing   **1.** In masonry work on stone walls, small stones embedded in cracks and small spaces. **2.** The material around the shaft of a value stem preventing water or fluid from leaking.

pad   The flattened stem of a cactus.

paddock   A relatively small field usually near a building that is meant to contain animals.

paenibacillus popillae *or* **bacillus popillae**   A biological (bacteria) control for the grub worms of Japanese beetles.

paint   A combination of liquid and pigment that adheres tightly to a surface when dried.

paintbrush   A tool comprised of long filaments bound together with a handle. The filaments are used to dip into paint, stain, etc. and spread it over a surface.

pale   **1.** Upright, usually pointed, flat, wooden, or round stakes set in a line to form a fence. **2.** An area enclosed by upright stakes set in the ground and forming a fence.

palea   The upper of two **bracts** (the other is the **lemma**) that enclose the flower of grasses. It is the bract closest to the point of the flower attachment.

paleaceous   A botanical term meaning chaffy.

palisade   A fence of trees, shrubs, or stakes fixed deeply in the ground in a close row. The French sometimes use this term to distinguish a hedge clipped to form a green wall, or a row of trees with bare trunks and the branches **pleach**ed to make a dense canopy. They are often found in formal gardens.

pallet   **1.** A series of planks nailed on larger wood members in a flat platform designed to accept the forks of a forklift. Materials are placed on the platform for easy handling and moving with the forklift. **2.** A piece of wood between brick or masonry unit joints used for fastening wood or other objects to the wall.

palmate   A botanical term applied to a leaf with three or more leaflets or divisions or with three or more main ribs (**veins**) all spread from a common point (as the apex of the petiole) like a hand with outspread fingers.

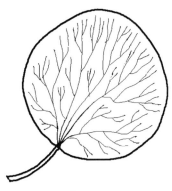

palmate veins

palmately compound

palmate

palmate leaf veins

palmately compound In botanical terms, a leaf with more than three leaflets arranged with a central point of attachment at the tip of a petiole. (Compare with **simple**, **pinnate**, **bipinnate**, **trifoliate**.)

palmately compound

palmately lobed *or* **cleft** *or* **parted** *or* **divided** In botanical terms, the varying depths of a palmate leaf's divisions that are not cut completely to the base.

palmatifid A botanical term describing a plant part that is more or less deeply cut in **palmate** fashion.

palustrine wetland Wetlands that are not dependent on streams, lakes, or ocean waters.

pane A small sheet of glass used for placement as a window. Large glass windows are usually referred to as sheets. These panes are often referred to as lights after they are installed. A window may be divided into several lights.

panel board A group of electrical **breaker switch**es controlling electrical circuits.

paneling Sheets of material placed as surface treatment on a structure or frame.

panel pin A very small finish nail.

panicle (inflorescence) In botanical terms, an open flower cluster like a raceme, but more or less compound (branched).

panicle inflorescence

paniculate A botanically descriptive term of a plant having flowers borne in panicles.

pannose A botanical term, densely and closely **tomentose**.

panorama **1.** A wide-range view of an expanse of land area usually wider than one's field of vision and usually requiring turning one's head to comprehend the entire view. **2.** A pictorial representation that is wide enough to make it difficult to see and comprehend all at once. **3.** An unobstructed and completely open view in all directions. (Compare with **vista** and **view**.)

pantile A roofing tile with a sectional shape like that of an S laid on its side. The tiles are laid by overlapping one another.

pantograph A handheld drafting instrument used to copy drawings, plans, etc. while increasing or decreasing the scale if desired.

papilionaceous In botanical terms, butterfly shaped. This is usually applied to a **corolla**, such as that of the pea.

papilla, papillae A botanical term used to describe a small, nipple-shaped protuberance.

papillate *or* **papillose** A botanical term, covered with short, rounded, blunt projections.

papillose In botanical terms, covered with **papillae**.

pappas The hairs or bristles of an **achene** that usually assist in dispersing the seed. Examples are dandelions and milkweed.

paradigm **1.** An example that is especially typical or outstandingly clear and understandable. **2.** A theoretical framework of a discipline in support of laws, generalizations, and experiments.

parallel A botanical term referring to plant parts that have a shape nearly equally distant at every part or edge or with markings running in the same direction nearly equally distant.

parallel bar An instrument providing the benefits of a T-square, but much easier and faster to move up and down a drawing board as it rides on cables with small pulleys at each end of the bar, keeping the bar parallel at any point up or down the cables.

parallel parking Vehicle parking that is parallel with the direction of traffic flow and adjacent to the traffic area.

parallel venation *or* **parallel-veined** A pattern formed by **veins** in a leaf where they run essentially the same direction and are often equally spaced apart. They may have several or many more or less parallel main veins.

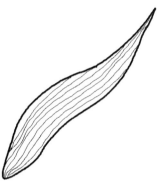

parallel venation

parapet **1.** A low protective wall at the edge of a sudden drop, as at the edge of a terrace, roof, overlook, deck, balcony, etc. **2.** That part of a building or a structure where the wall extends above the roof line.

parasite A pest, plant, or disease that lives on or in organisms of another species obtaining its life support from that organism known as the host. Parasites obtain their nutrients from hosts, but do not provide a useful return to their host plant. This can lead to the deterioration or death of the host.

parcel In the landscape this is a contiguous land area. It usually refers to a small piece of land with

parenchyma

one owner or a piece of land divided from another piece.

parenchyma   **1.** The tissue of plants consisting of thin-walled cells capable of division, and being used in photosynthesis, or for storage. This tissue comprises much of **leaves**, **stems**, **roots**, and **fruits**. **2.** An abnormal growth distinguished from supportive tissue.

parent materials   The portion of soils weathered from stone or bedrock, including the stone or bedrock itself.

parging   A **Portland cement** plaster applied over masonry.

park   Any public or private land set aside and available for recreational, educational, leisure, cultural, scenic, or aesthetic use, or for preservation of **open space** with vegetation or features. They are most often landscaped and made useful for active recreation or other activities.

park-and-ride lot   A parking lot for the temporary storage of automobiles on a daily basis. They are especially provided for commuters to park their automobiles and facilitate persons traveling together to and from work either through carpools, vanpools, bus-pools, or mass transit.

parking bay   A single row of contiguous **parking space**s without gaps or **island**s.

parking island   *See* **parking lot island**.

parking lane   A lane, usually located on the sides of streets, designed to provide on-street parallel parking for vehicles.

parking lot   An off-street area that is usually paved, for the temporary storage of motor vehicles not in use.

parking lot island   A raised planting completely surrounded by pavement within a **parking**

parking lot

lot and usually surrounded by a **curb**. They are placed to guide traffic, provide aesthetically pleasing surroundings, separate lanes, limit paving, cool and preserve paved areas with trees, cool automobiles parked beneath their trees, limit **heat island** effects, preserve existing vegetation or other features, etc. *See also* **center island**, **corner island**, **drive island**, and **end island**.

parking space *or* **parking stall**   A space available for the parking of one motor vehicle.

parking stall   *See* **parking space**.

parking well   A parking area where each parking space has direct access to a street.

park strip   Usually the area with open ground available for landscaping between the property

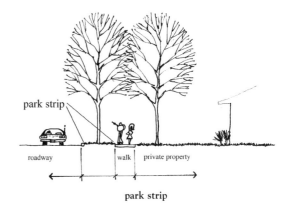

park strip

line and the curb, between the property line and the closest edge of the street paving, or between the sidewalk and the road curb.

parkway Usually the area with open ground available for landscaping between the property line and the curb or between the property line and the closest edge of the street paving.

part circle head A **sprinkler head** that distributes its water over an area less than a full circle (360°). Most sprinkler heads have adjustments for changing the pattern of the arc to a portion of a circle by twisting or turning a portion of the head, by placing a key in the top of the head and turning it, or by changing the **nozzle** on the head.

parted In botanical terms, a leaf with its edge (**margin**) having **lobe**s cut more than halfway (according to some sources) or more than three-quarters of the way (deeply cut, according to other sources) from its edge to its base or **midrib**. (Compare with **ciliate, pectinate, cleft, lobed, dentate, denticulate, serrate, serrulate, double serrate, incised, crenate, crenulate, entire.**)

parted leaf margin

parterre An ornamental garden with paths between planting beds; usually designed in a pattern.

parthenocarpic The ability to produce fruits with seeds without fertilization.

partial shade A planting spot that receives filtered sun and not direct sunlight. It may get a little direct sun early or late in the day.

partite Divided into a number of parts.

parts per million (ppm) A measure indicating minute amounts of materials, usually by weight. For soil, it is the number of units by weight of the substance per million units of oven dry soil (1 pound per million pounds; 1 gram per million grams; etc.). For solutions, it is the number of weight units of substance per million units of solution.

party fence A fence separating properties or land parcels at the boundary so that either or both parties may find it useful.

passive open space Land that is unimproved, or improved with no designated active recreational use reserved for public or private use and enjoyment.

passive solar energy system A system collecting solar energy and utilizing it by natural means instead of mechanical moving devices. Heat is distributed without active devices by radiation, convection, or conduction.

pasteurization A process that eliminates harmful **organism**s. This differs from **sterilization**, which eliminates all living organisms.

pasture A fenced or enclosed outdoor area with plant material suitable for particular animals to graze upon.

patch In **landscape ecology**, a relatively homogeneous nonlinear area (when viewed from the air) that differs from its surroundings.

patent hammer A hammer with a head having two sides made of parallel thin chisels so that it is useful in applying texture to stone or in dressing it with a finish.

path A walkway.

pathogen Any disease of a plant (i.e., bacteria, parasites, fungus).

patina *or* **patination** **1.** A greenish-brown crust that, when exposed over time, forms on bronze and is often thought of as aesthetically pleasing. **2.** A green surface forming on copper or its alloys that have been exposed to the atmosphere and weather for a sufficient period of time. This is often a desirable attribute.

patio An outdoor space made of concrete, masonry, or other hard surface for bar-be-ques, outdoor dining, entertaining outdoors, sunning, or other activities. They are common behind houses where people spend leisure time.

patio furniture

patio furniture Any furniture made for outdoor use and intended for placing on **deck**s, **patio**s, **plaza**s, etc.

patio tree A small tree meant to be grown in a container and often placed on a patio.

pavement light A heavy glass set in a paved surface and, while used as a walking surface, allows some light to a living or working space below grade.

paver **1.** A stone, brick, tile, etc. used in making a pavement surface. **2.** A machine that places concrete pavement while moving itself forward.

pavilion In a garden, fairground, or park, a structure or tent, usually open on all or most sides.

pavilion roof A steep roof, usually with a pyramidal shape.

paving aggregate Materials including, but not limited to, crushed stone, **gravel**, **sand**, slag, seashells, and **vermiculite** used in pavements, especially of **concrete** mixes.

paving unit Any prefabricated part laid or fit together in surfacing the ground.

PC Abbreviation for **Portland cement**; abbreviation for power connector.

pcf Abbreviation for pounds per cubic feet.

PE Abbreviation for professional engineer.

pea flower A descriptive botanical term referring to a plant's **flower** having a shape like a sweet-pea **blossom**.

pea gravel A fine, rounded, natural gravel of small diameter, about ¼ to ⅜ in (6.4 to 9.5 mm), usually gathered through **screening**.

pea gravel grout A **grout** containing pea gravel.

peak annual flow The most water flow produced by a stream or river during a year.

peak discharge The maximum flow of a stream or a river.

peak flow *See* **peak discharge**.

peak rate of discharge *or* **peak flow** The maximum rate of storm water flow at a given point in a channel, watercourse, or conduit resulting from a storm or flood. This can be calculated by assuming a flood or storm frequency size or by actual measurements of underwater flow.

pearlite *See* **perlite**.

pear slug The common name for the **larva** of a **sawfly**.

peat Partially decomposed, fairly stable organic matter formed from dead plants (usually mostly mosses) in areas that have been flooded.

peatland Land with predominantly **peat** soil.

peat moss Partially **decomposed** remains of several different types of mosses used as a growing medium, or an organic soil amendment. It is spongy, usually slightly **acid**, and has a high water retentive capacity.

peat pot A small container made of **peat** and often used for starting seedlings. It will break down in the soil and may be planted directly into the soil.

pectinate In botanical terms, divided into narrow and close divisions, like the teeth of a comb. (Compare with **ciliate, entire, cleft, lobed, dentate, denticulate, serrate, serrulate, double serrate, incised, crenate, crenulate, parted**.)

pedalfer Soils generally of humid climates where the **soil** is often or mostly moist from the surface to the water table, forests prevail, and

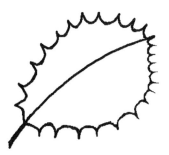

pectinate leaf margin

nutrients are frequently washed away. These soils are common in the eastern United States. *See also* **pedocal**.

pedate In botanical terms, **palmately divided** or **parted**. It may also mean footed.

pedestal **1.** An enclosure with a controller mounted on it that extends from the ground level to the controller and houses wires, etc. **2.** A stand or stable, load-bearing base for a column, sculpture, or display item.

pedestal

pedestal controller

pedestal

pedestal controller A **controller** of an irrigation system mounted upon a **pedestal** manufactured for the purpose of locating the controller closer to eye height. It also houses wiring and, sometimes, electrical components.

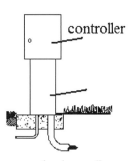

pedestal controller

pedestrian A human being traveling on foot without assistance of a machine or animal.

pedicel In botanical terms, a stalk that supports a fruiting or spore-bearing portion of a plant, the stalk of a single flower of an inflorescence, or the stalk of each flower in a cluster.

pedicle A **pedicel**.

pedocal Soils generally of dry climates where the **soil** is normally lacking water, the prevailing vegetation is composed of grasses and shrubs, and nutrients are often plentiful. These soils are common in the western United States. *See also* **pedalfer**.

pedogenisis The development and formation of **soil**.

pedology **Soil** science.

pedon The smallest volume that can be called or classified as a **soil**. It gives the soil profile three-dimensional form. The upper boundary is the soil's surface. The lower boundary is the arbitrary limit of effective rooting depth of perennial plants or horizons exhibiting pedogenic processes, whichever is deeper. The horizontal dimensions are large enough to exhibit natural variability of **horizon** thickness and continuity. The limits of the soil usually range from 1 to 10 sq m with the actual area determined by the variability of the soil. If the soil is homogenous, pedon size will be small; however, if the soil is highly variable the pedon may be quite large. A pedon is the unit of soil used for sampling, classifications, and study. Soil classifications are generally made up of many pedons.

peduncle A stalk that bears a flower cluster or a single flower.

pellucid A term used in botanical descriptions that means transparent or translucent.

peltate In botanical terms, shield-shaped; applied to a leaf, whatever its shape, when the **petiole** is attached at the undersurface of the leaf and inside the leaf's **margin**.

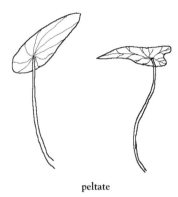

peltate

peltate-palmate   This refers to a **palmate** leaf **venation** with a circular shape and a **peltate** petiole location.

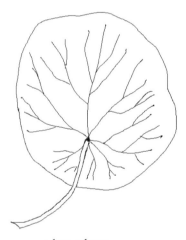

peltate-palmate

pen   **1.** An enclosure for animals. **2.** A permanent writing instrument useful in signing contracts, etc.

penal   A golf hole design style marked by numerous sand and water hazards placed in difficult spots for the playing ability of the average golfer. In this design, shots must be true, and in many cases long, to avoid a high score. *See also* **strategic** and **heroic**.

penal sum   The amount agreed to in a contract that shall be paid the owner as compensation by the contractor, should the contractor not complete the project or not finish the project on time.

pendant   In botanical terms, hanging down from its support.

pendulous   In botanical terms, somewhat hanging or drooping.

penicillate   A botanical term, a plant part with a tuft of short hairs at the end.

pennant   A lightweight plastic, fabric, or other material, suspended from a rope, fixed horizontal element, wire, or string, usually in a series, designed to move in the wind, or simply hang. They display aesthetic designs and color or messages.

penny   In the construction industry, a reference to the size of a nail by weight. One penny is the troy weight of 24 grains, which is equal to 0.05 oz or 1.555 g. Obviously, the higher the number given for this term, the greater the size and weight of the nail.

pennyweight   *See* **penny**.

penta-   A Greek prefix, meaning five; sometimes used before other botanical terms to identify the number of parts.

pentachlorophenol   A lumber preservative used to prevent wood from decaying. It is mildly toxic, and dangerous around the mouth and eyes.

percentage fee   Compensation for design work based upon a percentage of construction cost.

percentage of grade   The distance vertically from the horizontal in feet and tenths of a foot for each 100 feet of horizontal distance.

percentage of possible sunshine   The percentage of daylight hours in a specific location during which direct sun is bright enough to cast a shadow.

percent of slope   The steepness of a surface determined by vertical change in elevation from one point on the surface to another divided by the horizontal length. A slope on a 45° angle is 100% slope (1:1). A slope with a rise of 6 ft vertically (change in elevation) and having a horizontal difference between those same two points of 100 ft is expressed as 6% (6:100 = 0.06) slope.

perched water table   A layer of water-saturated soil that will not drain well even though the soils or material below it are dry. This situation often occurs when too much **organic material** is put in a **backfill mix**, the backfill mix is significantly different from the surrounding existing **soil**, or gravel is placed under the root ball without a **drainage** outlet from the planting pit. This often causes root rot and death for most transplanted trees surviving the initial **transplant** shock.

percolate   With regard to landscape work, the water moving by gravity through pore spaces of earthen material.

percolation   The movement downward of water through the soil when saturated or nearly saturated.

percolation test *or* **perc test**   A test on a site's soil to ascertain its rate of absorption so as to determine suitability for a septic drain field or effluent. The test basically consists of digging a hole, adding water, and measuring the rate at which the water level drops.

perennate   Living perennially from year to year.

perennial plant   **1.** A plant (usually in reference to herbaceous plants) that persists or resprouts year to year for several or many years. **2.** A plant whose life cycle is more than two years.

perennial stream   Stream channels that carry water all year.

perf.   Abbreviation for perforated.

perfect   In botanical terms, flowers with both **pistil**s and **stamen**s.

perfect flower   Any flower containing both female and male reproductive organs.

perfoliate   In botanical terms, a stem that appears to pass through a leaf base.

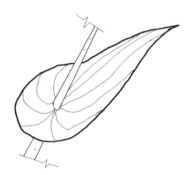

perfoliate leaf attachment

perforated pipe   A pipe with a hose in it to allow fluids to enter or leave its interior. It is used to distribute water such as in a septic leach field or to gather water as around a foundation.

performance bond   A legal document in which a surety guarantees to the owner of a project that the work to be performed by a contractor so covered will complete the work as per the **contract documents**.

performance guarantee   A security given to a municipality as a guarantee that improvements required as part of an application for development or construction are satisfactorily completed.

pergola A garden structure with an open wooden-framed roof, often latticed and covered by climbing plants while shading a walk, sitting area, or passageway.

perianth The outside envelope of a flower that protects its reproductive parts during development. In most **dicotyledons**, it is composed of two separate whorls, one being the **calyx** of **sepals**, and the other being the **corolla** of **petals**. In **monocotyledons** the sepals and petals are often indistinguishable and the segments of the perianth are known as **tepals**.

pericarp In botanical terms, the ripened and variously modified walls of a plant ovary usually comprised of the **exocarp**, **mesocarp**, and **endocarp**.

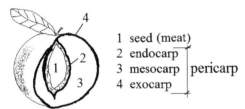

1 seed (meat)
2 endocarp
3 mesocarp } pericarp
4 exocarp

peach (cutaway illustration)

pericarp

perigynous The **perianth** and **stamen**s are united into a basal saucer or cup (the hypanthium) distinct from the ovary.

periphyton Microscopic plants and animals that grow on the surface underwater.

peristalith Upright stones encircling a burial mound.

peristyle **1.** A colonnade surrounding an open space area. **2.** The space enclosed by a colonnade.

perlite A siliceous volcanic mineral rock that is expanded by heat to form lightweight granules

approximately 15 to 20 times their original volume. They are lightweight and porous, and useful in making lightweight concrete or in making a soil mix. It can be used in synthetic soil formulas and as a substitute for sand in potting mixes. It has also been used (in a soil mix) on buildings or parking structures in planters as a lightweight soil to reduce weight on such structures. It is sometimes mixed with a heavy soil to assist in improving its structure, and conditioning it for better rooting.

permanganate of potash A mild **fungicide** and disinfectant with little potassium **fertilizer** value.

permeability **1.** In **soil**s or rock, their ability to **absorb** water, or the rate at which they allow water to pass through. Clays are generally least permeable, and any **compact**ed soil is less permeable when **friable**. **2.** In general, the ability of any substance to allow water to run into or through it; usually refers to preventing excess storm water runoff.

permeameter An apparatus used to measure permeability.

permit A document issued by a governing agency authorizing a particular work.

perron **1.** A formal terrace or green space often centered on a gate or doorway. **2.** An outdoor flight of steps, usually symmetrical, leading to a formal garden terrace, a gate, or a doorway of a large building.

persistant In botanical terms, remaining beyond the period when such parts commonly fall or remaining attached after the normal function has been completed.

perspective drawing A drawn representation, by hand or with a computer, using vanishing points to show depth. This type of drawing is useful in showing a project in a three-dimensional representation before construction.

pervious soil A soil with relatively free movement of water through its mass.

pervious surface A surface that allows or encourages precipitation to infiltrate into the ground where it falls or very nearly thereto.

P.E.S.B. Abbreviation for Pre-Engineered Steel Building.

pest In horticultural terms, an insect or animal that causes harm to plants or the **landscape (garden)**.

pest control The action or process of using various methods, devices, or chemicals to kill or repel insects and animals that cause harm to plants or other valuables.

pesticide A substance (most often a chemical) used to control **weed**s, **fungi**, insects, and other undesirable **pest**s.

pest management Regulating and monitoring pests and intervening in the natural processes of control only as necessary. The idea of pest control has meant in most cases destroying any and all pests.

petal A modified, usually brightly colored, leaf of the corolla of a flower.

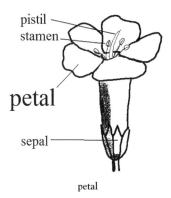

petal

petals

petaloid A descriptive botanical term referring to a plant part, such as stamens, being petal-like.

petaloides A botanical term meaning brightly colored and resembling **petal**s.

petiolate In botanical terms, having a **petiole**.

petiole The stalk portion of a **leaf** or a single flower of an **inflorescence**. It is the nonwoody portion of a leaf that arises from the woody portion and holds the leaf blade or leaflets.

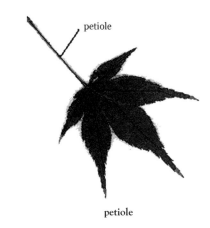

petiole

petiolule In botanical terms, a short **petiole**, or the stalk of a leaflet of a compound leaf.

petroleum asphalt Asphalt refined directly from petroleum.

PH Abbreviation for phase. It is often used on development or construction drawings where work will occur over an extended period of time. It is also used on electrical drawings to indicate single- or three-phase power. Their abbreviations are usually as follows: **1PH**—abbreviation for a **single phase** electrical **conductor**. **3PH**—abbreviation for a **three-phase** electrical **conductor**.

pH In soil, a measurement of the relative concentration of hydrogen ions; followed by a number. A pH of 7 is neutral. The higher the number is above 7, the higher the alkalinity of the soil. The lower the number below 7, the more acid the soil is. The pH scale is a logarithmic function. Each pH unit represents a 10-fold increase or decrease in relative alkalinity or acidity. A soil with a pH of 6.0 is 10 times more acidic than a soil with a pH of 7.0.

phenology Science dealing with the nexus (connection, link) between climate and periodic biological phenomenon such as flowering, breeding, and migration of plants.

phenotype In botanical terms, being of similar physical makeup as the **species**, but changed as influenced by **environment**.

Phillips head The top or driving portion of a screw or bolt that has an indentation shaped like an X to accept a screwdriver with a point that fits into the X indentation (Phillips screwdriver).

phillips screws and screwdriver

phloem The layer (outside of the **cambium** layer), or the portion of a plant, where tissues conduct organic substances (sugars, amino acids, **hormone**s, vitamins, stored food) from leaves to other portions of the plant. In woody plants, most **bark** is formed as this tissue dies and becomes hard.

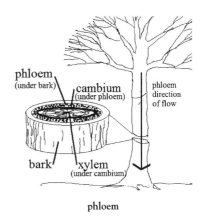

phloem

phosphate Any of numerous chemical compounds containing **phosphoric acid** or a **phosphorous** compound.

phosphate rock or **calcium-magnesium phosphate** A **fertilizer** with about 17% phosphoric acid and about 17% magnesium oxide.

phosphatic Of or relating to **phosphate**, **phosphoric acid**, or **phosphorus**.

phosphoric acid A syrupy tribasic acid used in preparing **phosphatic** fertilizers.

phosphorus A nonmetallic chemical of the **nitrogen** family that is a colorless semitransparent, waxy, soft solid; essential to plant and animal life. It is extremely rare in nature as a free form, but is instead found in various compounds, usually **phosphate**s. In **fertilizer**s, this is normally the second percentage listed on a label and has the symbol of P. Plants consistently need this nutrient to sustain growth. It does not leach easily through the soil and should be added to deficient soils. It promotes root establishment and formation as well as flowering. It is commercially available in many forms including triple superphosphate (**NPK 0-45-0**), superphosphate (NPK 0-20-0), and rock phosphate (NPK 0-25-0). It may be applied in natural forms such as **cottonseed meal**, **blood meal**, **bonemeal**, banana peels, etc.

photic zone   The area of a water body pierced by sunlight.

photoelectric cell   A device in an electrical circuit or incorporated into a **luminaire** (light fixture) that opens or closes the circuit (turns on or off electricity and/or light) as the device is affected by light striking a special portion of its surface. It is used most often to direct lights to automatically turn on at dark and off at morning light.

photoelectric control   An electrical control or switch that is actuated by light or a lack of it.

photometer   Any instrument capable of measuring luminance, luminous intensity, luminous flux, illumination, etc.

photometry   The measurement of light.

photopair   Overlapping aerial photographs that may be utilized in stereoscopic interpretation to determine such information as elevations and contours, heights of vegetation or structures, etc.

photoperiod   A recurring cycle of light and dark periods of consistent length.

photoperoidism   In horticulture, a reference to the alternating periods of lightness and darkness as they affect the growth of plants.

photosynthate   A product of photosynthesis.

photosynthesis   The process in **planting** of making **organic matter** from inorganic matter within their tissues containing chlorophyll when there is sunlight.

phototaxis   An orientational reflex stimulated by light.

phototropic   In plant material, a tendency to grow away from light (negatively phototropic) or toward it (positively phototropic). **Stem**s and **shoot**s are positively phototropic, and **root**s are negatively phototropic.

phototropism   The response of plants to light. *See also* **phototropic**.

photovoltaic   Creating electricity from **solar** energy.

phreatophyte   A deep-rooting plant that typically extracts its water from the water table or an area of soil just above it or a plant that usually has a major part of its root system in soil permanently saturated with water, usually below ground level. Examples are cottonwoods and willows.

phylloclade   In botanical terms, a flattened branch functioning as foliage, or a part of the stem having the general form and function of a leaf.

phyllode   In botanical terms, a flat expanded **petiole** with the form and functions of a leaf, or a more or less expanded, bladeless petiole.

phyllome   Part of a leaf or derived from a leaf.

phyllopodic   A botanical term meaning that the lowest leaves are well developed.

phyllotaxus *or* **phyllotaxy**   A botanical term referring to the leaf arrangement on a stem.

phylogeny   The evolutionary history of a plant group.

phylum   A group or family that shows unity in descent. (The broadest class in plant kingdom taxon is a **division**; the broadest class in animals is the phylum.)

physiography   The physical, mainly natural, character of a site or region.

phytobial   Combining plant-based systems and microbial-based systems to remediate contaminated land.

phytocap   Also known as **vegetative cap**, plants growing over contaminants to protect them from leaching.

phytodegradation   Also known as **phytotransformation**, the breakdown of contaminants in a plant or within its influence through the effect of compounds produced by the plant.

phytoextraction   The uptake of a contaminant from below ground level to above ground level where it is stored and available for harvesting. This is a type of **phytoremediation** most often used for remediation of metals.

phytohydraulics   A reference in **phytoremediation** to control of groundwater through plant transpiration also known as **hydraulic control**. It has the ability to contain groundwater-borne contaminants and prevent them from underground migration.

phytoplankton   Microscopic algae suspended in water and not attached to underwater surfaces.

phytoremediation   A technology that uses living plants to remediate or stabilize contaminants in soil, groundwater, or surface water.

phytostabilization   The immobilization of a contaminant in absorption and accumulation by roots.

phytotoxic   Descriptive of a substance poisonous to plants.

phytotransformation   Also known as **phytodegradation**. The breakdown of contaminants in a plant or within its influence through the effect of compounds produced by the plant.

phytovolitilization   The uptake and transpiration of contaminants through plants that allow the contaminant or a modified form of it into the atmosphere.

piano hinge   *See* **continuous hinge**.

pick *or* **pickax**   A hand tool with a 2½ to 3 ft long handle and a two-sided, steel, long (+/– 12 to 20 in each side) curved head having one side with a point and the other side with a flat chisel end. It is used to break up hard earth that is otherwise difficult to dig with a hand shovel.

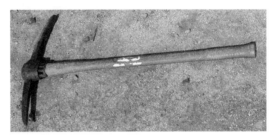

pick

picket   In landscape work, a pointed vertical member in a fence.

picket fence   A fence made of a line of vertical **post**s, **stake**s, **rod**s, etc. (often pointed at the upper end (traditionally about 4 ft high and painted white). It is usually made of wood and held together on horizontal **rail**s. There may or may not be space between the vertical members.

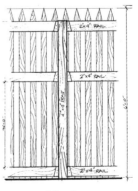

picket fence

pickup A light truck with a cab for the driver and passengers, and an open bed having low sides with a tailgate.

pickup truck

picnic table A table made of various materials (metal, plastic, logs, timbers, fiberglass) with benches or stationary seats, mostly used out of doors or under shelters for dining. In residential use they are usually moveable.

picnic table

picotee A flower with two colors and one of the colors only being present at the edges (margins). This color distribution is available in some tulips, carnations, etc.

picowatt (pW) A measured unit of power equal to one-millionth of one-millionth of a watt (i.e., 10^{-12}W).

pier 1. A column, post, or other vertical structural support carrying loads from above. 2. A structure built over or floating upon the water and used as a landing place for boats as well as for other marine transport, fishing, swimming, etc.

piezometric surface The surface elevation of pressurized groundwater in wells or springs.

pig iron Crude, smelted, high-carbon iron ore. It can be further refined to make steel.

pigtail A flexible conduit cord attached to an electrical component such as a sprinkler controller (instead of wiring direct) that can be plugged into an electrical outlet.

pilaster An architectural member usually projecting one-third or less of its width from a wall and being structurally a **pier**. It usually has the appearance of a **column**.

pile 1. A long slender column of wood, steel, or reinforced concrete driven vertically into the ground (partially or mostly embedded) for bearing a load (the weight) of a structure above it (bridge, deck, building, etc.). These are common and useful in areas of unstable ground where the pile can be driven to a stable substrate. 2. An accumulation and heaping of material such as soil, rock, wood, etc.

pile driver A machine that pounds vertical supports into the ground.

piling See **pile**.

pillar 1. A sturdy upright support for carrying a load such as **column, post**, or **pilaster**. 2. An ornamental or significant column that may stand alone.

pill bug The common name for an isopod crustacean (*Oniscoidea*) having an elliptical body with seven pairs of legs, sectioned shells, and the

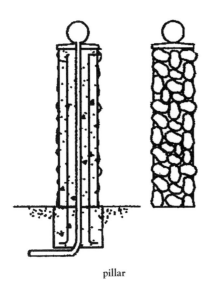

pillar

capability to roll up into a ball about the size of a pea. Other common names are sow bugs, roly-polies, or potato bugs. They feed mostly on decaying vegetation; however, they will feed on young tender plants, especially those just germinating or on fruits that are usually overripe or damaged. They are encouraged to proliferate by mulching and composting.

pilose   In botanical terms, long, straight, hairy; or shaggy with soft, spreading, slender hairs.

pilot hole   A punched or drilled shallow hole for guiding a nail, spike, or screw; or a guide for a larger drill bit to follow.

pin   Flowers with relatively long **styles** and short **stamens**. (Compare with **thrum**.)

pinch back *or* **pinch off** *or* **pinching back**   To use the thumb and forefinger to nip (pinch) off tips of new growth forcing side growth, delaying blooming, or making the plant produce a dense, more compact form. This is most useful with houseplants, flowers, herbaceous plants, and shrubs.

pine straw   A surface **mulch** often sold in bales consisting of pine needles and no straw. It makes weed-free mulch that assists in preventing weeds and gives a finished appearance to planted areas.

pine tar   A black substance made by distilling the wood from pines that is used to assist in waterproofing roofs.

pinna   In botanical terms, a primary division or **leaflet** of a **pinnate** leaf or **frond**.

pinnae   The leaflets of a **pinnate** leaf.

pinnate *or* **pinnately compound**   In botanical terms, a **compound leaf** with the **leaflets** on two opposite sides of an elongated axis. They are arranged like a feather with rows on each side of a stalk, spreading outward. A pinnate leaf can have veins or leaflets arranged in this manner. (Compare with **simple, bipinnate, trifoliate, palmate**.)

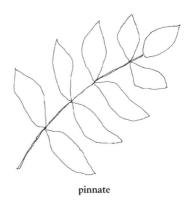

pinnate

pinnatesect   A leaf divided into opposite pairs of lobes that are cut nearly to the leaf midrib.

pinnate-trifoliate   A description of a leaf that has three **leaflets** arranged so that one is at the apex (end) and two split to either side opposite one another.

pinnate venation

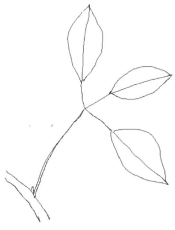

pinnate-trifoliate

pinnate venation   A leaf with **vein**s arranged off of either side of a central midrib vein.

pinnate venation

pinnatifid   In botanical terms, **pinnate**ly cleft, halfway cut to the midrib, feathered, or pinnate veins with lobes at each arranged as a feather.

pinnatifid leaf margin

pinnatisect   In botanical terms, a feathered leaf cut down to the midrib.

pinnule   In botanical terms, a secondary **pinna** or segment of a leaf or frond.

pint (pt)   English or U.S. capacity measurement comprised of 4 gills, or ½ **quart**, or 28.875 **c.i.**, or 473.176 **milliliter**s.

pip   **1.** A small fruit seed, especially a small seed of a fleshy many-seeded fruit. **2.** An individual rootstalk of the *Convallaria* (lily of the valley) plant.

pipe   A long, hollow, circular tube made of plastic, steel, copper, brass, iron, concrete, etc. for use as a conduit of fluids, wire, gases, etc.

pipe cross   A pipe fitting that can connect pipes as they cross at right angles.

pipe cutter   Any tool of various types used to make square cuts on the ends of pipes. Pipe cutters are different for pipes made of plastic, copper, cast-iron, etc.

pipe cutters

pipe die   A device that cuts threads into pipe.

pipe dope   A putty-like substance used to apply to threaded pipe, fittings, or equipment before screwing them together to facilitate a seal.

pipe expansion joint A device in a length of piping that compresses or extends to compensate for the piping expanding or contracting in length due to changes in temperature.

pipe fitter One who installs and joins pipe and its associated devices mostly outdoors.

pipe fitting A connection piece used in fitting pipe together. Examples are **elbow**s, **tee**s, **coupler**s, etc.

pipe hanger A device that hangs from a point of attachment and holds a pipe in place. They are useful when placing piping in or under structures such as buildings, bridges, and parking structures.

pipe joint compound A sealing material used on threaded fittings.

pipelayer **1.** A tool comprised of a winch and a boom with pulleys facilitating raising and lowering heavy pipes into trenches. They are usually mounted on a vehicle with tracks or wheels (usually tractors) to move along the pipe route. **2.** A person skilled in fitting, laying, and securing pipe systems.

pipe plug Any male fitting for a pipe that when inserted (glued or threaded) into an opening or a pipe end plugs it off, preventing flow.

pipe puller A motorized machine with at least four wheels and a blade used to cut the ground and having an attachment at the base of the blade where pipe is attached for pulling into the ground.

pipe pulling A method of establishing underground pipe lines by attaching pipe at the bottom of a steel blade behind a bullet-shaped head on a **pipe puller** that pulls the pipe into the ground.

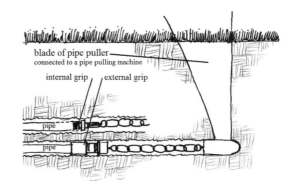

blade of pipe puller

pipe reducer Any fitting or device that facilitates changing sizes of pipes that are connected.

pipe ring A circular device for loosely holding a suspended pipe.

pipe saddle An upright support for pipes or devices attached to them.

pipe strap A thin metal strip wrapped around a pipe, allowing it to be hung from above.

pipe tee A **pipe fitting** with three openings for connections of **pipe**, **nipples**, or other devices.

pipe thread A V-shaped spiral cut on the inside or the outside of a pipe, or on a pipe fitting, coupling, or connector.

pipe tong A tool to screw or unscrew lengths of pipe or pipe fittings.

pipe vise A clamping device that has V-shaped jaws or a chain to hold pipe or devices firmly while being worked on.

pipe wrench A hand tool with a long handle, a movable jaw, and a stationary jaw. It is useful in pipe work with the jaws shaped to tighten when placed on a circular device or pipe and forced in a circular motion around the pipe. This allows

piping

for screwing together and tightening threaded pipes and devices.

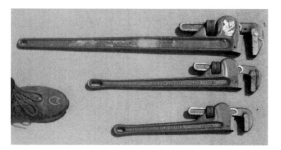

pipe wrenches

piping **1.** A reference to the action of runoff water or water from broken sprinklers passing through underground passages of eroded tunnels and back to the surface, or a reference to the passages themselves. **2.** Any system of connected **pipes** or hollow cylindrical tubes used to carry liquids, such as in an **irrigation system**. **3.** The migration of soil within the soil profile from one point to another.

pistil In botanical terms, this means the female ovule-bearing organ of a seed plant. This female portion of a flower is composed of an ovary, style, and **stigma**. *See illustrations under* **flower** and **perianth**.

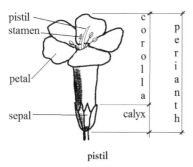

pistil

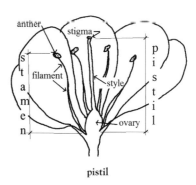

pistil

pistillate In botanical terms, provided with **pistils** (female); a term used when **stamens** are not present. This term is descriptive of a female flower or plant (only having female reproductive components).

piston pump A **pump** that moves and compresses fluids by use of a piston with an intake and outlet to the chamber allowing fluid in as it retracts the piston and forcing water out as the piston is pushed to the other end of the chamber.

pit The stone (seed) of a drupe fruit such as that of **stone fruit**.

pit boards Any lumber placed horizontally as sheeting to prevent caving in of an excavated bank of earth.

pitch **1.** The slope of a roof surface, often expressed as a ratio of a vertical drop or rise over a horizontal length such as 4:12, 3:12, etc. **2.** A dark distillate of tar or any of various resins. They may be useful in waterproofing, paving or caulking.

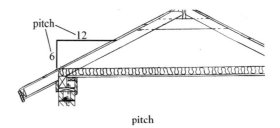

pitch

pitched roof   A steep roof, usually in reference to gabled roof.

pitcher plants   Carnivorous plants with leaves modified into organs shaped much like a pitcher.

pitch fiber pipe   A pipe made of cellulose fiber and coal tar with an advantage of being lightweight.

pitchfork   A tool with a long straight handle and several long, steel, pointed, and usually at least slightly curved pieces arranged in a fork-like manner. It is used for picking up loose intertwined material such as hay, straw, pine needles, or for aerating, etc.

pitch oil   Another name for **creosote**.

pitch pocket   **1.** A defect in softwood lumber where there is an opening in the grain containing pitch or resin. **2.** A metal piece around a member where it penetrates the roof. It is usually filled with pitch or sealant to prevent leaking.

pith   The soft, central core of trees or most plants. In herbaceous plants, it is the large central area used for support and storage. In a woody stem, it is the area of dead xylem cells at the center of a stem.

pith-faced   Stone masonry finished with a chisel at the edges and the center left rough.

pith fleck   A short dark streak in lumber caused by insects during growth.

pith ray   *See* **medullary ray**.

pit-run gravel *or* **bank-run gravel**   Ungraded gravel as it is taken directly from a bank of earth or pit.

pivot   In agriculture, an irrigation pipe on wheels that rotates around a point of connection to a water source. It is often used at sod farms.

PL, pl   **1.** Abbreviation for power line. **2.** Abbreviation for pipe line.

placenta   In plants, the tissue of the **ovary** to which the **ovule**s are attached.

plain ashlar   Stone with the face to be exposed having been smoothed with a tool.

plain concrete *or* **unreinforced concrete**   **1.** Concrete not containing reinforcement or reinforced only for shrinkage or temperature changes and not for load bearing. **2.** Concrete without an admixture or element added that is normally expected.

plain masonry   Masonry without reinforcement, or reinforced only for shrinkage or temperature change and not for load bearing, etc.

plain-sawn *or* **bastard-sawn** *or* **flat-grained** *or* **flat-sawn** *or* **slash-sawn**   A term used to describe lumber cut to size with the annual rings (seen from the end of the wood piece) intersecting its broadest face at less than a 45° angle.

plan   A drawing of an item, site, community, city, etc. as viewed from above.

planch   A British term for a floor of **plank**s or an individual plank.

planching   *See* **decking**.

plancier *or* **planceer** *or* **plancer** *or* **plancher**   **1.** The underside of a structure's projection, such as a soffit. **2.** A **planch**.

plan deposit   Money required to obtain bidding documents.

plane   **1.** An infinite number of contiguous straight lines forming a straight, flat surface. **2.** A tool used in removing imperfections of a wood surface, or in shaping and smoothing a wood surface. It is comprised of at least a handle and a slanted blade that is on or in a flat skid. The skid with its projecting blade is pushed over the wood surface to cut thin strips away.

plane ashlar A stone unit usually used in masonry having tool marks on its surfaces.

planed lumber Lumber having one or more of its surfaces **plane**d smooth.

plane surveying Surveying not taking the curvature of the earth into account in its calculations.

planimeter A mechanical device with an elbow and two parts to its arm; one part has a pin at its end to hold it steady on a drawing, and the other part is used to trace an area on the drawing. It is used for measuring the area of a plane surface within a perimeter on a map. A wheel usually near its elbow rotates as it is moved and yields a number that can be converted to the area at the scale of the drawing. It is useful in determining areas of odd shapes.

planing The process of smoothing a surface of a material by shaving off small thin sheets.

plank **1.** A board 2 to 4 in (5 to 10 cm) thick and usually 8 in wide (20 cm) or more. **2.** Any long, wide, reasonably thick piece of lumber, the dimensions of which vary depending on whether it is hardwood or softwood and depending upon lumber industry standards, etc. They are sometimes tongue-and-grooved at their edges.

plank fence **1.** Any fence made with lumber. **2.** A fence constructed with horizontal lumber attached to square posts.

planking **1.** A wood surface made of planks. **2.** The action of attaching planks. **3.** A log flattened on two sides, usually for use in a cabin. **4.** A reference to a quantity of planks.

planking and strutting Temporary wood members against the side of an excavation to prevent or redirect material caving in.

planned unit development (PUD) An area of contiguous land planned and developed as a single entity, containing one or more residential clusters and one or more public, quasi-public, commercial, or industrial areas, or nonresidential uses. They usually have an open space component and encourage pedestrian travel and access.

planning The process of studying and determining the layout of spaces, routes, structures, plantings, land uses, etc.

planning and zoning commission Within a government's jurisdictional area, a group of people (elected or appointed) that recommend boundaries of zoning districts and determine appropriate requirements relative to site plan review, including landscape requirements.

planning board *See* **planning and zoning commission**.

planning commission *See* **planning and zoning commission**.

plant available water (PAW) The quantity of water stored within the root zone between the conditions of field capacity and permanent wilting point.

plant classification An orderly, ranked system of similar plants that becomes less and less inclusive and from broadest to most specific is as follows: **kingdom, division, class, order, family, genus, species, variety** or **cultivar**, and **hybrid** or **strain**. *See also* **botanical name** and **taxon**.

plant community All of the plant species within a microclimate, habitat, or environment.

planted molding *or* **applied molding**   A molding fastened to a work instead of cut into the solid material.

planter   **1.** An area of ground for plants on a project. **2.** A container for plants.

plant hopper   *See* **leafhopper.**

planting   **1.** In landscaping, the act of placing plant material, roots, bulbs, rhizomes, or seed in soil or other growing medium anticipating or intending future survival or growth of a plant. (See appendix for construction details.) **2.** In masonry work, the placement of the bottom courses of masonry units as a foundation on a level bed.

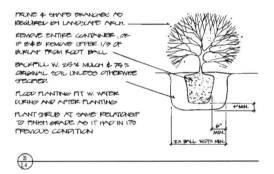

PRUNE & SHAPE BRANCHES AS REQUIRED BY LANDSCAPE ARCH.

REMOVE ENTIRE CONTAINER, OR IF B&B REMOVE UPPER 1/3 OF BURLAP FROM ROOT BALL

BACKFILL W. 25% MULCH & 75% ORIGINAL SOIL UNLESS OTHERWISE SPECIFIED.

FLOOD PLANTING PIT W. WATER DURING AND AFTER PLANTING

PLANT SHRUB AT SAME RELATIONSHIP TO FINISH GRADE AS IT HAD IN ITS PREVIOUS CONDITION

4" MIN.

6" MIN.

2X BALL WIDTH MIN.

B / 14

planting detail

planting detail   A drawing detailing the placement of a plant in the ground with information meant to facilitate its survival.

planting high *or* **planting proud**   Planting a tree or shrub slightly higher than the surrounding finished grade to avoid crown rot. This is often a good idea but is not as necessary in sandy soils.

planting legend   *See* **planting schedule.**

planting pit   A pit dug for the express purpose of placing a plant's roots, seeds, bulbs, or rhizomes in it along with **backfill** in expectation of a plant utilizing the space for growing. (See appendix for construction details.)

planting plan   A designed graphic representation of the location and type of **plant material** for a **site**.

planting schedule   A schedule for the installation and growth of plant material.

plant kingdom   In **taxonomy**, the broad category containing all living and extinct plants. The next category or unit of differentiation is the **division**. *See* **taxon.**

plant lice   *See* **aphids.**

plant material   **1.** Any or all plants. **2.** In landscape-related work, plants utilized in a planting plan or in actual construction.

plant palette   A list of **plant material** available for use; restricted by hardiness, government regulations, desired **aesthetic**s, **soil** type, pollutants, etc.

plant pit   A pit dug in soil for the express purpose of placing a plant within it along with backfill to secure for it a place to grow.

plant production   **1.** The amount of organic matter in the landscape over a day or year. **2.** The propagation of plants.

plant schedule   A combined legend and table referencing a planting plan usually identifying symbols (or labeled plants) on the plan to dictate attributes and requirements of plants represented on the plan for planting. It usually includes the symbol of the plant, the **botanical name**, the **common name**, the size it should be when planted (height, width, caliper, container size), its container type, and remarks such as spacing or whether clumped or single plants are desired, quality of plants, etc.

plant succession The change in plant material types and quantities on land over time due to competitiveness, amounts of water, amounts of light, changes in organic matter available, dispersal of seeds, etc.

plant taxon *See* **taxon**.

plantlet This term is often used to refer to a small young plant that is produced naturally by a parent plant and can be removed or separated to facilitate propagation.

plan view In reference to drawings, an aerial view or a view from above. Plan views are usually to scale. The scale should be referenced in writing or in a **bar scale** on the drawing.

plaque A small metal, plastic, etc. plate inscribed in some fashion to label or commemorate an item, person, historic event, dedication, etc. or to describe an exhibit, provide instruction, etc.

plastic **1.** An organic polymer that can be molded, extruded, or cut into shapes; is fairly lightweight and may be stiff or bendable. **2.** A term for concrete, mortar, or plaster that means easily spread or malleable. **3.** A description of wet soil that is sticky, malleable, and cohesive.

plasticity The ease of shaping or molding soils, freshly mixed cement paste, concrete, mortar, etc.

plasticizer An additive that increases plasticity of a concrete mix, mortar, etc.

plastic limit The least water content with which a soil exhibits plastic properties.

plastic pipe Pipe made of organic polymeric substances. It has low initial cost, is lightweight, with high flexibility and good corrosion resistance, but it also has poor resistance to solvents, low pressure ratings at high temperatures, and may break down when exposed to sunlight.

plastic soil A soil easily molded with little resistance to deformation.

plat A map, plan, or chart of record at a county, etc. indicating the location and boundaries of individual properties.

plate **1.** A thin, flat, rigid sheet of material. **2.** In wood frame construction, a horizontal timber connecting ends of posts, joists, rafters, etc. **3.** A timber laid on top of a wall, foundation, or ground to support other timbers or joists.

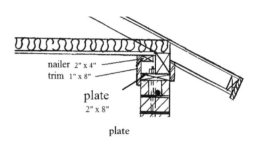

nailer 2" x 4"
trim 1" x 8"
plate
2" x 8"

plate

plate bolt A bolt that secures the **plate** on top of a foundation or wall and is usually embedded in the masonry or concrete.

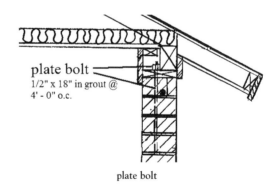

plate bolt
1/2" x 18" in grout @
4' - 0" o.c.

plate bolt

playfield An area designed for and/or large enough for field games.

playground **1.** An area with any apparatus for the amusement and recreation of children. **2.** A landscaped area for children to play out-of-doors.

playhouse A miniature house sized for children and built for their use.

play lot **1.** A small **playground**. **2.** An area or playground for children to recreate.

play structure An apparatus built for the use, entertainment, play, and recreation of children, usually with many play components (slide, swings, bridge, tower, balance beam, fireman pole, etc.) assembled and attached as one unit.

play structure

plaza A large open outdoor area or space frequented by pedestrians. These are usually urban spaces that are improved with landscaping or paving, and are most often encompassed by buildings, streets, or pedestrian corridors.

pleach *or* **pleaching** The interlacing of branches of one tree or shrub with another, often done to create a hedge, arbor, or dense canopy.

pleasance A pleasure garden used for enjoyment and relaxation; usually private and secluded.

plicate In botanical terms, folded lengthwise into plaits or pleats as in a fan or skirt.

pliers A hand tool with two handles and two jaws operating with a pivot much like scissors do. This tool allows one to grasp items and hold them or turn them. They also may be used for cutting wire.

plot **1.** A future or present building site. **2.** A plan for a present or future building on a parcel of land, usually showing accessory elements and often the dimensions thereto. **3.** The printing of a computer-generated drawing or the finished print of a computer-generated drawing, usually on large paper.

plotter A machine capable of printing wide sheets from computer-generated drawings, pictures, etc.

plow **1.** A device, whether pushed by hand, pulled by animals, or pulled by machinery, that turns over soil. It is useful in preparing for planting and loosening compacted soil. **2.** A router or carpenter's plane capable of cutting grooves. **3.** *See* **plow groove**.

plow-and-tongue **joint** *See* **tongue-and-groove joint**.

plow groove A groove parallel with the grain of wood in a piece of lumber, especially as within the indented side of a **tongue-and-groove** board.

plug **1.** Very small pots with starter plants (sometimes called **liners**) used for planting in the landscape, or for **potting up** in a **nursery**. **2.** Small pieces of **grass** used to start a **lawn**. **3.** A device for connecting electrical wires to an electrical outlet receptacle. **4.** Any male fitting for a pipe that, when inserted (glued or threaded) into an opening or a pipe end, plugs it off and prevents flow. **5.** *See* **plugging**.

plugging The act of drilling a hole in masonry and forcing into it wood, plastic, fiber, etc. to provide a spot for a screw to be driven into the wall, usually to attach something.

plumb **1.** A **plumb line**. **2.** Truly or exactly vertical. **3.** To install **plumbing**. **4.** A line pointed at the center of the earth (or its center of gravity) according to a **plumb line**.

plumb bob   A metal device usually with a point at the bottom suspended by a line indicating a vertical line or a point directly beneath another point from which it is held when dangled from a stationary point.

plumber   One who installs, repairs, or maintains mostly indoor **plumbing (3)**.

plumbing   **1.** The act of using a plumb. **2.** The trade or occupation of a plumber in which one installs mostly indoor pipe and its associated devices. Outdoors this work is referred to as **pipe fitting** and the trade is a pipe fitter. **3.** The fixtures, **pipes**, **fittings**, or other devices for conveying fluids, especially water. **4.** The installion work associated with a **plumber**.

plumbing hazard   According to the National Standard Plumbing Code, an internal or plumbing type of cross-connection in a consumer's potable water system that may be either a pollution or a contamination-type hazard.

plumb level *or* **pendulum level**   A bar with a plumb line; the bar can be placed horizontally by positioning it at a right angle to the dangling plumb line.

plumb line   A string, cord, etc. with a weight at one end able to be dangled to determine verticality.

plume   A body of contaminated groundwater moving or stationary that has originated from a source(s) and is moved by such factors as groundwater flow patterns, specific gravity, solubility of the contaminant(s), subsurface geology, and the influence of pumping wells.

plumose   In botanical terms, feathery; a description when any slender plant part is beset with hairs.

plunge   In landscape or nursery terms, piling material (soil, bark, peat, etc.) around a potted or b&b plant to moderate temperatures of the soil around roots, and affording a more uniform moisture for them.

plunging   Burying a potted plant in mulch to the top of the pot rim.

plywood   Wood sheets made of three or more layers of veneer (usually an odd number), joined and bonded with glue and pressure. They are most often sold in a 4 × 8 ft size.

pneumatic drill   A drill that operates on compressed air.

pneumatic riveter   A tool that installs rivets and is driven by compressed air.

PO   Abbreviation for purchase order.

pocket   **1.** A notch in masonry or concrete made to receive the end of a beam. **2.** An opening between the annual rings of a tree developing during its growth.

pocket gopher   A landscape rodent (family *Geomyidae*) pest (about the size of a rat) that burrows 6 to 18 in underground, surfacing and creating little dirt mounds. They eat roots, bulbs, and even some types of small plants which they pull into their burrows.

pocket rot   A type of decay in trees and lumber consisting of holes (pockets) surrounded by sound, healthy wood.

pocosin   A swamp of the coastal plain of southeastern United States. They usually occur on **poorly drained soils**, or level lands between stream drainages. They have peat soils with shrubs and trees adapted to periodic fires.

pod   **1.** The fruit of many **legume**s, of the *Bignonia* genus, etc. It is often long and always contains seeds. **2.** A botanical term identifying any kind of dry, **dehiscent** fruit.

podocarp A plant having fruits with stalks.

pointed ashlar A stone block for use in masonry having markings on its face produced by striking it with a pointed tool.

pointing **1.** The finishing treatment of **mortar** joints by troweling mortar. **2.** The act of filling gaps in mortar joints of brick or stone with mortar. **3.** Removal of mortar between joints of masonry units and replacement with new mortar.

pointing trowel A mason's trowel with a pointed tip used in **pointing** or removing mortar from joints in masonry.

point of connection (P.O.C.) The location where an irrigation system is connected to the water supply.

point source Water pollution emitted at a single source such as a sewage plant outfall.

pole foundation A foundation for support of a structure consisting of posts driven or partly buried in the ground.

pole pruner A tool with a **pruner** and sometimes a saw at the end of a long aluminum or fiberglass handle that may be unscrewed and extended. The pruning jaws are operated by a rope that extends down the handle for pulling to chop off branches, etc. It is handy for small cuts instead of using conventional pruners operated from atop a ladder.

pollarding A yearly pruning of **deciduous** trees to the same point on the same main branches each year to keep them at a modest size and give them a rather formal appearance. This gives a manicured style to trees. Branch ends become large and knobby. In summer they create a compact, leafy dome and a stark, odd, or interesting look during dormant months. London plane trees (*Platanus acerifolia*) have historically been a tree to which this technique has been applied.

pollen The microspores (fertilizing powder, gametophytes, or pollen grains) of the male organ (**anther**) of a seed plant that form a fine dust.

pollination In angiosperms, the transfer of pollen by gravity, wind, insects, birds, etc. from the **stamens** (**anther** portion) to the **pistil** (**stigma** portion) of a plant or plants to begin the process of creating seed.

pollinator Anything (**butterfly**, human, wind, **bee**, animal, etc.) that assists in transferring **pollen** from an **anther** to a **stigma**.

pollinizer **1.** A plant or flower that supplies pollen to fertilize another flower or plant. **2.** Any source of pollen.

pollution **1.** Contamination of any environment (for a particular organism or many organisms) from foreign or natural substances that have a negative effect. What is pollution to one organism may be a natural part of another organism's environment. **2.** In the human context, the presence of matter, gases, noises, unsettling visual images, or energy whose nature, location, or quantity produces undesired environmental, psychological, or physiological effects. Most any substance can be a pollutant (under this definition) if it affects a person negatively.

pollution hazard According to the National Standard Plumbing Code, an actual or potential threat to the physical properties of the water system or the potability of the public or the consumer's potable water system, but which would not constitute a health or **system hazard** as defined.

polyandrous A flower with multiple stamens.

polycarpic Descriptive of a plant that fruits and flowers multiple times in a life cycle.

polyethylene A low-cost, flexible plastic. In landscape work, it is most often useful in two forms. It is made into a somewhat bendable pipe, sheets, or rolls of plastic. As a pipe, it is useful because it generally does not break when frozen with water inside. As a sheet membrane, it is useful because it is waterproof. It has been used to line ponds, assist in roofing, and as a weed barrier. The difficulty of using it as a weed barrier is that it also is a barrier to gaseous exchange and water penetration. If it is watered by **drip irrigation** beneath the plastic it often develops **anaerobic** conditions detrimental to plant growth.

polyethylene pipe A plastic pipe made of a thermoplastic.

polygamous In botanical terms, having some **perfect**, some **staminate**, and **pistillate** flowers on the same plant or on different individual plants.

polymer concrete Any concrete utilizing an organic polymer as binder in the mix.

polymorphic A plant that is quite variable regarding habitat.

polypedon A group of similar pedons having edges defined by observable features such as changes in **slope** or soil properties like **horizon** texture or an easily observed color.

polypropylene pipe A tough plastic pipe with resistance to heat and chemicals.

polysepalous A botanical term describing sepals that are separate from each other.

polyvinyl chloride (PVC) A thermoplastic resin highly resistant to chemicals and corrosion used for pipe **fittings** and piping. **Pipes** of this material are classified for various pressures with either the pressure rating or a **schedule** (thickness) rating stamped on the side of the pipe. It is not resistant to impact, especially in smaller sizes. Connections may be made by solvent weld, threads, or by compression fittings with rubber gaskets, depending on the type of connection the pipe is manufactured for. It is a popular and dependable pipe for underground irrigation systems if installed properly.

pomace Spent seeds and skins of apples and grapes as a by-product of cider and winery operations. It has been shown to be valuable as a natural slow-release **nitrogen fertilizer**. It is also helpful in improving the **soil texture** of **clay** soils.

pome In botanical terms, a fleshy **indehiscent** fruit with an inferior ovary and more than one live seeds.

pome

pom-pom A reference to the pruning and shaping of a plant (usually a shrub) with all its main branches or stems exposed and no **foliage** for a distance extending to a small, rounded mass of foliage at each of its ends.

pompon The small, rounded flower head of a chrysanthemum or dahlia.

pond A natural or man-made water body smaller than a lake yet not a river or stream with moving water (though it may be a portion of one); a water body that is observed to be mostly still.

poorly drained soils Soils in which water is removed so slowly that the water remains wet most of the year. Water tables usually occur at or near the surface. Poor drainage is caused by the high water table, a slow permeable layer within the profile, or seepage.

popout The breaking away of small, usually conically shaped, portions of a concrete surface.

pop-up head An irrigation **head** designed to be placed with its top surface flush with ground level (generally at **finish grade**), and extending itself upward to shoot over plant material when it receives water pressure.

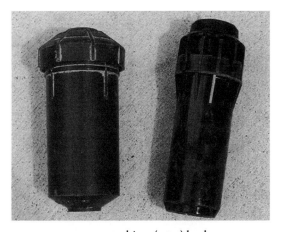

pop-up gear driven (rotor) heads

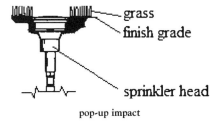

pop-up impact

pop valve A safety valve that normally keeps the valve closed except when the pressure of fluid on the valve overpowers the force exerted by a spring.

porch **1.** An exterior structure that extends along the outside of a building, is usually open or partially so, and is usually covered. **2.** The steps and landing at the door to a building entrance. **3.** A covered exterior entry to a building.

pore **1.** A small interstice allowing the **absorption** or passage of liquid. **2.** A minute opening in plants or animals that allows matter, liquid, or gases to pass.

porosity The amount of pore space in a material, especially soil that permits gases or liquids to pass through the material or soil. It is usually expressed as a ratio or percentage of the volume of voids in a material or soil to the total volume of the material or soil (including the voids). Pores in soil are essential for plants as they need oxygen, water, and gaseous exchange for their roots.

porous paving A surface used to facilitate traffic or storage of some kind out-of-doors and allows precipitation to infiltrate into the subsurface, preventing or reducing runoff.

porte cochere **1.** A roof usually attached to a building and erected over a driveway or street for shelter of those entering or exiting vehicles. **2.** An access through a screen wall to an interior court.

portico A covered area held up by columns, usually in a colonnade and usually at the entrance to a building.

Portland cement A cement-type binder used for structural concrete. It is manufactured by grinding and burning a mixture of limestone

positive displacement pump

with **clay** or shale and a smaller amount of **gypsum**. It is mixed with water and an aggregate to make a thick, heavy liquid that dries as concrete.

positive displacement pump A **pump** having pumping action created by displacement produced by a decrease in volume in the working chamber. Examples of this pump type are **rotary pump**s, gear pumps, **reciprocating pump**s, and vane pumps.

positive environmental impact Consequences in a realm involving interrelated or interdependent living things and their surroundings having influences of a beneficial nature, or being influenced in a positive way. It is most often used in the context of an anthropomorphic (human) cause of positive environmental changes and focuses on the effects of those changes. However, what is viewed as a positive impact upon one element or organism may be a negative impact to another. *See* **environmental impact**.

positive impact *See* **positive environmental impact**.

post A long, strong, stiff, vertical structural member (usually of wood or metal) or a column for a fence, etc. secured in an upright position to carry a load or give support to something.

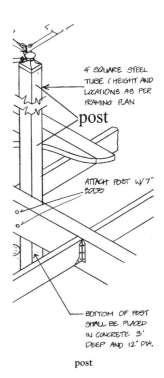

post

post (holding a beam supporting a ceiling and roof)

post and board fence A wood fence design of posts and rails spanning between them with space between the rails.

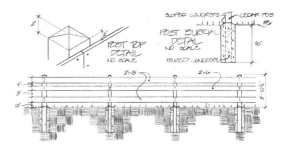

post and board fence

post base A steel device with a rod for pouring cement. At the end above grade a U-shaped bracket holds a post that is screwed or bolted to the bottom of a post or to the underside of a beam.

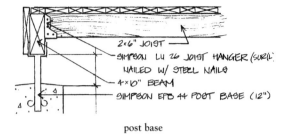

post base

post emergent An **herbicide** that will kill weeds after they have **germinate**d.

post hole A narrow hole in the ground dug to accept a fence column (post), or support post for a structure.

post hole digger A tool for digging narrow holes in the ground to accept posts. They have two long handles with curved jaws on their ends moving on a pivot point. The handles can be held together while the open jaws are thrust into the ground. The handles are then pulled apart to

post hole digger

squeeze the dislodged soil and allow it to be lifted and extracted from the hole.

post pounder A steel tool with two handles connected to a pipe with one end open and the other closed with a weight. It is useful to drive steel or wood posts into the ground by sliding the post into the tube, standing the post where it is to be driven, raising it by the handles, and dropping it on the stake.

post pounders

pot In the landscape industry, any free-standing container in which a plant is grown or placed. They are made of various materials including plastic, metal, fiberglass, clay, etc.

potable water Also known as **culinary water**, this water is of adequate quality to be used for human consumption. This water is usually treated to ensure purity for domestic or drinking purposes. It can be used as a source of irrigation if protection such as a **backflow preventer** is provided to prevent contamination to the domestic supply. Once water enters an irrigation system, it is not considered potable.

potager A French-inspired herb, vegetable, or flower garden of small size made with color, constant production, and low maintenance in mind.

potash

potash (K) Can refer to **potassium**, or various **potassium** compounds, but it is correctly used in reference to potassium carbonate (usually derived from wood ashes). It contains potassium, which is essential to plant growth. Potash can be obtained by washing wood ashes with water and evaporating the resultant solution until dry. This process used to be done in iron pots and thus the name derived from pot and ash. It is often used as the potassium in the basic components of a **complete fertilizer** and is usually indicated on fertilizer containers by the third percentage (number) listed on a label in the **NPK** ratio.

potassium (K) An alkali metal that is a light silver-white color, abundant in nature, and usually combined with minerals. It is highly reactive and thus readily forms various compounds. It is one of the three basic components of a **complete fertilizer** when it is in the form of potassium oxide, also known as **potash**. Plants consistently need this nutrient to sustain growth. It is represented by the letter K in the fertilizer **NPK** ratio. It is available in various compounds (i.e., **potassium nitrate**, **potassium sulfate**, etc.) for fertilizer or fertilizer manufacturing.

potassium carbonate A white salt that forms a strongly **alkaline** solution. *See* **potash**.

potassium chloride *or* **muriate of potas** A **chemical fertilizer** containing 48 to 62% water-soluble **potash** and 15% sodium. The salts can damage some soils and plants.

potassium magnesium sulfate A chemical fertilizer also known as double manure salts; supplies 30% water-soluble **potash** and up to 56% **magnesium**.

potassium nitrate A fertilizer with 14% **nitrogen** and 35% potash (14-0-35). *See* **nitrate of potash**.

potassium oxide The form of **potash** used in fertilizers.

potassium permanganate A mild **fungicide** and disinfectant with little potassium **fertilizer** value.

potassium sulfate A fertilizer also known as **sulfate of potash** containing 48 to 52% water-soluble potash.

potato bug An isopod crustacean (suborder *Oniscoidea*) having an elliptical body with seven pairs of legs, sectioned shells, and the capability to roll up into a ball about the size of a pea. They feed mostly on decaying vegetation; however, they will feed on young tender plants, especially those just germinating or on fruits that are usually overripe or damaged. They are encouraged to proliferate by mulching and composting. They are also known as sow bugs or pill bugs.

pot-bound A condition when a plant is in a smaller container than it needs or is left too long in a container. This is evident by roots that have begun to grow in circles. If planted in this condition they may not grow well, may become subject to windthrow, or may even die. Roots should be cut at the outside edges, or at least straightened and untangled.

potentiometric surface A surface that water will rise to as representing static head. In an aquifer, it is defined by the level to which water will rise in a well. A water table is a potentiometric surface.

potherb A plant grown for the use of its leaves, seeds, flowers, or other parts, especially as flavoring in foods, but also as a main dish.

potting Placing a plant and growing medium in a **pot** in such a way as to encourage growth.

potting mix The combination of materials used to support and sustain a plant growing in a pot. It may be comprised of **soil**, **sand**, decomposed manure, leaf mold, **perlite**, **vermiculite**, **peat**, or other ingredients in various combinations.

potting on   Moving a plant from a smaller container to a larger container when it has outgrown its container rooting space or shortly before.

potting up   Placing a plant that has been field grown and bare rooted, or grown as a cutting, etc. into a **pot**.

poultry manure   Excrement from poultry that is sometimes used as a fertilizer. It has an NPK ratio of 0.9–5, 0.5–1.5, 0.8–1.5. If not composted well, it can burn plants.

pound (lb) (#)   English or U.S. weight of 16 **oz** or 0.454 **kg**.

pour coat *or* **top mop**   On a built-up roof, the top coating of bitumen or final pouring of hot bitumen into which the gravel or such is embedded.

powdery mildew   Any of a number of fungal diseases acting as parasites, having a white, powdery, felt-looking appearance. They live primarily on the surfaces of plants and affect a wide variety of plants such as asters, calendulas, roses, zinnias, and lilacs. They are encouraged by damp areas with little air circulation, and are more prevalent when days are warm and nights are cool. Do not water infected plants late in the day.

PPAF   Abbreviation sometimes found on plant tags that stands for plant patent applied for.

ppm   Abbreviation for **parts per million**.

ppt   Abbreviation for parts per thousand.

PR, pr   Abbreviation for **precipitation rate** or **gross precipitation rate**. **2.** Abbreviation for pair.

praemorse   A botanical term describing a plant part that ends abruptly as if it were bitten off.

praying mantis   An insect much like a grasshopper that feeds on other insects and holds its prey in its forelimbs, much as if it were praying.

precast   *See* **precast concrete**.

precast concrete   A term describing concrete formed, poured, and finished at a location other than its final resting location or position.

prechill   A cold or freezing treatment given to seeds to break dormancy and allow them to sprout.

precipitation   Water from climatic events including rain, mist, snow, hail, sleet, or condensation. It is usually measured in inches or millimeters per day, month, or year.

precipitation rate   **1.** The rate at which rain, sleet or snow falls measured in water depth received per hour (inches/hour, or centimeters/hour). **2.** A measure of the rate at which water is applied, or is projected to be applied by a design layout, by sprinklers of an irrigation system as measured in the field or estimated by calculations in inches per hour or centimeters per hour. **3.** The rate water is projected to be applied over a given pattern of area by a single sprinkler head with a selected nozzle as given by a manufacturer in a catalogue based on field studies by the manufacturer. *See* **gross precipitation rate** and **net precipitation rate**.

precocious   In plants, something that appears early, such as flowers appearing before leaves on a plant.

predatory mites   A mite that eats the types of mites that are harmful to plants.

preemergent   Generally a chemical for treatment of soil to prevent weed seeds from germinating or emerging. It is also sometimes used after a crop is planted but before it emerges.

prefab Anything fabricated off-site and then installed at the construction site.

prefabricate The fabrication of components before their installation at the site.

prefabricated An item or its parts that are usually standardized; having been formed, cut, drilled, etc. or partially assembled off-site so that assembly consists of uniting the parts on-site to complete the construction of the desired structure, device, etc.

prefabrication The manufacture of components off-site for subsequent assembly at the site.

preferential assessment A form of **differential assessment** allowing eligible land to be assessed for its agricultural value instead of its development value. Taxes are then based on the potential revenue in crops or livestock, instead of its speculative value for development.

preferred angle **1.** An angle of the pitch on stairs between 30° and 35°. **2.** An angle of the pitch or slope of a ramp less than 15° from horizontal.

preliminary drawings Drawings not ready for construction that are produced during the early process of designing a project.

preliminary plan This term usually refers to a site plan for a project showing the layout and design of features in plan view to **scale** and usually colored.

premium fertilizer A complete fertilizer with several **micronutrient**s added.

premorse Abruptly ending as if broken off.

preplaced-aggregate concrete *or* **prepacked concrete** Concrete made by placing coarse

aggregate in a form before injecting a cement grout to fill the voids between aggregates.

preservative A substance that waterproofs, prevents rust, prevents decay, etc. With regard to lumber, a chemical that keeps moisture out of wood to prevent bacteria or fungi from getting nourishment, or a chemical that carries toxins to inhibit growth of these decay-causing organisms.

pressed brick Brick formed by pressing it to provide sharp edges and smooth surfaces before being fired in a kiln.

pressed steel Steel pressed into shape.

pressure **1.** The force exerted over a surface divided by its area. **2.** The force of a liquid or gas of uniform structure or composition per unit area exerted on the walls of its container. In sprinkler irrigation, the pressure of water exerted on walls of the pipe, etc. It is expressed in pounds per square inch (psi), bars, or kPa. It is the amount of energy available to move water through pipes, valves, sprinklers, or other equipment. **Static pressure** is the pressure measured when no water is flowing through a closed system. **Dynamic pressure** is the pressure measured when the system is open, and water is flowing.

pressure at the head In sprinkler design, the **dynamic pressure** as measured at the base of the sprinkler head.

pressure compensating Some **irrigation** emission components (**emitter**s, **spray head**s, etc.) that have devices within them that allow all emission points on the same line to operate at the same pressure by compensating for elevation change or pressure loss in flow of water through the system.

pressure-compensating emitter *or* **flexible diaphragm emitter** In drip irrigation, an emitter that is able to keep the emission of water fairly constant with variations in pressure within pipe supply lengths. This is accomplished by deformation of an elastomeric disc, diaphragm, or water passage. The drawback to these devices is that elastomeric materials have a tendency to absorb water, lose their elasticity, or creep under prolonged stress, which will change the performance of the emitter over time. *See also* **emitter**.

pressure gauge A gauge that measures the pressure of a liquid or gas.

pressure line A pipe line in a **sprinkler system** that distributes water from a source to **valves**. Also known as a **main line**.

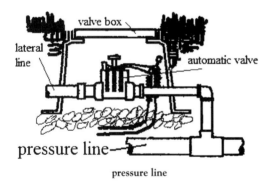

pressure line

pressure-reducing valve *or* **reducing valve** A valve that reduces pressure in a system, often adjustable to a range of pressure. They are used where pressure ranges for equipment (valves, heads) is excessive for proper operation, and on most **drip irrigation** systems.

pressure-regulating valve A valve designed to provide a preset downstream pressure in a hydraulic system.

pressure regulator A device in a pipe system that decreases the water pressure downstream, especially to allow sprinklers, emitters, etc. to operate optimally. It regulates available pressure to a preset maximum under static or flow conditions to downstream.

pressure-treated wood Any lumber that has been placed in a liquid under pressure to force it into the wood fiber. The liquid is often a preservative, and/or an insect- or fungal-retardant chemical. This is commonly performed on wood to be used in underground applications or where it may come in contact with water.

pressure vacuum breaker A backflow device with a spring-loaded float and an independent spring-loaded check valve. The check valve is designed to close with the aid of a spring when flow stops. It also has an air inlet valve designed to adequately open when the internal pressure is 1 **psi** above atmospheric pressure. This prevents nonpotable liquid from being siphoned back into the potable water system. This assembly includes resilient, seated shutoff valves and test cocks. It must be installed at least 12 in above all downstream piping and outlets, and it can be used to protect against pollutants or contaminants. It may only be used to protect against back siphoning and not against back pressure.

pressure zone An area or portion in a water system, such as for a city, where the pressure has a common origin not separated by a pressure regulator, pump, or other device for mechanically changing the pressure.

pretreatment In wetlands constructed for cleaning water, the initial treatment of waste water for removal of substances that might harm downstream treatment processes; to prepare waste water for more treatment, or cleaning.

pricking out Transplanting seedlings from their germinating tray, pot, or bed to a place where they have more room to grow.

prickle With regard to plants, a small pointed projection that is often like a small wire or stiff hair and usually is strong enough to puncture one's skin if pressed hard.

prick punch A pointed steel **punch** used to mark metal or make small indentations for a drill to follow, etc.

primary nutrient The most important nutrients needed in **soil**s for plant growth commonly shown on bags of **fertilizer**, including **nitrogen**, **phosphorus**, and **potash** uniformly indicated in that order on fertilizer supplies.

primary productivity The total amount of organic matter added to soils by plant **photosynthesis** daily or yearly.

primary treatment The first step in the process of cleaning storm water or waste water. It usually consists of removal of particulate solids through screening and sedimentation.

prime contractor A contractor on a construction project that has a contract directly with the **owner**.

prime professional A person or company having a professional services contract directly with the **owner**.

primer **1.** A first coat of paint applied to prepare for the finish coat by improving adhesion (especially on metal, plastic, etc.), sealing stains that may otherwise bleed, preventing rust, and/or filling small holes. **2.** In irrigation, a chemical liquid used to soften plastic pipe to prepare it for glue.

priming Applying a **primer** paint.

primocane A first-year raspberry cane.

principle of limiting factors The principle that the maximum rate of photosynthesis is limited by whichever basic resource needed for plant growth is least available to plants.

privacy berm A mound that obstructs view from one outdoor space to another.

privacy berm

privacy fence This term usually refers to any vertically constructed separation of outdoor spaces at least 6 ft tall, preventing views through it. It may be masonry, wood, plastic, etc.

Proctor compaction test A test determining the moisture content of a soil for optimum compaction.

Proctor penetration needle A needle, 0.05 to 1 sq in (0.32 to 6.45 sq cm) in area, used with a spring to measure resistance of fine-grained soil to penetration by the needle.

procumbent In botanical terms, along the ground, trailing, or low spreading.

production drawings Finished drawings for use in construction work.

progradation The process of growth of a shoreline toward the water due to sedimentation.

program In reference to a **dual programmable** sprinkler controller, a set time, day, and duration for operation of a **valve**(s) controlling **irri-**

gation of landscape areas with similar watering needs. Each area of different watering requirements is set on its individual program with its necessary start time, **run time**, and day(s) of operation.

progress payment   A payment made by a client for work in progress but not yet complete.

project   **1.** A design for a proposed improvement on land in the form of drawings, models, etc. **2.** A construction work of any kind, including the maintenance of facilities.

project manual   The specifications, bid requirements, contract conditions, etc.

promenade   A suitable place to enjoy walking for leisure, often with a dramatic, impressive, or beautiful view.

propagation *or* **propagating** *or* **propagate**   Multiplying **plant**s. In gardening, this refers to starting new plants (reproduction) from planting seeds (sexual reproduction), **division**s, **cuttings**, **budding**, **layering**, or **grafting**.

property line   A recorded **boundary** of land parcel, often having different ownership on each side of the line.

proposal   A term often used interchangeably with **bid**.

proposal form   A form to be filled in when submitting a **bid** for work.

prostrate   In botanical terms, laying flat on the ground. It is usually a description of a ground cover.

protected species   A plant protected by federal or state law.

protective covenant   A written agreement or legal document that restricts the use of real property.

protractor   An instrument usually shaped like a half circle connected at its ends by a straight piece, that is graduated in angular degrees along its curved edge for measuring angles, or to facilitate drawing angles.

provenance   The geographical area from which a plant originated.

proximal   A botanical term describing a plant part toward its base or its near end.

pruinose   A botanical term meaning very **glaucous**, or having a **bloom** or powder on a plant part, such as on grapes and plums.

prune *or* **pruning**   With regard to plants, the intentional cutting off of **root**s, **stem**s, or **shoot**s to make a plant more appropriate for its location, its purpose, to stimulate growth or flowering, or to improve its ability to survive.

pruner   A tool with two jaws and two handles on a pivot point allowing the handles to be squeezed and the jaws (at least one of which is sharp) to chop off woody plant growth when pruning. There are small pruners with handles that just fit in one hand and larger ones, often called loppers, with long handles and larger jaws.

pruners

pruning sealer   A substance, solution, or paint sprayed or brushed onto fresh cuts after pruning. There has been much controversy over its protective value, necessity, and potential harm.

pruning shears Long-bladed **pruners** used for shearing hedges, grass, or similar thin plant material.

pry bar A heavy solid steel bar with a point on one end and a chisel on the other. It is useful in prying, and in breaking up highly compacted soil, especially soils containing rocks.

pseudanthium A compact inflorescence with small individual flowers that together simulate a single flower.

pseudobulb A thickened, modified stem aboveground resembling a **bulb** (as in some orchids, *Cymbidium*) and serving as storage for nutrients.

pseudocarp Fruit that has considerable fleshy material, as with a peach or a strawberry.

psf Abbreviation for pounds per square foot.

psi Abbreviation for pressure expressed as pounds per square inch. In water pressure calculations, 1 psi is equal to 2.31 **feet of head** or the pressure at the bottom of a column of water 2.31 ft tall.

psp Abbreviation for plastic sewer pipe.

psyllids A jumping, sucking insect less than ¼ in long, much like **aphid**s and sometimes called jumping lice.

pt Abbreviation for **pint**(s).

p-trap A **drain** connection with a low point that is filled with water, preventing sewer gases from escaping into a **space** through a plumbing fixture.

puberulent In botanical terms, covered with almost imperceptible fine and short down. It is a very fine, almost imperceptible **pubescence**.

pubescence In botanical terms, the quality of being **pubescent**.

pubescent In botanical terms, covered with fine and soft short hairs.

PUD Abbreviation for **planned unit development**.

puddle With regard to soils, compacting loose soil by first soaking it, and then permitting it to dry.

puddled soil This is a reference to **soil** that is artificially compacted when wet by vehicle or foot traffic, or **clay** soils that are **till**ed when wet. It is dense, massive, compacted, and without **granular structure**. It does not allow good air or water movement in the soil.

puddling **1.** Reducing voids in mortar or concrete by the use of a tamping rod. This makes it more compact and assists in avoiding cavities. **2.** The act of coating with a mixture of wet clay that is water repellant.

pull box A box in which wire raceway sleeves open to allow pulling wires (conductors) through those conduits or sleeves.

pulling pipe A method of establishing underground pipe lines by attaching pipe to the bottom of a steel blade on a machine that pulls the pipe into the ground.

pull-string A string covered with chalk for stretching tightly over a surface where it is pulled from near the center and let go to snap a line on the surface marked by the chalk. This line is often used for cutting or marking.

pulp **1.** The pith of a plant **stem**. **2.** The soft part of a fruit.

pulverant A term used to describe **fertilizer**s that are not liquid, not granulated, but mostly powder.

pulvinus A botanical term referring to the swollen base of a **petiole**.

pumice A lava product with a lightweight, highly porous, loose, and spongy structure.

pumice concrete A lightweight concrete using pumice as **aggregate**.

pump **1.** A hand or motorized device used for causing water to flow or be compressed. They come in a large variety of types and sizes for various applications but can be classified into two basic types: the **positive displacement pump** (or static pump type) and the **dynamic pump** (or kinetic pump type). **2.** In excavation work, describes the ability of the ground to bring water to the surface when it is walked on or driven over. This is an unfavorable condition when attempting to compact an area.

pumping **1.** The action of fluid flow facilitated by a device used to move liquid (especially water) by mechanical means (a **pump**), usually through a pipe. **2.** In landscape and excavation work, the action of water movement to the surface when it is walked on, driven over, or an attempt is made to compact it. In this condition, soil is unfit for most work. In landscape work, if soil is worked in this condition, it becomes compacted, does not drain well, and is not conducive for most plants to thrive. Soil should not be worked when excess moisture becomes evident after stepping in the same spot several times (pumping occurs).

pump performance chart *or* **pump performance curve** *or* **pump performance graph** A graphical representation of a pump's performance characteristics based on water with a specific gravity of 1.0. These graphs provide information such as **total dynamic head**, brake horsepower, **efficiency curves**, and **net positive suction head required**.

pump speed The shaft rotational speed of a pump usually expressed in revolutions per minute. It is usually given on **pump performance charts**.

pump start circuit A feature on an irrigation controller allowing a connection to be made through a **relay**, with the pump starter, so the starter will be energized when a watering cycle begins.

pump start relay An electronic device that uses a signal current from the irrigation controller to actuate a separate electrical circuit that energizes the pump starter.

punch A short steel tool with a sharp point. It is struck with a hammer for centering, marking, or starting a drill in the right spot so that the drill bit does not wander as it spins.

punches A reference sometimes made in placing pipe underground where it must be bored or pushed under paved or sensitive ground areas.

punch list A written notice, list, and record of items observed on-site that are not complete, need correction, or need repair work by a contractor to meet design documents' intent and for the project to be completely finished. **Substantial completion** should occur before a punch list is created.

punctate In botanical terms, dotted with small, translucent glands, or with minute holes or apparently so.

pungent **1.** A bitter or sharp taste or smell. **2.** A botanical term referring to a plant part that is firmly sharp-pointed.

punkle *See* **midge**.

pupa The inactive, immature stage of many insects in the stage of metamorphoses to an adult stage.

purlin

purlin   A horizontal **beam**, strut, **timber**, or support in the framing of a roof system and usually supporting the roof **decking**.

purlins

pustule   A raised bump on a plant much like a blister.

putty   A heavy paste composed of pigment mixed with linseed oil and used to fill holes and cracks in wood prior to painting.

putty knife   A tool with a long handle and a flat-nosed blade used for spreading putty.

PVB   Abbreviation for **pressure vacuum breaker**.

PVC   Abbreviation for **polyvinyl chloride**, a common plastic material from which pipes are made, and is often the choice for use in constructing sprinkler irrigation systems. Pipes and fittings of this material are classified for various pressures with the pressure rating stamped on the side, or with the thickness of the pipe stamped by reference to schedule. It is not resistant to impact, especially in smaller sizes or with thin walls. It is sold in **schedule** or **class** sizes. Connections may be made by solvent weld, threads, or by compression fittings with rubber gaskets, depending on the type of connection it is prepared with.

pylon sign   A sign that towers above the surrounding landscape or buildings. (Compare with **monument sign**.)

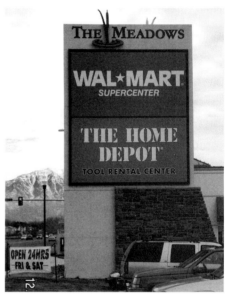
pylon sign

pyramidal   A botanical term describing a shape that resembles a pyramid: broad at the base and tapering to a point. It may describe a plant part or a plant outline of its head, such as many evergreen trees. (Compare with **round, columnar, fastigiate, oval, broadly spreading, upright spreading, weeping**.)

pyramidal tree forms

pyrethrin   The active ingredient of **pyrethrum**.

pyrethrum   A broad spectrum organic insecticide relatively harmless to warm-blooded animals, but lethal to insects. It is used as a powder or liquid made from *chrysanthemum, cinerariaefolium,* or *C. roseum.*

pyriform   In botanical terms, pear shaped.

pythium   A water mold, fungal **pathogen**, soil inhabitant, and cause of **damping off** and **root rot**.

Q

Q Abbreviation for quantity often used in referring to **gross precipitation rate**.

qt Abbreviation for **quart**(s).

quadrant sampling Gathering representative evidence of soils, plants, etc. from small plots in a landscape.

quadrate Nearly square.

quality of life A measure of the enjoyment or convenience experienced by residents living within a specific area. A myriad of influences plays a part in this measure, and some influences affect a portion of the population positively while affecting others negatively. **Open space**, landscaping, and **parks** generally play a part in this measure.

quantity survey A listing of the details of all materials and equipment needed for construction depicted on a drawing(s).

quarry-faced **Ashlar** only squared enough to fit in a wall with a rough, quarried surface.

quarry tile Fired clay tile often used in flooring or on outdoor **patio**s.

quart (qt) English or U.S. capacity measurement of liquid equal to 2 **pint**s, ¼ **gal**, 57.75 **c.i.**, or 0.946 **l**.

quarter section A square tract of land that measures ½ mi on each side.

quartz-halogen lamp A lamp with a tungsten filament in a quartz envelope.

quasi- A Latin prefix sometimes used in botanical terms meaning seemingly but not actually.

queen closer A brick that has been cut in half along its length. It is often used to complete a course.

quick coupler key A round key with a small knob that is inserted and turned into a **quick coupler valve** to allow water to escape.

quick coupler valve A valve with water pressure, which when a key is inserted into it allows water to escape, usually to a hose or a sprinkler head. Quick couplers were extensively used with sprinkler heads before automatically controlled systems became available. Sprinkler heads operated by quick couplers are expensive when labor is considered. They are also difficult to turn off in time to avoid overwatering, as many times they are forgotten and left in operation.

quoin *or* **coign** *or* **coin** In masonry, a hard stone or brick used to reinforce an external corner or edge of a wall.

R

R, r **1.** Abbreviation for radius. **2.** The symbol for the thermal resistance of a material. **3.** Abbreviation for electrical resistance.

rabbet, rebate A long channel, groove, or recess in one member to receive another as in a window or door edge, or as in **tongue-and-groove** lumber.

raceme In botanical terms, a flower cluster with one-flowered **pedicels** along the axis of **inflorescence**. It is a simple flower cluster with many stalked flowers about the same length coming from the same stem and usually opening in succession toward the apex.

raceme inflorescence

racemose Growing in the form of a **raceme**.

raceway A channel, pipe, or conduit for enclosing electrical conductors.

rachilla In botanical terms, the axis of a **spikelet**.

rachis In botanical terms, that which bears and is attached to **flowers** or **leaflets** of a plant. It may refer to an axis bearing close-set organs, espe-

cially the axis of a **spike**. It is also used in reference to the extension of the **petiole** or rib of a **compound** leaf from which the **petiole** meets the leaf **blade** to the tip of the leaf.

rachis radial A spine of a cactus where the spines originate from an **aerole**'s periphery instead of its center as is the case with a **central**.

radial Projecting outward from a center along a radius or in a circle, as rays projecting from a point.

radial-arm saw _or_ **radial saw** A saw that holds a rotating, circular saw blade above the work and has capabilities for tilting, rotating, or moving the blade.

radical Pertaining to the root.

radicle The lower part of a plant embryo. The root of a plant embryo or seedling.

radius of throw The distance from the sprinkler head to the farthest point of water application by the sprinkler.

rafter A structural support member extending from the ridge of the roof down to the eave.

raft foundation A thick, reinforced concrete slab used instead of wall or column footings or foundations to support and distribute the load of a structure to a soil with low-bearing capacity.

ragwork Thin, flat, undressed stones laid in a crude and random fashion, usually horizontally.

rail **1.** An elongated item of various materials used for grasping with a hand for stability and support, such as on stairs See **handrail**. **2.** Horizontal members of a fence extending from **post** to post.

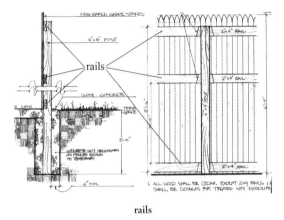

rails

railroad tie   A timber impregnated with creosote to prevent decay that had been used to hold railroad rails in place and then was salvaged for **site** work. They are often used for retaining walls, or separating various surface materials. They often ooze creosote, becoming offensive by staining clothes or tracking on shoes to other surfaces. Creosote contact with skin may raise health concerns.

Rails To Trails   A federal act affording interested governments the opportunity to use potentially abandoned railroad right-of-ways for recreational and aesthetic uses.

rainfall erosion index   Values representing the relative erosive power of rainfall from a 30 minute storm.

rainfall intensity   The amount of rainfall measured in centimeters or inches per hour or minute.

rain gauge   A device that collects rainfall information, particularly useful in computer applications of determining water needs. They are cup

shaped and gather rainfall usually allowing detection in $\frac{1}{100}$ in increments.

rain gutter   A channel at the edge of a roof for conveying water away.

rain sensor   A sensor that turns an **irrigation controller** off when rain has accumulated, and on when the water has evaporated.

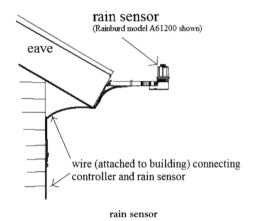

rain sensor

rainshadow   The dry area on the leeward side of a mountain where precipitation decreases.

rainsplash   The soil and water displacement occurring with raindrop impact, causing erosion.

rainwash   Water from rain gathering as a sheet and running over the land surface, causing erosion.

rainwater conductor   A pipe or tube, usually exposed on the surface of a structure, and usually made of **aluminum** or tin, for conveying **precipitation** from a roof or flat area of a structure downward.

raised planter   A **planter** with an elevation higher than the adjacent grade. The earth is usually retained by a retaining wall, boulders, etc.

rake   **1.** A sloping or inclined surface, especially a roof. **2.** A board along the sloping edge of a gable roof. **3.** Toothed, downward-turned, parallel bars or teeth, or fan-shaped spines on a long handle used for removing debris from a **ground** surface, for loosening soil, or for **grading** and smoothing.

raised planter

raking-out **1.** In landscape construction, the action of preparing a surface for planting or placement of mulch, etc. by raking it smooth and removing any unwanted debris. **2.** In brickwork, preparing mortar joints for pointing.

raking stretcher bond A pattern of bricks laid as stretchers in a flush wall where each brick overlaps the one underneath by one-quarter of a brick length.

rammed earth Earth and water compressed and then dried.

ramp A relatively short access from one elevation to another without any vertical rise, usually with a slope accommodating a particular type of traffic (i.e., wheelchair, automobile, golf cart, etc.).

rampant Wildness; absence of restraint; vigorous, aggressive growth.

rampart **1.** A wide embankment as fortification, usually having a parapet at its highest level. **2.** A wall-like ridge made of rock fragments, debris, or earth.

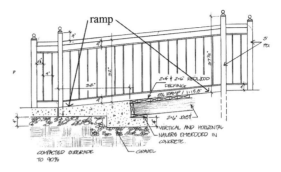

ramp

ramuliferous Densely or profusely branched.

random ashlar A masonry wall with rectangular stones not having continuous joints and without a fixed pattern.

rank foliage Leaves that have grown profusely or larger than normal.

rapid-curing asphalt Liquid asphalt cement and a petroleum-type diluting agent of high volatility, causing a quick cure.

rasp A coarse file with protruding, pointed teeth.

ratchet drill A hand-driven drill with ratchet-driven chuck.

rated horsepower The maximum horsepower provided under normal, continuous operation.

rate of slope *See* **slope ratio**.

rational formula *or* **rational method** A method of runoff calculation with a formula for computing the runoff volume of a given area. It is represented by $Q = CiA$ where Q is the peak runoff in cubic feet per second or cubic meters per second; C is the **coefficient of runoff**; i is the intensity of rainfall in inches per hour for design peak rainstorm adjusted to a duration equal to the **time of concentration** of the watershed; and A is the area of the watershed in acres or hectares.

rational method

rational method *See* **rational formula.**

ray In botanical terms, a branch of an umbel flower stalk.

RBM Abbreviation for **reinforced brick masonry.**

RC asphalt *See* **rapid-curing asphalt.**

RCP **1.** Abbreviation for residual current device. **2.** Abbreviation for reinforced concrete pipe.

rd **1.** Abbreviation for **rod**(s). **2.** Abbreviation for road.

reach The section of a sewer pipe between structures.

reaction wood Wood resulting from abnormal growth.

real property Land and everything growing on it or built on it (structures), and usually some space above it and everything beneath it.

reamer A tapered drill bit with sharp, spiral, fluted cutting edges along the shaft. This tool is used to enlarge an opening to cut burs from pipe, etc.

rear lot line Generally, the opposite and most distant line from the front lot line.

rear yard The yard across the full width of a parcel extending from the rear line of the main building to the rear property line.

rebar A steel bar used for reinforcing, having a pattern of raised areas on its surface to prevent moving concrete when temperatures change, or when pressure is applied.

rebloomer A plant that flowers more than once in a growing season.

receiving site *or* **receiving zone** *or* **receiving area** An area of land where dwelling unit numbers allowed (allowable density) is increased by transferring development rights (dwelling units) from a **sending site** by way of a **transfer of development rights**. This assists in preserving agricultural and natural areas.

receptacle A botanical term identifying the end of the stem (pedicel) to which the other flower parts are attached.

receptacle plug An electrical device capable of receiving a plug with a cord for supply of electrical current to appliances or portable, electrically powered devices. This device is mounted in a box, usually hidden behind a wall and the power is constantly supplied by a wire to the box and outlet.

recess A depression in a surface.

recharge In relation to water in the landscape, the replenishment of groundwater, or aquifers with water percolating from the surface of the earth.

recharge **1.** (**artificial**) The addition of water to groundwater by activities of man at a recharge rate greater than historically recorded. **2.** (**groundwater**) The replenishment of groundwater.

recharge zone *or* **recharge area** The portion of any area of land surface where **ground-water recharge** is naturally or historically significant.

reciprocating pump A **pump** that moves and compresses fluids by use of a piston with an intake and outlet to the chamber, allowing fluid in as it retracts the piston and forcing water out as the piston is pushed to the other end of the chamber.

reclaimed waste water Waste water that has been cleaned enough to be of beneficial reuse.

reclaimed water Water that has been collected (and sometimes treated as necessary) after an original use and then made available for reuse (often in an irrigation system).

reclamation The reuse or reclaiming of resources, usually in reference to natural resources. This term is often used for revegetation of an area that has been disturbed or denuded of vegetation.

record drawings The drawings prepared by a contractor before, during, and after completion of a project, showing the project as it was actually constructed with any changes from the original design drawings.

record sheet At a construction site, a sheet recording materials delivered, number of workers employed at the various trades, hours worked, weather, etc.

recreational vehicle (RV) A vehicle designed or used for living, sleeping, and recreational purposes and equipped with wheels to facilitate traveling. They include pickup coaches (campers), motorized homes, boats, travel trailers, camping trailers, four-wheelers, snowmobiles, etc.

recurved In botanical terms, bent backward, downward, outward, or toward its beginning.

recyclable material Waste materials or by-products processed and then returned to the economic mainstream in the form of commodities or products. Recyclable materials include metals, glass, plastic, paper, wood, etc.

recycling plant A facility that recovers resources, such as paper products, glass, metal, etc. to return them to use.

red brass *or* **rich low brass** A metal alloy containing about 85% copper and 15% zinc. It has high corrosion resistance, can be polished,

and is available in flat sheets, rod, wire, or tube.

red spider mite *See* **mites**.

reduced pressure backflow preventer *See* **reduced pressure principle assembly**.

reduced pressure principle assembly A **backflow preventer** with loaded, independently operating check valves and a mechanically independent, hydraulically dependent relief valve located between the check valves. The relief valve is designed to maintain a zone of reduced pressure between the two check valves. It contains tightly closing, resilient, seated shut-off valves upstream and downstream of the check valves along with resilient seated test cocks used for protecting the potable water supply from pollutants and contaminants and may be used to protect against back siphoning and back pressure.

reduced pressure vacuum breaker A device that protects upstream waters from downstream siphoning backward and contamination while under continuous pressure. It will stop water from moving backward even when it is under back pressure.

reducer **1.** Any fitting for piping facilitating a connection between two pipes of different sizes. **2.** A chemical such as a thinner or solvent that can be added to paints or varnishes to lower their viscosity.

reducer bushing A slip socket or threaded fitting that can be inserted into another fitting or flared end (bell end) of a pipe to allow the attachment of a smaller pipe or device with a male end by insertion into it.

reducing pipe fitting Any pipe **fitting** used to connect pipes of different sizes.

reducing valve A valve that decreases the upstream pressure of the pipe system it is installed onto. It assures less pressure for the pipe system downstream of it.

reduction ratio In stone crushing, the ratio of the maximum dimension of rock before crushing to the maximum dimension of rock after crushing.

reel mower A mower that has a spiral reel of blades that spin as the wheels turn and cut against a stationary sharp bar. They are drawn behind tractors or pushed by hand. They make a nice cut to lawn blades instead of tears as with a rotary mower. *See also* **rotary mower**.

refined tar Tar having its water evaporated or distilled to a desired consistency.

reflected radiation Solar light (radiation) reflected from surrounding objects.

reflecting pond An existing body of water or one often created to reflect or mirror images near it.

reflecting pond

reflection The change of direction of ray of light, sound, or radiant heat when it strikes a surface.

reflector Anything that redirects light or sound by reflection.

reflexed In botanical terms, bent outward, downward, or backward.

reforestation Replanting, encouraging, or allowing forest plant materials to increase where they once proliferated.

refraction The change in direction of a light ray or a sound ray in passing from one material to another.

refractory A material, usually nonmetallic, that can withstand high temperatures.

refuse Trash or debris.

region In spatial hierarchy (as defined in **landscape ecology**) of lands, a broad geographical area with common macroclimate and sphere of human involvement. It is smaller than a continent and larger than a **landscape**. It is tied together by human activities. Examples are northwestern United States, southwestern United States, and the Andes of Venezuela.

regolith In a **soil profile**, a layer of loose unconsolidated rock covering the parent material (bedrock), sometimes termed the **D horizon**. It is weathered overburden mostly made up of weathered rock that is disintegrating into **sand** and **clay** particles.

regular flower A flower that is radially symmetrical with **petals** and **sepals** arranged around a center like spokes of a wheel.

regulatory floodway A zone designated by U.S. federal flood policy as the lowest part of the floodplain where historically the deepest and most frequent floods have occurred.

REINF, reinf. Abbreviation for reinforce, reinforced, or reinforcing.

reinforced blockwork In masonry, **blockwork** containing steel reinforcement.

reinforced brick masonry (RBM) Brickwork that contains steel bars to impart tensile strength.

reinforced concrete *or* **ferroconcrete** *or* **steel concrete** Concrete containing reinforcement (usually rebar) to assist in resisting forces placed upon or working upon the concrete.

reinforced earth wall A granular matrix or fill reinforced with successive layers of metal strips to retain a slope.

reinforced grouted masonry A brick or block wall grouted solid throughout its entire height and having both vertical and horizontal reinforcing.

reinforced masonry Masonry with steel reinforcement.

reinforcing bar A steel bar used in concrete or masonry construction to improve its strength.

reinforcing fibers A synthetic fiber usually of polypropylene that is incorporated into a concrete or mortar mix for extra strength or elasticity.

reinforcing rod A long steel member placed or formed in concrete to give it strength.

relative humidity The percentage of the maximum amount of water vapor that air is capable of holding at any given temperature. Colder air takes less water vapor than warmer air to obtain the same relative humidity. Air saturated to the point it can hold no more water is at 100% relative humidity. The amount of water necessary to reach 100% of the capacity of air to hold it (complete saturation) is always more for warmer air and less for cooler air.

relay An electromechanical device that opens or closes electrical contacts in a circuit by changes in the current flow in another circuit.

release agent A chemical or substance sprayed in **forms** to facilitate easy removal with less sticking or chance of damage to the concrete when removed.

relief The difference(s) in elevation(s) and in spatial configuration(s) within a prescribed area of the surface of the earth.

relief valve A valve installed in a pipe system to relieve pressure in excess of a preset limit by discharging a portion of the water in the system.

remediation The act or process of remedying. In land planning and landscape architecture, it is used in reference to contaminated site cleanup to remedy hazardous wastes.

remolded soil Soil that has had its natural structure modified by dislocation and manipulation.

remote control valve A valve actuated by an automatic controller with electric or hydraulic means.

render **1.** In design work, to draw. **2.** To apply shades, textures, shadows, etc. to a line drawing. **3.** In construction work, to produce a smooth finish by covering a surface with **mortar** or **concrete**.

reniform In botanical terms, kidney bean shaped.

repand In botanical terms, wavy-margined.

repent A botanical term meaning creeping.

repot *See* **potting up**.

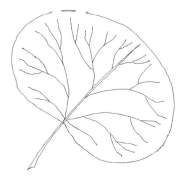

reniform leaf shape

req'd   Abbreviation for required.

request for information   An inquiry made by a participant in contractual obligations usually in the construction industry.

request for proposal   A solicitation normally from public agencies distributed to consulting, manufacturing, or development firms asking for a proposal for services or products. They are encouraged to contain a description of the project, program, or items, the amount budgeted, the type of contract (fixed price or time-and-expense, etc.), qualifications required, evaluation criteria, and a description of the materials to submit.

request for qualifications   A solicitation usually prepared by a public agency distributed to consulting and development firms requesting a statement of credentials associated with the firm. It usually requests contact information, a description of the organization, resumes of key personnel, a statement describing work completed on similar projects, availability for the work, a list of projects completed, and references.

reservoir   An artificial lake or pond created to retain and store water for later use.

reservoir pool   With regard to recirculating water features, the lowest pool which must have enough capacity to hold the water normally in transit when in operation as it will flow into it when pumps are turned off.

residence   A dwelling where a person(s) re-sides.

residence time   The time necessary to exchange the water in an aquifer or surface water body with new water.

residual fertilizer   The portions of fertilizer remaining in the soil after one or more crops or seasons.

resilient hanger   A pipe hanger with a resilient spring between the clamp or saddle and the point of attachment.

resistance   In electrical systems, the resistance or restriction to the flow of current measured in **ohms**. It can be compared to friction loss in an irrigation system. When electricity is flowing, resistance causes a drop in voltage along the length of a wire.

respiration   **1.** The chemical process in which a plant absorbs oxygen, then releases energy from the oxidizing of plant sugars to water and carbon dioxide. Plant soil should be sufficiently aerated to allow oxygen to be available to the plant's roots. **2.** The biochemical processes that consume oxygen and carbohydrates and release energy. It is the reverse of **photosynthesis**.

responsible bidder   *See* **lowest responsible bidder**.

resting   Said of a plant that grows for more than one season at the annual time it slows or stops growth.

restoration   The return by human intervention of an ecosystem from a disturbed or altered condition to a previously existing natural condition.

restrictive covenants   A restriction on uses, aesthetics, layout, design, or other items associated with a land or its potential. These are usually recorded with land records in the governing authority's records and are usually transferred from owner to owner when property is sold.

resupinate Upside down, or appearing to be so.

retail nursery A **nursery** that sells a majority of its products to the general public.

retainage Money withheld (usually a percentage) from progress payments to a contractor until completion.

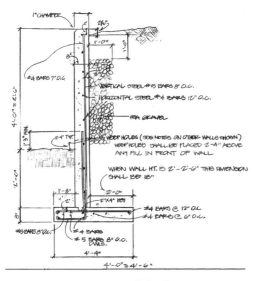

retaining wall detail

retaining wall

retaining wall **1.** A structure used as a vertical grade change to hold soil on the up-hillside from

moving downhill, slumping, sliding, or falling. They are made of concrete, brick, stone, block, etc. **2.** A wall with one side open to view and the other having earthen material piled against it.

retarder A chemical, etc. added to substances such as mortar and concrete to slow its hardening or wetting time.

retarding In nursery terms, delaying growth by prolonging a plant's **dormant** season (usually through the control of temperature).

retention **1.** A storm water management practice in which **runoff** is kept on-site in basins, underground, or released to infiltrate into the **soil**. *See* **retainage**. **2.** An amount withheld from payments on a contract and then paid at the end of work to assure its quality and completion.

reticulate A network (i.e., the veins in a leaf).

retrorse In botanical terms, directed back or downward.

retuse In botanical terms, a small terminal notch (the **apex** slightly indented) in an otherwise rounded or blunt leaf tip. (Compare with **emarginate, cuspidate, aristate, acuminate, acute, mucronate, obtuse**.)

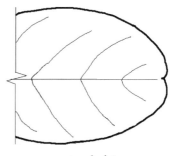

retuse leaf tip

reuniform In botanical terms, kidney shaped.

revegetation The replacement of plant material on a land area.

reversion   The occurrence of a plant of particular qualities reverting back (losing those qualities) to the parent plant qualities.

revet   The facing of stone, concrete, etc. against an embankment.

revetment   A wall facing over an embankment to prevent erosion or cave-ins.

revolute   In botanical terms, rolled backward, as the margins of many leaves.

RF, rf   On drawings, an abbreviation for roof.

rfg   Abbreviation for roofing.

RFI   In construction, a **request for information** by a participant of work under contract on a project.

RFP   Abbreviation for **request for proposals**.

RFQ   Abbreviation for **request for qualifications**.

rgs   Abbreviation for rigid galvanized steel.

rhiaomatous   A plant that spreads by **rhizome**s.

rhizanthous   Bearing flowers directly from the roots.

rhizobia   Small **heterotrophic** soil bacteria capable of making symbiotic nodules on roots of some leguminous plants that became **bacteroid**s fixing atmospheric nitrogen.

rhizobium   A species of bacteria that live in symbiosis with some plant roots (usually **legume**s) by forming nodules on them and deriving their energy from the root while in return **fix**ing atmospheric nitrogen for the plant and themselves.

rhizodegradation   Contaminant breakdown due to influence of the **rhizosphere** of a root.

rhizoid   A structure of a plant that is root-like, or a structure of root-like form and function but of simple anatomy, lacking xylem and phloem.

rhizome   In botanical terms, any prostrate, more or less elongated stem growing partially or completely beneath the surface of the ground. They may be thick, hard, and sometimes rather large, or in many grasses and such they are sometimes delicate and hair-like. Thicker, larger ones are sometimes considered a type of **bulb**, with the thickened underground stem utilized for food storage. They creep horizontally from their tips (and other growing points form along their length) with roots generally growing from its underside. The buds on the rhizome produce roots, foliage, and flower stalks. Cutting portions of the rhizome with new growth buds and transplanting them can produce new plants.

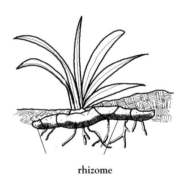

rhizome

rhizosphere   The area of soil influenced by plant roots that shows more microbial numbers, species, and activity than other soil. In flooded soils with some plants the rhizosphere can be oxidized, resulting in the presence of aerobic soil in an otherwise anaerobic soil environment. The volume of soil adjacent to the root that is under the influence of the root.

rhomboid   In botanical terms, a solid figure, rhombic (somewhat diamond shaped) in outline.

rhomboidal   A botanical term meaning roughly diamond-shaped.

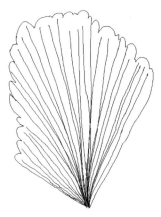

rhomboidal leaf shape

R horizon The bottom of a **soil profile** that is sometimes not considered part of the profile because it is **bedrock**. This consolidated rock is the parent material of the soil profile above it and may consist of sandstone, granite, limestone, etc. It is sometimes incorrectly called the **regolith**. Regolith is actually unconsolidated bedrock also referred to as the **D horizon**.

rich concrete Concrete with high cement content.

ridge **1.** A relatively narrow top of a steep slope, usually with an elongated crest, and sometimes having peaks significantly higher than the adjoining crest line. It is a linear, elevated portion of land with downslopes on either side. **2.** The horizontal line where the upper edges of two sloping roof surfaces meet.

ridgecap *or* **ridge capping** *or* **ridge covering** The covering on the ridge of a roof.

ridgeline *See* **ridge**.

riffle A segment of a stream channel or any water feature channel with rapid and at least somewhat turbulent flow.

right angle parking Vehicle storage spaces arranged at a right angle to the flow of traffic along the edge of a travel way.

right-of-way Any strip or area of land granted by deed, easement, reservation, dedication, prescription, or condemnation for any use other than the owner's personal use. They are often for utilities (usually linear) such as for power lines, telephone lines, roadways, gas lines, oil pipes, water lines, sewers, vehicular or pedestrian access or egress, etc.

rill Small, water-caused erosion channels made by a **rivulet**. These channels are usually small enough that they can be easily plowed out with a tractor disc. *See also* **rill erosion** and **gully**.

rill erosion The erosion that occurs with **runoff** water when it begins to move earth particles in shallow, narrow channels no more than a few inches deep and easily removed by agricultural tillage operations. They are indications of erosion to a moderate extent and over time will move a great deal of soil, eventually becoming gullies if not corrected.

ring nail This is a **nail** with tapered rings along its shank, which make it difficult to be removed from a material that it is pounded into. *See also* **annular nail**.

ring-shank nail A nail with ring-like grooves around the shank to increase its holding power.

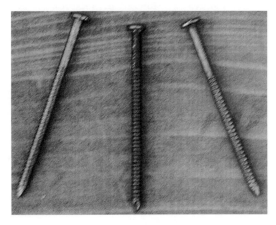

ring-shank nails

rink **1.** A bounded surface of ice used for skating, curling, or ice hockey. **2.** A bounded, smooth surface of wood, concrete, asphalt, etc. for roller skating, rollerblading, etc.

rip Cutting wood parallel to the grain.

riparian In landscape work, plant communities occurring in association with any spring, lake, river, stream, creek, wash, arroyo, or other water body having banks and a bed through which water flows at least occasionally.

riparian right The right of a landowner to use water from a river, lake, or other body of water that is contiguous to the owner's land or on the owner's land.

riparian wetland Wetlands on the edge of a large water feature such as a lake or stream.

ripe Mature, or fully developed.

ripper An attachment dragged behind a tractor with long, curved teeth extending below it for ripping compacted earth.

ripping size The size of lumber, as it comes from the operation of **ripsawing**.

riprap A layer of stones, broken concrete, or boulders placed on a slope to stabilize it against slope failure or **erosion** due to precipitation, natural drainage, waves, or wind.

ripsawing or **flat cutting** or **ripping** Sawing lumber essentially parallel to the direction of the grain.

rise **1.** The elevation difference between a supply point in any irrigation system and an elevated point of discharge or the highest point of discharge. **2.** The elevation difference in a flight of stairs from landing to landing. **3.** The elevation difference between successive treads of a stair. **4.** The vertical distance in a ratio used to express the height of a roof slope compared to horizontal distance or run.

riser **1.** The front vertical portion of a stair step which comprises the rise from one stair tread to another. **2.** In **sprinkler irrigation**, a vertical pipe, the **nipple**, rising above ground or **finish grade** from a **lateral line** with a water-dispensing device (**sprinkler head**, **shrub adapter**, etc.) mounted on its top. These are often used in shrub, ground cover, or flower areas to get the sprinkler above the plant material. **3.** Any vertical portion of pipe.

rived board or **riven board** **1.** A board shape obtained by splitting it along the grain instead of sawing it. **2.** The board making the vertical face of a step.

riverine wetlands Wetlands associated with rivers, streams, or creeks.

river rock A rock having a rounded form (or at least edges) and smoothed by the action of water flow or other forces of nature; most often available in water channels or in alluvium.

riverwalk A pedestrian path along a river edge.

rivet A short pin of a malleable metal with a head at one end that holds it in place against metal sheets while the other end extends through the sheets and is then smashed flat to hold it in place.

rivulet A small stream of water.

rivulose A pattern like a branching river, or a wavy serpentine pattern.

R/L Abbreviation for random lengths.

road A path or way meant for and in some way prepared for vehicles to travel.

road corridor The linear surface of a **road** and its associated linear vegetative **corridor**s.

rock A natural, solid, dense mineral material in large masses or fragments often requiring explosives or mechanical equipment to move. It is sometimes referred to as stone, and when fragmented can be any size. The word stone in most areas refers to small pieces used in masonry.

rock drill A machine or device used to drill holes in rock.

rockery Much like a **rock garden**, this is a **mound** or pile of rocks with planting dirt interspersed, usually formed to accommodate plants needing good drainage or for alpine-type plant material.

rock fill Loosely placed rocks in a layer or mass.

rock garden A constructed landscape with flowering or vine-type plant material amongst rocks. It is usually on sloping ground with rock used to retain soil or in an area containing natural-appearing rock or rock outcrops.

rock phosphate A naturally occurring mineral with varying **phosphorus** content from 14% (0-14-0) to 27% (0-27-0). In this state, this phosphate is only helpful in **acidic** soils. It is used to make **superphosphate**. It is available very slowly and not easily released, even when ground to dust. It is not effective on soils over 6.2 **pH**. It is more readily used by leguminous plants.

rockwork **1.** Any stacked-stone retaining wall, or free-standing wall. **2.** Rough, stone faced masonry.

rod English or U.S. length measurement equal to 5.50 **y**, 16.5 **ft**, or 5.029 **m**. **2.** A solid long piece of metal, wood, plastic, etc.

rodding **1.** The compaction of mortar or concrete by poking it with a rod. **2.** The action of clearing an obstruction in a drain by ramming.

rod target A target that slides up and down a leveling rod or range rod, making it easier to sight accurately from a transit, etc.

rogue or **rougued** or **rougueing** To weed out (remove) a crop, nursery stock, or field plants with diseases, inferior plants, or plants that are not typical.

rolling In landscape work, pushing or pulling a heavy (usually water-filled) roller over the ground to level small bumps or depressions. This is most often not effective as it requires a moist soil and any walking over the soil in this condition causes depressions in the footprints of one pulling the roller. In clay soils, it forces air from the soil, leaving it highly compacted.

rolock *See* **rowlock**.

roof The top covering of a building, space, shelter, or pavilion, including all materials that support the surface as well as the surface itself. It prevents precipitation and sun from disturbing an area.

roof drain A drain that receives water gathered on the surface of a roof to allow its drainage through an attached pipe or conduit.

roofing Material such as metal, tile, wood, asphalt, thatch, etc. used to cover the surface of a **roof**.

roofing felt A felt covered with asphalt and a mineral that is available in rolls.

roofing nail A short nail with barb or rings on its shank and a large flat head. It may have a neoprene, lead, or plastic washer to assist in securing roofing felt or shingles to the roof.

roofing paper *See* **asphalt prepared roofing, asphalt paper**.

roof overhang   A projecting area at the outer edge of a building or structure where it meets the roof.

roof pitch   The slope of a roof. It is expressed in degrees or a ratio of vertical rise to the horizontal run, such as 4:12.

rooftop gardening   Plants growing, usually in permanent containers, on top of a building.

root   The underground portion of a plant that provides support, obtains nutrients and water, stores food, and sometimes propagates by asexual reproduction for the plant.

root ball   The roots and the soil they hold when lifted from the soil, when removed from a container, or when in a **balled-and-burlapped** (**b&b**) condition.

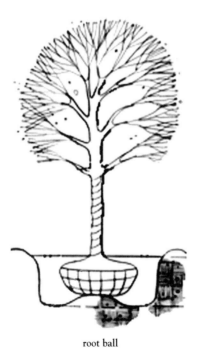

root ball

root bound   Plants whose roots have outgrown the space they have to grow within. This is common for trees in cities with much pavement and walls. It is also common for nursery plants grown for too long a period in a container. Root bound plants in containers may suffer for nutrients (especially if not supplemented) and usually exhibit roots circling the inside of the container. Before planting, the outside circling roots should be cut. Otherwise the roots will likely **girdle** themselves. This also causes trees to be stunted and can eventually cause **wind-throw**.

root cap   The arrangement of cells that acts as a protection to succeeding tissues of the root as it penetrates the soil pores.

root cellar   A structure partially or completely belowground used to store crops or foods at cool temperatures.

root collar *or* **root crown** *or* **crown**   The flared area at the base of a tree trunk (or main stem) at ground level and just above it. It is where roots change to trunk or stem. The trunk is not capable of resisting constant soil moisture. In most cases (except plants tolerant of **anaerobic** conditions such as poplars, willow, etc.), root collars are meant to be exposed to air, and not covered with soil or excessive mulch. Movement of oxygen and carbon dioxide in and out of the inner bark should not be inhibited. Lack of gaseous exchange will kill cells in the phloem tissue over a period of years, interfering with downward movement of food to the roots. Interference of the food supply eventually causes root dieback along with reduced water uptake in the xylem tissue. Plants in this condition are more susceptible to insects and diseases. When planting new trees and shrubs, place them at the same depth as the plant was originally grown, so that the root-collar area is above the surrounding grade after planting. The soil should taper away from the plant, facilitating drainage of surface water into the surrounding grade. Mulching practices that pile mulches against a root collar and stem should be avoided or mulch must be large, loose pieces, allowing air to the **crown** and not harboring moisture there (avoids disease).

root crown   *See* **root collar**.

root cuttings   Portions of fleshy roots cut from some perennials that are able to produce another plant from the cut-off portion.

rooter   A heavy-duty tractor attachment intended to assist in removing roots of trees.

root hair   The small thread-like roots of plants responsible for most of a plant's absorption of nutrients and water. They are tube-like extensions of the epidermal cells of roots.

rooting hormone   A chemical that stimulates root growth and development. It is especially useful on **cutting**s, and is available in a powder or liquid form.

rooting zone   The volume of soil encompassed by the entire root system of a plant.

root-knot nematode   *See* **nematode**.

root pruning   With regard to plants in containers or plants being prepared for field digging, a cutting of the outer roots. This fosters the development of a branched root system and in a field, it keeps roots within the dig zone, reducing shock when transplanted. The roots of plants that have been in containers too long begin to circle the container, and they need to be cut off after being pulled from the container before planting. This discourages the roots from continuing to circle and girdle, but instead encourages the roots to leave the planting pit and spread out.

root rot   A disease caused by **water molds**, which are encouraged and spread by standing water. Many times plants are overwatered when some negative symptom is observed. The only symptom that calls for more water is **wilting**. Too much water, which brings on water mold, is the most common cause of plant death. It is usually easily detected by digging in the root zone and smelling the soil and roots. Water molds occur in **anaerobic** conditions, causing the affected area to smell much like a sanitary sewer. When a dead plant is pulled completely out from the soil, the stench many times is unmistakable and obvious. Sometimes it is necessary to hold soil from the **root ball** in your hand and put it to your nose to detect the smell. The most frequent cause of water molds is the use of a different soil than the existing soil in the **backfill**, or **amendment**s to the soil backfill. This may cause a **soil interface** difficulty with water transfer.

rootstock   The portion of a **graft**ed or budded plant that furnishes roots and sometimes some branches for the plant. *See* **budding**.

root weevil   An insect that feeds on roots in its larval state and as an adult eats leaves of plants such as roses, rhododendrons, and azaleas.

rootworms   Larvae of beetles that feed on roots.

root zone   The area of a plant beneath the soil that performs absorption, aeration, and storage for plants.

rope   A strong, thick line made up of twisted or braided strands of fiber such as hemp or wire.

rope caulk   A preformed bead of caulking compound often containing twine reinforcement.

rosarian   One who cultivates and raises roses.

rose chafer *or* **rose bug**   A beetle of North America (*Macrodactylus subspinosus*) whose larvae feed on roots, and adults feed on leaves and flowers. They are fond of roses, grapevines, berry bushes, beans, cabbage, beets, etc.

rose hip   The fleshy seed enclosure (fruit) of a rosebush.

rosette

rosette   A description of the way a plant grows when its leaves are closely set around a crown or center. The leaves form a circular cluster usually near the ground.

rostrum   A raised platform, elevated area, pulpit, etc. for addressing an audience or performing in front of one.

rosulate   In botanical terms, having a **rosette** or **basal** cluster of leaves.

rotary mower   A lawn mower with a blade that spins horizontally and impacts grass blades, cutting or tearing them all at the same height. *See also* **reel mower**.

rotary pump   A **pump** that produces water by varying the volume in a cavity to force fluid in a desired direction. Depending on the type of **impeller**, a rotary pump may be a vane pump, a piston rotary pump, or a gear pump.

rotenone   An **insecticide** relatively harmless to humans and other warm-blooded animals, but deadly on contact with most insects and also effective as a stomach poison to them. It also kills fish and caution must be taken to keep it from infil-

trating into water bodies. It is derived from such tropical plant species as *derris* and *lonchocarpus*.

rotor head   A **sprinkler head** that irrigates by rotating smoothly instead of by a constant spray pattern (*see* **spray head**), or by a device impacting the stream of water to drive it in an arc (this term is also sometimes erroneously used in reference to **impact heads**). These are usually **gear-driven head**s and project a stream or spray of water in a full or part circle. Some brands or models of these heads are made separately full or part circle, but most heads usually allow adjustment of arcs by hand or with an instrument, without **nozzle** change. The various nozzles that are usually available with these heads often provide a change in water quantity output as well as a change in length of throw (radius). The radius can also usually be adjusted by rotating a screw down into the water pattern (this screw is often meant to only keep the nozzle in place), or by changes in water pressure.

rotor sprinkler head   The radius is usually controlled by interchangeable nozzles and a screw that disperses water by being screwed down into the stream of water. The arc may be controlled by hand adjustments to the head or by devices changed in and out of the head.

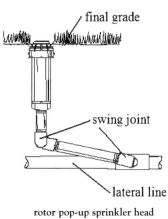

rotor pop-up sprinkler head

rototiller   A device used to turn up and pulverize soils, etc. with turning blades powered with an engine.

rough carpentry   The structural or formation framing, boxing, or sheeting of a wood structure.

rough-cut joint   A mortar joint in brick masonry work that is flush with the face of the brick.

rough grade   **1.** Approximate slope, drainage, and terrain formed, but not raked, rolled or finely bladed smooth, and ready for seed, sod, planting, etc. Sometimes this grade is a few inches below where **finish grade** will be to allow for placement of topsoil. **2.** Grading done before construction of structures, utilities, etc. begins.

rough sawn   Lumber that is cut to dimension, but not planed for smoothness or size reduction.

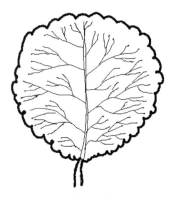

round tree form

round *or* **rounded** *or* **globe**   These terms are sometimes used to describe a plant (especially trees) with a roundish outline to its head. (Compare with **weeping, columnar, fastigiate, oval, broadly spreading, upright spreading, pyramidal**.)

roundabout   A circular road, usually with a round island at its center, at an intersection of streets. In many cases this allows for the flow of traffic without stopping as vehicles yield and merge (so long as they are not overly crowded with traffic).

roundhead wood screw   This screw has various indented shapes in its head for accepting a tool (screwdriver) to drive (turn) it into wood. Its head is larger than the shank and is a half circle at its top with its head's underside being flat immediately around its shank. Its shank has either a threaded taper from the underside of its head surface to its more slender pointed shank, or it is a slender shank of a constant diameter continuing to its threads where it then tapers with threads to its point.

roundabout

round timber   Logs that have not been sawn into lumber.

router   An electric machine with a rapidly turning cutter available in various shapes that cut to the shape of the cutter edge. They are used for routing, cutting mortises, making a decorative trim at the edge of a board, etc.

ROW, row   Abbreviation for **right-of-way**.

row cover   Semitransparent material over crops or nursery stock to extend the growing season or protect the plants. It is often laid over rows of plants, hence the name.

rowlock *or* **rolock** *or* **rollock**   A brick laid on its edge with its end exposed on a wall surface.

royal A cedar shingle with approximate dimensions of 24 in (61 cm) long and ½ in (1.25 cm) thick at the butt.

RP Abbreviation for **reduced pressure vacuum breaker**.

rpm Abbreviation for revolutions per minute.

R.R. **1.** Abbreviation for direct burial feeder conduit. **2.** Abbreviation for railroad.

rubble drain A trench filled with loose rock, rubble, or gravel for carrying away excess runoff or excess water.

rudenture Paving with pebbles or small stone and mortar.

rufus A descriptive botanical term referring to a reddish-brown color plant part.

rugby A field game played on a lawn with approximate dimensions of 450 to 480 ft long by 195 to 225 ft wide.

rugose In botanical terms, wrinkled, roughened with wrinkles, or leaf **veins** depressed with in between areas elevated.

rule A tool having straight edges marked off in inches or centimeters (and fractions thereof) for measuring distance or drawing straight lines.

rung A bar forming the step of a ladder.

runner In plant terminology, a slender stem sent out from the bases of certain perennials, which develops **offsets** at the joints (**nodes**) or at the ends. These horizontally spreading **prostrate** stems run aboveground. This term may sometimes refer to either offsets or **stolons**.

running grasses Any grasses that spread by creeping stems, and tend to form dense mats covering the ground. They may spread by stems on the surface of the ground (**stolons**), or by stems below the ground (**rhizomes**).

running ground Earth, **sand**, etc. that will not stand firm without sheeting.

run-of-bank gravel *See* **bank-run gravel**.

runoff **1.** In sprinkler systems, the water that is not absorbed by the soil and turf to which it is applied. Runoff occurs when water is applied at too great a precipitation rate for too long. **2.** In the natural landscape, it is excess water that flows during rain or snow melt and is not absorbed by soil, plants, or objects, does not evaporate, and drains off the surface of a land area. It usually contains suspended solids or dissolved material. **3.** Water that moves over the soil surface whether in sheet form or stream form.

run time **1.** The length of time necessary (designed or actual) for an **irrigation controller** to complete the entire watering it is programmed to accomplish. **2.** The length of time necessary (designed or actual) for an irrigation controller to complete one of its watering **programs**. **3.** The amount of time necessary for a **sprinkler zone** (sprinkler circuit, or station) to complete its programmed or selected amount of watering. This can be calculated by dividing the gross requirement in inches of water (desired or necessary over the landscape area) by the precipitation rate (**gross precipitation rate** or preferably **net precipitation rate**) and multiplying this quotient by 60. This is the amount of time necessary to run in minutes. Caution must be taken not to apply water faster than the soil **basic intake rate** or water will be wasted to **runoff**. *See* **maximum run time per cycle**.

R/W Abbreviation for right of way.

rust With regard to plants, a disease caused by any of a number of fungi (order *Uredinales*) producing lesions of a usually reddish brown color. The fungal diseases are specific in being contagious only to plants of the same type. Each rust fungus is specific to its host.

rustic brick Brick with a decorative effect created by being covered with sand on surfaces to be exposed before firing in a kiln.

RV Abbreviation for **recreational vehicle**.

R-value A measure of the thermal resistance of a material.

S

S **1.** Abbreviation on drawings for south. **2.** Abbreviation sometimes used for seamless. **3.** Abbreviation for second. **4.** A type of **mortar** used in exterior applications amounting to 1 part **Portland cement** by volume, 1 part hydrated lime by volume, and water in the amount of 2¼ to 3 times the sum of the volumes of cement and lime. It is useful for normal compressive and high lateral loads. It is the most common type used in reinforced masonry. Type **M** is stronger than type **N**.

saber saw A power-driven saw with an oscillating blade that acts similar to a jigsaw but has a wider and longer blade.

sabulous A sandy or gritty texture.

saccate In botanical terms, sack or bag shaped.

sack rub *or* **sack finish** A finish for concrete surfaces to produce even texture by filling pits and air holes. In this process, the surface is dampened, then mortar is rubbed over it, and then before it dries a mixture of dry cement and sand is rubbed onto it to remove surplus mortar and fill voids.

saddle **1.** A roof **cricket**. **2.** A floor support for a heavy pipe. **3.** A device that is clamped to a pipe so that a hole may be drilled into the pipe and a pipe attached for access.

saddleback A **coping stone** with a ridge at its upper surface sloped to direct water to either side of a wall.

saddle fitting A fitting that clamps over an existing pipe with a portion fitting the pipe much like a horse saddle and having a threaded hole in it for attaching another pipe. A hole is drilled into the existing pipe and the saddle is tightened to allow a leakproof attachment of pipe to the threaded hole.

saddle joint A joint for sheet-metal roofing; formed by bending up the edge of one sheet and folding it downward over the turned-up edge of an adjacent sheet.

saddle notch A rounded notch cut near one end of the lower surface of a horizontal log interlocking with another log below it.

safety net A woven, mesh fabric suspended below a place where people or materials may fall that protects from serious injury or damage in such a fall.

safe well yield The maximum pumping rate in a water well without lowering the well water level below the pump intake in the well.

safe yield The amount of water that can be withdrawn annually from a groundwater basin or **aquifer** without an undesirable result. Undesirable results can include reduction of groundwater, intrusion of poor quality water, violation of water rights, depletion of stream flows, and subsidence.

sagittate In botanical terms, arrowhead-shaped with **basal** ears turned downward or inward. (Compare with leaf base descriptions of **cuneate**, **obtuse**, **cordate**, **auriculate**, **attenuate**, **hastate**, **truncate**, **oblique**.)

sailor A brick placed on its end and having its wider face showing on a wall surface. (Compare with **soldier**.)

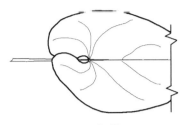

sagittate leaf base

saliens An artificial fountain with water shooting up through a constricted tube.

saline soil A soil containing enough soluble salt to impair plant health.

salinity The amount of salt in a substance. In landscape work, this usually refers to the salt content of soil or water. Excess salt can be toxic to plants, but more often symptoms are leaf scorch, stunted growth, yellow leaves, or withered leaf margins. Salt also interferes with germination of seeds, and can build up in the soil from softened water, green manure, fertilizers, chemical amendments, or salt applied for melting snow. Salt can best be removed from soil by **leaching** with water that is free of salt. This is most effective if the soil allows water to drain through it freely. Salinity is usually measured in parts per thousand (**ppt**). The salinity of seawater is about 35 ppt.

salinization The increased concentration of salt, especially in water or soil, which can result from lack of drainage and can reduce ability to sustain diverse plant life as well as a soil's ability to sustain crops.

sally port An underground passage or concealed gate linking the central and outer portions of a fortress.

salsuginous Grows in salt marshes or **brackish** areas.

salt damage In plants, injury caused by excessive salt in the soil or water. It is found most frequently in poorly drained lowlands, or in arid or semiarid lands, but it can occur anywhere. Salt accumulation in soil may come from fertilizers (including manure), deicing salts, spray from a nearby ocean, or other salt source carried by wind. Salts can be leached from the soil by frequent deep watering. It is a rule of thumb that 30 in of rain per year percolated into the soil (without **runoff**) is enough to leach the salts out. More water leaching may help, but one must avoid drowning plants, or causing root rot. Irrigation water can be used to leach salt from soil, but the water should be tested for salt content to make certain it does not add to salt accumulations in the soil. Salt damage in plants is usually evidenced by yellow leaves or yellow splotches on leaves, or dark brown leaf tips, or margins. Plant growth slows, stops, and plants may die. Excessive salt in soil may be evidenced by dark or white crusts forming on soil surfaces, especially in low dried spots. Some plants have higher salt tolerance than others.

salt-glazed brick *or* **brown-glazed brick** A brick with a glossy finish, obtained in a kiln by reactions between silicates of clay and vapors of salt, etc.

salt-glazed tile Facing tile with a lustrous, glazed finish obtained in a kiln by reaction of the silicates of the clay with vapors of salt, etc.

salt hay *or* **salt marsh hay** Hay from salt marshes useful in covering plants as a winter mulch, etc. It is desirable because of its wire-like makeup, which does not decompose easily, and because its seeds will not germinate or survive except in wet and usually saline conditions, so it does not promote weeds.

saltwater intrusion *or* **seawater intrusion** The migration of salt water into freshwater aquifers because of groundwater development (pumping drainage).

salvage Material once in place and then removed to be reused on the same site or another site.

salverform In botanical terms, a slender tube abruptly expanded into a widened, spreading limb. It is the shape of many flowers.

salverform flower shape

samara A dry, one-seeded, winged fruit found on maple, ash, elm, etc. Children call them helicopters.

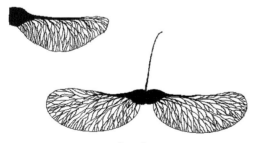

samara of maple trees

sand **1.** A mineral component of **earth** derived from fragmented and weathered rock made up of particles of a size between ⅟₅₀₀ and ⅟₁₂ in (0.05 to 2.00 **mm**) in size. It is classified by the U.S. Department of Agriculture as follows: very coarse sand—0.080–0.040 in; coarse sand—0.040–0.020 in; medium sand—0.020–0.010; fine sand—0.010–0.0040 in; very fine sand—0.0040–0.0020 in. It is smaller than gravel, but coarser than silt. It is used in mortar, glass, abrasives, foundry molds, etc. **2.** A **soil** textural class comprised of approximately 0 to 10% **clay**, with 0 to 15% **silt** and 85 to 100% sand. Individual grains of sand can readily be felt in this soil. When it is squeezed in the hand while dry, it falls apart as pressure is released, and when wet it will crumble if touched after being squeezed. These soils tend to be well drained or excessively drained, having little water-holding capacity, and little fertility.

sandbag A plastic, canvas, or nylon bag filled with sand, useful in temporarily containing floodwaters, or to hold down stands for temporary signs, etc.

sandblast Directing or shooting sand under air pressure at a surface to remove paint, dirt, or rust, to cut, to roughen, or to produce a desirable texture on the surface.

sand filter A layer of fine sand through which water is passed to remove small debris from the water.

sand interceptor *or* **sand trap** A small catch basin preventing passage of sand (and other solids) into a drainage system by allowing it to settle to the bottom of the basin before entering another pipe. It only functions if it is cleaned often enough to keep the collected sand and debris below the pipe inlet.

sandpile A sandbox or area of sand with boundaries for children to play or dig in, etc.

sand separator *See separator.*

sandstone Sedimentary rock composed of particles of sand with a high silica content bound in a natural cement. It is usually a relatively soft stone being easily eroded, but some are hard and durable. Some can even be polished.

sandy clay A **soil** textural class comprised of 35 to 55% clay, 0 to 20% silt, and 45 to 65% sand.

sandy clay loam A **soil** textural class comprised of 20 to 35% **clay**, 0 to 28% **silt**, and 40 to 80% **sand**.

sandy loam A **soil** textural class comprised of 0 to 20% **clay**, 15 to 50% **silt**, and 45 to 80% **sand**. Individual grains of sand can be felt and seen, but it has enough silt and clay to make it somewhat coherent. If it is squeezed while dry, it will form a cast that will fall apart readily. If squeezed while wet, it will form a cast that will fall apart unless handled carefully.

sanguineous A botanical term referring to a bloodred color.

sanitary sewer A pipe system conducting sewage, usually to a treatment facility.

sap The fluid flowing in the vascular tissue of plants.

sapling **1.** A young tree. **2.** A tree less than 4 in. in diameter at breast height.

saprophyte A plant that grows on dead or decaying organic matter.

sapwood Wood from the outer portions of a tree trunk between the bark and **heartwood** where there are active growth cells. It comprises the live cells of the **xylem** and **phloem**. It is generally more permeable, less durable, lighter in color, and less resistant to decay than heartwood.

sarment A **runner**.

saturated soil Soil in which all pore spaces are filled with water.

saturation coefficient Refers to the saturation coefficient for brick, which is the ratio of the percent absorption of a brick submerged in cold water for 24 hours to the absorption of a brick submersed in boiling water over a 5-hour period. The 24-hour cold water test is divided by the 5-hour boiling test. This value is a strength value that assists in measuring the durability of mason units. Durability of mason units may also be measured by conducting freeze/thaw tests. This is of prime importance in landscape work (especially in temperate climates) as brick in the landscape is exposed on one or both sides in nearly all cases. Most brick in the landscape should have a compressive strength of 3000 psi with a 5-hour boiling absorption at 17% maximum, and a maximum average saturation coefficient of 0.78. However, if a brick's minimum compressive strength is 8000 psi or greater, or in the cold water test of 24 hours absorbs less than 8% water, the saturation coefficient can be ignored.

savanna, savannah **1.** A treeless grassland or area of only low-growing plants. **2.** A tropical ecosystem with a consistent herbaceous ground cover (grasses or drought-resistant low growth) and scattered trees. **3.** A zone of transition between grasslands and forests, where there are scattered individual trees or clumps of trees and shrubs.

saw A cutting tool with a thin, flat blade, band, or stiff plate with cutting teeth or an abrasive that cuts as it slides through a material.

sawdust Fine, dusty wood shavings from cutting wood. This material is often used as a mulch, but the bacteria in the soil breaking it down then use most of the nitrogen in the soil preventing plants from gathering what they need. If used, it should be highly decomposed and **nitrogen** must be added to compensate for losses to bacteria. Watch for nitrogen deficiencies in plants with symptoms such as yellowing leaves, stunted growth, or no growth.

sawflies   A variety of flies whose **larvae** feed on plants. Adult females saw plant tissue open and lay eggs within it.

sawhorse *or* **sawbuck**   A four-legged narrow stand about waist height used for placement of material while working on it for sawing, gluing, etc. These are normally used in pairs.

saxicolous *or* **saxicoline**   In botanical terms, living on or among rocks.

scab   **1.** A fungal disease that makes disfiguring lesions. It is common to crabapples and apples. **2.** A short piece of lumber nailed onto two abutting pieces to splice them together.

scabrid   A botanical term meaning roughened.

scabrous   In botanical terms, rough, abrasive, or harsh to the touch. The roughness may be from the surface itself or from small stiff hairs.

scaffold   A temporary, elevated platform for standing upon while working, which supports workers and materials and is advantageous in providing access to work above the area reachable from the ground.

scaffold branch   **1.** A branch that grows horizontally from a main stem or trunk. **2.** The large limbs of a tree that intitiate its basic shape and form its structure.

scale   **1.** The ratio of difference in units measured (usually in a drawing or model) and the actual measurement of something that exists or is designed for building. In drawings, it is a short measurement of a representation of an item for construction that is, or will be in actuality, a larger dimension. Expressions of scale usually are written in such forms as follows: $1'' = 200'$, or 1 in = 200 ft, or 1:10,000. **2.** A ruler or device with units of measurement marked upon it for the purpose of measuring items, or spaces in scale to an existing or proposed item or space. **3.** Spatial proportion. A broad-scale example of spatial scale would be a **region**, whereas a fine-scale example would be for a building site. **4.** In botanical terms, a small leaf-like body that is usually dry and not green, but a rather chaffy or woody **bract**. **5.** Small insects much like **aphid**s, or **mealybug**s that form hard or soft waxy shells and feed on plants.

scalping   Removing particles larger than a size being screened.

scalp rock   Waste rock.

scandent   In botanical terms, a climbing growth habitat or a plant part that ascends.

scape   In botanical terms, this refers to a **peduncle** rising from the ground, naked (without ordinary **foliage**). The leafless stem of a single flower. Examples are daylilies, irises, etc.

scarcement   A setback or recess in an earthen embankment, etc.

scarf joint   Matching two board faces of fitted shapes for joining them and forming one continuous piece. This joint may be secured by glue, bolts, screws, or welding.

scarifier   A machine, a tractor attachment, or a part of a grader with long teeth that can be lowered to rip a soil surface, or pavement.

scarify   **1.** To run a **scarifier** over ground. **2.** To roughen a surface by sanding, etc. to improve adhesion of paint or glue, etc. **3.** Softening the outer coat of a seed to shorten germination time.

scarious   A botanical term referring to a plant part that is spoon shaped.

scarp   A steep slope or steep rock outcrop.

scenic area   Any area of significant scenic beauty.

scenic corridor   An area of land, right-of-way, or an area visible from a highway, waterway, railway, or major hiking, biking, or equestrian trail that provides aesthetically pleasing views of water, vegetation, farmlands, woodlands, coastal wetlands, mountains or hills, or even cities, etc. What is scenic to one may not be scenic to another.

scenic easement   The right for a public agency or other group to use an owner's land for scenic enhancement, such as roadside landscaping or vista preservation, by restrictions on the area of the easement

SCH   Abbreviation for **schedule**. This is a pipe of determined thickness regardless of the diameter of the pipe.

schedule   **1.** An outline of time needed in sequence or overlapping to accomplish tasks. **2.** In construction, a detailed table showing components, items, or parts to be furnished or installed for a design as per the drawings or the design it references. Irrigation schedules show symbols, give descriptions, manufacturers, sizes, remarks, etc. Typical planting plan schedules give such information as **botanical name, common name**, size, condition, spacing, remarks, etc. **3.** In reference to pipe, a pipe wall thickness based on a ratio of pipe size to pipe wall thickness.

schedule of values   A list furnished by the contractor showing portions of the **contract sum**

allotted for various portions of work. It is often used as the basis when reviewing the contractor's applications for progress payments.

scheduling coefficient (sc)   A measure of uniformity depicting water distribution in an area of irrigation based on a formula that does not treat underwatering or overwatering the same and assumes a landscape manager's water to the critical driest spot will be a number greater than one. This coefficient is an irrigation runtime multiplier and indicates how much longer one must irrigate to adequately water the critical driest spot. The formula is SC = average catch of all water **catchment** containers / average catch of water in the driest area of catchments.

scientific name   The **Latin name** (**botanical name**) of a plant.

scion   A bud or short stem of a plant that is grafted onto another plant **rootstock**.

sclerophyll   A firm leaf, with a large amount of strengthening tissue, that retains its firmness (and often also its shape) even when wilted.

scoop loader   *See* **front-end loader**.

scorch   *See* **sunburn**.

score   To cut, roughen, groove, or scratch a surface.

scorpioid   In botanical terms, a plant part that is curved or coiled at the end, reminiscent of a scorpion's tail.

scour   Erosion of a material. It is especially applicable to erosion of earth by water in a channel or ditch.

scouring action   The lifting or scrubbing of loose particles such as sediment and small pebbles during high flow in a drainpipe carrying the materials downstream.

S.C.R. Abbreviation for modular brick.

scraper A large, heavy, wheeled machine, with or without an engine, having a blade under its belly and a large hauling container useful for cutting, filling, and hauling earth.

scree Loose stone on a slope or at the base of a slope or cliff.

screed A long metal or wood rail used to slide along forms holding fresh concrete to pull off (strike off) the excess concrete and leave the surface at the intended level.

screen **1.** Something used to conceal from view one point or area to another. *See also* **berm, buffer, fence. 2.** A metal sheet of woven wire or other similar device with regularly spaced openings of uniform size, mounted in a frame and used in separating earthen material according to size. **3.** A see-through framed fabric (usually tiny metal or plastic wire mesh) used as protection over openings (windows, doors, etc.), in walls, etc. Protects from insects, debris blown by wind, etc. **4.** A machine used to separate earthen material into various sizes.

screening **1.** Visually shielding or obscuring an adjacent landscape, structure, or use from another by fencing walls, **berm**s, vegetation, etc. **2.** Removal from liquids of any large, heavy, floating, or suspended solids by straining through racks or screens. **3.** Separating earthen materials into various sizes, usually with a **bearclaw**, or **screen**.

screen wall An opaque wall preventing the ability to view through it.

screw In construction, a nail or rod-shaped device with a spiral groove or extended portion that when under pressure can be turned and inserted into a solid material for attaching materials.

screw clamp A clamp pressing two jaws or arms together by means of a screw, usually used in woodworking.

screwdriver A tool with a handle and a long shaft protruding from it with a tip that fits into a recess in the head of a screw so that by turning it a screw can be driven into place or removed.

screwdriver

SCS Abbreviation for **Soil Conservation Service** (now named the **National Resources Conservation Service**).

sculpture A three-dimensional form, prepared for decoration or artistic expression.

scupper **1.** An opening in a wall or **parapet** allowing water to drain from a roof. **2.** A device mounted in a drain opening having slotted openings or small holes to prevent debris from clogging the drain.

scurf In botanical terms, minute scales on the surface of many leaves.

scurfy A botanical term meaning beset with small, bran-like scales.

SDR Abbreviation for **Standard Dimensional Ratios**, used chiefly in the plastic pipe industry.

seal **1.** An embossing device to verify a corporate signatory or to show a registration in a state for a particular profession. **2.** A coating on a surface to repel moisture or prevent staining.

sealant In landscape construction, a compound used to waterproof such materials as **concrete** or wood.

seamless pipe A pipe not having a longitudinal joint or seam.

seawall A wall or embankment for stopping the encroachment of a water body.

seaweed Dried kelp. Used as an **organic fertilizer**. It has an **NPK** ratio of about 2.5-1.5-15.

secateur A mostly British term for **pruners**.

second Having flowers only on one side of a flower **spike**.

secondary nutrient In soils, these are the nutrients calcium, magnesium, and sulfur that are secondary (*see* **primary nutrient**) in importance for fertilizers because they are commonly already found in adequate amounts in most soils.

secondary treatment Generally refers to **storm water** treatment beyond initial screening or sedimentation. It usually includes biological changes in concentrations of oxygen-demanding pollutants.

section **1.** A drawing of a structure, landform, object, etc. as it would appear if cut by an imaginary plane, showing any internal portions and outer edges along the intersection. It often also shows the view of portions beyond the section as viewed in a particular direction. **2.** A subdivision of a division of construction specifications covering the work of only one trade.

section modulus A measure revealing the strength of a **beam**.

section view *See* **section** (1).

secund In botanical terms, the flowers or branches are all on the same side of the **axis**.

sedge A grass-like plant with triangular or hollow stems usually growing in wet areas.

sediment Mineral and organic solid particulate material that settles out from suspension in water having been removed from its site of origin, and deposited elsewhere. This is the material forming deposits along the courses of streams, rivers, etc. and at the bottoms of lakes, ponds, and reservoirs.

sedimentary rock Rock formed as the result of previously eroded and deposited sediments undergoing cementation with pressure, but not with high temperatures.

sedimentation The process of depositing suspended matter carried in water or air, accomplished by reducing the velocity of the water or air below the point where it can transport the suspended material, or by having the material contact a solid object.

seed **1.** In the active work of agriculture or horticulture, it means **seeding**. **2.** As a noun in agriculture or **horticulture**, it means the grains of ripened **ovule**s for sowing, or ripened ovules with a ripened **embryo** usually capable of producing a new plant.

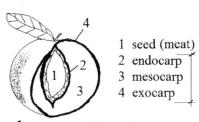

1 seed (meat)
2 endocarp
3 mesocarp
4 exocarp

peach (cutaway illustration)

seed bank The accumulation of live plant seed in soils available for germination under favorable conditions.

seedbed Soil prepared for planting seed.

seeding The act of placing, planting, grodcasting, etc. seed in anticipation of its **germination** and growth.

seedling   **1.** A small, very young plant. **2.** A young woody plant started from a seed.

seepage   Groundwater or **interflow** water oozing from the ground.

seepage bed   A wide trench containing distribution piping surrounded by clean, coarse, gravel material. Sewage from a septic tank that is partially treated flows through the pipes, and seeps into the ground via the gravel.

selected bidder   The bidder chosen by the owner for possible award of a contract for a project. *See also* **successful bidder**.

selective herbicide   An **herbicide** that only kills certain types of plants. *See also* **nonselective herbicide**.

selective pruning   Selecting branches to prune rather than shearing all branches to a particular length.

self-branching   A reference to certain perennials that produce many side growths, growing compactly and without having to be pinched back to form a dense plant.

self-cleaning valve   An **automatic valve** with a device that moves when turned off and on to clean portions of the inner valve.

self-fertile   The capability within a single plant of producing viable seeds by its own **pollen** fertilizing its own **ovule**s.

self-pollinating   *See* **self-fertile**.

self-seeding   A plant that will grow from seed deposited by a plant the year before without human aid.

self-sterile   A single plant not capable of producing viable seeds and fruit by its own **pollen** fertilizing its own **ovule**s.

self-tapping   Able to create its own screw threads on the inside of a hole as it is forced by turning.

semiarid climate   A climate where precipitation averages more than 20 in per year, but less than 40 in per year.

semidirect lighting   Light from luminaries distributing 60 to 90% of the emitted light downward onto a surface.

semi-double flower   A flower with two or three times the number of **petal**s necessary to form a circle; usually the petals appear in two or three rows.

semi-evergreen   A reference to plants that throughout winter retain some leaves, or lose only older leaves. Also descriptive of plants that retain nearly all leaves if the winter is mild.

semitransparent stain   This is a color pigment applied to wood that is not dark enough to cover the natural grain of the wood.

sems   A machine screw with a lock washer that was placed on the screw before threads were cut on it and which cannot be easily removed.

sending site *or* **sending zone**   An area of land where the number of dwelling units allowed by law can be purchased to keep the land from development. These units are usually sent or transferred to another site to increase the housing density allowed on that property (**receiving site** or zone).

senescence   The process of aging; growing older.

sense of scale   The feeling created or perceived when one is placed next to a very large object (such as a 50-story building 500 ft wide) or a small object (a toolshed 6 ft tall and 8 ft wide).

sensitive areas

One can be made to feel large or small, comfortable, or uncomfortable.

sensitive areas   In land development, areas not particularly suitable for development, areas that could have negative impacts if not carefully developed, or areas that have elements of concern to those surrounding or associated with the land. These land areas could be historic, part of a scenic corridor, **habitat** for endangered species, significantly influence property values, be polluted, have valuable resources, contain wetlands, be too steep, erosion prone, near fault line, subject to avalanche, flood often, have bedrock on or near the surface, be significant politically, have significant social interest, contain too high a pH, consist of salty soils, be made up of unstable soils, etc.

sepal   One of the modified leaves making up a **calyx** of a **flower** that is typically green or greenish.

separator *or* **desander** *or* **sand separator**   In irrigation systems, a device also called a desander or sand separator useful for removing sand from water.

septage   Solid and liquid wastes removed from sewage disposal systems.

septate   A botanical term meaning divided or with partitions.

septic system   An underground sewage-treatment system that includes a settling tank (**septic tank**) through which liquid sewage (domestic waste) flows and into which solid sewage settles to be composted and decomposed by bacteria. Flow through the tank exits to a leach field where it infiltrates into the subsurface soils. Septic systems are commonly used for individual home waste disposal where a sewer system is not available.

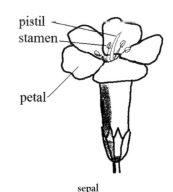

sepal

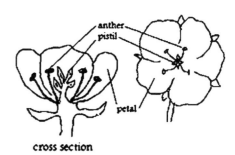

cross section

sepal

septic tank   A container that receives the discharge of sewage and permits the deposition of settled solids, the digestion of the matter deposited, and the discharge of the liquid portion remaining into a leaching field.

sericeous   A plant part covered with fine, soft hairs to the point it is often downy feeling.

series circuit   An electrical circuit connected so that the current passes through each device on the circuit in completing its path to the source of supply.

serrate   In botanical terms, a leaf with a margin cut into teeth pointing forward. It may look like a saw blade. (Compare with **ciliate**, **pectinate**, **cleft**, **lobed**, **dentate**, **denticulate**, **entire**, **serrulate**, **double serrate**, **incised**, **crenate**, **crenulate**, **parted**.)

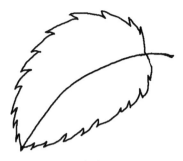

serrate leaf margin

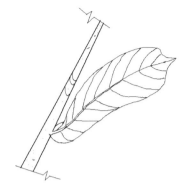

sessile leaf attachment

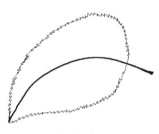

serrulate leaf margin

serrulate In botanical terms, the diminutive of **serrate** or finely serrated. (Compare with **ciliate, pectinate, cleft, lobed, dentate, denticulate, serrate, entire, double serrate, incised, crenate, crenulate, parted**.)

service conductors Electrical wire supply conductors between the street transformer or street main and the service equipment of the customer.

service connection The point where a customer's piping or wiring connects to a utility main service pipe or wire.

service equipment In electrical systems, a reference to all conductors and devices that are a part of transferring electricity from the power company's lines to the fuses or circuit breaker devices of an individual user.

sessile In botanical terms, a plant part sitting close without any stalk or **petiole**.

set **1.** A reference to an emission device (head, emitter, etc.) being at its proper elevation, orientation, and location. **2.** A nail that is pounded into place. **3.** With regard to concrete, masonry mortar, etc., a general point in time when it is no longer fresh enough to be loaded, or worked. Its condition is hard and no longer plastic or pliable. **4.** In landscape terms, to plant. **5.** Small bulbs, tubers, or other plant parts or starts used for **propagation**.

seta A botanical term meaning a bristle.

setaceous A botanical term meaning bristle-like.

setback The distance required by a governing authority from a line (usually a property line or easement line) to a structure, wall, sign, or another use, etc. that is usually specified by an ordinance, code, or restrictive covenants.

set heads *or* **setting heads** The action of placing or setting and stabilizing **sprinkler head**s during construction to assure their proper orientation and elevation for desired water dispersing.

setose A botanical term meaning beset with bristles.

setscrew   A screw placed through a collar shaft, etc. to hold a detachable or movable part in its place.

sett   A granite paving block that is often cube shaped.

setting bed   The layer of mortar on which tile is laid.

setting-up   **1.** The mobilization of equipment, obtaining sanitary facilities, establishing temporary office facilities, etc. to prepare for or begin a construction project. **2.** The hardening of concrete, mortar, paint, varnish, pipe glue, etc.

settlement   **1.** The sinking of earth, the fall in elevation of a ground surface in a backfilled trench or excavation, if not properly compacted or caused by underground erosion. **2.** The slow downward movement or change in elevation of a structure that is slightly sinking because of a poor bearing subsurface, or poor compaction beneath it, etc. **3.** An agreed upon compromise. **4.** The downward movement of solids in a liquid such as water due to gravity. When flowing water carrying sediment slows, it deposits material through this process.

sewage sludge   Recycled, dried product of municipal sewage treatment plants. Two forms are available: **activated sludge** (**NPK** 6-3-0.5) and **composted sludge** (**NPK** 2-2-0). The long-term effects of using sewage sludge are still under investigation. Heavy metals such as cadmium may be present in the soil where sewage sludge has been used, and they may build up after a period of time. There are possible negative effects depending on the origin of the sludge used.

sewer   A system of piping for collecting and disposing of waste waters. *See* **sanitary sewer** and **storm sewer**.

sewer main   A sewer line having sewer branches dispensing into it.

sewer pipe   A conduit or pipe used for carrying liquid waste.

SF, sf   **1.** Abbreviation for **square foot** (feet). This is an area equal to a square that measures 1 ft (12 in) long at each edge. **2.** Abbreviation for **surface flow**.

SH   Abbreviation for sheet.

shade   In consideration of access regulations regarding sunlight, the shadow cast by a structure, vegetation, etc.

shade cloth   A special cloth useful in placing above plant material to protect them from sun while in containers or greenhouses.

shade netting   A netting draped above plants to provide some shade. It has larger openings in the fabric to allow sun than **shade cloth** has.

shade tolerant   A plant that can grow well in shady conditions.

shade tree   Any tree planted or existing for the value of its shade.

shake   **1.** With regard to construction materials, a wood shingle split from a piece of wood (best formed by hand-splitting) and usually thinner on one end than the other. They are commonly made of cedar. **2.** With regard to lumber, a reference to cracks in the surface of the wood caused by drying and other effects.

shale   Sedimentary rock derived from clays or silts thinly laminated and easily split along planes.

shallow soils   **Soil**s that are generally less than 20 in deep to **bedrock**, unweathered parent material, or a **water table**.

shark fin   In roofing, this refers to an upward-curled felt **side lap** or **end lap**.

shear   To break off, clip off, or cut off. This is often done by chopping foliage and twigs to make a shape of the plant (especially espaliers, Christmas trees, hedges) or to confine a plant to space.

shear force The lateral force perpendicular to the **axis** of a member or structure, etc., causing it to be inclined to break, slide, deform, or be cut off. (Compare with **tensile force** and **compressive force**.)

shears Tools with handles and opposed cutting edges used for cutting plants by squeezing or drawing the handles together.

shear strength The maximum **shear stress** that a soil or other material (structural member, etc.) is capable of sustaining. (Compare with **tensile strength** and **compressive strength**.)

shear stress *or* **shearing stress** The force per unit area of cross section that can cause **shear**. (Compare with **compressive stress** and **tensile stress**.)

sheath A thin, usually tubular, covering over a plant part. In many grasses, this is the basal part of a leaf that wraps around the stem and holds it in place.

sheathing The surface material (usually wood boards, plywood, or wallboards) attached over exterior studs or rafters. *See also* **sheeting**.

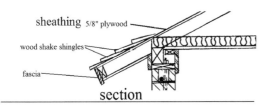

sheathing label: sheathing 5/8" plywood; wood shake shingles; fascia; **section**

sheathing

sheave In pulling cable, a grooved wheel or pulley assisting in pulling cable and often used for pulling underground cable between **manholes** or **pull boxes**.

shed A relatively small structure used for shelter, storage, or a workshop. It is often a separate building but is sometimes attached to another structure.

shed

shed roof *or* **pent roof** A roof surface having only one sloping side.

sheep manure Sheep excrement used as an **organic**, rapidly available **fertilizer** having an **NPK** ratio of 2-1.5-3.

sheepsfoot roller A self-propelled or towed large cylinder-like roller with projecting bumps or studs that penetrate the surface of the ground to facilitate a deeper compaction of fill material than facilitated by a smooth drum roller.

sheet In construction, a thin, flat, wide piece of material.

sheet asphalt Plant-mixed asphalt cement having a content of graded sand passing through a 2.00 mm (No. 10) sieve. Its use is usually confined to surface courses laid on binder courses.

sheet flow A relatively thin flow of water.

sheet glass Glass used in windows.

sheeting *or* **sheathing** **1.** Pieces of material (wood, steel) used to secure the vertical surface of an excavation. **2.** Material used in sheets. **3.** The boards forming the vertical surface of concrete formwork. **4.** Bedrock or stone with many fractures.

shell aggregate An aggregate composed of crushed seashells and sand.

shelterbelt *See* **windbreak**.

sherardize The process of placing a thin coating of zinc (usually with other materials) with heat (between 320 to 500°C) on steel to provide a corrosion- and abrasion-resistant surface.

SHGC Abbreviation for solar heat gain coefficient.

shifting *See* **shifting up**.

shifting up Removing a plant from a small container and placing it in a larger container. This is common practice in a nursery where plants are being grown up to size for sale. After this process, plants should be rooted into the **growing medium** before selling at the larger size.

shim A thin, tapered piece of stiff material (wood, metal, etc.) inserted under a member to adjust its height or vertical alignment, etc. They are often used to bring materials into flush alignment with one another.

shingle A roofing unit made of various materials and sizes used on an exterior surface. Each unit usually overlaps others to shed water.

shiplap A connection of boards side to side where the edges are **rabbet**ed to overlap flush from board to board.

shoot **1.** The young sprout of a plant. **2.** New growth of a plant. **3.** This year's growth of a plant usually identified on **deciduous** trees from **bud** to bud.

shop drawings The drawings, illustrations, schedules, etc. prepared by a contractor or any subcontractor, supplier, etc. that illustrate how specific items or portions of the **work** will be made, designed, or installed.

shore **1.** A board set temporarily at an angle to support a wall. **2.** The land immediately adjacent of, contiguous to, and influenced by a body of water.

shoring **1.** A number of boards set to temporarily support a wall. **2.** Material used and placed to support the earth on the sides of a trench or steep slope.

shoreland The land around a water body from which surface water drains directly into the water body instead of draining into streams and tributaries.

short circuit A condition in an electrical circuit when electricity escapes to a ground or returns, occurring when a hot wire of opposite phases touch each other, or a bare wire or connection touches a bare spot on a grounded wire or component, or a hot wire comes into contact with water or moist soil. This will usually blow a fuse or trip a circuit breaker if they are a part of the system.

shotcrete Concrete or mortar pumped through a hose onto a surface, sometimes with considerable force.

shot hole A fungus that causes spots on leaves that fall out, creating holes and looking like they have been shot with a shotgun.

shoulder nipple **1.** A **nipple** having threads at each end and a space along the pipe between the threads that are without threads. **2.** A short **nipple** just longer than a **close nipple**, but having only a short area without threads along its length.

shovel   A hand tool with a long, tubular handle and a broad, thin, metal blade. It is used for digging, scooping up, or cutting soil, sand, gravel, or any loose granular medium.

shovel prune   **1.** To prune a root system of a plant with a **shovel** by forcing the shovel blade completely into the ground at a consistent distance from the plant stem, usually completely around it. This prevents roots from extending to undesirable areas, prepares them for a more likely successful **transplant** by forcing more root growth closer to the stem, or in some cases encourages more top growth. **2.** A slang term meaning to dig up and throw away an undesirable plant.

shrinkage   The reduction in size of a member or material (pipe, timber, steel, concrete, etc.) as a result of drying, temperature change, etc.

shrinkage limit   With regard to soils, a point at which a reduction in water content will not cause a decrease in the soil mass, but an increase in water content will produce an increase in soil mass.

shrub   A plant with many stems or much branching near the ground; and is woody and forms new wood from old wood each year.

shrub adapter   An irrigation part that fits between a pipe threaded end and a nozzle mounted on top of it. It is usually mounted on top of a nipple aboveground to allow the watering of shrubs with a spray nozzle.

shrub head   A **shrub adapter** and nozzle.

shrub swamp   Swamps dominated by woody vegetation including shrubs, young trees, and trees that are stunted because of environmental conditions. The height of plants are less than 20 ft (6 m) tall.

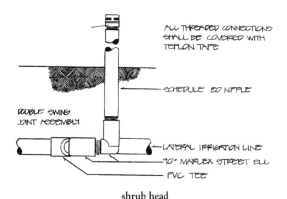

shrub head

shubunkin   A colorful variety of goldfish hardy in temperate climates for outdoor ponds. They are approximately 8 to 10 in long at maturity.

si   Abbreviation for **square inch**(es). It is an area equal to a square measuring one inch along each edge.

sickle   A hand tool with a short handle and a long, curved, sharp blade used to cut grain, grass, or brush.

SIDD   *See* **standard inside diameter dimension ratio**.

side-dressing   Fertilizers applied close enough to plants to provide the root zone with food.

side-dump loader   A tractor with a front bucket that can dump forward and to the side.

side lap   The amount that one sheet or roll of material overlaps another at its side edge.

side lot line   Generally any lot line that is not a front lot line or a rear lot line.

side shoot   A secondary stem that grows from the base of a main stem.

sidewalk   An improved footpath for pedestrian use that is usually paved (usually with concrete) and is typically located adjacent to a street. Its

side yard

name derived from how it allows pedestrians to walk beside a street, but this term is also used for any footpath located in any open space.

side yard The space to the right or left of a building as one faces it from the front. It includes the area between the building and the property line, along the entire side of the building. Most municipalities and counties specify a minimum side yard in their planning codes. The side yard as defined in codes for regulation usually includes a set minimum distance from a side property line extending from the front property line to the rear property line.

siding A covering finishing exterior walls made up of a series of horizontal strips or boards made of wood, aluminum, or such, usually applied horizontally with each strip overlapping the one immediately below it to prevent penetration of water as it drains off.

sieve A metal sheet of woven wire, closely perforated metal, or other similar device with regularly spaced openings of uniform size, mounted in a frame and used in separating earthen material according to size, cleaning, and sifting seeds, or separating any material for size.

sieve analysis *or* **screen analysis** The investigation and ascertainment of the proportions of particles and their size ranges in a granular material by using sieves (screens) with different-sized openings.

sieve method A method utilized in separating sizes of particles of a soil sample.

sight distance triangle The triangular area bounded by the street property lines of corners and a line joining points along said street lines a determined number of feet from their point of intersection. This area is kept free of visual obstructions from street to street to provide an open view of the intersection, providing more

safety for those traveling toward the intersection so that they can avoid intersecting traffic.

sight line The line from an observer to an object or area viewed.

sight rail One of a series of horizontal rails used to check the gradient of a pipe in a trench. The rails are adjusted to the desired gradient so that the bottom of the trench can be measured from them and ensure the proper gradient for a pipe.

sign A device that is usually flat with words, pictures, or drawings used for visual communication of commands, warnings, directions, advertisements, or anything intended to attract attention or communicate.

signage Visual communications in symbols, pictures, letters, drawings, photographs, or words whose function is to communicate directions, identifications, warnings, advertisements, etc. to passersby.

silica brick A brick baked at high temperature that is made from quartzite containing approximately 96% silica, 2% alumina, and 2% lime.

silicate An insoluble metal salt often contained in concrete, brick, glass, clay, etc.

silicone Many types of polymeric silicon compounds useful for water resistance, electrical insulation, heat resistance, binding, or as a lubricant.

silky In botanical terms, glossy with a coat of fine and soft, close-pressed, straight hairs.

sill **1.** A timber fastened to the top of a foundation useful in attaching a wood frame above it. **2.** The bottom horizontal portion of a frame, especially a window frame.

sill cock A water faucet that is threaded to provide a connection for a hose and often placed on the wall of a building just above the foundation at about the elevation of the sill.

silt   **1. Earth** with **soil** particles of a size between $\frac{1}{12,500}$ to $\frac{1}{500}$ in (0.05 to 0.002 **mm**) in size. It is a mineral component of soils that is a loose sedimentary deposit material derived from fragmented and weathered rock. It is smaller than sand particles and larger than clay particles. In high proportions in the soil it increases potential for compaction, but also increases water-holding capacity. **2.** A soil textural class comprised of approximately 0 to 12% **clay**, with 80 to 100% silt and 0 to 15% **sand**.

siltation   The deposition of sediment from erosion, storm water runoff, etc., but especially of particles of a size intermediate between **sand** and **clay**.

silty clay   A soil textural class comprised of 40 to 60% **clay**, 40 to 60% **silt**, and 0 to 20% **sand**.

silty clay loam   A soil textural class comprised of 20 to 40% **clay**, 4 to 73% **silt**, and 0 to 20% **sand**.

silty loam   A soil textural class comprised of 0 to 25% **clay**, 50 to 80% **silt**, and 0 to 20% **sand**. This soil may be cloddy when dry, but lumps can be broken easily or pulverized. It feels floury soft and when squeezed it will readily form a cast that can be handled without breaking whether wet or dry. When moistened and squeezed between the thumb and forefinger, it will not make a smooth ribbon, but will have a broken appearance.

silver orfe   *See* **golden orfe**.

simple   In botanical terms, of one piece; usually refers to leaves that are not made up of **leaflet**s, but instead have one single leaf **blade**. It may be deeply lobed, but it is not divided into separate blades. (Compare with **compound**.)

simple fertilizer   A fertilizer with only one of the three components (N, P, K) of a **complete fertilizer**. An example of a simple fertilizer is ammonium sulfate (18-0-0).

simple leaf   A leaf with its entire blade in one piece (although it may be deeply **cleft**) and not having **leaflets**. (Compare with **compound leaf**.)

simple vein   A **vein** in a **leaf** that extends from one end of the leaf to the other without branching.

single-acting pump   A reciprocal pump with a piston that causes pumping only as it moves either up or down, but not both.

single flower   A flower with the minimum number of flowers for its kind.

single grain soil   A soil without **structure** or **aggregation** that has individual particles of the same size.

single-hub pump   A pipe having a bell at one end and a spigot at the other.

single leg profile   In measuring water distribution of sprinklers, this refers to using a single row of **catchments** (catch cans) to obtain a **precipitation rate** profile of the throw of an individual sprinkler head.

single phase *or* **1PH** *or* **1ph**   Refers to electricity in **alternating current** with only one phase or **hot wire** and a **ground**. This is the most common type of electricity source used by landscapers when connecting a **sprinkler controller**, **pump**, or **low-voltage lighting** system to an electrical system. Large pumps and other heavy electrical equipment run more efficiently and economically on **three phase** electrical power.

single-stem   A description of a plant that has one trunk or stem arising from the ground. (Compare with **multi-stem**.)

sink

sink **1.** In landscape ecology, an area where input exceeds output of organisms or materials; nearly opposite of **source**. **2.** In terrestrial and aquatic environments, a place where natural or man-made debris collects.

sinker nail A slender nail having a flat head with a slight depression in it.

sinuate In botanical terms, leaves with a deep, wavy **margin**.

sinuosity The curviness of a stream or water feature channel numerically expressed by the ratio of channel length to the length of the meander water centerline.

sinus In botanical terms, the curve (or cleft portion, depression) between two lobes or teeth of a **leaf** or **leaflet**.

site **1.** A defined area of ground where (with boundaries) a building, project, **park**, etc. is located or proposed to be located. **2.** Any land area of reference.

site plan A plan of a site showing the positions, size, and types of elements such as roads, drives, parking lots, play areas, outdoor furniture, land uses, or structures existing or proposed for a **site**. It may or may not show **dimension**s, **contour**s, or have a legend.

sitework Construction work outdoors including earthwork, landscaping, and installation of fences, irrigation systems, utility services, retaining walls, etc.

size of pipe *or* **size of tubing** In drawing and specifications, the normal size by which the pipe (or tubing) is commercially designated. Sometimes specifically exact dimensions are given in specifications.

sizing Working (sawing, sanding, chipping, etc.) material to a desired size.

skeleton steps A staircase with treads supported on the sides and having no risers for support at the front of the **tread**s.

skewed Oblique, or twisted to one side.

skid steer loader *or* **skip loader** A compact tractor steering by direction of spin on wheels and with a front bucket that interchanges for various attachments such as a sweeper, an auger, a hydraulic hammer, etc.

skid steer loader

skimmer A device used in water features that collects material mostly from the surface of the water, depositing it in a basket or net as it flows through, usually to a pump.

skin **1.** The material covering a framework, especially on a building. **2.** An exterior wall bearing no weight from above.

skin friction Resistance due to friction between a soil and a structure.

skip **1.** With regard to surfaced wood, an area missed by the machine during surfacing operations of sanding or **planing**. **2.** In a finished painted surface, an area not finished or painted. These unfinished areas are sometimes referred to as **holiday**s.

skylight   An opening in a roof that has a covering of a transparent or translucent material. It is useful for admitting light into a space below.

slack side   The face of a board or wood veneer that was facing toward the tree's center before being cut.

slag   A gray aggregate residue of blast furnaces.

slag cement   A fine or powdery cementitious material made of a uniform blend of granulated blast-furnace slag and hydrated lime.

slant   A sewer pipe connecting a building's sewer to a main or common sewer.

slate   A hard, thin, flat, brittle rock made up mostly of clay minerals that were formed along parallel planes. It is used in roofing, flooring, patios, and even chalkboards.

slating nail *or* **slate nail**   A nail with a large, flat head and a medium, diamond-shaped point; useful in attaching slate to wood.

sledgehammer   A hammer with a heavy head used for pounding. Their heads are of various weights, and handles are of various lengths.

sledge hammer

sleeper   A timber at or near the ground that distributes load from other wood members above or from decking (flooring) attached to it.

sleeve   **1.** In irrigation, a pipe used to allow pipe(s) or wire(s) to be pulled or pushed through it. This is useful under pavements when the water pipes or wiring will be installed later. It also allows for access to wires or pipes housed in these conduits after paving is completed. **2.** In sprinkler irrigation, a vertical pipe that allows a long, solid shank key to be slid down it to the top of a valve to facilitate turning it off and on by turning a handle on the top of the shank.

sleeve fence   A short, decorative fence attached to a building often designed to complement the building design.

slip   **1.** A **cutting** of a plant. **2.** A description of the method of attachment of **PVC** fitting that slides together with glue as opposed to **compression** or **threaded fitting**s.

slip fix   A **PVC** device that slides into slip sockets (**tee**, **coupler**, etc.) with glue, and is capable of being extended so that it is particularly useful in repairing (fixing) damaged pipes.

slip fix

slip-joint pliers   A tool with curved, ribbed jaws and handles with a joint between them that slips to two different positions. When the handles are squeezed, the jaws can grip wide or narrow objects depending on the slip-joint setting.

slope   Ground that is not horizontal, but instead has an incline. The state of any surface not level or essentially perpendicular to a line from a

slope failure

given point on the earth's surface to its center. *See* **percent of slope** and **slope ratio**.

slope failure   A slope that fails by mass movement. *See also* **landslide** and **slump**.

slope map   **1.** A drawing showing land form (topography), allowing one to ascertain steepness of ground and surface drainage characteristics by use of contours (in most cases). **2.** A drawing showing various selected slope categories (i.e., 5 to 10%, 10 to 20%, etc.) in graphic form. These drawings are usually colored, but may also simply be labeled, or have various shades of gray to indicate steepness of slope as identified with a legend. These drawings may be generated by hand or computer by use of a **contour map**.

slope ratio   The steepness of a slope indicated by the rate at which it diverges from being vertical. It is a relationship of a horizontal distance to a vertical elevation difference. Examples are 3 to 1, sometimes shown as 3:1. In this example, the slope diverges three units horizontally for every one unit of vertical distance.

slough   A slow-moving creek or stream in flat terrain characterized by wetland vegetation.

sloughing   Loose material such as soil or **shotcrete** slipping, crumbling, or breaking loose from a vertical or steeply sloping face.

slow-release fertilizer   A fertilizer that releases its nutrients in regulated amounts. These are (1) fertilizers that very slowly dissolve in the soil, and (2) plastic-coated fertilizers through which water slowly penetrates, releasing the soluble fertilizer.

sluffing *or* **sloughing**   **1.** Material coming off at the edge or surface. **2.** Material in a pile, on a slope, or in an embankment, etc. that no longer

is stable and falls or tumbles from above under the force of gravity.

slug bait   A palletized or liquid substance attractive to slugs that is combined with a toxic substance to kill them.

slugs   Terrestrial mollusks found where moisture is high and temperature is cool. They feed on living plants, dead or decaying organic material, earthworms, and other slugs or snails.

slump   **1.** An indication of consistency of freshly mixed concrete, mortar, or stucco found by measuring the decrease in height to the nearest ¼ in (6 mm) of molded mass immediately after removal from a **slump cone**. **2.** *See* **slumping**.

slump cone   A truncated cone used to form freshly mixed concrete, mortar, or stucco that holds the fresh mix to the shape of the cone until it is removed to measure decrease in size as it slumps. *See also* **slump** and **slump test**. A concrete slump cone measures 8 in (20 cm) at the base, 4 in (10 cm) at the top, and 20 in (30 cm) in height. A mortar or slump cone measures only 6 in (15 cm) in height.

slumping   The movement of a mass of soil on a slope in response to gravity. This is often triggered by overly saturated, unstable soils, earthquake, vibration, or excavation.

slump test   A procedure for measuring the **slump** amount (the amount a fresh concrete mix sinks) after being placed in a slump cone, tamped, and then having the cone removed. It gives an indication of consistency and some idea of its workability. Aggregates should not be larger than 2 in when this test is performed.

smart controller   An **advanced irrigation control system** that controls irrigation by monitoring the weather or the soil moisture. They adjust **station** run time(s) or the frequency when there are changes detected in the soil moisture or the weather. Some will monitor wind, rain, or temperature. Another feature of some of these controllers is that they can monitor flow in pipes, determining if there is a break in the line. The features of these controllers are not all the same, but they include some method of automatically adjusting their schedules through the seasons of the year in an attempt to keep the optimum amount of moisture in the soil. These controllers are quite helpful in preventing waste of irrigation water. However, their accuracy and usefulness is only as good as their monitoring devices and their monitoring locations.

smart growth   A term used in land planning and landscape architecture referring to urban growth that serves the economy, the community, and the environment. The movement attempts to bring this about by basing itself on the following principles: mixed land uses, compact building design, ranges of housing choices, walkable neighborhoods, attractive neighborhoods, open space, farmland, natural beauty, strengthening existing communities, providing a variety of transportation choices, making fair development decisions, and encouraging community collaboration in development decisions. These offer general directions, but do not constitute an adequate theoretical construct for whole cities.

smut and white smut diseases   Fungi creating white or yellow blisters or galls with dark sooty-looking spores. These affect a variety of herbaceous plants.

snag   In pruning, an improperly pruned branch where a short stub remains.

snail   A terrestrial mollusk found where moisture is high and temperature is cool. They feed on living plants, dead or decaying organic material, earthworms, and other slugs or snails.

snake   **1.** See **fish tape**. **2.** A long, thin, wire-like metal strip with a crank handle useful for extending down pipes and rotating to remove clogs.

snecked rubble *or* **snecked masonry**   A masonry wall of rough, irregular stones fitting together well (tightly) to increase its strength.

snow fence   A usually horizontal **fence**-like linear structure, perpendicular to storm winds, that catches drifting snow and prevents it from accumulating where it is not wanted, such as on roads, driveways, etc.

snow mold   A disease of lawns caused by a variety of fungi with a variety of symptoms. It usually appears with the melting of snow. Poor drainage, excess thatch, and fast fall growth encourage these fungi.

soaker   An irrigation line that oozes water along its length.

soapinin   Any of various glucosides produced in plants characterized by a soapy lather.

soapstone   Soft rock containing large amounts of talc. It feels like soap.

soccer   A game played on a lawn where goals are at each end and players on 2 teams attempt to kick a ball or bounce it with their head to their goals (on opposite ends of the field). The field may be 255 to 300 ft long and 150 to 180 ft wide, depending on whether it is for girls, boys, men, women, college, high school, etc.

sod   **1.** A grass-covered surface of the ground including its roots and the soil they hold. **2.** A roll or sheet of grass (or other herbaceous plants), soil, and its roots cut from the ground in a thin piece for transplanting. It is produced by cutting an inch or two below the ground-surface and piling the slabs or rolls on **pallets**. It is important to get the sod laid down in place and watered before it undergoes **dessication**.

sod cutter   Any of various motorized machines used to cut and provide **sod** pieces in slabs or rolls of various sizes.

sodding   Laying **sod**.

sodic soil   A soil with a significant amount of sodium, usually characterized by poor **structure** and poor drainage.

sodium chloride   The salt found on tables for culinary use that is also used for melting snow and ice on pavements. It is toxic to roots; symptoms are scorched leaves, premature fall color, premature leaf drop, or twigs dying back.

sodium lamp   *See* **sodium vapor lamp**.

sodium light   Yellow-orange light produced by a low-pressure, **sodium vapor lamp**.

sodium nitrate   *See* **nitrate of soda**.

sodium vapor lamp   A lighting device using an electric discharge producing light by electric current flowing between electrodes in a sodium vapor container. They are usually used outdoors.

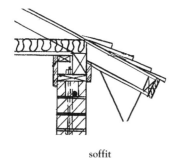

soffit

soffit   The narrow undersurface of an overhead structure such as a balcony, staircase, beam, cornice, roof, eave, arch, etc.

softball field   An outdoor playfield for the game of softball that starts at a point (home plate) and travels out in two base lines at right angles to one another, 60 ft to bases, and a 60-ft line bisects that angle. The distance to home plate from the pitcher's mound is 38 ft for women or 46 ft for men. The outfield fence is about 200 ft from home plate. These dimensions are for understanding scale, comprehension of shape, etc. and are for planning purposes only. Contact the appropriate league for their exact layout and dimensions and current information regarding different types of playfields.

softened water   Water that has been treated by reverse osmosis, filters, magnets, ultraviolet light, or use of salt (sodium chloride replaces calcium and magnesium ions), etc. to decrease dissolved minerals and their ability to form deposits. Water treated with salt can cause salt burn in plants, especially over a period of time. Some plants are highly susceptible, while others are tolerant of salt.

soft water   A water that has a low dissolved mineral (calcium, iron, magnesium, etc.) concentration (less than 100 ppm). Unlike **hard water**, it does not form insoluble deposits in pipes, valves, tanks, etc. It is common in alkaline soil areas and near limestone geological formations.

softwood   Wood obtained from an **evergreen** (**conifer**). It is often relatively soft and easily cut or worked, although some wood of evergreen trees is harder than many hardwoods (wood from deciduous trees). This term does not refer to the relative hardness of the tree.

softwood cutting A **cutting** from soft, succulent new spring growth.

softwood lumber Wood cut from **coniferous** trees.

soil The upper layer of the earth consisting of unconsolidated natural surface material above bedrock formed by weathering that can be dug or plowed. It is the natural medium in which plant roots survive. It is naturally a result of the interactions between geologic effects (weathered mantle existing on the earth's terrestrial surface), vegetation, and climate. It is comprised of mineral particles, air, water, living organisms, and **organic matter**. As the natural material for plant growth, it provides nutrients, water, and **environment** favorable to roots. **2.** A **soil mix**, or **growth medium**.

soil amendment Material such as lime, gypsum, sawdust, organic materials, or synthetic conditioners that is worked into the soil to improve it. Technically fertilizer is also an amendment, but the term "amendment" is most commonly used for added organic materials.

soil analysis *See* **soil test**.

soil bioengineering Soil stabilization and retention by use of plant roots or stems serving as structural and mechanical elements in a slope protection system.

soil boring **1.** Drilling earth horizontally to allow access of wire, pipe, etc., usually under a pavement, structure, etc. **2.** Drilling soil vertically to obtain information about the ground's subsurface.

soil cement Soil, cement, and water mixed to make a hard surface.

soil classification The systematic ordering of soils. This is usually accomplished by observing or finding physical or chemical property differences in soils. In the United States, the **Soil Conservation Service** is actively engaged in this work and has records in many areas of the country of soil types.

soil compaction The degree to which particles in the **soil** are compressed, filling pore space and increasing **soil density**. Compaction of soils is advantageous and usually essential to the stability of structures and paving, but is detrimental to plant growth. Plants are restricted by compacted soils because they afford little aeration, little gaseous diffusion, difficult root extension and penetration, and they usually lack water because it does not infiltrate well and has little **pore** space for its storage. *See also* **compact** and **bulk density**.

Soil Conservation Service In the United States, a portion of the federal government that has been assisting farmers, ranchers, and construction efforts by classifying, mapping, and analyzing soils for many years; now called the **National Resources Conservation Service** (NRCS).

soil creep A type of soil mass movement characterized by a very slow, often erratic and infrequent downslope displacement of soil not fracturing the soil mass. The impetus of soil creep is often freeze-thaw cycles or wet-dry cycles.

soil density *See* **soil compaction** and **bulk density**.

soil drainage Water drainage from the soil made up of three components: runoff, internal drainage, and permeability.

soil erosion The removal of soil by water or wind.

soil fabric Various-sized mineral particles derived from rock and arranged into geometric patterns.

soil fill   *See as* **fill** *or* **backfill**.

soil-heat flux   The rate of heat flow into, from, or through a soil.

soil horizon   In **soil** science, the reasonably distinct layers of soil or a land's underlying material in a profile as observed, studied, or found in a vertical section of land. Horizons are usually distinguishable by their change in color, or texture. Each layer or horizon is determined not only by color and texture, but also by **soil structure** type, **pH**, **root**s, and **organisms**. The master soil horizons are the **O horizon**, **A horizon**, **B horizon**, and **C horizon**. Sometimes a lowercase letter(s) will follow a soil horizon designation as follows: A1b. The letter(s) has a general meaning. Some of those meanings are as follows: b—buried soil horizon; ca—carbonate accumulation; cn—concretion accumulations; cs—calcium sulfate accumulation; f—frozen soil; g—strong gleying; h—humus and iron accumulation; m—cementation; sa—salt accumulation more soluble than calcium sulfate; se—silicious cementation that is soluble in alkali; t—illuvium clay, maximum clay; x—fragipan, a firm, brittle, and high density layer. The major soil horizons may also have differentiation of layers within them called **subhorizons**. They are usually labeled with the major soil horizon letter designation (O, A, B, C) followed by a number (1, 2, 3). The lower number is higher in the **soil profile** or the first subhorizon encountered when digging from the surface. There may be no subhorizons present in a soil profile, or several. *See also* subhorizons **A1**, **A2**, **A3**, **Oe**, **Oa**, **Oi**, and the **D or R horizon**s.

soil intake rate   **1.** The speed at which water infiltrates a soil. This changes significantly: it is a greater speed when precipitation first occurs and slows to a stopping point at complete saturation or at a point when the precipitation rate exceeds infiltration rate. **2.** The speed at which water infiltrates a bare soil at a specific time during the water application (irrigation) period. In irrigation, higher intake rates of soil assist in avoiding runoff, but the rate of infiltration significantly decreases with duration of water application. High soil intake rates are found in soils with good aeration (not compacted) and organic content.

soil interface   The area where two dissimilar soils meet. It will usually impede the flow of water, nutrients, and living things from one soil type to the other. This is dangerous because long periods of standing water usually bring on **water mold**, causing death in most plants.

soilless   Without **soil**. This term is often used in describing a **growth medium (soil mix)** that does not contain any soil as a part of its mix or composition.

soilless mix   A rooting or planting medium that has no soil, but instead is comprised of such materials as **perlite**, **vermiculite**, **sand**, **peat**, **fertilizer**, etc.

soil line   The circular line around a plant stem, or a structure where it contacts the earth.

soil mechanics   The laws and principles of mechanics and hydraulics in engineering as applied to soils examined as an engineering material.

soil mix   **1.** A mix of **soil**, **perlite**, **vermiculite**, finely ground bark, **peat**, or other **organic** or inorganic materials, used as a **growth medium** for plants. **2.** A **growing medium** mix for nursery **container** plants of the aforementioned ingredients except that **soil** is not normally a part of the mix. This is called a **soilless** growth medium.

soil pH   A measurement of the relative concentration of hydrogen ions in soil. It is followed by a number. A pH 7 is neutral. The higher the number is above 7, the higher the alkalinity of the soil. The lower the number below 7, the more acid the soil is.

soil pipe   A pipe carrying the discharge of toilets or other sanitary sewage.

soil polymers   Materials that absorb water hundreds of times their weight and that are used around plant material roots to provide water over a longer period of time. They are often called **superabsorbents**. They are most helpful in potting soils.

soil profile   The vertical assemblage of **soil** made up of layers that are called **horizon**s and lying between bedrock and the earth's surface. Soil profiles vary from region to region and usually from site to site in thickness and horizon types present. A soil profile may be as the accompanying illustration shows, but may also not contain some or many of these layers or may contain other layer combinations and **subhorizon**s.

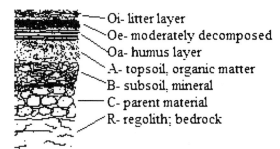

Oi- litter layer
Oe- moderately decomposed
Oa- humus layer
A- topsoil, organic matter
B- subsoil, mineral
C- parent material
R- regolith; bedrock

soil profile sample

soil reaction   Also known as **pH**, the hydrogen-ion concentration of a soil expressed in the form of the reciprocal of the log of the hydrogen-ion number. Neutral is a pH of 7.0. **Acid soil** is lower than 7.0, and **alkaline soil** is higher than 7.0.

soil reclamation   An effort to return a soil that was once arable back to an arable condition.

soil report   A document from a geological engineer providing information about the subsurface soil conditions. This report does not usually contain the information about a soil's capacity to grow plants but does tell about the composition of soil layers and gives information relative to its capacity and stability for construction purposes. *See* **soil test.**

soil salinity   The amount of salt in the soil. Excess salt can be toxic to plants, but more often symptoms are leaf scorch, stunted growth, yellow leaves or withered leaf margins. Salt also interferes with germination of seeds. Salts can build up in the soil from softened water, green manure, fertilizers, chemical amendments, or salts applied for melting snow. Salts can best be removed from soil by **leaching** with water that is free of salts. This is most effective if the soil allows water to drain through it freely.

soil series   A group of soils having similar profile characteristics and having been derived from the same parent rock material.

soil stabilization   The application of a chemical, biological (plants), or mechanical treatment to a soil to increase stability or desired engineering properties.

soil stabilizer   **1.** A machine with rotating tines that mixes surface soils in place with stabilizing materials (such as cement or lime) to increase soil-bearing capacity. Its rapidly rotating tines pick up and blend the soil with the stabilizing agent. **2.** A chemical or substance to improve the physical properties of **soil**, placed on or mixed in with soil to reduce or prevent erosion and sloughing, or to improve its bearing or structural qualities.

soil sterilant   A chemical that will kill all plants and prevent all plant growth in a soil.

They usually last for a number of years and should be used with caution. They may leach from points of initial application to adjacent areas as they travel with water moving through the soil.

soil sterilizing **1.** Heating soil to destroy organisms present. **2.** The application of chemicals to soil to prevent plants from being able to grow for a year or more. These chemicals should be used with extreme care.

soil structure The arrangement and degree of development of the primary soil particles into geometric patterns of natural aggregates. Various types of soil structure are recognized (massive, platy, prismatic, blocky, granular). Disturbance or excavation of naturally occurring soils tends to destroy its natural structure, which can lead to compaction and its associated problems of decreased gaseous diffusion, reduced water infiltration, and increase in resistance to root penetration.

soil survey An investigation of the soil, accompanied by a written report, usually including information concerning the type of soil, its thickness and strength, location of bedrock, depth to water table, shrink-swell capacity, stoniness, etc. that is prepared by a geotechnical firm, a government agency, etc.

soil test In **horticulture**, the necessary process and information obtained about a growing medium by analysis. This analysis of soil can be done with kits by individuals, but the most accurate information on **pH**, nutrient deficiency, texture, **salinity**, etc. is obtained by having a soil laboratory perform the analysis. Such laboratories can be found as private businesses, or they are often available at a university or at an agricultural extension service.

soil texture The size, shape, and proportional distribution of individual soil particles such as sand, silt, or clay into size classes, usually expressed by a percentage basis by weight into 12 classes of soils as defined by the USDA. It is not directly interpolated into the Unified Soil Classification System.

soil texture class The relative amounts of sand, silt, or clay in a soil. Sandy loam, loamy clay, and silty clay loam are examples of soil classes.

soil type *See* **soil classification**.

solar Relating to or derived from the sun.

solar collector A device made to absorb the sun's radiation and transfer the accumulated heat to a fluid passing through the collector.

solar constant The rate at which solar radiation is obtained on a surface facing directly at the sun on the edge of the atmosphere.

solar gain The amount of solar radiation absorbed by a landscape element or any surface.

solar heat coefficient The portion of incident solar energy transmitted through glazing under normal summer conditions.

solar heating Generating or using heat from absorbed solar radiation.

solarium A sunny room having a significant amount of glazing, allowing the sun's light and warmth to enter. These are often useful for growing indoor plants and for a person's leisure relaxation.

solar orientation The direction an object or formation faces in relation to the sun.

solar skyspace The space between a solar energy collector and the sun. It should be free of obstructions that shade the collector.

soldered joint A metal pipe joint made by heating the pipe and melting solder into the joint.

soldering gun An electrically heated soldering tool with a grip and trigger like a pistol.

soldering iron A tool with a tapered metal tip used to heat metal and melt solder to join the metals.

soldier A brick placed on end so that it is positioned vertically while having the narrower face showing on the wall surface. (Compare with **sailor**.)

soldier course A horizontal row of upright bricks with their narrow faces exposed on the wall surface.

solenoid In irrigation, an electrical device attached to a valve, which activates by signal through a wire from a controller opening or closing the valve.

solenoid valve A device preventing the flow of water (or other fluid or gas) through a pipe system until a small coil is electrically energized to move a plunger that allows the device (valve) to open and allow flow. This type of **valve** is the one most commonly used with **automatic controller**s in landscape irrigation work.

solid brick A brick without voids. *See also* **solid masonry unit**.

solid masonry unit (U.S.A.) A masonry unit with a net cross-sectional area in every plane parallel to bearing surface with at least 75% of its cross-sectional area being measured in the same plane.

solid state controller A **digital sprinkler controller**.

solid waste This term encompasses garbage, refuse, rubbish, and trash as classified and defined by the National Solid Waste Management Association.

solu-bridge A device that measures the electrical conductivity of a soil solution, facilitating a determination of the soluble salt concentration.

solum The soil above the parent mineral material comprising the **A horizon** and **B horizon**.

solvent-weld joint A connection made between plastic pipes or devices where substances (primers, glue) are placed in contact with each surface (usually with a brush or a dauber) to dissolve the surface of the plastics so that when placed in contact they can harden into a leak-proof joint.

somewhat excessively drained soil Soil in which water is removed rapidly. They are usually sandy and porous. After it rains, it is not long before optimum amounts of moisture for plant growth are no longer present.

somewhat poorly drained soils Soils in which water is removed or percolates slowly enough to keep it wet for significant periods, but not always.

sooty mold A mycelium growing on leaves, and twigs of trees and shrubs, caused by honeydew secretions from sap-sucking insects such as aphids and **scale**.

sordid A botanical term describing a plant part with a dull, dingy, or dirty hue.

sorus *or* **sori** A cluster of **sporangia** on a fern.

sough A surface water drain at the base of a hill or embankment that carries the water gathered to another drain, usually to one side.

sound wood Wood without decay.

source **1.** In landscape ecology, an area where output exceeds input of organisms or materials, and is nearly opposite of a **sink**. **2.** In irrigation design and construction, the supply of water for the irrigation system; it may be a city water main, lake, river, well, spring, etc.

south elevation **1.** A drawing, usually to scale, showing the south-facing portion of a structure or element as it would be seen standing to the south and looking north to view it. **2.** The **elevation** of a portion of ground, paving, or structure situated south of the remainder of it.

southern elevation *See* **south elevation**.

southern exposure **1.** A slope that from top to bottom slopes downward toward the south. In the northern hemisphere, it receives more light, and in the southern hemisphere, it receives less light. **2.** The south-facing portion of a structure. **3.** The area to the south of any nearly vertical surface that has a changed microclimate effected by it with regard to heat or cold, or brightness of sunlight or shadow.

southern grasses *See* **warm season grasses**.

southwest sunscald or **southwest sun scorch** Damage on tree trunks or sometimes branches of mostly young or recently planted trees that appears as split and exfoliating bark. This mostly occurs on the southwest-facing area of a tree trunk where on sunny days (especially with snow on the ground) the sap begins to flow, and then at night, if it is sufficiently cold, the sap freezes and the bark cracks or is exfoliated.

SOV Abbreviation for shutoff **valve**.

sow In landscape work, the placing of seed for future growth, especially by scattering, but also by covering with earth or **growth medium**.

sow bug An isopod crustacean (suborder *Oniscoidea*) having an elliptical body with seven pairs of legs, sectioned shells, and the capability to roll up into a ball about the size of a pea. They feed mostly on decaying vegetation; however, they will feed on young tender plants,

especially those just germinating, or on fruits that are usually overripe or damaged. They are encouraged to proliferate by mulching and composting. They are also known as potato bugs or pill bugs.

sowing *See* **sow**.

soybean meal Remains of defatted soybeans used as an **organic**, quickly available, fairly long-lasting **acidic fertilizer** having an **NPK** ratio of about 6–7-1.2–1.5-1.5–2.5.

SP, sp **1.** Abbreviation for **soil pipe**. **2.** Abbreviation for **standpipe**. **3.** Abbreviation for **species**. **4.** Abbreviation for static pressure.

space **1.** A defined area created indoors or outdoors by walls, **fences**, **hedges**, **berms**, buildings, trees, etc. that gives visual enclosure to an area. **2.** Any amount of area. *See also* **spacial**.

spacial A two- or three-dimensional area or space. A reference to an area, land, **site**, or anything regarding land that can be shown to have a defining edge whether sharp or vague. These relationships are those graphically shown and analyzed in **GIS** applications.

spade A **shovel** or hand-digging device that has a relatively thin blade and a handle.

spading Turning over soil for **sowing** seeds or **transplanting** plants.

spadix A long, fleshy, usually upright organ extending up from a flower (usually a **spathe**).

spall A chip or area removed from the surface of a stone, masonry unit, or concrete by a blow or by action of weather, etc.

spalling The flaking of a brick, stone, or concrete surface usually due to frost, chemical action, or in concrete work, too much water at the surface when it was finished. *See also* **laitance**.

span   The distance between two supports.

spandix   *See* **spadix**.

spangham   Mosses common to bogs, which, after harvesting and drying, are used in planting soils because of their moisture-retaining capacity and nutrients. See **peat moss**.

Spanish tile   A curved, red-clay roofing tile laid in courses, with adjacent tiles having their convex side laid alternately up and down.

spathe   In botanical terms, a flower-like or leaf-like **bract** partly surrounding the **inflorescence** that is usually colored and noticeably appealing. They usually enclose a **spadix**.

spathulate   *See* **spatulate**.

spatial element   In landscape ecology, each of the relatively homogeneous units in a mosaic at any scale.

spatulate   In botanical terms, shaped like a spatula, or druggist's spoon.

spatulate leaf shape

spawl   *See* **spall**.

special conditions   A section of contract documents that clarifies the general conditions of work, or a project's specific conditions.

specialty contractor   A contractor performing a particular trade such as sprinkler irrigation, deck building, installation of water features, flooring, windows, electrical work, etc. Landscape construction is often a specialty contractor's trade in reference to a building being constructed with its site to be improved.

species   A group of plants closely resembling each other and breeding freely. In a plant's **botanical name**, the first word used is the **genus**, the second word is species, and the third word, if any, is the **variety**. If there is a fourth word, it is a **strain**.

species factor (K_s) *or* **crop coefficient (K_c)**   In irrigation auditing, a plant's transpiration rate. A factor from 0.80 to 0.90 is generally high. Medium factors generally range from 0.50 to 0.70 depending on plant type. Low factors again depend on plant type and generally range from 0.10 to 0.60.

species richness   The number of species in a given area. In most cases, the more species found or available, the more it is thought to be rich. But compatibility and environmental survivability are issues for the actuality of species richness.

specifications   A written description of materials, systems, work processes, equipment use, etc. to be adhered to in order to enhance quality of construction on a project as part of the contract documents.

specific capacity   The discharge rate pumped from a well divided by the drawdown in the well water surface. It is a measure of the productivity or capacity of a well.

specific epithet   In botanical terms, the name of a plant in **binomial nomenclature**.

specific gravity   A ratio of the density of a substance to the density of a reference substance. For fluids, the reference material is usually water. For gases, the reference material is usually air.

specific name   A plant's botanical (scientific) name.

specific retention   The ratio of volume of water within rock or soil, after being saturated and retained against the pull of gravity, to the volume of rock or soil.

specific speed (Ns)   With regard to pumps, the value that centrifugal pump design engineers use to classify impeller design. It is not the **pump speed**.

specific yield   The ratio of the volume of water within rock or soil that moves with gravity after saturation to the volume of the rock or soil.

specimen   **1.** A term used to describe an ornamental plant of particular note for some attribute. **2.** A plant that is exemplary in form to the point of being an example of how plants of the same botanical name should appear. **3.** A plant specified for installation in a landscape construction project that should be healthy and true to form. It is usually for a conspicuous or important location in the landscape. **4.** A plant that is chosen, with purpose or at random, from many plants of the same type as a sample.

specular angle   An angle that is equal to the angle formed by a ray (such as light) striking a surface and a line perpendicular to the surface. The ray is reflected from the surface at the same angle it received the ray. The angle between the reflected ray and a line perpendicular to the surface is the specular angle.

spent   Flowers that have finished their blooming cycle, or an individual flower that has completed its bloom.

sperm   In reference to plants, a male gamete that can fuse with an egg to form a zygote.

sphagnum   Many mosses of the order *Sphagnum,* which grow in moist, acid areas where there are decaying remains with other plants become peat (**peat moss**).

spicate   In botanical terms, spike-like, in a spike, or arranged in a spike.

spider mite   *See* **mite**.

spigot   **1.** A **faucet** or **sill cock**. **2.** The end of a pipe made to fit into a **bell** end of another pipe of the same type.

spike   **1.** A thick, long, heavy nail, usually given this reference if over 3 in (7.6 cm) long. They are usually available up to 12 in (30.5 cm) long and are useful for attaching timbers. **2.** A grain plant head. **3.** A long inflorescence much like a **raceme** except that flowers are **sessile** (closely held) on an elongated **axis**. The flowers are directly attached without any stems along the main lower stem. Flowers open in sequence beginning with the bottom of the spike. Racemes are similar, but have a small stem supporting each flower from the main stem.

spike inflorescence

spikelet   In botanical terms, a small or secondary spike. It is a type or portion of a flower in grasses and sedges. It may be a flower or flower cluster, consisting of a flower or flowers and their enclosing bracts.

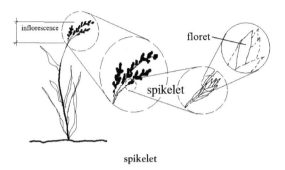

spikelet

spill stone   In a waterfall, the stone at the point where water falls; it shapes the sheet or dribble of water that falls.

spindle   In woodworking, a short piece shaped by turning and cutting on a lathe.

spindle-shaped   In botanical terms, tapered at both ends.

spine   In botanical terms, a sharp woody or rigid outgrowth from a plant **branch** or **stem**. A **thorn** or a stiff pointed portion of a plant capable of puncturing skin.

spinner sprinkler   A spinning sprinkler operated at low pressure with a small distribution pattern.

spirit level   A leveling device nearly filled with fluid utilizing an air bubble within a clear tube (or container) to allow determination of orientation to or from vertical or horizontal.

spittlebugs   Numerous insects (family *Cercopidae*) whose larvae secrete froth, protecting them from being seen. They feed on stems, strawberries, etc.

splash block *or* **splash guard**   A small **precast concrete** or plastic block laid below a **downspout**

to direct roof drainage away, and to prevent **erosion** of the surface on which it sits.

splash line   A noticeable line on a surface (such as a fence or a building) where water splashes or is sprayed consistently, causing discoloration from minerals in the water.

splice box   A box (often underground) made of plastic, fiberglass, or concrete, etc. where conductors (wires) are joined.

split-rail fence   A fence with openings between the horizontal rails that are made of split wood.

spoil   Material from excavating, trenching, or dredging.

sporangium, sporangia   In botanical terms, a case or capsule producing **spore**s on the underside of the fronds of **fern**s.

spore   A simple type of reproductive cell (taking the place of a seed) that can produce a new plant and is common to **algae**, **fungi**, ferns, and mosses. These plants are not seed producing.

sport   In **horticulture**, a **mutant** plant. It can be a plant or a portion of a plant exhibiting a sudden deviation from the norm for the plant type.

spot elevation   A point on a site, plan, or map with a known existing or specified future elevation.

spotted spurge   An annual weed with small leaves producing thousands of seeds within a month and is difficult to control, especially in lawns.

spp   Abbreviation referring to more than one species.

spray   The application of water or water mixed with fertilizer, insecticide, etc. by tiny droplets produced by pressure and coming from a nozzle that fans it out.

sprayed concrete *See* **shotcrete**.

sprayer A tank and nozzle in various shapes and sizes used to spray dyes for concrete, insecticides, liquid fertilizer, weed killers, etc.

sprayer

spray head A **sprinkler head** that sprays in a continuous spray pattern without rotating to irrigate. These heads usually allow change of nozzles for various trajectories, arcs, and water quantity outputs.

spray lime A hydrated **lime** made of fine particles, at least 9% of them pass through a No. 325 sieve.

spray sprinkler *See* **spray head**.

spreader A piece of equipment used to evenly broadcast **seed, manure, fertilizer, herbicide**, etc. over the ground.

spreading In the landscape industry, a plant that has a branching pattern or growing pattern that is more horizontal than vertical. Trees with this type of branching have horizontal trunks, or nearly so. (Compare with **ascending**.)

sprig **Stolon**s or small plant **division**s.

spreading branching patterns

sprigging The process of placing grass sprigs from running types of grasses (such as Bermuda grass) to create a lawn or stand of grass.

spring clamp A clamp with jaws that are normally kept closed by pressure from a spring to clamp materials or items. The jaws may be opened with two handles when they are squeezed.

springwood Growth of the **xylem** from the **cambium** layer that is formed in woody plants during spring and early summer. It is generally lighter in color than wood grown in late summer through fall.

sprinkler In landscaping, a device that emits, shots, sprays, or in any way distributes water.

sprinkler circuit The area covered by sprinkler heads operated by a single valve.

sprinkler controller A timing device used to turn on and off **sprinkler valves** or **heads**.

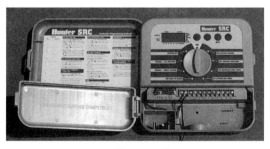

sprinkler controller

sprinkler flag   A small **flag** and thin wire or plastic staff, usually 12 to 18 in high, used to mark locations of existing or proposed **sprinkler head**s, **valve**s, etc. in the landscape.

sprinkler flag

sprinkler head   A device that delivers and distributes water for **irrigation** by a stream or spray projected above the area of irrigation via water pressure. The **nozzle** portion of the head determines the length, type (spray, stream), and distance of water distribution. Common types of sprinkler heads include **impact head**s, **spray head**s, and **rotor head**s.

sprinkler head profile   A graph showing the **precipitation rate** of a particular **sprinkler head** with a particular **nozzle** from the point of discharge to its farthest coverage point. These are quite telling of the areas within an arc or coverage area of the sprinkler that receive too little or too much precipitation. Sprinkler distribution is not usually even across the graph. Low and high points in the graph are usually overcome in sprinkler design by placing another sprinkler head no farther away than the farthest application of water by the next head. This is called **head-to-head coverage** and affords a better distribution and uniformity of applied water.

sprinkler irrigation   The watering of plants or seeds with **sprinkler head**s.

sprinkler key   A long metal device used for turning on or off valves on sprinkler systems. Some have a slot at their end (for **stop and waste valve**s), some have a box on their end (for large, water line, cast-iron valves), and some have a rounded fork at their end (for turning on **manual valve**s). The sprinkler key in the illustration fits over a manual angle valve.

sprinkler profile   *See* **sprinkler head profile**.

sprinkler program   Information entered into the controller's memory determining when the system will water. A program usually contains three pieces of information: days to water, time to start watering, and the length of each zone to be watered.

sprinkler schedule   **1.** A tabulation of materials for a sprinkler system including, but not limited to, such information as the type of equipment (i.e., sprinkler head, valve type, controller, quick coupler) size, gallons per minute, manufacturer, and model number. **2.** The timing and frequency of sprinkler operations including runtime, time of day for operation, and days to be operated.

sprinkler system   The composite of all elements to facilitate irrigation; usually refers to an irrigation system with sprinkler heads.

sprinkler valve   An **automatic valve** or a **manual valve** used for turning on and off a **sprinkler system**.

sprinkler valve key   *See* **sprinkler key**.

sprinkler zone   The area covered by sprinkler heads operated by a single valve.

sprout   **1.** The opening of a seed; the beginning of its growth. **2.** A **sucker** or **runner** from a plant.

spun concrete   Concrete compacted by spin-ning, as with the manufacture of pipes.

spur   **1.** Some fruits such as apples and cherries that bear their fruit on specialized short twigs. **2.** Projections from a flower (usually tubular) such as found in columbine (*Aquilegia*) flowers. They arise from sepals or petals. **3.** An offshoot or projection away from the main body.

sq. ft.   Abbreviation for **square foot** (feet).

sq. in.   Abbreviation for **square inch**(es).

sq. km.   Square **kilometer**(s); 1,000,000 square **meter**s, or 0.3861 square miles.

sq. m.   Abbreviation for **square meter**.

sq. mi.   Abbreviation for **square mile**(s).

square   **1.** Roofing materials equaling 100 sq ft (9.29 sq m). **2.** A steel, L-shaped tool used to draw lines to cut lumber perpendicular to an edge. *See* **steel square**.

square edge   In reference to lumber, wood cut with four edges at right angles. It is not tapered or tongue-and-groove.

square foot *or* **square feet** *or* **sq. ft.** *or* **ft^2**   English or U.S. measurement of area equal to a square measuring one foot along each edge. It is an area equal to 144 **sq in** or 0.093 **sq m**.

square foot gardening   A type of intensive gardening where plants are grown 1 ft apart, usually in raised beds, and by **organic** means.

square inch *or* **sq. in.** *or* **in^2**   English or U.S. measurement of area equal to a square measuring one inch along each edge. It is an area equal to 0.0069 **sq ft**, or 6.452 sq **cm**.

square kilometer   A metric measurement of area being one **kilometer** square; equal to 1,000,000 sq **m**, or 0.3861 sq mi.

square meter   A metric measurement of surface area equal to one **meter** square.

square mile *or* **sq. mi.** *or* **mi^2**   English or U.S. measurement of area equal to a square measuring one mile along each edge; equal to 640 **ac**, or 2.590 sq **km**s.

square spacing   A reference in sprinkler layout design in which **head-to-head coverage** is obtained by heads being laid out in a pattern that is square if imaginary lines were drawn between heads in **plan view**.

square yard *or* **sq. yd.** *or* **yd^2**   English or U.S. measurement of area equal to a square with each edge measuring one yard. It is equal to 9 **sq ft**, or 0.836 **m**.

squarrose   In botanical terms, a plant part abruptly spreading or recurved at some point above the base.

squash borer   A larva of a moth prevalent in the eastern United States that bores into squash stems, leaving a sawdust-like excrement while causing wilting and death.

squash bugs   A large blackish bug (*Anasa tristis* of the *Coreidae* family) that can cause plants of the gourd family to completely wilt. Damage is usually found on zucchini, winter squash, and pumpkin. Control is usually by chemicals.

sq. yd.   Abbreviation for square yard(s).

SSF   Abbreviation for **subsurface flow**.

SST   Abbreviation for stainless steel.

stability   In reference to composting, an indication of the relative state of decomposition. The more decomposed the compost material, the more stable it is. The process of decomposition may be temporarily harmful to plants, especially as nitrogen is robbed from the soil to assist in the process. **Humus** is fully or nearly fully decomposed **organic material** that is stable in or on the soil.

stabilization　**1.** The increase of stability of a sloped earthen mass. **2.** The securing, steadying, or establishment in place of, a construction item.

stable　A building for the sheltering and care of horses.

staging area　A **space** allowed for a **contractor** to place materials and equipment for constructing a project.

stain　**1.** An added color or a natural discoloration in the surface of a material. **2.** A chemical colorant (pigment) for enhancing wood grain during finishing. It may be a solid stain or a **semitransparent stain**. **3.** A pigment or dye in paint.

stair　A step or several steps.

staircase　A group of stairs or several groups (flights) of stairs with the associated framework, handrails, etc.

stake　**1.** A piece of metal, wood, etc. pounded into the ground to mark or support something. **2.** A reference to a **fertilizer** stake made of hardened fertilizer in the shape of a stake so that it may be forced into the ground. It is much like a fertilizer stick except that it is usually larger and has a point. It decomposes, and some materials leach, acting much the same as a **fertilizer tablet**.

stake-and-rider fence　A fence made of posts resting on the ground at an angle and fastened together where they cross near their ends; also has rails riding on these crossings extending horizontally between them.

staking　*See* **tree staking**.

staking out　The placing of stakes to give locations for construction work and placements.

stalk　**1.** The main stem of an **herbaceous** plant. **2.** The main stem of any plant. **3.** A slender support of a flower or leaf (**petiole, peduncle**).

stalked leaf　A leaf with a **petiole** for attachment of the leaf. (Compare with **sessile** and **perfoliate**.)

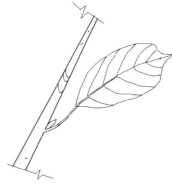

stalked leaf attachment

stamen　In botanical terms, the male organ of a flower consisting of an anther and a filament.

staminate　In botanical terms, a male flower with **stamens**, but no **pistils**.

staminode　In botanical terms, a modified **stamen** that does not produce **pollen**, or a structure resembling a stamen that is sometimes **petal**-like.

staminodium　A sterile stamen.

stamping　Shaping metal, concrete, etc. by forcing a hard device into its surface before it has hardened.

stand　A group of plants together in an area and usually touching one another or nearly so.

standard

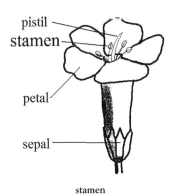

pistil
stamen
petal
sepal

stamen

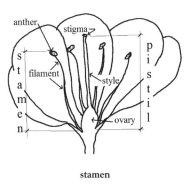

anther
stigma
stamen
filament
style
pistil
ovary

stamen

standard   In horticulture, a treelike form of a shrub or vine that is trained and pruned to have a trunk with a head like a miniature tree. Tree roses are the most common standards grown. Most standard forms have a **head** that starts at least 5 ft (1.5 m) from the ground surface. Some shrubs are grafted on a tall **stalk** for an interesting standard **specimen**.

Standard Dimensional Ratios (SDR)   The ratio of a pipe's outside diameter to its wall thickness (outside diameter/wall thickness). As the pipe diameter increases, there is a proportional increase in wall thickness. Pipes with the same SDR ratio will usually bear the same working pressure throughout all pipe sizes.

standard inside diameter dimension ratio (SIDR)   With regard to pipes, the ratio of the average inside diameter to the minimum thickness.

standpipe   A high vertical pipe or tank used for storing water and supplying pressure.

staple   A double-pointed, U-shaped metal wire or stiff steel often used for the same purposes as nails, but preferred for its potentially increased holding power. In smaller sizes, they are forced under pressure from a staple gun into construction materials, but in larger sizes they are usually forced by hand into such materials as **erosion control fabric** or **weed barrier fabric**.

start   A **set** or larger plant part used to propagate another.

starter solution   A chemical (usually vitamin A) fertilizer dissolved in water, and applied in the planting hole or around the roots of plants that have been newly transplanted. Sometimes bare root plants are soaked in such a solution before planting. This assists plants to withstand the shock of being moved and speeds up root development.

State Agriculture Experimental Station   In the United States, a government-sponsored resource for unbiased, current information regarding **hardiness**, **soils**, **fertilizers**, plant varieties, pest and disease control, etc. They are often associated with state agricultural colleges.

static head   The pressure in any water system not in use and not flowing when expressed as **head**.

static pressure   Within irrigation pipes, the pressure of water exerted when the system is at rest, in a closed system, with no water flow from or through pipes.

static suction head   A condition occurring when the pump is lower in elevation than the supply. It is the distance between the pump centerline and the water supply surface elevation.

static suction lift   The vertical distance from the pump centerline to the supply surface when the pump is above the supply.

station   **1.** A **circuit** on an irrigation controller that can be programmed with a runtime separate from other circuits and provides electrical power to open or close one or more remote valves. **2.** The coverage of a valve in combination with its watering devices.

statue   A three-dimensional representation of a person, animal, or mythical image (or a combination of such) created by sculpting, casting, carving, etc.

statue

STD, std.   Abbreviation for standard.

steam pasteurization   Treating a **growing medium** (**soil mix**) by heating with steam at a temperature of 160 F (56°C) to kill harmful organisms such as weed seeds, **nematode**s, insects, diseases, etc.

steam sterilization   Treating a **growing medium** (**soil mix**) by heating with steam at a temperature of 212 F (100°C) to kill all living organisms in the soil.

steel   An alloy of iron and steel refined from pig iron or from scrap steel.

steel square   A flat, steel, L-shaped tool with measurements (inches, centimeters) marked along its edge, used to mark perpendicular lines or check corners for being perpendicular (square) to each other.

stele   The primary **vascular tissue** structure of stems or roots together with any tissue (such as the **pith**) that it encloses.

stellate   In botanical terms, star-like; several similar parts radiating from a common center in various directions.

stem   **1.** A primary plant portion that develops buds and shoots rather than roots. **2.** The main trunk of a plant.

stemflow   Rainfall intercepted by plant leaves and branches conveyed to the ground via stems or the trunk.

step   A tread and a riser as a single unit or in a staircase.

stepped fashion   A horizontal flashing along a sloped roof against and intersecting a vertical face that steps up with the slope of the roof.

stepping stone   **1.** In landscape ecology, patches that are spatially arranged to act as cover or favorable conditions for an organism or element to move through the landscape from patch to patch. **2.** A hard surface piece placed in a lawn, ground cover, or surface mulch to allow pedestrians ease of access and prevent damage (soil compaction, damage to plants) to the landscape. They can be round, square, or any shape. Examples of materials used for stepping stones are brick, concrete, block, and wood rounds. They are usually laid in series with spaces between each. They are most often used in low-level pedestrian traffic areas.

stepping stone, detail

stepping stone

stereoscope A viewing device used to see a three-dimensional image using two **aerial photographs** overlapping (showing adjacent land areas) or side to side.

sterile 1. With regard to flowers (**inflorescence**), incapable of reproducing because of not bearing **spores**, **pollen**, or female reproductive organs (the **pistil**). 2. Not bearing flowers or not having seeds capable of germination. A description of the condition of a single plant that is not capable of producing viable seed. 3. A condition of soil when it contains no living organisms.

sterilization 1. The act of causing soil to be incapable of sustaining plant growth by use of heat, chemicals, etc. 2. The act of causing a flower or plant to not be capable of reproduction.

stick 1. A length of pipe. 2. A long, slender piece of wood. 3. A hardened **fertilizer** somewhat in the shape of a stake so that it may be forced into the ground. It is very similar to a fertilizer stake except that it is usually more slender and has no point. It decomposes, and some materials leach to the soil below, acting much the same as a **fertilizer tablet**.

stiffener plate A steel plate attached to structural members to add support against heavy loads, or to make a secure attachment.

stigma The part of the female portion of a flower (**pistil** or **style**) that receives **pollen**.

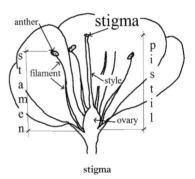

stigma

stile A vertical, structural member of a frame.

stinkbug Any of the family *Pentatomidae* that emits an unpleasant odor when disturbed. It can feed on fruits and vegetables and may become a nuisance.

stipe   In botanical terms, the stalk of a fern's frond.

stipple   A texture made of dots, points, or small bumps.

stipulate   A botanical term referring to the **stip-ule**s at the base of an attachment of a leaf.

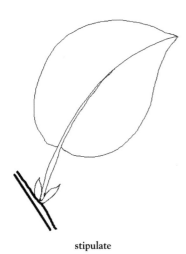

stipulate

stipule   In botanical terms, the appendages on each side of the base of some leaf **petiole**s.

stirrup   **1.** Same as a **hanger**. **2.** Bent rods or bars usually in W or U shapes, or any shape to resist shear in masonry or concrete.

stock   **1.** In construction, materials or plants on hand. **2.** The rooted plant on which a **scion** (**bud** or **shoot**) of another plant is placed in **budding**, **grafting**, or **inarching**.

stock plant   A plant from which **cutting**s are taken for production of more plants.

stock tank deicer   A floating heater designed to keep water a few degrees above freezing when the air is below freezing.

stolon   A long stem of a plant that creeps along the surface of the ground, or trails shoots above the ground, capable of rooting at the nodes or

rooting at some points where it contacts the ground, and forms new plants there. Examples of plants exhibiting this phenomenon are St. Augustine and Bermuda grasses. The term is sometimes loosely applied to slender **rhizomes** near the ground surface.

stoloniferous   In botanical terms, **stolons** or **plant material** producing or **propagating** itself by **stolons**.

stoma *or* **stomate** *or* **stomata** *or* **stomates**   Microscopic openings in plant tissues, usually in leaves (usually undersides) and stems, allowing for gaseous exchange and transpiration of water. Carbon dioxide enters the tissue through these pores, and water vapor is lost to cool the leaf. They occur between two adjoining specialized cells, called guard cells. Variation in the guard cell size by **turgor** adjusts the size of the opening. When pressure is low, the stomata are small to reduce loss of water, but they become larger when **photosynthesis** increases.

stone   **1.** A cut, shaped, or split rock for use in construction for facing or building walls, etc. **2.** Solid mineral matter of indeterminate size. A rock.

stoned   Removal of sharp edges of tile or masonry produced during cutting. This term comes from the use of a carborundum stone.

stone fruit   Fruit containing one seed in the center such as in plums, peaches, and apricots.

stonework   Any **masonry** work where rock is secured in place with a cement or mortar.

stool   A stump of a tree producing **sucker**s. **2.** A plant **crown** from which shoots grow.

stop and waste key   A long, T-shaped device with a slot on one end that fits over a valve to turn it off and on. They are typically used to slide down a vertical sleeve or curb box to access a valve below grade to operate it.

stop and waste valve

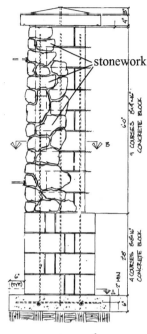

stonework

stop and waste key

stop and waste valve A valve that can be turned off and on with a long key that is extended down a sleeve to the valve. The valve stops the water flow in the pipe and opens a small hole in the valve to drain (waste) all water downstream and at a higher elevation. This is important in areas where the ground freezes in the winter to prevent freeze damage.

stope An excavation with a series of benches or tables.

storage tank A container that receives water from a source and holds it for distribution to the points of use.

storm cellar An underground space for shelter against violent storms such as tornadoes or hurricanes.

storm drain or **storm sewer** A conduit, pipe, natural channel, or structure used to convey waste water or storm water, but not industrial waste or sanitary sewage.

stormflow The significant increase in water traversing a stream channel due to storm water.

storm sewer A pipe system collecting and disposing surface water runoff.

storm water The water precipitated from clouds. It is usually in reference to rain but not sleet or snow and refers to its immediate **impact** or flow.

storm water detention 1. Any storm drainage technique that detains runoff. **2.** Storage of storm water runoff and its controlled release during and after a flood or storm.

stop and waste valve

storm water retention Storage of storm water runoff.

straightedge *or* **rod** **1.** A rigid, straight piece used to strike off a concrete, mortared, or plastered surface. **2.** A straight piece of lumber or metal used to align tile, or provide a straight or flush surface in aligning material. **3.** A metal, straight tool used to guide a straight line cut through paper, cardboard, etc.

straight fertilizer Those natural or synthetic **fertilizer**s that are not blended or mixed with other fertilizers or ingredients.

straight goods *See* **straight fertilizer.**

straight tee A pipe **tee** made with all three openings having the same size.

strain In a **botanical name**, strain refers to a population of plants within a **variety** that exhibits definite, usually attractive or improved characteristics, such as resistance to disease, improved yields, tolerance to environments, attractive growth, larger size, more vigor, etc.

stramineous A botanical term meaning straw-colored.

strap anchor A post attachment for a footing to support the post and its load. The metal strap is a U shape with its lower portion poured in concrete and the two upper ends bolted to two sides of a post for attachment.

strap leaves Leaves with margins partly or completely missing so that the leaves are narrower than normal and may resemble straps.

strap-shaped In botanical terms, long, flat, and narrow.

strap wrench A tool used for tightening large pipe, or pipe that may be broken with a pipe wrench, or pipes or devices that may be marred easily and that clamp with a strap that has a handle for tightening.

strategic A golf hole design allowing a golfer to play position to score well. Poor shots are not severely penalized. *See* **penal** design. Hazards are placed to give a golfer a reward if a risky shot is negotiated. *See also* **heroic.**

stratification **1.** Layers of soil. **2.** Treatment of seeds at low temperatures to assist in breaking dormancy and to promote germination.

stratified rock Rock layers that vary in composition.

stratify Freezing or chilling seed to assist in breaking dormancy and to promote germination.

stream bank The normal boundaries (defined by slope) of a stream channel, except when flooded.

stream corridor A strip of vegetation along a stream or river, which may be wider than the flood plain.

stream order The number assigned to a stretch between intersections or ends of a **dendritic** river system, determined by the number of upstream tributaries. Streams without any other streams contributing to them are first-order streams. Streams with one tributary are second-order streams. Second-order streams become third-order streams at the point downstream after the intersection of another stream, and so on.

street A public travelway.

street elbow *or* **street ell** A fitting accommodating a 90° turn, having one male opening and the other female.

street frontage The length of a property abutting one side of a street as measured between the property line and the street.

street furniture Items commonly furnished along streets such as trash receptacles, benches, movable planters, etc.

street lamp   A light on a pole alongside a street.

street noise barrier   A high wall, typically made of concrete, that parallels a street and reflects the noise of the traffic.

streetscape   **1.** The ground area adjacent to a street that may contain sidewalks, street furniture, landscaping, etc. **2.** The scenery viewed from a street and the visual positive or negative experience or feelings generated by such.

street tree   A tree that is currently located or proposed for planting along a street.

stress   In reference to plants, a condition brought on by any number of difficulties where the health of a growing plant is put at risk, or where external factors inhibit plant growth. It may be due to too little water, too much water, temperatures that are too low or too high, reflected light, chemicals, lack of aeration within the soil, lack of gaseous exchange within the soil, soil compaction, insects, fungus, etc. It is often noticeable by wilting leaves, brown-edged leaves, or a dulling in the color of leaves.

stretcher   A brick laid lengthwise in a wall or any masonry structure.

striate   A term often used to describe plant parts marked with fine, more or less parallel or longitudinal lines.

strict   A botanical term that means very straight and upright, not at all lax or spreading.

strigose   In botanical terms, beset with appressed, rigid bristles or hairs pointing in more or less the same direction.

strike   **1.** Finishing a mortar joint with a stroke of the trowel, at the same time removing extra mortar and smoothing the surface of the mortar to remain in the joint. **2.** A rooted **cutting** used in **propagation**.

strike off   **1.** To slide a straight wood or metal bar across a surface of fresh concrete, usually by extending one **form** across to another form so that excess concrete is removed, leaving a straight even surface. The long straight member is usually slid back and forth as it is pulled along the forms and moved forward, pulling the excess concrete. **2.** The straight edge used as indicated in (1).

strike plate *or* **strike** *or* **striking plate**   A metal plate and indentation that receives a bolt or latch of a lock on a door. It often has a curved lip at its edge toward the door opening, allowing a bolt with a sloped face to strike it as the door is closing, and then be forced by the plate to retract until the door closes far enough that a spring forces it back into the strike plate box. This holds the door shut until the bolt is removed by a door knob, etc.

string algae   An algae type that uses up oxygen and space in water features, choking out plants and fish. It forms a dense mat and can be removed by hand. Barley straw can retard its growth.

stringer   A long, narrow, horizontal timber between uprights for carrying the load of a floor, deck, or for making a frame.

stringing mortar   Spreading enough mortar to lay several masonry units at one time in place.

string trimmer *or* **weed eater**   A motorized gas or electric tool that spins a heavy plastic string to cut vegetation, especially at edges where a **lawn mower** cannot cut.

strip   **1.** Material that is long and narrow. **2.** To remove some or all of the threads on a nut or bolt. **3.** To remove old material from a surface, such as paint from a wall. **4.** To remove all vegetation from a site.

strobilus *or* **strobile** In botanical terms, this means a cone-like or head-like fruit, as in hop and pine.

strong mortar A cement mortar made without lime that has more shrinkage than usual.

structural A term describing a load-bearing member of a structure.

structural glass Glass cast in the form of cubes, rectangular (solid or hollow) blocks, tile, or rectangular plates.

structural plywood A plywood of the highest grade of structural exterior capability used between joists and such to create rigidity and provide a base for other surface finishes.

structural steel Steel used as load bearing or reinforcing material.

structure **1.** Anything built. **2.** The members giving stability to an object or conglomerate. **3.** The agglomeration configuration of soil. *See* **soil structure**.

strumose In botanical terms, covered with cushion-like swellings, or **bullate**.

strut Any structural member resisting thrusts in the direction of its length.

stucco An exterior finish made of some combination of **Portland cement, lime, sand**, water, and additives that dries to a hard, textured surface.

stud A vertical support member in a framed wall. There are usually several in a series to which sheathing for a wall surface is attached.

studio The workroom of an artist or designer.

stunt Smaller than normal. This can have many causes such as pollution, reflected light, soils low in fertility, or lack of water.

STW Abbreviation for storm water.

style An elongation of a plant ovary connected to a **stigma** at its apex.

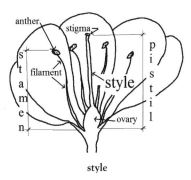

style

sub- A Latin prefix often used in botanical descriptions meaning under, almost, or not quite.

Sub *See* **subcontractor**.

subaqueous Existing or formed in or under water.

subbasin A small drainage basin within a larger watershed.

subcontractor A person or organization having a direct contract with a **prime contractor** to complete and perform a portion of the work at a site.

subcontractor bond A performance bond given by a **subcontractor** to a **general contractor** guaranteeing performance of a contract and the payment of bills for labor and material used on the project.

subcordate In botanical terms, not indented enough (but close) to be a heart shape; slightly indented.

subdivision **1.** The division of land into smaller parcels. **2.** A development of homes including the streets and adjacent land that typically has little or no open space, small lots, and similarly sized dwellings.

suberose   A botanical term meaning corky in texture.

subfloor *or* **blind floor** *or* **counterfloor**   A base floor for the finished floor material.

subgrade   **1.** A surface of earth or rock prepared to receive a foundation. This is applicable under paving and buildings, etc. **2.** The level of grade before **topsoiling** a landscape that is usually shaped and drained properly within $\frac{1}{10}$ of 1 ft. **3.** The prepared bed surface in a trench ready to receive piping.

subhorizon   A distinguishably different layer of soil within a major **soil horizon**. They are usually labeled with the major soil horizon letter designation (O, A, B, C) followed by a number (1, 2, 3). The lower number is higher in the **soil profile** or the first subhorizon encountered when digging from the surface.

submerged plants   Plants that grow below water surfaces for all or a majority of their life cycles.

submergent species   Species of plants that lie entirely beneath the surface of water.

submersible pump   A pump designed to be submerged in the liquid (usually water) that it pumps.

subshrub, sub-shrub   A more or less woody plant, usually shorter than 3 ft. **2.** A perennial. **3.** A permanently woody plant with soft, pliable, usually greenish stems.

subsoil   The layers of soil lying beneath the topsoil and above bedrock. They are often more **compact**ed, less fertile, of poorer **soil structure**, contain less **organic matter**, and have few but large roots.

subsoil drain   A pipe or conduit that collects water below the ground surface.

subspecies   A category in botanical classification that is a portion of a species with a variant characteristic observed in a locale. It is genetically different from others of the same species, but propagates well with the normal species if their range overlaps.

substrate   The base or surface on which an organism lives (soil for plants), grows, or is attached.

subsurface flow (SSF)   Flow of water beneath the soil surface.

subsurface investigation   Soil boring sampling and testing to determine subsurface soil profiles revealing relative strengths, compressibility, density, and other characteristics of the soils or rock to the depths necessary to establish viability of a proposed project or use.

subsurface sewage disposal system   Treatment and disposal of sewage via a septic tank and drain field.

subsurface utility   An underground gas, water, electric, or cable TV line, etc.

subsurface water   Any water below the surface of the **ground**.

substantial completion   The point at which work on a project (usually construction) is substantially complete. Other definitions are created within contract verbiage and are sometimes determined by date of occupancy, etc.

subtend   In botanical terms this means extend under, be opposite to, extend across, or directly below and close to.

subtropical plant   A plant found in the tropics, but capable of surviving cold better than tropical plants. Some even survive light frosts.

subulate In botanical terms, awl-shaped or tapering from a broad base to a sharp point or tip.

suburb *or* **suburban** An outlying area of predominantly residential land use in or near a city.

successful bidder The bidder selected to sign a contract for construction or supply of material.

succession The sequential changes of plants and animals in a given area following disturbance.

succulent **1.** Plants having **stem**s, or leaves, or both made up of fleshy tissue that stores water. This allows them to grow where water is scarce or infrequent. The most prominent members of this group are cacti. Other succulents include such plants as *sedum, agave, hoodia, crassula, senecio, caralluma, duvalia.* **2.** In botanical terms, juicy or pulpy.

sucker **1.** In reference to trees, a growth from the rootstock of a budded or grafted plant. Growth is instead desired from the intended portion of the plant, being the grafted or the budded portion. **2.** Underground stems that give rise to new plants. **3.** Strong, extremely vigorous, vertical green shoot growth from the stem, or sometimes the branches of a tree. The proper term for this is a **water sprout**.

suckering The process of producing **sucker**s.

suction entrance loss With regard to pumps, the velocity head (pressure) loss due to fluid moving in the direction of suction, and loss to any **foot valve**.

suction lift With regard to pumping, the vertical distance from the surface of fluid to be pumped to the centerline of the **pump**.

suction line *See* **suction pipe**.

suction pipe With regard to pumps, a pipe connected to the inflow of a pump, drawing fluid or air from another location.

suction pipe friction loss The is the loss of pressure in a **suction pipe** for a pump due to friction caused by interaction with the pipe walls. This is variable depending on flow rate, pipe materials (roughness), and pipe size.

suction pump A pump that raises water (liquid) by creating an area of low pressure or a partial vacuum that the fluid is drawn into.

suffrutescent A botanical term, half-shrubby, somewhat shrubby, or slightly shrubby.

suffruticose A botanical term indicating a plant or plant part that becomes somewhat woody.

sulcate In botanical terms, grooved, marked, or furrowed longitudinally.

sulfate A salt or ester of sulfuric acid having sulfur as a constituent. This is an element present in **fertilizer**s such as **ammonium sulfate** or **potassium sulfate**.

sulfate attack A chemical or physical reaction between sulfates and concrete or mortar.

sulfate of ammonia *or* **ammonium sulfate** A chemical **fertilizer** with an acidic reaction and about 20% nitrogen available to plants about 10 days after application.

sulfate of potash A fertilizer also known as potassium sulfate, containing 48 to 52% water-soluble potash.

sulfate-resistant cement A Portland cement (type V) that is low in tricalcium aluminate, giving it a reduced susceptibility to attack by dissolved sulfates in water or soils.

sulfur A micronutrient found in soils necessary for plant health. Plants lacking sulfur have similar symptoms to those lacking **nitrogen**. They are stunted and light green or yellow in color. It is seldom deficient in soils except where they are highly alkaline. Areas close to industrial centers may obtain sufficient sulfur in precipitation, and some irrigation water contains sufficient sulfur. Sulfur is an element present in sulfides, and sulfates and is a constituent of proteins.

summer **1.** A large **timber** or **beam** serving as a bearing surface. **2.** The warmest season of the year occurring between spring and fall. *See also* **summer solstice**.

summerhouse A garden structure of light, open design used during summer for protection from the sun.

summer oil A refined, powerful **horticultural oil** used as an insecticide for controlling insect pests during the growing season by spraying it on plants. It suffocates insects or their larvae and is not hazardous to other living animals.

summer solstice The longest day of the year (about June 22 in the northern hemisphere and December 22 in the southern hemisphere), which marks the beginning of **summer**.

summerwood Wood that is compact and has thick-walled cells denser than **springwood** because it is formed later in the growing season when growth is generally slower.

sump **1.** A depression, pit, tank reservoir, receptacle, etc. holding excess groundwater, sewage, or runoff, etc. to allow removal of the liquid to a higher elevation by pumping. **2.** A low point on a roof where a **roof drain** carries excess water away. **3.** An underground space filled with gravel where water is drained usually for disbursement into adjacent soils.

sump pump *or* **ejector** A pump for removal of the accumulated waste in a **sump**.

sunburn *or* **sunscorch** *or* **sunscald** With regard to plants, damage caused by sunlight to stems, branches, or leaves due to lack of water or excessive **transpiration**. This can be caused by planting in a location that is too sunny or too hot, sudden exposure in a previously shaded area, or because of improper **hardening off of** transplants. Sunburn may be evidenced by split bark, dead portions of leaves, leaves yellowing or fading to a whitish color, or wilting of leaves. It is most common with plants facing south or west, and with plants receiving reflected light.

sundeck An outdoor space with little or no shade oriented to take advantage of the warmth of the sun, and usually having a paved or wood surface.

sundial A device that casts a shadow on a dial capable of indicating the time of day. These must be designed for the longitude and latitude where they will be located. Accurately designed and placed, they will only give an accurate indication of time four days each year. For best results, place sundials on a level surface at noon on April 16, June 15, September 1, or December 25. On these days, position it so the shadow cast by its gnomon at noon points due north (not magnetic), adjust it so that the shadow is on the 12:00 mark, and fasten it in place.

sunken garden A **garden** that has a substantial portion of its space below the surrounding elevation, or that is surrounded by elevated terraces.

sun pocket A small space designed to take advantage of solar heating and light.

sunroom A room in a building allowing a substantial amount of natural light from glazing in walls or on the roof.

sunscald   *See* **sunburn**.

super-, supra-   Latin prefixes often used in botanical terms meaning above, upon, more than, or opposite.

superabsorbent   A polymer used to increase the water-holding capacity of soil. They come in natural starch-based polymers and synthetic formulations. The starch-based polymers absorb greater quantities of water, but are more easily broken down by soil organisms and lose their effectiveness. The synthetic polymers do not absorb as much water, but they are not as susceptible to attack by soil organisms. They are used most effectively in sandy soils of low water-holding capacity and dry regions.

superintendent   The **general contractor**'s representative responsible for field supervision, coordination, and project completion.

superior oil   *See* **horticultural oil**.

superior ovary   In botanical terms, having all **petals** and **sepals** below the ovary, or an ovary attached to the summit or center of the **receptacle** and free from all other flower parts.

superphosphate   This is **rock phosphate** treated with sulfuric acid to make it more soluble (about 90%) with a nutrient rating of about 0-14–20-0. It also provides the essential nutrients of sulfur and calcium (calcium phosphate usually in excess of 50%).

supplementary conditions   A portion of the contract documents supplementing and sometimes modifying provisions of the general conditions.

supplier   A person or firm that supplies equipment, plants, components, fixtures, materials, or parts for construction work.

supply bond   A bond guaranteeing that materials delivered comply with contract documents.

supply main   The pipes through which the water flows from the source to the user laterals.

surcharged earth   Any or all earth placed at a higher elevation than the top elevation of a retaining wall.

surcharged wall   A retaining wall holding back **surcharged earth**.

surety   A person or organization who contracts to insure the potential debt, performance, or default of another. An insurance company.

surety bond   A binding document with one party agreeing to answer to another party for any unpaid debt, default, or the failure to perform of a third party.

surface bleeding   With regard to lumber, a substance in the wood coming through the finished surface and causing discoloration or oozing. It may be moisture, a preservative, wood resin, etc.

surface course   The exposed surface of pavements intended to withstand wear, or provide aesthetic appeal.

surface flow (SF)   Flow of the water over the surface of the earth.

surface mulch   In landscape work, loose material (i.e., bark, rock, pine needles) spread on a landscape surface for aesthetics, moisture retention, weed control, etc.

surface pump   A water pump sitting on dry land and not submerged in water.

surface root   **1.** The plant roots within about 12 to 18 in of the soil surface, which gather most of the nutrients and water for a plant. They are also called **feeder roots**. **2.** The roots at the surface (usually tree roots), being visible above the ground, usually due to compaction. These are most often apparent around trees in heavy pedestrian traffic, or where soils are highly compacted around them due to construction or other activities. They are prone to be damaged or cause girdling. They are caused by the difficulty of roots attempting to penetrate highly compacted soil or by the lack of water percolating to soils beneath.

surface skimmer *See* **skimmer**.

surfaced size A reference to a piece of lumber's size that was **rough sawn** to a particular size and after being planed or surfaced for a smoother or more refined finish is then a different size.

surfacing The material used as a finished layer; covering.

surfactant A chemical that essentially makes water wetter by removing surface tensions. They allow liquids to penetrate better, spread out over a surface better, and dissipate better into a granular material such as soil. They are often used to help sprays spread out over leaves, and improve the wetting of new **growth media**.

surficial wetland A wetland producing local surface **runoff**.

surge A sudden voltage increase or decrease in an electrical current.

surge protector A device that protects electrical components and devices from damage caused by electrical spikes and surges.

surgical aquifer A water-bearing underground stratum that is not covered by a confining (impervious) bed and which can be replenished directly by rainfall or snowmelt.

survey **1.** Locating boundaries, easements, plans, buildings, pavements, topography, etc. on land. **2.** A map of the elements in (1). **3.** Acquiring information about a site, interest area, or project.

suspended load Sediment carried by wind or water above the ground surface.

sustainability **1.** The ability to sustain ecological integrity, including human needs throughout generations. Also, the ability to provide healthy human-influenced existences or processes symbiotic with, allowing, encouraging, or capturing stability with natural variances over generations. **2.** The ability to maintain with little deviation, with little waste, with renewable energy, etc.

sustainable agriculture **1.** The production of food stuffs over generations on the same ground without depleting its usefulness or ability to continue to produce. **2.** Farming that is ethically and environmentally sound while being productive for food and financial rewards. The quandary is how are such ethical uses defined and by whom.

sustainable development Development that maintains or improves economic, social, physical, spiritual, and cultural opportunity for the community's well-being, while preserving or protecting the natural environment upon which people depend. It satisfies the needs of the present without compromising the ability of future generations to meet their needs.

sustainable soil **1. Soil** capable of sustaining plant growth of various types presently and for future generations under present conditions. **2. Soil** comprised of recyclable products or with little mixture of useless soil material.

s & w valve A valve that can be turned off and on with a long key that is extended down a sleeve to the valve. The valve stops the water flow in the pipe and opens a small hole in the valve to drain all water downstream and at a higher elevation. This is important in areas where the ground freezes in winter to prevent **freeze damage**.

swale A linear depression in land. Usually describes smooth, low areas that gather water and direct it away at a slight **slope**.

swallowtail *See* **dovetail**.

swamp A wetland (completely, partially, or intermittently) dominated by woody plants (trees and shrubs).

sward Ground covered with grasses; turf.

sweating plants Forcing **bare root** plants to bud before planting. Some plants require this for best survival, but most do not.

sweep elbow *or* **long radius elbow** A term for a bent pipe portion or **fitting** changing a pipe's direction with a large sweeping radius assisting in avoiding pressure loss to resistance, improving flow characteristics, or facilitating the need to pull wire through it.

swing check valve A backflow preventer with a hinged gate that permits water flow through the valve in only one direction.

swing joint A type of joint used with threaded pipe and fittings that permits motion to occur in the configuration. These are often used in attaching heads to laterals so that heads can be run over by mowers, etc. without breaking the head, its attachment, or the lateral pipe.

swing pipe Polyethylene pipe, usually ½ inch in size, connected with barbed fittings. This pipe was originally and currently is most prolifically used to connect **sprinkler heads** to a **sprinkler system**'s **lateral lines**.

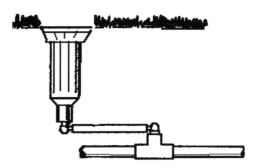

swing pipe   sprinkler head installation with a funny pipe (swing pipe) connection

swing set A usually free-standing frame suspending two or more swings and sometimes other play equipment. Some are portable and used in the backyards of single-family residences.

switch A device bridging or breaking the flow of electricity.

sy Abbreviation for square yards. It is an area equal to a square that measures 1 yd (36 in) along each edge.

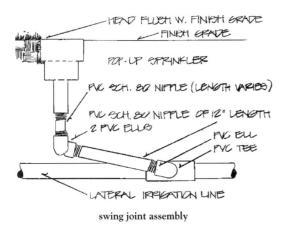

swing joint assembly

swing set

syd   Abbreviation for **square yard**(s).

symbiosis   Close physical association between two different kinds of organisms, which benefits both.

symbiotic   A mutually beneficial relationship between organisms.

sympatric   A plant or organism occupying the same geographic region. (Compare with **allopatric**.)

sympetalous   With the **petal**s connate (connected), at least toward the base.

symphylid   White, segmented, small (about ¼ in long) pests that kill plants by feeding on root hairs.

syn- *or* **sym-**   A Greek prefix used in botanical terms, meaning united.

syncarpous   A botanical term meaning with united **carpels**. (Compare with **apocarpous**.)

syngenesious   A plant that has connected **stamen**s or **anther**s.

synthesis   The combination of simple molecules forming another substance. Photosynthesis forms carbohydrates from water and carbon dioxide.

S.Y.P.   Abbreviation for southern yellow pine.

syringing   An old term mostly used in greenhouse work that refers to the process of washing dust, insects, grime, etc. from the foliage of plants. This term came about because originally a syringe pump was used to spray plants. Indoor plants should not be sprayed too late in the day as wet foliage at night may promote fungi.

system hazard   According to the National Standard Plumbing Code, this is an actual or potential threat of severe damage to the physical properties of the public or the consumer's potable water system, or a pollution or contamination that would have a protracted effect on the quality of the potable water in the system.

systemic   Spreading throughout the tissue of a plant. Some pathogens are systemic, as in a pesticide that is absorbed into the system and tissues of a plant, causing the plant juice to become toxic to targeted insects or fungi. This term can be found on container labels for weed killers, **insecticide**s, and **fungicide**s. It is also used for chemicals that, when absorbed, kill the plant itself.

T

T and G, T&G   **1.** Abbreviation for **tongue-and-groove**. **2.** Abbreviation for tar and gravel.

T, t.   **1.** Abbreviation for ton (English or U.S.). **2.** Abbreviation for **metric ton**(s). **3.** Abbreviation for **tee**.

tab   The lower portion of a shingle that is exposed.

table saw   A **circular saw** set below the surface of a table but having a portion of the blade extending through a narrow slot above the table surface. An adjustable straight edge to one side of the blade allows for boards to be slid along the edge, cutting them straight.

tablet   A plaque that is often etched, carved, or inscribed, placed in or on a wall or pavement, etc., often to commemorate an event or make a memorial.

tachifyer   A substance used in **hydromulching** or **hydroseeding** that acts as a glue with the mixture holding materials in place when dried. This is especially useful on steep slopes and in windy areas.

tack   Fastening in spots, often to temporarily hold. Fastening can be by gluing, welding, nailing, etc.

tack coat   *See* **asphalt tack coat.**

tackle   Rope or cable with a pulley block or assembly of pulley blocks that allows one to lift or move heavier objects than one could normally move alone.

tack rivet   A rivet temporarily placed to hold work for riveting, but not intended as a load-bearing rivet.

tack weld   **1.** A weld used to temporarily hold metal parts in position. **2.** A number of welds is not necessary to have a continuous weld.

tail   The lower portion of a slate shingle that is exposed on the finished roof.

tailing   **1.** The portion of a projecting stone or stones in a wall. **2.** Earthen spoils of a mine, usually in a pile, and often containing pollutants.

take off   Measuring and counting anticipated necessary materials and labor in preparation for bidding construction work.

taking   An illegal government appropriation, restriction, or use of private property or property rights. This is a government action that disturbs or interferes with an owner's use and enjoyment of real property without having a proportionate nexus between the reason for interference or disturbance and the owner or the real property.

talc   Hydrous magnesium silicate used to prevent rolls of roofing or rubber liners, etc. from sticking when in a roll. This is a mineral found chiefly in soapstone.

talus, tallus   A sloped surface or plane such as a wall face. **2.** Rock fragments, etc. at the base of a cliff or steep slope.

tamp   To compress firmly, usually with a tool.

tamper   A compaction device. Power tampers vibrate a plate up and down to facilitate compacting voids. With a hand tamper, one raises

tamping rod

and lowers a heavy metal plate while grasping a long handle extending up from the plate, so as to compact material.

tamping rod   A straight steel rod with a rounded tip at one end.

tankage   Dried animal residues used as an **organic fertilizer** with an **alkaline** reaction.

tap bolt   A completely threaded machine bolt that is screwed into a hole in a material without the use of a nut on its end because it is held tightly in the material.

tap root   *See* **taproot**.

tape measure *or* **tapeline**   A steel or plastic ribbon with graduated measurements along its length.

taproot   A main or primary root growing vertically or essentially straight down below some trees. It usually provides smaller lateral roots as it travels downward.

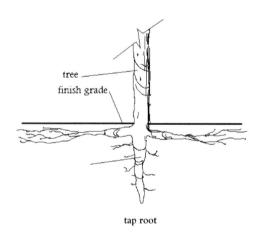

tap root

tarp *or* **tarpaulin**   **1.** A waterproof fabric often used to cover items exposed to wind or precipitation. **2.** Any thin sheet of plastic, canvas, etc. in a fairly large size, capable of being folded and tied around or over items, usually for protection or storage.

tautonym   A **botanical name** in which the **genus** and the **species** names are the same. According to the **International Code of Botanical Nomenclature**, these are not valid plant names.

taxon *or* **taxa**   **1.** A category or unit in taxonomy. In plant taxonomy, the taxa from broadest inclusion to most specific (descending order branching into many categories as it descends) is as follows: **kingdom, division, class, order, family, genus, species,** (sometimes **subspecies**), **variety** (or **cultivar**) and **strain** or **hybrid**. **2.** Relating to, or concerned with, taxonomic classification; **taxonomy**.

taxonomist   One who studies classifications of plants and animals based upon their attributes and relationships.

taxonomy   The theory, science, and practice of classifying biological organisms, including plants, into groups from the broadest to the smallest category by identifying features and abilities. *See* **taxon**.

tbc   Abbreviation for top back of curb.

T-beam   A **reinforced concrete** or rolled metal beam having a **cross section** in the shape of a capital T or combining with the beam a portion of the slab above as acting with it in load bearing.

TDH   Abbreviation for **total dynamic head**.

TDR   Abbreviation for transfer of development rights.

teak   A dark, yellowish-brown wood with a greenish or black cast that is often used for exterior construction or street furniture.

370

team dodge ball A game played with teams throwing a ball at the other team; one is knocked out of the game by being hit by the ball. The playfield space is 50 sq ft for girls and 60 sq ft for boys. The central circle area is a 35 ft diameter for girls, and 40 ft diameter for boys.

tear strength Resistance of material to being pulled apart.

tectonic **1.** Relating to construction or building, including the design or art associated therewith. **2.** The portion of geology concerned with structure of geological features such as faults and folds.

tectorial Covering, as with a roof.

tee In pipe work, a fitting accommodating the connection of one pipe to another at a 90° angle. **2.** The area of a golf hole where the first stroke is taken (usually with a driver), driving the ball toward the green and its flagged cup.

tee beam *See* **T-beam**.

teepee An upright, conically shaped dwelling of some American Indians. It was composed of animal skins, made waterproof, lashed together over poles, and set on the ground. The poles are held in place by being lashed together near the top of each pole where they all meet. An opening is left in the top, which can allow smoke to escape. They are sometimes useful in campgrounds, at special events, etc.

Teflon tape A type of tape wrapped around threaded pipe, fittings, or equipment before screwing together to facilitate lubrication and a better seal.

temper **1.** The act of mixing lime, sand, and water to make a **mortar** mix. **2.** To moisten and mix clay to a consistency ready for forming bricks. **3.** Impregnating wood with a drying oil or other oxidizing resin before curing with heat to improve its strength, hardness, water resistance, or durability. **4.** Heat-treating metal to bring it to a desired hardness.

temperate *See* **temperate zone**.

temperate zone The geographical area or region in the northern hemisphere between the Tropic of Cancer and the Arctic Circle and in the southern hemisphere between the Tropic of Capricorn and the Antarctic Circle. Temperate indicates that the climate is moderate, without extremes in hot or cold.

temperature inversion An atmosphere in which cold air is trapped beneath warm air.

temperature relay A relay that opens or closes at a predetermined temperature.

tempered glass *or* **toughened glass** (U.S.A.) Glass prestressed with heat and a sudden quenching in cool liquid to produce a compressively stressed surface layer, making a glass with a strength 2 to 5 times greater than ordinary glass.

tempered steel Hardened steel made by heating it to a high temperature and then putting it in water a number of times.

temping Firming loosened soil into which seeds or transplants have been placed.

template, templet **1.** A pattern used to guide repetitive construction work. **2.** A drafting tool made of a thin sheet of plastic, usually having shapes cut into it and facilitating the accurate and easy drawing of symbols, circles, squares, ellipses, etc. **3.** A drawing symbol used repetitively.

tender **1.** With regard to plants, usually refers to those with low tolerance to cold, freezing, or

tender plants

hot, dry temperatures. It is the opposite of **hardy**. It is any plant that is not completely hardy to the climate of an area. **2.** Sometimes used to refer to plants that need to **harden off** before being placed outdoors. **3.** A delicate or fragile plant. **4.** An offer, proposal, or bid for contract.

tender plants Those plants not capable of surviving a particular climatic condition. It usually refers to not being able to withstand cold temperatures. *See also* **tender**.

tendril In botanical terms, a thread-shaped, spirally coiling, twisting organ or appendage (shoot, or modified stem) of a vine-like plant used to hold or cling to objects for support in climbing.

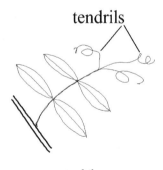

tendrils

tendrils

tennis court A playing surface for tennis made of clay, turf, concrete, asphalt, etc. They are approximately 60 × 120 feet.

tenon The shaped projecting end of a piece of wood or other material that is placed in the hole, notch, or recess (mortise) to secure a joint.

tenon saw A hand saw with a metal stiffening strip along the top of the blade and many small teeth along the bottom of its blade. It is useful in cutting miters, dovetails, etc. This saw is the same as a miter saw.

tensile force The force that tends to lengthen (pull apart) a member. (Compare with **compressive force** and **shear force**.)

tensile strength The resistance of a material to deformation or failure or being pulled apart when subjected to tension (**tensile force**). (Compare with **compressive strength** and **shear strength**.)

tensile stress The stress on a member caused by a force that tends to lengthen (pull apart) the member. (Compare with **compressive stress** and **shear stress**.)

tensiometer With regard to soils, a device that measures its moisture content. It has a long thin probe for inserting into the soil and a meter at its top to read the measurement.

tension The force or stress toward elongation; pulling or stretching apart.

tension wood Abnormal wood sometimes found on the upper side of hardwood branches with abnormally increased longitudinal shrinkage promoting warping and splitting.

tepal A **petal** or **sepal** where the **calyx** and the **corolla** are not well defined. They are the structures resembling petals of a flower without clearly defined sepals and petals. An example is a magnolia flower.

terete In botanical terms, circular in cross section. It is usually tubular and tapered.

terminal In botanical terms, at the apex or end of a shoot, or growing at the end of a **branch** or **stem**.

terminal bud A bud at the end of a branch or stem. *See also* **lateral bud**.

termite shield A projection around posts, pipes, foundation, etc. that acts as a shield preventing termites from gaining access to structures.

ternate A botanical term referring to plant parts or items found in threes. Arranged in threes.

terrace **1.** An embankment with a level area at its top. It is sometimes paved, planted, and furnished for leisure use. **2.** A flat roof or a raised space adjoining a building. It is often used for leisure enjoyment **3.** An essentially flat ground area with a vertical grade change separating it from surrounding ground elevations.

terraces

terra-cotta A reddish or reddish-yellow clayware or tile that is molded to shape and treated with heat in a kiln. Though hard baked, it is

sometimes easily saturated with water. Ornamental pots, floor tile, roof tile, or decorations are often made of this material.

terrain **1.** An area of land. **2.** The geographical land features of a **landscape**.

terrazzo *or* **terrazzo concrete** Marble-aggregate concrete that has been ground smooth.

terreplein **1.** An earth embankment that is flat on top. **2.** The level area behind the parapet of a **rampart**.

terrestrial **1.** Living on land not normally flooded or saturated. **3.** Growing in the ground.

tessellate **1.** A checkered or paving-block pattern. **2.** A mosaic-like pattern, as with veins of a leaf.

test plug In a drainage system, an inflatable plug able to seal off a pipe that is used to test for leaks.

test pressure In pipe systems, water pressure or air pressure that pipes and fittings are subjected to as they are tested for leaks.

tetra- A Greek prefix meaning four, sometimes used in botanical terms.

tetrad A group of four (often used in describing plant parts).

tetradinous Occurring in **tetrad**s.

tetradynamous A flower with four long and two short **stamen**s.

tetramerous In plant identification and descriptions, with four parts alike.

tetrastoon A courtyard having **portico**s or open **colonnade**s on all four sides.

Texas root rot A disease caused by a fungus (*Phymatotrichum omnivorum*) that destroys the outer portion of roots and cuts off water supply to the upper plant. It is common in arid and semiarid areas below 3500 ft in elevation. It thrives in areas and times of high temperatures, low organic matter, and alkaline soils.

texture **1.** In reference to soil, *see* **soil texture**. **2.** The fineness or coarseness of a visual image. **3.** The feel or appearance of smooth, grooved, bumpy, etc.

texture triangle A triangular chart assisting in USDA classification of soils based on percentages of sand, silt, and clay.

thallus A plant that lacks form or distinction into **roots**, **stem**, **leaves**, and does not grow from an apical point.

thatch In grasses, a layer at the soil surface composed of dead roots and grass blades. An essentially flat ground area with a vertical grade change separating it from surrounding ground elevations. Thatch over ½ in prevents water from reaching the soil and often harbors insects and fungi.

theodolite A surveying instrument used for measuring horizontal or vertical angles. It is made up of an alidade equipped with a telescope, a leveling device, and an accurately calibrated horizontal circle.

therm A quantity of heat equivalent to 100,000 Btu.

thermal break *or* **thermal barrier** A material of low heat conductivity placed to reduce or prevent the flow of heat.

thermal conductance The rate of heat flow through a unit area of material from one of its faces directly through to its other face under steady-state conditions.

thermal conductor A material readily transmitting heat by means of thermal conduction.

thermal expansion A material's change in length or volume when it is heated.

thermal insulation *or* **heat insulation** A material with high resistance to heat flow. It is often fabricated in batts, blankets, blocks, boards, granular fill, or loose fill. Blankets of foam, in the shape of a pipe, are often used to protect exposed pipes from freezing.

thermal load Pressure on a structure induced by changes in temperature.

thermal periodicity The response of flowers blooming to the alternation of warm and cold as in day and night.

thermal resistance *or* **R-value** The opposite of thermal conductance. These values are greatest with materials of good thermal resistance.

thermal shock Sudden stress in a material as a result of abrupt temperature changes.

thermal transmittance *or* **U-value** The rate of heat flow per unit area under steady conditions from a fluid on a warm side of a barrier to a fluid on a cold side (or visa versa), per unit temperature difference between the fluids.

thermosetting A material such as synthetic resin that has been heated and dried to become hard and will not soften when heated again.

thermostat An instrument with parts that move in response to changes in temperature, and thereby directly or indirectly controls temperature.

thickened edge Most often used in reference to the edge of a sidewalk where it would otherwise be next to a **curb**, but instead the edge of the walk is poured extra thick to become the curb.

thickened slab A reference often used in describing concrete flatwork (walks, patios, floors) where the concrete is thickened, usually for supporting weight from above.

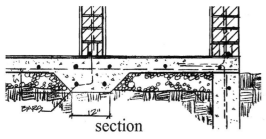

section

thickened slab

thicket   A dense stand (small patch) of shrubs or small trees.

thielaviopsis   A fungal disease inhabiting some soils, and can be a cause of **root rot**.

thinning   *See* **thinning out**.

thinning out   **1.** Removal of entire branches back to the main trunk, a side branch, or the ground. **2.** Removal of excess seedlings that are too close for healthy or normal development.

thin set   The suitable bonding material placed in a thin layer (usually about ⅛ in thick) underneath tile when it is laid.

thin soil   A soil that has **bedrock** near the surface.

thixotrophy   Loss of **soil** cohesion or in extremes the occurrence of **liquefaction** of wet or saturated soils under the stress of vibration. This can occur in all but the coarsest of gravely soils.

thorn   A spine, prickle, briar, or a stiff, woody, modified stem with a sharp point. (Compare with **prickle** and **spine**.)

thread   The small spiral ridges and valley (roots) forming a uniform helix on the external or inter-

nal surface of a cylinder such as a screw, nut, bolt, pipe, or fitting.

threaded fitting   A pipe **fitting** with inside or outside threads that allows it to be connected to another fitting or pipe with the opposite type of threads.

threatened species   According to the U.S. Endangered Species Act, a species rapidly declining in population that is likely to become an **endangered species** unless assistance or mitigation of circumstances is provided.

three phase *or* **3PH** *or* **3ph**   Refers to electricity in **alternating current** at the same frequency (U.S. 60Hz, Europe 50Hz) but with different phases. The phases are spaced equally at 120° (the maximum phase separation possible). A three phase conductor houses three wires, one with each phase, and a neutral or **ground** wire. It is the type of supply usually preferred for large pumps and motors as it is more efficient, less costly, and supplies the extra energy sometimes necessary to start them. It is usually the type of supply conductor to a building, with the individual circuits on-site usually being **single phase**.

threshold   A raised strip fastened to a floor under a door's bottom edge. It separates flooring types and can assist in making a seal to keep out wind, water, insects, etc.

thrips   Any of the order *Thysanoptera*, which is a very small insect that sucks the juices of plants. It may cause leaves to curl or discolor, and in severe infestations the leaves or flowers may not even open. Their presence is often noticeable by their black fecal pellets in affected areas. They may be controlled with chemicals, or with natural predators such as green lacewing larvae, or ladybird (**ladybug**) beetles.

throat **1.** In botanical terms, the open portion of a flower. **2.** A groove cut or formed on the underside of the face of a wall to prevent water from flowing back along the underside to the face of the wall.

throttling In a piping system, a valve that can control the amount of flow through it.

through bolt A bolt that passes entirely through the materials it fastens together.

through stone A stone with ends flush on each side of a wall and having its longest dimension perpendicular to the wall.

throw **1.** The distance between a light source and the area of illumination. **2.** The amount a bolt may extend beyond the surface it binds.

thrum In plant identification and descriptions, the type of flower that has a relatively short **style** and long **stamen**s. (Compare with **pin**.)

thrust The amount of force exerted by weight or momentum.

thrust block Anything that transfers water's energy within a pipe system to the earth rather than to a joint. This keeps gasketed and slip-pipe joints from coming apart under pressure. The most common material used for this purpose is concrete.

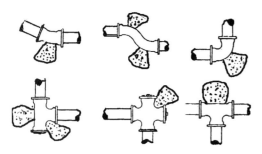

concrete thrust blocks

thumb In landscape construction and excavation work, a hydraulically operated attachment to an excavation bucket allowing the operator to grasp objects between them. They are commonly found on trackhoes, mini-excavators, and backhoes.

thumb latch A **lift latch** used to hold doors or gates closed.

thyrse An inflorescence with a long, narrow **panicle** consisting of a series of racemosely arranged small **cymes** similar to a lilac or horse chestnut. The main axis is **racemose** and the secondary axes are cymes.

tidelands Lands located between mean high tide and mean low tide.

tie **1.** A piece that connects materials, walls, branches, pipes, etc. **2.** In surveying, a connection from a point of known position to a point that is to be identified. **3.** The action of connecting pipes together.

tier A row or a group of rows positioned one above the other.

tie-rod A rod in tension, used to bind structural members together.

tie wall **1.** A wall built perpendicular to the rest of the wall to increase stability. **2.** A **railroad tie** wall.

tige The shaft of a column extending from the base moldings to the capital.

tile A ceramic or other clay-like material formed into varying shapes and uses, such as pieces for piping or thin flat pieces for finishing a floor, wall, or roof surface (ceramic tile, roof tile, quarry tile, etc.). Tile may be glazed or unglazed and is used both indoors and outdoors.

tile floor

till   *See* **tilling** or **glacial till**.

tillage   **1.** The process of **tilling**. **2.** The ground after it is conditioned by tilling.

tiller   *See* **rototiller**.

tilling   The act of turning over soil or mixing it by hand, with a shovel, a **rototiller**, a plow, etc.

tilth   A term used to describe the relative ease of tilling, or digging in, a soil as well as its impedance to seed emergence or root penetration.

timber   **1.** A tree or a group of trees. **2.** A large wood member in a structure such as a deck, roof,

timber steps

or trellis, etc. **3.** Any milled wood member with no dimension less than 5 in. These large wood members are often used in landscape construction to build retaining walls, planters, steps, etc. (see accompanying illustration).

timber connector   A metal connector of various types, usually with teeth, used with bolts, spikes, etc. to connect timbers in heavy construction.

timely completion   Completion of a project or a designated portion of it on or before the date required by contract.

time of completion   The date identified in the contract for substantial completion of the project.

time of concentration   In storm water drainage **runoff** calculations (i.e., **rational method**), the variable expressing the amount of time necessary for all areas of a watershed (including the most remote portion of the drainage basin) to contribute water to the watershed outlet, point of concentration, or drainage intersection.

time of haul   The amount of time from first mixing water and cement to the discharge from the cement mixer of the mixed concrete.

time-release fertilizer   A **fertilizer** with some provision that releases its nutrients or makes them available to plant roots in the soil over a lengthened period of time, as opposed to those that are soluble and released all at once or over a short period of time.

tin   **1.** A lustrous, soft, and malleable metal having a low melting point. It is often used for making **alloys**, solder, or in coating sheet metal, etc. **2.** To coat with a layer of tin.

tingle   **1.** A support that reduces sag in a long string pulled tight. This is useful to identify a horizontal line for laying a masonry course. **2.** A flexible clip used to hold a sheet of glass, metal, etc. in place.

tin snips   Shears used for cutting thin sheet metal or tin.

tin snips

tint   A light color made by mixing a small amount of color with a large amount of white.

tipi   *See* **teepee**.

tissue culture   In plant research, the aseptic culture (in flasks or test tubes) practice of growing plant cells into plant clones (for **propagation**) or for biochemical products, preservation, scientific research, genotype modification, etc.

TOD   Abbreviation for transit-oriented development.

toe   **1.** A piece of pipe threaded on one end only. It is usually used to connect threaded equipment or piping systems to glued piping systems. **2.** A nail driven on an angle. This is done to afford greater resistance from pulling out, or out of necessity. **3.** The bottom of a retaining wall footing, which projects in front of the wall (the side open to view and not retaining material). **4.** The base of an object, usually extending beyond the object. It is meant to give greater stability in standing upright. **5.** In excavation, the portion of sheeting below the **subgrade**. **6.** In welding, the area between the face of a weld and the face metal.

tocd   Two boards at right angles, nailed together with nails driven on an angle.

toe in   The slight reduction in the outside diameter of a plastic pipe at its cut end.

toenailing *or* **skew nailing** *or* **tusk nailing**   Surfaces fastened together by nailing on an angle into both surfaces (usually boards).

toggle bolt   A bolt having a nut with pivoted, flanged wings that close against a spring when it is pushed through a hole, and open after emerging on the other side of the hole. They are used to fasten objects to a hollow wall or to a wall that is accessible only from one side.

toilet   *See* **water closet**.

tolerance   The amount of stress or disturbance a plant can withstand before damage or before death.

tomentose   In botanical terms, clothed with matted woolly hairs.

tomentum   In botanical terms, matted woolly hairs.

ton   The weight of 2000 **pound**s (common or short ton), 907.2 **kg**, or 0.907 **metric ton**s.

tongue-and-groove, dressed and matched, t&g   In reference to lumber, this describes wood members cut with a ridge on one edge and a recessed area on the other edge so that boards can be interlocked for strength and tightness in **planking**, **decking**, etc.

tonne   A weight of 1000 lb (about 2205 lb). Also, a metric ton.

tooled joint   Any masonry joint where the mortar has been shaped with a tool before it sets sufficiently to resist tooling.

toothed   In botanical terms, furnished with teeth or short projections of any sort on the margin; used especially when they are sharp, like saw teeth, but do not point forward.

toothed plate *or* **bulldog plate**   A toothed metal plate used to connect timbers.

toothed ring   A metal ring with toothed edges used to connect timber.

top back of curb   The line or point on the line of the upper portion of a curb on the side away from the pavement of a road.

top dress   In landscape work, applying something to the surface of the ground or to a **lawn** such as a mulch or manure.

top dressing   **1.** Application of **mulch** to the soil surface. **2.** Application of **fertilizer** granules to a soil surface. **3.** *See* **surface mulch**. Most often refers to the need to filter nutrients from the mulch to plant roots rather than the need to suppress weeds or conserve soil moisture. Therefore, the type of mulch referred to in top dressing is more often (and more appropriately) a mulch capable of leaching nutrients to the soil and is most often an organic mulch such as ground bark, peat moss, soil conditioner, etc.

topiary   **1.** The art of training, shaping, pruning, and training plants into living sculptures of predetermined shapes of other objects of geometric form (**formal garden**), or animals, etc. Some plants often used for this purpose are boxwoods, yews, privets, rosemary, and hollies. **2.** A garden of topiary.

top lap   The overlapped portion or distance of shingles in place.

top of slope   A point or line where progressing up a slope it changes to horizontal or it begins to slope downhill.

topography   **1.** The physical features of the surface of the earth including those natural and

man-made. **2.** The detail and depiction on maps, charts, or plans of the surface of the earth by **contour lines**, or any means that shows the relative elevations, shapes, or steepness of grade, etc.

topsoil   **1.** The **A horizon** in the soil profile. It is the upper mineral horizon with **organic matter** incorporated into it, usually causing it to be darker than the **subsoil**s. It is usually of favorable **soil structure**, and contains many organisms favorable to plant growth. Usually 90% or more of the roots are found in this soil as it provides water, aeration, gaseous exchange, texture favorable to root penetration, nutrients, and organisms favorable to the **rhizosphere**. This soil may be nonexistent on some land, just a few inches thick, or several feet thick depending on the land's history and climate. This soil is what nearly all plants thrive in. In its ideal mixture for most plants, this soil is comprised of approximately 45% mineral material, 5% organic matter, 25% water, and 25% air. In construction work, it is usually stripped and stockpiled for future use in landscape construction. **2.** A soil prepared or mixed of various elements suitable for or preferred for plant growth and used in **container**s or to spread over the **subgrade** in **landscape**s.

topsoiling   The act of placing topsoil on an area of landscaping.

topsoil mix   A composition of several elements intended to imitate topsoil and provide for the necessities of the roots of a plant.

topsoil stripping   The clearing of vegetation and removal of the **A horizon** of soil. It is usually placed in a pile called a stockpile, for later use in spreading areas of new landscape on the site. Stripped soil seldom retains much of its original structure. For this reason, soil should not be stripped unless it is in a friable condition, or toward the dry range, but not when it is moist or flooded.

torching Lime mortar applied under roofing slate.

torii A monumental gateway that stands alone with two pillars holding aloft a horizontal, straight crosspiece and another crosspiece above it that usually curves upward at each end. These are common at entries to Shinto shrines.

torose In plant identification and descriptions, a plant part that is alternately contracted and expanded.

torque Force tending toward rotation.

torsel A timber, steel, or stone piece supporting one end of a beam or joist and distributing load.

torsion The twisting or rotating of a structural member around its longitudinal axis by two equal and opposite torques at each end of the member.

torsional strength The resistance of a material to being twisted or rotated.

torsional stress An increase in the potential for breaking, deforming, or in some way failing due to the force of twisting.

toshnailing Nailing at an angle to conceal the heads.

total dissolved phosphorous (TDP) A measure of total phosphorus (both organic and inorganic) in water.

total dynamic head Pressure in feet; the summation of suction pipe friction loss, suction lift, suction entrance loss, discharge pipe friction loss, discharge lift, sprinkler operating pressure, and miscellaneous fittings loss.

to the weather An expression describing materials or surfaces exposed to the weather and not protected by other material. An example is the outside of a brick wall as opposed to the framing it is attached to and protects.

tot lot A children's **playground**.

tower A structure or building much taller than wide.

townscape **1.** A view of a town or city from a particular point. **2.** The appearance of streets, landscapes, buildings, etc. within a town, city, etc.

toxic Descriptive of a substance that will cause harm or death to a living organism.

toxicity The ability of a substance to have a poisonous effect on growth, reproduction, or life of organisms.

toxin A poisonous substance.

trace elements Those elements necessary for plant growth, excluding the **macronutrient**s of **nitrogen**, **phosphorus**, and **potash**. They are also called **micronutrient**s.

tracing paper A translucent paper used for tracing and for original drawings.

track An oval path with run extensions at some corners where sprinting, running, hurdles, and other athletic field activities are often also accommodated. A common ¼ mi running track with its run extensions is usually about 670 ft long (oval 535 ft) with a 260 ft width.

trackhoe A tractor with a long hydraulically operated arm and bucket capable of digging much like an arm and hand, and moving about on steel or tracks. *See also* mini-excavator.

track loader A tractor with a bucket held in front of it by two arms that allow it to be tilted, raised, or lowered, and moving about on rubber or steel tracks.

track loader

tractor An engine-driven vehicle, on wheels or tracks, for pushing or pulling trailers, attachments, or tools, or for digging.

tractor loader *or* **tractor shovel** A tractor with a bucket for digging, elevating, and dumping its bucket load (usually at the height of a dump truck).

trade **1.** An occupation, skill, or craft usually involving manual skill. **2.** The classifications of work in the construction industry, such as masonry, carpentry, irrigation, landscaping, etc.

traffic calming A concept usually involving reduction of vehicle speeds, providing more space for pedestrians, or improving the local traffic environment.

traffic paint Durable paint made to withstand vehicular traffic, yet be visible at night. It is used to mark roadways, traffic lanes, crosswalks, parking lots, etc.

traffic signs Those signs directing motorized vehicles for safety and order, including stop signs, speed limit signs, etc.

traffic sign

trailing A botanical term meaning **prostrate** but not rooting.

training plants Applying procedures such as pruning (cutting, pinching, shearing) or tying shoots to supports to acquire a shape or desired effect. Training is most effective in a plant's formative stages.

trajectory In **sprinkler irrigation**, the measurement (in degrees) of the angle of the water projecting out from the sprinkler's **nozzle** to a horizontal surface. A trajectory of 0° would indicate a flat projection of water from the nozzle of the sprinkler.

transect sampling A field sampling method where samples are drawn from strips or parcels across a study area.

transfer of development credits *See* **transfer of development rights**.

transfer of development rights A process providing for relocation of potential development. Usually this relocation is from land areas where proposed land use or environmental impacts are considered undesirable (the **donor site** or **sending site**) to another (**receiving**) site chosen on the basis for its ability to accommodate additional units of development in excess of that for which it is zoned.

transfer of development rights easement
A legal covenant that protects the subject land in perpetuity from development beyond any development rights reserved subject to the underlying zone at the time the covenant is signed and provides for enforcement of the covenant in exchange for transferring development rights to another site.

transfer of development rights receiving area The area of land within which development rights transferred from **TDR sending site** can be used for increasing development opportunities (dwelling units or square footage).

transfer of development rights sending area A site from which **TDR**s can be transferred to a **receiving site**.

transformer An electrical device used for transforming, increasing, or decreasing the **voltage** of electrical **current**s.

transit A surveying instrument useful in measuring land to delineate angles, distances, and differences in elevation. It is usually set on a tripod and acts as a telescope capable of turning 360°.

transit light-rail The portion of passenger railroad operations that carries passengers within urban areas, or between urban areas and their suburbs. It differs from a railroad in that railroad passenger cars generally are heavier, the average trip lengths are usually longer, and the operations are carried out over tracks that are part of the railroad system.

transit-oriented development Moderate or high-density, usually mixed-use, developments located along transit routes that emphasize pedestrian-oriented environments or encourages the use of public transportation.

transit pipe A pipe made of asbestous cement material that is now difficult to use because of the contamination potential. It was once used for city mains and large irrigation systems in sizes of 4 in or larger.

translucent A material that passes light through it, but diffuses it so that images seen through it are not perfectly clear.

transmissivity The ability or potential of a material to transmit radiant energy.

transom A horizontal or **transverse** structural member in a structure.

transpiration The process by which water is drawn from **soil** by **osmotic pressure** of **root** systems of **plant material** and moved through the plant to the leaves where it is vaporized to the atmosphere. It is often thought of as simply the moisture released from a plant's leaves. This loss of water in the form of vapor is mostly from leaves through stomata or tiny pores, but it also occurs to a lesser extent through similar openings in **stem**s, called lenticels, and from other parts of the plant. Under favorable conditions this water is replaced by water absorbed by the roots when the relative humidity of the atmosphere is considerably below 100%. If the loss of moisture through transpiration exceeds replacement from the roots for any extended period of time, then soft tissues in the plant wilt and die and the firmer tissues dry and die. If wilting has not extended for too long and water becomes available to the roots the plant may live, but harm usually comes from this interruption of **photosynthesis**. The rate of water transpiration loss increases with exposure to wind, low humidity, or higher temperatures as well as other factors. Temperature and humidity are usually the most influential.

transplant   **1.** A plant that is being, will be, or has been **transplanted**. **2.** The act of **transplanting**.

transplanted   In the landscape and plant nursery industries, the past tense of **transplanting**, or digging up and moving a plant from one place to another, intending for it to grow in a new condition of rooting space or type.

transplanting   In the landscape and plant nursery industries, the act of digging up a plant and moving it from one place to another, intending for it to grow in the new condition of rooting space or type.

transplant shock   Any deterioration in the health of a plant due to its being **transplanted**.

transported soil   Soil deposits moved into place by water, glaciers, or wind.

transverse   In botanical terms, at a right angle to, across the main axis from, or directed across, such as something crosswise.

transverse load   Pressure applied perpendicularly to the longitudinal axis of a structure or member.

trap   In plumbing or a system of piping used for drainage, a device that maintains a water seal against sewer gases, air, odors, etc. by collecting water to prevent gases from traveling past its location.

trapeze hanger   A horizontal rigid member for supporting pipes that is suspended by rods from a structure above it.

trapeziform   In botanical terms, no two lines being parallel to one another.

trash   **1.** Any debris that is not useful. **2.** A mixture of combustible waste that may include paper, cardboard, wood boxes, combustible floor sweepings, etc. It may have up to 10% (by weight) of plastic or rubber scraps. It also can include 10% moisture, and about 5% incombustible solids.

traverse   A series of connected lines at various angles and directions on the earth's surface.

tread   The horizontal surface of a step.

tree   A **perennial** woody plant that grows or is capable of growing a trunk with a canopy of **foliage** generally high enough to walk under. Many trees will not assume this form without pruning and it is not necessary for them to be pruned to be referred to as a tree. Some shrubs grow tall enough to be trained and pruned into tree forms.

tree cart   A device with two wheels, a space for **b&b** plants, or plants in large containers, and two handles that assists in moving heavy plant materials by hand.

tree cart

tree-dozer

tree-dozer An attachment for a tractor with metal bars and a cutting blade useful for clearing small trees and bushes from a site.

tree grate A metal, decorative grate surrounding a tree in a paved area, flush with the surrounding paving. These are useful because they facilitate planting trees in paved areas by allowing air, water, etc. access to the tree roots.

tree guying The practice of attaching wires by several methods from a fixed object on the ground plane or below and to a tree a few feet above the ground to prevent the tree from blowing over. This method is usually used for large caliper trees, for clump trees, or for evergreen trees. When it is used for large **caliper**, single-**deciduous** shade trees, the wires are attached at about the first branching. Guy wires should always be attached at about the same height to avoid twisting the trunk or the root ball. Guy wires may be held in the ground with short ground level stakes, buried stakes, buried steel plates with eyelets, eyelets fastened in pavement, etc. The guy wires are usually marked with ribbon or **PVC** pipe to prevent pedestrians from tripping on them. Guy wires may be twisted to tighten them or they may make use of a turnbuckle. Where wires are attached to the tree they must be enclosed in a bendable protective medium where they are wrapped around the tree to protect the tree from the wire digging into the bark. Guying is not always preferred or necessary. *See also* **tree staking**.

treehopper A leaping homopterous (sucking) insect of the family *Membracidae*, *Melizoderidae*, or *Aetalionidae* that primarily feeds on the **sap** of shrubs or trees. It comprises about 3200 species.

tree line **1.** The upper elevation limit of tree survivability. **2.** The edge of a large group of trees where woods or forest ends, and meadow, grassland, or savannah begins.

tree staking The practice of pounding stakes (metal, bamboo, or wood) near trees and attach-

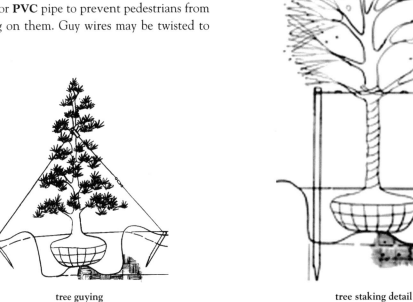

tree guying

tree staking detail

ing a wire or string to the tree to prevent the tree from moving or tipping in wind. This practice is common on small caliper trees, though it is not always necessary or desirable. Trees can be damaged by rubbing on stakes, the trees can become dependant on stakes or they can grow around the wire attachments if left too long. Also, they can be a hazard to pedestrians. Wires should be wrapped or placed in a protective medium where they are attached to the tree to protect the tree bark from damage. *See also* **tree guying**.

tree surgeon   One who is trained in treating damaged or diseased trees (usually an **arborist**).

tree surgery   Cutting or boring tree branches, trunks, or roots.

tree wrap   A 3 to 6 in wide strip, usually in a roll, of burlap or strong paper used to wrap the trunks of newly planted trees to protect against borers, or sunscald. *See* **southwest sunscald**. Tree wrapping can cause as much damage as it prevents. It can harbor sucking insects, encourage fungus by keeping the trunk wet, and hide activities of boring insects.

trellis   **1.** An open framework, latticework, or design of wood or steel in a vertical wall or horizontal overhead. **2.** A support of connected members for vines.

trench   A linear hole, channel, depression, long thin excavation, or a cut with steep sides dug in the ground. They are useful in irrigation, planting, or outdoor lighting. They are dug for irrigation and outdoor lighting systems for installing wiring or pipes underground. In planting they are used to plant seeds or plants. Trenches for tree planting in confined spaces with paving all around (restricting root growth) can be useful to prevent **windfall** or stunting of growth. Trenches are dug between trees and **backfilled** with rooting medium (usu-

ally a soil) allowing roots to extend and intertwine with other trees.

trench box *or* **trench shield**   A heavily constructed device with walls on each side used in deep trenches to protect workers in the bottom of the trench from cave-ins. It can be moved along as work proceeds in the trench.

trencher   **1.** One who digs trenches. **2.** A machine with a bucket conveyor, rotating cutting wheel, or a large rotating chain that can cut the earth as its cutting tool rotates and is lowered into the ground. It piles the earth to each side of the cut or in the direction of the cut it makes while propelling itself backward or forward to leave a **trench**.

trenching   Digging narrow linear holes in the ground usually for a piping system.

trenching shovel   A narrow shovel useful in trenching because it does not take as much effort to force through soil as wider shovels, and it disturbs less soil in trenching. This type of shovel is often preferred in digging trenches for underground **sprinkler system**s.

tri-, triplo-   A Latin or Greek prefix sometimes used in botanical terms meaning three.

triangular spacing   A reference in sprinkler layout design in which **head-to-head coverage** is obtained by heads being laid out in a pattern that is triangular if imaginary lines were drawn between heads in **plan view**.

tributary   In landscape concerns, a stream contributing water to another stream or water body.

trichotomous   A botanical term that refers to a plant part forking into threes.

trifoliate *or* **trifoliolate** *or* **trifoliately compound**   In botanical terms, three leaves or

trigeneric

leaflets grouped in threes. (Compare with **simple**, **pinnate**, **bipinnate**, **palmate**.)

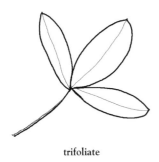

trifoliate

trigeneric Plants with parents representing three different **genera**.

trigonous A botanical term meaning with three angles.

trilocular A botanical term that means with three **locules**.

trim **1.** To lightly **prune** or **shear**, usually to a shape. **2.** A visible element that covers or protects joints, edges, or ends of another material. **3.** To slowly or finely adjust a device such as a flow in a gate valve. **4.** The visible woodwork or molding of a space including baseboards, cornices, casings, etc.

trimerous A botanical term that means with three similar parts.

trimmer Any tool used to **trim** plants.

trinomial With reference to a **scientific name** (**botanical name**), three names identifying a plant, usually the genus, species, and then a **variety**, **subspecies**, or **cultivar** name. *See also* **binomial** and **monomial**.

tripartite A botanical term, a plant part divided into three portions.

tripinnatifid Three times **pinnately** cleft.

tripod level A **level** composed of a telescope containing crosshairs (one being horizontal) and a frame attached to a usually three-legged, adjustable stand that allows the instrument to be turned in all directions while remaining level. This instrument is useful in determining **elevation**s and **grade**s.

triquetrous A botanical term that refers to a plant part with three sharp, acute, or projecting angles.

trivet A short support for a surveying instrument used where a tripod is too tall.

tropical A climate where temperatures remain above freezing all year, and the plants suited to the climate, receiving adequate moisture and nutrients to grow all year.

tropical plant A plant that is found native in regions of the earth having tropical climates.

tropism A plant's growth response or bending toward or away from a stimulus such as light or gravity. *See also* **phototropism**, and **geotropism**.

trowel **1.** A flat hand tool having a handle and a broad steel blade. It is used to apply, spread, or shape moldable materials such as mortar, green concrete, plaster, etc. **2.** A flat, thin sometimes curving or pointed, smoothing or digging tool with a handle.

troweling Working a moldable material with a **trowel**.

true In propagation, an indication that a plant can be reliably counted on to be similar to its parent when self-pollinated.

true breeding A description of a plant that can self-pollinate to produce offspring similar to the parent.

true bulb This **bulb** is an underground stem with an embryo near the basal plate surrounded

386

by fleshy scales that protect the embryo and store food for it. Dry scales forming a papery covering make up the tunic or outer covering. Examples are daffodils, tulips, and lilies. *See also* **rhizomes, roots, tubers,** and **corms.**

true north   The direction from any point on the earth to the geographic North Pole.

truncate   In botanical terms, ending abruptly, as if cut off, with the apex (or base) straight or nearly so. (Compare with leaf base descriptions of **cuneate, obtuse, cordate, auriculate, sagittate, hastate, attenuate, oblique.**)

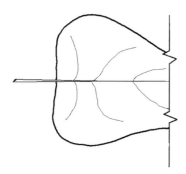

truncate leaf base

trunk   The woody portion (including bark) of a tree from ground level usually to the first significant live branch.

trunk line   A sewer line that has other sewer branches dispensing into it.

trunk sewer   A sewer with many contributing tributary branches that serves as an outlet for a large area.

truss   **1.** An assemblage of wood or steel members forming a rigid framework usually of triangular shapes. The most common trusses are those used to hold up a roof. **2.** A tight cluster of flowers or fruit.

try square   A square with its two arms fixed at 90° serving as a guide for marking lines at right angles to an edge or surface, as a measuring device, or as a tool for checking straightness or squareness of edges, faces, members, etc.

tube   **1.** A small container in which **cuttings** or **seedlings** are held. **2.** A pipe.

tuber   A type of **bulb** with a short, fat, underground stem flattened, rounded, or irregular in shape. It does not creep like a rhizome and is usually knobby with growth buds. Growth buds (eyes) are usually scale-like with a bud on its **axil.** Large tubers can be divided and replanted.

tubercle   In botanical terms, a small, wart-like or knobby projection or prominence on a plant that is usually distinct in color or texture from the organ on which it is found.

tuberculate   A botanical term meaning bearing tubercles.

tuberous   Thickened like a tuber.

tuberous roots   A type of **bulb** with thickened roots (not stems as with most bulbs) for food storage. They are much like **tubers** in appearance but do not have growth buds. They can be divided in the same way as **rhizomes** and **tubers** by cutting sections with a portion of the old stem base attached. The growth buds are in the old stems.

tubling   A small plant raised in a container called a **tube.**

tubs   Containers holding soil and plant roots that are moveable and usually placed for display of plants.

tubular   In botanical terms, a hollow cylinder form.

tuck pointing *or* **tuck and pat pointing** *or* **tuck joint pointing**   Finishing of old masonry joints by cleaning them out, and then filling them with mortar left projecting slightly from the **interstice**, or with a **fillet** of putty or lime.

tufa A porous limestone that holds moisture and is usually gray. It is often used in masonry construction and sometimes used for cultivating **alpine** plants.

tuff *or* **volcanic tuff** A porous low-density rock of volcanic particles.

tufted Grasses with spike-like foliage or grasses that have a fine texture with upright leaves originating at a basal clump and growing upward and outward without much arching or weeping. An example is Blue fescue. (Compare with **mounded (2)**, **upright grasses**, **upright divergent grasses**, **upright arching grasses**, and **arching**.)

tufted grasses

tumbled A metal or stone that has been finished by rotating in a drum.

tump **1.** A British term for a **mound**. **2.** A clump of any vegetation.

tundra A rolling treeless region usually in the arctic or subarctic climates where the subsoil is never fully thawed and the prevalent vegetation is moss, lichens, herbaceous plants, and low shrubs.

tungsten steel A gray to white, heavy, hard steel containing 5 to 24% tungsten and 0.4 to 2% carbon.

tunic In botanical terms, an enclosing or covering membrane or tissue such as around a seed, or the papery or fibrous membrane around a bulb or corm.

tunicate Covering or sheathing made up of leaf bases that form concentric circles when viewed in cross section like the bulb of an onion.

turbidity Water clarity or opaqueness determined by the amount of sediment suspended in the flow.

turbinate A botanical term meaning top-shaped or shaped like the top of an inverted cone.

turbulent flow A vigorous, fast water flow, usually caused by steepness of grade and bumps or projections (boulders, bedrock) underneath or to the sides of the flow. A turbulent flow in a water feature serves to aerate the water, assisting in control of algae growth, and providing air for aquatic plants and fish.

turbulent flow emitter In drip irrigation, an emitter of water droplets having a small tortuous path for the water to flow through that controls the amount of water emitted by dissipating energy in friction against the walls of the water passage and between the water particles themselves. Elevation differences and friction loss in pipe distribution can affect the output of emitters. These emitters are not highly sensitive to pressure or temperature variations. *See also* **emitter**.

turf A thick cover of grass that is usually maintained by mowing.

turgid Full of water; distended. Plant tissues that are naturally and normally swollen to a firmness and not limp, especially after watering.

turgor The normal state of plant cells when receiving sufficient water to provide a firmness instead of being limp.

turgid

turion   A botanical term identifying detachable winter buds.

turnaround   A space, path, or circular area that permits the turning around of a vehicle without the necessity of backing up.

turnbuckle   A device used between two cables, lines, etc. for connecting and tightening. It is made up of a right screw and a left screw coupled by means of a link.

turnkey job   A job where the contractor completely supplies all furnishings of a building, park, or project so that it is ready for immediate use.

turn under   The process of turning a portion of the soil surface upside down and burying any organic material (especially plants or remains)

as an **organic fertilizer** or soil improvement. It can be accomplished by shovel, tractor plow, disc, etc.

tussock   A slightly raised area in a marsh or bog that has a solid ground of intertwined roots, etc. They are often comprised of sedges or grasses.

twig   A small branch of a woody tree or shrub.

twine   A strong string of two or more strands twisted together. The most used and accepted type in landscape construction is that which is made of decomposable materials so that it may be used in **balled-and-burlapped** situations or in tying up palm fronds, etc. When it disintegrates, it is no longer binding to the plant parts.

twining   In botanical terms, ascending or climbing by coiling around a support, which is sometimes another plant, especially in a natural setting. Examples are the hop vine or Virginia creeper.

two-way reinforcement   Reinforcing bars set in a grid pattern with bars at right angles to one another.

type-DWV tubing   A copper tubing with thinner walls than other types of copper tubing. It is not generally used for liquids under pressure. It is generally used for drainage, vent lines, etc.

U

UBC Abbreviation for **uniform building code**.

U-bend A pipe **expansion bend** in the shape of the letter U.

UBG Abbreviation for **urban growth boundary**.

U-bolt A rod (iron bar) bent in the shape of the letter U with threads on each of the ends.

uf Abbreviation for underground feeder (wire for direct burial).

U-factor *See* **thermal transmittance**.

UL Abbreviation for **Underwriters' Laboratories, Inc.**

ULI Abbreviation for Urban Land Institute.

UL label Information affixed or inscribed on construction materials or devices showing evidence that the product has an approved rating by the **UL**. This approval is based on performance tests, from a production lot manufactured with materials and processes essentially identical to those of representative products that have been tested for fire hazard, electrical hazard, or other safety features. These products are also subject to reexamination services of UL.

ultimate strength The maximum value of tension, compression, or shear that a material can sustain before failure.

ultraviolet light (UV) A component of sunlight that is beyond the visible spectrum of light, having a wavelength less than that of visible light and longer than X-rays.

umbel In botanical terms, the umbrella-like form of inflorescence, or having flower stalks arise from the same point. Some umbels have a flat top to their flower head.

umbel inflorescence

umbellate In botanical terms, having **umbel**s.

umbo A blunt or rounded part or protuberance on the end or side of a plant organ, as with the scales of many pinecones.

unburnt brick A brick that is sun-dried instead of kiln-dried.

uncinate A hooked end, or bent like a hook at the tip.

unclassified excavation An excavation with a single unit price for removal, regardless of the proportion of earth material (common excavation) and solid rock material.

unconsolidated backfill Any fill material not properly compacted.

uncoursed Masonry having continuous horizontal joints.

underbrush Woody plants growing beneath taller plants.

undercloak A course of plain tiles or slate on a roof used under the first course at the eave edges.

undercourse An **undercloak**.

undercut **1.** In stonework, a drip edge made by various means. **2.** In earthwork, a dangerous area in a cut where there is earth or rock material directly above the cut. **3.** To place a cut in a tree trunk to direct the fall of the tree when cutting it down.

underdrain A drainpipe installed in porous fill, for draining water.

underfloor *See* **subfloor**.

underground feeder An electrical wire with a coating capable of withstanding the chemical forces of being buried underground.

underground guying The stabilization of a transplanted tree with guy wires tied to deadmen or anchor bolts underground and the wires passing at right angles over boards laid across the top of the root ball to distribute pressure across the root ball.

undergrown **1.** Plants with **underbrush**. **2.** An undersized plant or one that is not fully mature.

undergrowth **1.** Any plants growing beneath other plants. **2.** Any branches or growth on a plant below the level it is desirable or expected.

underlay In placement of waterproof liners for water features, material placed before the liner to assist in protecting the liner from puncture.

underlayment **1.** A material, often plywood, placed on a **subfloor** to provide a smooth, even surface for the finish. **2.** A material, usually felt, covering a roof deck before shingles are applied. **3.** A soft material such as wet newspapers, felt, or a rubber sheet laid on the bare surface of ground in preparation, and as protection, for laying a sheet of rubber or plastic (as a waterproof membrane) in constructing water features.

underpinning The rebuilding or deepening of an existing foundation to provide additional support.

underplant To plant small plants underneath the canopy or **crown** of larger ones.

underplanting Placement of one plant beneath another, especially those beneath trees.

undersanded concrete A concrete mix with an insufficient portion of fine aggregate to produce optimum properties for working and finishing fresh concrete.

understock The rooted plant on which a **scion** (**bud** or **shoot**) of another plant is placed in **budding**, **grafting**, or **inarching**. This portion of a grafted or budded plant furnishes roots and sometimes a branch or two for the plant.

Underwriters Laboratories, Inc. (UL) A nonprofit organization affiliated with the National Board of Fire Underwriters that classifies, tests, and inspects electrical devices for compliance with the **National Electrical Code**.

undeveloped land Land in its natural state.

understory **1.** Plants growing under the **crown** of a large **shade tree** or the canopy of a forest. **2.** Any plant other than trees. Sometimes **landscape architects** draw a **planting plan** for trees and a separate planting plan for all other **plant material** (understory plant material) to keep the **graphic**s easier to read.

undulate In botanical terms, wavy or wavy-margined. (Compare with **entire, crenate, dentate, serrate, lobed, pinnatifid**.)

undulate leaf margin

uni- A Latin prefix sometimes used in botanical terms, meaning one.

uniform building code A reference to the published Uniform Building Code (National Building Code in the United States). This is prepared by the Building Officials and Code Administrators International, whose address is 4051 West Flossmoor Rd., Country Club Hills, IL 60478.

uniform construction index An outline of building trades and products, separated into 16 divisions under the **uniform system** arranged by trade and construction sequence.

Uniform Federal Accessibility Standards (UFAS) U.S. standards for accessibility of disabled people available from: U.S. Access Board, 1331 F Street NW, Suite 1000, Washington, DC 20004-1111.

uniform grading A particle-sized distribution of aggregate with all pan fractions present and no size or group of sizes being overly represented.

uniformity coefficient A coefficient referencing the size distribution of a granular material.

uniform load A **load** evenly distributed over a structure or member.

uniform system Coordination of specification's technical data and construction opera-

tions organized in 16 divisions based on the relationship of place, trade, function, or material.

union **1.** In **graft**ing, the point at which the **scion** is joined to the stock. **2.** In sprinkler irrigation, a special coupler between pipes that allows the uncoupling of the pipe at a later date. It is made of two pipe portions that connect to the ends of each pipe to be joined and a third portion that is a **threaded fitting** over the two end pieces. It is held on the end of one pipe by a flange on the piece (fitting) on its end and screws onto the fitting on the end of the other pipe. When it is connected and turned, it pulls the two pipes together for a seal made by tightening (turning) it.

union joint A pipe joint made with a **union**.

unisexual In botanical terms, being of one sex (e.g., a flower being only male or female, with **stamen**s or **pistil**s, but not both).

United States of America Standards Institute *See* **American National Standards Institute**.

universal motor A motor that can operate either on alternating current or on direct current.

unit price A price per unit of measurement for materials or services.

unit water content **1.** The quantity of water per unit volume of fresh concrete. **2.** The amount of water on which the water-cement ratio is based, not including water absorbed by aggregates.

universal soil loss equation An equation for the prediction of soil loss from land. The equation is: $A = R \times K \times L \times S \times C \times P$. A is the computed soil loss per unit area (tons per acre per year). R is the rainfall factor, which is the number of erosion-index units in a normal year's rainfall. The erosion

unreinforced

index is a measure of the erosive force of a specific rainfall event. K is the soil-erodibility factor, which is the erosion rate per unit of erosion index for a specific soil in cultivated continuous fallow (the worst possible condition) on a 9% slope that is 72.6 ft long. L is the slope-length factor, which is the ratio of soil loss from a field slope length to that of a 72.6 length of the same soil-type slope. S is the slope-gradient factor, which is the ratio of soil loss from the field gradient to that from the 9% slope. P is the erosion-control practice factor, which is the ratio of soil loss with contouring, strip-cropping, or terracing in a pattern perpendicular (or nearly so) to the slope as compared to that with straight-row farming parallel to the slope (up and down the slope).

unreinforced   In construction, concrete not containing **reinforcing bars** or **welded wire fabric**.

unsound wood   Decayed wood.

UPC   Abbreviation for Uniform Plumbing Code.

upheaval   The upward push of an earthen mass.

upland   Land higher in elevation, upslope, and a significant distance from the ocean, a river, or other water body and its flood zone.

upright   A plant with a form that is vertical and usually having ascending branches. This form is found in trees, shrubs, and grasses. Trees of this

upright arching grass

form (and some shrubs) are often identified as **columnar** or **fastigiate**.

upright arching grass   A grass form with foliage that ascends vertically and arches or weeps at its top. (Compare with **mounded (2)**, **upright grass**, **tufted**, **upright divergent grass**, **arching**.)

upright divergent grass   *See* **upright spreading**.

upright divergent (spreading) grasses and shrubs

upright grass   Any grass that has an erect form with foliage growing vertically in a tight pattern.

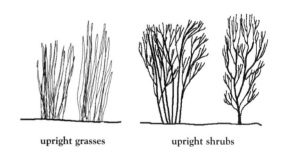

upright grasses   upright shrubs

upright spreading *or* **upright divergent**   Plants that have a somewhat narrow vase shape or V shape. Trees of this shape have branches that start at the ground or the first branching and spread further the higher they are from the ground. It is not broad (nearly as wide as tall), and usually has **ascending** branches and approaching **columnar** or **fastigiate**. (Compare with **round, columnar, fastigiate, oval, broadly spreading, weeping, pyramidal**.) Grasses of this form that grow up and out in a stiffly ascending pattern become more erect and tall than **tufted grasses**. (Compare with **mounded (2)**, **upright grass**, **tufted**, **upright arching grass**, **arching**.)

upright spreading tree form

upstand *or* **upturn**   The part of a roof surface that turns up against a vertical surface.

upzoning   A change in the zoning for a specific area creating higher residential densities.

urban   An area within a city, or an area that is comprised mostly of buildings and paving.

urban canyon   **1.** City street lined with buildings. **2.** Urban physical features that have an effect on airflow, sunlight, humidity, water percolation, heating, cooling of air, soils, etc.

urban climate   The climate in and near urban areas. It is often warmer, more or less humid, shadier, and has more reflected light than the climate of the surrounding land areas.

urban design   The designs of cities and their components. Those who often assist in this task are land planners, civil engineers, landscape architects, transportation engineers, and architects.

urban forestry plan   A plan for a highly developed land area (usually a city or town) that is prepared for the installation or maintenance of trees.

urban growth boundary   A perimeter line defined around an urban growth area preventing further growth of the urban form or defining a limited area to accommodate anticipated growth for a specific number of years. This is a management technique designed to prevent sprawl.

urbanization   The process of covering a significant portion of a land area with buildings or impervious pavements.

urceolate   In botanical terms, urn-shaped.

usable floor area   The floor area of a building after deducting the area of lobbies, corridors, rest rooms, utility rooms, etc.

USASI   Abbreviation for **American National Standards Institute**.

U.S. Customary Units   The system of units (inch, foot, pound, quart, mile, etc.) commonly used in the United States.

USDA   Abbreviation for United States Department of Agriculture.

utilities   Lines and facilities associated with the provision, distribution, collection, transmission, or disposal of water, storm, and sanitary sewage, oil, gas, power, information, telecommunication, telephone, etc.

utility pole   An outdoor post installed by or for a telephone or electric utility company to support conductors and other electrical or telephone distribution devices.

utility tractor   A low- to medium-horsepower tractor often used to pull attachments for rototilling, grading, spreading mulch, scarifying, etc.

utricle   A small, thin-walled, one-seeded, somewhat inflated, bladdery fruit.

U-value   *See* **thermal transmittance**.

UV filter   A filter on glass or plastic blocking or reducing ultraviolet light from sunlight passing through it.

V

V **1.** Abbreviation for volt. **2.** Abbreviation for valve.

vacuum circuit breaker An electrical circuit breaker with switch contacts enclosed in a vacuum.

vaginate In botanical terms, surrounded by a sheath, usually made up of leaf stems.

valley The trough, gutter, or low area formed by the intersection of two inclined planes of a roof surface.

valley flashing Sheet metal used to line a **valley** on a roof.

valley gutter An open gutter with a sloping side in a roof valley.

valley tile A special-shaped roof tile laid in a valley on a roof.

valute The stationary housing or casing of the **impeller** of a **centrifugal pump**.

valute with flexible coupling pump A **centrifugal pump** with the distinctive feature of the pump having its own impeller shaft mounted on one end of a frame and the electric motor on the other end with a flexible coupling connecting the two shafts.

valve An apparatus that controls flow, especially of water. It is capable of opening or closing and is often also capable of being adjusted to various amounts of flow. In irrigation, it may be operated by hand or by a **controller** via a **solenoid**.

valve adapter In irrigation, a replacement top to convert a manual valve to an automatic valve.

valve body The casing that attaches to pipes and surrounds valve components.

valve bonnet The top of a valve that is bolted or screwed onto the body.

valve box A box (usually concrete, plastic, or fiberglass) containing **valves**. In **irrigation systems**, they are usually buried with the lid showing.

valve box

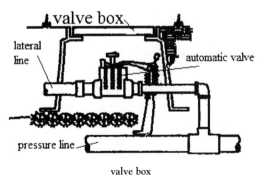

valve box

valve in head A sprinkler head in which the valve is actuated by the controller for turning the head off and on and is built into the sprinkler head. Most are currently electrically operated, but some are still hydraulically actuated. These types of heads are usually large and capable of spraying long distances. They are commonly used on golf courses and in large lawn areas of parks.

valve key A long, slender, metal rod with a handle forming a T shape and an end that is placed down on a **valve** in the ground to turn off, on, or adjust the flow of water or other fluids by turning. *See also* **sprinkler key** and **stop and waste key**.)

valve seat The opening edge of the port against which a disc or wedge sits to stop water flow within a valve.

valve stem The central threaded shaft within a **valve**.

vane A device designed to rotate in the wind, indicating wind direction. *See* **weather vane**.

vane pump A type of **rotary pump** capable of causing the flow or compression of a fluid.

vapor pressure The pressure exerted by a liquid's vapor or gaseous state when it is in equilibrium with its liquid state. When a liquid is at a temperature above its freezing point, it forms a vapor at its free surface, creating pressure. This pressure increases or decreases directly with temperature. When the vapor is at equilibrium, any additional pressure, decrease in temperature, or addition of vapor will cause the liquid to precipitate. This pressure is important with regard to pumps because if the pressure in the suction line falls below vapor pressure, it will cause the fluid to vaporize and produce bubbles of vapor. When these bubbles reach higher pressures in a pump, they collapse violently (**cavitation**), often doing harm to the pump.

variance An allowable exception to an ordinance or law. It is a waiver from compliance with a specific provision of a city ordinance granted to a particular property owner because of the practical difficulties or unnecessary hardship that would be imposed by the strict application of that provision of the ordinance. The granting of variances traditionally is the responsibility of the zoning board of appeals or board of adjustment.

variegated Leaves with markings of various colors not the same as the primary color of the leaf, but particularly leaves with yellow or white markings (especially at the edges).

variegated leaves

variety **1.** A subgroup of plants within a **species** having at least one identifiable characteristic that makes them distinctly different from others of the same species. This is the lowest or final botanical classification within a **botanical (scientific) name**. However, sometimes a **strain** of the variety is given afterward in the name. **2.** A naturally occurring variant of a wild **species** of plant.

varnish A protective cover for surfaces made of resinous matter dissolved in alcohol (or another volatile liquid) or in oil that is applied as a thin coating where it dries, becoming hard, transparent, and glossy.

varnish stain A **varnish** with a transparent coloring.

varved clay Thin layers of silt and clay deposited in water bodies during different times of year. When the clay becomes dry, there is usually some color variation between layers.

vascular A term used to describe plants that have **xylem** and **phloem**.

vascular plants Plants with cells arranged into a pipe-like system of tissue that conveys fluids (sap). Woody plants of this sort are composed of **xylem** and **phloem** vascular tissues.

vascular tissue The tissue of a leaf, root, stem, or flower stem including the **xylem** and **phloem** that conducts water and **organic** substances throughout the plant.

vault **1.** A spatially extended arch or interconnected, extended arches covering a space. **2.** In utility construction, a buried concrete space of various sizes, but usually large enough for a person to enter through a **manhole** to access equipment such as pumps, **backflow preventers**, **pressure reducers**, etc. They are also sometimes used for changing large storm sewer or sanitary sewer pipe directions. This term is sometimes used interchangeably with **manhole**, though they are separate items.

vault light *See* **pavement light**.

v.c. pipe Abbreviation for **vitreous clay pipe**.

V-cut **1.** Lettering inscribed in stone with acutely triangular cuts. **2.** A cut in wood that is V-shaped.

vegetation Any plant, or grouping of plants.

vegetative buffer **1.** An area extending landward from a lake, stream, or from the edge of wetland that provides adequate conditions and native vegetation for the performance of the functional properties of a stream corridor and other hydrological areas. **2.** An area of vegetation acting as a **buffer**.

vegetative cap Also known as a **phytocap**. Plants growing over contaminants to protect them from leaching.

vein The **vascular tissue** conducting a path (especially if easily visible), forming a thread-

vault

veins

vellum

like rib or channel framework or network as in a **leaf** or **flower**.

vellum   A slightly rough, translucent paper used for drafting or drawing upon.

velocity   In irrigation and water feature design, the speed of water flow within pipes in **feet per seconds (fps)**. The speed in a piping system must be controlled to avoid damage to the system. The common maximum flow designed for is usually 5 fps. A designer must use caution when designing a system where the water velocity exceeds 5 fps. *See* **water hammer**.

velutinous   A botanical term describing a plant part with a surface that has a fine, soft, short **pubescence**, or a velvety, dense, hairy covering (**indumentum**).

venation   A pattern, arrangement, or system of **veins** in a leaf.

vendor   A person or organization furnishing materials or equipment for a project.

veneered plywood   **1.** A thin layer of wood glued or attached over a less attractive wood. **2.** Any thin layer placed over another surface.

venous   Having to do with, or being comprised of, **veins**.

vent   In excavation and piping, a pipe providing airflow to or from a drainage system.

vental   In botanical terms, belonging to the anterior or inner face of an organ; the opposite of dorsal.

ventral edge   In botanical terms, belly side, on the lower side, or downside.

ventricose   In botanical terms, swollen on one side or mostly on one side.

vermicompost   A **compost** produced with the aid of **earthworms**.

vermiculite   A natural clay material (silicate clay) or mica product expanded by heat to produce a lightweight sponge-like material capable of holding water and air. It is used for insulation, soil conditioning, as a rooting medium for plants, as a product in synthetic soil formulas, in lightweight soil mixes (for use in planters on buildings or parking structures), or a lightweight concrete mix.

vermiculture   Raising and producing **earthworms**, including their by-products.

vernal   Relating to spring, or fresh like spring.

vernalization   A cold period necessary for some plants to grow or bloom, or for seeds to sprout.

vernation   Within a plant's bud, the pattern or arrangement of leaves.

verrucose   A botanical term that means warty, nodular, or covered with wart-like bumps.

vertical grain   A reference to lumber that is cut from a tree with its end's shortest dimension perpendicular to the growth rings. This produces a grain in the face (largest dimension) of the board that is mostly straight. Looking at the end of the board one will see grain lines parallel to its shortest dimension. *See also* **flat grain**.

vertical pump *or* **vertical turbine pump**   **1.** A long, slender pump designed to pump water from deep wells by being placed in an upright underground pipe. **2.** A **centrifugal pump** with the distinctive feature of the motor being mounted aboveground with a drive shaft extending down to the pump at the water source elevation.

verticil   A **whorl** of leaves or flowers as arranged in a circular pattern around a stem.

verticillate   In botanical terms, **whorled** or arranged in verticils.

verticillium wilt   A soil-borne **fungus** (genus *Verticillium*) that causes wilting of a plant by plugging the water-bearing tissues of the plant. It can infest a soil for years without a host plant. Growing wilt-resistant plants helps to avoid this disease.

very poorly drained soils   These are soils in which water is removed so slowly that the water table remains at or near the surface nearly all of the time. These soils occupy mostly level or depressed lands.

veseid   In botanical terms, glutinous, or sticky.

vespertine   In plant identification and descriptions, opening or functional in the evening.

vestibule   A small foyer leading into a larger space.

vest-pocket park   A park built on a small plot of land, usually within an urban setting.

V.G.   Abbreviation for vertical grain.

vibrating roller   A motorized heavy roller that rapidly, slightly jumps up and down. It is useful for compacting soils, base courses, etc.

view   **1.** To observe or examine. **2.** Within one's vision and capable of being seen; usually in context of a negative (undesirable) or positive (desirable) view. What is positive or negative in view is often different from person to person, but some views are almost universally good or bad. **3.** A pictorial representation or a picturesque setting or beautiful, or interesting area within sight.

villa   A historically Italian design of an estate with its dwelling, outbuilding, and decorative garden.

village green   An open space or park, historically located at the center of a village. They are still found in some towns today and were sometimes converted to a park from a common area where livestock were kept for the town.

villous   In botanical terms, shaggy with long, often bent or curved (not matted), soft hairs. (Compare with **hirsute**, **sericeous**, and **tomentose**.)

vine   A plant needing support for its stem that climbs by twining, or by tendrils, or creeps along the ground in a sprawling mass.

vinyl   A plastic of various types.

virgate   Plant parts that have a long slender shape like a rod or wand.

virus   An extremely minute entity only capable of reproducing within the cells of plants or animals. They cause a number of serious plant diseases including phloem necrosis, lily mosaic, etc.

viscid   Plant parts that are sticky, sweaty, greasy, or slimy.

viscidulous   Plant parts that are slightly or a little sticky, sweaty, slimy, or greasy.

viscometer   A device measuring viscosity that is often used to measure fresh concrete viscosity.

viscosity   The thickness of a liquid. This is important in pumping and pressure loss calculations as fluids such as water will require more pressure to move when they carry suspended particles.

vise   A tool that holds objects fast while they are worked on. Its rotating handle moves one jaw toward another, fixed jaw on a screw shaft so they can hold objects firmly.

vision light   A clear glass window.

vision-light door   A door with one small window in the upper portion.

vista **1.** An unobstructed distant view within one's range of vision without turning the head. **2.** A view that is framed by vegetation, buildings, a window, etc.

vitamin B₁ A vitamin that is essential for metabolism, widespread in plants and used as a stimulant to encourage root growth.

viticulture The growing and cultivating of grapes, especially in vineyards for wine making.

vitreous The degree to which a material is resistant to water **absorption**.

vitrified brick Brick that has been glazed in a kiln so that it is waterproof.

vitrified-clay pipe *or* **v.c. pipe** A pipe made of clay-type materials, glazed and hardened under heat, so that they are essentially impervious to water (5% or less) and resistant to chemical corrosion. They are often used underground for **drainage** systems or **sewer** pipes.

viviparous In botanical terms, germinating or producing young that are still attached to the parent plant. These are often produced instead of flowers.

V-joint *or* **vee joint** A V-shaped, recessed masonry joint formed in mortar with a V-shaped metal tool.

VOC Abbreviation for volatile organic compound.

void An unfilled space in materials or fluids.

void-cement ratio The ratio of air and water volume to cement volume.

void ratio The ratio of the volume of void space to the volume of solid particles in a soil, base course, etc.

vol. Abbreviation for volume.

volatile The condition of a substance that evaporates quickly and is flammable.

volatilization The transfer of a chemical from an aqueous state or liquid to a gas.

vole A small rodent of the *microtus* or related genera that is brownish with a short tail, short ears, and a blunt nose. They eat roots and stems of plants, and burrow underground to have young. They often follow **mole** tunnels.

volt (v) A unit of measurement denoting electrical pressure. It is the electrical pressure required to force one amp of current flow in a circuit against one ohm of resistance in the same circuit.

voltage The amount of **volts**. The potential difference or pressure of electricity caused by higher electric charge at one point in a conductor or electrical system than at another point.

voltage regulator An automatic electrical control device with an output of a constant voltage even when the supply line voltage may vary.

voluntary standard A standard with no obligation to comply.

volunteer plant A plant that germinates and appears without a landscaper or gardener having intended for it to do so.

vortex emitter In drip irrigation, an emitter with a whirlpool inside having a lower pressure at the center where there is provided a small hole (orifice) that controls the amount of water emitted by the size of the hole. Elevation differences and friction loss in pipe distribution can affect the output of emitters. These emitters are less sensitive than most to pressure variations. These emitters tend to clog with small particles and need high-quality filtration. *See also* **emitter**.

VP Abbreviation for vent pipe.

VS *See* V-joint.

W

W **1.** Abbreviation for wire. **2.** Abbreviation for watt. **3.** Abbreviation for west. **4.** Abbreviation for width. **5.** Abbreviation for with.

w/ Abbreviation for with.

wale, waler, whaler A horizontal timber used to brace an upright member.

walk **1.** A pedestrian path. **2.** A paved surface for foot traffic following a street.

walking-stick insects Grasshopper relatives with extremely thin bodies and legs. They usually do little damage to plants.

walkway A footpath.

wall An upright surface providing enclosure.

wall anchor **1.** A metal tie for anchoring beams or joists to a wall or larger structural member. **2.** A wrought-iron clamp, often decorative, on the exterior of a brick building connected to an opposite wall by a rod of iron to prevent the wall from moving apart. **3.** See **wall tie**.

wallboard A rigid sheet made of wood-pulp or gypsum used as a surface on walls.

wall bracket A bracket used to support piping, electrical components, or lighting fixtures.

wall garden Plants in the joints of a stone wall, where soil pockets are available.

wall thickness In pipes, the measurement of the thickness of the wall of the pipe usually given to three decimal places. Pipes of the same **nominal size** may have different wall thicknesses and different pressure ratings (maximums).

wall tie A metal strap or other device used to secure masonry facing to a backup wall, etc. It is

usually mortared into joints of masonry work and may also be attached with screws into the backup wall.

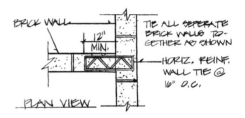

wall tie

walnut A tough, strong, dark brownish-black wood that does not split easily and takes a high polish.

wane With regard to lumber, a board that is not complete or true to its cut dimension because a linear piece of one corner of the board is missing.

warm season grasses Any grass that grows best in hot weather (80 to 95F), growing vigorously from spring to summer, after which it flowers and tends toward dormancy in the fall (i.e., Zoysia, Bermuda, St. Augustine, etc.). These grasses tend to change color in fall and are dormant during winter. The classification of grasses as cool or warm season is somewhat arbitrary as grasses perform differently from climate to climate. Grasses growing throughout the winter months in a mild climate may become completely dormant in a colder climate.

warm season plants Plants that thrive in warm weather such as some grasses, many vegetables, and most **annual** flowers.

warping Deviation of a surface from its original shape.

warping joint A joint allowing warping of pavement slabs when moisture or temperature changes occur.

warranty *See* **guarantee**.

wash The slope on outdoor steps facilitating water drainage. It is usually expressed in portions of an inch per foot (i.e., ¼ in/ft).

washer *or* **flat washer** A metal piece that is usually a flat ring shape used under a bolt head that surrounds its shank and extends beyond the bolt head to spread load, protects the surface from being crushed by the force of the bolt, ensures tightness, and relieves friction.

waste pipe A drainpipe receiving waterborne discharge, but not receiving fecal matter.

waste well **1.** *See* **leaching cesspool**. **2.** A well collecting surface waters, providing for the water to be dispensed and absorbed into the ground.

water-based paint A paint that may be thinned or diluted with water.

water basin A soil mound a few inches high usually formed at the drip edge of a plant for holding water to supply roots while preventing its runoff. These are commonly formed around plants at transplanting to aid in water retention.

water closet **1.** A fixture used to receive human excrement capable of flushing with water through a waste pipe. A toilet. **2.** An enclosure containing a toilet.

water cock A water outlet valve operated by turning a handle.

waterfall A flowing body of water (stream, river, etc.) falling through the air without its undersurface contacting the ground.

water farming *See* **hydroponics**.

water feature A water body or **fountain** that is often a **focal point** or of prominent importance in its surroundings. It may be still or moving water with fountains, waterfalls, and **informal** or **formal** designs.

water feature

water garden A garden of pools with aquatic and other water-loving plants.

water hammer *or* **water surge** A sudden rise in pressure usually caused by suddenly opening or closing a valve or valves, or by air in the pipe system, and by cycling of a pump. This stopping of water with momentum and usually higher than reasonable velocity causes pipes to jump, make banging noises, and will eventually cause damage to pipes and devices attached to them. It can be corrected by turning valves off slowly, by adding a shock absorber (a vertical pipe or pipes filled with air to act as a shock absorber), by adding a surge suppression device, by increasing pipe sizes to reduce the velocity of water, or by installing air vents on the piping.

water-hammer arrester A device utilized in a pipe system to eliminate **water hammer**.

water harvesting   Any technique or combination of techniques resulting in storm or flood waters being captured for later use or for return to the **water table**.

water horsepower (Whp)   The horsepower theoretically (does not take into account a particular pump's efficiency capability) needed for a **pump** to provide the required pressure and flow for a particular need. It may be found by multiplying the **total dynamic head** by the gallons per minute needed, and dividing it by 3960.

watering devices   Any number of items for the distribution of water, including, but not limited to, drip emitters, soaker hoses, root irrigators, sprinklers, etc.

watering programs   *See* **program**.

water meter   A mechanical device that measures the volume of water passing through a pipe or outlet. It is useful to suppliers of water as it allows them to assess and bill for water use.

water mold   Any of many fungi causing **root rot**. These molds are encouraged and spread by standing water. Many times plants are overwatered when some negative symptom is observed. The only symptom that calls for more water is **wilting**. Too much water bringing on root rot is the most common cause of plant death. It is usually easily detected by digging in the root zone and smelling the soil and roots. Root rot occurs in **anaerobic** conditions causing the affected area to smell much like a sanitary sewer. When a dead plant is pulled completely out from the soil, the stench many times is unmistakable and obvious. Sometimes it is necessary to hold soil from the **root ball** in your hand and put it to your nose to detect the smell. The most frequent cause of root rot is the use of a different soil than the existing soil in the **backfill** or **amendment**s to the soil backfill. Either may cause a **soil interface** difficulty with water transfer.

waterproof   Material or construction that is impervious to water.

waterproofing   A material applied to a surface that will not allow water to penetrate through it.

water pump   *See* **pump**.

water ramp   A series of pools with water flowing from one to another.

water repellant   A surface that sheds most of its water and is resistant to water penetration, but not completely.

water requirement   Generally, the amount of water required by plants for satisfactory growth during the season, the week, the month, or the day. Water requirements vary with climatic conditions, soil moisture, other soil characteristics, and with plant types.

water resistant   Material that will withstand limited exposure to water before allowing it to penetrate.

water retentivity   A mortar that prevents rapid loss of water by absorption in adjacent masonry units.

water seasoning   Preparing **lumber** by soaking it in water before air drying.

watershed   A drainage area. The surface drainage area defined by topographic boundaries that contributes storm water runoff to a lake, stream, river, pond, drainage system, estuarine waters, or oceanic waters.

water softener   A device that treats **hard water** by reverse osmosis, filters, magnets, ultraviolet light, use of salts (sodium chloride replaces calcium and magnesium ions), etc. to decrease dissolved minerals or their ability to form deposits. Water treated with salt can cause salt burn in plants, especially over time. Some plants are highly susceptible, while others are tolerant of salts.

waterspout   A duct, pipe, or device discharging rainwater from a roof or gutter.

water sprout   Strong, extremely vigorous, vertical green shoot growth from the stem, or sometimes the branches, of a tree.

water stop   A waterproof material placed across a joint to prevent the passage of water.

water table   The geomorphic plane at the upper limit (or transition zone in finer soils) of water beneath the surface of the ground. This elevation of water generally tends to follow the surface of the ground.

watertight   A material, container, pipe system, etc. that prevents the movement of water (moisture) out of it or through it.

water tank   An enclosed water storage container, usually elevated to provide constant pressure to pipes.

water test   A check of a water system under pressure to determine if there are leaks in the piping system.

water vapor transmission   The rate of water vapor flow through a unit area of material between two parallel surfaces under specified conditions.

water volume   Amount of water expressed.

water wand   An attachment to a hose that gives the user an extended reach with control of water volume, force, or pattern of water delivery for watering plants.

waterway   A shallow depression, usually of concrete, allowing water to cross a roadway or **driveway**, etc. instead of flowing across in a sheet pattern. These are common at street intersections where water gathered by raised curbs to corners must cross a paved surface. A waterway can carry water from one curb to another.

water wick   Glass, wool, nylon or other substances used to move water from a supply of water to the location of a plant. This is particularly useful for watering indoor houseplants.

watt (W)   A unit of measurement of electrical power. One watt of electrical power is equal to one volt of pressure times one ampere of current. Most electrical devices are rated according to the power they consume by this unit of measurement.

watt-hour   A unit of work equal to 3600 joules, or the power of one **watt** operating for one hour.

wattle   Poles intertwined with reeds or plants (willows, etc.) to create a fence, barricade, etc.

way   A street, alley, path, etc., usually with an easement established for the passage of persons or vehicles.

W.C.   Abbreviation for **water closet**.

WCV   Abbreviation for **butterfly** (wafer) **check valve**.

Wdr   With regard to lumber providers, an abbreviation for wider.

wearing surface *or* **wearing course**   The finished layer of surfacing that carries traffic or receives use.

weatherseal channel   An access with a top-closing channel set in **mastic** with its flanges oriented downward.

weathercock   A **weather vane** shaped like a rooster.

weathered   A term describing material that has been exposed to the elements of weather for an extended period causing it to change color, texture, etc.

weathering   **1.** Allowing or causing a material to become **weathered** in appearance or its surface to be changed by nature above- or belowground.

2. In soils, the physical and chemical disintegration or decomposition of rocks and minerals under natural conditions. **3.** Wear and change in color, texture, strength, size, cohesiveness, chemical composition, or other properties of materials exposed to weather.

weathering steel   A steel alloy that forms a self-protecting rust surface layer when exposed to outdoor elements and weather.

weatherproof   Protected from elements of the weather or not affected by them.

weather strip   A narrow piece of material applied to an exterior door or window to cover the joint made by it with the sill, casings, or threshold, to prevent rain, snow, cold air, etc. from entering.

weather-struck joint *or* **weathered joint**   A horizontal masonry joint in which the mortar is indented at the lower edge of bricks and slopes outward to meet the front edge of the brick below, facilitating the rapid shedding of water.

weathertight   Sealed from rain, snow, cold air, wind, etc.

weather vane   A thin, usually ornamental piece of metal on a pole or spindle capable of rotating with exposure to the wind and giving an indication of wind direction. It is usually located on top of a barn or other structure.

weaving   In shingled roofing, the alternate lapping of shingles on opposite faces in a **valley**.

web   The cross member of a truss or girder between the upper- and lower-span members.

webworms   Larvae of moths that feed on plants under silky webs.

weed   **1.** Any plant in an undesired location. Weeds compete for water, nutrients, and space. **2.** Plants that tend to overgrow and choke out

weather vane

more desirable plants. **3.** An undesirable, unattractive, or troublesome plant.

weed and feed fertilizer   A substance in liquid or granules that is both **fertilizer** and a chemical control of particular types of **weeds**.

weed barrier   A barrier placed to prevent or impede weeds from growing or germinating. Weed barriers are usually a fabric, plastic, or such. Plastic is no longer recommended in planting beds because it prevents **aeration** of the soil, causing **anaerobic** surface soil conditions that often kill plants.

weed barrier fabric   *See* **weed barrier**.

weed control   The spraying of chemicals or spreading of powders or granules to prevent weed seed germination, spreading of weed roots, or to kill weeds.

weed eater   *See* **string trimmer**.

weeding   Removal of unsightly, unwanted, out-of-place plants that are usually relatively small.

weep hole A small opening allowing water to drain from one side or surface of a material to the opposite side or surface. An example is a hole near the base of a retaining wall permitting water to drain to the outside of the wall. This assists in preventing buildup of pressure behind the wall.

weeping A description of a plant with a form that allows its branches to droop or hang downward and grow toward the ground. Ends of branches are pendulous. (Compare with **round, columnar, fastigiate, oval, broadly spreading, upright spreading, pyramidal.**)

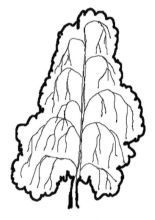

weeping tree form

weevil Any of many usually small **beetle**s (of *Rhynchophora*) with an elongated head that often curves downward forming a snout with jaws at its tip. Their **larva**e are destructive as they feed on roots, nuts, grain, and fruit. The adults chew on leaves and fruit at night and hide during daylight.

weir A shallow space or notch along a water's edge created of hard-surfaced materials (usually of a manufactured form) to allow water to pass over it and fall. It regulates the amount of water as it flows over it with its shape, width, and texture. It is often used to control or measure water or waste water flow. Common types of weirs are v-notch, parabolic, or trapezoidal, with each of them being either sharp-crested, round-crested, or broad-crested weirs.

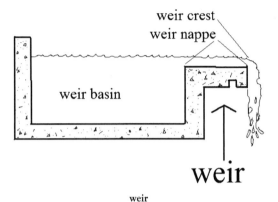

weir

weir basin The containment of water directly behind (upstream of) a weir.

weir crest The line directly over the weir edge where the water begins to bend and fall.

weir nappe The portion of a **weir** from the basin to the edge of the fall of water, including the entire width of the weir opening.

welded wire mesh *or* **welded wire fabric** *See* **wire mesh.**

well A hole, pipe, or pit sunk, drilled, or dug into the earth to reach and use a supply of water.

well-drained soil Any **soil** in which water is removed readily, but not rapidly. Well-drained soils usually retain optimum amounts of moisture for plant growth after rain.

well-graded aggregate An aggregate composed of particle-sizes to provide high density with little void space.

wellhead protection **1.** Methods utilized to prevent the contamination of a well within an area determined to be an influence upon the well waters. **2.** In land ordinances, a control of the area around a well by law to prevent contamination.

well house *or* **wellhead**   A protective enclosure over a water well.

wellpoint   Perforated vertical pipes in the ground for pumping out groundwater in lowering a **water table** or removing any unwanted water.

well-point system   Several **wellpoints** connected to a main pipe that is attached to a pump. It is often used to temporarily lower a water table in an area, usually so work below the water level can take place without flooding excavations.

welt   **1.** A seam in sheet metal where two edges are folded together and pressed flat. **2.** A strip of wood over a wood seam to increase strength.

west elevation   **1.** A drawing, usually to scale, showing the west-facing portion of a structure or element as it would be seen standing to the west of it and looking east to view it. **2.** The **elevation** of a portion of ground, paving, or structure situated east of the remainder of it.

western elevation   *See* **west elevation**.

western exposure   **1.** A slope that from top to bottom slopes downward toward the west. **2.** The west-facing portion of a structure. **3.** The area to the west of any nearly vertical surface that has a changed microclimate effected by it with regard to heat or cold, or brightness of sunlight or shadow.

western hemlock   A whitish-brown or yellowish-brown, fairly low density softwood used for general construction and plywood.

western larch   A reddish-brown, moderately strong, heavy softwood, used in general construction as timbers and flooring.

western red cedar   A durable, moderately low density wood, especially for shingles and shakes.

wet-bulb temperature   The temperature of a wick that is kept moist.

wet-bulb thermometer   The thermometer with a bulb that is kept moist in a **psychrometer**.

wetland   An area that is inundated or saturated by surface or groundwater at a frequency, duration, and depth sufficient to support predominance of **emergent plant** species (cattails, etc.) adapted to growth in saturated soil conditions.

wetland mitigation   Methods of eliminating potential damage or destruction to wetlands, or creation of wetlands from uplands to offset the loss of protected wetlands.

wetland mitigation bank   A preserved, restored, constructed, or enhanced wetland that has been set aside to provide compensation for losses of wetland functions caused by human activities as approved by regulatory agencies.

wetland treatment system   A wetland that has been designed for reducing concentrations of one or more pollutants in water.

wet rot   Decay in timber caused by fungi with a high moisture content.

wet sprinkler system   A sprinkler system with its pipes under water pressure, allowing immediate use upon activation.

wettable powder   A formulation of pesticide mixed with a finely ground clay to hold the pesticide in suspension when agitated with water.

wetted perimeter   The distance of a stream bottom measured from the surface of one side of the stream at a point in time to the surface of the stream on the other side at the same point in time.

wetting agents   A chemical in dry or wet form, also known as a **surfactant**. It assists water in penetrating soil more easily or causing such elements as ground bark or peat moss to absorb water faster. It seems to make water wetter.

W.F.

W.F. Abbreviation for wide flange.

wharf A structure built over or floating upon water and used as a landing place for boats as well as for other marine transport, fishing, swimming, etc.

wheelbarrow A handcart with a basin over a front wheel (or wheels) and two handles in back allowing it to be pushed, and also having two supporting legs in back to allow it to stand with the basin fairly level.

wheelbarrow

wheel stop An abrupt, short rise (4 to 8 in, usually about 6 in) at the end of a parking stall that stops the wheel of a vehicle when it is parking. It may be a curb or a specially designed long concrete piece placed at the end or toward the end of a parking stall.

whip A young tree that is usually not branched and more than 1 ft tall.

white cement A calcite limestone cement ground finer and of a higher grade than normal cement.

whitefly Any of numerous scale-like insects (family *Aleyrodidae*) with white wings whose young attach to the underside of leaves and suck on them while pupae and as adults. The pure white adults flutter erratically when disturbed. Adults are about ⅛ in long.

white oak A gray to reddish hard, heavy, durable wood used for flooring, paneling, trim, etc.

white pine A soft, light wood that resists splitting or swelling and is often used in building construction.

white Portland cement A **Portland cement** low in iron, hydrating to a white paste, and helpful in making a whiter than normal concrete.

white rot A type of fungus decay in wood that leaves a white residue.

whitewash A temporary white coloring brushed on surfaces.

wholesale nursery A **nursery** that sells a majority or all of its products to retail outlets or to landscape contractors and not to consumers.

whorl A cluster of three or more **bud**s, leaves, flowers, or **shoot**s arranged around a **stem** at the same level. In other words, a circle of leaves or other plant organs at a **node**.

whorled In botanical terms, arranged in a circle as with leaves around a **stem**.

whorled leaf arrangement

Whp Abbreviation for **water horsepower**.

wide-flange beam An **I-beam** with extended flanges.

wildflower The flower of a plant seeding itself by natural means in an uncultivated ground, or any flower not cultivated, or a flower from a native or wild condition planted in a cultivated garden.

wildlife Generally, animals that are not domesticated and are not aquatic.

wilt With regard to plants, this means to become limp because of lack of water.

wilting The state of a plant losing its leaf **turgor**, usually becoming a dull color, limp, and drooping because of lack of water supply.

wilting coefficient *See* **wilting point**.

wilting point The percentage of water in soil when permanent wilting of plants occurs. This is when the soil can no longer supply water at a rate sufficient to maintain the **turgor** of a plant, and it then permanently wilts. This is the point of moisture condition in the soil when the drainage and usage of water has reached a point that the remaining water cannot be drawn or moved to roots. The matric force acting on the water prevents molecule movement. *See also* **micropores**.

windbreak A dense growth of vegetation (usually trees) affording protection against wind.

windfall Trees blowing over in wind. It may refer to their tendency to do so because of their root structure, root confinement, root removal, or location.

wind load The force exerted by wind on a structure or part of a structure.

wind shake A crack or fissure in a log caused by wind strain during growth.

windthrow A condition in which plants (especially trees) are thrown to the ground by wind without breaking their main stem, but instead having their roots torn or lifted out of the ground.

window boxes Containers for growing plants, usually herbaceous, immediately below windows and usually attached to the building.

window head In framing, the upper horizontal member of the window frame.

window well A recess located below-grade to admit natural light to enter a below-grade window. They are often formed by a U-shaped corrugated metal sheet, but are also constructed of concrete, timbers, boulders, stone, etc.

windshield survey A rapid, extremely general sampling method for vegetation or land use wherein information is simply gathered by observations from a moving vehicle.

wing In botanical terms, any membranous expansion such as on a seed, or leafstalk, or along a stem or branch.

wing nut A nut having projections so that it can be tightened with fingers.

winter The coldest season of the year occurring between fall and spring. *See also* **winter solstice**.

winter annual An annual plant that germinates in the fall, spends the winter as a **seedling**, and then flowers in the spring or summer.

winter bud A fleshy bud that detaches from an aquatic plant and winters over at the bottom of the water and grows into a new plant the next spring.

winterization *See* **winterize**.

winterize To prepare an irrigation system for winter by removing water from the system. Commonly used in temperate climates where freezing temperatures in winter will burst pipes, fittings, or any device filled with water. This is commonly accomplished by forcing air through the system with a compressor, by allowing automatic drains at low points on pipes to drain, or by opening manual drains by hand.

winterizing *See winterize.*

winterkill Plants that die as a result of exposure to cold **winter** conditions.

winter solstice The shortest day of the year with the least amount of daylight hours. This day marks when **winter** officially begins. It is on or near December 21 or 22 in the northern hemisphere and about June 22 in the southern hemisphere.

wiper seal With regard to landscape sprinklers, **pop-up head**s that have a special seal preventing contaminants from being pulled into the head as it is retracted from extension.

wire basket In landscape construction and plant nursery stock, a steel mesh of wire holding in place a root ball of a plant. It usually has burlap or some other decomposable material inside the basket to assist in keeping soil in place around the roots. Wire baskets are usually left in place when transplanted. In planting, the upper portion of burlap or similar material should be folded back along with the wire to about one-third of the top of the root ball.

wire mesh A web of wires arranged at right angles to each other in sheets or rolls; often used as reinforcement in concrete or masonry.

wire nut A connector for small wires consisting of an insulating cap over a threaded metal insert. It is used by inserting wires stripped of insulation and turning until tight. It is best to twist wires together before inserting them into the nut. For waterproof coverings of connections, a variety of grease-filled caps may be used over the wire nut.

wire size The area of an electrical conductor in section perpendicular to its length. In the United States, this is usually referred to by sizes determined by the American Wire Gauge (AWG) or thousand circular mills (MCM).

wireworm A waxy, yellow worm about 1 in long that cuts roots, eats seeds, and bores into large roots, stems, and bulbs. The adult is a beetle.

witches'-broom Abnormal growth of plants with much branching; often caused by viruses of fungi.

withe **1.** A one-masonry-unit thick wall. **2.** A flexible twig used to tie roof thatching, as on some beach shade structures, etc.

wither To dry up and reduce in size by shriveling.

WOG A designation for plumbing components that are of sufficient quality to be rated for use with water, oil, or gas systems.

wood The **xylem** portion of a plant.

wood ashes The residue of burned wood. It is sometimes used as a **fertilizer**. It is highly alkaline and should not be used on alkaline soils or acid-loving plants. It supplies potassium in the forms of potash with a content varying from 5 to 25%. It contains about 30 to 35% lime and 2% phosphoric acid (**NPK** 0-2-5–25).

woodland A land area covered with woody vegetation (especially trees).

wood preservative Preservatives include tar, creosote, pitch, sodium fluoride, etc.

woods **1. Woodland. 2.** A reference to types of wood in lumber, such as pine, oak, etc.

wood screw A screw used for driving into wood or a similar material and used for attaching elements to the material. *See also* **oval-head wood screw, flathead wood screw, roundhead wood screw.**

woody Containing **wood** or wood fibers.

woolly In botanical terms, clothed with long and tangled soft hairs.

work **1.** Labor in construction, maintenance, production, etc. **2.** The finished or uncompleted product of a construction effort.

working drawings Finished drawings meant for construction use.

working pressure **1.** The water **pressure** exerted within a sprinkler pipe while one or more valves or heads allow water to escape. **2.** The maximum internal water pressure designed for a system to prevent damage.

workmen's compensation insurance *or* **workers compensation insurance** Insurance covering liability of an employer to employees for compensation of injury, sickness, disease, or death arising from work while employed.

worm Any of numerous, long, soft-bodied animals. *See also* **earthworm**.

worm fence *See* **zigzag fence**.

worms *See* **earthworms**.

woven-wire reinforcement *See* **welded-wire fabric**.

WP **1.** On drawings, abbreviation for waterproof. **2.** Abbreviation for weatherproof.

wrack **1.** The lowest grade of softwood. **2.** A cull.

wrecking The act of demolishing a structure.

wrought Objects that have been beat with a hammer to shape them.

wrought iron A commercially pure iron valued for its corrosion resistance and used for water pipes, water tank plates, forged work, etc.

wrought-iron fence Fencing made of **wrought iron** that usually has a decorative character (often with curved embellishments) but is minimally made up of **post**s, **rail**s, and vertical members that are often pointed.

wrt Abbreviation for **wrought**.

WT Abbreviation for watertight.

wt., Wt Abbreviation for weight.

wwf Abbreviation for welded wire fabric.

wwm Abbreviation for **welded wire mesh**.

wye A fitting for pipes allowing three pipes to be connected at an angle smaller than 90° forming a Y shape.

wye fitting *See* **Y-fitting**.

wye level A surveyor's leveling instrument with a telescope and spirit level, mounted in Y-shaped supports. It is useful for the measurement of differences in elevation.

wythe *See* **withe** (1).

x A symbol indicating a hybrid cross of two genetically different plants.

xanthophyll The yellow to orange carotenoid pigment in leaves, evident when **chlorophyll** is not present in a leaf or plant part.

xeric **1.** Descriptive of a plant requiring little water for survival. **2.** An area or soil that is deficient in moisture or is formed with little moisture (arid or desert). **3.** An extremely dry **habitat** or **ecosystem** such as a desert.

xerigation Minimizing irrigation with direct slow application of water to plants usually with a **drip irrigation** system.

xeriophytic In botanical terms, growing in dry situations and able to survive with little moisture.

xeriscape **1.** Any landscape requiring little water. The art of this type of landscape design is to make it pleasing for the user or viewer without lush **plant material**. **2.** Landscape design and landscape maintenance principles that promote good horticultural practices and efficient use of water. The term *xeriscape* is a registered trademark of the National Xeriscape Council. The meaning is there promoted as water-conserving, drought-tolerant landscaping.

xero- A Greek prefix that means dry, useful in botanical terms.

xeromorphic A plant that has the form or appearance of a **xerophyte** because it has some adaptation to reduce transpiration or survive desiccation.

xerophyte A plant that is adapted for life and growth with a limited water supply, usually by limiting its transpiration rate, or having extra water storage available within the plant. They are well suited to xerigation. An example of such a plant is a cactus.

xfer Abbreviation for transfer.

xfmr Abbreviation for transformer.

X HVY, xhvy Abbreviation for extra heavy.

XL Abbreviation for extra large.

XXH Abbreviation for double extra heavy.

xylem **1.** In woody plants, the inner portion of the **cambium** layer (live conductive tissue) and the woody portion to the center of the **stem**. This layer conducts water and some nutrients to other portions of the plant. This is the supporting structure of woody plants. **2.** The **vascular tissue** in any plant conducting water and nutrients primarily from the roots to the shoot and leaves. *See also* **phloem**.

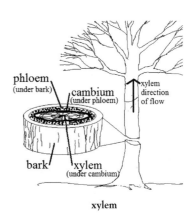

xylem

Y

Y Abbreviation for **wye**.

yard **1.** The outside area around a building. In commercial buildings, it is usually in reference to an outside storage or work area. In residential buildings, it is usually in reference to any area immediately surrounding the house. In land planning, it is usually made to a particular side of the building such as a side yard, front yard, or backyard. **2.** English or U.S. length measurement equal to 3 ft, or 36 in, or 0.9144 **ms**. Abbreviation is shown as **yd**.

yardage **1.** The cubic yards excavated or filled. **2.** An area expressed in square yards.

Y-branch *or* **wye branch** A pipe fitting branch in the shape of the letter Y.

yd. Abbreviation for **yard**(s).

yd^2 Abbreviation for **square yard**(s).

yd^3 Abbreviation for cubic yards. A cubic yard is a volume equal to a cube with each side measuring 3 ft and comprised of 27 **c.f.**

year ring *See* **annual ring**.

yellowing A loss of **chlorophyll** in a plant or its leaves caused by lack of water, plant diseases, or a fungi that is yellow in color.

yellow pine A hard, resinous wood used as flooring and in general construction.

yelm A bundle of reeds or straw used as thatching for a roof.

yet A term for a massive gate.

Y-fitting *or* **wye fitting** A pipe fitting, connecting pipes in a Y shape.

yoke The horizontal member forming the rough framing of a window, door, or other opening in a wood-framed wall.

yr Abbreviation for year.

Y-strainer *or* **wye filter** A device in the shape of a Y passing fluid through a strainer or filter before allowing it to enter the rest of a pipe system to remove particles or debris.

Z

zenith The point that is directly overhead to an observer.

zenith angle An angle formed between a line from the earth's center to a point directly overhead and a beam of incoming solar radiation. The angle created at this intersection is dependent upon the date and location of the measurement on the earth's surface.

zero-slump concrete Freshly mixed concrete with little water so it has no measurable slump.

zigzag fence A fence constructed of split rails that (in plan) alternates direction.

zinc **1.** A **micronutrient** found in soils that is necessary for plant growth. It assists in formation of growth-promoting substances in the plant. **2.** A blue, white, or bluish-white metallic substance that is malleable when pure but in the most available form is rather brittle at normal temperatures and becomes malleable when heated. It is often used to prevent rusting or disintegration of iron or steel by coating them with this material in galvanizing.

zinc chloride A caustic salt used as a wood preservative or as a drying agent.

zinc chromate *or* **zinc yellow** A yellow pigment used in paints and primers to inhibit rust.

zonal A soil, or relating to a soil or major soil group, characterized by well-developed features from climate and organisms, especially vegetation.

zonation A visible progression of plant or animal communities in response to water depth changes or other environmental factors.

zone **1.** In **sprinkler irrigation**, an area of landscape watered by one sprinkler valve. It may also be referred to as a **station** or a **circuit**. **2.** An area of land with similar normal annual temperatures in each season, allowing for the likelihood of certain plants being **hardy** to that area. **3.** A designation for allowable land uses given by a governing body having jurisdiction over such affairs with regard to a specific area of land.

zoological garden A park containing plant material, but primarily designed for exhibiting wild animals.

Z tie A Z-shaped reinforcing strip useful as a support bracket, tied (fastened) to a structural wall to a **masonry** veneer.

zygomorphic In botanical terms, capable of division into two symmetrical halves when cut lengthwise through the **axis** (middle or center).

zygote With regard to plants, a fertilized egg becoming an **embryo** in a **seed**.

APPENDIX

The meaning of botanical names other than the genus is often of interest and broadens one's understanding. They can be helpful in revealing a plant's area of native habitat and some significant feature that set a plant apart from other closely related plants, and they allow one to better identify or remember the plant. For those reasons, the meaning of some botanical names are provided below. Those reflecting the names of people and those used for genus are not listed. This is not a comprehensive list, but covers many of the most common names.

abbreviatus   shortened, abbreviated

abellophyllum   shrubs in the olive family

abrotanifolius, abrotanifolia, abrotanifolium   having leaves that resemble Southernwood

abruptus   abrupt

abyssinicus, abyssinica, abyssinicum   native of Abyssinia (Ethiopia)

acanthifolius, acanthifolia, acanthifolium   having leaves that resemble those of *Acanthus*

acaulis, acaule   stemless or almost stemless

acephalus, acephala, acephalum   without a head

acer, acris, acre   sharply pointed, or sharp and shocking to the taste

acerifolius, acerifolia, acerifolium   having leaves like a maple (acer)

acerosus   needle-shaped

achilleifolius, achilleifolia, achilleifolium   foliage like yarrow (*Achillea millefolium*)

acicularis, aciculare   needle-like, long, narrow, and pointed

acidissimus, acidissima, acidissimum   harshly acidic or sour

acidosis, acidosa, acidosum   acid or sour

aconitifolius, aconitifolia, aconitifolium   having leaves resembling monkshood (*Aconitum*) leaves

aculeatissimus, aculeatissima, aculeatissimum   tapered with a long, narrow point

aculeatus, aculeata, aculeatum   prickly

acuminatifolius, acuminatifolia, acuminatifolium   having leaves tapered to long, narrow points

acutangulus, acutangula, acutangulum   having sharp angles

acutifolius, acutifolia, acutifolium   having sharply pointed leaves

acutilobus, acutiloba, acutilobum   having sharp-pointed lobes

acutipetalus, acutipetala, acutipetalum   having sharp-pointed petals

acutissimus, acutissima, acutissimum   sharply pointed to an extreme; very acute

acutus, acuta, acutum   sharply pointed

adenophorus   bearing glands

adiantifolius, adiantifolia, adiantifolium
foliage like the Maidenhair fern (*Adiantum*)

adiantoides   like the Maidenhair fern
(*Adiantum*)

adnatus, adnata, adnatum   united, joined,
or attached

adonidifolius, adonidifolia, adonidifolium
foliage like that of *Adonis*

adpressus, adpressa, adpressum   pressed
together

adscendens, adscending   pointing or
moving upward

adsurgens   rising in an upright form, ascending

aduncus   hooked

aegyptiacus, aegyptiaca, aegyptiacum;
aegypticus, aegyptica, aegypticum
Egyptian

aequalis, aequale   equal

aequilobus, aequiloba, aequilobum
equally lobed

aequitrilobus, aequitriloba,
aequitrilobum   having three lobes that are
equal

aesculifolius, aesculifolia, aesculifolium
having leaves similar to a buckeye or horse
chestnut (*Aesculus*)

aestivalis, aestivale   of summer

aestivus, aestiva, aestivum   developing or
becoming ripened in summer

aethiopicus, aethiopica, aethiopicum
African or Ethiopian

aetnensis, aetnense   of Mount Etna, in Sicily

affinis, affine   related or similar to; of, or
related

africanus, africana, africanum   African

agavoides   resembling an *Agave*

ageratifolius, ageratifolia, ageratifolium
having leaves like *Ageratum*

ageratoides   resembling *Ageratum*

aggregatus, aggregate, aggregatum
grouped or clustered

agrarius, agraria, agrarium   associated with
fields

agrestis, agreste   of the fields

agrifolius, agrifolia, agrifolium   having
rough leaves

aizoides   resembling *Aizoon*

alabamensis, alabamense   from Alabama

alatus, alata, alatum   winged

albescens   whitish, or becoming white

albicans   off-white, becoming white

albicaulis   having white stems

albidus, albida, albidum   whitish, or white

albiflorus   white-flowered

albifrons   having white fronds

albiplenus, albiplena, albiplenum   having
double white flowers

albispinus, albispina, albispinum   having
white spines

albomaculatus, albomaculata,
albomaculatum   spotted with white

albopictus, albopicta, albopictum   painted
with white

albopilosus, albopilosa, albopilosum
white and hairy

alboplenus, alboplena, alboplenum   having
double white flowers

albovariegatus, albovariegata, albovariegatum   white variegations

albus, alba, album   white

alcicornia   elk-horned

aldenhamensis, aldenhamense   began at Aldenham, a garden near London, England

aleppicus, aleppica, aleppicum   of Aleppo (Haleb), Syria

aletris   blazing star

alexandrae   from Alexandria, Egypt

algeriensis, algeriense   of Algeria

alleghaniensis, alleghaniense   of the Allegheny mountain area

alliaceus, alliacea, alliaceum   onion-like flavor, scent, or resemblance

alnifolius, alnifolia, alnifolium   having leaves like alder

aloides or alooides   *Aloe*

aloifolius, aloifolia, aloifolium   having leaves like *Aloe*

alpestris, alpestre   of mountains at altitudes most often below timberline; nearly alpine

apicola   mountain dweller

alpinus, alpina, alpinum   of mountains at altitudes most often above timberlne; alpine

alternifolia   alternate-leaved

altissima   tallest

amarus, amara, amarum   bitter

amazonicus, amazonica, amazonicum   of the Amazon river area

ambiguus, ambigua, ambiguum   doubtful, ambiguous, vague, unsure

ambrosioides   looking like *Ambrosia*

amelloides   looking like amellus

americanus, americana, americanum   of North or South America

amethystinus, amethystina, amethystinum   amethyst colored (violet-colored)

ammophilus, ammophila, ammophilum   loving sand

amoenus, amoena, amoenum   pleasing

ampelopsis   woody vines

amphibious, amphibia, amphibium   able to grow on land and in water

amplexicaulis, amplexicaule, amplexicaulum   grasping

amplexifolius, amplexifolia, amplexifolium   grasping

amurenis, amurene   from the Amur river area

amygdaliformis, amygdaliforme   shaped like an almond

amygdalinus, amygdalina, amygdalinum   almond-like

amygdaloides   looking like an almond

anacanthus, anacantha, anacanthum   without thorns

anacardioides   looking like the cashew nut tree (*Anacardium*)

anagyroides   looking like *Anagyris*

anceps   two-headed, two-edged

anglicus   English from England

angularis, angulare   angular

angulatus, angulata, angulatum   angular, angled

angulosus, angulosa, angulum having many corners or angles

angustifolius, angustifolia, angustifolium having narrow leaves

anisatus, anisata, anisatum like anise

anisodorus, anisodora, anisodorum like anise

anisophyllus, anisophylla, anisophyllum having pairs of leaves, one larger than the other

annularis, annulare ring-like

annulatis, annulata, annulatum with rings

annuus, annua, annuum annual

anopetalus erect-petals

antarcticus, antarctica, antarcticum associated with the South Pole region

anthemoides resembling *Anthemis* (chamomile)

anthyllidifolius, anthyllidifolia, anthyllidifolium having leaves similar to Anthyllis

antiquorum of the ancients

antirrhiniflorus, antirrhiniflora, antirrhiniflorum having flowers like a snapdragon (*Antirrhinum*)

antirrhinoides looking like snapdragons (*Antirrhinum*)

apenninus, apennina, apenninum from the Apennine mountains

apertus, aperta, apertum bare, exposed, uncovered, showing, or open; not having petals

apetalus, apetala, apetalum not having petals

aphyllus, aphylla, aphyllum not having or apparently not having leaves

apiculatus, apiculate, apiculatum having a small usually sharp point

apifolius, apifolia, apifolium having foliage similar to celery

appendiculatus, appendiculata, appendiculatum having appendages

appressus, appressa, appressum pressed against

apricus, aprica, apricum loving the sun

apterus, aptera, apterum not having wings

aquaticus, aquatica, aquaticum; aquatilus, aquatile growing in or next to water

arabicus, arabica, arabicum; arabus, araba, arabum Arabian

arachnoides, arachnoideus, arachnoidea, arachnoideum with hairs like a spiderweb

araliifolius, araliifolia, araliifolium having leaves like *Aralia*

arborescens, arborus, arborea, arboreum somewhat like, or much like, a tree

arbusculus, arbuscula, arbusculum much like a small tree

arbutifolius, arbutifolia, arbutifolium having leaves looking like those of *Arbutus*

arcticus, arctica, arcticum from the North Pole region

arcuatus, arcuata, arcuatum curved, arched, or bent

ardens glowing

arenarius, arenaria, arenarium loving sand

argenteoguttatus, argenteoguttata, argenteoguttatum spotted with silver argenteomarginatus, argenteomarginata, argenteomarginatum   silver edged

argenteovariegatus, argenteovariegata, argenteovariegatum   having silver variegations

argenteus, argentua, argenteum   silvery

argentinus, argentina, argentinum   of Argentina

argutus, arguta, argutum   having sharp teeth or notches

argyraeus, argyraea, argyraeum   silvery

argyrites   having silver specks

argyrocomus, argyrocoma, argyrocomum   having silvery hairs

argyroneurus, argyroneura, argyroneurum   having silvery veins

argyrophyllus, argyrophylla, argyrophyllum   having silvery leaves

aridus, arida, aridum   growing in dry places

arifolius, arifolia, arifolium   having leaves like *Arum*

ariifolius, ariifolia, ariifolium   having leaves like *Sorbus aria*

aristatus, aristate, aristatum   having a beard or bristles

arizonicus, arizonica, arizonicum   of Arizona

armatus, armata, armatum   thorny, spiny, or with bristles

armeniacus, armeniaca, armeniacum   of Armenia

arnoldianus, arnoldiana, arnoldianum   from Arnold Arboretum, near Boston, Massachusetts

aromaticus, aromatica, aromaticum   aromatic or fragrant or sweet smelling

artemisioides   looking like *Artemisia*

articulatus, articulata, articulatum   having joints

arundinaceus, arundinacea, arundinaceum   reed-like

arvensis, arvense   of cultivated fields

asarifolius, asarifolia, asarifolium   having leaves like wild ginger (*Asarum*)

ascendens   sloping upward

asiaticus, asiatica, asiaticum   Asian

asper, aspera, asperum   rough, course

asperatus, asperata, asperatum   roughened, bumpy, jagged

aspericaulis, aspericaule   having rough stems

asperifolius, asperifolia, asperifolium   having rough leaves

asperrimus, asperrima, asperrimum   extremely rough or bumpily jagged

asphodeloides   looking like asphodel (*Asphodelus*)

asplenifolius, asplenifolia, asplenifolium   having leaves looking like those of spleenwort (*Asplenium*)

assurgens   ascending

assurgentiflorus, assurgentiflora, assurgentiflorum   having flowers in ascending clusters

asteroides   looking like *Asters*

astilboides   looking like *Astilbe*

asturicus, asturica, asturicum; asturiensis, asturiense   from Asturia, Spain

atlanticus, atlantica, atlanticum from areas close to the Atlantic Ocean or the Atlas Mountains, North Africa

atratus, atrata, atratum blackened

atriplicifolius, atriplicifolia, atriplicifolium having leaves like *Atriplex*

atropurpureus, atropurpurea, atropurpureum dark purple

atrorubens dark red

atrosanguineus, atrosanguinea, atrosanguineum dark blood red

atroviolaceus, atroviolacea, atroviolaceum dark violet

atrovirens dark green

attenuatus, attenuate, attenuatum narrowing to a point

aubrietioides looking like *Aubrieta*

augustifolium having foliage

augustissimus, augustissima, augustissimum majestic, outstanding, or prominent

augustus, augusta, augustum majestic, outstanding

aurantiacus, aurantiaca, aurantiacum; aurantius, aurantia, aurantium having an orange color

aurantifolius, aurantifolia, aurantifolium having leaves resembling orange (*Citrus aurantium*) plants

auratus, aurata, auratum decorated with gold

aureomaculatus, aureomaculata, aureomaculatum gold spots

aureomarginatus, aureomarginata, aureomarginatum having edges with gold

aureoreticulatus, aureoreticulata, aureoreticulatum having gold veins

aureovariegatus, aureovariegata, aureovariegatum having variegations of gold

aureus, aurea, aureum golden

auricomus, auricoma, auricomum having golden hairs

auriculatus, auriculate, auriculatum having an ear-like appendage or appendages

australiensis, australiense Australian

australis, australe southern

austriacus, austriaca, austriacum Austrian

autumnalis, autumnale of autumn

axillaries, axillare carried or produced in axils

axillary in an axil

azaleoides looking like azaleas

azoricus, azorica, azoricum of the Azores

azureus, azurea, azureum sky-blue, azure

babylonicus, babylonica, babylonicum from Babylonia

baccans berry-like or having berries

baccatus, baccata, baccatum berry-like

baccifer, baccifera, bacciferum bearing berries

bacillaris, bacillare stick-like

balcanicus, balcanica, balcanicum of the Balkan Peninsula

baldensis, baldense from Monte Baldo, Italy

balearicus, balearica, balearicum of the Balearic Islands

balsameus, balsamea, balsameum of balsam

balsamiferus, balsamifera, balsamiferum bearing balsam

balticus, baltica, balticum of the Baltic Sea area

bambusoides looking like bamboo

banaticus, banatica, banaticum of Banat, Romania

barbadenis, barbadense of Barbados, West Indies

barbatus, barbata, barbatum having beard-like long, weak hairs; bearded; barbed

barbigerus, barbigera, barbigerum possessing barbs or beards

barbinervis, barbinerve with barbed or bearded veins

barbulatus, barbulata, barbulatum lightly bearded or having a beard with short hairs

baselloides looking like *Basella*

basilaris, basilare concerning the base

basilicus, basilica, basilicum royal, princely, imperial

batatas the Carib Indian name for sweet potato

bavaricus, bavarica, bavaricum from Bavaria

belgicus, belgica, belgicum of Belgium or the Netherlands

belladonna beautiful lady (referring to the plant historically used to beautify the eyes)

bellidifolius, bellidifolia, bellidifolium having leaves like *Bellis*

bellidiformis, bellidiforme with the form of a daisy (*Bellis*)

bellidoides looking like *Bellium*

bellus, bella, bellum beautiful

benedictus, benedicta, benedictum blessed, having a good reputation

bengalenis, bengalense of Bengal, India; also spelled benghalensis

bermudianus, bermudiana, bermudianum of Bermuda

berolinensis, berolinense of Berlin, Germany

bessarabicus, bessarabica, bessarabicum of Bessarabia

betaceus, betacea, betaceum looking like beets

betonicifolius, betonicifolia, betonicifolium having leaves like betony (*Stachys betonica*)

betulifolius, betulifolia, betulifolium having leaves like a birch (*Betula*)

betulinus, betulina, betulinum betuloides, looking like bling birch (*Betula*)

bicolor of two colors

bicornis, bicorne; bicornutus, bicornuta, bicornutum having two horns

bidentaltus, bidentalta, bidentaltum with two teeth

biennis, bienne biennial

bifidus, bifida, bifidum divided into two parts; twice cut

biflorus, biflora, biflorum having twinned flowers

bifolius, bifolia, bifolium having twinned leaves

bifurcatus, bifurcate, bifurcatum forked with two usually almost equal branches; twice forked

bignonioides   like *Bignonia*

bijugus, bijuga, bijugum   two pairs united

bipinnatus, bipinnata, bipinnatum   twice-pinnate

bisectus, bisecta, bisectum   two equal parts

biserratus, biserrata, biserratum   two teeth

biternatus, biternata, biternatum   having three divisions

bivalves, bivalve   having two valves

blandus, blanda, blandum   mild, pleasant, bland

blepharophyllus, blepharophylla, blepharophyllum   leaves fringed like eyelashes

bolivianus, boliviana, bolivianum   of Bolivia

bombycinus, bombycina, bombycinum   silky

bonariensis, bonariense   from Buenos Aires, Argentina

borbonicus, borbonica, borbonicum   from Reunion Island, formerly Bourbon.

borealis, boreale   northern

borinquenus, borinquena, borinquenum   of Puerto Rico (formerly called Borinquen)

borneensis, borneense   of Borneo

botryoides   resembling a bunch of grapes, a cluster

brachiatus, brachiata, brachiatum   branching nearly at right angles

brachyanthus, brachyantha, brachyanthum   having short flowers

brachybotrys   short-clustered

brachycarpus, brachycarpa, brachy-carpum   having short fruits

brachycerus, brachycera, brachycerum   short-horned

brachypetalus, brachypetala, brachypetalum   short-petaled

brachyphyllus, brachyphylla, brachyphyllum   having short leaves

brachysiphon   having short tubes

bracteatus, bracteata, bracteatum   with bracts

bracteosus, bracteosa, bracteosum   having conspicuous bracts

brasiliensis, brasiliense   from Brazil

brassicifolius, brassicifolia, brassicifolium   having leaves like cabbage (*Brassica*)

brevicaulis   short-stemmed, brief stems

brevifolius, brevifolia, brevifolium   having short leaves

brevipedunculatus, brevipedunculata, brevipedunculatum   having a short flower stalk (peduncle)

brevipes   short-footed, or short (brief) stalked

brevis, breve   short

breviscapus, breviscapa, breviscapum   having a short flower stalk (scape)

brevistylus, brevistyle   having a short style

brilliantissimus   brilliant to a maximum

britannicus, britannica, britannicum   of Great Britain

briziformis, briziforme; brizoides   like quaking grass (*Briza*)

bronchialis, bronchiale   for treating bronchitis

bryoides   moss-like

buccinatorius, buccinatoria, buccinatorium; buccinatus, buccinata, buccinatum resembling a crooked horn

buddleoides like *Buddleia*

bulbifer, bulbifera, bulbiferum having bulbs

bulbiformis, bulbiforme bulb-shaped

bulbosus, bulbosa, bulbosum bulbous or quite swollen

bulgaricus, bulgarica, bulgaricum from Bulgaria

bullatus, bullata, bullatum blistered or puckered (bullate)

burmanicus, burmanica, burmanicum from Burma, now Myanmar

buxifolius, buxifolia, buxifolium having leaves like boxwood (*Buxus*)

byzantinus, byzantina, byzantinum from Istanbul (Byzantium)

cachemiricus, cachemirica, cachemiricum from Kashmir

caerulescens turning blue, or bluish

caeruleus, caerulea, caerulum dark blue

caesius, caesia, caesium bluish-gray

caespitosus, caespitosa, caespitosum clump making

calabricus, calabrica, calabricum of Calabria, Italy

calamifolius, calamifolia, calamifolium with reed-like foliage

calathinus, calathina, calathinum basket-like

calcaratus, calcarata, calcaratum having spurs

calcareous, calcarea, calcareum loving lime

calcicola growing in soil with lime

calendulaceus, calendulacea, calendulaceum orange-colored as with flowers of *Calendula*

californicus, californica, californicum of California

callianthus, calliantha, callianthum having beautiful flowers

callicarpus, callicarpa, callicarpum having beautiful fruit

callimorphus, callimorpha, callimorphum beautifully made or shaped

callistachyus, callistachya, callistachyum beautiful spikes

callistegiodes like *Calystegia*

callizonus, callizona, callizonum having beautiful bands or zones

callosus, callosa, callosum calloused, tough-surfaced, or thick-skinned

calocephalus, calocephala, calocephalum having a beautiful head

calophyllus, calophylla, calophyllum with beautiful leaves

calycinus, calycina, calycinum calyx-like

cambricus, cambrica, cambricum of Wales (Cambria)

camelliflorus, camelliflora, camelliflorum with flowers like *Camellia*

campaniflorus, campaniflora, campaniflorum flowers shaped like bells

campanuloides like *Campanula*

campestris, campestre of the fields, or plains

camphorates, camphorate, camphoratum
like camphor, or associated with camphor

campylocarpus, campylocarpa, campylocarpum   with curved or bent fruits

camtschatcensis, camtschatcense; camtschaticus, camtschatica, camtschaticum   of Kamchatka

canadensis, canadense   of Canada

canaliculatus, canaliculata, canaliculatum   grooved

canariensis, canariense   from the Canary Islands

cancellatus, cancellata, cancellatum
latticed or crossed

candelabrum   candelabra-like

candicans   shining or wooly-white

candidissimus, candidissima, candidissimum   very white

candidus, candida, candidum   shining or pure white

canescens   having off-white or whitish-gray hairs

caninus, canina, caninum   pertaining to dogs or inferior

cannifolius, cannifolia, cannifolium
having leaves like *Canna*

cantabricus, cantabrica, cantabricum
from Cantabria, Spain, or the Cantabrian mountains of Spain

cantabrigiensis, cantabrigiense   from Cambridge, England

capensis, capense   from the Cape of Good Hope, South Africa

caperatus, caperata, caperatum   wrinkled

capilliformis, capilliforme   hair-like

capitatus, capitata, capitatum   having dense heads

cappadocicus, cappadocica, cappadocicum   of eastern Asia Minor (Cappadocia)

capreolatus, capreolata, capreolatum
having tendrils

capreus, caprea, capreum   relating to goats

capsular, capsulare   resembling capsules

cardaminifolius, cardaminifolia, cardaminifolium   having leaves like *Cardamine*

cardinalis, cardinale   bright red, cardinal red

carduaceus, carduacea, carduaceum
like a thistle

cardunculus, carduncula, cardunculum
resembling a small thistle

caribaeus, caribea, caribaeum   from the Caribbean region

carinatus, carinata, carinatum   keeled

carinthiacus, carinthiaca, carinthiacum
from Carinthia (Austria)

carminatus   Carmine

carmineus, carminea, carmineum
carmine

carneus, carnea, carneum   flesh colored pink

carnosus, carnosa, carnosum   fleshy

carolinianus, caroliniana, carolinianum; carolinensis, carolinense; carolinus, carolina, carolinum   from North or South Carolina

carpaticus, carpatica, carpaticum
carpathicus of the Carpathian Mountains

carpenteria   *Philadelphus*-like shrub

carpinifolius, carpinifolia, carpinifolium
with hornbeam-like leaves

carthusianorum   from monks of the
Carthusian Monastery of Grande Chartreuse
of Grenoble, France

cartilaginous, cartilaginea, cartilagineum
like cartilage

caryophyllus, caryophylla, caryophyllum
having an aromatic smell like walnut leaves, or
cloves

**cashmerianus, cashmeriana,
cashmerianum**   from Kashmir

castaneus, castanea, castaneum
chestnut-colored

catalpifolius, catalpifolia, catalpifolium
with leaves like *Catalpa*

cataractae; cataractarum   from a waterfall
or waterfalls

catawbiensis, catawbiense   from the
Catawba area of the Blue Ridge Mountains of
North America

catharticus, cathartica, catharticum   with
purgative qualities

cathayanus, cathayana, cathayanum
from China (Cathay)

caucasicus, caucasica, caucasicum   from
the Caucasus

caudatus, caudata, caudatum   having a
tail or tails

caulescens   stemmed

cauliflorus, cauliflora, cauliflorum   having
flowers on the trunk or stem

cavus, cava, cavum   hollow

centifolius, centifolia, centifolium   having
many leaves

**centranthifolius, cetranthifolia,
centranthifolium**   having leaves like
Centranthus

cephalatus   bearing heads

**cephalonicus, cephalonica,
cephalonicum**   from the island of
Cephalonia in Greece

cephalotes   like a small herd

cerasifer, cerasifera, cerasiferum
cherry-like fruits

cerasiformis, cerasifore   shape resembling
cherries

cerifer, cerifera, ceriferum   waxy

cerinthoides   looking like *Cerinthe*

cernuus, cernua, cernuum   dropping

**chalcedonicus, chalcedonica, chal-
cedonicum**   Chalcedon (Asia Minor)

**chamaedrifolius, chamaedrifolia,
chamaedrifolium**   with leaves like
chamaedrys

**chasmanthus, chasmantha, chasman-
thum**   having wide-open, gaping flowers

cheilanthus, cheilantha, cheilanthum
having lipped flowers

chelidonoides   looking like *Chelidonium*

chilensis, chilense   from Chile

chiloensis, chiloense   from Chiloe Island,
off the coast of Chile

chinensis, chinene   Chinese

chionanthus, chionantha, chionanthum
having snow-white flowers

chlorochilon   with a green lip

chromatella   with color

chrysanthoides   looking like *Chrysanthemum*

chrysanthus, chrysantha, chrysanthum   with golden flowers

chrysocarpus, chrysocarpa, chrysocarpum   with golden fruit

chrysocomus, chrysocoma, chrysocomum   having golden hair

chrysolepis, chrysolepe   having golden scales

chrysoleucus, chrysoleuca, chrysoleucum   gold with white

chrysophyllus, chrysophylla, chrysophyllum   golden-leaved

cichoriaceus, cichoriacea, cichoriaceum   looking like chicory (*Cichorium*)

cicutifolius, cicutifolia, cicutifolium   having leaves like water-hemlock (*Cicuta*)

ciliata   margins with hairs, fringed

circinata   coiled

cirrose   bearing a tendril

cistiflorus, cistiflora, cistiflorum   having flowers like *Cistus*

cistifolius, cistifolia, cistifolium   having leaves like *Cistus*

citratus, citrate, citratum   looking like *Citrus*

citrifolius, citrifolia, citrifolium   having leaves resembling *Citrus*

citriniflorus, citriniflora, citriniflorum   having lemon-yellow flowers

citrinus, citrina, citrinum   lemon or yellow color or like a lemon

citriodorus, citriodora, citriodorum   lemon-scented

citroides   looking like *Citrus*

clandestinus, clandestina, clandestinum   hidden

clausus, clausa, clausum   closed

clavatus, clavata, clavatum   club-shape

clavellatus, clavellata, clavellatum   a small club shape

clematideus, clematidea, clematideum   looking like *Clematis*

clethroides   looking like *Clethra*

clypeatus, clypeata, clypeatum   with the shape of a Roman shield

clypeolatus, clypeolata, clypeolatum   shield-shaped

cneorum   *Daphne*, low evergreen shrubs

cocciferus, coccifera, cocciferum   having berries, or host to berry-like scale insects

coccineus, coccinea, coccineum   bright red

cochlearifolius, cochlearifolia, cochlearifolium   having leaves like *Cochlearia*

cochlearis, cochleare   spoon-shaped

cochleatus, cochleata, cochleatum   spiral shaped like the shell of a snail

coelestinus, coelestina, coelestinum; coelestis, coeleste   sky-blue

coerulescens   bluish or turning blue

coeruleus, coerulea, coeruleum   blue

cognatus, cognata, cognatum   closely related

colchicus, colchica, colchicum   from Colchis, near the Black Sea

collinus, collina, collinum from the hills

coloratus, colorata, coloratum colored

columbarius, columbaria, columbarium having to do with doves, or dove-like

columbianus, columbiana, columbianum from British Columbia or the Columbia River area

columnaris, columnare columnar

comatus, comata, comatum having a tuft

commelina plants like wandering Jew

commixtus, commixta, commixtum mixed

communis, commune common, general, or communal in habit

commutatus, commutata, commutatum changed or changing

comosus, comosa, comosum with a tuft, or long hair

compactus, compacta, compactum compact, dense

complantus, complanta, complantum flat

complexus, complexa, complexum complex, embraced, or circled

complicatus, complicate, complicatum complicated

compositus, composita, compositum compound, several parts

compressus, compressa, compressum compressed

concavus, concave, concavum hollowed, indented

conchifolius, conchifolia, conchifolium having leaves like seashells

concinnus, concinna, concinnum neat or elegant

concolor of one color, uniform in color

condensatus, condensata, condensatum; condensus, condensa, condensum crowded

confertiflorus, confertiflora, confertiflorum with crowded, pressed together, dense flowers

confertus, conferta, confertum crowded or dense

conformis, conforma, conformus to type; or similar to related types

confusus, confusa, confusum confusing

congestus, congesta, congestum congested

conglomeratus, conglomerata, conglomeratum crowded, or dense

conjugatus, conjugata, conjugatum; conjugalis, conjugale united in twos

conjunctus, conjuncta, conjunctum united

connatus, connata, connatum twin or having opposite leaves joined at bases

consanguineus, consanguinea, consanguineum related

consolidus, consolida, consolidum solid or stable

conspersus, conspersa, conspersum scattered

conspicuus, conspicua, conspicuum conspicuous, obvious

constrictus, constricta, constrictum constricted, tight, small

contortus, contorta, contortum twisted, contorted

contractus, contracta, contractum contracted

controversus, controversa, controversum controversial

convallaroides similar to lily-of-the-valley (*Convallaria*)

convolvulaceus, convolvulacea, convolvulaceum looking like Convolvulus

copallinus, copallina, copallinum gummy or with resin

corallinus, corallina, corallinum coral-red color

corchorus plants supplying jute

cordatus, cordata, cordatum heart-shaped

cordifolius, cordifolia, cordifolium with heart-shaped leaves

cordiformis, cordiforme a heart shape

cordyline plants resembling dracaenas

coreanus, coreana, coreanum from Korea

coriaceus, coriacea, coriaceum thick, leathery, tough

coriarius, coriaria, coriarium like leather, tough

corniculatus, corniculata, corniculatum having small horns

cornutus, cornuta, cornutum horned or shaped like horns

corollatus, corollata, corollatum looking like a corolla

coronans; coronatus, coronata, coronatum crowned

coronarius, coronaria, coronarium for garlands, belonging to a crown

coronopifolius, coronopifolia, coronopifolium having leaves like *Coronopus*

corrugatus, corrugata, corrugatum wrinkled, or in folds

corsicus, corsica, corsicum from Corsica

cortusoides looking like *Cortusa*

coruscans glittering, sparkling

corylifolius, corylifolia, corylifolium having leaves like *Corylus*

corymbiflorus, corymbiflora, corymbiflorum having flowers in corymbs

corymbosus, corymbosa, corymbosum with corymbs

costatus, costata, costatum ribbed, ridges

cotinifolius, cotinifolia, cotinifolium leaves like *Cotinus*

cotinoides looking like *Cotinus*

crassicaulis, crassicaule having thick stems

crassifolius, crassifolia, crassifolium thick-leaved

crassipes thick or big stemmed, or thick or big footed

crassus, crassa, crassum thick or fleshy

crataegifolius, crataegifolia, crataegifolium with leaves resembling hawthorn (*Crataegus*)

crataegoides resembling hawthorn (*Crataegus*)

crenatiflorus, crenatiflora, crenatiflorum having scalloped flowers

crenatus, crenata, crenatum having rounded teeth or scallops

crenulatus, crenulata, crenulatum being somewhat scalloped

crepitans rustling as with leaves in wind, or crackling

cretaceus, cretacea, cretaceum chalky or having to do with chalk

cretensis, cretense; creticus, cretica, creticum from Crete

crinita with long hairs

crinitus, crinita, crinitum having long, usually weak hairs

crispatus, crispata, crispatum; crispus, crispa, crispum curling wrinkles, or crisped close stiff curls, or wavy

cristatus, cristata, cristatum with tassel-like tips, or a showy tuft; a crest; comb-like

crithmifolius, crithmifolia, crithmifoilum leaves like *Crithmum*

crocatus, crocata, crocatum; croceus, crocea, croceum orange, saffron, or yellow

crotonifolius, crotonifolia, crotonifolium having leaves looking like *Croton*

cruciatus, cruciata, cruciatum resembling the shape of a cross

cruciferus cross-bearing

cruentus, cruenta, cruentum blood coloring, bloody

crustatus incrusted

crystallinus, crystallina, crystallinum like a crystal

ctenoides like a comb

cucullaris, cucullare; cucullatus, cucullata, cucullatum hood-like

cucumerifolius, cucumerifolia, cucumer-ifolium having leaves resembling cucumber

cultratus, cultrata, cultratum; cultriformis, cultriforme shaped like a knife's blade

cuneatus, cuneata, cuneatum shaped like a wedge

cuneifolius, cuneifolia, cuneifolium with wedge-shaped leaves

cuneiformis, cuneiforme wedge shaped

cupreatus, cupreata, cupreatum; cupreus, cuprea, cupreum color of copper or coppery appearing

cupressifolius, cupressifolia, cupressifolium having leaves like cypress (*Cupressus*)

cupressiformis, cupressiforme; cupressinus, cupressina, cupressinum; cupressoides looking like cypress (*Cupressus*)

curassavicus, curassavica, curassavicum from Curacao, Netherlands

curtus, curta, curtum made short

curvatus, curvata, curvatum curved

curvifolius, curvifolia, curvifolium with curved leaves

cuspidatus, cuspidata, cuspidatum having stiff, sharp points

cuspidifolius, cuspidfolia, cuspidifolium with leaves of a stiff, sharp point

cyananthus, cyanantha, cyananthum flowers of blue

cyaneus, cyanea, cyaneum blue

cyanocarpus, cyanocarpa, cyanocarpum
with blue fruits

**cyanophyllus, cyanophylla,
cyanophyllum**   leaves of blue

cyatheoides   looking like *Cyathea*

cyclamineus, cyclaminea, cyclamineum
looking like *Cyclamen*

cyclanthera   tender vines

**cylindraceus, cylindracea, cylindraceum;
cylindricus, cylindrical, cylindricum**
cylindrical

cymbiformis, cymbiforme   shaped like a
boat

cymosus, cymosa, cymosum   with flowers
in cymes

cynaroides   looking like *Cynara*

cyprius, cypria, cyprium   from *Cyprus*

cytisoides   looking like a broom (*Cytisus*)

dacrydioides   looking like *Dacrydium*

dactylifer, dactylifera, dactyliferum
looking like fingers

dactyloides   looking like fingers, finger-like

**dahuricus, dahurica, dahuricum;
dauricus, daurica, dauricum;
davuricus, davurica, davuricum**   from
Dahuria (Siberia)

dalmaticus, dalmatica, dalmaticum   from
Dalamatia

damascenus, damascene, damascenum
of Damascus

danaeifolius, danaeifolia, danaeifolium
having leaves like *Danae*

daphnoides   looking like *Daphne*

**dasyacanthus, dasyacantha,
dasyacanthum**   thick spines

dasyanthus, dasyantha, dasyanthum
having shaggy flowers

dasycarpus, dasycarpa, dasycarpum   with
hairy fruits

dasycladus, dasyclada, dasycladum   with
shaggy branches

dasyphyllus, dasyphylla, dasyphyllum
shaggy-leaved

dasystemon   having hairy stamens

daucifolius, daucifolia, daucifolium
leaves like a carrot (*Daucus*)

dealbatus, dealbata, dealbatum   whitened,
a coating of white powder

debilis, debile   weak or frail

decandrus, decandra, decandrum   with
10 stamens

decapetalus, decapetala, decapetalum
10 petals

decaphyllus, decaphylla, decaphyllum
having 10 leaves

deciduus, decidua, deciduum   deciduous

decipiens   deceptive, cheating, not true

declinatus, declinata, declinatum
declined or bent downward

**decompositus, decomposita,
decompositum**   more than one division

**decoratus, decorata, decoratum; decorus,
decora, decorum**   decorative or becoming
decorative

decorticans   having shedding bark

decumanus, decumana, decumanum
immense, gigantic

decumbens   having trailing stems with erect tips; reclining at base with tips erect

decurrens   running or extending down the stem

decussate   alternate leaf pairs at right angles

deflexus, deflexa, deflexum   bent down

deformis, deforme   deformed, not normal in appearance or function

dejectus, dejecta, dejectum   dejected, humbled

delectus, delecta, delectum   chosen

delicatissimus, delicatissima, delicatissimum   very delicate

delicatus, delicata, delicatum   delicate

deliciosus, deliciosa, deliciosum   delicious

delphinanthus, delphinantha, delphinanthum   having flowers like *Delphinium*

delphinensis, delphinense   from Dauphine, France

delphinifolius, delphinifolia, delphinifolium   with leaves like *Delphinium*

deltoides; deltoideus, deltoida, deltoidum   triangular shaped

demersus, demersa, demersum   submerged

demissus, demissa, demissum   hanging, fragile

dendroideus, dendroidea, dendroideum   like a tree

dendrophilus, dendrophila, dendrophilum   loving trees

densatus, densata, densatum; densus, densa, densum   compact in shape; dense

densiflorus, densiflora, densiflorum   flowered densely

densifolius, densifolia, densifolium   densely leaved

dentatus, dentata, dentatum; dentifer, dentifera, dentiferum; dentosus, dentosa, dentosum   having teeth

denticulatus, denticulata, denticulatum   lightly toothed

denudatus, denudata, denudatum   naked

dependens   hanging

depressus, depressa, depressum   flat

desertorum   from a desert

deustus, deusta, deustum   burned, scorched

diabolicus, diabolica, diabolicum   devilish

diacanthus, diacantha, diacanthum   having paired spines

diandrus, diandra, diandrum   having paired or two stamens

dianthiflorus, dianthiflora, dianthiflorum   having flowers like *Dianthus*

diaphanous, diaphana, diaphanum   transparent, see-through

dichotomus, dichotoma, dichotomum   many paired forks

dichromus, dichroma, dichromum; dichrous, dichroa, dichroum   having two separate colors

dictyophyllus, dictyophylla, dictyophyllum   with leaves with obviously netted venation

didymus, didyma, didymium   paired or in twos, or stamens in twos

difformis

difformis, difforme having unusual or strange form

diffusus, diffusa, diffusum loosely spreading

digitatus, digitata, digitatum a shape like a hand that is open

dilatatus, dilatata, dilatatum; dilatus, dilata, dilatum expanded, spread apart, dilated

dimorphus, dimorpha, dimorphum with two types of flowers having leaves or fruit on a plant

dioicus, dioica, dioicum; dioecious having male and female reproductive organs on a single plant

dipetalus, dipetala, dipetalum having two petals

diphyllus, diphylla, diphyllum with two leaves or leaflets

diplotrichus, diplotricha, diplotrichum having two kinds of hair

dipterocarpus, dipterocarpa, dipterocarpum having two-winged fruits

dipterus, diptera, dipterum two-winged

disciformis, disciforme disc-shaped

discoideus, discoidea, discoideum disc-like, not having ray florets

discolor two different colors

disperses, dispersa, dispersum scattered

dissectus, dissecta, dissectum deeply cleft

dissimilis, dissimile not like those typical of the genus

dissitiflorus, dissitiflora, dissitiflorum having flowers loosely arranged

distachyus, distachya, distachyum having two spikes

distans separated with space

distichous in two vertical ranks

distichus, disticha, distichum two-ranked

distortus, distorta, distortum poorly shaped

distylus, distyla, distylum with two styles

diurnus, diurna, diurnum flowering in the day

divaricatus, divaricata, divaricatum spreading, widely

divergens spreading wide from the middle

diversicolor diverse colors

diversiflorus, diversiflora, diversiflorum diversely flowered, variable leaves

diversifolius, diversifolia, diversifolium diversely leaved

diversiformis, diversiforme having various forms

dodecandrus, dodecandra, dodecandrum 12 stamens

dolabratus, dolabrata, dolabratum; dolabriformis, dolabriforme hatchet shape

domesticus, domestica, domesticum domesticated; used as houseplants

doronicoides looking like *Doronicum*

drabifolius, drabifolia, drabifolium leaves like *Draba*

dracaenoides looking like *Dracaena*

draco pertaining to a dragon

dracocephalus, dracocephala, dracocephalum dragon head shape

dracunculoides looking like tarragon (*Artemisia dracunculus*)

dracunculus a little dragon

drupaceous, drupacea, drupaceum; drupifer, drupifera, dupiferum bearing drupes (fleshy fruits)

drynarioides the genus of ferns *Drynaria*

dryophyllus, dryophylla, dryophyllum having leaves like an oak leaf

dubius, dubia, dubium dubious, or not conforming

dulcis sweet

dumosus, dumosa, dumosum brushy or shrubby

duplex; duplicatus, duplicatum double, two

durabilis, durabile lasting, continuing

dysentericus, dysenterica, dysentericum once used to treat dysentery

ebenaceus, ebenacea, ebenaceum ebony-like

ebenus, ebena, ebenum ebony, black, dark

ebracteatus, ebracteata, ebracteatum without bracts

eburneus, eburna, eburnum ivory or white

echinatus, echinata, echinatum hedgehog-like; surfaced with prickles or spines; bristly

echinocarpus, echinocarpa, echinocarpum having prickly or spiny fruits

echinosepalus, echinosepala, echinosepalum having prickly or spiny sepals

echinospermus, echinosperma, echinospermum having prickly or spiny seeds

echioides looking like *Echium*

edulis, edulise edible

effusus, effusa, effusum straggly or loosely spreading

elaeagnifolius, elaeagnifolia, elaeagnifolium having leaves looking like those of *Elaeagnus*

elasticus, elastica, elasticum elastic

elatior taller, or higher

elatus, elata, elatum tall

elegans; elegantulus, elegantula, elegantulum elegant, beautiful

elegantissimus, elegantissima, elegantissimum more elegant

ellipsoidalis, ellipsoidale ellipsoid

ellipticus, elliptica, ellipticum elliptical

elongatus, elongata, elongatum elongated, lengthened

emarginatus, emarginata, emarginatum notched at the apex

emeticus, emetica, emeticum inducing vomiting

eminens eminent or obvious

empetrifolius, empetrifolia, empetrifolium having leaves like *Empetrum*

enneacanthus, enneacantha, enneacanthum nine spines

enneaphyllus, enneaphylla, enneaphyllum with nine leaves or leaflets

ensatus, ensata, ensatum shaped like a sword

ensifolius, ensifolia, ensifolium having sword-shaped leaves

ensiformis, ensiforme resembling a straight sword; long and pointed

entelea corkwood

epigaeus, epigaea, epigaeum growing close to the ground

equestris, equestre associated with horses

equinus, equina, equinum of horses

equisetifolius, equisetifolia, equisetifolium leaves like a horsetail (*Equisetum*)

erectus, erecta, erectum upright

eriacanthus, eriacantha, eriacanthum wooly spined

eriantherus, erianthera, eriantherum wooly anthers

erianthus, eriantha, erianthum wooly flowers

ericaeus, ericaea, ericaeum relating to heaths (*Erica*)

ericifolius, ericifolia, ericifolium having leaves like a heath (*Erica*)

ericoides looking like a heath (*Erica*)

erigenia harbinger of spring

erigenus, erigena, erigenum originated in Ireland (*Erin*)

erinaceus, erinacea, erinaceum looking like a hedgehog

eriobotryoides *Eriobotrya*

eriocarpus, eriocarpa, eriocarpum wooly fruited

eriocephalus, eriocephala, eriocephalum wooly headed

eriophorus, eriophora, eriophorum wool-bearing

eriophyllum wooly sunflowers

eriostachys a wooly spike

eriostemon a wooly stamen

erosus, erosusa, erosusum a jagged margin; edge looking as if gnawed

erraticus, erratica, erraticum unusual, sporadic, or uncommon

erubescens blushing, red, or reddish

erythrocalyx a red calyx

erythrocarpus, erythrocarpa, erythrocarpum red fruit

erythrocephalus, erythrocephala, erythrocephalum red-headed

erythropeterus, erythropetera, erythropeterum with red wings

erythrosorus, erythrosora, erythrosorum with red spore cases

esculentus, esculenta, esculentum edible or having to do with eating

etruscus, etruscum of Tuscany (Etruria), Italy

eucalyptoides looking like *Eucalyptus*

euchlorus, euchlora, euchlorum good green

eugenioides looking like *Eugenia*

eupatorioides resembling *Eupatorium*

euphorbioides resembling *Euphorbia*

europaeus, europaea, europeaum European

evectus, evecta, evectum   extended, elongated

exaltatus, exaltata, exaltatum   very tall, high

exasperatus, exasperata, exasperatum   rough

excavatus, excavata, excavatum   hollowed

excellens   excellent, excelling

excelsus, excelsa, excelsum   tall

excisus, excisa, excisum   cut out or cut from

eximius, eximia, eximium   distinguished, prominent, unusual

exoniensis, exoniense   of Exeter, England

exoticus, exotica, exoticum   foreign, not native

expansus, expansa, expansum   expanded

exsertus, exserta, exsertum   exserted, projected

extensus, extensa, extensum   extended beyond

exudans   exuding, secreting

fabaceus, fabacea, fabaceum   looking like the broad bean (*Vicia faba*); bean-like

fagifolius, fagifolia, fagifolium   leaves like a beech (*Fagus*)

falcatus, falcata, falcatum; falciformis, falciforme   shaped like a sickle

falcifolius, falcifolia, falcifolium   having leaves shaped like sickles

falciformis   sickle-shaped

fallax   false, deceptive

farinaceous, farinacea, farinaceum   mealy, grainy, floury; containing starch

farinosus, farinose, farinosum   mealy, grainy, or powdery

fascicularis, fasciculare; fasciculatus, fasciculata, fasciculatum   clustered, in a bundle

fastigiatus, fastigiata, fastigiatum   of columnar form; close erect branches; erect

fastuosus, fastuosa, fastuosum   proud, stately

fatuus, fatua, fatuum   not good, lacking taste or interest

febrifugus, febrifuga, febrifugum   reducing fever

fenestralis, fenestrale   window-like openings

ferocactus   fiercely spiny gobular cacti

ferox   ferocious, extremely thorny

ferrugineus, ferruginea, ferrugineum   rust color

fertilis, fertile   fruitful, productive

festalis, festale; festinus, festina, festinum   festive

festivus   festive, gay, bright

ficifolius, ficifolia, ficifolium   having leaves like a fig (*Ficus*)

ficoides; ficoideus, ficoidea, ficoideum   looking like a fig (*Ficus*)

filamentosus, filamentosa, filamentosum; filarius, filaria, filarium   having threads, or being thread-like

filicaulis, filicaule   a thread-like stem

filicifolius, filicifolia, filicifolium   fern-like leaves

filiferus   bearing threads

filiformis, filiforme   thread-like

filipendulus, filipendula, filipendulum
looking like meadowsweet (*Filipendula*)

fimbriatulus, fimbriatula, fimbriatulum
with a small fringe

fimbriatus, fimbriata, fimbriatum   fringed

firmus, firma, firmum   strong, firm

**fissilis, fissile; fissuratus, fissurata,
fissuratum; fissus, fissa, fissum**   fissured,
or cut in two

fistulosus, fistulosa, fistulosum   pipe-like,
hollow

flabellatus, flabellata, flabellatum   like a
fan

flabellifer, flabellifera, flabelliferum   bearing
a fan

flabelliformis, flabelliforme   shape like a
fan

flaccidus, flaccida, flaccidum   weak, soft,
tender

**flagellaris, flagellare; flagelliformis,
flagelliforme**   like a whip

flammeus, flammea, flammeum
flame-colored, or resembling a flame

flavens   yellow

flaveolus, flaveola, flaveolum   yellowish

flavescens   yellowish, or becoming yellow

flavicomus, flavicoma, flavicomum   yellow
hair

flavidus, flavida, flavidum   yellowish

flavispinus, flavispina, flavispinum   having
yellow spines

flavissimus, flavissima, flavissimmum
intensely yellow

flavus, flava, flavum   yellow

flexicaulis, flexicaule   having yellow spines

flexilis, flexile   flexible

flexuosus, flexuosa, flexuosum   zigzag,
twisted, or tortuous

floccosus, floccose, floccosum   wooly

flocculosus, flocculosa, flocculosum
somewhat wooly

flore-albo   with white flowers

florentinus, florentina, florentinum   from
Florence, Italy

flore-pleno   with double flowers

**floribundus, floribunda, floribundum;
floridus, florida, floridum; florifer,
florifera, floriferum**   bearing flowers
abundantly; prolific flowers

floridanus, floridana, floridanum   from
Florida

floridus   flowering freely

floriferous   blooming freely

fluitans   floating

fluminensis, fluminense   from Rio de
Janeiro (*Flumen Januarii*), Brazil

fluvialis, fluviale; fluvialtilis, fluvialtile
having to do with running water

foemina   feminine

**foeniculaceus, foeniculacea,
foeniculaceum; foeniculatus,
foeniculata, foeniculatum**   like fennel
(*Foeniculum*)

foetidissimus, foetidissima, foetidissimum
very ill-scented

foetidus, foetida, foetidum   ill-scented, smelling badly

foliaceus, foliacea, foliaceum   leaf-like

foliates, foliata, foliatum   having leaves

foliolatus, foliolata, foliolatum; foliolosus, foliolosa, foliolosum   having leaflets

foliosus, foliosa, foliosum   leafy

follicularis, folliculare   having follicles

fontanus, fontana, fontanum; fontinalis, fontinale   from fountains or springs

formosanus, formosana, formosanum   from Taiwan (*Formosa*)

formosissimus, formosissima, formosissimum   very beautiful

formosus, formosa, formosum   beautiful

fourcroydes   looking like *Furcraea*

foveolatus, foveolata, foveolatum   slightly pitted

fragariflorus, fragariflora, fragariflorum   having flowers like those of strawberries; colored strawberry (*Fragaria*)

fragarioides   resembling a strawberry (*Fragaria*)

fragilis, fragile   brittle, fragile, or quick to wilt

fragrans   fragrant

fragrantissimus, fragrantissima, fragrantissimum   very fragrant

fraxineus, fraxinea, fraxineum   like the ash (*Fraxinus*)

fraxinifolius, fraxinifolia, fraxinifolium   having leaves like those of ash (*Fraxinus*)

frigidus, frigida, frigidum   from cold regions; frigid areas

frondosus, frondosa, frondosum   leafy

fructescent   fruitful

fructifer, fructifera, fructiferum   fruitful, bearing fruit

frutescens; fruticans; fruticosus, fruticosa, fruticosum   shrubby

fruticosus   shrubby

fucatus, fucata, fucatum   painted, dyed, or colored

fuchsioides   looking like *Fuchsia*

fugacious   withering quickly

fulgens; fulgidus, fulgida, fulgidum   shining, glistening, resplendent

fulvescens   turning yellowish-brown

fulvus, fulva, fulvum   reddish-orange, tawny

fumarifolius, fumarifolia, fumarifolium   leaves similar to fumitory (*Fumaria*)

funebris, funebrise   relating to or befitting a funeral

funiculatus, funiculate, funiculatum   a slender cord

furcans; furcatus, furcata, furcatum   forked

furfuraceus, furfuracea, furfuraceum   mealy or scurfy

fuscatus, fuscata, fuscatum   brownish

fuscous   grayish-brown

fusiformis, fusiforme   spindle shape

galacifolius, galacifolia, galacifolium   leaves like Galax

galegifolius, galegifolia, galegifolium   with leaves like goat's rue (*Galega*)

gallicus, gallica, gallicum   French

gandavensis, gandavense relating to Ghent, Belgium

gangeticus, gangetica, gangeticum from near the Ganges River, India

garganicus, garganica, garganicum from Monte Gargano, Italy

geminatus, geminate, geminatum paired, in twos

geminiflorus, geminiflora, geminiflorum paired or several flowers together

gemmatus, gemmata, gemmatum jeweled

gemmifer, gemmifera, gemmiferum having buds

generalis, generale usual, prevailing, most often

genevensis, genevense of Geneva, Switzerland

geniculatus, geniculata, geniculatum bent like a knee

genistifolius, genistifolia, genistifolium leaves like *Genista*

geometricus, geometrica, geometricum; geometrizans having formal markings

georgianus, georgiana, georgianum from Georgia, U.S.

georgicus, georgica, georgicum from Georgia of the former U.S.S.R.

geraniifolius, geraniifolia, geraniifolium having leaves like *Geranium*

geranioides looking like *Geranium*

germanicus, germanica, germanicum from Germany

gibberosus, gibberosa, gibberosum having a hump

gibbiflorus, gibbiflora, gibbiflorum flowers with a bump on one side

gibbosus, gibbosa, gibbosum; gibbus, gibba, gibbum enlarged, or swollen on a side

gibraltaricus, gibraltarica, gibraltaricum of Gibraltar

giganteus, gigantea, giganteum very large or tall, gigantic

gigas giant, immense

glabellus, glabella, glabellum; glabratus, glabrata, glabratum; glabrescens; glabriusculus, glabriuscula, glabriusculum mostly without hairs

glaber, glabera, glaberum without hairs

glaberrimus, glaberrima, glaberrimum having no hairs

glabra smooth, without hairs

glacialis, glaciale from areas of glaciers, or very cold regions

glandiformis, glandiforme gland-like

glandulifer having glands

glanduliflorus, glanduliflora, glanduliflorum having glands on flowers

glandulosus, glandulosa, glandulosum glandular, or having secreting organs

glaucescens gray, bluish-gray, or bluish-white from a light coating of waxy or thin powder; glaucous

glaucifolius, glaucifolia, glaucifolium foliage

glauciifolius, glauciifolia, glauciifolium leaves that look like *Glaucium* leaves

glaucophyllus, glaucophylla, glaucophyllum leaves that look like *Glaucium* leaves

glaucus, glauca, glaucum   gray, whitish, grayish, or bluish-grayish coating of thin, waxy powder that rubs off

globiferus, globifera, globiferum   globe-shaped clusters

globosus, globosa, globosum   a globe shape

globularis, globulare   small sphere or globe

globulifer, globulifera, globuliferum   having clusters of small globes

globulosus, globulosa, globulosum   small and shaped like globes; spheres

glomeratus, glomerata, glomeratum   clustered in somewhat spherical heads

gloriosus, gloriosa, gloriosum   glorious

gloxinioides   *Gloxinia*

glumaceus, glumacea, glumaceum   with glumes (chaffy bracts on flowers of grasses)

glutinous, glutinosa, glutinosum   sticky

glycinioides   looking like soybean (*Glycine*)

glyptostroboides   looking like *Glyptostrobus*

gnaphaloides   looking like *Gnaphalium*

gracilentus, gracilenta, gracilentum   slender, narrow

graciliflorus, graciliflora, graciliflorum   slender or graceful flowers

gracilior   more graceful

gracilipes   having a narrow stalk

gracilis, gracile   graceful, or gracefully slender

gracilistylus, gracilistyla, gracilistylum   having a narrow style

gracillimus, gracillima, gracillimum   most graceful

graecus, graeca, graecum   of Greece

gramineus, graminea, gramineum   grass-like

graminifolius, graminifolia, graminifolium   with leaves like grass

grandiceps   with a large head

grandicuspis, grandicuspe   having big points

grandidentatus, grandidentata, grandidentatum   having big teeth

grandiflorus, grandiflora, grandiflorum   having large flowers

grandifolius, grandifolia, grandifolium   large leaves

grandiformis, grandiforme   large

grandis, grande   large

graniticus, granitica, graniticum   growing in granite-like rocks or cliffs

granulatus, granulata, granulatum   tubercles or knobs like grain

granulosus, granulosa, granulosum   granular

gratissimus, gratissima, gratissimum   very gratifying

gratus, grata, gratum   gratifying

graveolens   very fragrant, heavy scented

griseus, grisea, griseum   gray

groelandicus, groelandica, groelandicum   from Greenland

guianensis, guianense   from Guiana, South America

gummifer, gummifera, gummiferum   producing, containing, or exuding gum

gummosus, gummosa, gummosum   gummy

guttatus, guttata, guttatum speckled, spotted, or splotched

gymnocarpus, gymnocarpa, gymnocarpum with naked fruits

gyrans in circles

haematodes color of blood-red

halimifolius, halimifolia, halimifolium blood-red flowers

halophilus, halophila, halophilum loving salt

hastatus, hastata, hastatum shape of a halberd or spear on spearhead

hebephyllus, hebephylla, hebephyllum downy leaves

hederaceus, hederacea, hederaceum like ivy (*Hedera*)

hederifolius, hederifolia, hederifolium having ivy-like leaves

helianthoides like Helianthus

hellenicus, hellenica, hellenicum from Greece

helveticus, helvetica, helveticum from Switzerland

helvolus, helvola, helvolum light brownish-yellow

hemisphaericus, hemisphaerica, hemisphaericum hemispherical

hepaticifolius, hepaticifolia, hepaticifolium having leaves like *Hepatica*

heracleifolius, heracleifolia, heracleifolium having leaves like *Heracleum*

herbaceus, herbacea, herbaceum herbaceous, with no woody growth

hesperus, hespera, hesperum of the West

heteracanthus, heteracantha, heteracanthum variously spined

heteranthus, heterantha, heteranthum variously flowered

heterocarpus, heterocarpa, heterocarpum variously fruited

heterolepis, heterolepe variously scaled

heteromorphus, heteromorpha, heteromorphum having variety of form

heteropetalus, heteropetala, heteropetalum variety of petals

heterophyllus, heterophylla, heterophyllum variety of leaves

hexagonus, hexagona, hexagonum hexagon shape (six)

hexapetalus, hexapetala, hexapetalum having six petals

hexaphyllus, hexaphylla, hexaphyllum having leaves in sixes

hians gaping

hibernalis, hibernale pertaining to winter, hibernation

hibernicus, hibernica, hibernicum from Ireland (*Hibernia*)

hibiscifolius, hibiscifolia, hibiscifolium having leaves like *Hibiscus*

hiemalis, hiemale of winter

himalaicus, himalaica, himalaicum; himalayensis, himalayense from the Himalayas

hippocastanum specific species name of horse chestnut, of the *Aesculus* genus

hippophaeoides like Hippophae

hirsutissimus, hirsutissima, hirsutissimum
very hairy

hirsutulus, hirsutula, hirsutulum   a little
hairy

hirsutus, hirsute, hirsutum   hairy, coarse
stiff hair

hirtellus, hirtella, hirtellum   rather hairy

hirtus, hirta, hirtum   hairy

hispanicus, hispanica, hispanicum   from
Spain (Hispania)

hispidus, hispida, hispidum   bristly or
bristly with hairs

hollandicus, hollandica, hollandicum
from Holland

holocarpus, holocarpa, holocarpum
whole fruits that are not lobed or split

holochrysus, holochrysa, holochrysum
wholly, or completely golden

hololeucus, hololeuca, hololeucum
wholly white

hondownsis, hondoense   from Hondo,
Japan

horizontalis, horizontale   horizontal form

horridus, horrida, horridum   prickly

**hortensis, hortense; hortorum;
hortulanus, hortulana, hortulanum**   of
gardens

humifusus, humifusa, humifusum
sprawling

humilis, humile   low or dwarf

humulifolius, humulifolia, humulifolium
having leaves like hops (*Humulus*)

hungaricus, hungarica, hungaricum
from Hungary

hupehensis, hupehense   from Hupeh,
China

hyacinthinus, hyacinthina, hyacinthinum
purplish-blue; resembling hyacinths
(*Hyacinthus*)

hyalinus, hyaline, hyalinum   transparent,
somewhat transparent, or partially transparent

hybridus, hybrida, hybridum   hybrid

hydrangeoides   like *Hypericum*

hyemalis, hyemale   of winter

hylocereus   a night-blooming cereus

**hypericifolius, hypericifolia,
hypericifolium**   having leaves like
Hypericum

hypericoides   like *Hypericum*

hypnoides   like *hypnum* moss

**hypochondriacus, hypochondriaca,
hypochondriacum**   somber

hypogaeus, hypogaea, hypogeum
underground, underneath

hypoglaucus, hypoglauca, hypoglaucum
glaucous

hypoleucus, hypoleuca, hypoleucum
white underneath

hypophyllus, hypophylla, hypophyllum
under a leaf

hyssopifolius, hyssopifolia, hyssopifolium
with leaves like hyssop (*Hyssopus*)

hystrix   bristly

ianthinus, ianthina, ianthinum
violet-blue

ibericus, iberica, ibericum   from the Iberian
Peninsula or from Georgia, former U.S.S.R., or
Iberia (Spain, Portugal)

iberideus, iberidea, iberideum   like *Iberis*

iberidifolius, iberidifolia, iberidifolium
leaves like *Iberis*

idaeus, idaea, idaeum   From Mount Ida in
Asia Minor

ignescens; igneus, ignea, igneum
fiery-red color

ilicifolius, ilicifolia, ilicifolium   having
leaves like holly (*Ilex*)

illecebrosus, illecebrosa, illecebrosum
enticing, attractive

illustratus, illustrata, illustratum   illustrated,
detailed

illustris, illustre   brilliant, shining

illyricus, illyrica, illyricum   from ancient
Illyria

imbricatus, imbracata, imbracatum
overlapping like tiles on a roof

immaculatus, immaculata, immaculatum
without spots or blemish, immaculate

immersus, immersa, immersum   growing
while immersed in water

impeditus, impedita, impeditum   tangled,
halted, or hindered

imperialis, imperiale   imperial, showy, royal

impressus, impressa, impressum
depressed, sunken, impressed

impudicus, impudica, impudicum
shameless, lewd

inaequalis, inaequale   unequal

inapertus, inaperta, inapertum   closed

incanus, incana, incanum   hoary, grayish,
or whitish, sometimes with age and sometimes
with hair

incarnatus, incarnata, incarnatum
flesh-colored

incertus, incerta, incertum   doubtful,
uncertain

incisifolius, incisifolia, incisifolium   cut
leaves

incisus, incisa, incisum   cut deeply and usually irregularly

inclinatus, inclinata, inclinatum   bent
downward, inclined

incomparabilis, incomparabile   incompa-
rable, excelling

**inconspicuous, inconspicua, incon-
spicuum**   not conspicuous

incurvatus, incurvata, incurvatum   curving
inward

indentatus   indented, toothed

indicus, indica, indicum   from India

indivisus, indivisa, indivisum   not divided

induratus, indurata, induratum   hard,
durable

inebrians   intoxicating, inebriating

inermis, inerme   without prickles

infectorius, infectoria, infectorium   colored
or dyed

infestus, infesta, infestum   troublesome,
infested

inflatus, inflata, inflatum   swollen, inflated

inflexus, inflexa, inflexum   bent inward,
flexed inward

infundibuliformis, infundibuliforme
funnel-shaped, or formed

ingens   enormous

indorus, indora, indorum   not scented, no odor

innoxius, innoxia, innoxium   harmless

inquinans   stained or flecked

inscriptus, inscripta, inscriptum   inscribed

insignus, insigna, insignum   remarkable, distinguished

insipidus, insipida, inspidum   insipid

insulanus, insulana, insulanum; insularis, insulare   from islands

intactus, intacta, intactum   intact

integer, integra, integrum   entire

integrifolius, integrifolia, integrifolium   with entire or undivided leaves

intermedius, intermedia, intermedium   intermediate

interruptus, interrupta, interruptum   not continuous, interrupted

intertextus, intertexta, intertextum   intertwined

intortus, intorta, intortum   twisted

intricatus, intricata, intricatum   tangled

introrsus, introrsa, introrsum   turned inward

inundatus, inundata, inundatum   growing in ground likely to be inundated with water, flood areas

involucratus, involucrata, involucratum   a circle of bracts surrounding a flower cluster

involutus, involuta, involutum   rolled inward

ioanthus, ioantha, ioanthum   violet-colored flowers

ioensis, ioensa, ioensum   from Iowa

ionopsidium   diamond flowers

iricus, irica, iricum   from Ireland

iridescens   iridescent

iridiflorus, iridiflora, iridiflorum   leaves like *Iris*

iridioides   like *Iris*

irritans   irritating

irroratus, irrorata, irroratum   minutely spotted, sprinkled

isabellinus, isabellina, isabellinum   yellowish

islandicus, islandica, islandicum   of Iceland

isophyllus, isophylla, isophyllum   leaves of equal size or form

istriacus, istriaca, istriacum   from Italy, Yugoslavia

italicus, italica, italicum   from Italy

ixia   hardy bulbous herbs

ixioides   like *Ixia*

ixocarpus, ixocarpa, ixocarpum   sticky fruits

jamaicensis, jamaicense   from Jamaica, West Indies

japonicus, japonica, japonicum   from Japan

jasmineus, jasminea, jasmineum; jasminoides   like jasmine (*Jasminus*)

javanicus, javanica, javanicum   from Java

junceus, juncea, junceum   like rushes (*Juncus*)

juniperifolius, juniperifolia, juniperifolium leaves like juniper (*Juniperus*)

juniperinus, juniperina, juniperinum like a juniper

kalmiiflorus, kalmiiflora, kalmiiflorum flowers like mountain laurel (*Kalmia*)

kamtschaticus, kamtschatica, kamtschaticum from Kamchatka

kansuensis, kansuense Kansu, China

kashmirianus, kashmiriana, kashmirianum from Kashmir

kermesinus, kermesina, kermesinum carmine, vivid red, scarlet, or crimson

kewensis, kewense from the Royal Botanic Gardens, Kew, England

kiusianus, kiusiana, kiusianum from Kyushu, Japan

koreanus, koreana, koreanum; koriaensis, koriaense from Korea

kousa Japanese for *Cornus kousa*

labiatus, labiata, labiatum; labiosus, labiosa, labiosum having a lip

laburnifolius, laburnifolia, laburnifolium leaves like *Laburnum*

lacer, lacera, lacerum lacerated, cut

laciniatus, laciniata, laciniatum; laciniosus, laciniosa, laciniosum shredded or cut into narrow divisions or cut strips; torn, fringed

lactatus milky

lactescens becoming milky, secreting a lactate-like substance

lacteus, lactea, lacteum milk-white

lactifer, lactifera, lactiferum milk-white-colored flowers

lactucifolius, lactucifolia, lactucifolium leaves like lettuce (*Lactuca*)

lacustris, lacustre of lakes

laetiflorus, laetiflora, laetiflorum bright flowers

laetivirens bright green

laetus, laeta, laetum bright

laevicaulis, laevicaule smooth stems

laevigatus, laevigata, laevigatum; laevis, laeve smooth

lagodechianus, lagodechiana, lagodechianum from Lagodechi, Kaukasus, in Georgia, Russia

lamellatus, lamellata, lamellatum layered

lanatus, lanata, lanatum wooly

lanceolatus, lanceolata, lanceolatum; lanceus, lancea, lanceum, lanceolate lance- or spear-shaped

lancifolium leaves lance-shaped

laniger, lanigera, lanigerum; lanosus, lanosa, lanosum lanceolate, lance or spear-shaped

lantanoides lantana-like

lanuginosus wooly, downy

lapponicus, lapponica, lapponicum from Lapland, above the Arctic Circle

laricinus, laricina, laricinum like larch (*Larix*)

lasiacanthus, lasiacantha, lasiacanthum wooly and spined

lasiandrus, lasiandra, lasiandrum wooly stamens

lasiocarpus, lasiocarpa, lasiocarpum wooly or rough fruit

lasiopetalus, lasiopetala, lasiopetalum
wooly petals

latiflorus   broad-flowered

latifolius   broad-leaved

latisquamus   with broad scales or bracts

latus   broad, wide

lenticularis, lenticulare; lentiformis, lentiforme   lens-shaped

lentus, lenta, lentum   tough and pliable

leonurus, leonura, leonurum   like a lion's tail

leopardinus, leopardina, leopardinum
spotted like leopards

lepidophyllus   scaly-leaved

lepidotus, lepidota, lepidotum   scaly

lepidus   graceful, elegant

leptocaulis, leptocaule   slender-stemmed

leptocladus, leptoclada, leptocladum
slender branching

leptolepis   thin scales

leptopetalus, leptopetala, leptopetalum
thin petals

leptophylus, leptophyla, leptophylum
thin leaves

leptosepalus, leptosepala, leptosepalum
thin sepals

leptostachys, leptostachya, lep-tostachyum   having slender spikes

leucanthus, leucantha, leucanthum
having white flowers

leucocaulis, leucocaule   having white stems

leucochilus, leucochila, leucochilum
having white lips

leucodermis, leucoderme   having white skin

leuconeurus, leuconeura, leuconeurum
having white veins

leucopetalus, leucopetala, leucopetalum
having white petals

leucophyllus, leucophylla, leucophyllum
white leaves

leucostachys, leucostacha, leucostachum
white spikes

leucotrichus, leucotricha, leucotrichum
white hairs

libani; libanoticus, libanotica, libanoticum
from Mount Lebanon, Lebanon

libericus   of Liberia

liburnicus, liburnica, libernicum   from Croatia (*Liburnia*)

lignosus, lignose, lignosum   woody, having lignin

ligularis, ligulare; ligulatus, ligulata, ligulatum   strap-like

ligusticifolius, ligusticifolia, ligusticifolium
leaves like lovage (*Ligusticum*)

ligustrinus, ligustrina, ligustrinum   leaves like privet (*Ligustrum*)

likiangensis, likiangense   from the Lichiang Mountains, China

lilaceus, lilacea, lilaceum   like a lily (*Lilium*)

lilacinus, lilacina, lilacinum   lilac-color

liliflorus, liliflora, liliflorum   flowers like a lily (*Lilium*)

lilifolius, lilifolia, lilifolium   leaves like a lily (*Lilium*)

limensis, limense   from Lima, Peru

limnophilus, limnophila, limnophilum   of swamps

limoniifolius, limoniifolia, limoniifolium   leaves like sea-lavender (*Limonium*)

limosus, limosa, limosum   of marshlands, or growing in wet ground

linariifolius, linariifolia, linariifolium   leaves like *Linaria*

linearifolius, linearifolia, linearifolium   having linear leaves

linearis, lineare   narrow, having nearly parallel, linear sides

lineatus, lineate, lineatum   lined, striped

linguiformis, linguiforme; lingulatus, lingulata, lingulatum   tongue-shaped

lingulatus   tongue-shaped

liniflorus, liniflora, liniflorum   flowers like flax (*Linum*)

linifolius, linifolia, linifolium   leaves like flax (*Linum*)

littoralis, littorale; littoreus, littorea, littoreum   from seashores, coastal, between high and low water marks

lividus, livida, lividum   bluish-gray, lead color

lobatus, lobata, lobatum   lobed

lobelioides   resembling *Lobelia*

lobulatus, lobulata, lobulatum   having lobes that are small

lomariifolius, lomariifolia, lomariifolium   leaves like *Lomaria*

longebracteatus, longebracteata, longebracteatum   having long bracts

longependunculatus, longependunculata, longependunculatum   having long peduncles (flower stalks)

longicaulis, longicaule   having long stalks

longicomus, longicoma, longicomum   having long hairs

longicuspis, longicuspe   long-pointed

longiflorus, longiflora, longiflorum   having long flowers

longifolius, longifolia, longifolium   having long leaves

longihamatus, longihamata, longihamatum   having long hooks

longilobus, longiloba, longilobum   having long lobes

longipes   having long stalks; long footed

longipetalus, longipetala, longipetalum   long petals

longisepalus, longisepala, longisepalum   having long sepals

longispinus, longispina, longispinum   having long spines

longissimus, longissima, longissimum   very long

longistylus, longistyla, longistylum   with long styles

longus, longa, longum   long

lophanthus, lophantha, lophanthum   having crested flowers

louisianus, louisiana, louisianum   from Louisiana

lucens; lucidus, lucida, lucidum   bright, shining, clear, lucent

ludovicianus, ludoviciana, ludovicianum   from Louisiana

lukiangensis, lukiangense   from Lukiang, China

lunatus, lunata, lunatum; lunulatus, lunulata, lunulatum   crescent shape

luridus, lurida, luridum   grayish-yellow, orange, pale, ghastly, or highly colored

lusitanicus, lusitanica, lusitanicum   from Portugal (Lusitania)

luteolus, luteola, luteolum   yellowish

lutescens   turning yellow or yellowish

luteus, lutea, luteum   yellow

luxurians   luxuriant

lychnidifolius, lychnidifolia, lychnidifolium   leaves like *Lychnis*

lycopodioides   like club-moss (*Lycopodium*)

lydius, lydia, lydium   from Asia Minor

lyratus, lyrata, lyratum   fiddle shape, lyre shape

lysimachioiedes   resembling Lysimachia

macedonicus, macedonica, macedonicum   from Macedonia

macracanthus, macracantha, macracanthum   large spines

macradensus, macradensa, macradensum   large glands

macrandrus, macrandra, macrandrum; macrantherus, macranthera, macrantherum   large anthers

macranthus, macrantha, macranthum   large flowers

macrobotrys   large grape-like clusters

macrocarpus, macrocarpa, macrocarpum   large fruits

macrocephalus, macrocephala, macrocephalum   large heads

macrodontus, macrodonta, macrodontum   large teeth

macrophyllus, macrophylla, macrophyllum   large leaves

macrorrhizus, macrorrhiza, macrorrhizum   large roots

macrospermus, macrosperma, macrospermum   large seeds

macrostachyus, macrostachya, macrostachyum   large spikes

maculatus, maculata, maculatum; maculifer, maculifera, maculiferum; maculosus, maculosa, maculosum   spotted, spots

madagascariensis, madagascariense   from Madagascar

magellanicus, magellanica, magellanicum   from near the Straits of Magellan

magnificus, magnifica, magnificum   magnificent, distinguished

majalis, majale   May flowers; of May

majesticus, majestica, majesticum   majestic

major; majus, maja, majum   big, large

malabaricus, malabarica, malabaricum   from Malabar, India

malacoides   soft or sticky or gelatinous, or mallow-like

maliformis, maliforme   apple shape

malvaceus, malvacea, malvaceum   like mallow (*Malva*)

malviflorus, malviflora, malviflorum   flowers like those of mallow (*Malva*)

mammiformis

mammiformis, mammiforme shaped like a nipple

mammillatus, mammillata, mammillatum; mammillaris, mammilare; mammosus, mammosa, mammosum breast-like or shaped like a nipple

mandshuricus, mandshurica, mandshuricum from Manchuria

manicatus, manicata, manicatum long sleeves

manipurensis, manipurense from Manipur, India

margaritaceus, margaritacea, margaritaceum; margaritus, margarita, margaritum pearly or like pearls

margaritifer, margaritifera, margaritiferum pearl bearing

marginalis, marginale; marginatus, marginata, marginatum margined, margins of different color

marilandicus, marilandica, marilandicum from Maryland

maritimus, maritima, maritimum of the sea

marmoratus, marmorata, marmoratum; marmoreus, marmorea, marmoreum marbled, mottled, splattered

maroccanus, maroccana, maroccanum from Morocco

mas; masculus, mascula, masculum masculine, male, sedate

masculatus masculine

matronalis, matronale relatively Roman festival of the matrons on March 1

mauritanicus, mauritanica, mauritanicum from North Africa (Mauretania)

mauritianus, mauritiana, mauritianum from Mauritius

maxillaries, maxillare jaws or jaw-like

maximus, maxima, maximum biggest

medicus, medica, medicum medicinal

mediopictus, mediopicta, mediopictum striped in the middle

mediterraneus, mediterranea, mediterranium from near the Mediterranean Sea

medius, media, medium intermediate

medullaris, medullare; medullus, medulla, medullum pithy

megacalyx having a large calyx

megacanthus, megacantha, megacanthum large spines

megacarpus, megacarpa, megacarpum large fruits

megalanthus, megalantha, megalanthum large flowers

megalophyllus, megalophylla, megalophyllum large leaves

megapotamicus, megapotamica, megapotamicum from the big river

megarrhizus, megarrhiza, megarrhizum big roots

megaseifolius, megaseifolia, megaseifolium leaves like *Bergenia* (*Megasea*)

megaspermus, megasperma, megaspermum big seeds

megastachyus, megastachya, megastachyum big spike

megastigmus, megastigma, megastigmum a big stigma

meleagris, meleagre   spotted like a guinea bird, speckled

meliodorus, meliodora, meliodorum   smell resembling honey

mellitus, melita, melitum   honey-sweet

meloformis, meloforme   melon shape

membranaceus, membranacea, membranaceum   membranous

meridianus, meridiana, meridianum; meridionalis, meridionale   of midday

metallicus, metallica, metallicum   metallic

mexicanus, mexicana, mexicanum   Mexican

micans   glittering

micracanthus, micracantha, micracanthum   small thorns

micranthus, micrantha, micranthum   small flowers

microcarpus, microcarpa, microcarpum   small fruits

microcephalus, microcephala, microcephalum   a small head

microchilus, microchila, microchilum   a small lip

microdasys   small and shaggy

microglossus, microglossa, microglossum   a small tongue

microlepis, microlepe   small scales

micropetalus, micropetala, micropetalum   small petals

microphyllus, microphylla, microphyllum   small leaves

microsepalus, microsepala, microsepalum   small sepals

microspermus, microsperma, microspermum   small seeds

militaris, militare   having to do with soldiers

millefoliatus, millefoliata, millefoliatum; millefolius, millefolia, millefolium   many leaves or leaflets

mimosifolius, mimosifolia, mimosifolium   leaves like those of *Mimosa*

mimosoides   looking like *Mimosa*

miniatus, miniata, miniatum   bright red

minimus, minima, minimum   smaller, dwarf

minor   smaller

minutiflorus, minutiflora, minutiflorum   minute or tiny flowers

minutifolius, minutifolia, minutifolium   minute or tiny leaves

minutissimus, minutissima, minutissimum   most minute or tiny

minutus, minuta, minutum   very small

mirabilis, mirabile   wonderful, extraordinary

missouriensis, missouriense   from Missouri

mitis, mite   mild, spineless

mitratus, mitrata, mitratum   a headdress; worshipful cap; mitered or turbaned

mitriformis, mitriforme   miter-like

mixtus, mixta, mixtum   mixed

modestus, modesta, modestum   modest

moldavicus, moldavica, moldavicum   from the Danube Basin

molle

molle   native of Peru

mollicomus, mollicoma, mollicomum
having soft hairs

mollis, molle   soft, or having soft hairs

mollissimus, mollissima, mollissimum
with much softness; very soft hairs

moluccanus, moluccana, moluccanum
from the Molucca Islands

**monacanthus, monacantha,
monacanthum**   having one spine

**monadelphus, monadelpha,
monadelphum**   having stamens'
filaments attached, in one bundle

monandrus, monandra, monandrum
one stamen

mongolicus, mongolica, mongolicum
from Mongolia

monilifer, monilifera, moniliferum   a
necklace

moniliformis, moniliforme   necklace-like

**monocephalus, monocephala,
monocephalum**   one head

monogynus, monogyna, monogynum
one pistil

monopetalus, monopetala, monopetalum
one petal

monophyllus, monophylla, monophyllum
one leaf

monosepalus, monosepala, monosepalum
one sepal

**monospermus, monosperma,
monospermum**   one seed

**monostachyus, monostachya,
monostachyum**   one spike

monostrosus, monostrosa, monostrosum
monstrous, not normal, or strange

montanus, montana, montanum   of
mountains

monticola, monticolus   inhabiting
mountains

morifolius, morifolia, morifolium   leaves
like mulberry (*Morus*)

mosaicus, mosaica, mosaicum   a mosaic
pattern, variegated

moschatus, moschata, moschatum   musk
scent

moupinensis, moupinense   from Pooksing
(Mupin), China

mucosus   sticky, slimy

mucronatus, mucronata, mucronatum
short terminal points, or ends; small, abrupt tip

**mucronulatus, mucronulata,
mucronulatum**   short, hard point

**multibracteatus, multibracteata, multi-
bracteatum**   having many or several bracts

multicaulis, multicaule   many or several
stems

multicavus, multicava, multicavum
many or several hollows

multiceps   many or several heads

multicolor   many or several colors

multifidus, multifida, multifidum   divided
many or several times

multiflorus, multiflora, multiflorum   having
many flowers

multijuga   in many pairs

multilineatus, multilineata, multilineatum
having many lines

multinervis, multinerve   many veins

multiplex   many or several folds

multiradiatus, multiradiata, multiradiatum   with many rays

multiscapoideus, multiscapoidea, multiscapoideum   having many naked flower stems

muralis, murale   growing walls

muricatus, muricata, muricatum   roughened, with strong points

musaicus, musaica, musaicum   a mosaic pattern

muscipilus, muscipila, muscipilum   catching flies

muscitoxicus, muscitoxica, muscitoxicum   poisonous to flies

muscosus, muscosa, muscosum   resembling moss

mutabilis, mutabile   changeable in color or variable in some other aspect

mutatus, mutata, mutatum   changed, mutant

muticus, mutica, muticum   blunt

myosotidiflorus, myosotidiflora, myosotidiflorum   flowers like forget-me-not (*Myosotis*)

myriacanthuss, myriacantha, myriacanthum   numerous thorns

myriocarpus, myriocarpa, myriocarpum   many fruits

myriophylloides   looking like *Myriophyllum*

myriophyllus, myriophylla, myriophyllum   many leaves

myrsinifolius, myrsinifolia, myrsinifolium   leaves like *Myrsine*

myrsinioides   resembling *Myrsine*

myrtifolius, myrtifolia, myrtifolium   leaves like myrtle (*Myrtus*)

myrtilloides   myrtle-like

mysorensis, mysorene   from Mysore, India

nankinensis, nankinense   from Nanking, China

nanus, nana, nanum   dwarf

napiformis, napiforme   shaped like a turnip

narbonensis, narbonense   of Narbonne, France

narcissiflorus, narcissiflora, narcissiflorum   flowers like *Narcissus*

narcissifolius, narcissifolia, narcissifolium   leaves like *Narcissus*

natalensis, natalense   from Natal, South Africa

natans   floating, swimming

navicularis, naviculare   shaped like a boat

neapolitanus, neapolitana, neopolitanum   from Naples, Italy

nebulosus, nebulosa, nebulosum   cloud-like; like a nebulous cloud

nectariferous   producing nectar

neglectus, neglecta, neglectum   neglected, overlooked, unnoticed

neilgherrensis, neilgherrense   from the Nilgiri Hills, India

nelumbifolius, nelumbifolia, nelumbifolium   having leaves like lotus (Nelumbo)

nemoralis, nemorale; nemorosus, nemorosa, nemorosum   from woodlands; of groves

nepalensis, nepalense   from Nepal

nepetoides   looking like *Nepeta*

neriiflorus, neriiflora, neriiflorum   flowers like oleander (*Nerium*)

neriifolius, neriifolia, neriifolium   leaves like oleander (*Nerium*)

nervosus, nervosa, nervosum   conspicuous veins, nerved

nevadensis, nevadense   from Sierra, Nevada, Spain; the Sierra Nevada Mountains of California; or the state of Nevada

nidus   a nest

nigella   love-in-a-mist

niger, nigra, nigrum   black

nigratus, nigrata, nigratum   from the area of the Nile River

niloticus, nilotica, niloticum   from the area of the Nile River

nipponicus, nipponica, nipponicum   from Japan

nitens; nitidus, nitida, nitidum   shining or bright

nitidus   shining

nivalis, nivale; niveus, nivea, niveum; nivosus, nivosa, nivosum   snow-white color, or from a snowy area

nobilis, nobile   noble, famous

noctiflorus, noctiflora, noctiflorum; nocturnus, nocturna, nocturnum   night flowering

nocturnus   of the night

nodosus, nodosa, nodosum   conspicuous nodes (joints), knobby, knotty

nodulosus, nodulosa, nodulosum   having small nodes (joints)

nonscriptus, nonscripta, nonscriptum   without markings

nootkatensis, nootkatense   from the region of Nootka Sound, British Columbia

norvegicus, norvegica, norvegicum   from Norway

notatus, notata, notatum   marked

novae-angliae   from New England

novaeboracensis, novaeboracense; novi-belgii   from New York

novae-caesareae   from New Jersey

novae-zelandiae   from New Zealand

nucifer, nucifera, nuciferum, nuciferus   bearing nuts

nudatus   nude, stripped

nudicaulis, nudicaule   naked-stemmed

nudiflorus, nudiflora, nudiflorum   naked-flowered, flowers without leaves

nudum   bare, naked

nummularius, nummularium   looking like a coin

nutans   nodding

nyctagineus, nyctaginea, nyctagineum   night-booming

nymphoides   floating heart

obconicus, obconica, obconicum   shaped like an inverted cone

obesus, obesa, obesum   fat, succulent, plump

oblatus, oblata, oblatum   flattened at the end

obliquus, obliqua, obliquum   oblique

oblongatus, oblongata, oblongatum   oblong

oblongifolius, oblongifolia, oblongifolium   oblong leaves

oblongus, oblonga, oblongum   oblong

obovatus, obovata, obovatum   an egg-shape with the broadest end upward or at the end

obscurus, obscura, obscurum   indistinct, dark or dusky, obscure

obsoleteus, obsoletea, obsoleteum   rudimentary, obsolete

obtusifolius, obtusifolia, obtusifolium   blunt leaves

obtusus, obtusa, obtusum   blunt, rounded

obvata   inversely ovate, shaped like an upside-down egg

occidentalis, occidentale   western, New World

ocellatus, ocellata, ocellatum   with eye-like spots or blotches, small eyes

ochraceus, ochracea, ochraceum   ochre-colored, yellowish-brown

ochroleucus, ochroleuca, ochroleucum   yellowish-white

ocimoides   looking like basil (*Ocimum*)

octandrus, octandra, octandrum   eight stamens

octopetalus, octopetala, octopetalum   eight petals

oculatus, oculata, oculatum   having an eye-like spot, blotch

oculiroseus, oculirosea, oculiroseum   a rose-colored eye

ocymoides   looking like basil (*Ocimum*)

odoratissimus, odoratissima, odoratissimum   very fragrant, having an odor

odoratus, odorata, odoratum; odorifer, odorifera, odoriferum; odorus, odora, odorum   fragrant, having an odor

officinalis, officinale   medicinal virtues (real or perceived)

oleifolius, oleifolia, oleifolium   leaves like olive (*Olea*)

oleoides   looking like olive (*Olea*)

oleraceus, oleracea, oleraceum   of vegetable gardens, edible

olifer, olifera, oliferum   oil-bearing

olitorius, olitoria, olitorium   associated with culinary herbs

olivaceus, olivacea, olivaceum   light greenish-brown, olive colored, olive-like

olympicus, olympica, olympicum   of Mount Olympus

omiensis, omiense   of Mount Omi, China

ophioglossifolius, ophioglossifolia, ophioglossifolium   leaves like adder's tongue fern (*Ophioglossum*)

oppositifolius, oppositifolia, oppositifolium   having opposite leaves

opuliflorus, opuliflora, opuliflorum   flowers like *Viburnum opulus*

opulifolius, opulifolia, opulifolium   leaves like *Viburnum opulus*

opuloides   leaves looking like *Viburnum opulus*

opulus   snowball, species of *Viburnum*

orbicularis, orbiculare; obiculatus, obiculata, obiculatum   disc-shaped

orchidaceae orchid family

orchideus, orchidea, orchideum; orchioides; orchoides orchid-like

orchidflorus, orchidflora, orchidflorum flowers looking like those of orchids

oreganus, oreganao, oreganum; oregonus, oregona, oregonum from Oregon

oreophilus, oreophila, oreophilum of mountains

orientalis, orientale of the Orient, Eastern

origanifolius, origanifolia, origanifolium leaves like marjoram (*Origanum*)

origanoides looking like marjoram (*Origanum*)

ornatus, ornata, ornatum showy, ornate, adorned

ornithocephalus, ornithocephala, ornithocephalum shaped like a bird's head

ornithopodus, ornithopoda, ornithopodum; ornithopus looking like the foot of a bird

orthobotrys erect clusters

orthocarpus, orthocarpa, orthocarpum erect fruits

orthocladus, orthoclada, orthocladum straight branches

orthoglossus, orthoglossa, orthoglossum a straight tongue

orthopterus, orthoptera, orthopterum straight wings

orthosepalus, orthosepala, orthosepalum straight sepals

osmanthus fragrant-flowered, or holly olive or devilwood

ovalis, ovale elliptic oval

ovatus, ovata, ovatum egg-shaped with a wide end at the base or lower end

ovifer, ovifera, oviferum; oviger, ovigera, ovigerum egg-shaped structures

ovinus, ovina, ovinum of or looking like sheep

oxyacanthus, oxyacantha, oxyacanthum sharp spines

oxygonus, oxygona, oxygonum sharp-angled

oxylobus, oxyloba, oxylobum having sharp-pointed lobes

oxyphilus, oxyphila, oxyphilum of acid soils

oxyphyllus, oxyphylla, oxyphyllum sharp-pointed leaves

pachyanthus, pachyantha, pachyanthum with thick flowers

pachycarpus, pachycarpa, pachycarpum having thick seed coats

pachyphloeus, pachyphloea, pachyphloeum having thick bark

pachyphyllus, pachyphylla, pachyphyllum thick-leaved

pachypodus, pachypoda, pachypodum having thick-based stems

pacificus, pacifica, pacificum of the Pacific Ocean

palaestinus, palaestina, palaestinum of Palestine

pallens; pallidus, pallida, pallidum pale

pallidus pale

palmaris, palmare a hand's or palm's breadth, high or wide

palmatus, palmata, palmatum shaped like a hand with outstretched fingers

palmifolius, palmifolia, palmifolium palm-like leaves

paludosus, paludosa, paludosum; palustris, palustre from marshes

palustris growing in the marsh

panduratus, pandurata, panduratum fiddle-shaped

paniculatus, paniculata, paniculatum flowers in panicles

pannosus, pannosa, pannosum tattered or shredded

papaveraceus, papaveracea, papaver-aceum looking like a poppy (*Papaver*)

papilliger, papilligera, papilligerum; papillosus, papillosa, papillosum having tiny, soft protuberances

pappus tuft of hairs attached to seed

papyraceus, papyracea, papyraceum papery

papyrifer, papyrifera, papyriferum useful in making paper

paradise; paradisiacus, paradisiacal, paradisiacum of Paradise

paradoxus, paradoxa, paradoxum paradoxical

parasiticus, parasitica, parasiticum parasitic

pardalinus, pardalina, pardalinum; pardinus, pardina, pardinum; pardinus, pardina, pardinum spots resembling a leopard or related to leopards' habitat

parnassi; parnassicus, parnassica, parnassicum from Mount Parnassus, Greece

parnassifolius, parnassifolia, parnassifolium leaves like those of *Parnassia*

paronychoides resembling whiteworts

parrotia short like witch hazel

partitus, partita, partitum small bracts

parviflorus, parviflora, parviflorum small flowers

parvifolius, parvifolia, parvifolium small leaves

parvus, parva, parvum small

pastoralis, pastorale associated with shepherds or pastures

patagonicus, patagonica, patagonicum from Patagonia

patens; patulus, patula, patulum spreading

patulus spreading

pauciflorus, pauciflora, pauciflorum few flowers

paucifolius, paucifolia, paucifolium few leaves

paucinervus, paucinerva, paucinervum few veins

pavoninus, pavonina, pavoninum peacock-blue, or with a colorful patch like one on a peacock's tail feather

pectinatus, pectinata, pectinatum resembling a comb

pectinifer, pectinifera, pectiniferum having a comb

pedatifidus, pedatifida, pedatifidum; pedatus, pedata, pedatum divided like the foot of a bird

pedemontanus, pedemontana, pedemontanum   from Piedmont, Italy

pedunculatus   stalked

pedunculosus, pedunculosa, pedunculosum   many or prominent flower stalks (peduncles)

pedunculuris, pedunculare; pedunculatus, pedunculata, pedunculatum   distinct flower stalks (peduncles)

pellucidus, pellucida, pellucidum   translucent or transparent

peltatus, peltata, peltatum   peltate shaped, like a shield with the stalk attached underneath and not of the margin of the leaf

pelviformis, pelviforme   like a shallow cup, pelvis-shaped

pendulinus, pendulina, pendulinum; pendulus, pendula, pendulum   hanging, pendulous

penindulstid, penindulstr   of a peninsula

pennatus, pennata, pennatum   pinnate or feathered

pennsylvanicus, pennsylvanica, pennsylvanicum   from Pennsylvania

pensilis, pensile   hanging

pentagonus, pentagona, pentagonum   five angles

pentagynus, pentagyna, pentagynum   five pistils, five fruits

pentandrus, pentandra, pentandrum   five stamens

pentaphyllus, pentaphylla, pentaphyllum   five leaves, or leaflets

pentapterus, pentaptera, pentapterum   five wings

peregrinus, peregrina, percgrinum   exotic, not native

perennans; perennis, perenne   perennial, lasting year to year

perfoliatus, perfoliata, perfoliatum; perfosus, perfosa, perfosum, perfoliate   the stem apparently piercing the leaf blade

perforatus, perforata, perforatum   with small holes or appearing as if so

perpusilla   very small

persicifolius, persicifolia, persicifolium   leaves like a peach (*Prunus persica*) leaf

persicus, persica, persicum   from Persia

persistens   persistent

persolutus   like a garland

pertusus, pertusa, pertusum   perforated

peruvianus, peruviana, peruvianum   from Peru

petaloideus, petaloida, petaloidum   petal-like

petiolaris, petiolare; petiolatus, petiolata, petiolatum   having leaves with distinct stalks, with petiole

petraeus, petraea, petraeum   rock-loving

phaeocarpus, phaeocarpa, phaeocarpum   dark fruit

phaeus   dusky

philadelphicus, philadelphica, philadelphicum   from Philadelphia

phoeniceus, phoenicea, phoeniceum   Phoenicia, or purple-red

phyllomaniacus, phyllomaniaca, phyllomaniacum   abundant leafy growth

picturatus, picturata, picturatum variegated, painted leaves

pictus, picta, pictum brightly colored or painted, variegated

pileatus, pileata, pileatum with a cap

pilifer, pilifera, piliferum with short, soft hairs

pilosus, pilosa, pilosum clothed with long soft hairs

pilularis, pilulare; pilulifer, pilulifera, piluliferum small spherical fruits

pimpinellifolius, pimpinellifolia, pimpinellifolium leaves like *Pimpinella*

pinetorum from pine forests

pinifolius, pinifolia, pinifolium leaves like a pine (*Pinus*)

pinnatifidus, pinnatifida, pinnatifidum pinnately divided

pinnatifolius, pinnatifolia, pinnatifolium pinnate leaves

pinnatinervis, pinnatinerve pinnate veins

pinnatus, pinnata, pinnatum feather-like

piperitus, piperita, piperitum pepper-like or hot taste, or peppermint fragrance

pisifer, pisifera, pisiferum pea-bearing

planiflorus, planiflora, planiflorum flat flowers

planifolius, planifolia, planifolium flat leaves

planipes flat stalked

planus, plana, planum flat

platanifolius, platanifolia, platanifolium leaves like a plane tree (*Platanus*)

platanoides like a plane tree (*Platanus*)

platyacanthus, platyacantha, platyacanthum wide spines

platyanthus, platyantha, platyanthum wide flowers

platycarpus, platycarpa, platycarpum wide fruits

platycaulis, platycaule wide flat stem

platycentrus, platycentra, platycentrum wide flat spur, wide center

platycladus, platyclada, platycladum flat branches

platyglossus, platyglossa, platyglossum a flat tongue

platypetalus, platypetala, platypetalum wide petals

platyphyllus, platyphylla, platyphyllum wide leaves

platypodus, platypoda, platypodum having wide stalks

platyspathus, platyspatha, platyspathum a broad or wide spathe

platyspermus, platysperma, platyspermum with wide seeds

pleniflorus, pleniflora, pleniflorum double flowers

plenissimus, plenissima, plenissimum very double

plenus, plena, plenum double

plicatus, plicata, plicatum pleated, folded like a fan

plumarius, plumaria, plumarium; plumatus, plumata, plumatum plumed or feathered

plumbaginoides

plumbaginoides like *Plumbago*

plumosus, plumose, plumosum feathery

pluriflorus, pluriflora, pluriflorum many flowers

podagricus, podagrica, podagricum swollen at the base

podocarpa with stalked fruits

podophyllus, podophylla, podophyllum leaves with stout stalks

poeticus, poetica, poeticum associated with poets

polifolius, polifolia, polifolium gray leaves like *Teucrium polium*

politus, polita, politum elegant or neat

polyacanthus, polyacantha, polyacanthum many thorns

polyandrus, polyandra, polyandrum many stamens

polyantha with many flowers; kind of rose

polyanthemos; polyanthus, polyantha, polyanthum many flowers

polybotryus, polybotrya, polybotryum many clusters

polycanthus many-striped

polycarpus, polycarpa, polycarpum many fruits

polycephalus, polycephala, polycephalum many heads

polychromus, polychroma, polychromum many colors

polygaloides like *Polygala*

polylepis many scales

polymorphus, polymorpha, polymorphum many forms

polypetalus, polypetala, polypetalum many petals

polyphyllus, polyphylla, polyphyllum many leaves

polyrrhizus, polyrrhiza, polyrrhizum many roots

polysepalus, polysepala, polysepalum many sepals

polystachyus, polystachya, polystachyum many spikes

pomaceus like a pome

pomeridianus, pomeridiana, pomeridianum of the afternoon

pomifer, pomifera, pomiferum apple-like fruits, bearing pome fruit

ponchirus trifoliate or hardy orange

ponderosus, ponderosa, ponderosum ponderous, heavy, massive

ponticus, pontica, ponticum from the area of the southern shore of the Black Sea

populifolius, populifolia, populifolium leaves like those of a poplar (*Populus*)

populneus, populnea, populneum associated with poplars (*Populus*)

porcinus, porcina, porcinum relating to pigs or their food

porophyllus, porophylla, porophyllum holes in leaves or appearing so

porphyreus, porphyrea, porphyreum a reddish hue

porphyrophyllus, porphyrophylla, porphyrophyllum purple leaves

porrifolius, porrifolia, porrifolium leaves like leeks (*Allium porrifolium*)

portulacaceus, portulacacea, portulacaceum   resembling *Portulaca*

poteriifolius, poteriifolia, poteriifolium   leaves like *Poterium*

praealtus, praealta, praealtum   extremely tall

praecox   very early, precocious

praestans   distinguished, excelling

praevernus, praeverna, praevernum   before spring

pratensis, pratense   of meadows

primuliflorus, primuliflora, primuliflorum   flowers like primroses (*Primula*)

primulifolius, primulifolia, primulifolium   leaves like primroses (*Primula*)

primulinus, primulina, primulinum   primrose-yellow

primuloides   like primroses (*Primula*)

princeps   most distinguished, princely, first

prismaticus, prismatica, prismaticum   like a prism, angled

proboscideus, proboscidea, proboscideum   snout-like

procerus, procera, procerum   tall

procumbens   prostrate, spreading horizontally, trailing

profusus, profusa, profusum   abundant

prolifer, prolifera, proliferum   flowering freely or propagating freely, many leaved

prolificus, prolifica, prolificum   free-fruiting, prolific

propinquus, propinqua, propinquum   related

prostratus, prostrata, prostratum   prostrate, lying flat

protrusus, protrusa, protrusum   protruding

provincialis, provinciale   from Provence, France

pruhonicianus, pruhoniciana, pruhonicianum   from Pruhonice, Czechoslovakia

pruinatus, pruinata, pruinatum; pruinosus, pruinosa, pruinosum   glistening, frosted

prunifolius, prunifolia, prunifolium   leaves like plums (*Prunus*)

pruriens   causing itching

psittacinus, psittacina, psittacinum   parrot-like

psittacorum   of parrots, parrot-colored

psycodes   butterfly-like

ptarmica   sneeze-producing

ptarmicoides   resembling sneezewort

pteridoides   like ferns of the *Pteris* genus

pubens; pubescens; pubiger, pubigera, pubigerum   downy

puberulus   somewhat pubescent

pubescens   pubescent; hairy, short, soft, and downy

pudicus, pudica, pudicum   bashful, shrinking

pulchellus, pulchella, pulchellum; pulcher, pulchra, pulchrum   pretty, beautiful

pulcherrimus   very handsome

pulverulentus, pulverulenta, pulverulentum   dusted, having powder

pulvinatus

pulvinatus, pulvinata, pulvinatum
cushion-like

pumilus, pumila, pumilum   dwarf

punctatus, punctata, punctatum   spotted,
depressions spotted

pungens   sharp points, piercing

puniceus, punicea, puniceum   purplish-
red

purgans   purgative

purpurascens   purplish

purpuratus, purpurata, purpuratum
becoming purple

purpureus, purpurea, purpureum   purple

pusillus, pusilla, pusillum   very small

pustulatus, pustulata, pustulatum
blistered appearance

pygmaeus, pygmaea, pygmaeum   small or
tiny, pigmy, dwarf

**pyramidalis, pyramidale; pyramidatus,
pyramidata, pyramidatum**   pyramidal

**pyrenaeus, pyrenaea, pyrenaeum;
pyrenaicus, pyrenaica, pyrenaicum**
from the Pyrenees

pyrifolius, pyrifolia, pyrifolium   leaves like
pears (*Pyrus*)

pyriformis, pyriforme   pear-shaped

pyxidatus, pyxidata, pyxidatum   having
a lid

**quadrangularis, quadrangulare;
quadrangulatus, quadrangulata,
quadrangulatum**   with four angles

quadratus, quadrata, quadratum   in fours

quadricolor   having four colors

quadrifidus, quadrifida, quadrifidum   cut
into four parts

quadrifolius, quadrifolia, quadrifolium
leaves in fours

quercifolius, quercifolia, quercifolium
leaves like an oak (*Quercus*)

quinatus, quinata, quinatum   in fives

**quinqueflorus, quinqueflora,
quinqueflorum**   flowers in fives

**quinquefolius, quinquefolia,
quinquefolium**   five leaves, or five leaflets

quinquenervis, quinquenerve   five veined

**quinquepunctatus, quinquepunctata,
quinquepunctatum**   five spotted

quintenis, quintene   from Quito, Ecuador

**racemiflorus, racemiflora, racemiflorum;
racemosus, racemosa, racemosum**
flowers in racemes

radiatus, radiata, radiatum   radiating

radicans   stems that root

radula   like a rasp or file

ramiflorus, ramiflora, ramiflorum
branched flowers

ramosissimus, ramosissima, ramosissimum
branched mulch

ramosus, ramosa, ramosum   branched

ranunculoides   resembling buttercups
(*Ranunculus*)

rapaceus, rapacea, rapaceum   associated
with turnips (*Brassica rapa*)

rapunculoides   looking like Rapunculus, a
group now included in *Campanula*

rariflorum, rariflora, rariflorum   scattered
flowers

reclinatus, reclinata, reclinatum bent backward

rectus, recta, rectum erect

recurvatus, recurvata, recurvatum; recurvus, recurva, recurvum curved backward

redivivus, rediviva, redivivum returning to life, surviving again, returned

reductus, reducta, reductum reduced

reflexus, reflexa, reflexum; reflexus, reflexa, reflexum bent backward

refractus broken

refulgens refulgent, brilliant, radiant

regalis, regale regal, splendid, suitable for a king

reginae related to the queen

regius, regia, regium royal

reinformis, reinforme kidney form

religiosums, religiosum, religios sacred, associated with religion or religions

remotus, remota, remotum scattered, distant parts

repandus somewhat wavy margins

repens; reptans creeping

resediflorus, resediflora, resediflorum having flowers like mignonette (*Reseda*)

resedifolius, resedifolia, resedifolium leaves like mignonette (*Reseda*)

resinifer, resinifera, resiniferum; resinosus, resinosa, resinosum resinous

resiniferous producing resin

reticulatus, reticulata, reticulatum netted

retroflexus, retroflexa, retroflexum; retortus, retorta, retortum twisted back, backward flexed

retusus, retusa, retusum rounded and slightly notched apex

revolutus, revoluta, revolutum rolled backward

rex king

rhamnifolius, rhamnifolia, rhamnifolium leaves like *Rhamnus*

rhamnoides resembling *Rhamnus*

rhizophyllus, rhizophylla, rhizophyllum leaves that produce roots

rhodanthus, rhodantha, rhodanthum with rose-pink flowers; flowers like roses

rhodora Azalea-like shrubs

rhombicus, rhombica, rhombicum; rhomboidus, rhomboida, rhomboidum diamond-shaped or rhomboidal

rhytidophyllus, rhytidophylla, rhytidophyllum wrinkled leaves

ricinifolius, ricinifolia, ricinifolium leaves like the castor-bean (*Ricinus*)

ricinoides looking like the castor-bean (*Ricinus*)

rigens; rigidus, rigida, rigidum rigid

rigidifolius, rigidifolia, rigidifolium having rigid leaves

rigidus stiff

ringens gaping

riparius, riparia, riparium of riverbanks

rivalis, rivale of streamsides, pertaining to brooks

rivularis, rivulare   brook or stream loving

robustispinus, robustispina, robustispinum   strong spines

robustus, robusta, robustum   strong or stout, vigorous

romanus, romana, romanum   of Rome

rosaceus, rosacea, rosaceum   rose-like

roseus, rosea, roseum   rose colored

rosmarinifolius, rosmarinifolia, rosmarinifolium   leaves like rosemary (*Rosmarinus*)

rostratus, rostrata, rostratum   beaked

rosularis, rosulare   with rosettes

rotatus, rotata, rotatum   resembling a wheel

rotundatus, rotundata, rotundatum; rotundus, rotunda, rotundum   rounded

rotundifolius, rotundifolia, rotundifolium   round leaves

rubellus, rubella, rubellum; rubescens   reddish

rubens; ruber, rubra, rubrum   red

rubescens   becoming reddish

rubiginous, rubiginoa, rubiginoum   rosy, rusty

rubioides   resembling *Rubia*

rubra   red

rubricaulis, rubricaule   red stem

rubrofructa   red-fruited

rufidulus   somewhat reddish

rugosus, rugosa, rugosum   wrinkled

rupestris, rupestre   rock loving

rupicola   living around rocks

rupicolus   growing on cliffs or ledges

rupifragus, rupifraga, rupifragum   rock breaking

ruscifolius, ruscifolia, ruscifolium   leaves like the butcher's broom (*Ruscus*)

rusticanus, rusticana, rusticanum; rusticus, rustica, rusticum   of the countryside

ruthenicus, ruthenica, ruthenicum   from Ruthenia, former U.S.S.R.

rutlians   reddish, becoming red

saccatus, saccata, saccatum   sack shape or resembling a bag

saccharifer, saccharifera, sacchariferum   source of sugar

saccharinus, saccharina, saccharinum   sugary

saccharoides   looking like sugar cane (*Saccharum*)

saccharum   sugar

saccifer, saccifera, sacciferum   bearing sacks or bags

sachalinensis, sachalinense   from Sakhalin Island, former U.S.S.R.

sacrorum   from sacred places

sagittalis, sagittale   arrowhead shaped

sagittifolius, sagittifolia, sagittifolium   leaves shaped like an arrowhead

salicaria   like a willow

salicifolius, salicifolia, salicifolium   leaves like willows (*Salix*)

salicinus, salicina, salicinum   willow-like

salicornioides   looking like *Salicornia*

salignus, saligna, salignum   willow-like

salinus, salina, salinum   in salty places

salpiglossis   painted tongue

salsuginosus, salsuginosa, salsuginosum   from salt marshes

saluenensis, saluenense   from the Salween River in China or Burma

salvifolius, salvifolia, salvifolium   *Salvia*-like leaves

sambucifolius, sambucifolia, sambucifolium   elder (*Sambucas*)–like leaves

sanctus, sancta, sanctum   holy, of a sanctuary

sanguineus, sanguinea, sanguineum   blood-red color

sapidus, sapida, sapidum   agreeable tasting, savory

sapientum   associated with wise (sapient) men, or authors

saponaceus, saponacea, saponaceum   soapy

sarcodes   flesh-like

sarmentosus, sarmentosa, sarmentosum   with runners

sarniensis, sarniense   from Guernsey (Saria) of the Channel Islands

sativus, sativa, sativum   cultivated

satureja   savory

saxatilis, saxatile; saxicola   inhabiting rocky areas

saxifrage   rockery plants

scaber, scabra, scabrum   rough

scabiosifolius, scabiosifolia, scabiosifolium   leaves like scabious (*Scabiosa*)

scabrous   climbing

scandens   climbing

scapiger, scapigera, scapigerum; scaposus, scaposa, scaposum   having scapes (naked, flowering stalks)

scariosus, scariosa, scariosum   shriveled, thin, and not green

sceleratus, scelerata, sceleratum   wicked, dangerous, associated with harm

schizopetalus, schizopetala, schizopetalum   cut petals

schizophyllus, schizophylla, schizophyllum   cut leaves

schollaris, schollare   school or scholarly associating

scilloides   looking like *Scilla* (squill)

sclerocarpus, sclerocarpa, sclerocarpum   with hard fruits

scoparius, scoparia, scoparium   brook-like

scopulorum   cliffs or crags (growing there)

scorpioides   scorpion-like

scoticus, scotica, scoticum   from Scotland

scutum   a shield

secundiflorus, secundiflora, secondiflorum   flowers on one side

secondus, seconda, secondum   one-sided; side-flowering

segetalis, segetale; segetum   from grain fields

segetum   of cornfields

selaginoides   looking like *Selaginella*

semperflorens   never-ending blooms

sempervirens   evergreen, always green

sempervivoides   resembling *Sempervivum*

senecioides   resembling *Senecio*

senescens   aging

senilis, senile   having white hairs, senile, old

sensibilis, sensibile; sensitivus, sensitiva, sensitivum   sensitive to touch or other stimuli, responding to and sensing touch

sensitivus   sensitive

sepiarius, sepiaria, sepiarium   associated with hedges

septangularis, septangulare   seven-angled

septemfidus, septemfida, septemfidum   seven cuts

septemlobus, septemloba, septemlobum   seven lobes

septentrionalis, septentrionale   northern

sericanthus, sericantha, sericanthum   having silky flowers

sericeus, sericea, sericeum   silky

sericifer, sericifera, sericiferum; sericofer, sericofera, sericoferum   bearing silk

serotinus, serotina, serotinum   blooming or ripening late

serpens   creeping, crawling, growing on the ground like a serpent

serpentinus, serpentina, serpentinum   relating to snakes or to serpentine shapes

serpyllifolius, serpyllifolia, serpyllifolium   leaves like *Thymus serpyllum*

serratifolius, serratifolia, serratifolium   saw-toothed leaves

serratulatus, serratulata, serratulatum   little saw-like teeth

serratus, serrata, serratum   saw-toothed, serrate

sessifolius   stalk-like leaves

sessilis, sessile   having no stalk

setaceus, setacea, setaceum   having bristles, bristle-like

setifer, setifera, setiferum; setiger, setigera, setigerum; setosus, setosa, setosum   bristly

setifolius, setifolia, setifolium   having bristly leaves

setigera   bristle-bearing

sexangularis, sexangulare   six-angled

siameus, siamea, siameum   from Thialand (Siam)

sibiricus   of Siberia

siculiformis, siculiforme   dagger-shaped

siculus, sicula, siculum   from Sicily

signatus, signata, signatum   clearly marked or vividly individualized

silvaticus, silvatica, silvaticum; silvestris, silvestre   of woodlands

similis, simile   similar

simplex   branchless

simplicicaulis, simplicicaule   having branchless stems

simplicifolius, simplicifolia, simplicifolium   a simple leaf, no compound leaves, or no leaflets

simulans   resembling, being similar to

sinensis, sinense; sinicus, sinica, sinicum   from China

sinuatus, sinuata, sinuatum; sinuosus, sinuosa, sinuosum   wavy margins, sinuous margins

sitchensis, sitchense   from Sitka, Alaska

smaragdinus, smaragdina, smaragdinum   emerald-green

smilacinus, smilacina, smilacinum   associated with Smilax

sobolifer, sobolifera, soboliferum   creeping stems that can root

socialis, sociale   forming colonies (societies), or clumps

solaris, solare   liking good solar (sun) exposure

soldanelloides   looking like *Soldanella*

solidus, solida, solidum   solid

somnifer, somnifera, somniferum   sleep producing

sorbifolius, sorbifolia, sorbifolium   leaves resembling the mountain ash (*Sorbus*)

sordidus, sordida, sordidum   dirty, sordid, wretched, dull; muddy color

sparsus, sparsa, sparsum   few, sparse

spathulatus, spathulata, spathulatum   looking like a spatula, spoon-shaped

speciosus, speciosa, speciosum   showy, deceptive, alluring, not genuine, specious, good-looking

spectabilis, spectabile   spectacular, remarkable

speculatus, speculata, speculatum   mirror-like

sphacelatus, sphacelata, sphacelatum   dead

sphaericus, sphaerica, sphaericum   spherical

sphaerocarpus, sphaerocarpa, sphaerocarpum   spherical fruits

sphaerocephalus, sphaerocephala, sphaerocephalum   spherical heads, rounded head

spicatus   spicate with spikes

spicifer, spicifera, spiciferum   having spikes

spiculiflorus, spiculiflora, spiculiflorum   flowers in small spikes

spinescens; spinifer, spinifera, spiniferum; spinifex; spinosus, spinosa, spinosum   spiny

spiniosus   full of spines

spinosissimus   most spiny

spinulifer, spinulifera, spinuliferum   small spines

spiralis, spirale   spiral

splendens; splendidus, splendida, splendidum   splendid

spurius, spuria, spurium   false, spurious, illegitimate

squalens; squalidus, squalida, squalidum   dirty looking, filthy, degrading, squalid

squamatus, squamata, squamatum   small scale-like leaves or bracts

squamosus, squamosa, squamosum   many scales

squarrosus, squarrosa, squarrosum   spreading or recurved ends

stachyoides   looking like *Stachys*

stamineus, staminea, stamineum   having conspicuous stamens, or stamens of interest

stellaris, stellare; stellatus, stellata, stellatum   star-like

stenocarpus, stenocarpa, stenocarpum   narrow fruit

stenocephalus narrow-headed

stenopetalus, stenopetala, stenopetalum narrow petals

stenophyllus, stenophylla, stenophyllum narrow leaves

stenostachyus, stenostachya, stenostachyum narrow spikes

sterilis, sterile sterile

stipulaceus, stipulacea, stipulaceum; stipularis, stipulare; stipulatus, stipulata, stipulatum stipules of interest or large size

stolonifer, stolonifera, stoloniferum with stolens

stramineus straw color

streptocarpus, streptocarpa, streptocarpum with twisted fruits

streptopetalus, streptopetala, streptopetalum with twisted petals

streptophyllus, streptophylla, streptophyllum with twisted leaves

streptosepalus, streptosepala, streptosepalum with twisted sepals

striatus, striata, striatum striped

strictus, stricta, strictum erect, standing up

strigillosus, strigillosa, strigillosum bristly hairs lying flat on a surface

strigosus, strigosa, strigosum stiff bristles, with few or no branches

strobilifer, strobilifera, strobiliferum cone bearing

strumarius, strumaria, strumarium; strumosus, strumosa, strumosum having swellings

stylosus, stylosa, stylosum having prominent or conspicuous style

suaveolens sweetly fragrant

suavis, suave sweet

subacaulis, subacaule with a short stem

subalpinus, subalpina, subalpinum from low alpine areas; nearly alpine

subauriculatus, subauriculata, subauriculatum partially or a little eared

subcaeruleus, subcaerulea, subcaeruleum partially or a little blue

subcanus, subcana, subcanum graying

subcarnosus, subcarnosa, subcarnosum somewhat fleshy

subcordatus, subcordata, subcordatum somewhat heartshaped

subdentatus, subdentata, subdentatum nearly toothless

subdivaricatus, subdivaricata, subdivaricatum spreading to some degree

subelongatus, subelongata, subelongatum lengthened to some degree

suberectus, suberecta, suberectum nearly upright

subglaucus, subglauca, subglaucum glaucous to some degree

subhirtellus, subhirtella, subhirtellum somewhat hairy

submersus, submersa, submersum submerged

subpetiolatus, subpetiolata, subpetiolatum short leafstalks

subscandens tends to climb

subsessilis   nearly stalkless

subterraneus, subterranea, subterraneum   underground

subulatus, subulata, subulatum   awl-shaped

subvillosus, subvillosa, subvillosum   soft hairs

succulentus, succulenta, succulentum   fleshy

suecicus, suecica, suecicum   Swedish

suffrutescens; suffruticosus, suffruticosa, suffruticosum   rather shrubby

sulcatus, sulcata, sulcatum   furrowed

sulfurus, sulfura, sulfurum; sulphureus, sulphurea, sulphureum   sulfur color or yellow

sumatranus, sumatrana, sumatranum   from Sumatra, Indonesia

superbus, superba, superbum   superb, showy

supinus, supina, supinum   prostrate, or leaning back

surculosus, surculosa, surculosum   having suckers or shoots

susianus   of Susa, an ancient Persian city

suspensus, suspensa, suspensum   hanging, dropping

sutchuenensis, sutchuenense   from Szechwan, China

sylvaticus, sylvatica, sylvaticum; sylvester, sylvestris, sylvestre; sylvicola   from forests, forest loving

syriacus, syriaca, syriacum   from Syria

syringanthus, syringantha, syringanthum   flowers like lilacs (*Syringa*)

syringifolius, syringifolia, syringifolium   leaves like lilacs (*Syringa*)

tabularis, tabulare   flat like a table or from Table Mountain, South Africa

tabuliformis, tabuliforme   flat or table shaped

taiwanensis, taiwanense   from Taiwan

taliensis, taliense   from the Tali Mountains, China

tamariscifolius, tamariscifolia, tamariscifolium   leaves like tamarisk (*Tamarix*)

tanacetifolius, tanacetifolia, tanaceti-folium   leaves like tansy (*Tanacetum*)

tanguticus, tangutica, tanguticum   from Kansu, China, or Tanget, Tibet

taraxacifolius, taraxacifolia, taraxacifolium   leaves like a dandelion (*Taraxacum*)

tardiflorus, tardiflora, tardiflorum   late flowers

tardivus, tardiva, tardivum; tardus, tarda, tardum   tardy or late in some aspect

tartaricus, tartarica, tartaricum   from Central Asia

tasmanicus, tasmanica, tasmanicum   from Tasmania

tatsienensis, tatsienense   from Tatsienlu, China

tauricus, taurica, tauricum   from the Crimea

taxifolius, taxifolia, taxifolium   leaves like yew (*Taxus*)

tectorum   of roots

tenax   strongly matted, or dense

tenera   slender, tender, soft

tenuicaulis, tenuicaule   having slender stems

tenuiflorus, tenuiflora, tenuiflorum   slender flowers

tenuifolius, tenuifolia, tenuifolium   slender leaves

tenuipetalus, tenuipetala, tenuipetalum   slender petals

tenuis, tenue   slender

terebinthinaceus, terebinthinacea, terebinthinaceum; terebinthininus, terebinthinina, terebinthininum   terpentine association

teres   cylindrical

terete   cylindrical

terminalis, terminale   associated with boundaries, or ending abruptly, at an end

ternatus, ternate, ternatum   clusters of three

terrestris, terrestre   of the ground

tessellatus, tessellate, tessellatum   checkered

testaceus, testacea, testaceum   brick colored, dull red, light brown

testicularis, testiculare; testiculatus, testiculata, testiculatum   looking like testicles

tetracanthus, tetracantha, tetracanthum   having spines in fours

tetragonus, tetragona, tetragonum   with four angles

tetrandrus, tetrandra, tetrandrum   four stamens

tetranthus, tetrantha, tetranthum   flowers in fours

tetraphyllus, tetraphylla, tetraphyllum   leaves in fours

tetrapterus, tetraptera, tetrapterum   four wings

teucrioides   resembling *Teucrium*

texanus, texana, texanum   from Texas

textilis, textile   used in textiles or for wearing

thalictrifolla   leaves like Thalictrum

thalictroides   resembling Thalictrum

theifer, theifera, theiferum   used in tea; fragrance like tea

thuyoides   looking like Thuja

thymifolius, thymifolia, thymifolium   leaves like thyme (*Thymus*)

thymoides   resembling thyme (*Thymus*)

thyrsiflorus, thyrsiflora, thyrsiflorum   arrangements of flowers called thyrses, like lilacs or horse-chestnuts

thyrsoides   thyrse-like

tibeticus, tibetica, tibeticum   from Tibet

tigrinus, tigrina, tigrinum   striped or decorated like a tiger; tiger-toothed

tiliaceus, tiliacea, tiliaceum   looking like a linden (*Tilia*)

tilifolius, tilifolia, tilifolium   leaves like a linden (*Tilia*)

tinctorium   of dyers

tinctorius, tinctoria, tinctorium   useful in dyeing with color

tingitanus, tingitana, tingitanum   from Tangiers, Morocco

tirolensis, tirolense   from the Tyrol

titanius, titania, titanium   bigger than large

tomentosus, tomentosa, tomentosum   dense, wooly, soft hairs

toringoides   like toringo carb

torridus, torrida, torridum   inhabits hot, dry places

tortifolius   leaves twisted

tortilis, tortile; tortus, torta, tortum   twisted

tortuosus   much twisted

toxicarius, toxicaria, toxicarium; toxicus, toxica, toxicum; toxifer, toxifera, toxiferum   poisonous, toxic

translucens   translucent

transparens   transparent

transylvanicus, transylvanica, transylvanicum   from Transylvania, Romania

trapeziformis, trapeziforme   formed of four unequal sides

tremuloides   looking like poplar (*Populus tremula*)

tremulus, tremula, tremulum   trembling

triacanthus, triacantha, triacanthum   three spined

triangularis, triangulare; triangulatus, triangulata, triangulatum   three-angled

tricanthophorus   bearing three spines

tricaudatus, tricaudata, tricaudatum   three tails

tricephalus, tricephala, tricephalum   three heads

trichocalyx   having hairy calyxes

trichocarpus   hairy-fruited

trichogynus, trichogyna, trichogynum   hairy ovaries

trichophyllus, trichophylla, trichophyllum   hairy leaves

trichospermus, trichosperma, trichospermum   hairy seeds

trichotomus, trichotoma, trichotomum   three branches

tricoccus, tricocca, tricoccum   fruits with three deep lobes

tricolor   three colors

tricornis, tricorne   three horns

tricuspidatus, tricuspidata, tricuspidatum   three points

tridens; tridentatus, tridentata, tridentatum   three teeth

trifidus, trifida, trifidum   cut or divided into three parts

triflorus, triflora, triflorum   flowers in threes

trifoliatus, trifoliata, trifoliatum; trifolius, trifolia, trifolium   leaves or leaflets in threes

trifurcatus, trifurcata, trifurcatum; trifurcus, trifurca, trifurcum   three forks

trilobatus, trilobata, trilobatum   three lobes

trimestris, trimester   of three months

trinervis, trinerve   three veins

tripetalus, tripetala, tripetalum   three petals

triphyllus, triphylla, triphyllum   leaves in threes

tripterus

tripterus, triptera, tripterum three wings

trispermus, trisperma, trispermum seeds in threes

tristachyus, tristachya, tristachyum spikes in threes

tristis, triste dull or sad

triternatus, triternata, triternatum three times in threes

triumphans triumphant

trivialis, triviale ordinary, trivial, common

trolliifolius leaves like a globe flower (*Trollius*)

truncatus, truncata, truncatum cut squarely across

tubatus, tubata, tubatum trumpet shape

tuberculosus, tuberculosa, tuberculosum; tuberculatus, tuberculata, tuberculatum covered with little warts or tubercules

tuberosus, tuberosa, tuberosum tuberous

tubifer, tubifera, tubiferum; tubulosus, tubulosa, tubulosum tubular

tubiflorus, tubiflora, tubiflorum tubular flowers

tulipifer, tulipifera, tulipiferum flowers like tulips; tulip-like

tumidus, tumida, tumidum swollen

turbinatus, turbinata, tubinatum top-shaped

turgidus, turgida, turgidum inflated, turgid, not limp

typhinus, typhina, typhinum resembling cattails (*Typha*), pertaining to fever

typicus, typica, typicum typical

uliginosus, uliginosa, uliginosum from swamps, or marshy places

ulmifolius, ulmifolia, ulmifolium having leaves like elms (*Ulmus*)

ulmoides resembling elms (*Ulmus*)

umbellatus, umbellata, umbellatum bearing umbels

umbraculifer, umbraculifera, umbraculiferum umbrella-like branching

umbrosus, umbrosa, umbrosum shade loving

uncinatus, uncinata, uncinatum hooked at ends

undatus, undata, undatum; undulatus, undulata, undulatum wavy, undulating

unguicularis, unguicularie; unguiculatus, unguiculata, unguiculatum claws contracting to an extended, narrow basal area

unicolor self-colored, one color

unidentatus, unidentata, unidentatum one tooth

uniflorus, uniflora, uniflorum one flower

unifolius, unifolia, unifolium one leaf, single leaved

unilateralis, unilaterale one side

uninervis, uninerve one vein

uniseriatus, uniseriata, uniseriatum one row

univittatus one stripe

urbanus, urbana, urbanum; urbicus, urbica, urbicum from towns, or urban environments

urceolatus, urceolata, urceolatum urn shape

urens stinging, burning

urophyllus, urophylla, urophyllum having leaves with long, tail-like apexes

ursinus, ursina, ursinum associated with a bear

urticifolius, urticifolia, urticifolium leaves like a nettle (*Urtica*)

urticoides looking like a nettle (*Urtica*)

usitatissimus, usitatissima, usitatissimum most useful

ustulatus, ustulata, ustulatum burned or scorched

utilis, utile useful; can be utilized

utriculatus, utriculata, utriculatum; utriculosus, utriculosa, utriculosum bladder-like

uva-ursi grape for bears

uvifer, uvifera, uviferum grapes or grape-like fruits

vaccinifolius, vaccinifolia, vaccinifolium having leaves like those of *Vaccinium*

vaccinioides resembling *Vaccinium*

vacillans variable, swaying

vagans wandering, spread widely about, vagrant

vaginalis, vaginale; vaginatus, vaginata, vaginatum sheathed or like such

valdivianus, valdiviana, valdivianum from Valdivia, Chile

validus, valida, validum strong, valid, good development

variabilis, variabile; varians; variatus, variata, variatum variable

varicosa swollen irregularly

variegatus, variegata, variegatum variegated, more than one color

vegetus, vegeta, vegetum vigorous

velutinus, velutina, velutinum velvety

venenatus, venenata, venenatum poisonous

venenosus, venenosa, venenosum very poisonous

venosus, venosa, venosum conspicuous vein

ventricosus, ventricosa, ventricosum swollen on one side

venustus, venusta, venustum charming, beautiful

vera true

verbascifolius, verbascifolia, verbascifolium leaves like *Verbascum*

veris of springs; true

vermicularis, vermiculare; vermiculatus, vermiculata, vermiculatum worm-like

vernalis, vernale of spring

vernix varnish

vernus, verna, vernum spring

verrucosus, verrucosa, verrucosum warty

verruculosus, verruculosa, verruculosum small warts

versicolor colored with variety

verticillaris, verticillare; verticillatus, verticillata, verticillatum parts in whorls or tiers; circled around stem

verus, vera, verum true to type, genuine, standard

vespertinus, vespertina, vespertinum of the evening

vestitus, vestita, vestitum clothed, usually with hairs, or scales

vexans irritating, wounding, harmful

vexillaris, vexillare flags or standards; standard petal in a pea flower

viburnifolius, viburnifolia, viburnifolium leaves like *Viburnum*

viciifolius, viciifolia, viciifolium leaves like vetch (*Vicia*)

villosus, villosa, villosum colored with soft hairs

viminalis, viminale; vimineus, viminea, vimineum long, wand-like shoots

vinifer, vinifera, viniferum producing wine

vinosus, vinosa, vinosum wine-red color

violaceus, violacea, violaceum violet colored

violascens somewhat violet-colored or turning that color

virens green

virescens turning green

virgatus, virgata, virgatum wand-like, twiggy

virginalis, virginale; virgineus, virginea, virgineum white, virgin white, fresh

virginianus, virginiana, virginianum; virginicus, virginica, virginicum; virginiensis, virginiense from Virginia

viridescens becoming green

viridiflorus, viridiflora, viridiflorum green flowers

viridifolius, viridifolia, viridifolium green leaves

viridissimus, viridissima, viridissimum very green

viridulus, viridula, viridulum somewhat green

viridus, viride green

viscidifolius, viscidifolia, viscidifolium sticky leaves

viscidus, viscida, viscidum; viscosus, viscosa, viscosum viscid, sticky, or gummy

vitaceus, vitacea, vitaceum like a grape vine (*Vitis*)

vitalba grape or vine family

vitellinus, vitellina, vitellinum resembling yolk of an egg, dull yellow

vitifolius, vitifolia, vitifolium leaves like a grape (*Vitis*)

vittatus, vittata, vittatum striped lengthwise

volubilis, volubile twining

vomitorius, vomitoria, vomitorium emetic, inducing vomiting

vulgaris, vulgare; vulgatus, vulgata, vulgatum common, vulgar

warleyensis, warleyense from Warley Place Gardens, Essex, England

wichuralana in honor of a Russian botanist named Wichuray

wolgaricus, wolgarica, wolgaricum from the Volga River region

xanthacanthus, xanthacantha, xanthacanthum having yellow spines

xanthinus, xanthina, xanthinum yellow

xanthocarpus, xanthocarpa, xanthocarpum   having yellow fruits

xantholeucus, xantholeuca, xantholeucum   yellowish-white

xanthonervis, xanthonerve   yellow veins

xanthophyllus, xanthophylla, xanthophyllum   yellow leaves

xanthorrhizus, xanthorrhiza, xanthorrhizum   yellow roots

xeranthemum   everlasting, immortal

yedoensis, yedoense   from Tokyo (Yedo), Japan

yunnanensis, yunnanense; yunnanicus, yunnanica, yunnanicum   from Yunnan, China

zanzibariensis   of Zanzibar, Africa

zebrinus, zebrina, zebrinum   having stripes like a zebra

zeylanicus, zeylanica, zeylanicum   from Ceylon

zonalis, zonale; zonatus, zonata, zonatum   having bands or stripes horizontally, having zones differentiated